The
Evolution of Arthurian Romance
From the Beginnings
Down to the Year 1300

by

James Douglas Bruce, Ph. D.
Professor of the English Language and Literature
in the University of Tennessee.

———

Second Edition
with a supplement by Alfons Hilka (Goettingen)

Volume II

GLOUCESTER, MASS.

PETER SMITH
1958 [c1928]

SECOND EDITION, 1928

REPRINTED 1958 BY PERMISSION OF
THE JOHNS HOPKINS PRESS

The announcement of Professor Bruce's death, five months ago, was a shocking surprise to his academic colleagues. He was widely known as a man of that well — poised physical vigor which warrants plans reaching far into the future; and Professor Bruce had eagerly entertained plans for a longer life than was to be his. The completion of the work now published brought to a close a period of a dozen years in which he almost exclusively devoted his study and research to the execution of the purpose he has briefly described in the preface to the first volume. He was attracted to this task by the conviction that by no less laborious undertaking could the complex history of the study of his chosen subject be surveyed and made available as a stimulating guide to future investigation and interpretation.

Professor Bruce was stricken, while in his class-room, on Wednesday, February the fourteenth, and remained unconscious until his death five days later, February the nineteenth. Of the work now published the proofs of the second volume had not been corrected, and the manuscript of the Index of Subject-Matter and Index of Critics, in unrevised form, remained to be extended to include the references to the second volume. What was thus left to be done was also attended by delays and complications in bringing together the material for the second volume as it was found in Professor Bruce's library. This considerable task of seeing the second volume through the press has been almost entirely performed by Dr. Morris Edmund Speare. He has exercised the required technical skill, and especially shown an admirable devotion to the memory of a true scholar.

16. July, 1923.

JAMES W. BRIGHT

Contents of Vol. II.

Part III: The Prose Romances (concluded).

Chapter X.
Prose Romances in which Perceval is the Grail Hero.

Besides the Pseudo-Robert cycle, in which, just as in the Vulgate, Galahad is represented as the Grail hero, there are two other romances, also, posterior in date to the Vulgate cycle,[1] in which Perceval is restored to his old place of preeminence, which Galahad had usurped. The romances in question are the so-called *Didot-Perceval* and the *Perlesvaus*.[2] Leaving for another section of this work[3] the justification of the views here expressed in regard to the respective dates of these romances and their relations to the Vulgate cycle, we shall now proceed to outline, as far as seems necessary, the contents of these works.[4]

1. The Didot=Perceval.

This brief romance[5] commences where Robert's *Merlin* left off — namely, just after Arthur's coronation as king of Logres

---

[1] The opposing views of Miss Weston, Brugger, etc., on this subject will be discussed, Part IV, below.

[2] The first of these romances was, in a certain sense, cyclic, inasmuch as its author attached it to Robert's *Joseph* and *Merlin;* the latter, in the opinion of the present writer, was not cyclic. Cp. Part IV, below.

[3] Cp. Part IV, below.

[4] A pretty full analysis of the *Perlesvaus* is necessary, to make comprehensible the subsequent discussion Part IV, concerning its true place in the evolution of the prose cycles.

[5] In my analysis I follow the Modena MS. text, as published by Miss Weston, *Legend of Sir Perceval,* II, 9—112 (London, 1909). The *Queste* proper ends, p. 84. The remainder is a *Mort Arthur.* — For a fuller discussion of the problems concerning the place of the *Didot-Perceval* in the evolution of the Arthurian romances, see Part IV, below.

(Britain).[6] Merlin now appears on the scene and informs the barons
that the new king is really the son of his predecessor, Uther Pen-
dragon. They, in turn, recommend Merlin to Arthur as the prophet who was his father's friend and the originator of the Round
Table. Merlin predicts to Arthur that the latter will be the third
king of Britain to become, also, king of France and emperor of
Rome,[7] but declares that he (Arthur) must first render the Round
Table glorious. The sage, then, tells briefly the history of the
Grail and its wanderings and how its keeper, the Rich Fisher
King, now sick, is awaiting the coming of the Grail Knight. This
knight is to be a knight of the Round Table, and he is to ask
the question that will heal the sick king of his infirmities and
put an end to the enchantments of Britain. Having thus delivered
himself, Merlin goes off to Northumberland — to Blayse, who
had been the confessor to his (Merlin's) mother and who was
accustomed to record Merlin's sayings (p. 13).[8]

The fame of Arthur's court reaches Alain le Gros, Perceval's
father, and the latter wishes to send his son thither, but dies,
before he can do so. After his father's decease, however, Perceval goes there on his own account. Arthur dubs him knight, and,
inspired by love of Elaine, Gawain's sister, he proves himself
superior to all of Arthur's other knights, in a great tournament
at Pentecost. After this, he occupies the vacant seat[9] at the Round
Table, whereupon a great cry is heard and darkness fills the hall.
A voice, then, denounces Perceval's hardihood, foretells sufferings
for him and for his fellow-knights of the Round Table, because
of this act, and avers that, but for the merits of his father and
grandfather (Bron), he would have been cast down into the abyss,

----

[6] Sommer's *Vulgate Version*, II, 88.

[7] According to the Didot MS. (Miss W. II, p. ll, note 1), the
Sibyl and Solomon had already made this prediction about Arthur
before Merlin.

[8] This *motif*, adopted from Robert's *Merlin*, is repeated more
than once in the romance. Cp. pp. 68, 84, 85 and, in its Mort Arthur
section, pp. 102, 111, 112.

[9] As he does this, the seat — which is of stone — splits (p. 21),
but joins together later on, when he wins the Grail (p. 84).

as a punishment therefor. The voice announces, too, the presence of the Grail in the land, and repeats what Merlin had already said in regard to the Grail Knight, the Rich Fisher King, and the enchantments of Britain. Perceval and the other knights now vow that they will go on a quest for the Grail, never staying two consecutive nights in the same place. Arthur and his barons grieve sorely at their departure (p. 22).

The writer narrates only Perceval's adventures on this quest, and these, which, in the main, are mere variations of *motifs* furnished him by Chrétien's *Perceval* and Wauchier's continuation of that work,[10] have, in reality, little to do with the Grail. During his wanderings, however, he returns to his father's house and hears from his sister of their mother's death (p. 38). Having learned his identity, his sister takes him for confession to their hermit-uncle (Alain's brother), who has told her that God had pre-ordained Perceval to be the Grail Winner. The hermit confirms what she had said and warns his nephew, as the scion of a holy family, against the killing of knights and against other sins. The very next day, however, Perceval, in defending his sister, is compelled to kill a knight (p. 43). After two victorious encounters on the way,[11] he is told the direction of the Grail castle by two naked children (each six years old), whom he found disporting themselves in the branches of a tree at the crossing of

---

[10] For the correspondences in detail, cp. Part IV, below. At the commencement of the quest the adventures are 1. the episode (pp. 23 ff.) of Perceval's combat with Orguelleus de le Lande — Knight of the Tent — taken from Chrétien. 2. the first part of the long complex of Perceval's adventures (pp. 31 ff.) which began at the castle of the magical chessboard and of the girl who grants him her love on condition that he will bring her a certain stag's head — taken from Wauchier. These imitations of the poets in question are typical of the rest.

[11] In the second of these — the adventure of the Perilous Ford (pp. 50 ff.), suggested by Wauchier — we have the striking incident of the sorceress transforming herself and her maidens into birds and coming to the assistance of Perceval's adversary, her lover. For parallels to this incident in the Welsh *Dream of Rhonabwy* and other Celtic sources, cp. Miss Weston, II, 207 ff.

four roads (pp. 55f.). Proceeding towards the castle, he comes
upon his grandfather (as it later turns out), the Rich Fisher (Bron),
in a boat with two men. Despite his grandfather's directions
about the road to the castle, Perceval only finds it with much
difficulty. Whilst they are at dinner, the Grail procession — a
girl, with a cloth about her neck and carrying two small silver
plates, a valet bearing a bleeding lance, and another valet holding
aloft the Grail in his hands — pass twice through the room, but
Perceval, from a variety of motives (fear of troubling his host,
remembrance of his mother's warnings not to ask too many questions, and, lastly, fatigue), failed to ask the necessary question
(p. 59). The next morning the castle is empty, and when Perceval goes forth into the forest, he comes upon a weeping girl, who
upbraids him for the failure just mentioned and his consequent
responsibility for the Grail king's continued infirmity, but tells
him that this is the castle of his grandfather, the Fisher King,[12]
and that he must return there for another trial. Perceval, however, is unable to discover the Grail castle again. During the
seven years of his continued wanderings that now follow, his adventures are altogether secular in character, save that we have the
motif repeated from Chrétien of his neglect of religion, his meeting
with the penitents, the rebuke which he received from them for
riding armed on Good Friday, and his subsequent confession to
his hermit-uncle (p. 68). From this uncle, besides, he learns of
his sister's death. After other adventures, he comes upon Merlin,
who reproaches him for violating his vows in regard to the quest
and puts him on the road to the Grail castle (p. 81). Perceval
reaches this castle the same day and the Grail procession again
passes through the hall, but this time he asks the fateful question
and his grandfather, Bron, the Fisher King, is healed. After
imparting to Perceval the secrets of the Grail which Christ had
taught Joseph in prison, Bron places the vessel in his nephew's
hands and passes away. The enchantments of Britain now cease
and henceforth Perceval is the Grail king.

---

[12] All this is, of course, drawn from Chrétien.

The insignificant *Mort Arthur* which follows immediately upon this Perceval-*Quest* differs so little from the account of the last phase of Arthur's career which we find in Wace[13] that any further analysis of it seems unnecessary. The most striking departure from the Geoffreyan tradition which the narrative offers is in placing the scene of Arthur's last battle on an island[14] near

---

[13] On this subject cp. F. Lot, *Bibliothèque de l'École des Chartes*, LXX, 568 (1909) and Bruce, RR, IV, 448 ff., including notes (1913).

[14] Such seems to be the meaning of the passage, Miss Weston, II, 111, not Ireland. That the king of this isle should be a Saxon is not surprising; for *Saxon (Saisne)*, as is well-known, was used as a general term in the mediaeval romances for "heathen". The heathen of a somewhat later time, — viz. the Scandinavian vikings — did spread themselves all over these Western isles.

In *Romania*, XLV 16 ff., F. Lot contends that this departure from the Geoffreyan tradition is due to a misunderstanding of Geoffrey's *Vita Merlini*, l. 1115, where, after Mordred's usurpation, Arthur is represented as returning to Britain and driving his nephew *trans aequora diffugientem*. Lot interprets *aequora* as referring to the river, Cambula, (Geoffrey, Book XI, ch. 2.), on which Arthur fought his last battle with Mordred. But, in the opinion of the present writer, there is no need of putting this (to say the least of it) unusual construction on the word, for in the context *aequora* can well mean the seas that lie between Britain and Germany. In Geoffrey's *Historia* (Book XI, ch. 1.), Mordred had sent Cheldric to Germany to gather together Saxon troops; in the *Vita Merlini*, he goes there, himself, for this purpose. The lines, 1112 ff., of the *Vita* with which we are most immediately concerned are the following:

> Ast ut fama mali tanti sibi venit ad aures
> Distulit [Arthur] hanc belli curam patriamque revertens
> Applicuit multis cum milibus atque nepotem
> Obpugnans pepulit trans aequora diffugientem.
> Illic collectis vir plenus proditione
> Undique Saxonibus, coepit committere pugnam
> Cum duce, set cecidit, deceptus gente prophana
> In qua confisus tantos inceperat actus.

The true reason, then, we believe, for the change was the one stated in the text above. Lot, indeed, *Lancelot*, p. 195. note 1, already recognizes this. Possibly, too, the vague description in Robert's *Joseph*, ll. 3122, of the lands adjacent to Avalon (Avaron) may have had some influence with the author in this passage, as in the beginning of his

Ireland, instead of in Britain — probably, for the reason that
the author wished to bring this scene nearer to the supposed site
of Avalon (in the Western seas), whither the wounded Arthur
was to be borne after the battle.[15]

The *Didot-Perceval* was undeniably composed as a continuation of Robert de Boron's *Joseph-Merlin*, and several distinguished
Arthurian scholars have even regarded it as simply a prose rendering of a lost work of that writer's,[16] although no such claim is
made for it in the two extant MSS. of the romance. Certain conflicting conceptions, however, between its narrative and that of
Robert's genuine compositions prove that the assumption is unwarranted — e. g. 1. In Robert's *Merlin* it is said that the knight
who was to fill the vacant seat at the Round Table must first
have filled the vacant seat at the Grail Table. But the order of
things here indicated is exactly reversed in the *Didot-Perceval*.
2. In Robert the Grail Table and the Round Table are kept clearly
apart; in the *Didot-Perceval* they are confused. 3. In the *Didot-
Perceval*, owing to the influence of Chrétien's continuators, the

romance, p. 12, where the Fisher King's habitation is placed "en ces
illes d'Irlande". Altogether, we see no necessity of assuming with Lot,
Romania, *loc. cit.*, that the *Vita Merlini* was a source of the Mort
Arthur section of the *Didot-Perceval*, unless we assume, also, that
Morgan's attendance on Arthur in Avalon was an invention, pure and
simple, of Geoffrey in this poem. But that is not probable. Cp. Vol. I,
79 f., note, above. Contrary to Lot, *Lancelot*, p. 195, note 1, we
believe that the location of the Fisher King's dwelling, just mentioned,
was suggested rather by Robert than by the *Vita Merlini*.

[15] About the end of this *Mort Arthur* (p. 111), it is said that
Arthur told the Britons that he would return — hence they waited
forty years for him, before they elected a new king. Then the author
adds: "Mais tant sacies vous que li auquant l'ont puis veu es fores
cacier, et ont oi ses chiens avuec lui, et li auquant i ont eu esperance
lonc tans qu'il revenist".

It will be seen from this last sentence that here, as elsewhere,
the departed king has usurped the place of the Wild Huntsman in
the famous storm-myth. On Arthur in this rôle, in general, see
J. D. Bruce, RR, III, 191ff., and Archer Taylor, "Arthur and the
Wild Hunt", *ibid.*, XII, 286ff. (1921).

[16] Cp. Part IV.

Grail is more imposing than in Robert.[17] 4. Doubtless, under this same influence and under that of Chrétien, himself, the lance, which was wanting in Robert, appears in the Grail procession.[18] More telling, however, than even these inconsistencies is the difference of style. For the present romance, as stated above, is, in incident and outlook, like its chief sources, Chrétien and Wauchier, romantic, and, for the most part, secular, whereas Robert's sober genius, to judge from his undisputed works, keeps within the bounds of Christian legend (in the *Joseph*) and pseudo-history (in the *Merlin*). Altogether, the *Didot-Perceval* is an unoriginal composition, in respect to both style and contents. As far as the latter are concerned, they are drawn, in the main, as we have seen, from Chrétien and Wauchier, although varied, naturally, in the re-telling. It is, accordingly, not the intrinsic merit of the romance that has made it the centre of so much discussion, but the place which it has filled in the theories of certain scholars concerning the evolution of the prose romances.[19] There is, really, no valid reason, however, for viewing it as the archetype, so to speak, from which the *Queste* and *Mort Arthur* branches of the great Vulgate cycle developed. It is rather an independent romancer's completion of the prose Robert,[20] and, in its brevity, it conforms to the latter.

---

[17] Cp. pp. 59, 82.   [18] *Ibid.*

[19] Cp. Part IV, for a full discussion of these matters. The motives which have led the scholars in question to give the romance this relatively early dating are, 1. their identification of it with the continuation of Robert's work which, as appears from the latter part of the *Joseph,* he was planning at the time that he wrote that poem. 2. their reluctance to acknowledge that Perceval could again become the Grail Winner, after having been once superseded by Galahad. On this subject, however, see Part IV.

[20] In the *Didot-Perceval,* Alain (Perceval's father) is always called *Alains li Gros.* Cp. pp. 12, 14, 17, 40f., 69, 82. This is an indication that its author used the (secondary) prose version of Robert, not the original metrical version, for the epithet, *li Gros,* is attached to the name only in the former.

Lot's discussion, *Lancelot,* pp. 183ff., implies that the *Mort Arthur* of the *Didot-Perceval* must have been composed before the

2. The Perlesvaus.

The story opens[21] in Arthur's palace at Carduel on Ascension
Day, when the king discovers Guinevere in tears and learns, on
inquiry, that her distress is caused by the decline in the splendor
of the royal court. Formerly, on festival days, the knights that
assembled there could hardly be numbered. Now they were shame-
fully few and adventures seemed a thing of the past. Arthur
acknowledges that he is to blame for the decline, since he has

---

battle of Bouvines — Aug. 27, 1214 — since the French play such
a submissive part in it. But the writers of the time recognized that
Arthur's continental conquests belonged to a world of the imagination
and not of reality, so that our author may have very well followed
the Geoffreyan tradition in these episodes, without feeling that patriotic
susceptibilities were involved in the matter.

Evidence is wanting to determine even the relative date of the
present romance, but I see no obstacle to regarding it as subsequent
to the Vulgate cycle, and belonging, say, to the third decade of the
thirteenth century. An old line of tradition, as I have often had
occasion to remark, frequently persists by the side of one of later
origin, so that the absence of any certain influence on the romance
from the Vulgate does not necessarily possess any significance. The
prominence given to Lancelot, pp. 15 ff., may, after all, be due to the
influence of the prose *Lancelot*. See further on this subject Part IV,
below.

[21] Up to the present time there has been but one edition of the
Perlesvaus, viz. C. Potvin's, in Vol. I (Mons, 1866) of his *Perceval
le Gallois ou le Conte du Graal*. Another, however, is being prepared
by W. A. Nitze and others, including J. T. Lister, who has already
published, on his own account, the opening section of the text with an
introduction — in the form of a University of Chicago dissertation, *Perlesvaus, Hatton Manuscript 82, Branch 1* (Menasha, Wisconsin, 1921).
For descriptions of the *Perlesvaus* MSS. see E. Wechssler, "Handschriften
des Perlesvaus", *Zs. f. rom. Ph.*, XX, 80 ff. (1896) and the dissertations
of Nitze and Lister. In the last-named the earlier literature of the
subject is given. For errors in H. O. Sommer's article, "An unknown
MS. and two early printed editions of the Prose-Perceval", MLN, XXI,
225 f. (1906) see Nitze, "Dr. Sommer's alleged discovery of a new
MS.", *op. cit.* XXII, 27 (1907) and Sommer's "A note on the Prose-
Perceval", *ibid.* pp. 94 f. On the early prints (Paris) of 1516 and
1523, cp. Nitze, *loc. cit.*

lost the spirit of largesse and has fallen into "a feebleness of
heart." On his wife's advice, he decides to go to a chapel of
St. Austin (Augustine) in the forest and pray to God that he
may be reformed. Accordingly, he bids Chaus, a young man at
court, the son of Yvain the Bastard, prepare to accompany him
thither in the morning. That night, however, Chaus dreams that
the king has already gone ahead of him and that, in hurrying
to overtake him, he (Chaus) comes upon a chapel in a cemetery,
dismounts, enters it, and finds therein the dead body of a knight
covered with a rich cloth and surrounded by burning candles. The
intruder carries off one of the golden candlesticks, but encounters
in the forest a hideous, black man, of giant stature, who challenges
him to surrender the stolen article. He refuses, and, intending
to deliver it, instead, to Arthur, endeavors to outspeed the challenger. He fails, however, and his enemy thrusts a knife into
his side. At this point the young man awakens, and calls out
that he has been slain. He tells the king his dream and, on
examination, it is discovered that he has really received a mortal
wound from a knife that is still sticking in his side, and, sure
enough, when this knife is drawn out, the wounded man expires.
At his father's request the golden candlestick is presented to St.
Paul's church in London, in order that prayers might be said there
for the dead man's soul.

Warned by this marvellous incident, Arthur makes his journey to St. Austin's chapel, alone, but on the way thither he has
an experience which illustrates the wonder-working power of Our
Lady: In the chapel of a hermitage where he has turned in for
the night, he over-hears a strife between angels and devils concerning the soul of the hermit, who, after forty years of a robber's
life and five years of repentance and penance therefor had died
that night. The devils argued, plausibly, that the forty years
of crime outweighed the few years of atonement, but Our Lady
intervened, and, declaring that the decision in such cases depended
on the character of the man's life at the time of his decease, drove
the fiends away. Similarly, when the king arrives at St. Austin's,
he sees the Christ-child and his mother assisting the hermit of

the chapel in the celebration of the mass. Then, when the hermit is about to perform the sacramental rite, Our Lady places her son in his hands and the child becomes the bleeding Christ of the crucifixion, although later he resumes his former shape.

During all this scene in St. Austin's chapel, Arthur is not permitted to cross the threshold, because of the sin of his recent decline in chivalry, as he learns from the hermit. He promises amendment, however, and learns from the holy man of the misfortunes which Perceval has latterly brought upon the land of the Fisher King by his failure to ask the questions concerning the Grail — what purpose it served and whence it came. Among other adventures, too long to recount here, which he has on his return to Carduel, Arthur again meets a girl who had directed him to St. Austin's chapel and she relates to him the story of Perceval's youth up to the time that he was knighted by Arthur.[22]

----

[22] His father's name, as given here by Perceval's sister, is "Vilein le gros des vaus de Kamaaloth", according to Potvin's text (p. 19), which is based on the Brussels MS., but the form, *Vilein,* which occurs frequently in this text (pp. 139. 142, 145, *et passim).* is certainly a mere corruption of *Alein.* Another frequent corruption of the name in Potvin's text is *Julien,* pp. 3 *et passim.*

Perceval's mother is Ygloas, (Yglai, Iglais): Cp. pp. 2 f. In this text, moreover, the hero's own name is generally *Percevax* or *Perceval* (cp. pp. 105, 106, 181, 302, etc.), but sometimes *Perlesvax (Perlevax,) Perllesvax* or *Pellesvaus.* Cp. respectively, for the latter pp. 19, 87 and 43, 56. The romance is entitled *Pellesvaus* in the *explicit* at the end. Perceval's sister explains to Arthur the origin of the name, *Perlesvax,* as follows (p. 19): "Sire, fet-ele, quant il fu nez, si demanda (on) son pere commant il auroit non an droit bautesme. Et il dist qu'il vouloit qu'il eust non Perlesvax; quar li sires de Mores li toloit la greignor partie des vaus de Kamaaloth, si voloit qu'il an souvenist son fil par cel non, se Diex le monteploiot, tant qu'il fust chevaliers". Cp. too, p. 181.

Furthermore, Perceval is called *Par-lui* by his valet (p. 61) and *Par-lui-fez (fet)* by his hermit uncle pp. 87, 105. The first is probably a mere MS. error for the second, which means "self-made", — por ce qu'il c'estoit fet par lui memes (p. 105). — for Perceval had no regular training in knight hood. P. 87, however, his sister declares that his true name is *Perllesvax,* not *Par-lui-fez. Par-lui-fez* is

She begs the king, moreover, to apprise Perceval, should he meet him, of the straits to which their mother has been reduced by the King of the Moors and the brother of the Red Knight whom Perceval has slain. Arthur goes on his way, but before he reaches his destination, a voice proclaims to him in the depths of the forest (p. 22) that he must hold court as soon as possible; for the world which had deteriorated through his fault, is about to take a turn for the better.

As a result of his late miraculous experiences, Arthur undergoes now a thorough change of heart. His love of honor and of largesse return to him in full measure, and, obeying the injunction of the voice, he appoints the next meeting of his court for St. John's Day at "Pannenoisance qui siet sor la mer de Gales" (p. 24) — doubtless, Penzance, on the English Channel. The barons and knights assemble in great numbers and the new era of Arthur's glory opens with a greater adventure than his court had ever known before — namely, the adventure of the Grail. It commences in the following manner (pp. 24ff.):

Whilst the king and his retinue were seated at the table and only the first course had been served, there rode into the hall a damsel on a white mule. It turned out that this damsel was bald — only she concealed her baldness with a chaplet — having lost her hair because of Perceval's neglect to ask the questions touching the Grail, and that she would not recover her tresses until the Grail Winner should come to the Fisher King's castle. A second damsel, who accompanied her, carried on horseback a *brachet* (hound) and a richly bejewelled shield, which was striped with silver and azure bands and bore also a red cross. Still a third damsel, the most beautiful of all, was on foot and was constantly urging on the mounts of her companions with a whip. As is later disclosed, the shield is that of Joseph of Arimathea, and, in compliance with the damsel's directions, it is attached to a column in the hall, where it is to await the coming of the Grail Winner. The dog, too, is to remain in Arthur's castle;

shortened, p. 63, to *Parfez* by the uncle, who declares here already that Perceval is self-made.

it will never show signs of joy until the Grail Winner arrives.
The bald damsel now delivers to Arthur the greetings of the Fisher
King and explains to him, also, how Perceval's failure to ask
the questions had caused the illness of that mysterious monarch
and plunged his dominions in strife. Still further she calls Arthur's attention to a strange wagon outside, drawn by three white
stags, on which there lay the heads of one hundred and fifty
knights, some sealed in gold, some in silver and some in lead.[23]
These men had all been slain in consequence of Perceval's failure
(p. 27).

Having concluded their mission, the three damsels, followed
by the strange wagon, disappeared into the forest. Here, however, they soon meet Gawain (p. 30), whose steed and equipment
were in wretched condition from his long wanderings and numerous
combats. He, too, is on his way to the Fisher King's country,
and he grants the request of the bald damsel when she prays him
to act as their escort until they have passed the Black Hermit's
castle. Gawain is touched by the sufferings of the damsel on
foot and when he hears that these sufferings and other afflic-
tions of the land would end, if he should ask the fateful questions
and thereby undo the spell which rests on the land, he resolves
to undertake the adventure.

Space fails us to recount the exploits and experiences of
Gawain on his journey to the Grail castle, in the company of
the damsels and, afterwards, alone. Some of these episodes have
no real connection with the Grail story. Of those that do have
such a connection, the most important is the one (pp. 84 ff.) which
tells how Gawain obtained through the gratitude of the pagan
king, Gurgalan,[24] the sword with which St. John was beheaded.

---

[23] Nitze points out, MPh., XVII, 161, note, that this is imitated
from *Revelation*, VII, 3.

[24] The name is probably an alteration of *Murgalan(t)* — a
common name for pagan kings in the *chansons de geste*. Kittredge,
Arthur and Gorlagon (Harvard *Studies and Notes in Philology
and Literature*, VIII, pp. 203 f., tries to identify it with *Gorlagon*,
which he derives from the Welsh.

This sword (the Grail sword) bled every day at midday, since it was at that hour that St. John was executed. No one could enter the Grail castle without it (p. 86), says the Fisher King, when Gawain presents it to him.

On his arrival at the Grail castle, Gawain finds the Fisher King, as in Chrétien, reclining on a bed, and his niece, Perceval's sister, is, also, in the hall (pp. 86ff.). The king tells his visitor how his illness was due to Perceval's omission in regard to the questions, and begs him not to commit the same mistake. Perceval's sister, furthermore, thanks Gawain for the protection which he had recently afforded her mother against the assaults of the Lord of the Moors, but declares that this warfare is on the point of being renewed. Whilst they are at dinner, a girl bearing the Grail and another bearing the bleeding lance pass through the hall, two angels with candlesticks accompanying them. They disappear in a chapel, but soon return through the hall — only this time, it seemed to Gawain that the number of both girls and angels had increased to three. Moreover, he thinks now that he sees a child in the Grail, who soon undergoes the same transformation into the crucified Christ that Arthur had witnessed at St. Austin's chapel. This grievous sight had the unfortunate effect of so touching Gawain's heart that he forgot all about the questions — to such a degree, indeed, that when the Grail procession has again disappeared in the chapel and dinner is over, he indulges in an inopportune game with the chessmen of the magic chessboard[25] which he observes at the end of the room. After he had suffered two defeats at the hands of the automatic chessmen, a damsel enters the room and has the chessboard taken away, and he falls into a profound slumber, which lasts until mor-

---

[25] For a discussion of this *motif*, which occurs in five other Arthurian romances, cp. especially, Bruce, RR, IX, 375f. (1918). Cp., also, Vulgate *Merlin*, II, 246, taken from *Lancelot*, V, 149ff. The source of the present passage is, doubtless, Wauchier de Denain's continuation of Chrétien's *Perceval*, ll. 22442ff. The insertion of the incident at the most solemn point in Gawain's Grail quest is a proof of our author's bad judgment.

ning. He hears in the early morning the services that are held
in the Grail chapel on account of the sword of St. John, which
Gawain has brought to the Fisher King, but he is not allowed
to enter this chapel, and a damsel reproaches him with his neglect to ask the unspelling questions. Still further, a voice bids all
that are in the castle depart; the drawbridge, it declares, must
now be raised on account of the king of the Chastel Mortel, through
whom "the lion" (Fisher King) is to die (p. 90). Thus, like
Perceval, Gawain has failed in his quest.

After Gawain's quest of the Grail (pp. 30—90) follows that
of Lancelot (pp. 91—132), which is even more futile. The transition from the one to the other is formed by an incident in which
Gawain comes to Lancelot's rescue in an unequal combat of the
latter against four knights. The narrative of Lancelot's quest,
however, contains an even larger proportion of matter that is ex-
traneous to the main theme than is the case with Gawain's quest.[26]
Lancelot finally reaches the Grail castle and is introduced there
to the Fisher King (p. 130), who inquires of him about Perceval
and informs him that they (Lancelot and himself) are relatives.
Owing, however, to his sinful love for Guinevere, Lancelot is not
privileged to behold the Grail (p. 132).

The two knights who were most highly prized in Arthur's
court having failed in the Grail quest, it is now the turn of the
successful hero of this adventure to occupy the stage. Apart from
allusions — particularly to his abortive first visit to the Grail

---

[26] Cp., for example, the episodes (pp. 109ff.) in which Clamados
des Ombres and Melyot de Logres figure — also, the incident of
Lancelot and the beheading game (p. 103), which is not concluded,
however, until much later in the romance (p. 233). On this incident
cp. G. L. Kittredge, *Study of Sir Gawain and the Green Knight*,
pp. 52ff. (Cambridge, Mass., and London 1916). Cp., too, the episode
of the Castle of Beards (Ritho *motif*, Geoffrey's *Historia*, X, 3) pp.
97ff. In his "Spenser and Two Old French Grail Romances", PMLA,
XXVIII, 539ff. (1913), E. A. Hall maintains (wrongly, I believe) that
Spenser used this episode of the *Perlesvaus* in his *Faerie Queene*,
Book VI, Cantos 1—2.

castle[27] — Perceval had already figured in the story (pp. 105ff.) as suffering pangs of distress at the house of his hermit uncle (King Pelles) on account of his failure on that occasion and consequently confessing himself to his uncle, at the same time that he disclosed to him his identity. Then, on quitting Pelles' hermitage, he had fought an indecisive combat with his cousin, Lancelot (pp. 106f.), neither recognizing the other at first.

After many adventures, including those that render evident Perceval's identity with the long expected "Good Knight", who is to undo the spell of the Grail castle, he learns from his sister (p. 178) that the Fisher King is dead and that their wicked uncle, the King of the Chastel Mortel, has seized the Grail castle. She has just been informed of this by a miraculous voice at the chapel of the Perilous Cemetery, and the news is afterwards confirmed by a message from King Pelles (p. 185). Perceval, however, first slays his mother's oppressor, the Lord of the Moors (pp. 183f.), and achieves still other adventures,[28] before he settles down in

---

[27] Pp. 26, 30, 80, 86. Important, too, is the description of Perceval, though he is left unnamed, p. 37: "Il a chief d'or, et regart de Lion, et nombril de virge pucele et cuer d'acier et cors d'olifant, et tesches sans vileinnie." With some slight difference this description is repeated, too, pp. 197f. It has been taken over from the *Perlesvaus* into the *Livre d'Artus* of MS. 337 (Sommer, VII, 52). In the prose *Lancelot*, III, 27, besides, an interpolator has applied it to Galahad. Cp. Bruce, RR, IX, 267 (1918). This adaptation of the *Perlesvaus* passage to Galahad is not surprising, for two Paris MSS. adapt the opening episodes of that romance to the Galahad *Queste*. Cp. Nitze's dissertation, p. 7.

[28] Especially noteworthy are his deliverance (pp. 200ff.) of the Castle of the Golden Circlet (Cescle d'Or) from the Knight of the Burning Dragon and his conquest of the Copper Castle (pp. 202ff.). The golden circlet is really Our Savior's crown of thorns, which is awarded to Perceval as the prize of his victory. The Burning Dragon is the image of a dragon on its owner's shield, but this image emits real flames. The Copper Castle was an enchanted stronghold of evil spirits and its entrance was defended by two copper men with iron mallets. The author had a fondness for such automatic and other magical contrivances of a mechanical kind. For example, compare the two copper men who defend the entrance to the Fisher King's land

earnest to the redemption of the Grail castle. Nevertheless, he finally besieges the place and the King of the Chastel Mortel, driven to despair by the slaughter of his knights, commits suicide (p. 215). The knights of the Fisher King now return to the castle — also, the priests and damsels that were there before their lord's death.

After the recovery of the Grail castle, Perceval's mission was fulfilled and our author should have taken example from the *Queste* and transported his hero at once to the New Jerusalem on the Ille Plenteureusse (p. 330). On the contrary, he now plunges afresh into a series of adventures — many of them pointless and wholly out of harmony with the spirit of a true romance of the Grail — the heroes of which are, in turn, Arthur, Gawain and Lancelot, and not merely Perceval. Especially prominent among such adventures is the episode of Brians des Illes' intrigues — temporarily successful — to undermine Lancelot with Arthur (pp. 273 ff.). At last, however, the ship which was destined to bear Perceval away from human sight appears at the Grail castle, where his mother and sister had already died and were buried. He embarked in this vessel and the writer avers (p. 347) that no earthly man knew after that what had become of him. Moreover, the Grail disappeared from its wonted place and was seen no more. Notwithstanding these declarations of our author, it is manifest that the voyage of both the Grail knight and the Grail, according to his conception, was to the mysterious isle which Perceval had visited before (pp. 328 ff.). Its inhabitants were all of one age and clad in white garments, marked with red crosses, that are reminiscent of the Knights Templars. Thence, doubtless, they passed to the adjacent isle, the Ille Plenteureusse (Bounteous Isle), where the good were separated from the wicked. These islands constitute, it would seem, a sort of mystic abode for the Grail

---

(p. 64) and the turning castle invented by Virgil (pp. 197 f.). There are still other automata, pp. 71—73. On turning castles see G. Huet, "Le Chasteau Tournant dans la suite du *Merlin*" *Romania*, XL, 235 ff. (1911), and on copper men, Bruce, "Human Automata in Classical Tradition and Mediaeval Romance", MPh., X, 511 ff. (1913).

company [29] — an ante-chamber, as it were, to the New Jerusalem — but even here it was possible to miss eternal joy and there was another isle reserved for the wicked who had been expelled from the Bounteous Isle and filled with weeping and lamentation as that was with bliss.

The *Perlesvaus,* like the Vulgate *Queste,* was evidently written by an ecclesiastic and is strongly ascetic in its tendencies. Love is, accordingly, totally excluded from its pages. Owing to his abhorrence of adultery, the author, as we shall see, makes only brief allusions to the loves of Lancelot and Guinevere and rejects the whole traditional conclusion of the Arthurian story. It was, indeed, this abhorrence, no doubt, that caused him, in the first instance, to dethrone the newcomer, Galahad, the child of an adulterous connection, and restore Perceval to his original place — a Perceval, however, wholly chaste, as was not the case with Chrétien's hero — at least, in the earlier phases of his career.

Apart from the ascetic, we observe a specifically ecclesiastical bias in every part of this romance. Not only are the Grail and the objects pertaining thereto here thoroughly Christianized,[30] but in the Grail chapel there are still other holy relics (p. 217), and the hermits of the forest hold regular mass there three times a week (p. 249), as they might have done in any other church. Similarly the ideal island realm [31] whither Perceval and the Grail are

---

[29] Two white-haired old men, who greeted Perceval there on his first visit, show adoration on beholding Perceval's shield and tell him (p. 328) that they knew its former owner (Joseph of Arimathea) even before the crucifixion of Christ.

[30] It is not definitely stated anywhere in the romance whether the Grail was identified with the cup or the dish of the Last Supper. Probably the author, himself, had formed no clear conception on the subject. P. 54, the Grail receives the blood that flowed from the lance; p. 88, Gawain sees the Christ child in the sacred vessel, and later (p. 89) the vessel seems to have turned into the crucified Savior. The lance is obviously the lance of the crucifixion, but the Grail sword is here the weapon with which St. John was beheaded (pp. 74f. 86, 217). Our Lord, it is said (pp. 216f.) loved the Grail chapel.

[31] Heinzel, p. 172, has plausibly surmised that the conception of the isles and the monastery was suggested by the legend of St. Brendan.

transferred at the end of the romance and where they are to abide
henceforth (pp. 330, 347) is plainly a monastic state, although
the realm is a spiritual one.

Furthermore, the hero of the romance is a propagator of the
Christian faith (New Law), even at the point of the sword (p. 217),
and Arthur and his knights exhibit an equal zeal in proselyti-
zation (p. 3).

On the other hand, the *Perlesvaus* differs from the *Queste,*
inasmuch as a large proportion of the narrative is given up to episodes that are purely secular in character and that have no real
bearing upon the Grail quest. This is true especially of the portion
that follows upon the death of the Fisher King (pp. 176f.) —
that is to say, the second half of the romance. After that event
there was no valid reason why the story of the quest should not
have been concluded in relatively few pages with Perceval's capture
of the Grail castle, but so brief an entertainment would have,
doubtless, disappointed the expectations of the author's noble patrons, so that he is obliged to extend his narrative by imitating
Chrétien and his continuators and adding to the Grail story, which
he had really exhausted, a series of virtually disconnected episodes,
many of which not only have no relation to the Grail, but no
relation even to the hero, himself. Thus an analysis that limits
itself to the Grail episodes of the *Perlesvaus* gives a false idea
of the work. Nevertheless, the writer evidently intended his romance as primarily a Grail romance, for not only is the quest
of the sacred vessel incomparably the most important element in
the work, but he begins it with the Grail and ends it with the
Grail, and it is the current interest in this theme, obviously, that
prompted him to the composition of his romance. Through the
prominence which he gives to the Grail theme, he attains a comparative unity of design that is wanting in Chrétien's poem, as in
the other Arthurian romances of the biographical type.

From the point of view of style, the *Perlesvaus* is inferior
to the *Queste,* not only in sombre strength, but in unity of spirit
and design. A large proportion of its adventures are, in essentials,
repetitions of well-known *motifs* of the Arthurian romances. More-

over, these adventures are not merely of a secular nature, and hence out of harmony with the deep mysticism of the central theme, as has just been remarked, but they are insipid in themselves and manifestly inserted simply to lengthen out the romance.

As a good illustration of the author's want of judgment and of the low level on which his imagination moves, one might cite the conclusion which he has given to the Grail *Quest;* for the Fisher King — the mystical figure who is the guardian of the sacred vessel and whose health is bound up in so strange a manner with the fateful questions — perishes here in war like any ordinary monarch and the final achievement of the Grail adventure contains no mystical elements, but consists merely of the capture of a castle (the Grail castle) by force of arms — such an incident as occurs in scores of other episodes in Arthurian romance, as well as in the actual life of the age. The magical *motif* seems hardly worth inventing, if this was to be the end of the adventure.

Even worse is the writer's rejection of the time-honored tradition concerning the destruction of Arthur and his knights as the consequence of Guinevere's adultery — one of the finest tragical themes in European literature. Probably, reprobating, as an ecclesiastic, the interest which this conception had generally inspired and the dominant place which love had held in Arthurian tradition, the author sets it aside altogether and represents Guinevere as dying from grief whilst her consort's glory is at its height — because of the murder of her son, Lohot, by Kay.[32]

---

[32] Cp. *Perlesvaus*, pp. 169f., 219, 221f. For a discussion of Lohot in Arthurian romance (including the *Perlesvaus* passages) cp. Bruce, "Arthuriana", RR, III, 179ff. (1912), and (less fully) G. Huet, "Deux Personnages Arturiens", *Romania*, XLIII, 100ff. (1914). — For the sources of the *Perlesvaus*, in general. cp. Part IV, below.

Chapter XI.
Palamedes and Other Late Romances.

1. The *Palamedes*[1] is an offshoot of the prose *Tristan,* and, in respect to date, it falls, apparently, between the composition of that romance in its original form, and the cyclic redaction of the same.[2] Owing to the insignificant rôle which Palamedes plays in the work, as it has survived to us, Paulin Paris[3] was led to conjecture that the current title of the romance became attached to it through

---

[1] For the MSS. and early prints of this romance cp. Löseth, *Le roman en prose de Tristan,* pp. 433 ff. and *Le Tristan et le Palamède des manuscrits français du British Museum,* pp. 29 ff. Of the MSS. twelve are in the Bibliothèque Nationale, three in the Arsenal Library (Paris) and two in the British Museum. Only two — MS. 350, Bibl. Nat. and Arsenal 3325 — go back to the thirteenth century. For the early prints of the two divisions of *Palamedes* see note 5, below. The work has not been printed since the sixteenth century, so that we are dependent for our knowledge of it on Löseth's analysis in his *Le roman en prose de Tristan,* etc. pp. 436 ff. For a briefer analysis cp. Dunlop-Wilson, I, 188 ff., 233 ff.

[2] The character, Palamedes, is drawn from the *Tristan.* So, too, Meliadus and many others. The dependence of the romance on the original prose *Tristan,* indeed, is not open to question, although, as G. Paris, *Huth-Merlin,* I, pp. XXXV ff., has shown, the epilogue found in certain MSS. of the latter, which attribute the authorship to Helie de Borron, is modelled after the prologue to *Palamedes.* This epilogue, however, was plainly of late origin. — *Tristan* influences in the *Palamedes,* as far as has been pointed out, are none of them derived from the cyclic version of the former.

[3] *Manuscrits François de la Bibliothèque du Roi,* II, 351 (Paris, 1838). He, consequently, always calls the romance *Guiron le Courtois,* since Guiron is the most prominent character in the book, and many scholars have followed him. In its prologue, however, the work is expressly named *Palamedes.* Cp. Hucher, I, 159. — Even the MSS. do not preserve to us the romance in its original form; the earlier prints give us merely a selection of episodes from the MSS.

some misunderstanding. Even if this conjecture, however, is correct, the error is one of long standing, for in a letter of the year 1240,[4] the German emperor, Frederick II, refers to it by that title. In any event, at an early date, the work was divided into two parts, known, respectively, as *Meliadus de Leonnoys* and *Guiron le Courtois*, which in the sixteenth century were printed as separate romances.[5] The author of *Palamedes* is unknown, for the ascription to a pretended Helie, which occurs in the prologue, is, without doubt, fraudulent.[6]

---

[4] In this letter, dated Feb. 5, the emperor thanks the Segreto of Messina for sending him a book that had formerly belonged to one Johannes Romanzorius. The passage which concerns us — quoted in Ward's *Catalogue*, I, 366 — reads: "De LIV quaternis scriptis de libro Palamidis qui fuerunt quondam magistri Johannis Romanzori, quos nobis per notarium Symonem de Petramajore mictere te scripsisti, gratum ducimus et acceptum."

[5] *Guiron le Courtois* was published at Paris by A. Verard about 1501, *Meliadus* in 1528 by Galliot du Pre, and in 1532, by D. Janot. P. Rajna, *Le Fonti dell' Orlando Furioso*[2], p. 61, mentions two other editions of *Guiron*, one of them from about 1501, the other from 1529.

In the 1528 edition of *Meliadus* the prologue described above, I, 486 f., is attributed by the publisher to Rusticien de Pise, instead of to Helie de Borron. The substitution is due to the fact, no doubt, that this publisher found in his MS. the preamble of Rusticien's compilation inserted at the beginning of *Guiron* and inferred from this circumstance that the above-mentioned prologue was, in reality, by the Italian writer. On these matters see, especially, Löseth, p. 435.

[6] Cp. G. Paris, *Huth-Merlin*, I, pp. XXXIII ff. The prologue has been printed in full by Hucher, I, 156 ff. Cp., too (more briefly), P. Paris, *Manuscrits François de la Bibliothèque du Roi*, II, 346 ff. and Ward's Catalogue, I, 365. On its relation to the *Tristan* epilogue, cp. I, p. 486, note 9, above. For a variant form of this prologue in a Turin MS. cp. P. Rajna, *Romania*, IV, 264. As G. Paris, *loc. cit.*, note 3, remarks, the "Gasse li blons", referred to in the prologue vaguely as a writer of Arthurian romance, is, doubtless, Wace (Guace), author of the *Brut*.

Rusticien de Pise has been frequently spoken of by scholars as the author of *Palamedes (Guiron le Courtois)*. Cp., for example, Dunlop-Wilson, I, 188, 233, Gröber, *Grundriss*, Band II, Abt. I, p. 1008, Golther, *Tristan und Isolde*, p. 130. But, as we have seen,

According to the romance, the father of Palamedes is a Babylonian nobleman, named Esclabor, who, as part of a tribute, is sent to the imperial court at Rome and wins the good graces of the emperor there by saving his life, but, in so doing, excites the jealous ill-will of certain courtiers. These same courtiers murder the emperor's nephew and try to fix the blame of the affair on the Babylonian. After the real murderer, however, has been exposed and executed, Esclabor, with the emperor's consent, sails for Logres (Britain), disembarks in Northumberland, saves the life of Pellinor (Perceval's father), king of that country, and goes on to Camelot. This was not long after the coronation of Arthur. At this point we are regaled with the adventures of Pharamont, King of Gaul, an enemy of Arthur's, who comes to his court in disguise, displays his prowess there, and, although finally recognized, continues to be treated with the greatest courtesy. Furthermore, we are told here of the brilliant exploits of Meliadus (who gives his name to the first division of the romance), King of Leonois and father of *Tristan* — especially, how he had repulsed Uterpendragon's army, when it was besieging Pharamont. We learn here, likewise, of Meliadus's rival, Le Chevalier Sans Peur — one of the chief characters in the book —

Palamedes was already in existence by 1240 and Rusticien merely incorporated the romance into his compilation. Cp. G. Paris, *Manuel*, p. 110, and Löseth, pp. 432 ff. Rusticien, himself, wrote the *Travels of Marco Polo* in 1298, so belonged to the next generation. In its preamble and epilogue — cp. Löseth, pp. 433, 472, respectively — his compilation is called *Meliadus* — but that is, no doubt, in consequence of an error, like the one which has caused Malory's compilation to go under a name *(Morte Darthur)* that belongs properly to only a part of the whole.

Having regard to the date of the composition of *Palamedes (Guiron le Courtois)* — the second quarter of the thirteenth century — we should naturally identify with Henry III, the "noble roi Henry d'Engleterre", who is referred to as the author's patron in the prologue to that romance (Hucher I, 156). The reference, however, is, doubtless, purely fictitious and imitated from the end of the Vulgate *Queste* or opening of the Vulgate *Mort Artu*, where the King Henry referred to is Henry II.

a knight from the border of Gaul and Little Britain, on whom
Uterpendragon had bestowed the kingdom of Estrangorre. Incidents of a supernatural character are entirely excluded from the
first division of *Palamedes* — otherwise, however, the adventures
are of the usual type. Especially prominent in this first division
are the abductions of noble ladies. Thus Meliadus, who is a skilful poet and musician, like his more famous son, *Tristan*, woos
the queen of Scotland in lays, carries on a clandestine love-affair
with her at Arthur's court and when the husband discovers her
adultery and tries to take her back to Scotland, waylays them
and bears her off to Leonois. In the war that follows this abduction, Arthur joins the enemies of Meliadus and the abductor
was on the point of being made captive, when the hero of the
second part of the romance, Guiron le Courtois, intervenes and
saves the situation. After this the figure of Meliadus is secondary in the story.

In this first part of *Palamedes*, it was, of course, the romancer's aim, in the manner which was general with the authors
of the cyclic romances, to exploit the interest of his public in
an older popular hero — Tristan — in favor of his own inventions,
by making the central character in his work the father of that
hero. The influence of the *Tristan* poems, whether directly or
indirectly (through the *Mort Artu*), is, moreover, manifest in detail even in the meagre outline given above. Similarly, the author
introduces into his narrative the fathers of other famous characters of Arthurian romance — e. g., Lac (Erec's father), Pellinor
(here, as in the prose *Tristan*, represented as Perceval's father)[7] —
or confers on older knights in his story names that had been already rendered illustrious in romance by heroes of the next generation — e. g. Perceval and Lamorat.[8]

In the creation of Guiron le Courtois,[9] the author of *Pala-*

---

[7] Cp. e. g. pp. 450, 444, respectively, *et passim.*
[8] Cp. e. g. pp. 444, 443 ff., respectively, *et passim.*
[9] Guiron enters the story at Löseth, p. 447. His name is probably derived from the hero, Goron (Gurun, etc.), of the famous lay.
Cp. Bédier's edition of Thomas's *Tristan*, I, 51 ff.

medes set himself the praiseworthy task of drawing a type of
perfect fidelity in love and friendship. The hero demonstrates
his perfection in the latter relation by the self-restraint which
he exhibits in his conduct towards the wife of his unworthy friend,
Danain of Maloaut (Maloanc). When she has been consigned to
his care by her husband, in the latter's absence, he not only protects her against the violence of an importunate lover (Lac), but,
what was far more difficult, he was able to resist the temptations
of his own and her passion and preserve his loyalty to his friend.[10]
It is true that he was on the point of succumbing, when an accident drew his attention to the hilt of his sword and he read there
the fortifying inscription: "Loyalty surpasses everything; falsity
dishonors everything." Overcome with remorse at the thought of
the act of disloyalty which he had been about to commit, he plunges
his sword into his own bosom, but, fortunately, without fatal
effects. At this juncture, Danain, having heard a false report
concerning the relations of his friend and his wife, returns. Guiron
avows his part in the affair, whilst suppressing that of the lady,
and so receives the husband's pardon. Unaffected, however, by
this example of loyal friendship Danain does not scruple some
time later to carry off Bloie, Guiron's lady-love. In rescuing her,
Guiron again gives a proof of his generosity by dismissing his
false friend unharmed — a favor which the latter subsequently
requites in a more honorable fashion than might have been expected by delivering the former as well as Bloie from an enemy.

Guiron, on his father's side, was a descendant of Clovis, King
of Gaul, through Febus, a famous warrior, who abandoned the
throne of that country to pursue the life of a knight-errant. On
his mother's side, he belonged to the Grail family. The scene in
the cavern of the aged anchorites — Guiron's grandfather, father,
and cousin (once king of Gaunes) — where these revelations concerning the hero's ancestry are made to Brehus sans Pitie is one
of the most striking in the book and serves to connect the hero
with the most hallowed traditions of Arthurian romance.

---

[10] Pp. 449 ff.

Dunlop has spoken of the earlier part of *Guiron le Courtois*
as "perhaps the finest of all the old fabulous histories of Britain."
Certainly, it was one of the most popular of the Arthurian romances, being exceeded in this respect, if at all, only by the *Tristan*
and *Lancelot*. Like these romances, it supplied materials to the
genius of Boiardo[11] and Ariosto[12] in the age of the Renaissance.
Indeed, it was Ariosto's favorite among all the Arthurian romances.[13] Still further, it furnished the basis for a poem[14] by
another Italian poet of the same period, Luigi Alamanni, which
was undertaken at the request of Francis I, King of France,
Even as late as the eighteenth century this expression of the ideals
of a society that had vanished centuries before still had the power
to captivate the fancy of Wieland and inspire him to one of the
most charming narrative efforts[15] of the Romantic Revival in Germany.[16]

---

[11] All the chief Old French Arthurian romances in prose were
accessible at the library of the princes of Este in Ferrara in the
fifteenth and sixteenth centuries. For the fifteenth century catalogues
of this library cp. Giulio Bertoni's *Nuovi Studi su Matteo Maria
Boiardo*, ch. VII (Bologna, 1904), and for the indebtedness of Boiardo's
L'Orlando Innamorato to *Palamedes (Guiron le Courtois)* see *ibid.*,
ch. VIII.

[12] Cp. the Index to Pio Rajna's *Le Fonti dell' Orlando Furioso*[2]
(Firenze, 1900) under *Palamedes*.

[13] Cp. Rajna, pp. 60 ff. First came *Palamedes*, next *Tristan*,
thirdly, *longo intervallo*, *Lancelot*.

[14] *Gyrone il Cortese* (1548). The author followed almost sla-
vishly the 1501 print (A. Verard). For everything pertaining to this
poem cp. H. Hauvette, *Luigi Alamanni*, pp. 319 ff. (Paris, 1903).
For two early Italian prose translations of *Guiron le Courtois* cp.
Rajna, p. 62. Only one has been printed (Firenze, 1855, edited by
F. Tassi). *Meliadus* was, also, translated into Italian prose and
published at Venice, 1558—1560.

[15] *Geron der Adelige* (1777), based on the version of the Old
French romance as given in Comte de Tressan's *Bibliothèque Uni-
verselle des Romans* (1775—89).

[16] Another offshoot of the prose Tristan, which, since it was
composed in the fourteenth century, falls outside of the limit of the
present work is *Isaie (Ysaye) le Triste*. On the date of the romance,

2. The Compilation of Rusticiano da Pisa.

The bulk of this vast compilation,[17] in the fragmentary form
in which it has come down to us, is made up, in a large measure,
of the *Palamedes,* so that, as has already been stated above,[18]
through misunderstandings, the compilation has appropriated to
itself even in the MSS. the name — *Meliadus* — of the first
division of that romance, and, *vice versa,* the *Palamedes* has been
often ascribed to the author of the compilation.

According to its preamble[19] the work was compiled by Rusticien de Pise (Rusticiano da Pisa) — designated here, also, "le
maistre" — who "translated" it from a book of "my lord, Edward, King of England, at the time that he [Edward I] went
overseas in the service of our Lord God to conquer the Holy Se-
pulchre." It is further declared that the author is going to deal
especially with Lancelot and Tristan, since they were the most
distinguished knights of their age, and that he will tell a good
deal more about them than one will find in any other books.

The Rusticien de Pise, here mentioned, is, obviously, identical with the person of that name who, whilst a fellow-cap-
tive of Marco Polo's at Genoa in 1298, wrote down in French

---

cp. Julius Zeidler, *Der Prosaroman Ysaye le Triste,* p. 6 (Halle diss.
1901). Zeidler has, also, given a full analysis of this romance in
the *Zs. f. rom. Ph.* XXV, 175 ff., 472 ff., 641 ff. (1901). For briefer
analyses cp. Dunlop-Wilson, I, 212 ff., and Golther, *Tristan und Isolde,*
pp. 131 ff., and for the critical literature pertaining to it cp. Gröber's
Grundriss, Band II, Abt. I, p. 1010, note 2. On the early prints of
this romance see, especially, *Romania,* XXIII, 86. — Isaie le Triste
is the son of Tristan and Iseult of Cornwall. He is born shortly after
his mother has heard of the fatal wounding of Tristan by Marc. In
her sorrow she directs that her son shall be baptized with the above-
mentioned name, which is suggestive of the names of both parents,
and, at the same time, suits the sorrowful circumstances of his birth.
A few days later both Tristan and Iseult die. A hermit rears the
hero, whose adventures, of course, make up the romance.
[17] For an analysis of it cp. Löseth, pp. 423 ff. For indications
regarding the MSS. and regarding the early prints of *Meliadus* and
Guiron that contain parts of the compilation, cp. *ibid.,* p. 423, note 1.
    [18] Pp. 21 f., note 6.   [19] Löseth, pp. 423 f.

the latter's recital of his Oriental travels. Moreover, Edward I, here referred to, went on his crusade in August, 1270, and did not return to England until August, 1274, although he became king on the death of his father, Henry III, in November, 1272. He was in Palestine from May, 1271 to August, 1272. Now, there is no reason to question the accuracy of the statement which we have just quoted or to doubt that Rusticien, writing certainly after November, 1272, and most probably after August, 1274,[20] had before him one of the Arthurian compilations that had begun to come into existence about the middle of the thirteenth century.[21] He probably acquired it during Edward's stay in Sicily in 1271. To what degree, however, he may have modified his original or how much he may have added to it either from other works or from the resources of his own imagination must remain a matter of conjecture. We know that his compilation, as it stands, embraces, besides the *Palamedes,* considerable portions of the *Tristan.*[22] On the other hand, what is not taken over from these two romances, whether it be the production of Rusticien, himself, or another's, is so destitute of originality that the question of its provenience possesses little or no importance. Perhaps, the episode of most interest in the work is the curious one with which it opens[23] — the adventures of Branor le Brun, the giant knight, one hundred and twenty years old, who wishes to test the valor of the younger generation and so appears at Arthur's court with a crowned damsel, beautiful and richly clad, challenges Arthur's

---

[20] We have no means of determining the downward limit of date. One would judge, however, from the tone of the reference to Edward's crusade that that expedition already belonged to a rather distant past. The compilation, however, doubtless, antedates the *Travels of Marco Polo* (1298).

[21] The cyclic *Tristan* is, in reality, such a compilation. MS. 112 (Bibl. Nat.) and Malory are fifteenth century specimens of the same *genre.*

[22] Cp., for example, Löseth, p. 468.

[23] Löseth, pp. 424 ff. The preamble states expressly that the episode is taken from the "livre d'Engleterre" -- i. e. King Edward's book.

chief knights to enter into a contest with him for this damsel, and
vanquishes them all in succession — Gawain, Tristan, Lancelot,
along with the rest. By a singular fortune, this extravagant
episode is the only specimen of Arthurian romance, as far as we
know, that penetrated into Byzantine literature. There, in a version of about the year 1300,[24] we find it presented in Greek verses
(306 lines), which are so strongly colored with Homeric phrasing
and imagery that the lines produce the impression of a bombastic
travesty of the style of the *Iliad*.

3. Les Prophécies de Merlin.

The prose work which bears the above name, although usually referred to as a romance,[25] is entitled only in part to that

---

[24] It was first edited (with a Latin translation) from the unique
Vatican MS. (about 1300), under the title of *Poema graecum de
rebus gestis regis Arturi Tristani Lanceloti, Galbani Palamedis
aliorumque equitum Tabulae Rotundae*, by F. H. von der Hagen,
Berlin, 1821. The text has since been reprinted by 1. its first editor
(Berlin, 1824), 2. F. Michel, in his edition of the *Tristan* poems,
II, 267 ff. (1835), 3. L. G. Visscher, in his edition of the thirteenth
century Dutch romance, *Ferguut*, pp. 198 ff. (Utrecht, 1836),
4. A. Ellissen: *Nachtrag zum ersten Teil des Versuchs einer Poly-
glotte der europäischen Poesie* (Leipzig, 1846), under the title,
῾Ο πρέσβυς ἱππότης. Ellissen gives the most correct text and his
introduction is very valuable. The poem is written in the so-called
„political" verse (catalectic iambic tetrameter), the favorite metre of
Greek popular poetry. The first person to point out the true source
of the work was L. K. Struve, in a review of von der Hagen's edition,
Kritische Bibliothek. For an analysis of the poem see M. A. C. Gidel:
*Études sur la littérature grecque moderne; imitations en grec de
nos romans de chevalerie depuis le XIIe siècle*, pp. 79 ff. (Paris,
1866). The Greek poet has altered and shortened his French original.
See, still further, on this work Krumbacher, *Geschichte der Byzan-
tinischen Literatur*[3], pp. 866 f. (Munich, 1897). Both Gidel and
Krumbacher, however, wrongly assign the French romance to the
twelfth century.

[25] So, for instance, in Miss L. A. Paton's "Notes on Manuscripts
of the *Prophecies de Merlin*", PMLA, XXVIII, 121 ff. (1913), which
is much the most instructive study of the book that has yet appeared.

designation, and, consequently, a summary description of its contents will suffice for our purpose. It is not to be confounded with Geoffrey of Monmouth's *Libellus Merlini* (later incorporated in his *Historia* as Book VII) or with the numerous pseudo-prophetic writings of a political nature, ascribed to Merlin and imitated from Geoffrey's *Libellus*, that were issued during the Middle Ages.[26] According to the principal authority on the subject, "the *Prophecies* consists of historical prophecies and teachings derived from the stock of encyclopaedic material of the Middle Ages, delivered by Merlin either in dialogue form or in writing to various definitely named personages; among these prophecies and teachings are interspersed anecdotes usually designed to set forth the weaknesses of the clergy or to illustrate the supernatural gifts of Merlin, and also romantic episodes recounting adventures of Arthurian heroes — a unique production even in an age of extraordinary compilations."[27]

The items that make up this strange medley differ very considerably in the different MSS. and early prints.[28] This applies, particularly, to the romantic episodes that are interspersed among

---

Cp., too, Ward's *Catalogue*, I, 371 ff. (1883), and Ireneo Sanesi, *Storia di Merlino*, pp. LVII ff. (*Biblioteca storica della letteratura*, III, Bergamo, 1898). For MSS. and early prints see Paton, pp. 122 ff. It was first printed in 1498 (Paris, A. Verard) as Vol. 3 of the *Romans de Merlin* — so, too, likewise, in the sixteenth century. For the fifteenth and sixteenth century Italian translations, cp. Paton, p. 124. One of them has been edited by Sanesi, *op. cit.* Miss Paton cites, also, as a Spanish version, *Las Profecias del sabio Merlin*, printed by A. Bonilla y San Martin in the *Libros de Caballerias Primera Parte: Ciclo — arturico = ciclo carolingio*, pp. 155—162 (Madrid, 1907). This, however, is very brief. She enumerates, pp. 122 ff., twelve MSS. of the French work, the earliest of which seems to belong to the latter part of the thirteenth century.

Miss Paton in her study mentions that she is preparing an edition of the *Prophecies*, but it has not yet appeared.

[26] For those of English origin, cp. Rupert Taylor, *The Political Prophecy in England* (New York, 1911).

[27] Paton, *op. cit.*, p. 122.

[28] Cp. Paton, pp. 125 f.

the prophecies, although they have no real connection with the latter. The only portions of the book that have been printed since the sixteenth century are two such episodes — viz., the adventures of Alexandre l'Orphelin (Alexander the Orphan) and the great tournament of Galehaut (Lancelot's friend).[29] In both Palamedes plays a part and both are, by origin, merely, late additions to the prose *Tristan*.[30] In the first—which alone possesses any interest — we have a narrative of the adventures in fighting and in love of Alexander, a nephew of King Marc of Cornwall, whose father (Marc's brother) had been killed by the latter and whose own life that monarch, also, vainly endeavored to take through a series of years.

The book purports to be a translation from a Latin original by a certain Master Richard of Ireland at the command of the Emperor Frederick II (1215—1250). The first assertion is merely the customary fiction which we meet with in virtually all the prose romances and the declaration as to the author and the circumstances under which the work was written may be equally untrustworthy. Some color of credibility, however, is given to this declaration by the fact that the prophecies which the compilation contains, when they are not purely romantic, usually relate, for the most part, to Italy and the Holy Land.[31]

---

[29] Sommer has edited them, from the British Museum MSS. Add. 25434 and Harley 1629, in his edition of Malory's *Morte Darthur*, III, 295ff. (1891). The episodes in question are, also, to be found in Malory, Book X, ch. 32—39 and *ibid*, ch. 40, etc., respectively.

[30] For *Alexandre l'Orphelin* in *Tristan* and *Palamedes* MSS., cp. Löseth, pp. 186, 481.

[31] Cp. Ward, p. 371. We know, too, that there was a Magister Riccardus attached to Frederick's court. But many of the prophecies, as Miss Paton observes, p. 128, would have been unpleasing to Frederick. Whether we accept the above-mentioned declaration as authentic or not, the work was probably composed in the second quarter of the thirteenth century. The two episodes edited by Sommer are, beyond question, dependent on the prose *Tristan*. With our present information, however, one cannot say positively that they belonged to the book in its original form.

4. Le Chevalier du Papegau.

This insignificant romance[32] is to be numbered among the later prose romances of the Arthurian cycle. The only MS. in which it has survived belongs to the fifteenth century and there is little likelihood that the date of its composition was much earlier. In the main, we have here a mere rehash of the old familiar *motifs* — the deliverance of distressed damsels, the slaying of giants and dragons, etc. — and almost the only originality to which the work may lay claim is through the occasional addition of some new absurdity. Two such additions are, perhaps, especially worth recording — namely, (1) the conception of the Fish-Knight, a sea monster which is made up of a knight, his horse and equipment — all of flesh, and all of one piece, so that when the shield, for example, is pierced, it drips blood, (2) the dwarf's son who becomes a giant, because he is suckled in the forest by a kindly unicorn. The hero of the romance is King Arthur himself — here represented as going forth just after his coronation and having the same sort of career as a knight-errant that in the other Arthurian romances is ascribed to his knights. He acquires his nickname (Knight of the Parrot) from a parrot which he captures from a knight and which, with a dwarf as its keeper, he carries about with him in his travels. Both the parrot and the

---

[32] In the unique MS. 2154 (f. fr., Bibl. Nat.) it is entitled, in a later hand, *Le Conte du Papegaulx qui contient les premieres Aventures qui auindrent au bon Roy Artus.* G. Paris was the first person to call attention to it — viz. in his analysis of the romance HLF, XXX, 103 ff. Since then it has been edited by Ferdinand Heuckenkamp under the title of *Le Chevalier du Papegau* (Halle, 1896). In this edition the text covers 90 pages. The editor (p. LVI) is inclined to assign the work to the fourteenth century. The author seems to have drawn, in part, from a lost French metrical romance, which was used, also, by the German poet, Wirnt von Grafenberg, in his *Wigalois*, Cp. F. Saran, "Über Wirnt von Grafenberg und den Wigalois", PBB, XXI, 253 ff. (1896) — especially, pp. 336 ff. — and Heuckenkamp, pp. XXIX ff. — The romance, doubtless, falls in a period later than that with which the present treatise deals, but I include it here because G. Paris discusses it in his well-known work on the Arthurian romances.

dwarf are great cowards and there is some humor in the reproaches of the bird, when the dwarf takes to his heels at the first scent of danger, forgetting completely his charge, which, however, is fully as much frightened as its keeper. In ordinary times, however, the parrot regales Arthur in his wanderings with the most beautiful songs that were ever heard.

Chapter XII.
Historia Meriadoci and De Ortu Waluuanii.

We may assign to the middle or second half of the thirteenth century the above-named romances in Latin prose,[1] both of which reveal, clearly a dependence on the prose *Tristan* — more particularly, in respect to nomenclature.[2] That they are the productions of a single author — probably an Englishman — is manifest, still further, from considerations of language, style and narrative method.[3] Just as in the later stages of the devel-

---

[1] Edited by J. D. Bruce in *Ergänzungsreihe*, 2. Heft, of the Johns Hopkins Press series, *Hesperia* (Göttingen and Baltimore, 1913). This edition supersedes, in every respect, the same editor's previous editions of these romances in PMLA, XIII, 365 ff. (1898) and XV, 327 ff. (1900). In the former place, the *De Ortu* was published; in the latter the *Historia Meriadoci*, under the erroneous title, *Vita Meriadoci*. Both romances are preserved in the Cottonian MS. of the British Museum, Faustina B. VI, (early fourteenth century); the *Meriadoc* is contained, also, in the Bodleian MS., Rawlinson — B. 149 (written about the year 1400).

[2] Leaving aside names of Welsh origin, the author of the *Meriadoc*, imitating the opening episodes of the prose *Tristan*, draws the names of his characters partly from Arthurian sources, partly from early French history. It is particularly significant that both the French and the Latin romance should, each, contain a king of Cornwall, named Meroveus and a subject of Meroveus named Sadoc. These names, of course, do not occur in the authentic history of Cornwall. On the name, *Sadoc*, cp. I, 492, note 26, above.

Similarly the names *Nabor* and *Buzafarnan* (corruption of *Nabuzardan*) in the *De Ortu* are derived from the prose *Tristan*.

On these questions of nomenclature, cp. Bruce, pp. XXI ff. — H. Suchier, *Literarisches Zentralblatt* for 1898, col. 980, derives the name *Egesarius* (alternative name of the pagan chieftain, Buzarfarnan, from the Eishere of the Monk of St. Gall (ninth century). Eishere was a giant who spitted his foes on a spear, like little birds.

[3] Cp. Bruce's edition, pp. VII ff. The Welsh mountains give the background of the *Meriadoc*, and the distinctive names in this romance

opment of the Charlemagne epic, the theme of the *Chanson de
Roland* acquires standing in learned circles and receives at the
hands of a cleric, in the poem, *Carmen de Proditione*, a Latin
dress, so here in the decline of Arthurian romance we find certain
themes of this species of literature passing, likewise, into similar
hands. In both cases, very likely, the authors were inspired with
the mistaken notion that, by clothing these subjects in a learned
language, they would impart to them a dignity and permanence
which they could not attain in the vernacular. In any event, the
author of the two Arthurian fictions is intoxicated with the exu-
berance of his own rhetoric and is quite unaware of the fact that the
main interest of his compositions is that they preserve for us in
translation the materials of romances in the vernacular which otherwise would have perished. It must be said, too, that they possess

---

are Welsh (cp. Bruce, p. XXVIII, note 1) but, as Ward, *Catalogue*,
I, 375, points out, the author could not have been a Welshman, since
he says that *Snowdon* is the Welsh name of the famous mountain.
As a matter of fact, in Welsh it is called *Eryri*. On the other hand,
the following circumstances favor the supposition that the work originated in Great Britain: 1. The only extant MSS. are in England.
2. The word *chiula*, for *ship*, which is here employed (*De Ortu*,
p. 74), occurs apparently only in writings of British origin.

   In the sixteenth century John Bale, *Index Britanniae Scriptorum*,
pp. 384f. (edited by R. L. Poole and Mary Bateson as Part IX of the
Anecdota Oxoniensia: Mediaeval and Modern Series, Oxford, 1902),
ascribed these romances to Robertus de Monte or Robert de Torigni,
as he is variously called — the well-known chronicler and abbot of
Mont Saint Michel in Normandy from 1154 to 1186. An attempt to
establish the correctness of this ascription was made by Miss M. S.
Morriss in her paper, "The authorship of the *De Ortu Waluuanii*
and the *Historia Meriadoci*", PMLA, XXIII, 599ff. (1908). The
difference of language, style, etc. and the dependence of the Latin
romances on French prose romances of the thirteenth century — *Tristan*
and *Lancelot*, in particular — prove, however, that her thesis is
untenable. Cp. Bruce, *op. cit.*, pp. Xff. It is a pity that so erroneous
an idea — for, in that case, these Latin romances would be the
earliest of all extant Arthurian romances — should have found acceptance in a standard work, like the Suchier-Birch-Hirschfeld, *Geschichte der französischen Literatur*[2], I, 112 (Leipzig, 1913).

no little value as literary curiosities, for they are the only Arthurian romances, properly speaking, in Latin that have descended to modern times.[4] *Arthur and Gorlagon*[5] is a striking Welsh folk-tale in Latin form, but it does not fall in the category of the romances.

In the *Historia Meriadoci,* Meriadoc and his sister, Orwen, are the children of Caradoc, king of Wales, who is murdered on a hunt by his brother, Griffith. The latter succeeds his brother and orders them to be secretly taken to the forest of Arglud and hanged there. Out of compassion, however, the executioners fail to carry out their wicked master's commands, and the children finally get into the hands of Ivor, the king's huntsman, and his wife, Morwen, both favorable to the royal orphans. Whilst they are all hiding in the forest, Urien, king of Scotland, who happens to be passing that way, carries off Orwen and marries her, whilst Kay, Arthur's seneschal, conveys Meriadoc to his sovereign's court. Later, Morwen and Ivor, however, rejoin Orwen and Meriadoc, respectively. Arthur and Urien besiege Griffith at Mount Snowdon, capture him and slay him, and make Meriadoc king in his place. The young prince, however, turns over his kingdom to Urien and himself goes forth in search of adventure. He first aids the Emperor of Germany in his war with Gundebald "King of the land from which no one returns,"[6] who had abducted the emperor's only daughter. In pursuit of the enemy he and his followers cross a river and enter a vast forest, haunted by wild beasts and

<hr/>

[4] Cp. Bruce, p. XXXV, note 3.

[5] Edited by G. L. Kittredge, [Harvard] *Studies and Notes in Philology and Literature,* VIII, 149ff. (1903). It is, primarily, a werewolf tale, affiliated with *Bisclavret* and *Melion,* but contains, besides, other folk-tale elements. Kittredge's edition contains an elaborate study of the sources. There is only one known MS. of the work — the Bodleian MS. Rawlinson B. 149 (about 1400) which, as we have seen, also, includes the *Meriadoc.* The date of composition is undetermined.

[6] This *motif* comes to our author, ultimately, from Chrétien's *Lancelot,* L. 645, but it is here thoroughly rationalized, since Gundebald's stronghold is represented (p. 43) as an island in the Rhine Cp., on these matters, Bruce, pp. XXXIV f.

phantasms — a sort of Otherworld. Here he has a series of fantastic adventures — mainly in splendid fairy castles with supernatural inhabitants. In the end, by a stratagem, he gets into communication with the imprisoned princess and, with her assistance, overcomes Gundebald and liberates her. The Emperor now proves faithless to his promises and wishes his daughter to wed the King of Gaul in order to settle a war with the latter. On learning, however, of the princess's condition in consequence of her secret relations with Meriadoc, the king declines the honor, and, assisted by his rival, renews the war, in which Meriadoc soon slays the Emperor. Nevertheless, he later marries the princess. Moreover, the King of Gaul establishes our hero next to himself in authority in his dominions and the latter enjoys a long and prosperous life.

According to the second of these romances, Gawain was the offspring of a secret love-affair between Loth, nephew of the King of Norway, and Anna, daughter of Uther Pendragon, during the former's sojourn as a hostage at the British court. To save the princess's reputation, as soon as the child is born, it is committed to some foreign merchants, along with certain valuables, which include, *inter alia,* the means of its future identification. On disembarking near Narbonne, after their voyage from Britain, the merchants unwarily leave their ship in charge of a boy and go off to the city. The boy forthwith falls asleep and a neighboring fisherman, Viamundus, uses the opportunity to steal the child and the valuables. He brings up the boy as his adopted son, and, after seven years, goes to Rome with his ill-gotten wealth, and, pretending to be of a noble Roman family, receives from the Emperor the former palace of Scipio Africanus as his dwelling and becomes a leading citizen of Rome. Only when he is on his death-bed does he confess to the Emperor and the Pope Sulpicius his true history and beg them to take charge of the child and educate him for knighthood. The Emperor accepts the care of the boy and knights him when he is fifteen years old. Up to that time the dying injunction of Viamundus had been obeyed and no definite name had been conferred upon the hero, so that he was known merely as the "Boy Without a Name." On the day, however, that he was knighted, he appeared wearing a surcoat — the first person ever to do so — and so won the nickname by which he is known up to the closing scenes of the romance, viz. "The Knight of the Surcoat."

Soon after this Gawain sails for Jerusalem in order to assist the Christians there in their war with the Persians. On the way out, however, the expedition stops at an island in the Aegean Sea, whose pagan inhabitants, as Gawain and his companions had ascertained, were planning to intercept the Roman fleet. In the course of this episode, we have, what is unique in Arthurian romance, a description of a naval engagement — moreover, an account of the terrible effect of Greek fire, together with a prescription for its preparation. It is, perhaps, needless to say that the Romans were victorious in this affair and that Gawain led all the rest in valor. Similarly, on his arrival at Jerusalem, as the champion of the Christians, in a duel which, according to agreement, was to determine the issues between the opposing hosts, he slew the Persian champion and delivered the city.

After receiving appropriate honors on his return to Rome, Gawain resolved to seek further adventures at Arthur's court. On his departure the Emperor turns over to him the documents which are to identify him, but commands him not to look at them until he has seen the British king. On the night before our hero reaches Caerleon, Arthur's wife, here called Gwendolen,[7] foretells that a knight who is superior to the king, himself, is on the point of arriving. Whilst the queen is asleep, Arthur goes forth to test, according to his custom, the strength and skill of strange knights. He happens to encounter Gawain in the night and suffers a humiliating overthrow at his hands. In a later affair before Maidens' Castle in North Britain the latter subjects the king to an additional humiliation, but all soon ends happily, when the true story of the young knight's birth is brought to light and he is acknowledged by his parents to be their son.

---

[7] The name is probably taken from Geoffrey's *Vita Merlini,* where Merlin's lady-love is so called.

The discovery of the *Enfances Gauvain*,[8] a fragmentary poem on Gawain's youth, a few years ago, has confirmed the conjecture, which had been already advanced,[9] that the *De Ortu* was based on a lost romance in that language. Both of these romances, it would seem, go back to still a third French romance, which is no longer known to exist.[10] The distinctive feature of the lost romance, which has been inherited by its descendants, is the rationalized adaptation to Gawain of the legend of Pope Gregory, who was set adrift on the sea in a cask, was picked up by fishermen, and brought up by an abbot, who gave him his own name. The author has also appropriated ideas from Geoffrey's *Historia* and from various French romances, some of them lost, and he has effected the union of these disparate elements with no little skill.

The sources of the *Historia Meriadoci* are of the same general description as those of the *De Ortu* — only, in this case, more plainly than the other, Arthurian names have been used to give *éclat* to stories that, originally, had no real connection with Arthurian tradition.[11] The pseudo-historical account of Meriadoc's youth is as purely fictitious as that of his adventures in the fairy forest, and, indeed, seems to be a mere variant of the *Havelok* story.[12]

---

[8] Two fragments were discovered and edited by Paul Meyer, *Romania*, XXXIX, 1 ff. (1910). The MS. (Bibl. Nat.) belongs to the middle of the thirteenth century and the poem, itself, probably, to the beginning of the century. H. Gelzer has shown, *"Zu den Enfances Gauvain"*, *Zs. f. rom. Ph.* XXXVIII, 614 (1914), that, contrary to Meyer, no third fragment ever existed.

[9] In my first edition of the romance.

[10] Cp. Bruce, pp. XLVff. On its connection with the Gregory legend and with the cognate episodes of the *Perlesvaus*, pp. 252 f. and *Huth-Merlin*, I, 204 ff. cp. *ibid.* pp. XXXVf. — The motive of incest which is so important in the Gregory legend is here omitted, although utilized, as we have seen, in the *Huth-Merlin* passage and in the *Lancelot*, V, 284 f., with reference to Mordred.

[11] For the sources of the *Meriadoc*, cp. Bruce, pp. XXIVff.

[12] Cp. Bruce, p. XXX — also, Max Deutschbein, *Studien zur Sagengeschichte Englands, Teil I, Die Wikingersagen*, pp. 134 ff. (Cöthen, 1906).

Chapter XIII.
The Influence of the prose Romances on subsequent Literature.

The subject which is indicated in the above heading is too large a one to dilate upon here and would require, indeed, a separate volume for adequate treatment.[1] We cannot conclude our long discussion of the prose-romances, however, without adding a brief note on the momentous influence of these romances upon the development of narrative literature throughout Europe in later ages — more especially, during the Renaissance.

As has been already remarked above, long before the end of the Middle Ages the prose romances had completely eclipsed the metrical romances in popularity, and it was not until the Romantic Revival in the latter part of the eighteenth century that interest in the latter began to be reawakened. On the other hand, during the period of the Renaissance, the prose romances continued to enjoy an undiminished favor with the readers of the time, as is sufficiently attested by the numerous editions, which have been recorded in the notes above.[2] The *Lancelot, Tristan,* and the other prose romances determined, indeed, the character of subsequent prose fiction of the larger sort in France far on into the sixteenth century, and, to a certain degree, indirectly, beyond.

---

[1] F. Lot, *Lancelot,* pp. 280 ff., has given a chapter to the subject, as far as the Vulgate cycle is concerned.

[2] On this subject, see, too, A. Tilley, "Les romans de chevalerie en prose", *Revue du seizième siècle,* VI, 45 ff. (1919). It appears from this article, however, that the popularity of the Arthurian romances in the Renaissance was confined to the noble and *bourgeois* classes. On the other hand, the prose versions of the *chansons de geste* were much more popular, generally speaking, and, accordingly, were much more frequently reprinted. Tilley gives the dates of the first editions of the fifteenth and sixteenth century prints of the various prose romances, but only of the first.

Many a Frenchman, doubtless, agreed with Clément Marot[3] that
Lancelot was a "très-plaisant menteur". Still more important,
however, was the influence which these romances exercised outside
of France.

First in Italy: The French prose romances, — more particularly, the *Lancelot, Tristan* and *Guiron le Courtois* — were the
direct models of Boiardo's great romance-epic in verse, the *Orlando Innamorato*[4] (1486 *et seq.*). Moreover, as is well-known,
Ariosto's still more famous *Orlando Furioso* (first edition, 1516) is
a mere continuation of Boiardo and in the features which most
concern us here, the incoherence, the abrupt transitions, the interweaving of a whole series of narratives that have no vital connection with one another, it is similar to his predecessor's poem.
In its turn, the *Orlando Furioso* served as a model for Spenser's
Faerie Queene, for it was the English poet's ambition, as we
know from Gabriel Harvey, even to "overgo" the excellence of
his great Italian original. Hence those features of Spenser's narrative which have proved so often a stumbling-block to the modern
reader are due, in the last analysis, to the tradition which was
established by the *Lancelot* and its companion-romances.

Hardly less fateful than the relation of Boiardo and Ariosto
to the prose romances in the history of Italian literature was
Luigi Alamanni's innovation — the most audacious, perhaps, in
European literature — in his *Avarchide* (1570), of Arthurizing
the *Iliad.*[5]

Although the poet retains the main outlines of the Homeric
epic, despite the change in the name of the besieged city,[6] we

---

[3] *Elégie,* XVI.
[4] The main characters were drawn from the Charlemagne cycle,
but the whole spirit of the work is that of the Arthurian romances.
Cp. A. Gaspary, *Geschichte der Italienischen Literatur,* II, 281 ff.
(Berlin, 1888).
[5] On the *Avarchide* and its sources and on Tasso's debt to
Alamanni, cp., especially, H. Hauvette, *Luigi Alamanni,* pp. 357 ff.
(Paris, 1903).
[6] In Alamanni the city is called *Avarco* — Latin *Avaricum*
(i. e. modern *Bourges*). The action is laid about 500, A. D.

have here the heroes of the Arthurian romances — Lancelot, Tristan, and the rest — stalking in the shoes of Achilles, Ajax, etc. It was on the model of the *Avarchide* that a few years later, Torquato Tasso, in his *Gerusalemme Liberata* (1581), offered to the world a far happier combination of classical and romantic elements.

Secondly, in Spain: The influence of the prose romances is also of the first importance in the literature of Spain and Portugal. The immense body of romances of chivalry which was produced in the Iberian peninsula from the thirteenth to the sixteenth century — from the *Amadis de Gaula*[7] (late thirteenth) to the *Espejo de Principes y Caballeros* (1580) — simply continues the tradition of the French romances, and it is undeniable that *Don Quixote* (Part I, 1605), itself, though one of its objects was the extinction of the *genre*, inherits its narrative technique, in a large measure, from these same French romances. In any event, the Spanish romances of chivalry and their offspring, the pastoral romances, like Cervantes' *Galatea* (1585) and the *Diana* (about 1588) of Montemayor, exerted an influence on contemporary France and England, and even later. Apart from translations the latter especially influenced the huge French romances of the seventeenth century — the productions of La Calprenède, Scudéry, and others, which found their echo in England — more particularly, in the Heroic Drama of the Age of the Restoration.[8]

---

[7] For the immense indebtedness of the *Amadis* to the *Lancelot,* see Miss G. S. Williams, *The Amadis Question,* in the *Revue Hispanique,* XXI.

[8] Comprehensive studies on the influence of the prose romances on the literature of the Renaissance are still wanting. I have mentioned in the text the great outstanding examples of this influence. It penetrated, however, even the Italian *novelle.* Three such instances have been recently noted (not all, for the first time, to be sure) by E. Winkler, in the second section — "Die Quellen der Lanzelot-Erzählungen der Cento Novelle Antiche" — of his article "Arturiana", *Zs. f. rom. Ph.,* XLI, 193ff. (1921). In the first section of the article, the author points out an imitation of the storm-making spring of Chrétien's *Yvain* in King René of Anjou's *De la Queste de la tres Doulce Merci au Cuer d'Amours espris* (1457).

PART IV.

DISCUSSIONS.

Chapter I.
Date of the Battle of Badon Hill (Mount Badon).

The date of the battle of Badon Hill is of prime importance
for fixing the date of the historical Arthur, and hence of the
legends that are connected with his name. Gildas, to whom we
owe the first mention of the battle, says, ch. 26, in regard to
the wars between the Saxons and the Britons after the time of
the British leader, Ambrosius Aurelianus:

"Ex eo tempore nunc cives, nunc hostes, vincebant, ut in
ista gente experiretur dominus solito more praesentem Israelem,
utrum diligat eum an non; usque ad annum obsessionis Badonici
montis, novissimaeque ferme de furciferis non minimae stragis,
quique quadragesimus quartus, ut novi, orditur annus, mense iam
uno emenso, qui et meae nativitatis est."

These words have been variously interpreted. Some modern
scholars have followed Bede, *Historia Ecclesiastica*, Book I, ch. 16,
in taking the ambiguous passage to mean that the battle of Badon
Hill was fought in the year of the author's birth, forty-four years
after the coming of the Saxons. Cp., for example, A. de la Borderie, *Revue Celtique*, VI, 1ff. (1885), and E. Windisch, *Das
keltische Britannien bis zu Kaiser Arthur*, p. 39 (1912). On
the other hand, a more likely interpretation is that Gildas means
that Mount Badon was fought forty-four years before the time
when the author penned this passage (and in the year of his nati-
vity). This is the interpretation, for instance, of H. Zimmer,
Nennius Vindicatus, p. 286 (1913), Mommsen, in his edition of
Gildas, III, 8 (1896), C. Plummer, edition of Bede, II, 31 (Oxford, 1896), and Hugh Williams, p. 63, note 1, of his edition of
Gildas (London, 1899—1901) in the Cymmrodorion Record Series,
No. 3. Mommsen, however, emends the text and substitutes for
"ut novi" "est ab eo qui", whilst Williams merely puts "ut

novi" in brackets. Inasmuch as, according to the *Annales Cambriae*, Gildas died in 570 and Maglocunus, one of the British princes whom he inveighs against in the *De Excidio* as still living, died in 547, it is probable that Gildas's birth, and hence the battle of Badon Hill, fell in the first years of the sixth century.

On the other hand, if Gildas meant that the battle was fought forty-four years after the coming of the Saxons, it would not be possible to fix the date with quite the same certainty; for the date of this coming is in dispute. Bede, *Historia Ecclesiastica*, Book I, ch. 15, V, ch. 24, who is followed by the Anglo-Saxon Chronicles, places it in, or about, the year 449 A.D.[1] But Bede's dating has no genuine authority; for, as R. Thurneysen has shown in his article, "Wann sind die Germanen nach England gekommen?", *Englische Studien*, XXII, 174f. (1895), the Anglo-Saxon historian arrives at this date by merely combining the statement of some continental source that the Roman rule in Britain ended in 409 with the statement of the lost *Annales Romanorum* (cited by Nennius, ch. 10, and apparently of Irish origin) that the Saxons invaded Britain forty years after the Roman rule terminated, although this latter source, doubtless, like Nennius, who is dependent on it, dated the end of the Roman power with the death of Maximus in 388. The date in Nennius thus indicated for the beginning of the Anglo-Saxon conquest (i. e. the landing of certain Anglo-Saxon bands at the invitation of a British king to aid him in his wars against the Picts and the Irish), viz. 428, is, doubtless, correct, since the *Annales Romanorum* to which he refers was of a considerably earlier time. Cp. Thurneysen, *Zs. f. d. Ph.*, XXVIII, 92f. (1896), (review of Zimmer's *Nennius Vindicatus)* and *Zs. f. celt. Ph.*, I, 166f. (1896), (review of Mommsen's edition of Gildas and Nennius). The contemporary *Chronica Gallica*[2] (p. 660), which was compiled before 452, re-

---

[1] Elsewhere in Bede's history (e. g. I, 23, V, 23) other dates (447 or 448) are implied, and in his *Chronica*, 452. See Williams' edition of Gildas, p. 53, note.

[2] *Monumenta Germaniae Historica. Auctorum Antiquis-*

cords that Britain passed under Saxon rule in 441 or 442.[3] This record is, no doubt, accurate, as applied to the part of Britain with which the author would be naturally best acquainted, namely, the southeastern coast. Taken in this sense, the statement would harmonize well enough with 428, as the date of the first permanent landing of the Anglo-Saxon tribes. On this subject compare, besides, Thurneysen's articles already cited. Of less value is the discussion of these matters by N. J. Krom in his Leiden thesis: *De populis Germanis antiquo tempore patriam nostram incolentibus Anglosaxonumque migrationibus*, pp. 115 ff. (Leiden, 1908). Strange to say, Krom seems entirely ignorant of Thurneysen's article in *Englische Studien*, XXII.

The enemies against whom the Britons appealed to Aetius for help in the letter of 446 A.D. were, no doubt, really the Anglo-Saxon invaders, and not the Picts and Scots, as Gildas (ch. 20) thought.[4] Cp. Thurneysen, *Englische Studien*, XXII, 177.

If we take 428, then, as the date of the arrival of the Anglo-Saxons in Britain, the battle of Badon Hill was fought in 472 or 473. As I have stated above, however, the alternative interpretation of the passage in Gildas is preferable, and the real date of the battle probably falls in the first four or five years of the sixth century.[5]

simorum, Tomus IX. Chronicorum Minorum Saec. IV, V, VI, VII. Vol. I, edited by Theodor Mommsen, Berlin, 1892.

  [3] V. H. Friedel, in his article, "L'arrivée des Saxons en Angleterre d'après le texte de Chartres et l'Historia Britonum", *Foerster-Festgabe*, pp. 280 ff. (1901), argues for the date 418/419, but Thurneysen's argument is to me the most satisfactory on the subject. — The worthlessness of the traditional dates in relation to the Anglo-Saxon conquest of England has been recently emphasized by F. Lot in his valuable article, "Les migrations saxonnes en Gaule et en Grande-Bretagne du IIIe au Ve siècle", *Revue Historique*, vol. 119, pp. 1 ff. (1915).

  [4] This correction of Gildas is much more acceptable than Anscombe's *Zs. f. celt. Ph.*, VII, 435 (1907). He thinks that the "Britanni" who addressed the appeal to Aetius were really Armorican "Britons".

  [5] A. Anscombe, "Date of the First Settlement of the Saxons in

Turning now from the question of the date of the battle of
Badon Hill to that of the place where it was fought, we are con-
fronted with a hopeless uncertainty.[6] It has been customary to
identify the site of the battle with Bath,[7] and in Nennius (ch.
68) there is, indeed, a mention of "balnea Badonis", which seems to
mean the battle at the city of Bath; but the old Roman Aquae Solis
could only have received the Anglo-Saxon name of "Bath" after
the battle of Deorham (a few miles distant) in 577, through which
the Anglo-Saxons for the first time got possession of the place and
surrounding district — hence, the identification is obviously baseless. The same thing may be said of the identification of Badon
Hill with Badbury in Dorset;[8] for, as W. H. Stevenson has pointed
out,[9] the latter derives its name from some Anglo-Saxon, the

Britain", *Zs. f. celt. Ph.*, III, 492 ff. (1901), VI, 339 ff., XII, 419 ff.,
tries to reconcile the two dates. Bede's 449, he says, really means
450, for in those ages, he contends, chroniclers often designated the
year by the sum of years, completed up to date. Moreover, this 450
was the annuary number, not according to the orthodox (Dionysian)
system of computation, but according to that which is called the
system *secundum evangelicam veritatem* by the person with whom
it is commonly identified, Marianus Scotus (11th century), which would
involve a retardation of 22 years. He tries to show by examples that
Marianus's system of computation was really in use before Bede's time.
E. W. B. Nicholson, *ibid.*, VI, 439 ff., VIII, 121 ff., replying to Anscombe, shows that the instances with which he supports these conten-
tions are merely chroniclers' blunders. Besides, Thurneysen, as we
have seen above, explains satisfactorily Bede's date, 449. Anscombe
has written still further on the subject in *Eriu*, III, 117 ff. (1907).

[6] The best brief summary of the discussion as to both place and
date is that of W. H. Stevenson in *The English Historical Review*,
XVII, 632 ff. (Oct. 1902). The date given by the *Annales Cambriae*,
516, is now accepted by no one. For further discussion of the date
of the Anglo-Saxon invasion, see H. M. Chadwick, *The Origin of the
English Nation*, 35 ff. (Cambridge, 1907).

[7] The most elaborate defence of this view is E. W. B. Nicholson's,
in his articles, "Mons Badonicus and Geoffrey of Monmouth", *The
Academy*, March 14 (pp. 220 ff.) and April 11 (pp. 305 ff.), 1896.

[8] Proposed by E. Guest, *Origines Celticae*, II, 189 (London,
1883), and accepted by the historians, Freeman, J. R. Green, etc.

[9] *English Historical Review*, XVII, 634 (1902).

Anglo-Saxon form, "Baddanbyrig", being, of course, a combination of the genitive form of "Badda" (a personal name) with the Anglo-Saxon word for "town". Now, no town in Dorset could have received an Anglo-Saxon name until the conquest of that part of England — that is to say, until at least as late as the above-mentioned battle of Deorham.

For different reasons the identification with Acornbury (Aconbury), in Herefordshire proposed by A. Anscombe, *Zs. f. celt. Ph.*, V, 116 (1905), is, likewise, to be rejected. His line of argument is that *Badonicus* is really a mere scribal corruption of an hypothetical *Hagonis, Mons Hagonis* being the Latin equivalent of *Mynydd Agned* (= Hill in the land of Agon or Acon), which is in some MSS. of Nennius the name of the eleventh in the list of Arthur's twelve battles. The scribe of the archetype of these MSS., according to this view, did not recognize the identity of *Mynydd Agned* with *Mons Badonicus,* so made two battles out of one. The corruption, Anscombe thinks, began in the MSS. of Gildas, passed thence into MSS. of Bede, and from Bede into Nennius. All this, however, is too purely speculative for acceptance. One can, at most, only admit that Anscombe's identifications of the scenes of Arthur's eleven other battles with places in Upper Britain, in this same article,[10] if

---

[10] "Local Names in the 'Arthuriana' in the *Historia Brittonum*", *Z. f. celt. Ph.*, V, 103ff. (1905).

[11] It is, perhaps, advisable to mention that Anscombe, and, later, A. W. Wade-Evans, have attacked, although futilely, the authenticity of Gildas's *De Excidio Britanniae.* For the argument of the former on the subject, cp. his articles in *The Academy,* Sept. 14, 28, Oct. 5, 19, Nov. 16, 1895. He bases his criticism on supposed inconsistencies of statements in the work with sixth century conditions, e. g. Gildas's allusion, ch. 24, to the Saxons having reached already the west coast of Britain. A raid, however, extending to that coast is not unlikely even in the first half of the sixth century. See the excellent replies to Anscombe by W. H. Stevenson, *ibid.,* Oct. 26, Dec. 14, 1895 — also, E. W. B. Nicholson, Nov. 2. Stevenson lays stress on our meagre knowledge of the Anglo-Saxon conquest. Besides; why should any one between 640 and 641 (limits of the date of the *De Excidio* according to Anscombe, *ibid.,* Oct. 5, 1895) be interested in inveighing so bitterly

correct, would go to prove that Badon Hill, too, was in that part
of the island.[11]

---

against British princes of the fifth and sixth centuries? Wade-Evans's
main articles on the subject appeared in *The Celtic Review*, I, 289 ff.
(1905), II, 46 ff., 126 ff. (1905), IX, 35 ff. (1913), 314 ff. (1914), X,
215 ff. (1915), 322 ff. (1916). — See also his "The Chronology of
Arthur", *Y Cymmrodor*, XXII, 125 ff. (1910). For a reply to the
earlier articles of this long series, see E. W. B. Nicholson, *The Celtic
Review*, II, 369 ff. (1906). This answers pretty well the whole series;
for, in the main, the argument is merely repeated. Wade-Evans's final
result (X, 329 f.), is that Mount Badon (Badon Hill) was fought in 665
and the *De Excidio Britaniae* written in 708. The only real battle
of Mount Badon, he argues, was that which is entered as the second
of the name in the *Annales Cambriae* under the year CCXXI (i. e.
665 or 666 A. D.). This is the battle mentioned in Gildas (ch. 23)
— "Badonici Montis". The battle of this name, entered under the
year LXXII (i. e. 516 or 517 A. D.) in the *Annales Cambriae*, according to Wade-Evans, never occurred, the name being adopted from
Gildas, or "pseudo-Gildas", as Wade-Evans calls the author of the
De Excidio. Arthur really flourished and died, he maintains, in the
latter part of the fifth century.

Most of Wade-Evans's argument hinges on his interpretation of
the prophecy which Gildas (ch. 23) mentions as firmly relied on by
the Saxons, when they invaded Britain, viz. that they should occupy
the country for three hundred years, and that for one hundred and
fifty years of this period they should make frequent devastations ("sae-
pius devastaret") in it. Wade-Evans assumes that this is a prophecy
after the event. Gildas (ch. 26) represents that active hostilities ceased
after the battle of Mount Badon (the year of Gildas's own birth) and
that forty-three years of peace had already passed at the time that
he was writing. Consequently, Wade-Evans concludes that the *De
Excidio* was written 150 plus 43 years after the Anglo-Saxon invasion
began. But Gildas explicitly says that the prophecy in question was
a Saxon prophecy and he neither expresses nor implies any belief in
it, himself. Wade-Evans's conclusion, therefore, is unwarranted. So,
too, I may add, is his assertion that Gildas implies a long interval
between the appeal to Aetius and the landing of the Anglo-Saxons.

Chapter II.
Brutus, Eponymus of the Britons.

Brutus, as the eponymus of the Britons, Geoffrey found already in Nennius, ch. 18 (Mommsen's edition, p. 161). For the manner in which this notion grew up with the growth of the *Historia Brittonum* see, especially, G. Heeger: *Über die Trojanersage der Britten,* 9 ff. (Munich, 1886), H. Zimmer, *Nennius Vindicatus,* 245 ff. (Berlin, 1893), and, above all, R. Thurneysen, *Zs. f. d. Ph.,* XXVIII, 86 ff. (1896). W. W. Newell, PMLA, XX, 628 ff. (1905), is largely based on Thurneysen.

The starting-point was given by an entry in the chronicle of Eusebius-Jerome, which was a popular historical handbook in the Middle Ages. Here, under the date of the year of Abraham 1875 (i. e. 138, B. C.), it is stated: "Brutus Hiberiam usque ad Oceanum subigit." This Brutus was a Roman consul of the year in question, D. Junius Brutus, surnamed Callaicus. The compiler of the *Historia Brittonum* in its earliest form (679), tempted by the similarity of the names *Brutus* and *Britannia,* — and few mediaeval chroniclers could have resisted the temptation — tacitly extended the conquests of this consul to Britain, also, and inserted in the *Historia* the statement (ch. 7): "Britannia insula a quodam Bruto consule Romano dicta." The author of this etymology may or may not have known the uncomplimentary derivation of "Britones" from the Latin adjective "brutus" (stupid, brutish), which had already been incorporated into another popular handbook of the time, the *Etymologiae* (written in 628) of Isidore of Seville, who says, Book IX, ch. 12: "Britones quidam Latine nominatos suspicantur, eo quod bruti sint."

This same compiler added (ch. 17), still further, a genealogy of the Britons, the origin of which is as follows:

In the pseudo-learned genealogy of the Romans and the Germanic nations which was drawn up in France somewhere about 520 A. D. and which has been best edited, under the title of "Die fränkische Völkertafel", by K. Müllenhoff, in the *Abhandlungen der Königlichen Akademie der Wissenschaften zu Berlin, aus dem Jahre, 1862,* pp. 532ff., these nations are said to be descended from three brothers, Erminus, Inguo and Istio (i. e. the eponymi respectively of the Herminones, Ingaevones, and Istaevones, the three great divisions of the Germanic tribes according to Tacitus, *Germania,* ch. 2, and Pliny, *Naturalis Historia,* Book IV, ch. 14.). In the text as printed by Müllenhoff it is said of the third of these brothers: "Istio frater eorum genuit Romanos, Brittones, Francus, Alamannus." Now in ch. 17 (Mommsen, pp. 159ff.) of the *Historia Brittonum,* we have an attempt in the true mediaeval style to run the genealogical line of the Britons back to Adam. The author follows the method of the genealogies in the Bible, which had also, no doubt, been the model of the Frankish "Völkertafel", and boldly connects the Istio of the latter, through his father, Alanus (already included in the Frankish document) and a few intervening fictitious ancestors, with the Old Testament genealogies. He carries out the system of his sources, however, still further, and partly influenced by the Old Testament and partly adopting, perhaps, the suggestion of the "Francus, Alemannus" of the Frankish document,[1] gives the name of each of the nations concerned in the singular as that of a national eponymus. Thus he says *ibid.*: "Hissitio [MS. corruption for *Histio = Istio]* autem habuit filios quattuor: Francus Romanus Britus Albanus [MS. corruption for *Alemannus*]."

The Romans and Britons now stood together in this genealogical list, and this fact stimulated later interpolators to still further inventions connecting the two more intimately, which resulted in

---

[1] In the barbarous Latin of the time, *u* often stood for long *o.* Cp. M. Bonnet, *Le latin de Gregoire de Tours,* pp. 126ff. (Paris, 1890). Hence these accusative plurals had the same forms as nominative singulars.

ch. 10—11. For these inventions the chronicle of Eusebius-Jerome again furnished the starting-point:

In that chronicle, under the year of Abraham 878 (cp. Thurneysen, pp. 87f.), the compiler makes certain statements about the "reges Albanorum, Sylvii", descendants of Aeneas, the Trojan leader, who was so well-known through Virgil as an ancestor of the Romans. The author of the *source* of the part of the *Historia Brittonum* with which we are now dealing (apparently, an Irishman) misinterpreted (wilfully, it may be) these "Albani" (who were, of course, really Italians of the region near Rome) as the inhabitants of "Albion" (Britain). The author of ch. 10—11 in the *Historia*, itself, on the strength of this confusion, identifies Brutus, the first Roman consul — whom, as the *first* consul, he chooses to make a brother of Romulus and Remus, the founders of Rome, and hence a descendant of Aeneas and the "Albanorum reges" — with the Brutus after whom, according to ch. 7, already Britannia had been named. Consequently, we have Silvius Ascanius, Aeneas, and their Trojan ancestors now introduced into the genealogy of Brutus.[2] Lastly, he makes this Brutus, after whom Britannia was named, absorb also the function of the Britto (Britus) who had developed as the eponymus of the Britons out of the Frankish genealogy of the nations in the manner that we have seen. Henceforth, we shall hear, then, in the mediaeval chronicles only of Brutus.

---

[2] This part, doubtless, underwent expansion at different times.

Chapter III.
Supplementary Observations on the Question: Were there Arthurian romances before Chrétien?

Many eminent Arthurian scholars have answered this question in the affirmative — e. g., G. Paris, *Manuel*, pp. 100f., E. Brugger, *Zs. f. frz. Spr. u. Litt.*, XXXI², 143f. (1907) and Miss J. L. Weston, *The Legend of Sir Perceval*, I, 230f., (1909).[1] Let us now examine the evidence on the subject.

We have already considered the bearing on this question of the Italian names to which P. Rajna called attention, and of the figures on the Cathedral at Modena, — also, of the Wolfram-Guiot and *Mabinogion* controversies.[2] Leaving these matters aside, we may say that, perhaps, the best statement which has been presented of the reasons for believing that there were romances before Chrétien is that of Eduard Wechssler, *Sage vom heiligen Gral*, pp. 156f. (Halle, 1898).[3] Of the five reasons advanced by Wechssler two are obviously of little force. The first indeed, rests on a blunder. He cites as evidence of a French *Lancelot* romance before Chrétien a supposed episode in Malory's *Morte Darthur* of the woman who is turned into a dragon for not obeying the requirements of the *amour courtois*. But the episode here referred to is really in the Middle High German *Lanzelet*, not in Malory. Gaston Paris, to be sure, expresses the belief, *Romania*,

---

[1] The chief representatives of the opposing view have been W. Foerster in the prefaces to his various editions of Chrétien's works — especially, the *Lancelot*, W. W. Newell, *The Legend of the Holy Grail* (Cambridge, Mass., 1902), and W. Golther in numerous reviews.

[2] Cp. I, 12ff., 313ff., above.

[3] Foerster has subjected Wechssler's argument to an elaborate refutation in the Introduction to his edition of Chrétien's *Lancelot*, pp. XCIIff.

XII, 503 ff. that in his Book XIX, where Lancelot rescues Guinevere from Mellyagraunce, Malory was following a more primitive version than Chrétien's of the incident which we may call the Rape of Guinevere. But this is surely an error, for Malory's work is based on the prose romances, and, in no ascertained case, on any French poem, whether early or late.

Wechssler's second reason has hardly greater force than his first — namely, Chrétien's mention of a book as the source of his *Perceval*. But, even if the statement is not intentionally misleading, the term "book" is indefinite and does not necessarily imply a French romance.

The following points cited by Wechssler are the ones that have most weight:

1. The list of Round Table heroes given by Chrétien in his *Erec*, 11. 1691 ff., implies a fully developed literature on the subject already. When Erec brings his bride to Arthur's court, the poet introduces this long list of the knights who were there — Gawain, Lancelot, and a host of others.

2. The supposed fact that the Tristan legend had already been treated in French verse.

3. The supposed priority over Chrétien of the French original of the Middle High German poem *Lanzelet* by Ulrich von Zatzikhoven, who wrote at the end of the twelfth century.

Now, the third point is so doubtful that it can hardly be used in the controversy. For the considerations that tell against this assumed priority, cp. I, 210 ff., above.

As far as the first point is concerned, Foerster (p. XCI of Introduction to *Lancelot*) has rightly urged that there is no reason to suppose that Chrétien was here using written sources of any kind. At the beginning of the *Erec* he says: "The story is of Erec, the son of Lac. Those who wish to live by telling stories are in the habit of tearing it to pieces and perverting it before kings and counts." These words evidently refer to oral recitation.[4]

---

[4] It should be mentioned here that the eminent Celticist, J. Loth, has tried to show by the forms of the French names *Yvain, Loth,* etc.,

The one point in Wechssler's list that has real force is, in my judgment, the second. If we grant that a great poem on Tristan existed in the first half of the twelfth century, that would create, undeniably, a presumption that there were Arthurian romances before Chrétien, for it is not at all likely that such a poem stood isolated in the poetical literature of the time. Foerster, *Lancelot,* p. xciv, meets this point with the observation that the Tristan saga had originally nothing to do with the Arthurian cycle and was first connected with it after Geoffrey of Monmouth and Wace had established the stories of this cycle in contemporary literature. So this is no argument, he says, for the supposed Arthurian romances before Chrétien.

It is undoubtedly true that Tristan was originally unconnected with Arthur, yet if similar poems were written about the characters whom we find associated with the great king in Chrétien, these would constitute substantially Arthurian romances. We need not suppose that the lost poems exhibited the artificial ideal of the *amour courtois* like Chrétien or followed his methods of psychological analysis — they would, nevertheless, remain Arthurian romances — that is, narrative poems embodying romantic tales concerning Arthurian heroes.

As a matter of fact, however, Miss Schoepperle's investigations (cp. I, 152f., note, above) prove that the lost romance on Tristan from which our extant versions are descended was not composed before the second half of the century, and only a short time, if at all, before Chrétien began to write.[5] Chrétien's own knowledge of the

in relation to their Celtic originals, that Chrétien must have used written Welsh sources. Cp. his articles, "Des nouvelles théories sur l'origine des romans arthuriens" in the *Revue Celtique,* XIII, 475 ff. (1892) and "Le roi Loth des romans de la Table Ronde", XVI, 84 ff., (1895). But his arguments have been successfully refuted by Zimmer. See Foerster, pp. CXXIII ff. These names had been long current among the French-speaking populations who transmitted the *matière de Bretagne* from Brittany to the French poets, and apparent coincidences with Welsh in slightly differentiated matters of pronunciation, such as *b* against *u* in twelfth century Breton, in *Caradoc Briebras (Brechbras)* and the like, can claim no importance.

[5] Cp. I, 152 f., note 1, above.

Tristan story need not, then, have been derived from a formal romance — it may have come from oral recitations. Consequently, in this case, as in the case of his other works, there is no convincing proof that he drew on poems earlier than his own — or, in any event, on a narrative poem of considerable extent.

It would be special pleading, however, to deny that the lost *Tristan* romance may have been anterior to Chrétien. But this relatively late work is the only definite romance of which, on the basis of positive data, one may maintain not unreasonably that it was composed before Chrétien began to write. There may have been a few more such narrative poems of whose existence we possess now no evidence, but in the present writer's opinion, in any event, there is nothing to justify the assumption of a fully developed *genre* of Arthurian romance before the great master whom we have just named.[6]

In addition to Wechssler's arguments in favor of the existence of Arthurian romances before Chrétien, it is well to mention the following also: 1. A. Jeanroy's (cp. Faral, p. 395) to the effect that the love-episodes in the romances of antiquity (absent from their main Latin sources) must have been suggested by pre-Chrétien Arthurian romances. E. Faral, however, has shown that certain Latin writings, especially Ovid's, are the true sources of these episodes. Cp. his *Recherches sur les sources latines des contes et romans courtois du moyen age*, pp. 406ff. (Paris, 1913). 2. The supposed French origin of the forms *Walgainus, Hiderus*, in Geof-

---

[6] In my edition of the *De Ortu Waluuanii*, p. 111, I have pointed out a detail towards the end of Chrétien's *Perceval*, ll. 8057ff. (Baist's edition) which would lead one to infer that Chrétien was using here a lost romance on Gawain's youth — the common source of the *De Ortu* and the *Enfances Gauvain* — whose existence seems assured. The episode in the *Perceval* takes it for granted that Gawain was separated from his mother from his infancy onwards, but how this came about and its consequences constitute the theme of the two romances just named — so the common source of these romances was, doubtless, older than the *Perceval*. It may have been later, however, than some of Chrétien's other romances.

frey's *Historia*. Cp. Lot, *Romania*, XXV, 2ff. But this conjectured French origin is too little assured to be used as evidence.

Latterly, W. Meyer-Lübke in his "Crestien von Troyes Erec
und Enide," *Zs. f. frz. Spr. u. Litt.*, XLIV[1], 129ff., especially,
pp. 159ff., has re-examined the question of pre-Chrétien romances,
taking the *Erec* as the basis of his investigation. He is inclined
to answer the question affirmatively, but his results seem to me
wholly indefinite. His discussion of the names, pp. 163ff., strikes
me as the best part of the work.

Chapter IV.
The Mabinogion Controversy.
I.

It may be said, in general, that the scholars who look upon the Welsh tales as independent of Chrétien have based their argument mainly on the ground that the former, in some important points, exhibit a more logical narrative than the latter and hence represent a more primitive form of the story — in other words, are not derived directly from Chrétien, but from a common source. Apart from the fact that opinions differ very much in individual cases, as experience abundantly shows, as to which of two variants in any given narrative is the more logical, the whole principle must be regarded as possessing only a limited validity. Even great writers have been occasionally guilty of inconsistencies or inadequate motivation which an adapter of far inferior powers might remove or improve. The line of argument which is taken by the above-mentioned scholars — and at the same time, I believe, its weakness — can best be illustrated, however, by a concrete example:

In the case of *Geraint and Enid* the main objection urged is that, unlike Chrétien, the Welsh here offers a satisfactory motive in respect to the matter which is, as it were, the very *raison d'être* of almost the whole story, viz. the hero's harsh treatment of his wife (Enid), from the time that he is awakened by her lament over his neglect of knightly activities, for which she has, as she repeats to him, heard him blamed by other knights and for which she recognizes his excessive affection for herself as the cause, down to the point (near the end of the tale) where after her display of devotion to him in many trying circumstances he changes his mood. The motive for the hero's conduct in *Geraint and Enid* is

expressly stated to be jealousy;[1] in Chrétien we are left to infer
for ourselves what it is.[2] A few lines of explanatory comment
would undoubtedly have helped to clarify Chrétien's handling of
the situation at this point. In the main, however, in his narrative
the motives of Erec's conduct are sufficiently clear. His wife's
implied criticism of his sloth in arms has awakened his suspicions
of her love for him, and, it may be added, also, of her conformity
to the spirit of obedience which the men of the Middle Ages,
high and low, were, as a rule, accustomed to exact from their
womenkind. Jealousy was not in question, for there is nothing
in the story to suggest it, and, besides, Chrétien distinctly says
that Erec was not jealous.[3] That the harshness with which he
treats his wife was undeserved goes, of course, without saying;
but there is plenty of precedent in actual life for this picture
of a man who vents the self-dissatisfaction which springs from
the stings of his own conscience upon an innocent victim — especially, upon the wife who has unwittingly aroused him to a sense
of his delinquencies. The whole story of Enid's trials, then, is
a characteristic test of a woman's love by her husband in the
mediaeval vein. In the case of the Patient Griselda, who, like
Enid, was raised from poverty to high station by her marriage,
three leading writers of the Middle Ages, in succession — Boccaccio, Petrarch and Chaucer — took even less pains than Chrétien to supply a plausible motive for the hero's brutality.[4] It

---

[1] Loth, II[2], 152.   [2] ll. 2576 ff.   [3] l. 3304.

[4] I had written the above lines before I observed that E. Philipot had already drawn the comparison (*Romania*, XXV, 264) between
Enid and Griselda. The same scholar declares, *Annales de Bretagne*,
XXVII, 149 (1911) — in a review of Edens's dissertation — that he
would be suspicious of any form of the Griselda story that would justify
the Marquis's conduct to his wife. This seems to me to be a just
observation.

In arguing against the fairy mistress origin of the Erec-Enid
story, M. B. Ogle, "The Sloth of Erec", RR, IX, 1 ff. (1918), has
shown by numerous examples that the opposition of endeavour and
marital love was a commonplace in Latin literature, both in antiquity
and in the Middle Ages. He is right, I believe, in his criticism of

was on the *incidents* of the test and the pathos of the victim's patience and devotion that they concentrated the resources of their art. These were the matters that really interested them. The only passages in Chrétien which, at first blush, would appear to conflict with the interpretation of Erec's conduct towards Enid that I have just given are one in which Erec acknowledges the justice of the criticism of his uxorious indolence (2576f.) and another in which on setting out on the journey that is to test Enid's love and constancy, he recommends her to the care of his father-in-law, in case he, himself, should die (2725ff.). A modern writer here would, doubtless, have added in each instance some two or three lines to prevent the impression of inconsistency. In the first passage, he would have explained that, in confessing his fault, the hero was revealing only a part of his true mood. As it is, Chrétien leaves us to draw this inference from the fear of the consequences of her imprudence which the unfortunate Enid feels (2484ff.) after that confession has been made as well as before. In the second passage, he might have added, though the addition would not have been imperative, that, in spite of the test to which he was about to subject her, the husband did not desire in any event to leave his wife an outcast on the world.

It will be seen from the above that from the point of view of the readers or hearers of twelfth century France, for whom Chrétien was writing, the story of Erec's conduct towards Enid called for little explanation. But what judgment shall we pass on the treatment of the same theme in the Welsh tale which Zenker and his followers find so logical and satisfactory? As a matter of fact, nothing could be more illogical than the conception here of jealousy as the cause of the hero's conduct. There is not the trace of an incident in the story that might arouse such a passion, and the author who did not understand the more complex emotions of Chrétien's characters in this central situation is simply falling back on the motive which will nearly always pass muster in pic-

Nitze, Sheldon and B. R. Woodbridge. For the interpretation of the first two, pp. 68—9, below. For Woodbridge's interpretation see his "Chrétien's Erec as a Cornelian Hero", RR, VI, 434ff. (1915).

tures of matrimonial discord — namely, jealousy. But did any
one ever hear of a story of jealousy in which there is not even
the slightest allusion to the identity of the third party? The
introduction of this motive into the economy of the tale, as it
stands, is merely a crass blunder.

II.

For a review of the debate, in its earlier phases, on the relations of the Welsh tales to Chrétien cp. R. Edens, *Erec-Geraint;
Der Chrétien'sche Versroman und das wälsche Mabinogi*, pp. 1ff.
(Rostock diss., 1910). San Marte and H. de la Villemarqué, the
first scholars to consider the matter, regarded the *Mabinogion*
as Chrétien's source for his *Erec, Yvain* and *Perceval*, and this
untenable opinion prevailed for many years. The view, however,
that the two sets of works had a common source was advanced
at an early date, notably by W. L. Holland, the editor of Chrétien, but first gained prominence, when G. Paris espoused it, *Romania*, X, 467f. (1881), in connection with his well-known hypothesis of the Anglo-Norman origin of the Arthurian romances.
In a more detailed study of the matter than had hitherto appeared,
Karl Othmer, *Das Verhältnis von Christian's von Troyes "Erec
et Enide" zu dem Mabinogion (sic) des roten Buches von Hergest "Geraint ab Erbin"* (Bonn diss. 1889), maintained that the
Welsh tales were directly derived from Chrétien. This study led
G. Paris, *Romania*, XX, 166 (1891),[5] to modify his previous
opinion and acknowledge Chrétien's *Erec* as a source of *Geraint*

---

[5] Paris is reviewing Foerster's edition of the *Erec* (1890). The
review is very important as expressing the writer's estimate of the
literary value of the *Erec* as well as his opinions in regard to its
sources.
 In an important article, "Une épisode *d'Erec et Enide:* La Joie
de la Cour", *Romania*, XXV, 258ff. (1896) E. Philipot expresses
agreement (p. 294) with Othmer as to the relations of the Welsh tale
and *Erec*. In this article Philipot discusses the relations of the Joie
de la Cour episode in *Erec* to the similar episode of the *Bel Inconnu*
romances and concludes that the latter is not dependent on the former.
The conclusion, however, is very questionable.

and Enid, but he still assumed that the author of the Welsh tale drew, also, from another lost French source. In his editions of Chrétien's romances, and, especially, in his edition (1899) of Chrétien's *Lancelot (Karrenritter),* pp. cxxviiff., W. Foerster held to Othmer's position. With the appearance of Edens's above-mentioned dissertation, however, the debate on the relation of the *Erec* to *Geraint and Enid* passed into the stage of a furious controversy. Following are the titles of the publications that pertain thereto, arranged in chronological order:

1. Edens's dissertation (1910).
2. Foerster's review of Edens, *Literarisches Zentralblatt* (LZ), Aug. 26, 1911, cols. 1120 ff.
3. Edens's reply to Foerster, LZ, Nov. 18, 1911, cols. 1522 ff. and Foerster's rejoinder *ibid.,* cols. 1525 ff.
4. Foerster's more elaborate reply to Edens in his article, "Noch einmal die sogenannte Mabinogionfrage," *Zs. f. frz. Spr. u. Litt.,* XXVIII¹, 149 ff. (Dec. 1, 1911).
5. Joint reply of Edens and R. Zenker to Foerster, LZ, Dec. 2, cols. 1590 f. and *ibid.,* col. 1591, Foerster's answer thereto.
6. R. Zenker, *Zur Mabinogionfrage* (Halle,, 1912).
7. A. Smirnov, review of Edens, *Revue Celtique,* XXXIII, 130 ff. (1912).
8. P. A. Becker's review of No. 6 in *Literaturblatt für germ. u. roman. Ph.* (LB), Jan., 1913, cols. 19 ff.
9. Zenker's reply to Smirnov in "Nochmals Erec-Geraint," *Zs. f. frz. Spr. u. Litt.* XL¹, 186 ff. (Feb. 17, 1913).
10. Zenker's reply to Becker, LB, May, 1913, cols. 180 f.
11. Zenker's fuller reply to Becker in "Weiteres zur Mabinogionfrage, I," *Zs. f. frz. Spr. u. Litt.,* XLI¹, 131 ff. (Nov. 10, 1913).
12. W. Gaede, *Die Bearbeitungen von Chrétien's Erek und die Mabinogionfrage,* Münster diss., 1913, in substantial agreement with Foerster.
13. Zenker's reply to Gaede, "*Weiteres zur Mabinogionfrage,* II," *Zs. f. frz. Spr. u. Litt.,* XLIII¹, 11 ff. (1914).

14. Foerster, Chrétien *Wörterbuch*, 139*(1914).

In the course of the controversy Zenker yielded some points, and No. 13 represents his maturest conclusions on the subject. Sifting this article, then, we find that he rests his case for the independence of the Welsh substantially on the following evidence: 1. pp. 33 ff. In W *(Geraint and Enid)*, as, partly, in Hartmann von Aue's *Erek*,[6] the equipment which Enid's father lends

---

[6] For the relation of Hartmann to Chrétien cp. K. Bartsch, "Über Christians von Troyes und Hartmanns von Aue 'Erec und Enide'", Pfeiffer's *Germania*, VII, 141 ff. (1862). He concludes that, despite differences, Chrétien was Hartmann's sole source, although the MS. which the latter used did not always offer the same readings as any of our extant MSS. of Chrétien's poem. E. Kölbing arrived at similar conclusions with regard to the Norse version of this poem. Cp. his "Die nordische Erexsaga und ihre Quelle", *ibid.*, XVI, 381 ff. (1871), — also, Foerster's large *Erec*, pp. XVIII ff., XLIII ff. (Halle, 1890). As against Bartsch, Foerster, *op. cit.* pp. XVII f., attributes to Hartmann's invention the variations in his narrative. For a continuation of the controversy concerning Hartmann's relation to Chrétien see (in addition to articles cited above, which deal primarily with the question of the *Mabinogion*) Karl Dreyer: *Hartmanns von Aue Erec und seine altfranzösische Quelle*. Programm Königsberg, 1893 — also, Paul Hagen, "Zum Erec", *Zs. f. deutsche Ph.*, XXVII, 463 ff. (1897), and F. Piquet, *Étude sur Hartmann d'Aue* (Paris thesis, 1898). Dreyer's conclusion is that Hartmann's source is Chrétien's poem, but in a different redaction from that which we possess. Hagen and Piquet believe that he used some other (unknown) source, in addition to Chrétien, and G. Paris, in reviewing Piquet, *Romania*, XXVIII, 167 (1899), regards that scholar's result as plausible, though not assured. For a criticism of Piquet by Foerster cp. the latter's edition of Chrétien's *Lancelot*, pp. CXLIV ff., note 1. In my opinion, Foerster is nearer the truth than any of the other participants in this controversy.

Since Foerster's death, Zenker, "Weiteres zur Mabinogionfrage: II, Die Bearbeitungen von Chrétien's *Erec* in ihrem Verhältnis zu diesem, und zu dem kymrischen Mabinogi", *Zs. f. frz. Spr. u. Litt.* XLV[1], 47 ff. (1917), has argued that Hartmann used a form of the Erec story which was, in many respects, different from Chrétien's. Some of his points are worthy of attention, but, on the whole, they are, in my opinion, susceptible of explanation on the same principles as the instances which I have discussed in the text. The *Anhang* (pp. 95 ff.) to this article consists of a reply to W. Meyer-Lübke,

Erec for the sparrow-hawk contest is poor and rusty, as accorded with the owner's poverty; in Chrétien it is fine and bright. The Welsh is more logical and hence preserves a more primitive form of the incident.

In reply one might say that armor is the last thing that a knight would neglect, and, as Zenker concedes, there is no absolute reason for condemning Chrétien's version. On the other hand, the Welsh author might naturally have changed Chrétien, in order to harmonize the armor with the general poverty of Erec's host. This is all the more likely, inasmuch as the suggestion lay ready to hand in the terms of Erec's request for arms (ll. 609f.):

> D'unes armes viez ou noveles.
> Ne me chaut ou leides ou beles.

As regards the partial agreement with W in H (Hartmann), who represents the armor as bright, but the shield, spear, and covering of the horse as obsolete and unsuitable, on which Zenker lays stress, this is, no doubt, a half-hearted attempt on the part of the German poet in the same direction as W. Zenker's explanation, however, seems to me forced, viz. that H had two versions before him, one like Chrétien's, the other like W's, and that he took the description of the shield and spear from the latter and the rest from the former.

2. pp. 35 ff. In the duel between Erec (Geraint) and Yder, according to W and H, both break several lances, before they begin the fight with swords on foot, and in the end the hero only unhorses his opponent with a lance given him by Enid's father. In Chrétien, too, the old man gives Erec a lance (implied in *le*

"Chrestien von Troyes Erec und Enide", *ibid.*, XLI, 129 ff., who, among other things, had expressed his agreement with Foerster and Becker as to the direct dependence of the Welsh *Gereint* on Chrétien.

The present work was about to go to press, when Zenker's *Forschungen zur Artusepik I. Ivainstudien* (Halle, 1921) reached me. In this volume he maintains, of course, the same side in the *Mabinogion* controversy as in his previous writings — more especially, with reference to the *Yvain*. As I have said above, I regret that his book arrived too late for me to take account of it in the present treatise.

soreplus, l. 629) beforehand, but the weapon is not mentioned specifically in the account of the combat. Moreover, after a single tilt both combatants are unhorsed and resume the fight with swords on foot.

The agreement between W and H is not perfect, for in the former Ynywl steps forward during the fight and presents the spear to the hero, whereas in H Erec already has it and merely reserves it to the last. Descriptions of combats in the Arthurian romances are rarely so brief as this one in Chrétien, and it was quite natural for two writers independently to try to enhance the interest of the narrative by the device of retardation. There is always the possibility, too, which Foerster emphasizes, *Karrenritter*, pp. cxxxvf., that they were using MSS. that contained variant readings not preserved in our extant MSS. In view of the wholesale agreement of W and Chrétien throughout their narratives, it would be unjustifiable to attach any importance to this partial coincidence in respect to a minute detail between W and H.

3. pp. 39ff., 62ff. The motive of jealousy which is found in W, but not in C. I have already discussed this above.

4. pp. 44ff. When the importunate count in Chrétien (ll. 3522ff.) comes to abduct Enid, he finds that she and Erec have departed and he sets out in pursuit, but nothing is said of his questioning the host in regard to their flight. In both W and H, however, we have a dialogue of this sort, although different in detail. In W the count asks in anger why the innkeeper did not warn him of their departure, to which the man replies that the count had not ordered him to do so. Moreover, he can only tell the nobleman that the pair took the high road on leaving the inn. In H the host is as high-tempered as the count, and a heated colloquy ensues, in which the former denies any knowledge as to the whereabouts of the supposed fugitives. The dialogue here is longer and the count more suspicious of the host.

It is quite possible that Foerster's theory, mentioned in the discussion of No. 2, applies also in this case. But, after all, such a dialogue is naturally suggested by the situation, and Chrétien's treatment of the count's descent upon the inn is, perhaps, unduly abrupt. There is, consequently, nothing arbitrary in assuming with Gaede that W and H hit upon their additions independently here. As a parallel example, take the coincidence between W and the Old French prose version (cp. Zenker, p. 55) in respect to the dwarf at the beginning of the story. Chrétien (ll. 225ff.) says that when the dwarf struck Erec, the latter failed to resent it, because the dwarf's master, standing by, was armed, as Erec was not. In addition, both W and the Old French prose declare that he was also restrained by the feeling that for a knight to slay a dwarf would have done dishonor to the knight. Now, no one has ever maintained that the prose had any other source than Chrétien, yet here it agrees with W. The reason is that the situation suggested this appeal to what was a common mediaeval sentiment.

5. pp. 48ff. In Chrétien (ll. 4045ff.), Erec, with the butt of his spear, unhorses Kay (Keu), but when he learns that the horse which Kay was riding belonged to Gawain he at once surrenders it. Kay takes the steed back to court and recounts the affair there. Arthur's curiosity is aroused, and he sends Gawain to fetch the stranger to him. Erec, however, being wounded and, generally, in bad condition, declines, but Gawain sends a "vaslet" to tell the king to pitch his tent at a point on the road where he will have the chance of making the acquaintance of "the best knight, of a truth, that he might ever expect to see." Presumably, because of his armor, Gawain does not recognize Erec. On the contrary, in W he does recognize him, and so Zenker contends that here again we have in W a logical, primitive trait which proves its independence of Chrétien; for how could Gawain speak of a knight that he did not know in such terms? The expression, however, is obviously hyperbolical -- purposely so on Gawain's part, probably, as Becker, LB, XXXIV, 25, has observed, in order to excite Arthur's curiosity all the more — and is not at all unnatural, when one considers the impression which Kay's report of the stranger's prowess and courtesy (the latter, *nota bene*, shown especially to Gawain) had made at court and how this impression was deepened by the sight of Erec, himself. We may take the

alteration in W, then, as simply another example of the literal tendency of the author's mind.

It will be observed that only Nos. 2 and 4 among Zenker's objections are based on concrete evidence. The rest are, to all intents and purposes, subjective. The controversy is continued, in part, by W. A. Nitze in "The Romance of Erec, son of Lac," MPh., XI, 445 ff. (1914), especially, pp. 471 ff., where the author, though believing that Chrétien was using a Celtic source, maintains, *versus* Edens, that *Erec* is more primitive than *Geraint*. For the rest, Nitze explains Erec's treatment of Enid as due to his desire to assert the principle of the husband's "sovereignty" in marriage, at all costs (p. 448). I cannot agree with Nitze (pp. 459 ff.) in accepting the theory of E. Philipot, *Romania*, XXV, 264,[7] (1896) and M. Roques, *ibid.*, XXXIX, 379 ff.[8] (1910), that the story of Enid is simply an adaptation of the Joie de la Cort story near the end of the *Erec*.[9] There is not a trace of the supernatural in the former, as we have it, and where the incidents are so totally different, there is no basis for the idea that Chrétien gave a new and rationalized shape to the original Joie de la Cort story with the aim of pre-

---

[7] In the article "Un épisode d'*Erec et Enide*: La Joie de la Cour-Mabon l'enchanteur", *Romania*, XXV, 258 ff. The author discusses its relations to the *Bel Inconnu* romances, especially. He regards (pp. 293 f.) *Geraint* as derived directly from *Erec*.

[8] In his review of Myrrha Borodine's *La femme et l'amour au XII siècle d'après les poèmes de Chrétien de Troyes* (Paris, 1909), where, p. 76, Erec's conduct to his wife is explained on the principle that the duties of knighthood must be superior to love. Roques objects to the current view that the Joie de la Cort episode is an "hors-d'oeuvre"; but the looseness of structure of the Arthurian romances permitted such an episode.

[9] In his article, "The Sloth of Erec", *Romanic Review*, IX, 1 ff. (1918), M. B. Ogle, answering Nitze, disputes (rightly, I believe) any connection between the Erec-Enide story and the fairy mistress theme. He cites (pp. 9 ff.) examples from Latin literature and from mediaeval works that continue the classical tradition to prove that the opposition of love to endeavor was a commonplace of such literature. Cp. Nitze's rejoinder, "Erec's Treatment of Enide", *ibid.* X, 26 ff. (1919).

senting an intentional contrast "entre la sage Enide et sa romanesque cousine" (Roques). A brief summary of the story of
the "cousine" (ll. 6052ff.) will reveal the difference: A knight
(Mabonagrain) unwarily binds himself, by a *don*, to his lady-love
never to leave the marvelous garden, in which his uncle Evrain
had conferred on him the order of knighthood, until he is overcome by some challenger. She did not believe that this would
ever happen, and, on the other hand, she told him that she would
abandon him, should he violate his pledge. He slays many knights
who attempt the adventure, but is, at last, vanquished by Erec,
who then blows a magic horn and dissolves the enchantment, thereby
liberating the knight. A wall, as it were, of air (ll. 5739ff.),
created by necromancy, had cut off the garden from the surrounding
world.

We have evidently here in partly rationalized form the story
of a fay who keeps her mortal lover in her power by a spell,[10]
but in what point has it any relation to the story of Enid?

Furthermore, in RR. V, 115ff. (1914), in his article, "Why
does Chrétien's Erec treat Enid so harshly?," E. S. Sheldon rejects Nitze's solution and argues that in the passage, ll. 2493ff.,
Erec only heard Enid's "Con mar i fus!" (l. 2507) and, observing her weeping, asked her the cause, and that, when she evaded
a direct answer, until she was forced to give one, her husband's
confidence in her sincerity was shaken — hence his harsh conduct
towards her. This, however, seems hardly an adequate motive,
even from the mediaeval point of view, for so long a course of ill-
treatment.[11]

---

[10] The Calypso-Ulysses *motif*, which is frequent, too, in Celtic
tales. Foerster, *Wörterbuch*, p. 116*, interprets it as a variant of
the *motif* of the liberation of a girl whom a giant has made captive,
but the girl here is evidently the dominant figure.

[11] J. H. Kool: "Le problème *Erec-Geraint*", *Neophilologus*, III,
167ff. (Groningen, 1918), examines Chrétien's method of paraphrasing
Ovid in his *Philomena* and tries to apply the results to the *Erec* problem.
This is all beside the mark, however, and the article is negligible.
In MLN, XVIII, 220ff. (1903) A. J. Morrison has pointed out an
apparent imitation of *Erec* — decayed gentleman *motif* — in *Sone*

The name, "Erec", is *Breton*. Cp. J. Loth, *Revue Celtique*, XIII, 482ff. (1892), and *Mabinogion²*, I, 56 (1913).¹² F. Lot, *de Nausay*, ll. 12673ff. and *ibid.*, XX, 222f. (1905), a Modern Welsh parallel, in Allen Raine's *Heart of Wales* (London, 1905), pp. 2ff., for the same *motif*.

¹² Zimmer, *Zs. f. frz. Spr. u. Litt.*, XII¹, 26ff. had wrongly argued that "Erec" was a Germanic name and had identified the character with Eoric, King of the Westgoths (466—485), who were established in Southern Gaul. Zimmer wished still further to discard *Outre-Gales*, the name of Erec's conntry, which Foerster adopts in his edition of the poem (ll. 1874, 3881), and substitutes therefor *Estregales*, which in some MSS. takes the place of *Outregales* (l. 3881). This *Estregales* Zimmer derives from an hypothetical *Dextra Gallia*, which he interprets as Southern Gaul. Through a misunderstanding of the original, *Destregales*, he thinks, came to be interpreted as *d'Estregales* (*Estregales* meaning "Beyond Wales") — hence in the MSS. just referred to we have (l. 3881): "Rois est mes pere d'Estregales". Space prevents me from summarizing the "evidence" with which he supports this hypothesis. Suffice it to say that it is of the flimsiest character. *Destregales* is not found anywhere, except once (continuation to Chrétien's *Perceval*, l. 13725), and that in a passage so corrupt that nobody knows what it means. The only thing certain about the line is that the form *Destregales* in it is due merely to a scribe's blunder. On the other hand, *Dextra Gallia* is purely hypothetical. F. Lot, *Romania*, XXV, 7ff. (1896), accepts, however, Zimmer's *Destregales* and *Dextra Gallia* — only he interprets them as referring to South Wales and cites in favor of his interpretation from Welsh writings, *dextralis Walliae pars, dextralis Kambria, dextralis Britannia*. G. Paris, however, in a note at the end of Lot's article (p. 32), disputes the whole basis of his and Zimmer's speculations, viz. that *d'Estregales* in *Erec*, ll. 1874, 3881, is not the correct reading. His own suggested reading, *d'Osteregales* (= *Australis Wallia* of Giraldus Cambrensis), however, has no manuscript authority. Lot's interpretation is, no doubt, a consequence of his theory that Chrétien's source for *Erec* was Welsh. I have commented, above, on the other supposed evidence for this theory which he has adduced.

In the *Zs. f. frz. Spr. u. Litt.*, XXVII¹, 78ff. (1804) E. Brugger has offered some effective criticism of Zimmer and Lot, and would himself identify Estregales with Strathclyde ("Valley of the Clyde"), the old Celtic kingdom, which extended from the Derwent (in England) to the Clyde (in Scotland). He derives the name, *Estregales*, from

Romania, XXV, 588 ff. (1896), has identified him with an actual Count of Nantes of the same name who died about 990, but
historical conditions render it probable that the Bretons regarded
this personage as an enemy, rather than as a national hero, and
so Lot thinks that he is a substitute for the original hero, Geraint, who ruled (cp. *ibid.*, pp. 10f.) over Devon and Cornwall
in the latter part of the seventh century. In Foerster's edition,
however, of Chrétien's 'Karrenritter (*Lancelot*, pp. cxvf.), Zimmer
points out that there were two earlier princes named "Weroc"
(= "Erec") in the sixth century in south-east Brittany (including
Nantes) and that the second (last quarter of the century) was
famous on account of his battles with the Franks. The objection to the tenth century Erec would not apply in these cases.
In any event, the substitution of the unpopular Erec of the tenth
century for an earlier hero would be hard to explain.

In *Romania*, XXX, 21 (1901), Lot, also, identifies Enide
with "enit", the Welsh word for "woodlark", which he says does
not exist in Breton, as far as he knows. In the absence of early
Breton records, however, one cannot say whether this was true
of the period with which we are particularly concerned or not,[13]
and, besides, the similarity between the forms just named may
be purely accidental.[14]

According to Lot (*Romania*, XXV, 9ff.) certain names of
places in Chrétien's poem (Rotelan-Ruddlan, Caradigan, etc.) prove

Celtic *Stratcloith* through an hypothetical *Estregalo(u) (-i)*. His
conclusions, however, depend on the validity of a long chain of speculations (pp. 97ff.) and are anything but convincing.

[13] In *Romania*, XXIV, 321ff. (1895) F. Lot, also, interprets the
name, "Mabonagrain", as a combination of "Mabon" and "Evrain",
names of two magicians who figure in *Le Bel Inconnu* (which is,
itself, of course, of much later date than the *Erec*), "Evrain" being
really a distortion of "Euuain" (= "Owain"). It seems to me, however, more likely that the author of *Le Bel Inconnu (Li Biaus
Descouneus)* took the name "Evrain" direct from Mabonagrain's uncle
in the *Erec* and that he shortened Mabonagrain's own name into
"Mabon", because the latter was easier to handle in the verse.

[14] Cp. Brugger, *Zs. f. frz. Spr. u. Litt.*, XXVII[1], 89 (1904)
— also, W. Meyer-Lübke, *ibid.*, XLIV[1], 144f. (including note 19).

that the story came from Cornwall to Brittany by way of Wales —
which, one may remark, would accord with the (now) abandoned
theory of Anglo-Norman origin of the Arthurian romances, but
would be a singularly indirect route for a tale actually to take
in passing from the one country to the other. Besides, as Lot
five years later himself observes, *Romania* XXX, 19 f. (1901),
Cardigan (Caradigan), as the name of a town, is not Welsh, but
Norman, the place to this day being known to the Welsh as
Aberteivi.

These names play, also, an important part in the argument
of Edens and Zenker. Chrétien, however, would naturally locate
the plot of an Arthurian romance in Great Britain and consequently make the place-names, in some degree, conform with this
conception. Similarly, the Welsh, in adapting Chrétien's romances, would cymricise names of all kinds more completely, substituting, for example, "Geraint" for "Erec", with which they
were not familiar.

In addition to the scholars who have taken an active part in
this controversy, J. Loth and A Nutt have also accepted the hypothesis of a common French source for W and Chrétien. Cp.,
respectively, *Les Mabinogion*[2], I, 53 ff. (Paris, 1913), and the reprint of Lady Charlotte Guest's *Mabinogion* (London, 1902), with
notes by Alfred Nutt, pp. 351—354. Nutt here expresses the opinion that G. Paris's earlier theory of common Anglo-Norman
sources for Chrétien and the so-called *Mabinogion* is "probably
very near the truth" (p. 353). F. Lot, *Romania*, XXV, 8, 12
(1896), seems disposed, also, to believe in the complete independence of the *Mabinogion*, and E. Windisch, in the work already
cited, pp. 221 ff., goes furthest of all in taking up the impossible
position that the *Mabinogion* show no French influence at all.

J. Loth was unfortunate in declaring, *op. cit.*, I, 51, that
"En dehors de l'école de Foerster, dont le plus remarquable tenant
est W. Golther, on ne voit plus dans les romans gallois une traduction des romans francais." (One has to take "traduction" here
in the sense of "adaptation", since it is not contended that the
Welsh stories were literal translations of Chrétien.) For certainly

Brugger and Nitze, to say nothing of P. A. Becker, do not belong to Foerster's school, and yet within a few years of the publication of Loth's work (the second edition) both had expressed the opinion that *Peredur* was merely an adaptation of the *Conte del Graal.* For the articles in question see my discussion of *Peredur*, above. Every probability of course, favors the supposition that, if one of these tales is derived from Chrétien, the others are, too.[15]

The controversy which has been carried on with such ardor and, frequently, with such acrimony, in regard to the relations of Chrétien's *Erec* and the Welsh *Geraint and Enid* has extended, of course, to the similar question in regard to the relations of his *Yvain* to the Welsh *Owain* (i. e. *Lady of the Fountain*). It is impossible for us, however, in this place, to discuss the questions at issue so fully as we have done in the case of *Erec*. Suffice it to say that the following are the most important contributions to the *Yvain-Owain* controversy: 1. Foerster's large edition of the *Yvain*, pp. xix ff. (1886). 2. A. C. L. Brown, "On the independent character of the Welsh Owain," RR., III, 143 ff. (1912), advocating a common source, an Anglo-French metrical or Latin prose romance (p. 157). 3. A. Smirnov's review of Brown's article in *Revue Celtique*, XXXIV, 337 ff. (1913). 4. Walter Greiner's Leipzig diss.,[16] *Owein-Ivain: Neue Beiträge zur Frage nach der Unabhängigkeit der Kymrischen Mabinogion von den Romanen Chrestiens. Erster Teil* (Halle, 1917). 5. R. Zenker, *Ivain-Studien* (Halle, 1921).

Both nos, 4 and 5 conclude that Chrétien and the Welsh go back independently to an ultimate common source.

No. 2 is valuable for the parallels (pp. 157 ff.) which the author has collected from Celtic literature to features of *Owain*. This does not conflict, however, with the hypothesis that *Owain*

---

[15] The sparrow-hawk adventure (ll. 342 ff.) was borrowed from *Erec* by some of the later romances. Cp. W. H. Schofield, *Studies on the Libeaus Desconus*, 164 ff. (Boston, 1895) and W. A. Nitze, MPh. XI, 450 ff. (1914).

[16] This has been published, also, in the *Zs. f. celt. Ph.*, XII, 1 ff. (1918).

is dependent on *Yvain*. We should simply have here the same method of cymricisation of the French original that is observable in a somewhat more marked degree in *Peredur*. Brown's effort to prove that the Welsh tale is more primitive than *Yvain*, because it is (supposedly) more logical in some points, has been successfully refuted, in my opinion, by Smirnov. Moreover, as Foerster has remarked, *Zs. f. rom. Ph.*, XXXVI, 734, note 1 (1912) and Chrétien *Wörterbuch*, 140ff. (1914), if Laudine, the easily consoled widow, is imitated from Jocaste in the *Roman de Thèbes*, then, *Owain* is certainly dependent on *Yvain*. Now, the imitation in question seems undeniable, and has been accepted as such by a number of especial students of the subject. Cp. *Wörterbuch*, 107*, note 1.

In closeness to the corresponding romance of Chrétien, *Owain*, though much condensed, stands midway between *Geraint* and *Peredur*, the last-named showing (in certain sections) the widest departures from the French, through the addition of new materials. The episode of the Pesme Avanture (*Yvain*, ll. 5109ff.) is in *Owain* placed at the end of Yvain's exploits, but the story is the same.[17]

For the relation of *Peredur* to Chrétien's *Perceval* and its continuations, cp. I, 342ff., above.

---

[17] The three romances of Chrétien discussed above have come down to us, also, in mediaeval Scandinavian versions: *Erexsaga, Iventsaga, Parzivalsaga*, edited by E. Kölbing in his *Riddarasögur* (Strassburg, 1872). Chrétien is generally acknowledged to be the sole source of these Old Norse prose tales. For detailed comparisons with the French, besides the work just named, see E. Kölbing, "Die nordische Erexsaga und ihre Quelle", Pfeiffer's *Germania*, XVI, 381 ff. (1871), and on the *Parzivalsaga, ibid.* XIV, 129ff. (1869) — also, introductions to Foerster's large editions of the *Erec* and *Yvain*, respectively. The analogy of these Norse sagas has been often cited in support of the view that Chrétien was, likewise, the only source of the three Welsh tales.

Chapter V.
The Sources of Chrétien's **Yvain**.

As Nitze has observed,[1] we have in Laudine's story neither
the heroine's luring on of the hero to the adventure (enticement
motif) nor the liberation of the heroine by the hero, which are
fundamental characteristics of the fairy mistress theme. Yvain
goes to the fountain to avenge his cousin, Calogrenant (l. 589).
He knows nothing of Laudine, and she knows nothing of him,
until he invades the castle under the circumstances which we have
seen, and, as the story stands, she is not in need of liberation.
Then, we have the complete divergence between the *Yvain* and
Cuchullin's Sick Bed concerned in respect to accessory details.

---

[1] MPh., VII, 160, note 5 (1909). G. Ehrismann, PBB, XXX,
14 ff. ("Märchen im höfischen Epos") distinguishes as the most important *motifs* in the Arthurian romances (1) the *Verlockungsmotiv*
(the fairy's enticement of the hero into fairy-land), (2) the *Befreiungs-
motiv* (liberation from the fairy's power), and regards both as drawn
from Celtic — more particularly, Irish — *Märchen*. For a list of
scholars, beginning with Osterwald in 1853, who have derived the
Yvain from a Celtic fairy tale cp. Brown, *Iwain*, pp. 19 ff. and MPh.
IX, 109, note 4 (1911). Especially noteworthy is G. Paris's idea,
Romania, XVII, 334 f. (1888) that the *Yvain* story is of the same
type as that of *Guingamor, Ogier le Danois, Tannhäuser* etc.: A
mortal marries a fay, leaves her, intending to return, but forgets his
promise or breaks her commands. In Chrétien, however, Laudine is
not called "the lady of the fountain", as Paris asserts. This epithet
is found only in the corresponding Welsh tale. Ahlström makes the
same mistake in his "Sur l'origine du Chevalier au Lion", *Mélanges
de Philologie romane dédiés à Carl Wahlund*" (Macon, 1896),
p. 297. His interpretation (p. 301) of Laudine as a "femme-cygne"
(cp. the Wieland saga) is entirely baseless. G. Baist interprets her as
a "Wasserfrau" whose story Chrétien attached to the spring in the
forest of Broceliande. Cp. Baist's article, "Die Quellen des Yvain",
Zs. f. rom. Ph., XXI, 402 ff. (1897).

In rejecting Professor Brown's solution of the problem,[2] one must confess that none of the alternate hypotheses are wholly satisfactory. The basis of the plot is, no doubt, a *märchen*. Chrétien, however, has altered his source to such a degree that the outlines of the original are no longer recognizable. Professor Nitze[3] had endeavored to explain the fountain story as derived from the myth of the Arician Diana, whose armed priest guarded the grove and lake[4] of the goddess in the Alban hills near Aricia.

---

[2] Cp. I, 94 ff., above. — In his article, "Chrétien's 'Yvain'", MPh., IX, 109 ff. (1911), Brown adds to his original theory of the fairy mistress theme a feud motive. The "Hospitable Host, to whose party doubtless were attached both Lunete and Laudine, was oppressed by a tyrannical fairy foe, Esclados the Red, who had got Laudine into his power. Lunete went to Arthur's court in the interests of the Hospitable Host to persuade some mortal into undertaking the adventure of the Fountain Perilous" (p. 111). But, this is substituting for the actual story preserved in Chrétien's text one so entirely different that I see no profit in discussing it.

Even in his comparison of the *Yvain* with the *Serglige Cuchulain* Brown has been criticised by G. Ehrismann (who, in the main, agrees with him) for stressing the resemblances between the two and neglecting the differences. Cp., too, PBB, XXX, 42, and more strongly A. Jeanroy, *Revue Critique*, for Jan. 2, 1905, p. 4. For a similar criticism of this defect of Brown's method *in re* Holy Grail, cp. A. Nutt, *The Academy*, May 7, 1910, and *in re Yvain*, Windisch, *Das Keltische Britannien bis zu Kaiser Arthur*, p. 181 (Leipzig, 1912).

[3] First in his review of Brown's *Iwain* in MLN, XIX, 84 (1904), and more fully in his articles, "A New Source of the *Yvain*", MPh., III, 267 ff. (1905) and "The Fountain Defended", *ibid.* VII, 145 ff. (1909). In the latter article (p. 160), however, he assumes that the myth was combined or confounded with the fairy mistress theme. In this new form, then, his theory would relate only to the ultimate source of the *Yvain*. In MPh. IX, 116 ff. Brown has offered some good criticism of this theory. I agree with Brown, *ibid.*, p. 127, that in attempting to go behind the immediate sources of the *Yvain* (whatever they may be) Nitze is undertaking the impossible.

[4] Not fountain. The interpretation of this myth forms, of course, the starting-point of Sir J. G. Frazer's famous treatise, *The Golden Bough*.

until some intruder — usually a runaway slave — challenged the priest by breaking a sacred bough near her temple, and, if victor in the combat that ensued, became the defender of the lake. Apart, however, from the fact that there is no storm-making quality associated with the Arician lake, there is no evidence that this myth was ever localized in Brittany or that any native Gallic fountain-cult ever assumed this form, under the influence of the Arician myth, and, in the absence of such evidence, the theory is unacceptable. On the other hand, according to the interpretation of Foerster,[5] the *märchen* involved is the familiar one of the girl whom a giant has captured and who is liberated by the hero — a *motif*, of course, which is, in no way, specifically Celtic. The storm-making spring was then foreign to the original story, but was introduced by Chrétien from the description which Wace gives in his *Roman de Rou*, ll. 6395 ff., of the spring of Berenton in the famous Breton forest of Broceliande,[6] just as he

---

[5] Cp. his *Yvain*, pp. XXXIV ff. (1902) and Chrétien *Wörterbuch*, pp. 109 * ff. (1914). Pp. 95 * ff. of the latter work offer a comprehensive discussion of all *Yvain* problems and the critical literature pertaining thereto down to 1914. So, too, — from the opposite point of view — does R. Zenker's *Ivainstudien* (Halle, 1921), which reached me too late to be used in this book.

[6] Wace, *loc. cit.*, says that, according to the Bretons, huntsmen would pour water from the spring on a *perron* by its side and a rain would fall on the forest and surrounding region. He says scornfully, however, that he went to Berenton and that he did not see verified this or any of the other marvels which the Bretons tell of the forest. For the passage in Wace and other testimony to this Berenton fable cp. Foerster, Chrétien *Wörterbuch*, pp. 99 * ff. For parallel stories elsewhere, cp. Louise B. Morgan "The Source of the Fountain Story in *Ywain*", MPh., VI, 331 ff. and Nitze, *ibid.*, 148 ff. (1908). G. L. Hamilton is bringing out in the *Romanic Review* a study entitled "Storm-making Springs: Studies on the sources of the Yvain", in which he is to deal with all such stories in popular tradition throughout the world. He has published two sections of the study, *ibid.*, II, 355 ff. (1911) and V, 213 ff. (1914), but has not yet reached the more immediate parallels to the *Yvain* spring. In his "Christian von Troyes *Yvain* und die Brandanuslegende", *Zs. f. vergl. Litteraturgeschichte,* N. F., XI, 442 ff. (1897), E. Kölbing thinks that the birds in the

also introduced from the *Roman de Thèbes*, ll. 223ff., the *motif* of the widow, easily consoled, who marries her husband's slayer almost immediately after the event.[7] Like Jocaste, the widow

---

Yvain, ll. 460ff., who sing their "servise", after the storm at the spring has passed away, were taken from a similar description in the legend of the Irish St. Brendan, and Nitze, MPh., III, 274, note 2, agrees with him. But the ecclesiastical image involved (the birds singing a service) might occur to a writer in any age or country. Cp. the elaborate use of the *motif* in the pseudo-Chaucerian *Court of Love*, ll. 1352ff. An example from the *Arabian Nights* is given by John C. Hodges, MLN, XXXII, 282, (1917). It is a similar conception when Salvator Rosa, condemning in his First Satire the custom of the Italian princes of the seventeenth century in maintaining eunuchs in their households as singers, says:

> "E in vece di un castrato ingordo e rio
> Tenete un rusignol che nulla chiede,
> E forse i canti suoi son inni a Dio."

[7] A. G. Van Hamel first pointed this out in *Romanische Forschungen*, XXIII (volume entitled *Mélanges Chabineau*), 911ff. (1907). His observation, which, I believe, is certainly right, has been widely accepted. Cp. Foerster, *Wörterbuch*, p. 107*, note 1. In his first small edition of *Yvain*, pp. XVf. (1891), Foerster had compared the character of Laudine with that of the Widow of Ephesus, so well-known from Petronius's *Satyricon*, ch. 111—112, and studied in all the variants of the *motif* by E. Grisebach, *Die Wanderung der Novelle von der treulosen Wittwe durch die Weltlitteratur* (2nd. ed. Berlin, 1889). The characters unquestionably are very much alike, but the circumstances of their stories are too widely different to be connected historically, since in the Widow of Ephesus group, to mention only one fundamental divergence, the second husband is not the slayer of the first. Foerster's idea that Chrétien's picture of Laudine's fickleness was suggested by some contemporary incident is not very probable. In his article, "Byzantinisch-Geschichtliches im Cliges und Yvain", *Zs. f. rom. Ph.*, XXXII, 400ff. Franz Settegast goes so far as to identify her with the Byzantine empress, Eudoxia, and Yvain with this empress's husband, Romanos IV Diogenes (1068—1071); but there is really no analogy between the two sets of incidents. Nitze, MPh. XI, 459, note, pertinently calls attention to the actual practice of Chrétien's contemporaries in regard to re-marriage. Even women of the highest birth were less squeamish than is usually the case now in such matters. One does not have to go back to Irish analogues like that which

of Laius in the *Roman de Thèbes*, who marries Oedipus, her first
husband's slayer, Laudine, too, is aware of the identity of her
first husband's slayer, as her vassals are not, but she pretends
to yield to their entreaties to marry him, because she wants to
have a defender for her possessions.[8] For the rest of the story,
Foerster argues that in conscious contrast to Erec, who, from uxori-
ousness, fell into a neglect of arms, Chrétien makes his new hero
scorn such slackness and continue to devote his life to deeds of
knighthood. It is true that the fickle lady, being angered by his
neglect, breaks with him and so throws him into a state of mad-
ness, but after his marvelous cure he still devotes himself to knightly adventure up to the reconciliation at the end. The particular
adventures had no original connection with one another and are
here linked together for the first time.[9] One of them, indeed,

---

Windisch, *Das keltische Britannien bis zu Kaiser Arthur*, p. 167,
points out: Cuchullin marries Aiffe, whose husband he had just slain.

[8] As I have said in the text, I believe that Foerster is right in
his identification of Laudine with the heroine of the *märchen* indicated
above, but I cannot agree with him when he reads this same *motif*,
Yvain[4], pp. XXXIVff., and *Wörterbuch*, pp. 109*ff. into the Joie de
la Cort episode of *Erec*. The predominance of the girl in the latter
shows, it seems to me, that we have here a real instance of the fairy
mistress theme. Moreover, I cannot share Foerster's opinion (*loc. cit.*)
as to the importance of the passages in the *Lanzelet* and *Huon de
Bordeaux*. Nitze, MPh., VII, 161, note (1909) has already remarked
that the *Huon* passage is clearly an imitation or reminiscence of the
Yvain, and believes that the same thing is true of the *Lanzelet* —
a third-rate poem that is made up of borrowings from every quarter,
including Chrétien's romances, as Foerster, himself, *loc. cit.* observes.

[9] This is the view expressed by Baist in the article, cited above.
The first part (the fountain-story) he thinks (pp. 404f.) "hat stofflich
den Charakter eines Lais, nicht den eines Romans". In contrast with
Baist and Foerster, — and, I may add, Golther, *Zs. f. frz. Spr. u. Litt.*,
XXVIII[2], 36 (1904) — we have A. C. L. Brown's effort, "The Knight
of the Lion", PMLA, XX 673ff. (1905) above-mentioned to force all
the varied incidents of the part that follows the fountain story into the
pattern of a single Celtic fairy tale (type of *Cuchullin's Sickbed*),
which, in my judgment, is impossible. As far as *Yvain's* love-madness
is concerned, one does not have to go to Irish saga for this *motif*. In-

the episode of the Pesme Avanture (= Worst Adventure) is, indeed, merely a variant of the *märchen* on which the first part of the poem is based — viz. that of a girl, the captive of a giant, who is liberated by the hero. There can be little doubt that Foerster

sanity on account of love was a regularly recognized disease in mediaeval practice. Cp. J. L. Lowes' well-known article, "The Lover's Maladye of Hereos", MPh., XI, 491 ff. (1914). As Baist says *(loc. cit.)* Chrétien, no doubt, really took the conception from the *Folie de Tristan*.

Baist is also, no doubt, right in deriving the *motif* of the grateful lion, which gave its name to the poem, from the classical story of Androclus and the lion. In the original form of the story the cause of the beast's gratitude was that the hero had drawn a thorn from his paw. Already by the first half of the eleventh century, a serpent had superseded the thorn, and it is in this form that Chrétien uses the story. Cp. on the whole subject G. Baist "Der dankbare Löwe", *Roman. Forsch.*, XXIX, 317 ff. (1910). He quotes an example from *Petri Damiani Epistol.* VI, 5 (first half of the eleventh century). The best account of this *motif* (including cognate forms) has been given by O. M. Johnston, "The Episode of Ivain, the Lion and the Serpent in Chrétien de Troyes", *Zs. f. frz. Spr. u. Litt.*, XXXI[1], 157 ff. (1907). Whether the *motif* is of oriental origin (as Johnston maintains) or not, is, I believe, of little consequence with reference to Chrétien, for he knew it, no doubt, merely in its (modified) classical form. The story was told, indeed, of an actual knight, Golfier de las Tors (from the Limousin), who participated in the first crusade. Various legends attached themselves to his name — among others, that of the grateful lion whom he delivered from a serpent. This last-named legend was connected with him, it would seem, at least, as early as the latter part of the twelfth century. The earliest record of it is found in the Latin chronicle of Jaufré, prior of Vigeois, and is quoted by P. Meyer, *Chanson de la Croisade contre les Albigeois*, II, 379, note 1 (Paris, 1879). For repetitions of this story about Golfier and his lion and allusions thereto see Meyer, *loc. cit.*, A. Thomas, *Romania*, XXXIV, 55 ff. (1905), XL, 446 ff. (1911) — also, A. Pillet, *Beiträge zur Kritik der ältesten Troubadours*, (Breslau, 1911). The story passed into the Italian, too. Cp. "Unpublished Manuscripts of Italian Bestiaries", by K. Mackenzie, PMLA, XX, 395 f. (1905).

Brown had contended that Chrétien's lion came· from the Celts. Cp. his list of lions and guiding beasts in Celtic Otherworld tales, PMLA, XXV, 688 ff. (1905).

is correct in crediting Chrétien with the combination of this series of adventures which make up the greater part of the *Yvain.* If the poem were, indeed, developed from a single source, it would constitute an exception among the Arthurian romances. As regards the cardinal episode of the poem, Yvain's combat at the spring and his winning of the heroine, it will be objected here again that in the actual story, as told by Chrétien, there is no suggestion that Laudine required liberation. This is, of course, true, yet on no other *märchen motif* could the somewhat cynical idea of the easily consoled widow, borrowed from the *Roman de Thèbes,* be so easily grafted as on this one. In such *märchen* the girl captive passes at once, of course, from the possession of her captor into that of the hero, as is the case in Chrétien's poem, although the treatment of the incident in the former instance is, of course, purely naive.

W. Foerster, who suggested this interpretation of the story of Laudine, denies that Chrétien's source was Celtic. The setting of the story, however, seems Celtic, and so, in all probability, it was a Celtic form of this wide-spread *motif* that Chrétien employed.[10]

---

[10] The closest parallel to the capital episode of *Yvain* — the fountain story — is to be found in the Irish tale, *In Gilla Decair,* where we have a fight between the hero and a water-spirit who defends his fountain. This was first pointed out by F. Lot, "Le Chevalier au Lion: comparaison avec une légende irlandaise", *Romania,* XXI, 67 ff. (1892). Cp. Brown's *Iwain,* pp. 104 ff. for an analysis of the tale. In other respects, however, the two stories are unlike. We have no copy of this tale earlier than the eighteenth century, and so I agree with Nitze, MPh., VII, 155 f., as against G. L. Hamilton, RR, II, 355 and Brown, MPh., IX, 122 ff., in regarding the story as too late to afford a safe basis for the study of *Yvain* origins, although he is wrong in asserting that we have preserved an Irish translation of Chrétien's romance, also from the eighteenth century. Cp. Brown, *loc. cit.,* p. 120, note 4. For Welsh marvellous springs, see, especially, G. Dottin, *Annales de Bretagne,* XXIII, 469 ff. (1907—8).

Brown, *Iwain,* pp. 70 ff., lays stress on the parallel of a similar herdsman in the Irish *Imram Maelduin (Voyage of Maelduin).* But Brugger, *Zs. f. frz. Spr. u. Litt.,* XXXIII °, 62 (1908), asserts that this figure is not peculiar to Celtic Otherworld tales — that it is even commoner in similar stories in the Germanic languages. I do not find, however, anything quite similar in Hans Siuts's *Jenseitsmotive im deutschen Volksmärchen* (Leipzig, 1911), which contains a pretty exhaustive list of everything pertaining to Otherworld conceptions in specifically German territory. Giants of one sort or another, filling such rôles, are, of course, frequent (cp. *ibid.*, pp. 161 ff.), but there appear to be no herdsmen among them. Only the tale, W 269 (p. 163), is a possible exception.

Recently, in the Dutch journal, *Neophilologus*, III, 122 ff. (1918), "Über die Laudinefigur", H. Sparnaay has argued that the fountain *motif* (combat with fountain guardian) was originally separate and was only later combined with the fairy mistress theme (Laudine story). If Chrétien was to combine the two, says Sparnaay, he had to represent the heroine of the latter as an easily consoled widow. This scholar acknowledges, however, the influence of Jocaste on the characterization of Laudine.

Sparnaay in his "Laudine bei Crestien und bei Hartmann", *ibid.* IV, 310 ff. (1919), has compared in detail the French and German poems in all that relates to Laudine. He concludes that Hartmann made changes in his original (Chrétien) for the purpose of elevating the character of this heroine from the moral point of view, but was not always successful.

In her "Die künstlerische Stoffgestaltung in Chrétien's Ivain", *Zs. f. rom. Ph.*, XXXIX, 385 ff. (1918), Elise Richter maintains that Chrétien, in his portrayal of Laudine, tried to adapt the theory of the *amour courtois* to everyday conditions — more especially, to conditions of *bourgeois* married life. The poem was to contrast with the same poet's *Lancelot*, in which the above-mentioned theory operates in an ideal world, without any of the restrictions of actual life. The article is an interesting one, but I question whether Chrétien was consciously drawing any such contrast.

Miss Richter (pp. 393 ff.) also contends that Chrétien purposely duplicates all the chief features of the narrative in the *Yvain*, his object being to heighten the effect: Lunette twice advises Laudine (ll. 1666 ff. and 6586 ff.), Laudine is twice angry with Lunette (ll. 1710 ff. and 6760 ff.), etc.

Chapter VI.
Date of Chrétien's **Perceval.**

1. For the date of composition of Chrétien's *Perceval* see especially A. Birch-Hirschfeld, *Die Sage vom Gral*, pp. 81f. (Leipzig, 1877), G. Paris, *Mélanges de Littérature Française du Moyen Age, publiés par Mario Roques*, I, 263ff. (Paris, 1910) and W. Foerster, *Kristian von Troyes: Wörterbuch zu seinen sämtlichen Werken*, pp. 38f., 151f. of the Introduction (Halle, 1914). In view of the considerations which I have urged in my text, I believe that Foerster, p. 173, is unjustified in declaring that Chrétien's *Perceval* may just as well have been written about 1190 as about 1180. In his *Die Sage vom Heiligen Gral*, 148ff. (Halle, 1898), E. Wechssler has given interesting details concerning the life and character of Philip of Flanders, in connection with the question of Chrétien's relations to him and the date of the *Perceval* — also, a useful list of authorities for Philip's life — but his argument that Chrétien must have written his dedication whilst Philip was regent of France (1180—1182), during the minority of his godson, Philip II of France, is, as Gaston Paris (*loc. cit.* p. 264, note 1) has remarked, anything but convincing — as little so as his previous argument, 146ff., that the poet was a Cancellarius or Magister Scholae at the Cathedral of St. Peter in Beauvais. The substance of Wechssler's argument is that Chrétien's extravagant laudation of his patron as surpassing even Alexander the Great could not have been applied to a simple count: Philip must have occupied the quasi-royal position of regent, when he was extolled in this style, and Chrétien's assertion that no such tale was ever told in *court roial*, he thinks, confirms this supposition. But Chrétien's assertion is obviously a mere piece of *réclame* which might have been employed anywhere — even in a recitation in the market-place — and as for the praise lavished on Philip, who has

ever discovered in the literature of dedications down to the nineteenth century any sense of proportion in flattery? Besides, it is to be remembered, after all, that Philip of Flanders was a powerful nobleman. G. Paris remarks justly, too, p. 164, that Chrétien would doubtless have alluded to the fact, if his patron had, indeed, occupied such a high position as that of regent of France at the time that this prologue was written. Paris observes, still further, that the poet's silence in regard to Philip's expedition ("assez ridicule d'ailleurs") to Palestine in 1177 would seem to show that Chrétien wrote his *Perceval* before that affair. This, however, seems to me about as feeble as anything in Wechssler's argument.

It has been suggested that Gerbert's statement, Potvin, VI, 212, that Chrétien died before he could finish his *Perceval* may be a mere guess based on the incomplete condition of the poem. But this is not likely. The statement is made in the most positive form and appears to be confirmed by the fact that we have no work from Chrétien's pen of later date than the *Perceval*. There is no ground for believing that he was an old man when he composed this poem. On the other hand, he had been a prolific writer. Why, then, after such productivity should he have suddenly stopped writing? There is no parallelism here with the case of the *Lancelot*, which, likewise, Chrétien did not finish; for, as Foerster, *loc. cit.*, p. 152, remarks, another poet, Godefroi de Leigni, did carry that romance to a conclusion and with Chrétien's consent.

Chapter VII.
The Elucidation and Bliocadrans-Prologue.

In the Mons MS. of Chrétien's *Perceval* and its continuations, which has been printed by Potvin, we have a spurious introduction[1] of 1282 lines, which consists really of two independent parts: (a) ll. 1—484, (b) 485—1282. These parts had, doubtless, different authors. It is convenient to call the first, as Miss Weston does, by the name which it bears in its prose form,[2] found in most copies of the 1530 print of the prose *Perceval*, viz. *Elucidation*, and the second by the name which scholars have generally adopted for it, viz. the *Bliocadrans-prologue* (Bliocadrans being the name which is here given to Perceval's father).

The first part is very obscure, and the title, *Elucidation*, affixed to it in the 1530 print, might well strike the reader as ironical. It would seem to be the introduction to some compilation concerning the Grail which the author was planning, and

---

[1] In his review of Potvin's edition of Chrétien's *Perceval*, *Revue Critique* (No. 35) for Sept. 1. 1866, Paul Meyer accepted ll. 485—1282 as Chrétien's, whilst rejecting ll. 1—484. Birch-Hirschfeld, pp. 69 ff., has shown, however, by a detailed examination of language and style that this, too, is spurious, and his conclusions have been generally, approved. In Potvin's edition the genuine prologue of Chrétien has been relegated to the notes, II, 307 ff.

In the above-mentioned review P. Meyer declares (p. 130) that of all the MSS. of Chrétien's poems the one chosen by Potvin (i. e. the Mons MS.) is least suited to constitute the basis of an edition. Nutt, p. 8, note, rejects this introduction as spurious, but believes that it embodies a genuine tradition.

[2] This prose form (from the edition of 1530) has been reprinted by Ch. Potvin, *Bibliographie de Chrestien de Troyes*, pp. 171 ff., (Bruxelles, Leipzig, Gand, Paris, 1863).

we infer that he intended to make it embrace seven branches[3] — each corresponding to a separate visit to the Grail Castle by some knight who participated in the Grail quest. He gives in the passage just cited hardly intelligible indications as to the subjects of the individual branches, but only one of them (the reference to the dead knight in the swan-drawn boat that came to Glamorgan, Pseudo-Wauchier, ll. 20857ff.) can be positively identified with an incident in the extant romances.[4] On the other hand, in ll. 215ff. the writer speaks of Gawain's visit to the castle of the Fisher King (here represented as a magician, as nowhere else) and, also, at considerably greater length, of Perceval's experiences there. The reference in the former case is to Gawain's visit in Chrétien — only among the sacred objects of the procession we have here included certain things (broken sword, *denie[r]s*, silver cross) that are not found in Chrétien's description. It is obvious that the author knew both Pseudo-Wauchier and Chrétien, and when he shows departures from the narrative of either in various details, it is because, like all other Arthurian romancers, he gave the reins to his own invention, whenever it pleased him. In her article, "Wauchier de Denain, as a continuator of Perceval and the Prologue of the Mons MS.," *Romania*, XXXIII (1904), 333ff., Miss Westōn speaks (p. 334) of the "account of Gawain's visit to the Grail Castle . . . related in close accordance with the version of

---

[3] Instead of "branches", the writer employs the terms, "souviestemens" (ll. 341, 343) — "formes que *revêt* le conte" (as Potvin explains) — and "gardes" (ll. 344, 345, 349). But "gardes" properly applies to the heroes of the branches, — "guardians" of the Grail — not to the branches themselves, and is actually so used in ll. 17—22. — F. Lot, *Étude sur le Lancelot en prose*, p. 285, note 3, has pointed out that the prose *Lancelot* is, also, used in the *Elucidation*.

[4] Miss Weston, *Legend of Sir Perceval*, I, 280, is probably right in identifying "l'aventure de l'escu" (l. 379) with the magic shield episode in Wauchier, ll. 31598ff., but one cannot decide positively, since the reference is so indefinite. See also Heinzel (p. 80) and Miss Weston (279 f.) for conjectures as to the references to "l'ire et le perte de Huden" (l. 360) and to Lancelot, "la ou il perdi sa vertu" (l. 374).

Wauchier," and even of the "close verbal correspondence" in certain lines, but, as she does virtually always in such instances,
explains this close agreement on the hypothesis of a common source
(her Chastel Orguellous complex). The direct dependence of the
Elucidation on Pseudo-Wauchier here, however, has been recognized by Heinzel (p. 71) and is too plain to require argument.[5]
The most interesting feature of ll. 1—484 is the account of
how the blight fell upon the land of the Grail Castle: Formerly
there were "puceles" in this land who lived in the springs (evidently, water-fairies) and who refreshed travellers with whatever
food they might ask for. Each of them, moreover, bore a cup
of gold. After a while King Amangon[6] ravished one of these
"puceles" and carried off her golden cup. Many of his men
followed his evil example, and the girls retired to the springs
and ceased their benevolent offices. In consequence of the crimes
of Amangon and his men the country fell into a decline, the king
himself had a bad end, the kingdom became a desert, etc., and
the court of the Fisher King could no longer be found. — In the
course of time Arthur's knights went forth to redress the wrongs

---

[5] Cp., too, G. Gröber, *Zs. f. rom. Ph.*, XXIX, 148 (1905) in his
review of Miss Weston's book. Brugger, *Zs. f. frz. Spr. u. Litt.*,
XXXI [2], 149 (1907), accepts Miss Weston's theory that the *Elucidation*
is derived from her hypothetical Chastel Orguellous complex. When
he regards the allusion to Lancelot and (apparently) to the dog Huden
(in the Tristan legend), as interpolations (p. 148), that is simply because these allusions conflict with this theory. There is, however, no
ground for considering them interpolations.

[6] Heinzel has pointed out, p. 78, note 1, that Amangon is a
character in the following romances: *Le Bel Inconnu*, *Meraugis de
Portlesguez*, *Vengeance Raguidel* (as "Amangins"), *Chevalier as Deus
Espees* (as king of the land whence no one returns). He should have
included Chrétien's *Erec*, 318, 1726, whence the romances that he
cites, doubtless, derived the name (Amaugin, Amangon). The present
author, no doubt, derived the name from one of these romances. —
F. Lot, *Romania*, XXIV, 325 ff. (1895) identifies "Amargon", a variant
of "Amangon" in *Meraugis*, with "Amorgen", name of Conall Cernach's
father in the Irish saga of Conchobar. Even if this identification,
however, is correct, it would not affect the question we are now
dealing with.

of the above-mentioned "puceles" and to destroy all who had harmed them. As it turned out, they could not discover the "puceles"
whom they sought. They came upon others, however, who were
accompanied by knights, and they engaged in combats with the
latter. In some instances Arthur's men were killed; in others
they were victorious and sent their vanquished adversaries, in the
approved style of the romances, to report at Arthur's court. One
of these, named Blihos Bliheris,[7] whom Gawain had conquered,
relates at the court that the knights and the girls whom Arthur's
knights had encountered in the forests have sprung from the
damsels that were ravished by King Amangon and his followers,
and that they were destined to wander thus up and down through
the forests and elsewhere, until they discover the Fisher King's
court. This story of Blihos Bliheris pleased Arthur's knights
greatly and after a meeting on the subject they go forth in search
of the Fisher King's court. Gawain and Perceval find it.

There is no need to seek beyond the *Elucidation*, itself, for
the origin of this tale of how the Grail country fell under an evil
spell. Whether the account of the water-fays was an invention
of the author of the *Elucidation* or not, the very imperfect welding
of the story with the Grail theme proves that it had originally
no connection with that theme. The writer seems to imply (ll.
201 ff.) that the discovery of the Grail would be enough to lift
the spell, but, as Heinzel (p. 71) has observed, when we have,
ll. 225 ff. an allusion to Gawain's undoing of this spell, the author
evidently has in mind here Pseudo-Wauchier (ll. 20238 ff.,
20339 ff.), where, after all, it is not the mere discovery of the

---

[7] In *Romania*, XXXIII, 338 f., and *Legend of Sir Perceval*,
I, 288 ff., Miss Weston identifies this person with "Blihis" of l. 12
and "Bliheris" of Pseudo-Wauchier (l. 19434) in MS. 794 (Bibl. Nat.).
As she points out, *Legend of Sir Perceval*, I, 241, note, two MSS.
have "Bleobleheris" in the line from Pseudo-Wauchier. No doubt,
Brugger is right, however, *Zs. f. frz. Spr. u. Litt.*, XXXI [2], 154, in
asserting that we have here a case of substitution — Bliobliheris (and
variants) being the name of an Arthurian knight, who is found in several romances —, just as the Mons MS. substitutes in the same line
the name of another Arthurian knight, Brandelis.

Grail Castle, but the asking of the question that produces the happy result. There is, besides, no real logical connection between the cause of the blight that afflicted the land (the wrong done the "puceles") and the means of its removal (the discovery of the Grail Castle).

As we have seen, the author of the *Elucidation* knew pseudo-Wauchier, as well as Chrétien. There is no sign, however, that he knew Chrétien's other continuators, except, perhaps, Wauchier.[8] It would be hasty, however, to conclude from this circumstance with Heinzel (p. 81) that he wrote earlier than Gerbert, to say nothing of Manessier. His manuscript of the *Conte del Graal* may have happened to contain merely Chrétien and the first continuation.

In ll. 12f. our author cites "Maistre Blihis" as authority for the assertion that nobody should tell the secret of the Grail. Miss Weston, *Legend of Sir Perceval*, I, 281f., assumes that this is a reference to her hypothetical common source of Wauchier (or Pseudo-Wauchier) and the *Elucidation*. But, as has been observed above, other passages make it plain that the author of the *Elucidation* drew directly from Pseudo-Wauchier, and the present line is merely another instance of this borrowing. To be sure, the "Bleheris", of Pseudo-Wauchier l. 19434, is here shortened to "Blehis", but that might be easily due to faulty recollection or even to arbitrary mutilation of the name to suit the exigencies of this particular line.[9]

The second part of the spurious introduction to Chrétien's *Perceval*, viz. ll. 485—1282, is not marred by the obscurities and

---

[8] See note above. (p. 86, note 4).

[9] Similarly, Pseudo-Wauchier, when he wishes to get a rhyme, does not hesitate to change the name of Gifflet, one of the best known knights in the Arthurian romances, to "Giefloi", "Gyfloi". Cp. ll. 16259, 19542. Cp., too, the shortening of "Abrioris" to "Brioris" and "Escavallon" to "Cavallon" in Wauchier, and of "Hebron" to "Bron", which I have discussed pp. 130f. — In addition to the alternatives which I have stated above, there is also the possibility, suggested by Brugger, *Zs. f. frz. Spr. u. Litt.*, XXXI[2], 150, that the-*er* in "Bleheris" was represented by a sign of contraction in the MS. used by the author of the *Elucidation*, and chanced to be overlooked.

inconsistencies of ll. 1—484; on the other hand, it is not bright-
ened by the same gleams of the romantic spirit.   It is a perfectly
commonplace account of how Bliocadrans, Perceval's father, was
slain in a tournament and of how his wife thereafter, with all
the retinue of a feudal dame, moved to the Waste Forest, her purpose being to bring up there in seclusion and security her son,
Perceval, her only child, to whom she had given birth only a
few days after Bliocadrans's departure for the fatal tournament.
She tries to rear him in the belief that there are no houses and
people except those that he sees about him in the Waste Forest.
When he is old enough, she permits him to hunt goats and stags
in the forests, but warns him against men clad in iron — for she
avers they are devils.

This so-called Bliocadrans-prologue is the invention of a third-
rate poet who wishes to explain how Perceval and his widowed
mother came to be living in the Waste Forest, as we find them
at the beginning of Chrétien's *Perceval*. The *Tristan* poems and
Chrétien's *Cliges,* not to mention other romances, might have suggested to him the idea of supplying such an introduction concerning the hero's parents. The author knew nothing of Perceval
except what he found in Chrétien, and there is not a trace of folk-
lore sources in the whole composition.[10]

---

[10] The name of Perceval's father here, *Bliocadrans,* is puzzling,
as is the case with many Arthurian names.   It is probably, like
Bliobleheris (Bliobleris, Blioberis), ultimately, of Welsh origin.
J. Loth, *Contributions à l'Étude des Romans de la Table Ronde,*
pp. 36 f. (Paris, 1912), connects the latter with an hypothetical Old
Welsh *Bled-cobret,* which is the same as *Bled-cuurit* of the *Book
of Llandaff* (eleventh century) and *Blegobred (Bredgabred)* of Geoffrey
of Monmouth, III, 19.   The corresponding Modern Welsh form is
Blegwryd (Blegywrd) or *Bleddgwryd.*   On the other hand, in *Y
Cymmrodor,* X, 219, note 1 (1891) and XI, 45 f. (1892), E. Phillimore identifies the forms just enumerated (and the *Bledkenred* of
Annales Cambriae, anno 1018) not with *Blioberis,* but with *Bliocadrans,* the hypothetical Old Welsh original form which he postulates
being *Bledcabrat* (not *Bledcobrit*). Phillimore's derivation, however, does
not appear to me satisfactory. *Bliocadrans* has probably suffered corruption
at the hands of the scribes, until the true form is no longer recognizable.

Chapter VIII.
Miss Weston's Gawain=Complex.

In her *Legend of Sir Perceval*, I, ch. VI—X, Miss Weston develops a vast speculation concerning the sources of the continuation (or continuations) of Chrétien's *Perceval* from the point where he left off down through l. 34394, with which Wauchier's contribution to the *Conte del Graal* ends. She is inclined (p. 215), as we have seen, to ascribe to the copyists what precedes the episode of Arthur's war against Brun de Branlant (which begins l. 11597) and everything (barring interpolations) from there on through l. 34934 to Wauchier. The main sources of these additions (from the conclusion of Chrétien through l. 34934), in her opinion, are two (p. 178) — both, of course, purely hypothetical — 1. "a group of short episodic poems," which she designates "the Chastel Orguellous group," 2. "an elaborate poem of considerable literary merit," which she designates the "Chastel Merveilleus." Both were "independent versions of the Gawain legend", and the Perceval story, before Chrétien wrote his poem, had already been contaminated with both. This theory of Miss Weston's is, of course, intimately connected with her idea that Chrétien, whose romances are the earliest of the Arthurian cycle that we possess, came after the period of the really great Arthurian romances, all of which, in her opinion, have perished. Miss Weston is unable to produce a single item of objective evidence in support of this theory of hers concerning the sources of the continuations which I have attributed to Pseudo-Wauchier and Wauchier respectively, and, for my own part, I regard the whole speculation as baseless and unnecessary. Though restricted by considerations of space, I will endeavor to deal with the main points of Miss Weston's theory. It will be more convenient to discuss No. 2 first. 1. The section of the *Conte del Graal* for which her hypothetical *Chastel*

Merveilleus is here supposed to be, especially, the source consists
of ll. 6125—11596 and deals with Gawain's visit to the fairy-
castle, where he finds his mother and sister and Arthur's mother,
and the incidents connected therewith. Chrétien began this episode, but he broke off in the middle of it (l. 10601), and it was
completed by some one else. This continuator would, of course,
complete it according to the indications of Chrétien's unfinished
portion and there is no need to conjure up any imaginary source.[1]
Within the lines 10602—11596, as, indeed, throughout the division of the *Conte del Graal* which has been commonly assigned
to Pseudo-Wauchier, the MSS. show some considerable variants;
but when Miss Weston wishes to see in certain of these variants
(p. 198) remnants of her hypothetical *Chastel Merveilleus* poem,
this is, on the face of it, purely subjective, and even if we should
concede that her genealogy of the MSS. is correct, the cross agreements between different versions (longer and shorter) which she
speaks of (p. 213) would merely show the contamination of different lines of manuscript tradition — one of the commonest phenomena that editors of mediaeval texts have to deal with.[2]

   As regards the supposed coincidences (pp. 210ff.), between
Wolfram's *Parzival* and ll. 10602ff. of the *Conte del Graal*, they

---

[1] Miss Weston rightly rejects G. Paris's suggestion (*Manuel*,
p. 105) that Chrétien's first continuator used notes left by Chrétien
which indicated how the story should develop. As Brugger, *Zs. f.
frz. Spr. u. Litt.* XXXI[2], 141, well says, this method of composition
is not mediaeval, but modern.

[2] I am discussing here merely the relation of Chrétien's continuator to this incident of the so-called Chastel Merveilleus. The
question of Chrétien's own sources for the incident is another matter.
In my *Historia Meriadoci and De Ortu Waluuanii*, p. LII (Göttingen
and Baltimore, 1913), I have pointed out that in this final episode
Chrétien seems to have used, *inter alia*, a lost French romance on the
subject of Gawain's youth. This hypothetical romance, however, could
not have been of popular origin, since it contained conceptions borrowed
from Geoffrey of Monmouth and the legend of Pope Gregory. The
marvellous castle, moreover, unquestionably has Other-world features,
but there is no reason to believe that before Chrétien Gawain was
connected with this conception.

are so slight as to be negligible. When two writers are completing an unfinished episode on indications furnished by that episode, there are bound to be some coincidences in their respective works. If Martin, as Miss Weston notes (p. 212, note 1), in his edition of Wolfram, merely records these parallels without comment, it is, no doubt, because he very properly attached no significance to them.

Since the basis of her theory concerning this hypothetical *Chastel Merveilleus* poem, as set forth in her Chapter VII, which I have just examined, has so little solidity, there is no need of going into her more hazardous speculations in Chapter VIII as to still other drafts on this imaginary poem which she supposes to have been made in the continuation of Chrétien's *Perceval*.

2. According to Miss Weston's hypothesis, the Gawain adventures of ll. 15795—21917 (end of Pseudo-Wauchier) and ll. 31520—33754 (point in Wauchier where the narrative turns to Perceval's adventure at the Grail castle) are derived from the "Chastel Orguellous group" of episodic poems. "This group," she says (p. 178), "represents, I believe, the earliest stratum of the Arthurian romantic tradition we as yet possess, and may not improbably go back as far as the tenth century."

It is a mistake, in the first place, for Miss Weston to group together ll. 15975ff., on the one hand, and ll. 31520ff., on the other. They do not belong in the same category, properly speaking, the difference between the two being in conformity with the usual difference between Pseudo-Wauchier and Wauchier. The passage, ll. 31520ff., is really made up of threadbare Arthurian commonplaces — the Little Knight who defends the shield that hangs on a tree by a fountain, Gawain *incognito* at the tournament etc.[3] On the other hand, whatever one may think as to the sources of ll. 15795ff., we have here at any rate, incidents of a distinctive character, which are, besides, admirably told. Take,

---

[3] The Little Knight, with whom we may compare Guïvret le Petit in Chrétien's *Erec*, defends the fountain, ll. 32130ff. (here shield by the fountain), like Chrétien's Yvain; the Pensive Knight (ll. 32906ff.) is plunged in revery about his *amie*, like Chrétien's Perceval, and so on.

for example, Gawain's narrative (ll. 15885ff.) of his affair with
Brandelis's sister and the dramatic manner — hard to parallel
elsewhere in Arthurian romance — in which he gradually reveals
the strange story only under constant pressure from Arthur (ll.
17011ff., 17137ff.). Really, it is only in its relation to
ll. 15795—21917 (all in the Pseudo-Wauchier section) that Miss
Weston's theory requires discussion.

In the case of these lines, there is in ll. 16626ff., as Miss
Weston, p. 238, has noted, an appeal, it would seem, to a definite source. The author tells how Arthur took his companions
along with him on the expedition to Chastel Orguellous, but, in
the midst of his narrative, says:

> Desor est li romans trop lons,
> Mais je le vos voel abreger.
> II. jours errerent sans mangier
> C'onques ne peurent liu trover
> U il eussent .i. disner
> Jusqu'el vergier des sepoutures
> U on trueve les aventures;
> La mangierent avoec enclus
> Dont il i avoit. XXX. u plus,
> La mervelle del cimentire
> Ne me loist ore mie dire
> Dont les sepoutures estoient
> N'establissement qu'il trovoient
> Des enclus, car trop longement
> I metroie, mon ensient.

The first line of this quotation, by itself, would not mean
much, for the romancers often speak of their own works as "li
romans" etc., but in connection with what follows it would seem
that the writer is really here referring to an external source. If
so, that source, however, was, doubtless, a regular Arthurian romance, with the siege of the Chastel Orguellous as the main subject — that is to say, it was a formal literary production like
Chrétien's romances, and not an episodic poem, or group of episodic poems, such as Miss Weston supposes, that had lived in oral
tradition for centuries. Certainly, the narrative that follows in
Pseudo-Wauchier obviously derives one of its cardinal incidents

from Chrétien's *Perceval*, viz. that which forms the starting-point for the whole story of Gawain's affair with Brandelis's sister (ll. 16954ff.). He finds her alone in a tent and, despite her warnings of the consequences, deflowers her. This is plainly imitated from the incident in Chrétien's *Perceval*, ll. 1829ff., about the *amie* (in a tent) of Orguellous de la Lande, whom Perceval kisses by force, despite similar warnings — only in Pseudo-Wauchier Gawain actually justifies the suspicions expressed by the jealous lover in the former case (ll. 5031ff.) and the combat that ensues develops differently in the two instances. The only question here is whether the borrowing is due to Pseudo-Wauchier or his source. The question is not of the first importance, but for my own part, I think that it was probably Pseudo-Wauchier, himself, that made the combination, for in the cases where we can control with precision his use of sources, actually extant, viz. in the case of the *Bel Inconnu* episode (based on *Li Biaus Desconneus*) and the incident of the swan-drawn boat (from *Le Chevalier au Cygne*) we do not find him following his original through any long stretch of narrative.

It is to be observed that, after all, there is not a great deal to connect this Chastel Orguellous episode with popular tradition, even in respect to ultimate origin. The castle of Brandelis, where most of the action develops, is given fairy-tale features (the girls by the fountain who disappear so suddenly, the rich feast laid in the hall, yet no one visible etc.),[4] in order to render the setting more romantic, but otherwise there is nothing supernatural about the story, and above all, the effort of Brandelis's sister to induce

---

[4] Arthur's revery (ll. 15892ff.) over Gifflet's vacant place and his cutting himself heedlessly with the knife, whilst plunged in thought, may belong to folk-lore. The passage has been imitated in the prose *Lancelot*, III, 272, and in *Li Atre Perillos*, ll. 298ff. (Herrig's *Archiv*, XLII, 151).

It should be remarked that Chrétien (cp. his *Perceval*, ll. 6099ff.) planned an episode which was to deal with an adventure of Gifflet's at the Chastel Orguellous, but, of course, never came to it. This, in itself, was an invitation (so to speak) to later romancers to make it the theme of their inventions.

her brother and her lover (Gawain) to stop their duel by bringing
forth the little child of Gawain and herself — the fruit of the
violence done her by Gawain which has so enraged her brother
against him — is obviously not of folklore origin. Still further,
the incident[5] of Le Riche Sodoier (ll. 18997ff.), which is the
culmination of the whole Chastel Orguellous episode, evidently has
no basis in folklore, for we have here a most fantastic exhibition
of the chivalric courtesy which formed a part of the French ideal
of conduct in the aristocratic society of the time. Nothing could
be more artificial or further removed from primitive simplicity.

After the adventure of the Chastel Orguellous has been disposed of with the liberation of Gifflet and Lucan and the acceptance of Arthur as his suzerain by Le Riche Sodoier (ll.
19355ff.), we have next (ll. 19735ff.) the Grail adventure. As
I have elsewhere remarked, the starting-point — illustrating the
power of Gawain's courtesy as contrasted with Kay's rudeness —
is imitated, beyond dispute, from the similar incident in Chrétien's
Perceval, ll. 5796ff., where Perceval plays the rôle that is here
played by the unknown, wounded knight. In the further narrative
of Gawain's journey to avenge this strange knight and of his stay
at the Grail castle the author employs folk-tale *motifs* (the Black
Hand in the Forest Chapel, the Grail which supplies food etc.),
but, in dealing with matters that involved the supernatural, this
was, of course, necessary. There is no reason, however, to doubt
that our poet was the first to combine these particular *motifs*.

Miss Weston, *Romania*, XXXIII 342 (1904) and *Legend of
Sir Perceval*, I, 282ff., 323 (1906), makes much of the supposed
relation of certain Middle English Gawain poems to the first continuation of Chrétien's *Perceval*, as evidence of the earlier existence of the episodic poems which she postulates as Bleheri's source.

---

[5] Gawain vanquishes this character, who begs him, however, to
pretend that he (Gawain) is vanquished and to present himself to his
(Le Riche Sodoier's) *amie* under that pretence, because he fears lest
she may die, if she hears the truth about her lover's defeat. Gawain
consents and surrenders his sword to the girl. Arthur, believing that
Gawain has been really vanquished, is plunged in woe.

The Middle English poems which she names are: 1. *Sir Gawayne and the Grene Knyghte*, 2. *Golagros and Gawayne*, 3. *Awntyrs of Arthur at the Tarne Wathelyne*, 4. *The Weddynge of Syr Gawayne*, 5. *The Jeaste* [i. e. Geste] *of Syr Gawayne*, 6. *Syr Libeaus Desconus*. The authors of these poems, she thinks, drew not from the Chrétien continuation, but from the ultimate sources of that continuation.[6] We may drop No. 6 at once from the discussion, for as Miss Weston, herself, says, it stands "apart from the collection" [i. e. of Gawain episodes represented in the continuation to Chrétien].

It is a mere English redaction of the Old French romance of the same name (or, as some scholars believe, of a romance which was the latter's source), and its only connection with the Chrétien continuation is that they both show use of this romance, which is, of course, not episodic.

As far as the other romances are concerned, it is to be observed that only the first antedates the fifteenth century — which is pretty late for independent derivation from hypothetical lost French poems of the middle of the twelfth century (at the la-

---

[6] Besides the poems cited by Miss Weston, there are others in Middle English with Gawain as the hero. 1. *The Turke and Gawin* (preserved only in a MS. of the sixteenth century, but composed probably in the latter part of the fourteenth century). 2. *Syre Gawene and the Carle of Carelyle* (fourteenth or fifteenth century). 3. *The Grene Knight*. No. 1 (in this list) probably is not based on a French original (cp. Kittredge, p. 280); No. 2 is a mere adaptation of *Sir Gawayne and the Grene Knight* (cp. *ibid.* p. 134). No. 2, as Kittredge, p. 95, thinks, has a French source, which is also the source of the *Chevalier à l'Épée* (thirteenth century). The examples, however, which he gives, pp. 257 ff., show how widespread the *motif* was, and its relation to the *Chevalier à l'Épée* must remain doubtful. Brugger, *Zs. f. frz. Spr. u. Litt.*, XXXI[2], 149 ff., accepts Miss Weston's theory, except that he derives these poems from the hypothetical Gawain compilation of Bleheri. Despite the authorities, however, to which Brugger appeals (p. 149), Miss Weston is right in asserting that these English poems are from different times and places. One is Scotch, others are North Midland, still others, South Midland. Some are of the fourteenth century, others of the fifteenth.

test). Nos. 2 (a Scottish poem) and 5 are undoubtedly based on
stories which we find in Pseudo-Wauchier, and the editors have
drawn the natural conclusion that Pseudo-Wauchier was their
source. There is not the slightest reason to reject their judgment
in this matter. Miss Weston, herself, remarks (p. 283) that the
adventure of Kay and the Spit in no. 2 is "related in close agreement with the version of the *Perceval*" and that the events before
Chastel Orguellons "agree closely with the French text." If the
conclusion of no. 5 shows a departure from Pseudo-Wauchier, this
is simply an example of the liberty which poets in the Middle
Ages, as in all other ages, permitted themselves. The only reason
which Miss Weston gives for denying a relation of direct dependence on Pseudo-Wauchier in the case of these poems she states
in the following words, where she is speaking of the whole group
of Middle English poems named above: "Gawain is undoubtedly
a far older Arthurian hero than Perceval, Lancelot or Tristan.
A group of poems which regard him as the exclusive protagonist
[i. e. the Middle English group] is *prima facie* likely to be earlier
than a similar group in which he shares the honours with one or
more of these knights." Apart from the fact that "a similar
group" is an incorrect description' of Pseudo-Wauchier's continuation, this *a priori* generalization has little weight in the ba-
lance as compared with the "close agreement" which she herself acknowledges in the case of no. 2.

The only point which Miss Weston mentions (pp. 284f.) as
connecting no. 3 with the continuation of Chrétien is that in the
former Gawain is represented as temporarily in possession of Galloway. He receives it as a fief from Arthur, but later exchanges
it with its proper ruler who has lost it through conquest. "This
is an interesting testimony to the tradition of Gawain's association
with Galloway preserved in the Chastel Merveilleus story," she
observes (p. 285). But the extant romances were amply sufficient to suggest such a connection with Galloway[7] ("Galvoie",

---

[7] In the *Gesta Regum Angliae* of William of Malmesbury (who
wrote in the first half of the twelfth century), in connection with the
well-known description of Gawain's tomb, it is said of him (Book III,

"Gauvoie" of the Old French romances) as we find here. In *Erec* (ll. 6815ff., 6827ff.) we already find Gawain appearing in company with the King of Galloway, and in the *Perceval* (ll. 7966ff.), despite warnings, he undertakes to penetrate into that land. The "Galvoie" of this latter poem has indisputably attributes of the Otherworld, but there is every likelihood that Chrétien was the first to endow it with these mysterious features. In any event, the episode[8] in which Galloway is named in No. 3 is a perfectly commonplace one, illustrating the courtesy of Arthur's court: the dominions of the lord of Galloway are returned to him, notwithstanding his defeat at Gawain's hands. Chrétien could have easily supplied the author of this romance with the name of the land and the suggestion of the hostility of its lords. This author would be all the more disposed to use this particular name from the fact, which has often been observed, that he evidently had a close acquaintance with the neighborhood of Carlisle, from which Galloway is not far distant. The alliteration of the verse would offer a still further temptation to employ the name in the story with Gawain's.

There remains only no. 1. But according to the careful investigation of G. L. Kittredge, *op. cit.*, pp. 38ff., in the part

under the year 1087): "Regnavit in ea parte Britanniae quae adhuc Walweitha (i. e. Galloway) vocatur." The passage is, doubtless, an interpolation (based on the romances), but it is an early one. — In *Romanische Forschungen*, XXIX, 320, G. Baist interpreted *bogue* in *bogue de Galvoie* (Potvin's edition of Chrétien's *Perceval*, l. 7966, as representing *bog* (= *quagmire*), which comes from the Irish, and as a mark of Celtic origin in this episode. In his *"Keltismus in der Monser Percevalhandschrift"*, *Zs. f. rom. Ph.* XXXVI, 611 (1912), Foerster, however, pointed out that the *bogue* of Potvin's MS. was merely a corruption of *bone* (a frequent variant for *borne = boundary* in Old French) — very likely through *bogne* — and that MS. 794 (B. N.) actually has *bone* here. For the *bones* (or *bornes*) *Artu* in Old French literature, cp. R. Weeks, *Mélanges offerts à M. Emile Picot, Membre de l'Institut, par ses amis et ses élèves*, I, 209ff. (2 vols., Paris, 1913).

[8] The first part of the poem is based on a legend concerning Pope Gregory: *The Trental of Gregory.*

which he accepts as alone connected originally with Gawain (the Beheading Game), this romance has the same source as the *Livre de Caradoc*, so that it does not testify to any additional episodic poem concerning that hero.

As regards Miss Weston's "Gawain legend," then, which, it seems, she would date back to the tenth century, neither here in her *Legend of Sir Perceval* nor in her *Legend of Sir Gawain* (with its misleading title) has she brought forward any proof that it ever existed. Gawain is extolled in Geoffrey of Monmouth as a valiant nephew of Arthur. From Geoffrey, or, more probably, from his translator, Wace, Chrétien and the other romance-writers took their cue, and it is to them, exclusively, as we may reasonably conclude, that the character owes his further adventures and his fame. We have no early "short episodic poems" about Gawain and no evidence that there ever were any.

Brugger, *Zs. f. frz. Spr. u. Litt.*, XXXI^2, 127ff., 148, regards the adventures related of Perceval in the Chrétien continuations, as having been brought into connection with that hero in these continuations for the first time. But the same thing is, no doubt, true of the adventures that are imputed to Gawain in the episodes under discussion, although Brugger (p. 159) would make the hypothetical Bleheri (Bledri) responsible for this.

In connection with her theory which I have been discussing, Miss Weston (p. 177) expresses the view that it is strange that the writer who undertook to complete Chrétien's *Perceval*, "instead of returning to the original subject matter of the poem, the story of *Perceval*, confined himself instead to that of Gawain." But, aside from what I have already said on the general disregard of conformity which is exhibited by the writers of Arthurian romance, it is to be observed here that, after all, in Chrétien's own poem the space occupied by Gawain's adventures does not fall far short of that which is devoted to the adventures of Perceval[9] — only no visit to the Grail castle had been related of

---

[9] Gawain is so prominent that Heinrich von dem Türlin, in *Diu Crone*, either mistook him for the Grail hero or wilfully transferred

the former, although it was probably Chrétien's intention to introduce, sooner or later, such an episode into his poem. For the continuator to describe a visit of Gawain to the mysterious castle would have, then, of course, the advantage of novelty. The circumstances just enumerated, combined with the fact that Chrétien broke off his work in the midst of a Gawain episode, would give a sufficient answer to the question which Miss Weston raises.

The fact, too, that the Pseudo-Wauchier section shows such extensive interpolation or redaction, as compared with the other continuations of Chrétien, can, I believe, be, also, satisfactorily explained. This first continuation was, of course, recognized as such, and it was not protected from alteration by a distinguished name, as Chrétien's own poem was. Copyists or other persons, therefore, would not hesitate to introduce what they considered improvements, if they saw fit to do so. By the time that Wauchier and the rest made their additions, to continue Chrétien's *Perceval* was no longer a novelty, and, indeed, such additions might be looked upon very properly as really a mere continuation of his continuator (or continuators), so that the incentive to interpolation was naturally weaker.

In rejecting the theory of Miss Weston which I have outlined above, it will have been observed, of course, that I make no assertion that the sources of Pseudo-Wauchier and Wauchier did not include, to some extent, lost Arthurian romances. We have seen that both writers made use of an extant romance of this cycle, *Li Biaus Descouneus (Le Bel Inconnu)* by Renaut de Beaujeu, and that the former borrowed from *Le Chevalier au Cygne* his swan-drawn boat (ll. 20357ff.). We have seen, too, in ll. 16626ff. a reference to a lost source. Otherwise, as far as I know, no convincing case has been made out so far for any definite borrowing from a lost romance in these two continuations. Brugger, *Zs. f. frz. Spr. u. Litt.*, XXXI[2], 127, believes that he can prove that Perceval's stag-adventure (ll. 22393ff.) was derived from such a lost romance (of which Perceval, however, was not the hero). But

---

him to that rôle. Cp. on the subject G. Paris, *Histoire Littéraire,* XXX, 44.

the hunt for a marvellous stag, like the castle of the fairy-mistress, who imposes the execution of a task as the price of her love, with which it is here combined, is an old *motif*,[10] and I see no reason to suppose that Wauchier was not just as capable as Brugger's hypothetical author of effecting the combination and interweaving with it, still further, the *motif* of the self-playing chessmen. Mennung[11] pointed out many years ago that the incident in the stag-hunt tale when the "puciele de malaire" (l. 22604) carried off Perceval's "braket" (lent by his fairy mistress) and refused to surrender it was borrowed from *Le Bel Inconnu*, i. e. *Li Biaus Desconneus* (ll. 1291ff. of G. P. Williams' edition), where the girl, Helie, does the same thing with the "braket" of Orguillous de la Lande. This seizure of the dog is an essential feature of the whole episode, and tends to show that Wauchier was the first to combine the *motifs* that make up the complex of incidents in question.

The group of strange incidents which are connected with the name of Caradoc in the Pseudo-Wauchier section of the *Conte del Graal* and which make up the so-called *Livre de Caradoc* are of a very different character from the Gawain episodes which surround them. Unlike the latter they bear plainly the stamp of folk-tale origin, not merely in occasional details, but in every essential particular. This *Livre de Caradoc*, however, not only does not relate

---

[10] Cp. the very full collection of examples in Carl Pschmadt's *Die Sage von der verfolgten Hinde* (Greifswald diss., 1911), and M. B. Ogle's "The Stag-Messenger Episode", *American Journal of Philology*, XXXVII, 387ff. (1916). Ogle, who discusses the episode we are here considering, pp. 398f., opposes the hypothesis of Celtic origin for this *motif* of the marvellous hind or stag.

Miss Weston's idea (p. 117) that the stag here is a woman transformed is rightly condemned by Brugger, in the article cited above, pp. 128f., and Pschmadt, p. 107, note 3, condemns her similar interpretation (p. 113) of the lay, *Tyolet*.

[11] Albert Mennung: *Der Bel Inconnu des Renaut de Beaujeu in seinem Verhältniss zum Lybeaus Disconus, Carduino und Wigalois*, p. 17 (Halle diss. 1890).

Miss Weston's Gawain-Complex 103

to Gawain, but it is generally admitted to be an interpolation,[12] so that we need not discuss it here.

[12] Cp. G. Paris, *Romania*, XXVIII, 230 f., note (1899), Miss Weston, *Legend of Sir Perceval*, I, 309 ff. (1906), G. L. Kittredge, *A Study of Gawain and the Green Knight*, p. 26 (1916). Kittredge (p. 224) does not believe that the head-cutting challenge incident was ever connected in Celtic tradition with Caradoc. It belonged, he believes, exclusively to Cuchullin. Even literary tradition, however, I would remark, is not very consistent in these matters, as we see from the history of this very incident in Old French literature, where it is ascribed in different works to Caradoc, Gawain, and Lancelot, respectively. Accordingly, the Celtic treatments of the theme may have displayed the same inconsistency. In any event, when Kittredge supposes (p. 50) that Gawain was the hero of the incident in the sources of the *Livre de Caradoc* which he reconstructs, this does not strike me as very convincing. It is in the natural order of things that the great hero of Arthurian romance, Gawain, should annex the achievements of minor personages, but it is not so easy to understand why one of the less important heroes of Celtic saga, Caradoc, should first have these Celtic stories attached to his name, many years after they had passed into French literature.

R. Heinzel, *Über die französischen Gralromane* (pp. 32 ff.), is the only scholar, as far as I am aware, who denies that the *Livre de Caradoc* is interpolated. He shows very clearly the chronological inconsistencies which its introduction produces in the narrative, but argues that the chronological inconsistencies of this same continuation of Chrétien are just as great in the case of the *Bel Inconnu* episode. On the whole, however, the evidence supports the generally accepted conclusion with regard to the *Livre de Caradoc* being an interpolation.

In concluding this excursus on the sources of the continuations to Chrétien's *Perceval*, I will recall to the reader that G. Baist, *Parzival und der Gral*, p. 39, numbered among these sources his *Liber Glastoniensis* (hypothetical source of *Perlesvaus*, etc.), through which, according to his theory, the Grail story first became Christianized. I have discussed this adversely below.

Chapter IX.
The Didot=Perceval.

The so-called *Didot-Perceval* is preserved in only two MSS.:
1. the Didot MS., now in the Bibliothèque Nationale, Nouvelles
Acquisitions, 4166 (dated 1301); and 2. MS. E. 49 of the Biblioteca Estense in Modena (latter part of the 13th century. Cp.
Miss Weston, II, 6). The first of these MSS. (formerly the only
one known — hence the current title of the romance) was printed
by E. Hucher in *Le Saint Graal*, I, 415 ff. (1874); the second,
which offers a much superior text, by Miss J. L. Weston, *The
Legend of Sir Perceval*, II, 9 ff. (1909).[1] The *Didot-Perceval*, as
intimated above, has been the centre of an unusual amount of discussion, owing to the fact that in both of the above-mentioned
MSS. it follows on the prose rendering of Robert de Boron's *Merlin*,
which, in turn, in each of these MSS., is preceded by the prose
rendering of his *Joseph*. Moreover, indications within the romance itself make it evident that the *Didot-Perceval* was intended
to continue this series.[2] E. Hucher, the first editor of the romance,
left the question of authorship open, I, 375, although subsequently he always refers to it as if it were Robert de Boron's work; but
inasmuch as Robert at the end of the *Joseph* announces his purpose of telling the story of Alein "et ques oirs de li peut issir"
(1. 3467), it was natural that many Arthurian scholars should

---

[1] A fragment of the romance is, also, preserved in a MS. of the
prose *Tristan*, but has no particular value. Miss Weston has printed
it, *ibid.*, II, 118 ff.

[2] It is not a continuation, however, of the *Merlin*, especially, as
Sommer (*Zs. f. rom. Ph.*, XXXII, 323) asserts. One has only to
compare it with the genuine *Merlin* continuations, viz. the Vulgate,
the *Huth-Merlin*, the one in MS. 337, to see that this is not so.
These carry on the narrative of Robert's *Merlin*, as the *Didot-
Perceval* does not.

have regarded the *Didot-Perceval* as a prose rendering of the (hypothetical) lost verse form of the continuation of the *Joseph* and *Merlin* thus announced. So, for example, G. Paris, *Huth-Merlin*, I, p. ix, *et passim*, speaks of the *Perceval* (i. e. *Didot-Perceval*), without qualification, as Robert's work. See, too, his *Manuel*, p. 109, as well as G. Gröber in his *Grundriss der Romanischen Philologie*, II, 997 and F. Lot, *Lancelot*, pp. 182ff. But apart from the fact that in neither MS. is Robert named as the author, there is satisfactory internal evidence that he is not responsible for the romance.

The main arguments in favor of accepting the *Didot-Perceval* as the prose rendering of an hypothetical poem[3] by Robert de Boron have been presented by A. Birch-Hirschfeld, *Die Sage vom Gral*, 180 ff. (1877), and E. Wechssler, *Zs. f. rom. Ph.*, XXIII, 144 ff. (1899). These arguments rest on what the two scholars in question regard as the numerous points of agreement between the narrative of the *Didot-Perceval* and that of Robert's *Joseph* and *Merlin*. Wechssler distinguishes between supposed references of the *Perceval* (of the Didot MS.) to the *Joseph, Merlin*, and *Mort Arthur*, on the one hand, and of the *Joseph, Merlin*, and *Mort Arthur* to the *Perceval* (of the Didot MS.), on the other, and he ascribes to agreements of the first kind greater force than to agreements of the latter. Leaving aside, however, the assumption that the *Mort Arthur* of the Didot MS. is by Robert, I will

---

[3] There is no certain indication in Robert's authentic work that he intended to give the name "Perceval" to Alein's heir, who was to succeed Bron as Grail-keeper, or even that he conceived of "li tierz hons" (1. 2790) as a knight. Most scholars assume this, it would seem, because they believe that in the pre-Chrétien oral Grail legend of their theory the Grail hero already bore that name. As W. W. Newell, *Journal of American Folklore*, X, 221, however, says, Robert's poem is religious, and in the style of the Christian apocrypha, so that there is no likelihood that he would have represented "li tierz hons" as a knight of the Round Table. Cp., too, what I have said above I, 145, note 36, concerning the passage in the prose rendering of Robert's *Merlin* (*Huth-Merlin*, I, 98 and Sommer, II, 56). The unnamed knight of that passage is usually identified with Perceval.

say that there is really nothing to choose between the two classes
of references; for a writer who was supplying a continuation to
Robert's unfinished work would, of course, not only exploit his
predecessor's actual narrative, but would develop into incidents any
hints which he might observe in that work as available for use
in the continuation. As a matter of fact, the union of the prose
rendering of Chrétien's *Lancelot* (Sommer's *Vulgate Version of
the Arthurian Romances,* IV, 155 ff.) with the narrative that precedes it in the huge prose *Lancelot* romance is much smoother
than is the case with the *Perceval* of the Didot and Modena MSS.
in its relation to the branches to which it is joined, and yet we
know that in that instance the parts in question are certainly by
different authors.

On the other hand, there is as has been stated in the text above,
a fundamental conflict between the conceptions of the *Didot-Perceval* and Robert's *Joseph* and *Merlin* — "ein Widerspruch aller-
dings von tiefschneidender Art," as Wechssler, p. 147, himself,
acknowledges — which alone would be sufficient to disprove the
contention that the *Didot-Perceval* is a poem of Robert's in prose
dress — viz. that, contrary to the declarations of Robert's *Merlin*
(*Huth-Merlin,* I, 98 and Sommer, II, 56) that the person who is
to fill the vacant seat at the Round Table must first have filled
the vacant seat at the Grail Table (cp. *Joseph,* ll. 2790 ff.), Perceval takes the seat at the Round Table at the very beginning of
this romance (p. 21 of Miss Weston's text), before he has started
on his quest for the Grail. The awkward attempt to identify Round
Table and Grail Table, which Robert keeps clearly apart, though
he models the former after the latter, is another sign that we
have before us here a work that is not from his hand; and so, too,
with the warning (unheeded, and, as the event proves, unnecessary)
which Arthur addresses to Perceval, the Grail-hero.[4] I may add

---

[4] If we accept as genuine the passage preserved in MSS. 747
(B. N.) and Add. 32125 (B. M.) at the end of the *Merlin* which I
have quoted below, this does not accord with the theory that the
Didot-Perceval is based on a poem of Robert's, for the *Didot-Perceval* does the opposite of what is there stated, inasmuch as it does

that the episode of the tourney (pp. 17ff.), where Perceval appears
in the commonplace rôle of the *galant* knight of Arthur's niece,
Elainne (Aleine), is simply inconceivable in a work of the mystic
Robert de Boron. To throw back the responsibility of the episode
on the source is unavailing, for poets do not wholly renounce the
power of selection in dealing with their sources, and Robert would
surely not have taken the trouble to turn into his heavy and laborious verse a piece of trivial *galanterie* like this, which was so
foreign to his own genius. The same thing is true of the whole
complex of episodes — magical chessboard, stag-hunt, and tomb-
knight — of which we shall hear later. Indeed, it would be difficult to imagine anything more different from the ultra-romantic
Didot-Perceval than Robert's *Joseph*, which is based mainly on
Christian legend, or his *Merlin*, which is pseudo-historical.[5]

I may remark that the careless adjustment of the beginning
of the *Didot-Perceval* to Robert's *Joseph* and *Merlin* reminds one
of the similar exhibition of negligence and clumsiness on the part
of the author of the conclusion of the prose *Lancelot*, which was
expressly composed to effect the transition to the *Queste del Saint
Graal*, yet contradicts the latter in some serious points.

Wechssler, p. 148 (following in part Heinzel, p. 121), has
discerned a contradiction within the *Didot-Perceval* itself, in the
following circumstances: Perceval (p. 14) sets forth on his adventures, being enjoined thereto by his dying father, but no mention is made of his mother; yet (pp. 38ff.) he returns to his
home and learns from his sister that his mother has died from
grief on account of his departure, likewise "der Vater und sechs
ältere Söhne aus derselben Ursache." But the statement which
I have quoted in the original German here is an error of Wechss-

---

tell of Arthur and speaks also of Alein's death. Cp. Heinzel, p. 118.
As Heinzel remarks, pp. 118f., also, the *Didot-Perceval* does not
fulfill Robert's promise to tell of Moyses and Petrus — still further,
the appearance of the Grail is much more pretentious in this romance
than in Robert's.

[5] W. W. Newell, *Journal of American Folklore*, X, 309 (1897),
has properly characterized the difference in these terms.

ler's own — there is nothing to support it in the texts. For the
rest, the implication that Perceval was one of six brothers is due
to a scribal blunder in the Didot MS. (Hucher, I, 446), which
has "vii" for "un" (Modena MS., Miss Weston, p. 38) — an
error, I may remark, that is repeated later in the same MS. in
another connection (Hucher, I, 459). The supposed contradiction
thus reduces itself to this: Perceval's mother is not mentioned when
he goes forth on the Grail quest; she is mentioned in the episode
of his return to his home. But in a condensed narrative like
that of the *Didot-Perceval* there is nothing surprising, much less
contradictory, about this. As a matter of fact, the difference is
due to the circumstance that in the first passage, where the Grail
quest was the main thing, the author is adapting his work to
Robert's *Joseph,* in which neither the mother nor the sister of
the prospective Grail-keeper were named, whereas in the latter
he was following Wauchier (ll. 25880ff.), where the sister tells
Perceval of her mother's death, just as here.[6]

From the start it was really impossible to maintain that the
Didot-Perceval in the form in which we have it was a prose-
rendering of Robert's hypothetical poem; for its dependence on
Chrétien's *Perceval* and Wauchier's continuation to that poem is
manifest. Nutt, *Studies on the Holy Grail,* p. 94, had an inkling
of this, but in the end (pp. 127ff.) resorts, as usual, to an (imaginary) lost saga source.[7] Heinzel, whose whole discussion of the
Didot-Perceval is most valuable, came nearer (pp. 119f.) to the
expression of the full truth, when he rejected Birch-Hirschfeld's
theory (pp. 183ff.) of later interpolation in the case of a matter
where the *Didot-Perceval* agrees with Chrétien and Wauchier as

---

[6] By a blunder the scribe of the Didot MS. (Hucher, I, 426)
calls "Moys" the man who perished when he tried to take his seat at
the Round Table (Sommer, II, 57). It was the vacant seat at the
Grail table (prose *Joseph,* p. 118) which Moys tried to occupy. Cp.,
also, *Didot-Perceval,* p. 12.

[7] Some years later, *Legends of the Holy Grail* p. 34 (London,
1902), he comes nearer to the truth in describing the *Didot-Perceval*
as an "incongruous jumble of hints from de Borron's work and a confused version of the *Conte del Graal"*.

against Robert, viz. in making the lance appear in the Grail procession, as it does not in Robert — and suggesting direct dependence of that romance, even in its earliest form, on these writers as sources. It was left, however, to W. Hoffmann, *Quellen des Didot-Perceval* (Halle diss. 1905) to furnish the detailed proof of this dependence: e. g. with reference to Chrétien, p. 18 (Great Fool *motif, Didot-Perceval*, p. 15 of Miss Weston's edition), pp. 58ff. (Perceval's wanderings and second visit to the hermit, *ibid.*, pp. 67ff.), 62ff. (the three days tournament, *ibid.*, pp. 70ff.), 68ff. (lance in the Grail procession, Fisher-King's father, form of the Grail question, *ibid.*, pp. 81ff.), besides pp. 12, 16, 20, etc.; with reference to Wauchier, pp. 26ff. (Orgoilleus de la Lande episode, *ibid.*, pp. 23ff.), 29ff. (Perceval's return to his home and episodes involving his sister, *ibid.*, pp. 37ff.), p. 36 (episode of Li Biaus Mauvais and Rosete, *ibid.*, pp. 44ff.), pp. 52ff. (the series of episodes combining magical chessboard, stag-hunt and tomb-knight adventures, which make up a considerable part of the whole *Didot-Perceval, ibid.*, pp. 31ff., 62ff.), 58ff. (Perceval's wanderings and second visit to the hermit, *ibid.*, pp. 67ff.). In the case of Wauchier, particularly, there is no possibility of the incidents having passed from his work to the *Didot-Perceval* through an intermediary poem of Robert's, for the close verbal correspondences noted by W. Hoffmann (pp. 23, 36, 52) between Wauchier and the *Didot-Perceval* demonstrate the immediate dependence of the latter upon the former beyond the shadow of a doubt. These correspondences really render superfluous the further proof which he furnishes (pp. 57f.) of the falsity of Wechssler's theory (*Zs. f. rom. Ph.*, XXIII, 161ff.), that Wauchier, the *Didot-Perceval*, and Gerbert drew independently from a lost romance concerning Perceval's Grail-quest and stag-hunt.

Hoffmann's demonstration of the dependence of the *Didot-Perceval* on Wauchier relegates to the limbo of oblivion Birch-Hirschfeld's theory, pp. 194ff., that the former romance was the source of both Chrétien and Wauchier. That theory, to be sure, I believe, had never found an echo in Arthurian discussions.

W. Hoffmann's excellent dissertation put into clear, accurate, and compact form convincing proof that the *Didot-Perceval* does not represent a lost poem of Robert de Boron's. Miss Weston, however, owing to her invincible prejudice against acknowledging that any extant work could be used by the author of any other extant work, speaks (*Legend of Sir Perceval*, II, 185, note 3, and 190, note) with the greatest contempt of his investigations and tries to rehabilitate this discredited thesis by new arguments of two different kinds: In the first place she tries to explain (*ibid.*, pp. 333ff.) the complete change of plan and tone between the *Didot-Perceval* and Robert's authentic works on the gratuitous hypothesis that, before beginning the *Didot-Perceval,* the poet had changed his patron and was adapting himself to a new lord. We know, of course, virtually nothing of Robert's life and nothing whatever of this second hypothetical patron — little enough, indeed, of the first — and it is therefore, impossible to take seriously so unfounded a suggestion. In the second place, Miss Weston has endeavored to prove that the *Didot-Perceval* is based on a poem of Robert's by actually reconstructing, out of the extant prose, specimens of the original lost metrical romance which she assumes. But she has convinced nobody, and Brugger, especially, by his searching criticism[8] of her reconstructions from various points of view, *Zs. f. frz. Spr. u. Litt.*, XXXVI[2], 32ff. (in his review of the Second Volume of her *Legend of Sir Perceval*), has demolished them once for all. He rightly sums up Miss Weston's whole effort in this direction as a "müssige Spielerei" (p. 41). The same judgment, of course, would apply to any reconstruction of "traces of verse" which Sommer may have imagined that he detected in the Modena MS. Cp. his *Vulgate Version of the Arthurian Romances*, Vol. I, p. xi. And so whatever argument for a metrical original for the *Didot-Perceval* that scholar may have based on these imaginary "traces of verse" — and he has not even suggested any other argument — is valueless. It is true that, unlike Miss Weston, Sommer does not identify this metrical original with any supposed work of Robert de Boron's, but with an hypotheti-

---

[8] Cp. also W. Foerster's Chrétien *Wörterbuch*, p. 236*.

cal lost poem of about the year 1200, which had among its sources
Chrétien and Wauchier. See his *Messire Robert de Borron und
der Verfasser des Didot-Perceval*, p. 39 (Halle, 1908) — also, *ibid.*,
note 3, the obscure hint which appears to refer to the "traces of
verse" more definitely spoken of in the passage which I have
just cited. Sommer, as I have intimated, has not even attempted
to bring forward any evidence as to the existence of this hypothetical poem, unless we are to take this hint as such, and he
has gained no adherents to his theory, so that we may dismiss
it from our discussions.

Brugger acknowledges (*Zs. f. frz. Spr. u. Litt.*, XXIX[1], 69 ff.,
XXXVI[2], 53 ff.) that Chrétien and Wauchier are sources of the
Didot-Perceval in the only form in which we have it — for instance, for the long complex of episodes that relate to the magical
chessboard, the search for the hound, the stag-hunt and the tomb-
knight, taken from Wauchier, ll. 22393 ff., but still contends that
the work is a prose rendering of a lost *Perceval* by Robert de Boron
and that passages based on these writers were interpolated — most
probably by a redactor of the original prose rendering. But Hoffmann has shown in a perfectly objective manner that the borrowings from Chrétien and Wauchier (very frequently from the
former, though in larger measure from the latter) are observable
virtually in every part of the *Didot-Perceval*, from beginning to
end, and where the author is not drawing upon the two poets, as,
for example, in the episode of Perceval's taking his seat at the
Round Table, near the beginning of the romance, he still stands
(as we have seen) in flagrant contradiction with the conceptions
of Robert. In view of these conditions, Brugger's modification
of the theory that the *Didot-Perceval* is a lost poem of Robert's
turned into prose[9] is as untenable as Miss Weston's unqualified

---

[9] Brugger shows a weakening, *Zs. f. frz. Spr. u. Litt.*, XXXVI[2],
55, in regard to this theory, when he says: "Robert's Autorschaft
scheint mir auch für den ursprünglichen Didot-Perceval nicht absolut
erwiesen." He hastens, however, to reaffirm his faith in it.
   Contrary to his former opinion, F. Lot, in his *Étude sur le
Lancelot en prose*, pp. 133 f. (including notes), *et passim*, accepts the

hypothesis. Furthermore, in view of these same conditions, it is in the highest degree improbable that the invective against Chrétien and "li autre troveor qui en ont trove por faire lor rimes plaisanz" (p. 68) did not belong to the romance in its original form.

If the *Didot-Perceval* is not by Robert, then, there is no reason to attribute to him the insignificant *Mort Arthur* which is attached to that romance in both of our MSS. These MSS. do not ascribe it to him and in his *Joseph* and *Merlin* he gives no indication that he intended to write a *Mort Arthur*. The fact that the author of the actual *Mort Arthur* of the *Didot-Perceval* MS. follows closely a bald verse-chronicle account of that division of Arthurian story, which he found in Wace's *Brut* or in some slightly modified version thereof, is additional proof that it is not by Robert, for in neither of this writer's authentic works do we observe this slavish adherence to sources. (Cp. on the sources of the *Didot-Perceval Mort Arthur*, F. Lot, *Bibliothèque de l'École des Chartes*, LXX, 567f. and J. D. Bruce, RR., IV, 448ff.) [10]

In the Didot MS. the *Joseph* begins (Hucher I, 277) with "Ci comence le romanz des prophecies Merlin," and the *Mort Arthur* ends (Hucher I 505): "Ci finist le romanz des prophecies Merlin" (in the Modena MS. Miss Weston, II, 112: "Ici fine li romans de Merlin et del Graal"). But this designation is unquestionably due to the error of a scribe, who probably took it (cp. Sommer's *Messire Robert de Borron*, etc., p. 16) from a French translation of Geoffrey's *Prophecies of Merlin*, which in this MS. is inserted into the prose *Merlin*. Sommer, *ibid.*, p. 39, has expressed the opinion that the small cycle (or trilogy, as he regards it) contained in the Didot and Modena MSS. was formed about

Didot-Perceval as relatively early and as a prose rendering of Robert's (hypothetical) lost *Perceval*.

[10] Brugger and Miss Weston, who believe that the *Perceval* section of the *Didot-Perceval* is based on Robert's verse, believe the same thing of the *Mort Arthur* section. For the former, cp. *Zs. f. frz. Spr. u. Litt.*, XXIX[1], 60f. 71, XXX[1], 182ff. XXXVI[2], 55f.; for the latter, cp. *Legend of Sir Perceval*, II, 326. If the source of the *Mort Arthur* section was indeed Martin of Rochester's chronicle, this chronicle must have differed very slightly from Wace.

1230 on the model of the larger cycle (which in the MSS. is falsely ascribed to Robert de Boron) as a protest against the substitution of Galahad for Perceval as the Grail hero. The "protest" would be coming pretty late — for Galahad by that date must have been holding the field for something like two decades — and the theory also involves the common assumption, which I believe to be unwarranted, that the authors of the Arthurian romances took these creations of their contemporaries more seriously than has been true under similar circumstances with the fiction-writers of other periods, but otherwise the suggestion possesses a certain plausibility, and has, in my judgment, the great merit of recognizing that because Galahad through the Vulgate cycle had become the popular Grail Winner, there was no reason why a writer seeking novelty in his own fashion should not revive Perceval in that function. Nevertheless, I believe, for my own part, that this smaller cycle may have been modelled directly after the Vulgate (instead of the Pseudo-Robert) cycle with the *Lancelot* left out. A writer may have very well thought that by the side of that huge cycle there would be among the aristocratic patrons of the time a public for a Grail cycle of moderate dimensions. With the prose versions of Robert's *Joseph* and *Merlin* already at hand, such a cycle was, of course, easy to compose, and the temptation to try one's hand at such a work was accordingly all the stronger.[11]

---

[11] For important additional evidence that tells against the theory of Robert's authorship of the *Didot-Perceval* (in its hypothetical verse-form), see next discussion.

Chapter X.

Robert de Boron, his Origin, the Date of his Poem and its Relation to the Didot=Perceval.

In the references to Robert de Boron (Borron), he is always called *messire (mesire, missire)*, so he was a knight, not an ecclesiastic. For his origin and the date of his poem, cp. especially, A Birch-Hirschfeld, pp. 238ff. (1877), G. Paris, *Huth-Merlin*, vol. I, pp. viiiff. (1886), R. Heinzel, pp. 113ff. (1892), H. Suchier, *Ps. f. rom. Ph.*, XVI, 269ff. (1892) (i. e., his review of Heinzel's Grail treatise), and W. Foerster, Chrétien *Wörterbuch*, 167*ff. (1914) — also, I, 220ff., above.

Francisque Michel in his edition of the *Tristan* poems (London and Paris, 1835—1839), vol. I, p. III, brought to light a Robert de Burun from an Essex document of the twelfth century, and H. L. D. Ward communicated to Suchier, *loc. cit.*, p. 274, information concerning still another, who, with his wife and son granted eighty acres in Cockenhatch, Hertfordshire, to a monastery of S. Salvius or S. Winwaloeus of Mosteriol (Picardy), now Montreuil-sur-Mer. Robert, abbot of the monastery from 1177 to 1203 "presently transferred" the grant to the chapel of S. Winwaleus in Saffron Walden, Essex. In the *Geschichte der französischen Literatur*, p. 137 (second edition, Leipzig, 1913), written by himself and Birch-Hirschfeld, Suchier is inclined to identify this second Robert de Burun with the poet. In the above-cited article in the *Zs. f. rom. Ph.* he had already argued from the language that the poet was an Anglo-Norman. But the more detailed examinations of the linguistic evidence in M. Ziegler's dissertation, *Über Sprache und Alter des von Robert de Boron Verfassten Roman du Saint Graal*, p. 92 (Leipzig, 1895) and in Foerster's *Wörterbuch*, pp. 168*f. (including note) point to the conclusion that Robert belonged, at least, originally, to Picardy — the rhyme *e: ie* constituting the only distinctively Anglo-Norman feature of his language.[1] To be sure, Brugger, *Zs. f. frz. Spr. u. Litt.* XXXVI, 33 (review section, 1910) denies that the *e: ie* rhyme in Robert is really Anglo-Norman. The *e*, he says, merely rhymes with the second element in the rising diphthong, *ie*. Before accepting this view, however, I would await confirmation from authorities on Old French metre and dialects. In any event, Brugger's explanation evidently did not occur to Foerster, for he offers the following alternative hypotheses to account for the somewhat conflicting phenomena: 1. That the second redaction of Robert's poem was by a person whose dialect was different from Robert's own. 2. That Robert's language, though originally Picard, may have been affected by a long stay in England. The second of these suppositions, which, *per se*, with regard to the conditions of the time, is a very likely one, seems to me preferable. The evidence which G. Paris, *loc. cit.*, has adduced to prove that the poet, personally, was ignorant of Great Britain and drew on a defective memory of Wace for all that he says about it is, I believe, reconcilable with this assumption. For Paris points out only one positive geographical blunder in Robert's work, viz: that of making Winchester a port. But one can easily conceive of a foreigner, who, in the twelfth or thirteenth century, if not in the twentieth, should continue under this erroneous impression, even after he had resided in Great Britain for several years, if his residence were in some other part of the island. It is not necessary to ascribe the error to the author of the prose version, as Foerster, *Wörterbuch*, p. 171*, is inclined to do. The other matters which Paris, pp. XIf. (including notes) calls attention to as showing ignorance of Great Britain on the part of the author are, in my opinion, compatible with this theory of Robert's life, for none of them would be strange in an Arthurian romance by a native of Picardy, even if he had sojourned for some time in England.

---

[1] In his review of Birch-Hirschfeld's *Sage vom Gral, Zs. f. rom. Ph.*, II, 617 ff. (1878), E. Koschwitz, on the basis of the rhymes, had already decided that Robert did not write in Anglo-Norman, but Ziegler and Foerster present fuller evidence.

The slightly conflicting evidence as to the date of Robert's language, noted by Foerster, may be explained by a taste for archaic forms on the part of the author. P. Paris's attempt (*Romania* I, 477) to connect Robert with Belfort and E. Hucher's (*Le Saint Graal*, I, 41 ff.) to connect him with a commune, now called "Bouron", on the southern edge of the forest of Fontainebleau, are both rendered nugatory (despite Birch-Hirschfeld, p. 240) by the evidence of the language. On the other hand, the passage in the prose *Tristan* (E. Löseth, *Le roman en prose de Tristan*, p. 216) which speaks of Robert's having seen at Oxford a silver image, made at King Arthur's command, of a certain hideous damsel in that romance is, on the face of it, like other citations of the same writer in this work, certainly a mere invention. Cp. Foerster, *Wörterbuch*, p. 169*, on the subject.

The much-debated lines at the end of Robert's *Joseph*, on which the dating of the poem depends, are so important that it is desirable to reprint them here (from F. Michel's *Le roman du Saint Graal*, 145 ff., Bordeaux, 1841) in their entirety.

> Ainsi Joseph se demoura.   3455
> Li boens Pescherres s'en ala
> (Dont furent puis meintes paroles
> Contees, ki ne sunt pas foles)
> En la terre lau il fu nez,
> Et Joseph si est demourez.   3460
> Messires Roberz de Beron
> Dist, se ce ci savoir voulun,
> Sanz doute savoir couvenra
> Conter la ou Aleins ala,
> Li fiuz Hebron, et qu'il devint,
> En queu terre aler le couvint,
> Et ques oirs de li peut issir,
> Et queu femme le peut nourrir,
> Et queu vie Petrus mena.
> Qu'il devint n'en quel liu ala,   3470
> En quel liu sera recouvrez;
> A peinnes sera retrouvez;
> Que Moyses est devenuz,
> Que fu si longuement perduz:

Trouver le couvient par reison
(De parole ainsi le dist-on)
Lau li riches Peschierres va;
E a quel liu il s'arrestera,
Et celui sache ramener,
Qui orendroit s'en doit aler.   3480
Ces quatre choses rassembler
Couvient chaucune, et ratourner
Chascune partie par soi
Si comme ele est; meis je bien croi
Que nus hons ne's puet rassembler
S'il n'a avant oi conter
Dou Graal la plus grant estoire,
Sanz doute, ki est toute voire.
A ce tens que je la retreis
O mon seigneur Gautier en peis,   3490
Que de Mont-Belyal estoit,
Unques retreite este n'avoit
La grant estoire dou Graal
Par nul homme qui fust mortal;
Meis je fais bien a touz savoir
Qui cest livre vourrunt avoir,
Que, se Diex me donne sante
Et vie, bien ei volenté
De ces parties assembler,
Se en livre les puis trouver.   3500
Ausi cumme d'une partie
Leisse, que je me retrei mie,
Ausi couvenra il conter
La quinte, et les quatre [2] oublier,
Tant que je puisse revenir
Au retreire plus par loisir
Et a ceste uuevre tout par moi,
Et chascune m'estu[et] par soi;
Meis se je or les leisse a tant,
Je ne sai homme si sachant   3510
Qui ne quit que soient perdues
Ne qu'eles serunt devenues,
Ne en quele senefiance
J'en aroie feit dessevrance.

---

[2] In *Bausteine zur romanischen Philologie: Festgabe für Adolfo Mussafia zum 15. Februar 1905*, p. 617 (Halle, 1905),

P. Paris, RTR., I, 152, note, proposes rightly, I believe,
that ll. 3459 and 3460 should exchange places. Suchier's conjectural restoration (p. 271) in l. 3508, *mestrai,* is preferable to
Michel's *m'estuet,* and I accept also his emendation of *ierent* (future) for *furent* in l. 3457, a scribe having probably mistaken
ierent, the future, for the imperfect of the same form. Moreover,
Suchier is certainly right *(ibid.)* as against Heinzel, p. 117, in
interpreting ll. 3479 ff. as applying to the Rich Fisher and not
to Gautier de Montbelyal, and the Grail history of ll. 3487, 3493
as meaning Robert's own *Joseph* (or rather, as I should, myself,
say, his *Joseph* plus his proposed continuations of the story of
the Grail), instead of some other book — for example, the *Estoire
del Saint Graal* as P. Paris, *Romania,* I, 481 (including note 1)
and *Romans de la Table Ronde,* V, 356, conjectured. See, too,
Heinzel, p. 112. It is merely a characteristic awkwardness of
expression that makes the poet, l. 3486, put himself for the moment
at the point of view of the reader.

P. Paris, *Romans de la Table Ronde,* 1, 109, *Romania,* I,
481, and G. Paris, *Huth-Merlin,* I, p. IX, note 1, have expressed
the view that the sole text of Robert's poem that we possess is
that of a second redaction, differing, as their words would imply,
from the first;[3] but their statements are merely of a general nature.

E. Freymond defends *troi,* the reading here of MS. Riccardiana 2759
(the MS. which he is describing). That MS. (of the prose *Joseph*),
however, has no value (cp. Brugger, *Zs. f. frz. Spr. u. Litt.,* XXIX [2],
33 ff.) and there is no reason for rejecting the usual reading. Freymond (so, too, P. Paris and Gröber) thinks *(ibid.,* pp. 619 f.) that
Alain, his son, and Bron were to be the heroes of the postponed three
branches. He regards Moyses and Petrus as merely *episodenhaft* and
remarks that the figure, three (the number of the Christian Trinity),
runs all through Robert's poem. Robert's words here, however, are
too plain to be argued away.

[3] So, too, E. Freymond, *op. cit.* p. 617, especially with reference
to ll. 3481 to the end of the poem. He expresses uncertainty as to
whether these lines represent the working over (by Robert or another)
of an older passage, or whether they constitute an addition to the first
redaction. So too, with ll. 3455 f. He suggests that a copyist substituted
l. 3460 for a lost line, reading probably "Et Joseph est mort et finez"

The puzzling lines, 3489 ff., one may accept with practical certainty as a later addition. They furnish no ground for the belief, however, that the poem, as a whole, was recast, or "abridged and arranged," as Nutt, p. 95, puts it. Heinzel, who adopts the opinion of P. and G. Paris, gives it a somewhat more definite form, inasmuch as he cites (p. 88) as an addition of the second redaction, ll. 881—938, besides 3481—3514 (last paragraph of the poem). In these lines, 881 ff., Christ, speaking to Joseph in the prison, promises that those that believe in him shall be saved and that Joseph's memory will always be connected with the sacrament — then recounts briefly the Last Supper, and interprets his own entombment in terms of the eucharist. At the end, the poet says, ll. 929 ff.:

> Je n'ose conter ne retreire,
> Ne je ne le pourroie feire,
> Neis, se je feire le voloie,
> Se je le grant livre n'avoie
> Ou les estoires sunt escrites,
> Par les granz clers feites et dites:
> La sunt li grant secre escrit
> Qu'en numme le graal et dit.

The three points which Heinzel makes, in arguing that, ll. 881—938, did not belong to the original redaction, are, 1. that just before this passage we have, ll. 879 f.:

> "Joseph, qui a genouz estoit,
> Prist le veissel [i. e. Grail] que Diex tenoit",

and immediately after it we have the same thing virtually repeated, ll. 937 f.:

> "Adonc le veissel li bailla,
> Et Joseph volentiers pris l'a."

But there is no reason *per se* why the intervening lines should not have stood in the first redaction, and, if that is true, even a poet who was not afflicted with Robert's proverbial clumsiness might have found it advisable, after so long a digression, in resuming his narrative, to repeat the last *incident* which he had given in that narrative. 2. Heinzel thinks that the words, l. 941, *ces trois vertuz*, referring to the Trinity, could not have been sepa-

rated so far in the original redaction from the last mention of the
Trinity, ll. 877 f.   But after Christ's previous description of the
Trinity, ll. 873 ff., as three persons in one, in whose name the
Grail-keepers will guard the vessel, there could be no misunder-
standing of his words, ll. 939 ff.:

> "Joseph, quant vouras
> Et tu mestier en averas,
> A ces trois vertuz garderas,
> Q'une chose estre ainsi creiras."

Joseph would have had a short memory, indeed, if he had forgotten these tremendous teachings in so brief an interval. 3. Heinzel sees a contradiction in regard to the Grail story between l. 934
(about the Grail book of *les granz clers*) and ll. 3489 ff. (quoted
above), where Robert implies that he was the first to write about
the Grail. To begin with, it seems a very questionable exegesis
to try to hold down to strict accuracy an obscure, negligent writer
in a reference to a purely fictitious book (*pace* Wechssler, *Zs. f.
rom. Ph.*, XXIII, 169). But, even waiving this objection, it is
surely more likely that the poet, writing or recasting the epilogue
to his poem some years after the poem itself was composed (as
the use of the preterite, *retreis*, compels us to assume) and on
the point of beginning the *Merlin*, should have forgotten his lines
about the Grail book of the great clerks, than that he should
have inserted these two more or less contradictory passages in his
new redaction — for, if Heinzel's theory is true, this is what
must have happened.

   If I have been successful in refuting the main points raised
by Heinzel, there is no need of considering his suggestion (p. 89)
as to the supposed modification of ll. 2448 ff. in the extant version.

   W. Foerster's acceptance of a second redaction, *Wörterbuch*,
p. 161*, is connected with his theory that the first redaction an-
tedated Chrétien's *Perceval;* this theory, however, has found no
adherents.

   In the *Zs. f. rom. Ph.*, XXIII, 170, note 2 (1899), E. Wechssler has already, in general terms, rejected the theory of a second
redaction of Robert's poem, and specifically, with reference to the

passage which I have just been discussing, but the "verlorene
mystisch-symbolische Graallegende" which he assumes to have been
Robert's source for this passage as for others in his poem is a pure
myth.

Brugger, *Zs. f. fr. Spr. u. Litt.*, XXIX[1], 64, note 13, has
also rejected the theory of a second redaction on more general
grounds than those which I have adopted in my argument above.
I agree with Brugger that *en peis* is put in merely for rhyme's
sake, but the suggestion that *retreis*, the preterite which rhymes
with it, should have been substituted by Robert for *retrei*, the
present (which would have expressed his real meaning), is incredible. — It would remove all difficulties, if we could assume
that the poet was here writing from the point of view of his reader,
as was the custom, for instance, in Roman letter-writing. In that
case the past tense would be appropriate. But as far as I know,
there are no parallels to this in medieval usage.

H. O. Sommer and F. Lot are to be added to the list of scholars who have refused to accept the theory of two redactions for
Robert's *Joseph*. For the former cp. *Messire Robert de Borron
und der Verfasser des Didot-Perceval*, p. 13 (Halle, 1908), and
for the latter, *Bibliothèque de l'École des Chartes*, LXX, 565,
note 4. As I have said already, however, Lot's rejection of the
whole reference to Gautier de Montbéliard as a falsification seems
unjustified. Believing that Robert advanced this impudent claim
only after Gautier's death, Lot puts the composition of the *Joseph*
after 1212. But this is virtually impossible, for the prose romance of the Vulgate cycle which has been commonly called the
Grand St. Graal is indisputably dependent on Robert's *Joseph* and
yet, was certainly in existence by 1216, and, in all likelihood,
several years earlier. See my article in *The Romanic Review*,
III, 185ff. (1912). Wauchier de Denain, I may add, may have
written before Robert, as Lot appears to think, but Brugger has
shown conclusively, *Zs. f. frz. Spr. u. Litt.* XXXVI[2], 45ff., that
there is no reason why we should limit his literary activity to
the thirteenth century.

Wechssler, *Zs. f. rom. Phil.*, XXIII, 149ff., maintains that

Robert actually composed the branches on Alain, Petrus, Moises,
and Bron which he speaks of, 346 ff., though they are no
longer extant, and that these branches came just after the
Merlin. But no trace of any such branches, if they ever existed,
has reached us; for the incidents attached to the four characters
in the latter part of the *Grand St. Graal (Estoire del Saint Graal)*,
I, 260 ff. (Sommer's edition), which Wechssler cites, cannot be
taken in this sense. He, himself, notes the want of correspondence
between the part of the *Grand St. Graal* in question and such indications as we have of Robert's intentions in his extant work,
and draws the familiar inference that the two are not directly
related, but go back to a common lost source. This is a very disputable conclusion, but I will not argue the matter here, since,
in granting that this part of the *Grand St. Graal* is not dependent
on Robert, Wechssler yields the essential point. The part of his
argument which is based on supposed references to these branches
in the *Didot-Perceval* is only valid on the assumption that that
romance is really the prose rendering of a lost poem by Robert;
but this assumption is, in my judgment, erroneous, as the evidence which I shall review in a moment appears to prove.

In two MSS. of the prose *Merlin* (747 of the Bibliothèque
Nationale and Add. 32625 of the British Museum) we have at
the end of that romance the following passage: "Et je, Robers de
Boron qui cest livre retrais . . . . ne doi plus parler d'Artus, tant
que j'aie parle d'Alain, le fils de Bron, et que j'aie devise par
raison, por quelles choses les poines de Bretaigne furent establies.
Et ensi com li livres le reconte, me convient a parler et retraire,
ques hom fu Alain, et quele vie il mena, et ques oirs issi de lui,
et quelle vie si oir menerent. Et quant tems sera et leus, et je
aurai de celui parle si reparlerai d'Artu et prendrai les paroles
de lui et de sa vie a s'election et a son sacre."[4]

---

[4] I have given the text of MS. 747 (Bibl. Nat.), as it is reproduced
by P. Paris, I, 357. Nearly every one who has discussed the problems
of the *Didot-Perceval* has reprinted it. The text of Add. 32125
(B. M.), which is not quite so correct, can be best consulted in Sommer's

This passage has been accepted as genuine by P. Paris, I, 357, who first printed it (from MS. 747), by Birch-Hirschfeld, pp. 179f., who points out its coincidences of phrasing with lines in Robert's poems, and by G. Paris, *Huth-Merlin*, I, pp. XXIf. — also, by Wechssler, *Zs. f. rom. Ph.*, XXIII, 138f., and Brugger, *Zs. f. frz. Spr. u. Litt.*, XXIX[1], 67f., XXXVI[2], 12f. On the other hand, W. Hoffman, *Quellen des Didot-Perceval* (Halle, 1905), pp. 12f., and Sommer, *Messire Robert de Borron und der Verfasser des Didot-Perceval*, pp. 2f. (Halle, 1908), have objected to its authenticity. The latter, especially, has argued the question at some length. Brugger, *Zs. f. frz. Spr. u. Litt.*, XXXVI[2], 9ff., has answered convincingly three of the four arguments which Sommer has advanced, but the second of these arguments, viz. that the passage is a mere repetition, in condensed form, of the end of the *Joseph*, still seems to me to possess weight. More decisive, however, in favor of the position of Hoffmann and Sommer than anything which they themselves urge are, I believe, the following considerations: 1. the peculiar use in this passage of "poines", in the phrase, "poines de Bretagne" — "por quelles choses les poines de Bretaigne furent establies." Hoffmann's interpretation of the "poines de Bretagne," as referring to the wars that are related in the *Merlin* continuations (between Arthur and his barons, Arthur and the Saxons, Arthur and the Romans), is hardly admissible. The word "establir" does not accord with this interpretation. Men do not "establish" wars. "Poines" that are "establies" must mean "adventures" and the passage implies the establishment of adventures (or *coutumes,* which are to be overcome by adventures) such as we meet with at every turn in the Chrétien tradition. The connotation of the word here is identical with that of "poine" in the *Didot-Perceval* (Hucher, I, 448),[5] where Perceval tells his sister that he would stay, "se je avoi acomplie la poine ou je sui entre," and it is similar to that of the "enchante-

---

Vulgate Version of the Arthurian Romances, II, 86, note 1. It is there given with its context.

    [5] The Modena MS. has here "queste". Cp. Miss Weston's text, II, 39.

ments" of the same romance, Hucher, I, 419, 428, 467, 484f.[6] —
which end (pp. 484f.), after Perceval has achieved the Grail adventure — although not quite identical, I believe, as Wechssler and
Brugger assume. Now in Robert's verse, as far as it has been
preserved, the word *poine* (*peine* and other variants) occurs only
four times, viz., *Joseph*, ll. 130, 214, 3472, and *Merlin*, l. 3619.
The first two times it is in the singular, the last time in the plural.
In the third case it means "difficulty" *(à peinnes)*, in the rest,
"suffering" (twice with reference to Christ). In the portion of
Robert's work which is preserved to us only in the form of a prose
rendering — that is to say, in the remainder and greater part of
the *Merlin* — it occurs only once, viz. Sommer's *Vulgate Version
of the Arthurian Romances*, II, 54, in the plural *(painnes)*, and
here again it means "sufferings", being used this time of the
sufferings of Christ's apostles. It is found, also, in the singular
(paine) six times in the prose-rendering of Robert's *Merlin*, viz.
Sommer, II, 19 (twice), 20 (twice), 24, 54, and always with the
meaning of "labor expended in achieving a task."[7] Thus it will
be seen that Robert's undisputed works, as far as the extant MS.
tradition permits us to judge, contain no instance of *poines* in the
peculiar use of the passage under discussion. 2. Furthermore, the
conception of romantic adventure implied in the phrase "por
quelles choses les poines de Bretaigne furent establies," — fairy-
tale tasks to be achieved by the hero — which came to the Arthurian romancers from folk-tales, is entirely foreign to Robert,
whose mind moves altogether in the realm of legend (whether
Christian or oriental) and chronicle. 3. There are indications that
the passage is a mere imitation of the epilogue to the *Joseph* and
was inserted by a scribe who wished to indicate at this point what

---

[6] The corresponding passages in the Modena MS. will be found
in Miss Weston's text, II, 13, 22, 62, 84. The word, "encantement",
is found here, too, in all but the first passage.

[7] In his *Vulgate Version of the Arthurian Romances*, I, p. XXII,
Sommer seems to regard Merlin's address to Blaise, II, 19f., in which
the first four instances of *paine* in the singular occur, as a scribal
interpolation. But its very clumsiness and obscurity, which recall so
strongly the *Joseph* epilogue, testify to its genuineness.

he knew from that epilogue to have been Robert's original intention. As bearing on this point, I would call attention to the fact that in exactly the same MSS. (747, B. N. and Add. 32125 B. M.) that preserve this passage we have in the body of the *Merlin*, Sommer, II, 20, note 1, another (brief) insertion which, likewise, harks back to this epilogue and which is plainly unauthorized. It is, of course, derived by the two MSS. from a common ancestor in the MS. tradition. The situation is this: Blaise has taken down from Merlin's dictation the narrative of the events which have been related up to that point in Robert's *Merlin,* and Merlin then tells him that his (Blaise's) book, which is, of course, really Robert's *Merlin,* is going to be joined to the *Joseph.* He continues: "Et quant li doi liure seront ensemble, si i aura .j. biau liure, & li doi seront .j. misme chose, fors tant que ne puis pas dire ne retraire les priuees paroles de ihesu crist & de ioseph [i. e. as is done in Robert's *Joseph*][8] ne en engleterre nauoit onques este rois crestiene [i. e. at the time of the events related in the *Joseph*]. Et des rois qui i aucient este deuant ne me chaut de retraire fors tant comme a cest conte amonte."

Now after the word "ioseph" in this passage, MS. Add. 32125 (B. M.), fol. 214a, intercalates, "Elsi [for *eisi*=*ensi*] dit mi sire Robert de Borron qui cest conte retrait [o] mi sire Gauter de Montbeliart qi cist conte se redoble [i. e. the *Merlin* is added to the *Joseph*] et ensi le dita merlin qil ne pot sauer le conte du graal." MS. 747 (B. N.), fol. 82b, as Sommer tells us, has "a similar passage but 'mi sire Gauter de Montbeliart' is not mentioned." The variant from MS. Add. 32125, fol. 213d, which Sommer gives, II, 19, note 2, in its allusion to Bron (Alain's father) which is not found in the other *Merlin* MSS., shows the same harking back to the epilogue of the *Joseph.*[9] It is obvious from these pas-

---

[8] My interpretation differs slightly from that which Brugger has given of this passage, *Zs. f. frz. Spr. u. Litt.,* XXIX[1], 82, note 34. Moreover, when he says there that Robert may have meant to include a *Perceval* in the *Merlin* which is here indicated, this is obviously unjustified.

[9] I have tried to prove that the passage (in the two MSS.) which

sages that the scribe (or redactor) of the archetype of these MSS. drew from the *Joseph* epilogue on his own account, and, no doubt, he was doing the same thing when he inserted the passage under discussion at the end of the *Merlin*.

The question has been asked: Why did Robert postpone completing the story of the four characters, Alain, Petrus, Moyses and Bron, whom he had introduced in the *Joseph*, and take up the *Merlin*, instead? Brugger, *Zs. f. frz. Spr. u. Litt.*, XXIX[1], 64, thinks that he wanted to wait in order to learn what impression his innovation — the introduction of Christian legend into the Arthurian romances "on a large scale" — would produce. To me the most plausible explanation is that he was drawn away from his immediate theme by the story of Merlin, partly on ac-

---

I have been discussing is spurious. But even if we accepted it as genuine, it would not justify the inferences which have been drawn from it. In that event, it would merely show that Robert now intended to compose an *Alain*, as a separate branch, in conformity with his statement as to the omitted branches in the *Joseph*, l. 3483 *(chascune partie par soi)*. In the face of the author's own express declaration of his intentions, Brugger's argument, *Zs. f. frz. Spr. u. Litt.*, XXIX[1], 67, that what the above-quoted passage announces about Alain was to constitute a part of the *Perceval* branch is of no avail, for the poet puts Alain first and not his heir. Similarly, the theory which the same scholar adopts (pp. 59f.) that Robert planned his work as a trilogy is contradicted by Robert's own words, who, himself, speaks (l. 3504) of the *Merlin* as the fifth branch. Later in the same journal, XXXVI[2], 8, 55, Brugger changes "trilogy" to "tetralogy", but that is open to the same objection.

The idea that Robert cast his work in the form of a trilogy, which has been adopted by Birch-Hirschfeld, I, 181, Miss Weston, *Legend of Sir Lancelot*, I, 126, and others, is entirely natural for anyone who regards the *Didot-Perceval* (including its insignificant *Mort Arthur* section) as a prose rendering of Robert's verse. But the maintenance of this idea depends wholly on one's ability to establish the thesis just mentioned. It derives no support from Robert's own declaration on the subject. It would seem from Sommer, II, 19f., as if Robert, when he wrote this passage, had already decided to content himself with the *Joseph* and the *Merlin*, and had renounced his original ambitious plan.

count of the intrinsic interest of the latter (to which something may have attracted his attention, whilst he was composing the *Joseph*) and partly because a work on the great magician, as he may have come to feel, was sure to gain him a wider hearing than the adventures of the four shadowy characters named above. He might well shrink from pursuing the latter further in their wanderings and have taken a short cut to what from the beginning had been his ultimate goal — namely, Britain, as the stage of the actions of King Arthur and the celebrated characters who surrounded him. I have no doubt, too, that the poet was deterred from following out the careers of Alain, Petrus, Moyses and Bron by the effort which the invention of adventures for these characters would have entailed, whereas the remarkable story of Merlin's conception (probably an adaptation of a rabbinical tale) and other similar stories, together with the metrical chronicles — especially, Wace's *Roman de Brut*, or, it may be, the lost expansion of the same — furnished him with ample materials for a romance concerning Merlin.

It has, of course, been assumed quite commonly that the story of Alain and the rest in Robert's *Joseph* is derived from hypothetical lost sources. In the *Zs. f. rom. Ph.*, XXIII, 161 ff. Wechssler, for example, has conjured up a number of such imaginary sources — "Percevals Gralsuche und Hirschjagd," "Pseudo-blasius," "Die Graallegende von Joseph und seinem Geschlecht," "Die mystisch-symbolische Graallegende," "Die Legende vom Graal als der Abendmahlschüssel." But this is all purely subjective. The critic has simply analyzed the various elements in Robert's poem and assigned to each an imaginary writing as a source. He has produced no evidence, beyond these subjective impressions, to prove that any such sources ever existed.

So, too, when Brugger, *loc. cit.*, p. 67, note 15, interprets *li livres*, in the passage (at the end of the prose *Merlin* in the two MSS. named) which I have quoted above, as referring to Robert's source, there is no cogency in his interpretation, since it is a commonplace for the writers of Arthurian romance — indeed, a sort of formula — to appeal to *li livres, li contes, li escris,* as authorities for what are really their own inventions. In his continuation to Chrétien's *Perceval*, Gerbert (Potvin, VI, 193), in the same manner, plainly speaks of his own work, as if he were speaking of its *source:*

"Si com Gerberts le nous tesmoigne
En son conte que il en fist!"

I wish to devote a few pages to this question of Robert's source, which though, in my judgment, satisfactorily answered, in the main, by Birch-Hirschfeld, still requires some elucidation, as regards the last division of the *Joseph*.[10]

The *Vindicta Salvatoris* and *Gesta Pilati*, as the German scholar, just named, has shown, are the sources of the first part of Robert's poem. I believe that we can fix with equal certainty the sources of the latter part — the part (ll. 2307ff.) in which Bron, Alain etc. appear. To be sure, as Birch-Hirschfeld, p. 224, has remarked, the story here moves very slowly and consists of a few simple incidents, without the complications of the earlier narrative. Religious instruction, which is imparted especially in dialogues between Joseph and the Holy Spirit, takes, as he says, the place of action, in a large measure. The action here is more meagre, no doubt, for the reason that the source of this part was poorer in incident. Now, as regards the identity of this source, Birch-Hirschfeld, *loc. cit.*, has observed that the incidents of this last part of the *Joseph* "sind im ganzen nur biblischen Vorgängen nachgebildet." More specifically, Heinzel has noted (pp. 99, 102f.) that the wanderings of the Children of Israel in the Wilderness formed the model for the similar journey of Joseph and his companions in Robert's poem. He has, besides (pp. 102f.) pointed out the many resemblances between the Ark of the Covenant in the Old Testament narrative and the Grail in the *Joseph*. All

---

[10] P. Paris in his article, "Le Saint Graal", *Romania*, I, 457ff., observed the dependence of the Early History of the Grail in the romances on the *Vindicta Salvatoris* and *Gesta Pilati*, but he made the mistake of dating the *Estoire del Saint Graal (Grand St. Graal)* as earlier than Robert's *Joseph,* and hence regards the author of that work as the first of our romance-writers to use these materials. But Birch-Hirschfeld, pp. 162ff., proved that the *Estoire* is dependent on Robert's poem.

of this is so obvious that the author of the *Estoire del Saint Graal (Grand St. Graal)*, I, 20, whose work is, of course, based on Robert's, really, makes Joseph (following God's command) put the Grail in an ark. Even Heinzel, however, I believe, has not discerned the true significance of Robert's poem in its relation to the Old Testament narrative. In order to establish what that significance is, let us consider the following circumstances:

The conclusion of Robert's *Joseph* indicates clearly enough that he, like all other writers of Arthurian romance, connected the Grail with Britain, and that, in the event of his carrying out the programme which he outlines, ll. 3461ff., he intended to transport it and its keepers thither, as his imitator, the author of the *Estoire del Saint Graal*, I, 211ff., actually does. If this is so, it seems strange that he should not have done this immediately after Joseph, liberated and in full possession of the Grail, had been avenged on the Jews. Instead, he sends Joseph and his companions off to journey, like the Israelites, "in distant lands," l. 2363. Britain was surely distant enough and the test of the powers of the Grail could have been made there as well as anywhere else. As a matter of fact, in my opinion, he was influenced in the course which he has adopted by the motives of religious symbolism which we find governing him everywhere in his poem (cp. particularly, ll. 893ff.). His interest in the Grail was primarily religious, and he desired to express symbolically through his narrative the doctrine which Christ proclaimed in His institution of the Holy Communion that the New Covenant which was symbolized by His blood, was to supersede the Old Covenant of the Mosaic dispensation, which was symbolized by the Ark of the Covenant: *St. Matthew*, XXVI, 27—28. "Et accipiens calicem gratias egit: et dedit illis, dicens: Bibite ex hoc omnes. Hic est enim sanguis meus novi testamenti, qui pro multis effundetur in remissionem peccatorum." So, too, *St. Mark*, XIV, 23—24. Even nearer to Robert's conception, however, is the corresponding passage in *St. Luke*, XXII, 20, where Christ says: "Hic est calix novum testamentum in sanguine meo, qui pro vobis fundetur." The Grail in Robert's poem is, of course, the *calix*

of the Last Supper, and all that the poet does is to send these new
chosen people of God into the Wilderness, with this symbol of
the New Covenant[11] substituted for the Ark which was the symbol
of the Old Covenant. It would not have been sufficient, if he had
located these wanderings in Britain. It was necessary that they
should be, in a general way, in the same region, hallowed by the
Scriptures, as the wanderings of the Israelites — only the matter
had to be left somewhat in the vague, for Joseph of Arimathea
and his people were, of course, not fleeing from the land of Egypt.

This interpretation of the later episodes of Robert's *Joseph*
is confirmed by the author's adoption of the name, Hebron, as
that of the Grail-keeper, who is to succeed Joseph. We find the
full form,[12] "Hebron" in the poem thirteen times, the shortened

---

[11] In our Authorized Version we have "testament" in the passages
just quoted from the Gospels, where the Vulgate has "testamentum".
In the Old Testament, on the other hand, where the Authorized Version
has "covenant", the Vulgate has usually "foedus", e. g. *Genesis*, VI,
18, IX, 13, *Exodus*, VI, 4, etc.; more rarely, "pactum", e. g. *Genesis*,
IX, 11, *Leviticus*, XXVI, 15, *Deuteronomia*, IV, 13, etc.; only once
"testamentum", as far as I have observed, viz. *Numeri*, X, 44 (arca
testamenti). To be sure, in the New Testament the Vulgate has, *Ad
Hebraeos*, IX, 15, 16, 17, "testamentum", where the Authorized
Version has "covenant". The Greek Bible uses the same word
throughout in all cases, viz. διαθήκη. So, too, the English Revised
Version uses "covenant" everywhere.

[12] The full form is undoubtedly the original form; for shortened
forms of proper names by the side of the full forms, owing to various
causes, are, of course, frequent in all ages. On the other hand, what
motive would one have had to prefix the syllable, *He*, to „Bron", if
that had been the original form of the name? For the rest, the
attempt of the Celticists to identify Robert's *Bron* with the *Bran* of
Celtic legend is on a par with Rhys's attempt (*Arthurian Legend*,
pp. 321 f.) to identify *Nascien, Natien* (Galahad's ancestor) with the
Nwython (Bede's *Naiton*, it seems) of Welsh legend. But, as I have
pointed out, MLN, XXXIII, 134 f., *Nascien* is indisputably the *Naasson*
of *St. Matthew*, I, 4 and *St. Luke*, III, 32 (genealogies of Christ),
and has nothing to do with the Celts.

In Old French the *H* in *Hebron* being silent and the accent
falling on the second syllable, the aphaeresis of the initial unaccented

form, "Bron", twenty-three times. The variation in the form of vowel was no great liberty to take for a poet who was evidently not a ready writer and who accordingly desired the alternative of a monosyllabic form, because it was often easier to accommodate to his line. The phenomenon just mentioned (aphaeresis of initial vowel or syllable in proper names) is frequent in all languages, but, especially, so in French. Cp. K. Nyrop, *Grammaire Historique de la Langue Française*, I, 390 (Copenhagen, 1899), where we have, for example, *Colin* (common already in Old French) from *Nicolin*, *Chardin* from *Richardin*, etc. Such forms, it is true, are generally hypocoristic in origin, although later they lose this sense.

An example of double forms, parallel to *Hebron* and *Bron*, occurs in Wauchier's continuation to Chrétien's *Perceval*, ll. 23 707 ff., where we have *Abrioris* (the name of a knight) and *Brioris* within two lines of each other and both assured by the metre:

"Frere", ce dist Abrioris,
"Bien estes enseignies de dis."
Brioris a tant chemine, etc.

The longer form occurs again ll. 23 720, 23 771. In the MSS. of Manessier's continuation, ll. 35 608, 44 762, 45 292 etc., we have sometimes *Agloval*, sometimes *Gloval* as the name of Perceval's brother. Without a critical edition, however, one cannot say whether these forms are purposely made to alternate or whether we have here simply the common phenomenon of the loss of initial letter or syllable through scribal errors, which was of such frequent occurrence in mediaeval MSS. and which occasionally causes double forms to appear side by side in the same MS. It is possible, of course, that, through some such corruption, Robert's MS. of the Vulgate may have already contained the double forms, *Hebron* and *Bron*.

Perhaps it is, also, advisable to note the occurrence of forms of proper names with and without initial *Es-*, which are used side by side in Old French verse. Thus *Escavalcn*, name of a kingdom in Chrétien's *Perceval*, occurs in Wauchier's continuation, l. 33 625, as *Escavillon*, but ll. 33 625, 33 631, as *Cavillon (Kavillon)*. So in Wace's *Roman de Brut* Arthur's sword is *Calliborc* in l. 13 291, but *Escaliborc* in l. 13 330. For other examples cp. Zimmer, *Zs. f. frz. Spr. u. Litt.*, XII [1], 236 (1890), and E. Brugger, ibid., XXVII [1], 103 (1904).

Where shortened forms of proper names from various causes, as illustrated by the different kinds of examples which I have just cited, were so frequent, by the side of the longer forms, it is not surprising that Robert's poem should also show such double forms, even if we concede that he was the first to abbreviate *Hebron* to *Bron*.

the name is not due to the scribes, for the correctness of both
forms is established by the metrical requirements, and both occur
throughout the last episodes of the poem. The shortened form
is the more frequent, simply because it was easier to fit into the
verse than the dissyllabic form.

"Hebron" being unquestionably the original form, let us see
whence Robert derived it. The name is undoubtedly taken from
the Old Testament, where it is not only the name of a city, but
of a person[13] — one of the grandsons of Levi, to say nothing of
a later character. As all the world knows, the Levites (descendants of Levi) constituted the priestly caste among the Hebrews.[14]
It is not so generally known, however, that the guardianship of
the Ark of the Covenant was exclusively entrusted to the descendants of just one of the sons of Levi, viz. Kohath, grandfather
of the most illustrious of the Levites, Moses and Aaron, who were,
accordingly, among the Kohathites. On the subject cp. *Numeri*,
III, 31: "Et custodient arcam, mensamque et candelabrum, al-
taria et vasa sanctuarii in quibus ministratur, et velum, cunc-
tamque huiuscemodi supellectilem."[15] Cp., too, *ibid.* IV, 4, 15,
X, 21. Now, according to *Numeri*, III, 19, Caath (Kohath of
our Authorized Version) had four sons: "Filii Caath: Amram et
Iesaar, Hebron et Oziel." So, too (except for the variant spelling,
"Isaar") in *Exodus*, VI, 18, I *Paralipomenon*, VI, 2, 18, XXIII,
12. It would seem from *Numeri*, III, 30, that the first chief of
the descendants of Caath (Kohath), after they began to exercise
their sacred functions, was "Elisaphan, filius Oziel," but it would
have been impossible for Robert to fit this name into his verse,

---

[13] Heinzel, p. 94, noted this, but he made no use of the fact.
In offering a conjecture (which he, himself, at once rejects) that
"Alain" was suggested by "Eliel", he quotes, I, *Paralipomenon
(Chronicles)*, 5 (misprint for 15), 9, in which the name, Hebron,
occurs, but does not comment on it.

[14] Cp. *Numbers*, ch. 3—4, and the book called *Leviticus*.

[15] This passage and the other passages concerned in the Old
Testament substantiate the statement of *The Jewish Encyclopaedia*,
New York, 1904, (under *Kohath*): "The division of the Kohathites
was more important than the other two Levitical divisions."

and the same thing applies, in almost equal measure, to the names
of all the sons of Caath except "Hebron," which, besides, would
lend itself more easily to rhyme in French verse than the rest,[16]
and would also make a presentable name, as we actually see in
Robert's poem, in the abbreviated form. This Hebron, it will
be observed, was an uncle of Moses (son of A.nram), whose rôle
in the wanderings, described in Robert's poem, is taken by Joseph.[17]

The words of Christ in instituting the Holy Communion which
I have quoted above from the Gospels are not the only passages
of the Scriptures, however, that connect the doctrine of the Atonement with the Old Covenant and its symbols, as they appear in
the Old Testament narrative of the wanderings of the Israelites
in the Wilderness. In his discourse at Capernaum, *St. John*, VI,
26—58, the day after he had performed the miracle of the loaves
and fishes, Jesus emphasizes in the strongest manner that the
miracle by which his flesh and blood are to give eternal life is to
supersede the miracle by which the Children of Israel were sus-
tained with manna in the desert. Furthermore, in the *Epistle to
the Hebrews*, ch. 9, we have the substitution (under the New Dispensation) of the blood of Christ for the Ark of the Covenant with
its attendant sacrifices set forth in an elaborate comparison.

It is plain, then, I believe, that Robert framed the narrative
of the peregrinations of Joseph and his companions with the religious purpose which I have described above in view, and that
he selected the name of the second keeper of the symbol of
the New Covenant from the family which was especially charged
with the guardianship of the symbol of the Old Covenant.[18]

---

[16] It is actually found in rhyme only twice in the poem (both
times, the full form), ll. 2310, 2510; but when the poet chose the
name on beginning this part of his poem, he would not know, of
course, how often it might prove convenient for him to use it in rhyme.

[17] Since Joseph filled the part of Moses, Robert gives the name,
Moses, to the hypocrite who is destroyed in trying to occupy the empty
seat at the Grail table.

[18] In the Kittredge *Anniversary Papers*, p. 236, note 1 — a

The author of the *Estoire del Saint Graal,* which is based on
Robert's *Joseph,* recognized, as has been noted above, that Robert
was imitating the story of the Israelites in the Wilderness. There
are indications, too, that he was aware of the true relation of the
Grail in Robert's scheme to the Ark of the Covenant in the Bible
narrative; for not only does he connect the Grail with the Ark
by putting the former in the latter, I, 20, but in the list of the
Grail-keepers which he compiles, I, 289, it would seem that he
drew upon the genealogical lists from which Robert had drawn
the name, "Hebron". Between Alain, Bron's son, and Pelleam,
father of Pelles (the Fisher King of the *Queste* and Galahad's
grandfather), according to the *Estoire,* there were the following
Grail-keepers: Josue, Aminadap (Aminadab), Catheloys (Carte-
lois, Carcelois), Manaal (Manael, Manuiel), Lambar (Lambor,
Labain, Labran, Lambart).[19] Now "Josue" is, of course, the Vulgate equivalent for "Joshua", the name of Moses' successor in
leading the Israelites out of the Wilderness in our modern versions,
and "Lambar" is very probably a mere manuscript corruption
of "Laban" (cp. the variant "Labain"), name of Jacob's father-
in-law. As for the remaining names, "Aminidab" occurs, *Exodus,* VI, 6 (one of the passages where the Levite genealogy is
given) as the name of Aaron's father-in-law, just five verses below

passage which is important from the point of view of those who ad-
vocate the Celtic origin of the Grail — A. C. L. Brown remarks: "If
the phrase 'rich fisher' meant in origin one who converted many, Peter
ought to be the original Fisher King, certainly not Joseph of Arimathea
or any other figure like Brons." But Joseph, being the preserver of
the Grail according to the story, of course, had the first claim to the
title which Chrétien applied to the Grail-keeper, and, even if Bron's
name did not originate in the manner I have described, he would be
a proper inheritor of the title, since he was destined to convert the
Britons to Christianity.

[19] The last three of these names are greatly corrupted, but not
more so than scores of others in our MSS. of the Vulgate cycle, to
say nothing of mediaeval MSS. in general. Thus on the page following this list of the Grail-keepers, I, 290, Lambar's slayer is called
in different MSS. "Brulans", "Valan" and heaven knows what else,
besides.

the enumeration of the sons of Caath (Kohath). "Catheloys" is most likely connected with "Caath" in some way. It is to be remembered that in mediaeval MSS. proper names are, as a rule, not distinguished by capitals, and, on the other hand, *e* and *o* are constantly confused, so that "Cathelois" may represent a corruption of "cath fil leui(s)."[20] As for the fourth of the Grail-keepers, we have in the Old Testament genealogical lists already quoted a name which appears in *Exodus*, VI, 15, as "Iamuel", but as "Namuel" (the same person) in *Numeri*, XXVI, 12. Is not this probably the original of "Manaal", "Manael", "Manuiel"? I would point out, too, that "Alphasan" (*Estoire*, II, 289), name of the holy father-in-law of Josue, the first of the Grail-keepers in the above list, suggests a connection with "Elisaphan", *Exodus*, VI, 22, who, according to *Numeri*, III, 30, was the chief of the Kohathites, when they took charge of the Ark of the Covenant.

Returning to Robert's *Joseph*, we see, then, that the only Celtic name employed in the poem is Alein,[21] and that, obviously, because its bearer was to be the apostle of the extreme West[22] (i. e. Britain). To Bron, who is to succeed Joseph as Grail-keeper, the term, "the Rich Fisher" (ll. 3387, 3416, 3431, 3440, 3477), or "the Good Fisher" (l. 3456), is applied, because that was the epithet of the Grail-keeper in Chrétien's *Perceval* (l. 3482).

---

[20] "Cathiles" for "Cathites" (descendant of Caath) with the second *t* changed to *l*, might, also, form the basis of the corruption. In the Vulgate the descendants of Caath are called "Caathitae". Cp. *Numeri*, III, 27, I. *Paralipomenon*, VI, 54.

[21] Enygeus (Enyseus), the name of Bron's wife (Joseph's sister), still constitutes a puzzle, but the form — manifestly corrupted — suggests Greek or Latin origin, not Celtic. Heinzel, pp. 93 f., tries to derive it from "Phenicienne" ("Venicienne"). The argument, however, depends on a whole chain of hazardous assumptions and is anything but convincing.

[22] Cp. ll. 3100 ff.

Chapter XI.

The Theories of Brugger and Lot Concerning the Origin of the Vulgate cycle.

We have explained above[1] what appears to us to be the true nature of the influence of Robert de Boron's *Joseph-Merlin* on the formation of the Vulgate cycle. We have, also, endeavored[2] to prove that the *Didot-Perceval* is not a prose rendering of a lost *Perceval* of Robert or any other poet, but a late original (prose) composition of its author. The assumption, however, that Robert did add a *Perceval* to his *Joseph* and *Merlin* has led some Arthurian scholars to adopt a different view of the evolution of the prose cycles from that which the present writer has set forth in the text above. These scholars believe that the earliest (hypothetical) Arthurian prose cycle developed directly out of the prose renderings of Robert's poems[3] and that the Grail hero in this earliest (hypothetical) prose cycle must have been Perceval, and not Galahad, who is actually the Grail hero in all the extant MSS. of the Vulgate and so-called Robert de Boron cycles of the prose-romances.[4] Indeed, Brugger has assumed that an extant *Per-*

---

[1] Pp. I, 456f.   [2] Pp. II, 104 ff.

[3] Miss Weston, *Legend of Sir Lancelot*, pp. 126 ff. (1901), and, more fully and clearly, Brugger, in his articles named below, note 6. In her later book, *Legend of Sir Perceval*, II (1909), however, the former makes the connection of the prose cycles with Robert much less direct. Cp. her schema, *ibid.*, p. 328 — also, her "Notes on the Grail Romances: the *Perlesvaus* and the Prose *Lancelot*", *Romania*, XLVI, 314 ff. (1920). On Wechssler's theory of the origin of the prose cycles, summarized in his *Sage vom heiligen Gral*, pp. 126 ff., cp. note 10, below.

[4] Besides Miss Weston and Brugger cp. Sommer, below, p. 146, note 3.

ceval romance — namely, the *Perlesvaus* — was actually the *Queste* branch in this earliest prose cycle.[5]

On the basis of the above-mentioned view that the prose-cycles were the result of a direct and orderly evolution from Robert de Boron's cycle, Brugger has worked out an elaborate theory of the development of the prose-cycles with that assumption as his starting-point.[6] According to this scholar, Robert's cycle in its prose, as well as in its verse, form, consisted of the following branches: *Joseph, Merlin, Perceval,*[7] *Mort Arthur,*[8] and the first step in the evolution of the cycle was the substitution of the *Perlesvaus*[9] for the *Perceval* in the series. Into the cycle, as thus constituted, was next imported the *Lancelot* — hitherto an independent romance. The *Lancelot* having been incorporated into the cycle, the next step taken was to supplant the *Perlesvaus* (= Perceval-*Queste*) by the Galahad-*Queste*. From the cycle, when it had attained this (hypothetical) form, he supposes that the extant Vulgate and Robert de Boron cycles of the prose romances were now developed independently. As I have observed (p. II, 153), it is Brugger's unwillingness to acknowledge that a romancer could again enthrone Perceval as the Grail hero, after the character had been once displaced by Galahad, that has caused him to evolve this complicated theory of successive series of cycles of which there is

---

[5] That is, earliest after the prose renderings of Robert. In this respect Miss Weston (last passage cited) agrees with Brugger. G. Paris, *Manuel,* § 60, dates the *Perlesvaus,* also, before the Galahad *Queste,* although he does not make it actually a part of the cycle.

[6] In the series of articles entitled *L'Enserrement Merlin,* which were running in the *Zs. f. frz. Spr. u. Litt.* from Vol. XXIX[1] (1905) to Vol. XXXV[1] (1909). Most important for the statement of the theory is the first of the series, viz. XXIX[1], 56ff., with the schema of the supposed development of the prose cycles at the end (p. 138). See, too, the author's summary of his theory, *op. cit.,* XXXVI[2], 206f. (1910).

[7] In the main, identical with the extant *Didot-Perceval,* according to Brugger. See II, p. 111 above.

[8] Represented in a somewhat shortened (prose) form by the *Mort Arthur* at the end of the *Didot-Perceval.* Cp. *op. cit.,* XXIX[1], 70f.

[9] In a different form from the extant text.

no evidence in the manuscript tradition.[10]   I need not linger over the matter here, however, since I have attempted elsewhere (I, 468ff., II, 145ff.) to prove (1) that the *Didot-Perceval* is not a prose-rendering of a lost *Perceval* by Robert de Boron and that we do not know, indeed, whether Robert ever wrote such a poem, (2) that the *Perlesvaus* is later and not earlier than the Galahad *Queste*. If my conclusions in regard to the *Perlesvaus* are true, this, of itself, would be fatal to Brugger's theory.

With regard to this scholar's assumption that the Pseudo-Robert-de-Boron cycle of the prose romances is not based on the extant Vulgate cycle, but is derived from a common (lost) source,[11] it may be remarked that the *Mort Arthur* branch of the latter is demonstrably a mere modification of the corresponding branch in the former.[12]   The same relation prevails, also, as between the *Merlin* branches of the two cycles.[13]   Furthermore, as we have

---

[10] For virtually every stage in the evolution of these hypothetical lost cycles Brugger assumes that redactions of various branches are different from those that have been actually preserved in our MSS. What likelihood is there of a theory's being correct, when it requires the acceptance of such a number of unprovable assumptions? The difficulty of any fruitful discussion of Brugger's theory is increased by the fact that its author gives us no definite idea as to the supposed forms of these various hypothetical redactions.

The same is true, in an even larger measure, of Wechssler's theory, summarized in his *Sage vom h. Gral*, pp. 126ff. This deals to such an extent with purely hypothetical works that it furnishes no real basis for discussion. For comment on his similar assumptions in regard to Robert cp. p. 127.

[11] So, too, before Brugger, Heinzel, in his Grail treatise, pp. 168ff. (1892) and Wechssler, Habilitationsschrift, p. 5 (1895).

[12] For the proof cp. RR, IV, 429ff.   The Spanish *Demanda* contains the Pseudo-Robert *Mort Arthur*.   Sommer has, also, recognized the undoubted dependence of Pseudo-Robert on the Vulgate in respect to this branch.   Cp. *Romania*, XXXVI, 585 (1907) and *Zs. f. rom. Ph.*, Beiheft 47, p. LII, note 1 (1913).   The fact that the Pseudo-Robert *Mort Arthur* is derived, beyond question, from the Vulgate *Mort Arthur*, of itself, makes an irreparable breach in the theory of Brugger, etc.

[13] G. Paris, Introduction to the *Huth-Merlin*, p. LXIV, asserted

seen,[14] there is no reason to believe that the Pseudo-Robert cycle ever contained a *Lancelot*, or that its lost branch on the early history of the Grail differed materially, if at all, from the Vulgate *Estoire*. Lastly, the contamination of the *Queste* of the pseudo-Robert cycle with the prose *Tristan*, which, in turn, presupposes the Vulgate cycle, shows that, in respect to this branch, too, the Vulgate cycle is the earlier.[15]

---

that the Merlin continuation in that work, is entirely independent of the Vulgate *Merlin* continuation and that the authors of these two continuations executed them "sans se connaître". So, too, Wechssler, *op. cit.*, p. 5, and Brugger, *Zs. f. frz. Spr. u. Litt.*, XXIX[1], 109. (For some remarks on this theory cp. Bruce, MPh., XVI, 341f.) But E[lla] Vetterman, in her *Die Balendichtungen und ihre Quellen (Zs. f. rom. Ph.*, Beiheft 60), pp. 271ff. (Halle, 1918), has shown from the episodes concerning Arthur's wars with Rion, Lot and their allies and from the Escalibor episodes that the *Huth-Merlin* continuation is dependent on the Vulgate. It would have been strange, indeed, if this had not been the case, since the author of the former displays an intimate familiarity with the other members of the Vulgate cycle. Cp. Vetterman, pp. 226ff.

[14] I, 468ff.

[15] On this subject cp. particularly A. Pauphilet "La Queste du Saint Graal du MS. Bibl. Nat. Fr. 343", *Romania*, XXXVI, 591ff. (1907). G. Paris, *Huth-Merlin*, I, pp. LIXf. and *Manuel*, § 60, was, doubtless, led to regard the *Queste* of the Vulgate as a recasting of the Pseudo-Robert *Queste*, instead of *vice versa*, by the fact that the latter bore Robert's name, which, however, it really had no right to. The only argument which he advances is based on the circumstance that the Vulgate *Queste* (VI, 22f., 184) gives the affair of the killing of Baudemagus by Gawain in a mutilated form which renders it virtually unintelligible, whereas the Pseudo-Robert *Queste*, as Paris was able to infer even before the publication of the Portuguese *Demanda*, relates this incident clearly and in full. In the Vulgate, it is true, no narrative is given of the fatal combat between Gawain and Baudemagus; only from the inscription on the tomb of the latter at the white abbey (p. 184) do we learn that Gawain slew him. In Pseudo-Robert, on the other hand, the whole story of the combat is told. In the opinion of the present writer, however, the deficiency in the Vulgate narrative must be due to an omission in the archetype of the extant MSS. of the Vulgate *Queste;* for it is inconceivable that the

According to Brugger's hypothesis, no attempt was made to modify substantially any individual romance, by itself — the modi-

author of that romance would have left his account of the death of Baudemagus, one of the oldest characters in Arthurian romance, purposely unintelligible. The situation is probably the same as in the Spanish *Demanda,* ch. 393, and the Harleian *Morte Arthur,* ll. 933 ff., where injudicious condensation on the part either of the authors of these works or of the scribes of the MSS. which they used has produced an unintelligible narrative — only, in these cases, the (approximate) original narratives of the incidents in question have survived, so that we are not left to conjecture on the subject. Cp. on the two passages — respectively, RR, IV, 429 f. and *Anglia,* XXIII, 85 f. On the other hand, the author of the Pseudo-Robert *Queste* probably had before him a copy of the Vulgate which was not marred by the deficiency indicated above. If not, then he made good the deficiency from his own invention.

Apart from the contamination with the prose *Tristan,* Heinzel, *op. cit.,* pp. 169 f., mentions the following additional features of the Pseudo-Robert *Queste* as pointing to a late origin: 1. its tendency to mix up with the Grail adventures other adventures that are commonplaces and have nothing to do with this main theme of the romance. 2. the tendency to introduce incidents from the general stock of stories current in the Middle Ages — especially, incidents of a sensational nature, as of rape or incest. Nevertheless, he denies the dependence of the Pseudo-Robert *Queste (Demanda)* upon the Vulgate on the following grounds: 1. it contains the account of the slaying of Baudemagus, as the Vulgate does not. 2. the greater prominence of Lancelot in the Vulgate *Queste* seems to show that this was later than Pseudo-Robert. 3. the Vulgate *Queste* evinces a more perfect adjustment to the narrative of the *Estoire.*

As regards these points, No. 1 I have already dealt with, and No. 2 is a purely subjective ground for deciding a question of relative date. With respect to No. 3, the *Estoire* of the Pseudo-Robert cycle is lost and the *Queste* of this cycle was adjusted to that version of the Early History of the Grail, not to the *Estoire* of the Vulgate, with which Heinzel made his comparison. In any event, a less perfect adjustment does not necessarily mean earlier composition. Even the greatest writers, like Tasso and Keats, have spoiled their own work in re-writing it, so that there is no reason to imagine that a mediaeval author of no remarkable genius, in rewriting an earlier romance — the composition of another man — may not have neglected such matters of adjustment as those referred to by Heinzel. There is no

fication in the successive stages took place all along the line, and the development was always by cycles.[16] He recognizes, however, that the *Lancelot* was originally by a different author from the other members of the cycle[17] and he seems to imply that different redactors took part in the development of the successive cycles of his theory which finally resulted in the Vulgate cycle (to say nothing of the Pseudo-Robert cycle).[18] Thus, according to this scholar, as well as his predecessors, the Vulgate cycle is of composite authorship, although he supposes that the redactors of each of his hypothetical cycles aimed at preserving a unity of design for the whole.[19]

Recently, however, a theory concerning the origin of the romances of the Vulgate cycle which involves the assumption of an even more perfect unity of design than is assumed in Brugger's has been advanced by one of the most eminent of Arthurian scho-

---

reason, then, to conclude with Heinzel that the Pseudo-Robert *Queste* was derived not from the Vulgate, but from a common source.

[16] It is to be remembered that these cycles are altogether hypothetical.

[17] Cp., e. g., *Zs. f. frz. Spr. u. Litt.*, XXXVI², 205.

[18] He observes *loc. cit.*: "die Gralzyklen sind nicht einfach das Werk von Kopisten, die ein paar selbständige Romane zusammengestellt hätten, sondern das Werk von Redaktoren, die ein Ganzes schaffen wollten." It is not clear, however, whether he means that there was just one redactor for each of his hypothetical cycles or whether there were more. In view of the enormous extent which one is compelled to assume for these hypothetical cycles after the *Lancelot* became incorporated into them and the labour which the expansion of this branch and the composition of the new Galahad branches *(Estoire* and *Queste)* involved, it appears necessary to postulate more than one redactor for each stage in the later stages of the development of the cycles — yet the cooperative composition of fiction on this scale has no parallel in literary history. For a fuller discussion of these matters, cp. RR, IV, 462ff.

[19] Cp. the quotation in the preceding note. How little such a unity is really preserved in the Vulgate version is manifest from the inconsistencies, repetitions, etc., mentioned Part III, above.

lars — Ferdinand Lot.[20] Contrary to the theory of plural authorship, which had been held hitherto by all students of these matters,
Lot has endeavored to prove that the whole of the Vulgate cycle —
the *Merlin*, alone, excepted — is the work of one author, who
planned and composed the different branches of the cycle as parts
of a single design. He bases his theory on the following obser-
vations: [21]

1. Throughout the *Lancelot* the different episodes of that
romance are intimately interwoven with each other in a way that
is inexplicable on the hypothesis of interpolation or multiple
authorship. Moreover, the various branches are bound together
in a similar manner: For example, cross references between the
Lancelot and the other branches are frequent, and, in some cases,
episodes that are begun in one branch of the cycle are only completed in a later branch. 2. The *Lancelot* exhibits throughout
a systematic chronological scheme. 3. A unity of plan, spirit,
language and style is manifest throughout the Vulgate cycle.
4. All the different branches show the use of the same sources.

---

[20] In his *Étude sur le Lancelot en prose* (Paris, 1918): fascicule No. 226 of the Bibliothèque de l'École des Hautes Études. For
the opinions of scholars heretofore on the subject of the plural authorship of the cycle, cp. Bruce, RR, IX, 241 ff. (1918).

[21] These points are made the subjects of successive chapters in
Lot's treatise. It is impossible to deal adequately here with his detailed and elaborate arguments on the points in question. What follows
in the text above is merely a summary of the objections to the theory
of single authorship which I have already offered in fuller form at the
beginning of my article entitled, "The Composition of the Old French
Prose Lancelot", RR, IX, 241 ff., 353 ff. (1918), X, 48 ff., 97 ff. (1919),
and in my review of Lot's book, *ibid.* X, 377 ff. (1919). In the first
of these articles (the proofs of which I had corrected before the publication of Lot's work) my criticism, it is true, was directed against the
theory of single authorship for the *Lancelot* alone, but what I urged
there tells, of course, with even greater force against the theory of
single authorship for the whole cycle *(minus the Merlin)*. Lot's
theory is, also, rejected by A. Pauphilet in his important review of
the above-mentioned treatise, *Romania*, XLV, 514 ff. (1919), and by
Miss Weston, *ibid.*, XLVI, 314 ff. (1920).

There are grave *a priori* objections, however, to Lot's theory, for it is to be remembered that, unless we accept an earlier date for the brief prose-renderings of Robert de Boron's *Joseph* and *Merlin*, these romances of the Vulgate cycle are the first specimens of prose fiction in any of the great literary languages of Modern Europe, and that, on the other hand, with the exception of one or two of the vast French romances of the seventeenth century (e. g. Mlle. de Scudéry's *Le Grand Cyrus* and *Clélie*) the four branches combined would constitute the longest and most intricate work of fiction in all European literature. Now, it is extremely improbable that the first work of modern prose fiction should, also, be the longest and most intricate in the whole history of European prose fiction, with the exceptions just indicated. Such length and intricacy are inconsistent, too, with the circumstance that not only French prose fiction, but French prose of any kind, was then in its infancy, and that, as a matter of fact, the only other French prose work of even moderate length which had been written down to the time that the Vulgate cycle was composed — viz. Villehardouin's chronicle of the conquest of Constantinople in 1204[22] (which was finished certainly not earlier than 1207) — was considerably less than one twentieth the size of the abovementioned four branches combined. Much nearer the truth, then, on *a priori* grounds, would seem to be the theory, generally held, that the central romance of the series, the *Lancelot*, as we have it, is the product of a long evolution and the work of different hands, and that still other authors are responsible for the remaining branches of this cycle.

As regards the specific arguments, indicated above, which the French scholar has brought forward in support of his hypothesis, it may be remarked of the first two, that, if in the primitive *Lancelot* (which was probably, the first, or so-called *Galehaut* section of the romance, in a somewhat shorter form)[23] these two

---

[22] In N. de Wailly's edition (Paris, 1874), it fills only 150 octavo pages, which is the equivalent of considerably less than 75 of the quarto pages in Sommer's edition of the *Lancelot*.

[23] Cp. Bruce. RR, X, 48ff. — What follows in the text above is summarized from my review of Lot's treatise, *ibid*. X, 377ff.

structural devices were found, naturally the continuators of that romance would, likewise, adopt them, and it would not be hard for such interpolators or continuators to fit their work so exactly to that of their predecessors as to render the points of juncture of the two, so to speak, invisible.[24]

Furthermore, it is difficult to concede Lot's contention that the cycle, as a whole, exhibits a unity of plan, spirit, language and style. On the contrary, there are, as has been already noted, flagrant inconsistencies and contradictions between certain branches, and, also, in some cases, within the individual branches. One may observe, moreover, every variety of style within the limits of the cycle, from the baldest rubbish, as in the long quest for Lancelot which follows upon the adventures of Bohort in the *Lancelot* — where we have scores of pages of unsurpassed insipidity, or even absurdity — to the grand mystic vision of Galahad and his companions at the Grail castle in the *Queste*, or the sublime epic of the destruction of Arthur and the knights of the Round Table, together with the translation of the wounded king to Avalon, at the end of the *Mort Artu*. Still further, as we have seen, the individual branches, taken as a whole, differ from each other. In the *Queste* there is not a trace of the dramatic power that distinguishes the *Mort Artu;* in the *Estoire* there is a love of romantic and sensational incident of a purely secular kind which is not found in the *Queste* — and so on. Finally, as regards the alleged use of the same sources in the four branches, this is true only to a limited extent, the observation being admissible only with reference to such sources as Wace's *Brut* (or a lost expansion of the same), the *Tristan* poems, and Chrétien's romances (especially his *Perceval* and its earlier continuations), which were the chief Arthurian works at the time that the Vulgate cycle was composed, and which, therefore, naturally served as sources to more than one member of that cycle.

---

[24] As a matter of fact, Miss Weston, *Romania,* XLVI, 327 ff. (1920), has pointed out some chronological inconsistencies in the series.

Chapter XII.

The Relation of the Perlesvaus to the Vulgate Cycle.

A question of fundamental importance in the study of the prose romances is the following: Was there ever a stage in the formation of the Vulgate cycle when Perceval, and not Galahad, was the hero of the Grail quest? For, of course, Perceval, as Chrétien's poem shows, to say nothing of Pseudo-Wauchier and Wauchier or of Wolfram von Eschenbach, was, undoubtedly, the original hero[1] of this quest.

As a matter of fact, it has been very commonly assumed that a *Queste* of which Perceval was the hero once actually occupied in the series the place which in the Vulgate, as we have it, is filled by the *Queste*, of which Galahad is the hero. Some distinguished Arthurian scholars have gone still further and identified this supposed Perceval *Queste* with the *Perlesvaus.*

The main basis for the above-mentioned assumption is the fact that in three passages of certain MSS. of the prose *Lancelot* — the number of MSS. supporting the reading in question varies for each passage[2] — Perceval is still alluded to as the Grail Winner,

---

[1] Wechssler, in his *Sage vom heiligen Gral* (Halle, 1898), inspired by Heinzel, Grail treatise, p. 135, tried to give this distinction to Galahad, but his theory has been universally rejected.

[2] The passages in question are quoted by Sommer, *Vulgate Version of the Arthurian Romances*, I, pp. XIIIf. In the case of two of these passages the Perceval allusions are limited to two MSS. and one MS., each, respectively. Obviously, these MSS. have no authority as against the overwhelming mass of MSS. that stand out against them. Moreover, the sole MS. authority (Bibl. Nat. 754) for one of the Perceval allusions is vitiated by another blunder of its own, viz. the statement that Perceval achieved the Grail quest after Lancelot's death, which does not accord with any known version of Perceval's story. — I have discussed these matters in detail in RR, IV. 468ff. (1913) and in the notes below.

although, generally speaking, as we have seen, Galahad enjoys that honor in the Vulgate cycle. Such allusions have been interpreted by certain scholars[3] as survivals, through the negligence of scribes, from an earlier (hypothetical) stage in the evolution of the Vulgate cycle, when, as has just been said, they imagine a Perceval-*Queste* to have filled the place which is actually filled in our extant MSS. by the Galahad-*Queste*. In only one of these passages,[4] however, — and that an extremely corrupt one — is

---

[3] This view is implied in P. Paris, *Romans de la Table Ronde*. So, too, with G. Paris, *La littérature française au moyen age* § 60, 63 (Paris, 1888 et seq.). For his meagre and vague expressions of opinion regarding the relation of the *Perlesvaus* to the Vulgate cycle, cp. Nitze's summary in his *Perlesvaus* dissertation, pp. 27 f. It is Brugger, however, who has developed this theory most fully. Cp. *Zs. f. frz. Spr. u. Litt.*, XXIX[1], 77 ff. (1905). Somewhat similar to this theory is that of Sommer, *Romania*, XXXVI, 369 ff., 543 ff. (1907) and MPh., V, 291 ff. (1908). He postulates a lost Perceval-*Queste*, in prose, — which was different from the *Perlesvaus* — as once occupying the place of our Galahad-*Queste*. Similar, it would seem, to Sommer's theory is Miss Weston's *Legend of Sir Lancelot*, pp. 120 ff. The theories of these scholars are, also, based on the Perceval allusions in the *Lancelot* MSS., but the want of harmony between the *Perlesvaus* and the Vulgate cycle, doubtless, deterred them from identifying their hypothetical *Perceval* with the *Perlesvaus*.

[4] The three passages are quoted by Sommer, *Vulgate Version*, Vol. 1, p. XIII. I have given two notes below the reading of No. 1 — the only passage of real importance — according to MS. 768 (Bibl. Nat.). The other two respectively are as follows: No. 2. We have a reference to "li conte de Perceval" in two *Lancelot* MSS. — Lansdowne 757 (British Museum) and MS. 751 (Bibl. Nat.). The words are:

"Et le grant conte de lancelot couuient repairier en la fin a perceval qui est chies et la fin de toz les contes as autres cheualiers. Et tuit sont branches de lui por ce quil acheua le grant queste. Et li contes de perceval meismes est une branche del haut conte del graal qui est chiez de tout les contes. Car por le graal se traueillent tuit li bon cheualier dont lan parole de celui tans."

For the inferences which Miss Weston has drawn from this passage cp. her *Sir Lancelot*, p. 125. No one, however, can account for the whims and blunders of individual scribes. There were, of

the Perceval allusion backed by manuscript authority that is sufficient to render it worthy of serious consideration — namely, the passage (Sommer, III, 29), where, in connection with the praise of the beauty of Pelles's daughter, Perceval is called Pelles's son and, also, the Grail Winner. The MS. followed by Sommer in his edition of the *Lancelot* has *Galahad,* in this place, and not *Perceval,* but a large majority of the MSS. here read *Perceval.*[5] On the other hand, even the most intelligible MS.[6] of this majority

course, several romances in which Perceval was the Grail Winner and these monkish scribes — granting that they are independent of each other — may have taken his side against *Lancelot,* because of the latter's notorious adultery.

No. 3. A single MS., No. 754 (Bibl. Nat.) has, also, the following passage in which Perceval is said to have delivered Merlin from the confinement to which he had been committed by Vivien through the spell which she won from him. Here it is declared that no one ever saw Merlin after his confinement until he was delivered by Perceval "qui vit la grant merueille del graal apres la mort de Lancelot si com li contes vos devisera ca auant."

This passage does not really conflict with the Galahad-*Queste,* for in that *Queste,* VI, 189, Perceval did actually see the marvel of the Grail. For the rest, however, the scribe has blundered in making Perceval survive Lancelot. He dies at the end of the *Queste,* VI, 198, whilst Lancelot is still alive.

[5] For the readings of the individual MSS. and early prints cp. Sommer, MPh., V, 293 ff. (1908). That Sommer here attaches an exaggerated importance to the *Parceuau* of the British Museum MS., Royal 19, C. XIII, has been shown by Brugger, *Zs. f. frz. Spr. u. Litt.,* XL[1], 47, note 11.

[6] MS. 768 (Bibl. Nat.), fol. 12, verso, col. b. The text has been printed by G. Bräuner, *Der altfranzösische Prosaroman von Lancelot del Lac.* I Branche, p. 48: *Marburger Beiträge zur romanischen Philologie,* Heft II (Marburg, 1911), whence it has been reprinted by Bruce, RR, IV, 469 and Lot, *Lancelot,* p. 112. Like MS. 768 are MS. 118 and its dependent, Arsenal 3479. Only two ladies, it is said in this passage, could compare with Guinevere in beauty. The one was Heliene-sanz-per, "Et l'autre fu fille au Roi Mehaignie, ce fu li rois Pelles, qui fu peres Perlesvax a celui qui vit apertement les Granz Mervoilles del Graal, et acompli lo Siege Perilleus de la Table Reonde, et mena a fin les aventures del Reiaume Perilleus Aventureus, ce fu li regnes de Logres. Cele fu sa suer, si fu de si

makes Perceval a son of Pelles — a conception of their relationship which is found nowhere else in Arthurian romance. Moreover, as in all other MSS., whether the reading of the passage be *Galahad* or *Perceval*, we have in this text Pelles (the Fisher King of the Vulgate cycle) identified with "the Maimed King," which contradicts the whole tradition of the Vulgate cycle.[7] Still further, the alternative names here given to Perceval's sister do not, either of them, appear attached to her any where else in Arthurian romance.

It will be observed, then, that this passage on which the theory in question is based, even according to the reading of the most intelligible MS., is so marred by contradictions of the fixed traditions of the cycle, and of Arthurian romance, in general, as to suggest the hand of a blundering interpolator. If we examine the other MSS., however, the same thing is suggested with even greater force — for nearly all of these MSS., whether they read *Perceval* or *Galahad* here, contain the absurdity of making the mother of the Grail hero at the same time his sister.[8]

The passage, then, swarms with errors, and even if *Perceval*

---

grant biaute que nus des contes ne dit que nule qui a son tens fust, se poist de biaute a li aparellier, si avoit non Amide en sornom, et an son droit non Heliabel." (MS. 768, Bibl. Nat. fol. 12, verso, col. b). This reading of the passage, though still open to the objections which I have mentioned in the text above, makes at least good sense, and has been accepted by Lot, *op. cit.*, pp. 112ff., as representing accurately the original text of the *Lancelot*, but cp. my criticism of his views in RR, X, 386f.

[7] In certain MSS. of the *Queste*, VI. 150, we have a similar blunder. This is the only exception. Cp. Bruce, MPh., XVI, 122ff.

[8] Take, for example, the reading of the British Museum MS. Additional, 10293, printed by Sommer, III, 29: "Et l'autre fu fille au Roi Mahaignie. Che fu li rois Pelles qui fu peires a Amite meire Galaat chelui qui vit apertement les grans meruelles del graal. Et acompli le siege perillous de la Table Reonde. Et mena a fin les auentures del roialme perelleus & aventureus. Che fu li roialmes de Logres. Cele fu sa suer si fu de si grant biaute que nus des contes ne dist que a son tans fust ne se peust de biaute a lui apparellier. Et si avoit non Amite en sornon & en son droit non Helizabel."

were the reading of all MSS., instead of simply the majority, it is very questionable whether, under the circumstances, we should be justified in drawing the far-reaching inference which is implied in the hypothesis that a Perceval-*Queste* once held the place in the Vulgate cycle which in the extant MS. tradition is held exclusively by a Galahad-*Queste*.[9] What is virtually a single corrupt passage cannot outweigh the testimony of the whole remainder of the vast manuscript tradition.

As a matter of fact, however, this same incurably corrupt passage, itself, contains an indication that, despite the numerical preponderance of the MSS. that offer the reading, *Perceval*, the Grail hero who is referred to, must, after all, have been originally Galahad. This indication lies in the double naming: "Et si avoit non Amite en sornon & en son droit non Helizabel." For this 'double naming has no meaning as applied to Perceval's sainted sister, but it is strictly in accord with the conceptions of the Galahad *Queste*. Just as Lancelot, in baptism, was given a name with sacred (Biblical) associations, viz. *Galahad (Galaad)*, but lost it through unchastity and received the secular name, *Lancelot* (Sommer, III, 3), so, for a similar reason, after losing her virginity to Lancelot, Pelles's daughter, who was christened *Elizabeth* (*Helizabel*, etc.), the name of the mother of John the Baptist, received a secular name, *Amite (Amide)*.[10]

---

[9] I have suggested, RR, IV, 470, certain possibilities in the case and more recently, *ibid.*, X, 387, that a scribe who knew of Perceval as the Grail Winner through romances outside of the Vulgate cycle and who possibly had only a superficial acquaintance with the Vulgate cycle, itself, as a whole, may through inadvertence or actual ignorance, have introduced Perceval for Galahad here into the manuscript tradition, in the first instance. The variants of Perceval's name that are commonest in the MSS. at this point, viz., *Pelesvaus* etc. (cp. MPh., V, 293, note 1) appear to show that he had the *Perlesvaus* in mind. We have, too, the same form in the other isolated MSS.

[10] For a fuller discussion of these matters cp. RR, IX, 259f. Most MSS. do not have the name of Pelles's daughter spelt *Elizabeth*, but the *Helizabel, Heliabel*, etc. which they offer are obviously mere corruptions of that name. I have suggested that *Amite* and *Amide* are variants of *Amice*, the name of a character in the *Meraugis de*

It would seem, then, after all, that this much debated passage did not belong to the original text of the *Lancelot*, but, like the other Grail materials in that romance, was of later introduction.[11]

Portlesguez. An even earlier scribal blunder in this passage, I believe, was the substitution of *suer* ("Cele fu sa suer") for *mere*. Cp. *op. cit.*, X, 386f.
The double naming was, no doubt, imitated from the *Estoire del Saint Graal.* Cp., on the subject, RR, IX, 250. In that romance, as in actual life, pagans, when converted, were re-named. Hence the chief characters have double names. Seraphe is renamed *Nascien*, Evalac, *Mordrain*, etc. In the case of Lancelot and Amide, we have the process reversed. Instead of acquiring new names by baptism, as a sign of regeneration from sin, they lose their baptismal names and are given others, because of their lapses into sin.
[11] The introduction probably occurred very late, for the whole passage is obviously imitated from the eulogy of Guinevere in the Vulgate *Merlin* continuation, Sommer, II, 159. For a better text of this eulogy (printed first by Sommer, MPh., V, 305) and my discussion of the question involved cp. RR, IV, 257f. This *Merlin* continuation is generally recognized as the latest part of the Vulgate cycle.
If my refutation of the inference that has been drawn from these Perceval allusions in the *Lancelot* MSS. is sound, there is no need of any further discussion of Brugger's hypothesis, *Zs. f. fr. Spr. u. Litt.*, XXXIII[1], 192ff. (1908), XXXVI[2], 198ff. (1910), and elsewhere, that it was not the extant *Perlesvaus* to which the *Lancelot* was adjusted in this hypothetical stage of the evolution of the Vulgate cycle, but a (supposed) lost later version of the romance. He is driven to this hypothesis, of course, by the fact that the extant version does not fit in with the Vulgate cycle in the slightest degree. Since it makes Guinevere die long before Arthur's wars with Mordred — the latter's name not even occurring in the romance — it is irreconcilable with the only *Mort Artu* that is preserved to us in the MSS. of the Vulgate cycle or, indeed, in any other version of the *Mort Arthur* theme. For Guinevere is in every one of them, and, except in that of the *Didot-Perceval*, is the great moving force in them all. Brugger recognizes this, of course, and postulates, accordingly, *op. cit.* XXIX[1], 81, an hypothetical *Mort Arthur*, in which there was no Guinevere to harmonize with his hypothetical *Perlesvaus*. But this setting aside of the uniform manuscript tradition in favor of one's own theories cannot be taken seriously. — Still further, the conception of the con-

As regards the specific identification of the *Perlesvaus* with the hypothetical Perceval-*Queste* in question, a passage which stands at the end of a single MS. of this romance,[12] and that not the best,[13] has often been taken, also, as an indication that it originally constituted merely one branch of a cycle[14] — either the Vulgate (in an earlier form) or some other. The passage in question states

---

clusion of the Grail is entirely different in the *Perlesvaus* and Vulgate *Queste*. — But where so little is alike, it is useless to point out further differences between the versions. Brugger, *op. cit.*, XXXVI[2], 199, cites as portions of this hypothetical *Perlesvaus* actually preserved what he calls the Perceval *Enfances* in Sommer, V, 377 ff. and MPh., V, 322 ff. (*Tristan* MS. Brit. Museum, 5474). But there is no reason to assume this. There is no ground for doubting that the second of these texts is anything more than an individual variant of the conclusion of the *Lancelot*. Sommer's edition shows that we have variants for other portions of this branch. As for the usual text of this conclusion, V, 377 f., it betrays familiarity with other branches of the Vulgate cycle. Cp. RR, IX, 391 ff. On the other hand, the introduction of Perceval adventures at the end of the Lancelot means nothing. The writers who expanded the primitive *Lancelot* introduced any characters or any adventures where they pleased. The detail which Brugger cites, *loc. cit.*, from the *Venjance Nostre Seigneur* is manifestly too slight to have any value in proving that the *Perlesvaus* underwent an entirely new redaction.

[12] The MS. is the Brussels MS. Bibliothèque de Bourgogne, No. 11145, on which Potvin's edition is based. For this passage see Potvin, p. 348: It runs as follows:

"Apres iceste estoire, conmence li contes si conme Brians des Illes guerpi le roi Artus por Lancelot que il n'amoit mie et conme il aseura le roi Claudas, qui le roi Ban de Benoic toli sa terre. Si parole cis contes conment il le conquist et par quel maniere, et si com Galobrus de la Vermeille Lande vint a la cort le roi Artus por aidier Lancelot, quar il estoit de son lignage. Cist contes est mout lons et mout aventureus et poisanz; mes li livres s'en tera ore atant trusqu a une autre foiz."

[13] Hatton 82 (Bodleian Library) is the best. Cp. Nitze, MPh., XVII, 152, 166 (1920). The passage is, also, wanting in the Welsh translation of the *Perlesvaus* and in the early prints.

[14] Cp. e. g., Heinzel, p. 177, Brugger, *Zs. f. frz. Spr. u. Litt.*, XXIX[1], 77 ff.

that after the *Perlesvaus* follows the tale of how Brians des Illes, on account of his hostility to Lancelot, deserted Arthur and joined Claudas — the story of whose war against Ban it also contained — and how Perceval's cousin, Galobrus de la Vermeille Lande, came to Lancelot's aid. The writer lauds this continuation of the *Perlesvaus*, but, after all, postpones the relation of these matters.[15]

Even if we grant, however, that this passage is not the later addition of an unauthorized scribe and that such a narrative as that which is indicated in it was really executed,[16] this would not justify the hypothesis that our romance was merely a branch of a large cycle. The author might simply have decided — possibly as an afterthought — to take as a starting-point adventures of Brians des Illes which he had related already and add, for the entertainment of his patrons, a continuation of his romance of a more secular character. All the Lancelot materials of the *Perlesvaus* accord perfectly well with the Vulgate *Lancelot* in the form in which the latter has come down to us[17] and there is no ground for supposing that the author of the passage under discussion had in mind anything more than a new series of adventures such as make up that work.[18]

---

[15] Nitze gives MPh., XVII, 612, note 2, the romances in which Brians des Illes occurs. He observes that the "Vulgate form of the Prose *Lancelot*" is not among them. I am inclined to think that the author of the *Perlesvaus*, however, really had in mind here Lancelot's enemy in the prose *Lancelot*, the Lord of Dolerous Gard, whose name was *Brandins (Brandis, Branduz) des Illes.* Cp. Sommer, III, 151 ff. The confusion of *Brians* and *Brandins* would have been easy. But even if this conjecture is incorrect, the fact that Nitze calls attention to it would have no significance. If the writer in question was going to try his hand at new Lancelot adventures, he did not have to limit himself to the characters or incidents of the existing *Lancelot.* Compare, for example, the procedure of the author of the *Livre d'Artus* of MS. 337 with relation to the Vulgate *Merlin*-continuation.

[16] It had not been composed at the time that the passage under discussion was written and we have no reason to believe that it was ever actually composed.

[17] On this subject Cp. p. 162 below.

[18] The question is essentially the same as that which I have

In regard to the questions of date and sources of the *Perlesvaus*, two influences have led certain scholars[19] to assign a relatively early date to this romance: 1. the exaggerated view that has generally prevailed concerning the seriousness with which the mediaeval romancers and their patrons took the inventions of the former[20] and the consequent reluctance to concede that Perceval could be restored to the position of Grail hero, when Galahad had once supplanted him.[21] 2. the Perceval allusions in the *Lancelot* MSS.,

argued, p. 150, above. Despite the requirements of Brugger's theory, it is obvious that an author who desired to compose a new version of some branch of the cycle did not have to provide new branches of all the cycles. Thus it is not necessary to assume that the allusions in the *Perlesvaus* (pp. 26, 30, 43, etc.) to Perceval's previous, abortive, visit to the Grail castle were drawn from a lost previous branch of a *Perlesvaus* cycle. A man can refer to other people's books as well as his own and this visit had been related by Chrétien. If he chose to alter Chrétien's conceptions, in some respects, that was his own affair. Similarly with the allusions to the sinful passion of Lancelot and Guinevere (pp. 130, 132). This all stood in the Vulgate *Queste* and *Mort Artu*.

[19] G. Paris, *Manuel*, § 60, 63, and Brugger in the passages cited above, p. 146, note 3. So, too, Nitze, for the latest expression of whose views see his article, "On the Chronology of the Grail Romances", MPh., XVII, 151 ff. (1919), 605 ff. (1920). W. Golther, *Zs. f. fr. Spr. u. Litt.*, XXVI[2], 12 f. (1903) accepts Nitze's results. Cp. too, Suchier, in his and Birch-Hirschfeld's *Geschichte der französischen Literatur*[2], p. 169 (1913).

[20] I have already discussed this matter, which is fundamental for our interpretation of mediaeval romance, above.

[21] Brugger expresses himself strongly on this point, *Zs. f. frz. Spr. u. Litt.*, XXIX[1], 78 (1905). As Lot has observed, *Étude sur le Lancelot en prose*, p. 286, note 2, it is primarily Brugger's reluctance to make the concession referred to in the text that has driven him to evolve his intricate theory concerning the development of the prose cycles. But in Arthurian romance, as in other forms of literature, older traditions about any given characters often survive by the side of those of later origin. See the present writer's reply, RR, IV, 250, note 66 (1913), to Miss Weston, whose views, *Sir Perceval*, II, 340 (1909), are similar to Brugger's, although she does not date the *Perlesvaus* so early. As especially pertinent to the question, note

which we have discussed above, and which, in most cases, present Perceval's name in its *Perlesvaus* forms.[22]

On the other hand, the majority of scholars[23] have regarded the *Perlesvaus* as among the very latest of the Grail romances. First, with respect to the question of date, the indisputable evidence leaves us still within very wide limits — 1191, on the one hand, and 1250 on the other — so that any nearer dating must depend on the conclusions which we reach as to the sources of the romance.[24] Now, the author of the *Perlesvaus* states quite

---

that Gerbert and Manessier, although familiar with the Galahad-*Queste* and using it as a source, nevertheless, stick to the Perceval tradition and add continuations to Chrétien's poem.

[22] It should be remembered, however, that, according to Brugger's theory, these allusions refer not to the actual *Perlesvaus,* but to his hypothetical later redaction. For the importance of these allusions in his theory, cp., especially, *op. cit.* pp. 87f.

[23] Cp. Birch-Hirschfeld, *Sage vom Gral,* pp. 135ff. (1877), Nutt, *Studies on the Legend of the Holy Grail,* p. 64 (1888), Gröber, *Grundriss,* II, Abt. I, 726 (189), A. Jeanroy, *Revue Critique,* Oct. 10, 1904, J. L. Weston, *Sir Perceval,* II, 259, 274 (1909), W. Foerster, Chrétien *Wörterbuch,* p. 186 (1914), F. Lot, *Étude sur le Lancelot en prose,* p. 286, note 2 (1918), Bruce, MPh., XVI, 117, note 1, (1918), ånd above. Heinzel, *Über die französischen Gvalromane,* p. 172 (1892), was inclined to accept Gerbert's continuation of Chrétien's *Perceval* as a source of the *Perlesvaus,* which implies, also, a late dating.

[24] Much the most elaborate studies of the date and sources of the *Perlesvaus* are Nitze's. Cp. his Johns Hopkins dissertation, *The Old French Grail Romance Perlesvaus* (Baltimore, 1902) and his articles, "The Glastonbury Passages in the *Perlesvaus*", University of North Carolina *Studies in Philology,* XV, 7ff. (1918) and "On the Chronology of the Grail Romances", cited two notes above. Nitze is, doubtless, right in inferring from the *Perlesvaus,* pp. 261f. (Lancelot finds in a chapel at "li leus d'Avalon" two tombs, one containing Guinevere's remains already, the other destined to contain Arthur's), that its author knew of the fraud of the pretended discovery of the tombs of Arthur and Guinevere at Glastonbury in 1191 — which gives 1191 as the *terminus a quo* for the composition of the romance. This, however, involves no great gain, for no one has ever proposed to date any prose Arthurian romance earlier than that. The present

writer had already established the same date as the *terminus a quo* for the dating of the Vulgate *Mort Artu*, whose author, likewise, shows a knowledge of the new notion about Arthur's being buried at Glastonbury. Cp. T. Lewis and J. D. Bruce, "The pretended exhumation of Arthur and Guinevere", *Revue Celtique*, XXXIII, 432, note (1912), and Bruce, RR, IV, 454 (1913). There is, however, absolutely nothing whatever to show in the one case any more than in the other that the particular author was writing shortly after the above-mentioned fraud was perpetrated.

The *terminus ad quem* for the dating of the *Perlesvaus* is fixed by an allusion to Perceval's father (with the distinctive name given to him in this romance) in the metrical romance, *Chevalier as Deus Espees*, ll. 2604f. The latter romance was composed certainly before 1250. Cp. Nitze, MPh., XVII, 166. Probably as early as 1230 is the Vulgate *Merlin*-continuation, in which, Sommer II, 316, we have, it seems, an allusion to the *Perlesvaus*, pp. 189f. (Kay's killing of Arthur's son, Lohot). Cp. Brugger, *Zs. f. frz. Spr. u. Litt.*, XXXIII[1], 192 and Bruce, RR, III, 183f. — Sebastian Evans, *High History of the Holy Grail*, II, 290, points out another allusion to the *Perlesvaus* in the Old French romance *Fulk Fitzwarin* (late thirteenth century), but this is later than the *Chevalier as Deus Espees*.

The following passage which is found at the end of the Brussels MS. of the *Perlesvaus* (p. 348) and no other, and which has furnished the basis for much of the discussion concerning the date of this romance, may help us to reduce the *terminus ad quem* to something like 1235. It runs:

Por le seignor de Neele fist li seignor de Cambrein cest livre escrire, qui onques mes ne fu troitiez que une seule foiz avec [error for *avant*] cestui en roumanz; et cil qui avant cestui fust fez est si anciens qu'a grant poine an peust l'an choissir la lestre. Et sache bien misires Johan de Neele que l'an doit tenir ceste conte cheir, ne l'an ne doit mie dire a jent malentendable; quar bone chosse qui est espendue outre mauvesses genz n'est onques en bien recordee par els."

On this passage and previous criticism of it, cp., particularly, Nitze, MPh., XVII, 605ff. (1920). According to Nitze's interpretation, the opening words refer to the Brussels MS., not to the original composition of the romance, and the old book was really the particular MS. of the *Perlesvaus* which the scribe of the Brussels MS. was transcribing, although he is trying to convey the impression that he is translating independently from the supposed Latin source. But that any MS. of a Grail romance should have been so old as to be illegible to a scribe of the first third (say) of the thirteenth century is most

definitely that he translated his romance from a Latin original,[25]

---

unlikely. For my own part, I regard the passage rather as one of the ordinary mystifications of the Middle Ages — in this case of a scribe — through which a writer — or in this case, no doubt, a scribe — endeavored to heighten the interest in his work by ascribing to it a great antiquity, as Geoffrey of Monmouth, for instance, did in the case of the pretended original of his *Historia*. The only thing genuine, accordingly, in the passage, in my opinion, is the statement that a lord of Cambrein presented the Brussels MS. to a lord of Nesle. The lord of Cambrein (i. e. Cambrin, arrondissement de Béthune, in Northern France — not Cambria, as some scholars have assumed), to be sure, has not been identified. Nitze, pp. 608f., suggests that he was Hellin de Wavrin, seneschal of Flanders, but this is merely conjectural. Doubtless the Johan de Neele of this passage was Jean II, who, as Nitze has established, p. 607, was already lord of Nesle by 1202. In this year he participated in the Fourth Crusade (against Constantinople). In 1212 he pledged his service to Philip Augustus, in 1214 he probably took part in the battle of Bouvines, and in 1225 he definitely parted with his Flemish possessions (Nitze, p. 610). Nitze thinks (611) that the presentation of this copy of the *Perlesvaus* took place "between 1200 and 1212, which covers the period of Jean de Nesle's crusading activities and of his Flemish connections", and hence that the *terminus ad quem* for the composition of the romance must lie between these two dates. The grounds on which he bases this opinion, however, seem to me insufficient. Nothing is said about the crusade in the passage and one nobleman might present a copy of a romance to another in one period of the latter's life as well as another, barring early childhood and, possibly, extreme old age. As a matter of fact, Jean II's connection with Flemish affairs was weakened, no doubt, after 1212, but it did not end until 1225. Besides, even after he entered into closer relations with France, it is not reasonable to suppose that he threw overboard all the friendships of his previous life. Then, too, it is always possible that this lord of Cambrein sided likewise with the French.

The date of Jean II's death would, of course, give a true *terminus ad quem*, but that, apparently, is unknown. In view of the fact that the *Perlesvaus* has been used, apparently, by the author of the Vulgate *Merlin*-continuation, I should be inclined to date it somewhere about 1225.

[25] Cp. p. 306: Josephus nos dist, par l'escriture qui le nos recorde de quoi cist estoires fu traite de latin en roumanz, que nus ne doit estre en doutance que ces aventures avenissent a cel tans an la

but, as is obvious from the whole passage in which the statement occurs, this is merely one of the common appeals of mediaeval writers to fictitious Latin sources for the purpose of imparting an air of authority to their inventions.[26] The name which is given to the author of this supposed Latin original — *Josephus* (and variants) — is of course equally fictitious, and the only question that can arise is as to the motive which prompted the real author of our romance to choose this name for his imaginary authority. The scholars who, owing to the influences which I have stated above, assign an early date to the *Perlesvaus* and — what most concerns us here — put its composition before that of the Vulgate *Estoire del Saint Graal*, have adopted the theory that the writer

Grant Breteingne et an touz les autres roiaumes, et plus i avint ancore assez que je ne recort; mes cestes furent les plus seures.

It is possible that this appeal to a Latin original may be imitated from the *Estoire*, I, 195, where it is said that Robert de Boron translated that work "en franchois de Latin".

[26] Baist (*Prorektoratsrede*, p. 15), we believe, is the only scholar who still believes in this Latin source of the *Perlesvaus*. He identifies it with his hypothetical "liber Glastoniensis", on which, as he surmises, Robert de Boron drew, also, for his *Joseph*. But in regard to this hypothetical work, see I, p. 263, note 54, above. Nitze, too, once believed in the Latin source, MPh., I, 257 (1903), but has latterly given up this belief. Cp. *ibid.*, XVII, 165 (1919), 605, note 2 (1920). As to the authorship and date of the two Latin romances, *Historia Meriadoci* and *De Ortu Waluuanii*, to which Nitze refers, the dependence of the former on the prose *Tristan* is beyond question. Not only does it adopt from the *Tristan* the trick of drawing names for its characters from early French history, but, like that romance, it gives a Cornish Meroveus a subject, Sadoc (the latter name is taken from the genealogy of Christ, *St. Matthew*, I), as is done nowhere else in literature. It draws from the same source other names, also, besides those which were connected with the early history of France. On these matters, cp. pp. XXIff. of my edition (Göttingen, 1913) of these Latin romances.

Nitze, it should be remembered, still further, is not justified in asserting MPh., XVII, 165, that "the demands of the case are amply satisfied by referring the expression *Li latins de coi cist estoires fust traite an romanz* to Glastonbury records about Arthur as preserved in chronicle sources". The author of our romance says quite definitely (cp. previous note) that it was drawn from an "escriture".

had in mind the well-known Jewish historian, Flavius Josephus. But in our romance the author[27] of the supposed Latin original is definitely said to have been "the first priest to sacrifice the body of our Lord" — that is to celebrate the mass. Now, nowhere is there recorded any legend to this effect concerning the historian, Josephus.[28] Indeed, if we except the present passage of the *Perlesvaus* and the *Estoire del Saint Graal*, nowhere is any such legend recorded concerning any person whatever. But this passage in the *Perlesvaus*, as we have observed, contains a mere allusion. On the other hand, the long and elaborate episode of the *Estoire* in which Christ initiates Josephe(s), son of Joseph of Arimathea, into the mysteries of the mass, consecrating him the first bishop of the church (p. 35),[29] — the Grail being the centre of the sac-

---

[27] Cp. p. 113. *Joseph* is here the variant of this supposed author's name. The passage is as follows: "Cist hauz estoires nos tesmoigne et recorde que Joseph qui nos en fet remembrance fu li premiers prestres qui sacrefiast le cors Notre Seignor, et por itant doit l'an croire les paroles qui de lui viennent."

In view of this definite identification, there can be no force in the objection that our author does not call him the son of Joseph of Arimathea.

[28] At most, he was represented as having been converted to Christianity. Cp. the *Venjeance Nostre Seigneur* (a poem written shortly before or after 1200), cited by Brugger, *Zs. f. frz. Spr. u. Litt.* XXIX[1], 82, note 33 a. Josephus's history is an actual source of this poem. It would seem that among the Christians of Syria there was, also, a legend that he was really the Jewish priest, Caiaphas, (*St. Matthew*, XXVI, 3) and afterwards, being converted to Christianity, resumed his original name of Josephus. Cp. Heinzel's Grail treatise, p. 107.

Nitze supposes, MPh., XVII, 160, that the idea of citing Flavius Josephus as his authority was derived by the author of the *Perlesvaus* from a copy of Freculf's chronicle in Glastonbury abbey, in which work Josephus is mentioned.

[29] Cp. Sommer, I, 30 ff. This contradicts, to be sure, an earlier statement in the *Estoire*, p. 19, where St. Philip is called the first bishop of Jerusalem, at the time that he baptizes Joseph of Arimathea. The inconsistency, however, is unimportant.

According to Brugger, *op. cit.*, p. 101, the author of the *Estoire* is merely working up a long story out of the hint contained in the single sentence of the *Perlesvaus*. Not only would the reverse be

ramental service — and Josephe now celebrates the first mass, is of cardinal importance in that work, since Josephe here typifies the church in the execution of its mission to carry the Christian faith to the ends of the earth for the salvation of mankind, in which mission its authority is mainly based on its possession of the mysteries that are embodied in the mass. The whole scheme of the book, then, requires that he should be the first priest to be inducted into these mysteries and that he should be inducted by Christ, himself.

The author of the *Estoire*, moreover, had implied unmistakably that the hermit who copied the *Estoire* from the book that Christ handed him was a member of the Grail family; [30] hence the author of the *Perlesvaus* does the same thing and accredits his own work to a member of that family who not only enjoyed the highest authority, but had already been exalted in the *Estoire* for his learning [31] — namely, Josephes. There is, accordingly,

more natural, but the fact that, as I have stated above, there is not the remotest reason for believing that Flavius Josephus was ever regarded as the first celebrant of the mass proves that this contention is baseless. A writer who propounded such a startling novelty as this about the holiest of Christian rites would surely have to justify it. Obviously, he is alluding here to something well known through another book (the *Estoire*), just as in the cases of his allusions to Perceval's abortive first visit to the Grail castle (Chrétien's *Perceval*) and Lancelot's sin with Guinevere (Vulgate *Queste*).

Brugger, himself, confesses *op. cit.* pp. 82 ff., that it would be strange even for a mediaeval romancer to ascribe a history of the events of King Arthur's reign to a man who lived some four hundred years earlier, and he tries to get over this by a series of the most intricate and improbable speculations, into which we need not follow him here.

[30] Sommer, I, 3, 5. The author of the Vulgate *Merlin*-continuation II, 222, says that it was Nascien. This identification is his own, but, like the author of the *Perlesvaus*, he had the passage in the *Estoire*, of course, before him.

[31] His father extols his learning, p. 27. Moreover, he succeeds in refuting the pagan clerks, I, 43 ff., where Joseph had failed, and all through the *Estoire*, he is the chief representative of the Christians, when it comes to expounding doctrines and allegorical dreams. For example, cp. I, 43 ff., 221 ff. 247 ff. 250 ff. 257 ff. This justifies the

no ground for doubting that the fictitious authority to whom our
author ascribes the composition of his pretended source and whose
name is usually spelt *Josephus* in the only MS. of his work that
has been printed, is really the Josephe(s) of the *Estoire* — the
first Christian bishop, according to that romance. The Latinized
form of the name, if not due simply to manuscript corruption,³²

---

epithet, "bon clerc", applied to him in the *Perlesvaus*, pp. 79, 107,
174, and in the variant version of a *Lancelot* episode, Sommer, V;
465. It is doubtless in imitation of the *Estoire* that we find Josephus
(Joseph) giving similar expositions of allegorical matters in the *Perlesvaus*, pp. 79—81.

³² This explanation may easily be the true one, for, although
everyone agrees that, according to the *Perlesvaus*, Perceval's father
was named *Alein,* the name does not occur with this (its true) spelling,
a single time in Potvin's text. We have, instead, *Julien, Vilain* and
(only once, p. 332) *Elein.* On the other hand, we do have *Josephe(s)*
twice (pp. 315, 348) and *Joseph* (which in the MSS. of the *Estoire*
is not infrequently confounded with *Josephe(s)* thrice (pp. 79 —
twice — and 348). Everywhere else, the character is named *Josephus,*
save in a single passage (p. 197), where he is called *Joseus* — by
confusion, no doubt, with the knight (also of the Grail lineage) who,
to expiate the sin of slaying his mother, abandoned knighthood for a
hermitage. Joseus's name, in turn, is once (p. 152) written *Josephus.*
Josephes is, of course, merely the French form of *Josephus.*
In the Vulgate, *Joseph,* like other Hebrew names, is not declined,
but in the Middle Ages the name was also used with the Latin inflection. *Joseph* and *Josephus* then formed separate names, but they
were not always kept apart. Thus the Carolingian poet was generally
called Josephus Scottus, but again *Joseph Scottus.* Cp. *Monumenta
Germaniae Historica: Poetarum Latinorum Medii Aevi* Tomus I,
149f. 159 (Berlin 1881). *Ibid., Diplomatum Karolinorum* Tomus I,
471f. (Hannover, 1906), we find *Joseph* and *Josephus* as variant
names of the same person in the same document. The document (a
forged one) purported to be of the eighth century, but the editors
(p. 470) assign it to the twelfth. Similarly, *ibid., Scriptorum Rerum
Merovingicarum,* VI, 550 (Hannover and Leipzig, 1913), *Josephus,*
Bishop of Freising, who died in 760, is called *Joseph* in the metrical
inscription on his tomb. A similar confusion, as we have seen, exists
in some MSS. of the *Estoire* between the French equivalents of the
two names. Indeed, the author of the *Lancelot* episode, V, 465, says
outright that Joseph of Arimathea and his son bore the same name.

was probably adopted to conform with the author's statement regarding the language of his fictitious original. That Josephus should record this story of the Grail in obedience to a message conveyed by an angel (p. 1) is probably a reminiscence of the visit of the angel to the author of the *Estoire* (I, 7) in the introduction to that work, when the divine messenger took this author (the hermit) up to the seventh heaven and revealed to him there the mysteries of the Trinity, in order that he might be fitted to relate the history of the Grail and its servants.

If the *Josephus* of the *Perlesvaus,* then, is derived from the *Josephes* of the *Estoire,* the former work must be not only of later date than the latter, but of later date than the *Lancelot* and the *Queste,* and doubtless, also, the *Mort Artu,* for the *Estoire* presupposes unquestionably the first two of these works, and apparently, also, the last-named.[33]

There is, however, independent evidence to the same effect — first of all, in the off-hand references to Lancelot's sinful relations with Guinevere (pp. 130, 132), as a thing that is well-known to all the world.[34] But the conception of these relations as sinful originated with the *Queste,* spread thence to the *Lancelot,*[35] and was incorporated in the beginning of the *Mort Artu,*

---

[33] Since sending this chapter to press, I have observed that in the 1516 and 1523 prints of the *Perlesvaus* Josephe's name appears regularly as *Josephus.* This clinches my argument in the text above.

[34] It would be absurd to maintain that the elaborate use of this *motif* in the *Queste* was suggested by these brief allusions in the *Perlesvaus.* Note similarly the author's habit, remarked on by Nitze, diss. pp. 47f., of retelling in condensed form long episodes of his sources.

[35] That is to say, in the only extant form of this branch. It is the opinion, however, of the present writer, as of most scholars, that the *Lancelot* in its primitive form contained no allusions to the Grail.

Birch-Hirschfeld, p. 141, has cited many important parallels in the *Perlesvaus* and the Vulgate *Queste,* respectively, in which he supposes that the former is the borrower. I agree with him in regard

when that romance came to be written. There is not a trace of it in Chrétien's *Lancelot*. Similarly, the conception of Claudas's defeat of Ban and of his wars with Arthur and Lancelot (pp. 277 ff., 324), — also, alluded to as if they were matters with which everybody was familiar — belongs to the *Lancelot*. The fact, then, that we have here allusions that accord with the *Queste* and the *Lancelot* of our extant MSS. renders it most probable that it was in cyclic redactions of substantially the same character [36] that the author of such allusions knew these branches.

---

to these parallels, but even more telling, I believe, are those about the adultery of Lancelot and Guinevere cited above. Here, in the *Ferlesvaus* we have mere off-hand allusions, in the *Queste*, a whole romance in which this adultery constituted an essential *motif*. The parallels cited by Birch-Hirschfeld are: 1. The white shield marked by a red cross, originally Joseph of Arimathea's, *Queste*, VI, 21 ff., *Perlesvaus*, pp. 25, 144. 2. The hero opens a tomb and finds the corpse of an armed knight therein, Q. VI, 27, P. p. 179. 3. Pelles is a character in both, in Q. as Galahad's maternal grandfather, in P. as Perceval's uncle. 4. The mysterious ship in which the heroes make voyages, called in the *Queste* Solomon's ship, Q. VI, 143 ff., P. pp. 142 ff., 146, 330, 347. 5. At the end of each romance the hero passes in a ship with the Grail to his eternal abode, Q. VI, 192 ff., P., p. 347. 6. The rôle of Lancelot in both as an unsuccessful Grail-quester.

To these should be added the idea that the Grail questers *par eminence* should be three in number, in Q. Galahad, Perceval, Bohort, in P. Perceval, Gawain, Lancelot.

The connection between these passages in the two romances is indisputable. In view of the unquestionable superiority of the *Queste* to the *Perlesvaus*, in respect to literary quality, and in view of the other evidence bearing on their relative dates, how can one doubt that the latter is the borrower?

[36] The contamination of the primitive *Lancelot* with the conceptions of the *Queste* must have begun very soon — probably, at once — after the composition of the latter. Consequently, there is no reason to doubt that the author of the *Perlesvaus*, in any event, knew the *Lancelot* as it was after this contamination had taken place, since he was evidently familiar with the *Queste*. The *Lancelot*, to be sure, may not have reached the final stage of its evolution, represented by the extant MSS.

That our author numbered among his sources Robert's *Joseph,*
Chrétien's *Perceval,* and, at least, the first two continuations of
the latter (viz. Pseudo-Wauchier and Wauchier) is generally agreed,[37] but his indebtedness to the romances of the Vulgate cycle

---

[37] Cp. Nitze's dissertation, pp. 102 ff. and review of earlier
opinions on the subject, pp. 20 ff. — also, Bruce, MPh., XVII, 117 ff.
I agree with Nitze that it is impossible to determine whether Manessier
is, also, among these sources. The Craven Knight episode (*Perlesvaus,*
pp. 52 ff., 189, 301, and Manessier, ll. 42 125 ff. and 43 719 ff.) the
chief one involved, may well have been derived from a common lost
source. On the other hand, Nitze's ground (p. 103) for rejection of
Birch-Hirschfeld's views, *Sage vom Gral,* pp. 139 f., as to Gerbert's
being a source of the *Perlesvaus* is inadequate; for, as we have seen
above, the dating of the latter from external evidence between 1200
and 1212 is, by no means, established. The two romances have in
common the following episodes: 1. Perceval sees two priests before a
cross, one striking it with a stick, the other worshipping it. 2. Perceval chases the *beste glapissante,* whose young within it are constantly barking. 3. Perceval's combat with the Dragon Knight. —
The *Perlesvaus* inverts the order of 1 and 2, but both romances
interpret them allegorically. The close connection of the two romances
in respect to these episodes is undeniable and I am inclined to agree
with Birch-Hirschfeld. Gerbert's citation of "li livres" is not necessarily decisive, as Nitze (p. 96) thinks, for the romancers habitually
speak of their own works as "li livres", "li escris". — For minor
sources of the *Perlesvaus* cp. *Vengeance de Raguidel,* ll. 1880 ff.
(episode of the damsel of Gaut Destroit, source of the Proud Damsel
episode in *Perlesvaus,* pp. 55 f.), pointed out by Nitze, dissertation,
p. 48, note — *Enfances Gawain* or variant of the same (story of
Gawain's early life in *Perlesvaus,* pp. 252 f.). The fragmentary *Enfances Gauvain* was edited by Paul Meyer, *Romania,* XXXIX, 1 ff.
(1910), and its relation to the *Perlesvaus* episode discussed by Bruce,
Historia Meriadoci and De Ortu Waluuanii, pp. LIII f. (Göttingen,
1913). Both the *Vengeance* and the *Enfances* belong, it seems, to
the beginning of the thirteenth century.
On the relations of Lancelot's beheading game in the *Perlesvaus,*
pp. 103, 233, to the treatment of the same theme in *Syr Gawayne
and the Grene Knight* cp. Kittredge, *Sir Gawain and the Green
Knight,* pp. 52 ff. Still other notes on the minor sources will be
found in Nitze's dissertation, pp. 104 f., and for parallels see Lister's
diss., pp. 12 ff. With the episode of Marin le Jalous (pp. 48 ff.) cp.

seems to the present writer equally clear and of far greater importance. Many features of the romance, besides those that have been mentioned, betray its late origin[38] — especially, such features as are marked by violent and illjudged change from the general Arthurian tradition: e. g. the conception that the hero's father was still alive when he himself first went out into the world (p. 20) — a conception which cuts at the very root of the whole Perceval legend — the appropriation to the castle of Perceval's mother of the time-honored name of Arthur's capital, *Kamaalot* (pp. 19, *et passim*), and the addition (pp. 24, 40 etc.) of a new capital Pannenoisance (Pannennoiseuse) — most likely, Penzance — to that monarch's list of capitals, the three-fold (allegorical) naming of the Grail castle (p. 249), the excessive number of additional relics (Christ's crown of thorns, portions of his blood and garment, the implement which was used in taking him down from the cross, Joseph's shield, banner and mule, the sword used in the decapitation of St. John) which the author introduces into the Grail story and which, as a German scholar has remarked,[39] make his Grail chamber, as it were, a museum of curiosities.

that of the jealous lord of Beloe in the *Mort Artu*, Bruce's edition, pp. 215 ff. — In his article, "The Schwanritter — Sceaf Myth in Perceval le Gallois ou le Conte du Graal", *Journal of English and Germanic Philology*, XIX, 190 ff. (1920), P. S. Barto derives from "Germanic mythology" *Perlesvaus*, pp. 142 ff. (Arthur from the window of his castle at night sees a mysterious boat with an armed and sleeping knight — really Perceval — on board drawing to land) and 333 ff. (Perceval observes the approach of the Red Cross ship which is to bear him away on his last voyage). The first of these episodes, however, is based on pseudo-Wauchier, ll. 20857 ff. So, too, the latter, in all probability, with an additional reminiscence of Arthur's translation to Avalon. Like Sebastian Evans, his authority, Barto is unaware of the existence of the early MSS. of the *Perlesvaus*, barring the insignificant Bern fragments.

In her recent article, "The *Perlesvaus* and the *Vengeance Raguidel*", *Romania*, XLVII, 349 ff. (1921), Miss Weston argues (wrongly, I believe) that these two works drew on a common source for the Mysterious Ship and Proud Lady episodes, respectively.

[38] Cp. the list of such features enumerated by Heinzel, pp. 175 f.

[39] Birch-Hirschfeld, *Sage vom Gral*, p. 143. In the same pas-

Altogether, as we have seen, the *Perlesvaus* is a mediocre patchwork of *motifs* drawn from a great variety of earlier Arthurian sources, prose as well as verse, and it bears all the marks of a period of decline. In the minds of English-speaking readers it has gained an artificial importance, inasmuch as it is the only one of the Old French Arthurian romances in prose which has been translated into English since the Middle Ages.[40] Owing to the translator's skilful revival of the style of Malory and to the fact that the version appeared in a popular series, the *Perlesvaus,* in its English dress, has had a circulation much beyond its merits.

Even for especial students of the Arthurian romances, however, this romance would possess a peculiar interest, if it were true, as has been contended,[41] that it was written in the interests of Glastonbury Abbey. As a matter of fact, the author was, doubtless, acquainted with the notion which the monks of Glastonbury so sedulously cultivated from the latter half of the twelfth cen-

---

sage he enumerates the relics named above. This is all a mere effort to outbid previous Grail romancers.

[40] The same is true of German. Cp. the German translation of the *Perlesvaus* by G. Gietmann: *Ein Gralbuch* (Freiburg, 1889). The English version, referred to, is by Sebastian Evans and is entitled *The High History of the Holy Grail* (2 vols. London, 1898). It appeared in *The Temple Series.* The discussion of the Grail Legend which Evans appended, II, 283 ff., to his work is worthless. As intimated above, in his translation he employs an archaic style modelled on Malory's, and if one accepts the general method, it must be acknowledged that the work is well done. In the opinion of the present writer, however, this general method is of disputable value, for the factitious archaic style leaves on the reader's mind an impression of artificiality which is not produced by the French original or by Malory. Especially, there is an oppressive solemnity about Evans' version which the natural style of the *Perlesvaus,* itself, is free from.

[41] Cp. especially Baist, *Literaturblatt,* 1892, col. 160, *Prorektoratsrede,* p. 39 (1894), and *Zs. f. rom. Ph.,* XIX, 326 ff. (1895) and Nitze, "Glastonbury and the Holy Grail", MPh., I, 247 ff. (1903), "The Glastonbury Passages in the *Perlesvaus*", University of North Carolina *Studies in Philology,* XV, 7 ff. (1918) and "On the Chronology of the Grail Romances. I", MPh., XVII, 151 ff. (1919), 605 ff. (1920).

tury[42] namely, that Glastonbury was identical with the Isle of
Avalon (really the Celtic Elysium) — and, also, with the other
baseless invention of these same monks in 1191 to the effect that
Arthur and his consort were buried in this abbey. The author of
the Vulgate *Mort Artu* had already shown familiarity with these
matters[43] and, from the time that the last-named fraud was perpetrated, they were, no doubt, widely known among all that had
an especial interest in Arthurian traditions and, particularly, among
ecclesiastics, like the author of the *Perlesvaus*, who cherished such
interests. The description of "li leus d'Avalon" (pp. 261f.), however, which has been taken to be a description of St. Mary's chapel
at Glastonbury[44] — even if we grant that the identification is

---

[42] Cp. above.   [43] Cp. I, 428ff.

[44] So Nitze in the second of his articles just named p. 12 —
on which I offered some critical comments in MPh., XVI, 117f., note,
and in the third, pp. 158f.

The place is described, pp. 261f. on the occasion of Lancelot's
chance visit there. This passage and the others relating to Avalon in
the *Perlesvaus*, viz. pp. 222, 270, 348, are reproduced by Nitze in
his second and third articles.

The chapel is said to be situated in a valley, ten "lyeues
galesches" long, with forests on each side. "Desus la montaigne de
la valee", on the right, he sees a rich chapel newly made. By the
side of this chapel and each joining it separately were "iii messons
mult richemant herbergiees" (i. e. fitted up as dwellings, I take it).
"Il avoit mout biau cimetire a la chapele anviron, qui clos estoit a la
rende de la forest, et descendoit une fontaine, moult clere, de la hautece
de la forest, par devant la chapele, et coroit an la valee par grant
ravine; et chascune des messons avoit son vergier et li vergier son
clos. Lancelot oi vespres chanter a la chapele |et| il vit. i. santier
qui cele part tornoit; mes la monteingne estoit si roiste que il n'i pot
mie aler a cheval, ainz descendi; si le trest par la rene apres lui tant
qu'il vint pres de la chapele." In the chapel there were three hermits
singing vespers. They come forth, greet Lancelot, and have his horse
stabled. Inside he finds two tombs. In one Guinevere is interred, in
the other the head of her son Lohot, pending the death of Arthur,
who is himself to be buried therein, according to the written directions
of Guinevere, kept in the chapel. She had had the place renovated
("renoveler") before her death.

Lancelot did not know before of the queen's death. He refuses food and spends the night in lamentation and prayer by the side of her tomb and the next morning after attending services, departs for Carduel.

In a previous passage (p. 222) it is said that Arthur had had Lohot's head borne "en l'ille de Valon, en une chapele qui estoit de Nostre Dame ou il avoit un seint hermite preudome qui mout estoit bien de Nostre Seignor". Later (after Lancelot) Arthur, accompanied by Gawain, also, went to l'ile, d'Avalon" (p. 270) and grieved there over his wife and his son, saying that he ought to love this holy chapel more than all others in his land.

Obviously, the main objection to the view that we have here a description of St. Mary's chapel at Glastonbury by an eye-witness is the fact that the chapel of the romance is situated on a very steep mountain (or hill), but the actual St. Mary's was not situated on high ground at all. In *Studies in Philology*, XV, 12, Nitze was inclined to think that the romancer had deliberately disregarded the actual conditions and put the chapel on top of Glastonbury Tor (the steep cone outside of the town, which rises some 500 feet above the surrounding country), because St. Mary's was the leading church of Glastonbury and the Tor was "the most prominent place of the scene he is describing"; in MPh., XVII, 156, note, he believes that the words "desus de la montaigne" need not imply more than that the chapel was on the slopes of the Tor. But there is nothing to choose between the interpretations, for, in either case, the statement of the romancer would stand in flat contradiction to the historical truth, and we cannot conceive what motive an ecclesiastic who had lived at or visited Glastonbury Abbey and who was "writing in its interests" would have in deliberately perpetrating such a gross inaccuracy. Moreover, even if we put St. Mary's in an imaginary position on the lower slopes of the Tor, where alone *vergers* are possible, what stream descending from the mountain before the chapel did the author have in mind? There is none mentioned in the descriptions of Glastonbury.

The first of the points just mentioned is sufficient, in my opinion, to invalidate Nitze's theory and to show that the description of St. Mary's is anything but "precise" (MPh., XVII, 614, note 1). Indeed, the whole passage is about as vague as the fanciful descriptions of the romances usually are, and, in some points, suggests comparison with previous descriptions in the *Perlesvaus*, itself, e. g. p. 6. The author says at the end of his work (p. 348), "Li latins de coi cist estoires fust traite an romanz fu pris an l'ille d'Avalon en une sainte messon de religion qui siet au chief des mores (Hatton MS. *mares*), la ou li rois Artus et la roïne Guenievre gissent par le tesmoing de prodomes

religieus qui la dedanz sont qui tote l'estoire en ont vraie des le con-
mancemant tresqu'a la fin", and he is, doubtless, availing himself of
the current idea that Arthur and his wife were buried at Glastonbury
("ille d'Avalon") to give authority to his romance by pretending that
he got it thence.   The whole statement is, of course, a fiction, for
there is not the slightest reason to believe that the *Perlesvaus* ever
existed in Latin form.   Especially noteworthy, however, is the fact
that, when he comes to describe Avalon in full (pp. 261f.), he appears
to have forgotten the actual Glastonbury altogether, for he mentions
no monks there, but only three hermits.   The "clerc" (p. 263) probably assisted the hermits in the chapel.   He does not mention, either,
the abbey; he merely speaks of three houses, which are obviously the
houses of the three hermits.   But the historical records tell us nothing
of three houses being attached to St. Mary's.   On the other hand, the
author of our romance was obsessed with the number, three (the
number of the Trinity), and introduces it and its multiples at every
turn.   Thus there are three Grail questers, three names for the Grail
castle, thirty-three companions on the Bounteous Isle (p. 330) etc.
There is nothing about the chapel in which Arthur and Guinevere
are buried that is different from the other hermits' chapels, described
in the romance, except that its richness is strongly emphasized —
even more so than that of Pelles' chapel (p. 62) — and that three
hermits are connected with it, instead of one, and, accordingly, that
three *messons* (hermits' habitations) stand next to it, instead of one.
There is no intimation that there is any other building nearby.   In
Chaus's dream-adventure at the beginning of the *Perlesvaus* (p. 6),
like Lancelot, he penetrates a great forest, follows what he imagines
to be the tracks of the king's horse as far as a glade *(lande)* in the
woods "si resgarde a destre et vit une chapele enmi la lende et voit
anviron un grant cimetiere ou il avoit mout de sarquenz, ce li estoit
avis".   The chapel is later (p. 12) said to be situated "el regort de
la forest".   Cp. the one described p. 169, "el regort d'une montaigne".
That the three hermits' lodgings should be richly furnished may seem
strange, but so it is with the one which Gawain visits (p. 61) as well
as with that of King Pelles (p. 62), and this hermitage too had its
enclosed *vergier.*   The hermits, moreover, always have attendants to
look after the steeds and armor of their visitors (pp. 59, 62, 102, 108,
126).   It will be seen from this comparison that there is little left in
the picture that would suggest an identification of the chapel with
St. Mary's at Glastonbury's.   That the author of the romance represents
his edifice as having been renovated may be well accounted for by the
fact that it was destined to receive the body of the sovereign and his

correct — is too inexact to have been written by a person who had first-hand knowledge of the spot. At most, one can only maintain that the author derived some vague idea of the topography of the abbey and its environs from hearsay or from books and filled out the rest from his imagination. The legends, then, which we find connected with St. Austin's chapel at the beginning of the *Perlesvaus* — the slaying of Chaus by invisible hands and the vision of the Virgin Mary, who offers her son in the mass — and which were, also, localized at Glastonbury, as we learn from John of Glastonbury,[45] the fifteenth century chronicler of the abbey, were more probably drawn by the monks from the romance rather than *vice versa*. Certainly, we know from this same chronicler that they had localized materials from the Vulgate *Estoire del Saint Graal* there and that he, himself, continued, in the same spirit to draw freely on the Grail romances of the Vulgate cycle,[46]

---

consort. It is implied in the *Perlesvaus,* moreover, that only Arthur and Guinevere have tombs in this chapel, which there is no reason to believe was true of St. Mary's.

[45] *Johannis, confratris & monachi Glastoniensis Chronica sive Historia de Rebus Glastomiensibus,* edited by Thomas Hearne, 2 vols. Oxford, 1726. The legends in question will be found I, 77 ff. Nitze has reprinted the passage MPh., XVII, 616 ff. (1920). Here it is not St. Austin's chapel, but the hermitage of St. Mary Magdalen of Beckery (at Glastonbury) that Arthur visits. Moreover, he goes there not on his wife's advice, but because he is warned by an angel in a dream. Gawain belittles the significance of the dream. At the time the king was staying in Wirale nunnery at Glastonbury.

[46] Thus, in the first volume, Joseph of Arimathea and his son, Josephe (the latter invented by the author of the *Estoire*), are represented, p. 17, as being buried in the church at Glastonbury. Mention is also made, p. 51, of Josephe's being consecrated bishop in "Sarath" — that is, Sarras. Cp. Sommer, I, 30 ff. The author cites, p. 52, directly the book "qui *Sanctum Graal* appellatur" (i. e. Sommer, I, 211) as his authority as to how the converters of Britain made the voyage thither, Josephe and his companions on Josephe's shirt, the rest in Solomon's ship. He relates, also, pp. 52 f., how Mordrain, warned in a vision by Christ, took his army, which was led by Nascien (not Vespasian, as Nitze, MPh., I, 249, note, interprets *Vaciano*) to Britain and overcame the king of North Wales (Norgales). Cp. Sommer, I,

and even on the *Lancelot*,[47] for still other materials in compiling
the history of the foundation, so that there is no reason why the
monks of Glastonbury, who nearly three centuries earlier had begun
exploiting the popularity of the Arthurian romances in the interests of their abbey, should not have included the *Perlesvaus* in their
depredations as well as the other Grail romances.[48]

230—241. On p. 53, the chronicler quotes some lines from "quidam
metricus" in regard to Josephe's accompanying Joseph of Arimathea to
Britain, which shows that he (John of Glastonbury) was not the first
to localize these materials from the Grail romances at Glastonbury.
Pp. 56, 73 we find Arthur numbered among the descendants of Joseph
of Arimathea, whose genealogy is given in the *Estoire* (Sommer, I,
286—290). This idea of Arthur's descent from Joseph, however,
which is not found in the *Estoire* or any other Arthurian romance, is
more likely to have been an invention of the Glastonbury monks before
John of Glastonbury than of a sober historian (according to his lights),
like John. See, too, in this chronicle (p. 59) the list of Pierre's
descendants taken with much mutilation of names from *Estoire*, I, 280.

In a similar manner, the chronicler refers definitely to an incident
in the Vulgate *Queste* — "in inquisicione vasis quod ibi vocant *Sanctum
Graal*, refertur fere in principio", etc. (p. 55) — namely, the one (*Queste*,
VI, 24 ff.) where the White Knight (Christ) gives the marvellous shield
to Galahad.

[47] The "liber de gestis incliti regis Arthuri" (p. 55), is the
Lancelot. The whole passage in John of Glastonbury runs: "Joseph
ab Armathia, nobilem decurionem cum filio suo, Josephes dicto & aliis
pluribus in majorem Britanniam quae nunc Anglia dicta est, venisse &
ibidem vitam finisse testatur liber de gestis incliti regis Arthuri in
inquisicione scilicet cujusdam illustris militis, dicti Lanceloth de Lac, facta
per socios rotundae tabulae, videlicet, ubi quidam Heremita exponit Wal-
wano misterium cujusdam fontis, saporem et colorem crebro mutantis,
ubi et scribebatur quod miraculum illud non terminaretur, donec veniret
magnus leo qui & collum magnis vinculis haberet constrictum."

The fountain which changed its color and taste and the hermit's
interpretation of it will be found in the unique *Lancelot* variant contained in MS. Harley 6342 (fifteenth century), which Sommer has
printed as an appendix to Vol. 5 of his series. Cp., particularly,
pp. 455, 464 ff. of that text.

[48] For the opposite interpretation of these matters cp. Nitze,
MPh., I, 248 f., note, and XVII, 164 f.

The first of the incidents of the St. Austin's chapel episode,

named above, has approximately parallels elsewhere in mediaeval literature. Of very common occurrence is the second (miracle of St.
Gregory, as it is called). The two combined, however, occur only in
the *Perlesvaus* and in the Glastonbury chronicle, as far as I know.
The one text, then, doubtless, derived them from the other, or both
derived them from a common source. The fact that Gawain appears
in the Glastonbury version is an indication that its source was an
Arthurian tale of some sort. That character, it is true, does not
appear in the *Perlesvaus* in these incidents, but immediately after
them. The localization would account for the other changes. The
monks were eager to localize miracles of Our Lady at their abbey.
See the chapter in the chronicle, I, 45 ff. It should be noted, moreover,
that between these two incidents, the *Perlesvaus* has a third: Arthur
comes to a hermit's chapel on his way to St. Austin's chapel and
overhears Our Lady's decision in the dispute of the angels and devils
over the hermit's soul. If the author of the *Perlesvaus* were really
drawing from the Glastonbury legend, and not *vice versa,* his motive
for inserting this incident would not be apparent.

Sebastian Evans, *High History of the Holy Grail,* II, and Miss
Weston, *Romania,* XLIII, 420 ff. (1914), believe that the author of
the *Perlesvaus* drew Chaus's fatal dream-adventure at St. Austin's
chapel (pp. 6 ff.) from a local Shropshire legend. They regard the
passage about this adventure in a prophecy of Merlin's in the *Histoire
de Fulk-Fitzwarin* (end of the thirteenth century) as proving that the
legend came from this locality. The *Histoire* identifies the St. Austin's
chapel of the *Perlesvaus* with one in a district which he calls
"Blaunche-Vile". Miss Weston indulges in some hazardous speculations,
but she really fails to connect the story with any Shropshire locality,
or, indeed, to find it actually localized anywhere. The *Histoire's*
localization, such as it is (it occurs in a prophecy of Merlin's!) was,
no doubt, the individual fancy of its author.

It should be added that Nitze takes *Glais,* the name of Perceval's
paternal grandfather in the Berne MS. of *Perlesvaus* (p. 3) — he is
only named once in the romance — as certainly derived from *Glast,*
name of the eponymic founder of Glastonbury Abbey according to the
De Antiquitate Glastoniensis Ecclesiae. Is there any assurance,
however, that *Glais* is the correct form of the name? The Brussels
MS. here gives him the common Old French name, *Gais* (Latin *Gaius*).
Just a few lines before, this same Berne MS. has the name of Perceval's mother as *Iglais.* It is possible that some confusion with this
name may have caused the scribe to change *Gals* to *Glais.* In any
event the names of the *Perlesvaus* in our only printed text (Potvin's)

are incredibly corrupt. I have already referred to the fact that the name of the hero's father *Alein le Groos* (which the author evidently took from the prose *Joseph*, since the epithet does not appear in Robert's verse) is not spelt correctly a single time in this text, although it occurs often there. Moreover, one, at least, of the names of this Alein's brothers in the same text (p. 3) is so corrupt as to be unintelligible, viz. *Melaarmaus*. It tells against the correctness of Nitze's derivation, however, that the names of the sons of *Gais (Glais)* have no connection with the names of Glast's descendants as they are given in the mediaeval chronicles of Glastonbury or relating thereto. Apart from *Alein (Julien*, etc.), the name of Perceval's father, the names, *Bruns (de) Brandalis, Bertholez, Brandalus (Brandelis) de Gales, Elinaus de Gavalon, (Elinaus d'Escavalon), Meralis (Mariales* of the prose *Lancelot). Frommers* (in the *chansons de geste, Gaydon* and *Gaufrei), Alibans* — corrupted to *Aliliaus* in the Brussels MS. (*Alibon, Aliblon* of the prose *Lancelot* and Vulgate *Merlin* continuation) — are drawn from various French romances. Of the rest *Galobrutes* is plainly manufactured by combining *Galo* (from *Gales* = Wales, but also a personal name in Arthurian romance) with *Brutus*, name of the eponymus of Britain. Probably manufactured, also, from *Gales* are the *Galiaus (Galians)* and *Gorgalians* of this list, which differ only by the prefix *Gor-*. In any event, there is no reason to doubt that these and the certainly corrupt *Melaarmaus* are names drawn from French romance. On *Pelles,* name of Perceval's maternal uncle, cp. p. 15, above. The author of the *Perlesvaus* probably discarded it as the name of the Fisher King, because to leave this monarch with no definite name seemed more impressive. On the shiftings of names in the *Perlesvaus,* see Bruce, MPh., XVI, 128.

Nitze, MPh., I, 255, on the suggestion of Prof. H. A. Todd, has plausibly identified *Pannenoisance (Pannenoiseuse)* — the new capital which is given to Arthur in the *Perlesvaus* (pp. 24, 140 *et passim*) — with Penzance on the South Cornish coast. *Ibid*. XVII, 161, he cites the introduction of this place (hitherto unknown in Arthurian romance) as tending to confirm the theory of the connection of the *Perlesvaus* with Glastonbury. There is no sign, however, that our author really knew where Penzance (if we accept the identification) was, for he says in one place (p. 24) that it is "sor la mer de Gales" and in another (p. 140) that it is in "Gales" (i. e. Wales). These statements are, of course, incorrect and cannot be taken as showing any real knowledge concerning the town on the part of the author.

PART V.

ANALYSES AND BIBLIOGRAPHIES.

Chapter I.
Narrative Lays: Analyses and Bibliography.

The standard edition of the lays of Marie de France is that of Karl Warnke: *Die Lais der Marie de France (2te verbesserte Auflage*, Halle, 1900). This has completely superseded the earlier edition by B. de Roquefort in his *Poésies de Marie de France*, I (Paris, 1819). Comparative notes on the stories of which Marie's lays are variants were supplied to Warnke's edition pp. lxxvff., by Reinhold Köhler, the great master in this branch of study.[1]

Roquefort's edition included a Modern French prose translation of the lays. W. Hertz, *Spielmannsbuch*[4] (Stuttgart and Berlin, 1912 contains German metrical paraphrases of *Lanval, Yonec, Deux Amans, Le Fraisne, Eliduc.* Hertz's notes, *ibid.* are, also, very valuable. Eugene Mason's *French Mediaeval Romances* (Everyman's Library) includes a prose translation (English) of the lays. For another partial translation see Edith Rickert, *Marie de France: Seven of her Lays* (New York, 1901).

For the literature of the narrative lays of the Middle Ages in general (editions, etc.) cp. Warnke, pp. iiif. Among the general discussions of the subject which he names, especially noteworthy for sources is Axel Ahlström: *Studier i den Fornfranska Lais-Litteraturen* (Upsala, 1892), and for the literary valuation of Marie, in particular, J. Bédier, *Revue des Deux Mondes*, CVII, 853ff. (Oct. 15, 1891). Important, too, is Brugger's discussion of the lays, *Zs. f. frz. Spr. u. Litt.*, XX, 120ff. (1898).

---

[1] Since the above was written, E. Hoepffner has reedited the lays of Marie de France in the Bibliotheca Romanica, Nos. 274, 275, 277, 278 (Strasbourg, 1921). The edition includes a glossary (two pages) and variant readings, but no notes.

We have seen what the story of the first of Marie's twelve lays, viz. *Guigemar*, is. The *motifs* of the remainder may be briefly indicated as follows:

2. *Equitan:* A king of this name, practising adultery with his seneschal's wife, is scalded to death in a tub of hot water which he and the adulteress had prepared for the seneschal. The last-named, who has detected the two in the act of adultery, throws his wife into the tub, and she, too, dies.

3. *Le Fraisne:* Based, in part, on the superstition (common in primitive society) that twins are always children of different fathers. A lady in Brittany makes malicious remarks to that effect about a neighbor who has borne two sons. Shortly thereafter she herself gives birth to twin daughters. To conceal the fact, she gives one to an attendant to kill. This woman, however, deposits the child, with costly coverlet and handsome ring on its arm, on an ash-tree (hence the heroine's name) near a nunnery, the abbess of which brings the child up as her niece. Le Fraisne elopes with a lord and lives with him unmarried. The lord is later about to marry her sister. Like the patient Griseldis, under similar circumstances, Le Fraisne acts meekly as attendant, lays the coverlet on the bridal bed. Mother of the bride recognizes it, Le Fraisne's identity is revealed, and she (not her sister) is married to the lord.

4. *Bisclavret:* A knight under a spell becomes a wolf (were-wolf) three days every week. His wife worms the secret out of him and her lover seizes his clothes in the forest, so that he cannot become human again. King hunts in the forest and the wolf, acting humanly, is permitted to attach himself to the king. Attacks his wife's lover at court on sight, and later his wife. She confesses, the knight's clothes are restored, he becomes human again, and the adulteress and her paramour are banished.

5. *Lanval:* Lanval, a poor knight, neglected by King Arthur in the distribution of gifts, is lying, dejected, in a meadow by a brook. A fay summons him to her tent, grants him her love and the power to have every wish fulfilled, provided he will keep their relations concealed. Lanval is rich and happy, until Ar-

thur's queen falls in love with him. He rejects her proposals, and, stung by her insinuations as to the causes of his coldness, tells her that he has already as his lady-love the most beautiful woman in the world, whose lowest maid surpasses the Queen in beauty. The Queen (like Potiphar's wife) accuses Lanval to the king of soliciting her love, and repeats his depreciation of her beauty. Lanval denies the first charge, but admits the truth of the second. Arthur and the barons say that he must prove his assertion or die. Lovely attendants of the fay arrive, but Lanval declares that none of them is his lady-love. At the climax of the judges' impatience the fay arrives. Lanval's assertion has proved true, and the king acquits him of blame. The fay, however, will not remain, and, Lanval having sprung upon her horse behind her, they ride away to Avalon (the Celtic Elysium).

6. *Les Dous Amanz (The Two Lovers):* A father will give his daughter only to the man who can carry her to the top of a certain hill (in Normandy) without stopping. On the girl's advice, her lover gets from her aunt at Salerno a magic drink which will give him the necessary strength. He fails to use it, however, and dies of exhaustion, as he reaches the top. The girl, too, will not use it, and dies with her lover. The hill is named "The Hill of the Two Lovers."

7. *Yonec:* A beautiful young woman of high birth is kept in a tower by a jealous husband. A fairy prince, in the form of a falcon, flies into her room. Resuming his human form, he becomes her lover. She regains now her beauty and happiness. The husband, suspicious of the change, has her watched. Having discovered the truth, he has spear-heads fixed in the window, which give a fatal wound to the falcon on its next visit. The transformed prince tells the lady that his wound is mortal, but that the son whom she will bear to him is destined to avenge his death. He then flies away, but she springs through the window, follows him by the traces of his blood into the hollow of a mountain, where his fairy kingdom is situated, has a final interview with her lover, who gives her a magic ring and sword as well as directions as to how the death of her husband is to be compassed by their son

(yet to be born). These directions are in the course of time carried out, and Yonec (the son) avenges his father.

8. *Laustic:* A young woman is accustomed to lean out of her window at night to talk with her lover in the adjoining house. Her jealous husband asks why she is so fond of going to this window at night. She replies, "to hear the nightingale." The husband has the nightingale caught, kills it and throws the bleeding bird on her breast. She no longer has an excuse for stolen conversations with her lover — sends the bird, however, to her lover, who has it set in a case, and carries it about on his person in memory of his lady-love.

9. *Milun:* In a secret intrigue with a lady of his land (South Wales) Milun begets a son, who is brought up in Northumberland by the lady's sister. The lady is compelled to marry another man against her will, but by means of letters concealed under a swan's wing, and in other ways, maintains communication for years with her lover. The son grows up, knowing the story of his parents, but has not met his father. The two have an encounter in a tournament. The father is unhorsed, but recognizes a ring on his son's hand. There is a recognition-scene and the son takes his father to his mother, whose husband has died in the meanwhile. The parents are married.

10. *Chaitivel:* Four knights try to win a lady's favor by valiant deeds. Three are killed; the fourth is maimed. The lady grieves that she should have been the cause of these misfortunes and has a lay composed about it. It is called *Li Chaitivel* after the surviving knight, who thinks that he is the unluckiest of the four.

11. *Chievrefeuil (Honeysuckle):* Tristan communicates with Iseult of Cornwall by messages inscribed on a stick of hazel, which he lays in the road where she is to pass. In this way they arrange a meeting and Tristan learns that King Marc regrets having banished him. In memory of this message Tristan composed a lay named *Chievrefeuil*.

12. *Eliduc:* Eliduc of Brittany loves his wife and vows fidelity to her, when his enemies cause him to be banished from

the land. In Great Britain, where he greatly distinguishes himself, he meets a king's daughter, Guilliadun, who falls in love
with him. His lord in Brittany needs him and regrets his banish-
ment — summons him to return. When he leaves, Guilliadun
is in despair. He promises, however, to return and take her with
him to his native land. He does so, after peace in Brittany has
been restored, but on the voyage back to the continent a storm
arises and a sailor says that the cause is his lord's conduct with
Guilliadun. Eliaduc throws the sailor into the sea, but Guilliadun
falls into a trance. Her lover takes her to a church in Brittany
and is going to bury her there. Eliduc's behavior on his previous
return to Brittany had aroused his wife's suspicions, which were
still further confirmed by his present behavior. She accordingly
watches him and understands what is the matter, when she discovers Guilliadun in the chapel. She is the means, however, of
bringing the apparently dead girl back to life, for she has observed a weasel resuscitate its dead mate by putting a leaf of a
certain herb in the latter's mouth. She has a leaf of this same
plant put into the mouth of Guilliadun, who is likewise restored
to life. Still further, the self-sacrificing wife renounces her claim
to Eliduc, founds a convent, and becomes a nun. Eliduc lives
happily for years with Guilliadun, but they, too, ultimately adopt
the monastic life, and so end their days.

To the discussions of the individual lays which are recorded
in Warnke's second edition (1900) should be added the following
which have appeared since the publication of that edition:

4. *Bisclavret.* Cp. G. L. Kittredge's edition of *Arthur and
Gorlagon:* Harvard *Studies and Notes in Philology and Literature*, VIII (Boston, 1903). *Arthur and Gorlagon*, preserved only
in the MS. of the Bodleian Library, Rawlinson B. 149 (end of the
fourteenth century), is a Welsh folk-tale (a sort of *mabinogi*) in
Latin prose. It is, in part, a werewolf tale, closely akin to *Bisclavret* and the anonymous lay of *Melion*. Owing to its kinship
with certain Irish tales, Kittredge concludes (p. 261) that the
story of *Bisclavret* reached Brittany from Ireland.

5. *Lanval.* C. W. Prettyman, MLN, XXI, 205 ff. (1905),

shows that *Lanval* is a source of the Middle High German poem
(of about 1310), *Peter von Staufenberg,* last edited by Edward
Schröder (Berlin, 1894). For Celtic parallels cp. T. P. Cross, "The
Celtic Fée in Launfal," Kittredge *Anniversary Papers,* pp. 377ff.
(Boston and London, 1913) and "The Celtic Elements in the Lays
of Lanval and Graelent," MPh., XII, 585ff. (1915). The latter
is the fullest discussion of *Lanval* and cognate tales and contains
in the notes very abundant references to the literature of the subject. Cp., also, *Anmerkungen zu den Kinder- und Hausmärchen
der Brüder Grimm, neu bearbeitet von J. Bolte und G. Polivka,*
II, 327ff. (Leipzig, 1915).

6. *Les Dous Amanz.* This has been reedited by A. L. Durdan: *Le Lai des Deux-Amants, Légende Neustrienne de Marie
de France* (Macon, 1907), but the edition has no value. Durdan
appears ignorant of the existence of Warnke's standard edition.
O. M. Johnston's "Sources of the Lay of the Two Lovers," MLN.,
XXI, 34ff. (1906) is the most valuable study of the subject.
As Johnston says, the lay combines two folk-tale *motifs,* for each
of which he adduces parallels: 1. A king, on losing his wife,
wishes to marry his own daughter. 2. A girl can be won only
by performing some difficult task, set by her father.

7. *Yonec.* Edith Rickert, *Marie de France; Seven of her
Lays* (London, 1901), 184, cites parallels from the *Wooing of
Etain* and other Irish sagas. P. Toldo, *Romanische Forschungen,*
XVI, 609ff. (1904) cites still others from the Orient. Cp., too,
O. M. Johnston: "Sources of the Lay of Yonec," PMLA. XX,
322ff. (1905) and "The Story of the Blue Bird and the Lay of
Yonec," *Studj Medievali,* II, 1ff. (1905) and Bolte and Polivka,
II, 261ff. (1915). According to Johnston, *Yonec* combines two
folk tale *motifs:* 1. *The Jealous Stepmother* (perhaps, of Celtic
origin). 2. *Inclusa* (perhaps, of Oriental origin): A jealous hus-
band shuts up his young wife, but in the end a lover carries her off.
Through the first of these elements it is related to the story of
L'Oiseau Bleu in the collection (seventeenth century) of fairy tales
by the Comtesse d'Aulnoy. Cp., still further, T. P. Cross, "The
Celtic Origin of the Lay of Yonec," *Revue Celtique,* XXXI,

413ff. (1910). Cross reviews preceding discussions and tries to establish by Irish parallels (mainly), Celtic derivation. Features of the tale can be paralleled in classical and oriental tradition, but Cross thinks (p. 471) that the cumulative evidence favors the theory of Celtic origin, although the revenge *motif*, with its corollary of the gift of sword and ring, is wanting in the Celtic Stories. Bird-lovers are found in folk-tales everywhere, but when one considers the Celtic names in *Yonec*, it seems to me better to accept this element of the lay as of Celtic (Breton) origin.[2] On the other hand, the *Inclusa* element, as Cross (p. 455) seems willing to concede, is, doubtless, ultimately of Oriental origin. Taking *Yonec* as a whole, one must confess, nevertheless, that much the closest parallel that has ever been adduced is not Celtic but Russian (doubtless Oriental in the last analysis), viz. *Le faucon resplendissant*, which Toldo, *op. cit.*, pp. 629 f., cites from Leon Sichler: *Contes Russes*, 24ff. (Paris, 1881). We have here among other things, what is wanting in Cross's Celtic parallels of bird-lover tales, namely, the heroine's search for the wounded bird-prince until she finds him in his fairy realm. To be sure, the Russian tale ends happily.[3]

9. *Milun.* M. A. Potter, *Schrab and Rustem* (London, 1902) is the best study of the theme of the combat between father and son in literature and popular tradition.

11. *Chievrefeuil.* Cp. Lucien Foulet, in his "Marie de France

---

[2] In the *Annales de Bretagne*, XI, 479 (1895-6), J. Loth, reviewing F. Lot's "Études sur la provenance du cycle arthurien", *Romania*, XXIV—XXV, expresses the opinion that *Yonec* is of Welsh origin. He observes, however, that the mention of St. Aaron in it means nothing, for Aaron figures, also, among Breton saints. He founded a monastery at St. Malo.

[3] Since the above was written, M. B. Ogle's article, "Some Theories of Irish Literary Influence and the Lay of Yonec", RR, X, 123 ff. (1919), has appeared. Ogle points out classical and oriental parallels to *motifs* in *Yonec* and denies that the lay is derived from Celtic sources. The nomenclature, however, is Breton, and, whatever the ultimate sources of the tale may be, it seems to me that the immediate source was, most likely, Breton.

et la legende de Tristan," *Zs. f. roman. Ph.*, XXVIII, 273 ff.
(1908). He concludes (p. 283) that the incident in this lay was
taken by Marie from the (lost) primitive *Tristan* poem. In MLN,
XXIII, 205 ff. (1908) he shows as stated above, that Marie's
apparent appeal (1. 5) to an oral, as well as a written, authority·
for her tale is "a meaningless mannerism." The numerous parallels which he cites from her other writings puts this beyond doubt.
— In the article cited I, 66, note 61 above, Ezio Levi, pp. 137 ff.,
argues unconvincingly that this was one of the primitive *lais* about
Tristan — anterior to the romances on that hero. He argues,
pp. 150 ff., the same thing with reference even to *Guirun* and
Jgnaure.

12. *Eliduc*. René Basset: "La légende du mari aux deux
femmes," *Revue des Traditions Populaires*, XVI, 614 ff. (1901),
cites a parallel from a tale of the Prussian Altmark and two
parallels from *the Arabian Nights*. Cp., too, A. Bayot: *Le Roman
de Gillion de Trazegnies* (Louvain and Paris, 1903). This romance deals, also, with the theme of the "man with two wives."
Bayot believes that it is based on a lost French poem (which he
dates about 1365) and traces the theme to India. — J. E. Matzke
has discussed *Eliduc*, also, in his article "The Source and Composition of *Ille et Galeron*," MPh. IV, 471 ff. (1907). He disputes the position, which Foerster had taken in his edition (Halle,
1891) of this poem, that it is based on *Eliduc* — argues that the
lay and the romance are derived independently from a common
tradition. — In his Göttingen dissertation (1910), *Der Einfluss
des Gautier d'Arras auf die altfranzösische Kunstepik, insbesondere
auf den Abenteuerroman*, pp. 11 ff., W. M. Stevenson accepts
Foerster's view that *Ille et Galeron* is wholly dependent on *Eliduc*,
but he offers no new argument.

So much for the undisputed *lais* of Marie de France. As we
have seen above, the term became conventional and was applied
even to narrative poems that had nothing to do with the *matière
de Bretagne* — as Warnke, p. xxxvii, says, simply because it
carried with it a greater distinction than the terms, *fableau* and *dit*.
In MS. 1104, Nouvelles Acquisitions, Fonds Français (Biblio-

thèque Nationale), which dates from the end of the thirteenth
century, we have a considerable number of such pieces mixed with
genuine *lais bretons* (by Marie de France and others) and all
headed: *lays de Bretaigne.* See the list of its contents given by
G. Paris, *Romania,* VIII, 31 ff. (1879). Páris had already edited
two of the spurious lays in this collection, *ibid.,* vol. VII —
Épervier (pp. 1 ff.), *Amours* (pp. 407 ff.). Warnke, pp. xxxvii f.,
has enumerated the lays of this character. I would add to his
list *Ignaure, Cor, Havelock, Trot, Nabaret* (for all of which see
Foulet, *Zs. f. rom. Ph.,* XXIX, 54 f., note 1) — also, *L'Espine,*
which has no real connection with Celtic matters (Cp. Brugger,
Zs. f. frz. Spr. u. Litt., XX¹, 139, and Foulet, *Zs. f. rom. Ph.,*
XXIX, 36). What has been said of *L'Espine* is true, too, of the
Lecheor. This so-called *lai* is merely a cynical joke on the true
source of inspiration in chivalry — too gross for repetition. I cannot take seriously, either, its introduction — as G. Paris and
Warnke have done — which tells us that on St. Pantelion's day,
"as the Bretons relate," people used to assemble in honor of the
saint and the men would recount adventures of love and knighthood,
whilst the ladies listened to them. The adventure which pleased
them most was turned into a lay by the company. This, however, is evidently a piquant invention, and nothing more, to introduce with mock seriousness the vulgar joke that follows. There
is no reason to imagine that any one in France or elsewhere ever
imagined that Breton lays really came into existence in this
manner.

The mysterious title, *Gumbelauc,* given to the lay in the Old
Norse version of the lays (*Strengleikar,* p. 68, edited by Keyser
and Unger, Christiania, 1850), has been interpreted as Welsh and
as affording proof of the Celtic origin of the lay. Cp. on the
subject E. Philipot and J. Loth, *Revue Celtique,* XXVIII,
327 ff. (1907). This position, however, is disputed by L. Foulet,
"Les Strengleikar et le lai du Lecheor," "*Revue des Langues
Romanes,* LI, 97 ff. (1908).

Apart from the recognized compositions of Marie de France,

following are the lays which appear to have some genuine connection direct or indirect, with the *matière de Bretagne:* [4]

1. *Tyolet.* Combines the *motif* of Perceval's childhood (hero is brought up in forest by his widowed mother in complete ignorance of arms, but meets knights in the forest and goes to Arthur's court) with that of the false claimant in Thomas's *Tristan* — that is to say, the hero being wounded, an impostor gets possession of some symbol of his achievement — here the white foot of a stag — and claims, himself, the credit for this achievement until he is exposed. The author is obviously merely drawing on Chrétien and Thomas. Foulet, *Zs. f. rom. Ph.,* XXIX, 48ff., notes, too, verbal echoes of Marie's lays.

2. *Guingamor:* The hero has rejected a queen's love and she tries to dispose of him by provoking him to an impossible enterprise — the killing of a certain wild boar in the neighboring forest. He crosses a perilous river (boundary of fairyland), has an adventure with a fay, lives in her castle in such joy that he thought the time three days, though it was really three hundred years. She permits him to return for a visit to his friends, but warns him against eating anything, whilst in his own country. Being hungry, however, he eats some wild apples, whereupon he shrivels up into an excessively old man. The fay, however, sends her messengers, who take him back to fairy-land, and he is heard of no more. — *Guingamor* may very well be by Marie. Foulet, *op. cit.* p. 303, assumes this. Cp. too, G. Paris, *Manuel,* p. 98, and R. Zenker, *Litteraturblatt f. germ. u. rom. Ph.,* XIII, 149 ff. For a study of this beautiful story, which is undoubtedly of Celtic origin, see W. H. Schofield, "The Lay of Guingamor," Harvard *Studies and Notes in Philology and Literature,* V, 221ff. (Boston, 1896). Cp., also, T. P. Cross, MPh., XII, 590ff. (1915). The hero's name is really identical with that of the hero of Marie's first lay — *Guigemar.* Cp. on the subject, H. Zimmer, *Zs. f. frz. Spr. u. Litt.* XIII[1], 7ff. (1891). For further instructive notes on this lay cp. W. Hertz, *Spielmannsbuch*[3], pp. 382ff. F. Lot compares

---

[4] G. Paris, *Manuel,* p. 98 ascribed nos. 2 and 4 to Marie.

(*Romania*, XXV, 590 f.) the White Boar of this lay with the Twrch Trwyth of *Kulhwch* and *Olwen* and the sow, Henwen (Old White), of a Welsh triad (Loth, Mabinogion², II, 271).

3. *Doon.* An heiress who lives at Daneborc (Edinburgh) fixes as the price of her hand that the successful suitor in one day should ride from Southampton to Edinburgh. Several accomplish this feat (!), but they are so tired at the end of the journey that they fall into a profound sleep and the girl kills them before they awaken. Doon sits up the whole night after his arrival and wins the heiress. A second part of the poem is based on the same *motif* as Marie's *Milun* (combat of father and son).

4. *Tydorel.* A queen of Brittany has no child by her husband— has one, Tydorel, however, by a supernatural lover (water-sprite). Tydorel becomes a powerful king, but betrays his supernatural origin by never sleeping. People have to sit up with him all night to entertain him with stories. A young man, unwillingly impressed for this duty and instructed to say what he does by his mother, tells the king that a person who cannot sleep is not human. The king takes the taunt to heart, goes to his mother, who confesses the circumstances of his paternity, whereupon he mounts his steed, proceeds to his father's lake, plunges in, and is heard of no more.

For a study of this theme (hero who is the son of a woman and a supernatural lover) cp. Florence L. Ravenel, "The Lay of Tydorel and Robert le Diable," PMLA, XX, 152ff. (1905). See, too, W. Hertz, *Spielmannsbuch*³, pp. 389ff.

5. *Melion.* A werewolf story closely akin to *Bisclavret*. For a study of this story in connection with *Bisclavret*, etc., cp. Kittredge, *Arthur and Gorlagon*, pp. 167ff. He derives *Bisclavret* and *Melion* from a common source. It seems to me, however, more likely that the latter is based on the former. This is the conclusion of L. Foulet's examination of the subject, *Zs. f. rom. Ph.*, XXIX, 40ff. (1905). He points out Marie's influence on the phraseology of the anonymous lay — also, Wace's.

6. *Graelent.* A variant of the *Lanval* story with the incidental *motif* added, of the knight who captured a girl (fay) by seizing her clothes, whilst she is bathing in a pool. For a study of this and

cognate stories cp. W. H. Schofield, "The Lays of Graelent and
Lanval and the story of Wayland, "PMLA, XV, 121ff. (1900)
— also, T. P. Cross, "The Celtic Elements in the Lays of Lanval
and Graelent," MPh., XII, 585ff. (1915). Schofield and Cross
regard *Lanval* and *Gréalent* as coming from a common source.
Moreover, Schofield derives the clothes-stealing incident from the
Norse saga of Wieland (who seizes the swan-garments of a swan-
maiden under the same circumstances). This, however, is very
doubtful. Cp. M. B. Ogle, *American Journal of Philology*, and
Cross, loc. cit., p. 621, note 4. Foulet argues plausibly, *Zs. f. rom.
Ph.*, XXIX, 19ff. that *Graelent* is based on *Lanval*. On the name,
Graelent, cp. H. Zimmer, *Zs. f. frz. Spr. u. Litt.*, XIII[1], 1ff.
(1891).

7. *Désiré.* An unskilful and still further rationalized version
of the *Lanval* theme, and as Foulet, *op. cit.*, pp. 37f., says, doubtless, based on Marie's *Lanval*. For supposed points of contact between this lay and Chrétien's *Yvain*, cp. A. Ahlstrom, *Mélanges-
Wahlund*, pp. 296f. (Macon, 1896).

The first four of these anonymous lays were edited by G.
Paris, *Romania*, VIII, 29ff. (1879), no. 5 by W. Horak, *Zs. f.
rom. Ph.*, VI, 94ff. (1882), no. 6 by Roquefort, *Poésies de Marie
de France*, I, 486ff. (Paris, 1819), Barbazan and Méon, *Fabliaux
et Contes*, IV, 57ff. (Paris, 1808), in the 1829 (Paris) edition of
Le Grand D'Aussy's *Fabliaux ou Contes*, I, App., 16ff., and by
G. Gullberg, *Deux lais du XIIIe siècle*, 1ff. (Kalmar, Sweden,
(1876), no. 7 by F. Michel, *Lais inédits des XIIe et XIIIe siècles*,
pp. 5ff. (Paris and London, 1826).

On the language of nos. 1, 2, and 4 cp. K. Warnke, *Marie de
France und die anonymen Lais*, Programme no. 699 (1892) of
the Gymnasium Casimirianum in Coburg. It is the same as Marie's
own language, according to Warnke, p. 7. No. 5 is Picard, no. 6
originally Norman. Cp. Warnke, *ibid.* pp. 18ff.

In addition to the French lays already enumerated one should
add the lay on the classical harper, Orpheus, which is preserved
only in its English form, *Sir Orfeo;* but the English poem, edited
by O. Zielke (Breslau, 1880), is indisputably based on a lost French

original. For a study of this and other supposed Breton lays in
English, cp. Kittredge, *American Journal of Philolgy*, VII, 176 ff.
(1886). Foulet, however, *Zs. f. rom. Ph.*, XXX, 704 (1906)
seems to show that the Celtic coloring of *Sir Orfeo* is due to imitation of Marie. See, also, his article, "The Prologue of *Sir
Orfeo*," MLN, XXI, 46ff. (1906). — For notes on *Sir Orfeo*, cp.,
too, W. Hertz, *Spielmannbuch*³, pp. 357ff. — Gabrielle Guillaume,
"The Prologues of 'Lay le Freine' and 'Sir Orfeo'," MLN,
XXXVI, 458ff. (1921), disputes Foulet's conclusions.

1. Analyses and Bibliography of the French Arthurian Romances in Verse.

The following romances were all composed in octosyllabic couplets. A full list of the editions is given in the case of each romance.
Nothing is said of the manuscripts, except where the work survives in only a single copy. The most ample information in regard to the sources, date, etc. of any romance is to be found, of
course, nearly always in the introductions to the editions of the
work. It is not necessary, therefore, to repeat this statement under
each heading in the following list — which, I may add, is complete for the metrical romances, now extant.

In the brief bibliographies that precede the analyses of the
various romances below, we have cited all publications of value with
regard to the poems (excepting those that relate merely to textual criticism), but have not otherwise tried to make the citations
exhaustive. The critical literature thus cited, supplemented by
the introductions of the editions of the individual works, will
enable any one that so desires to follow up the study of any particular romance. The comment with which we have concluded each
article in the list consists for the most part of informal notes on
the general literary value of the respective romances for the guidance of students who have not as yet read these works. References
to "G. Paris, HLF, XXX," are to that scholar's standard treatise,
"Romans en vers du cycle de la Table Ronde," *Histoire Littéraire
de la France, ouvrage commencé par des religieux Benedictins de*

la congregation de Saint-Maur et continué par des membres de l'Institut," Tome XXX, pp. 1—270 (Paris, 1888). It is hardly necessary for me to say that this treatise is still fundamental in the study of the verse-romances. References to "Gröber" are to Gröber's *Grundriss der romanischen Philologie* (Strassburg, 1888—1901).

In arranging this list of the metrical romances I have adopted the chronological order, as far as that is ascertainable. In many cases, of course, even the relative dates of the works concerned are doubtful. The reader, however, is referred to the editions of the individual romances for the discussion of such questions.

I have included in my list even the metrical romances that were composed after the year 1300, but, since these works lie beyond the limits which I have set for this treatise, I have refrained from any save the most general indications as to their contents.

It is, perhaps, advisable to state, in conclusion, that the following analyses, except in the case of the two or three romances that have not yet been printed, are all based directly on the original texts.

1. *Erec et Enide.* Edited by Immanuel Bekker, *Zs. f. d. A.*, X, 373ff. (1856) and by W. Foerster, in octavo, Halle, 1890, in duodecimo, ibid., 1896 and 1909. 6958 lines — For author (Chrétien de Troyes), dialect, bibliography, and date cp. I, 108ff., above.

Whilst holding court at Caradigan at Easteride, Arthur proclaims the chase of the white hart, according to custom, notwithstanding Gawain's objection that to do so will produce envy and discord among the courtiers, for whoever should kill the beast would have to select the girl at court whom he considered the prettiest and kiss her. Guinevere joins in the chase, accompanied by one female attendant and by Erec. The rest of the party had gone on some distance ahead, when the queen sights a knight, a girl, and a dwarf, and sends her damsel to inquire who the knight and the girl are. The dwarf, however, rudely bars the way, and, when the damsel insists on executing her commission, he strikes her with his whip. The queen now despatches Erec to order the knight and girl to come to her, but he receives the same treatment as the damsel. Nevertheless, he feels unable to resent the blow, for he notices that the knight is armed, whilst he himself is unarmed. He resolves, however, to avenge the insult, and leaving the queen keeps the trio in sight and follows them to a castle in the neighborhood of which the greatest activity prevails. — In the meanwhile the hart had been killed, but Guinevere persuades Arthur to postpone the function of the kiss three days, so that Erec may be present. Having observed where the knight had turned in, Erec finds lodgings for the night with a vavassor, who had once been rich, but now was poor — so much so, indeed, that his beautiful daughter had to act as ostler to Erec's horse. Erec learns from the vavassor that the bustle which he had observed was due to a contest over a sparrow-hawk, as the prize of beauty, which was to take place the next day. The knight whom Erec had followed had, the two preceding years, borne off the prize unchallenged and awarded it to his lady. Erec next obtains equipment for the contest from his host and, also, permission to fight for the latter's daughter in this contest. He is the son of King Lac and wishes to marry this daughter, should he carry off the prize. Erec, of course, wins the prize for his lady — vanquishes the knight with the insolent dwarf, but spares his foe's life on the condition that he, the girl, and the dwarf shall present themselves to Guinevere as her captives. The knight is named Yder, son of Nut. On his arrival at court, as we learn later on, Yder is pardoned by the king and enrolled in the royal retinue. Erec is now made much of by everybody, including his host's brother-in-law, the count of the district. Nevertheless he will not stay even with this nobleman, but takes the vavassor's daughter off to Arthur's court to marry her. Moreover, he will not allow her to accept rich attire, in the place of her poor garments, save from Guinevere. When she has been clad in fine rainment (presented to her by the queen), Arthur makes her sit by himself and his consort and chooses her for the kiss which was required by the custom of the chase of the white hart. Her preeminence in beauty, however, is so indisputable, that no discord results from this choice.

Erec now sends money, clothing, etc. to his future father-in-law, and after this the wedding is celebrated with due splendor at Arthur's court. In the course of the marriage service the bride for the first time discloses her name as "Enid". A month later Erec attends a great tournament at Tenebroc (Edinburgh) and wins the highest honors of the occasion.

Our hero now returns to his father's court, where he and his bride meet with the most cordial welcome. In the course of time, however, he becomes so uxorious that he neglects feats of arms and is generally criticized for his slothfulness. Enid overhears these murmurings, and, knowing that she is the cause of the change, is greatly disturbed over it. One morning, accordingly, whilst they are lying in bed together, she gives feeling expression to her regret, thinking that her husband is asleep. He is half-awake, however, and makes her tell the whole story. Vexed by her recognition of the truth of the criticism, he then orders her to array herself in the best manner, puts on his armor, and, without revealing to her or anyone else his purpose, he rides away, accompanied by her. As a culmination to her unhappiness, he bids Enid under no circumstances to speak to him. They had not journeyed far, however, before Enid, observing that three robber knights — one of whom wanted her horse — were about to attack her husband, and unable to restrain her fears for his safety, breaks his command, in order to warn him of the danger. Though he rebukes her for speaking, he takes advantage of the warning. Now, in those days, two or more knights would never assail a single adversary together in a joust — consequently, Erec is able to dispose of all three, in succession, and make his wife lead away their three horses in front of him. Just after this we have a repetition of this incident — only, in the second case, there are five robber knights. That night Erec proposed to his wife that she should sleep, whilst he remained awake, but she refuses, and, by way of penance for having angered her husband, insists on guarding the horses all night long. whilst he sleeps. — Next day a squire gives the husband and wife food and conducts them to the house of a citizen near his lord's castle. Furthermore, he extols the pair to his lord so highly that the latter goes to this house, falls in love with Enid, and importunes her to become his paramour, whilst Erec is out of hearing. In order to escape from her unwelcome wooer, she pretends to consent, but puts him off until the next day. Early in the morning, however, she awakes Erec and warns him of their new peril. They ride away, therefore, after having requited the host for his entertainment with seven of their horses. When the count and his men the next day follow after them, Enid first sights their pursurers, and warns her husband, who, as in the previous instances, upbraids her for speaking to him, but gets ready to defend himself. He slays, then, the seneschal and unhorses the count — the two men who lead the rest. The remainder of the band stop to look after these two, which enables Erec and Enid to get away. Moreover, the count now penitent, calls off his followers from the pursuit.

Erec's next encounter is with Guivret le Petit, who defends his tower, surrounded by a moat over which a drawbridge is thrown. Erec wins, but is, himself, badly wounded in the combat. Nevertheless, the adversaries become friends, when the fighting is over, and bind up each other's wounds. Continuing his journey, the hero arrives at a plain where Arthur is hunting. Kay, on observing him, springs upon Gawain's steed, the Gringalet (Guingalet), asks who he is, and wants him to come to the king and queen. Erec refuses, whereupon there is a quarrel and a joust in which Kay is unhorsed. On learning, however, that Kay's steed belongs to Gawain, Erec gives him back the animal to be returned to its owner. Arthur now sends Gawain to fetch Erec to him. When Erec declines to come, Gawain despatches a secret message to the king to shift his tents to a place on the road by which Erec would have to pass. He, himself, stays with the young knight and delays him, until Arthur has had time to make the change. Thus our hero is trapped and is compelled to accept the king's hospitality and tell his name. His wounds are, also, healed with a lotion which Morgan le Fay had presented to her brother, Arthur. Erec, however, insists on resuming his journey with Enid the next day. In a forest through which they pass they find a girl in despair over her lover, Cadoc de Tabriol, whom two giants have carried off.

Erec follows and slays the giants and restores Cadoc to the girl and sends him to Arthur, whilst he, himself, rejoins Enid. The heat of the day and the weight of his arms, however, cause his wounds to burst open again, so that he faints before his wife. She thinks that he is dead and is about to kill herself with his sword, when Count Oringle of Limors comes up and tries to comfort her by offering himself as her husband in Erec's place. She repels this offer, but he takes her back to his castle with him — also, the (supposedly) dead body of her lord. Moreover, he forces her to go through the form of a marriage with him, but, when at the marriage feast that follows, she still shows herself obdurate, he strikes her in the face. His own barons protest against this brutality, and, in the midst of the ensuing uproar, Erec regains consciousness, draws his sword, and slays the count. The barons are panic-stricken with the apparent spectacle of a dead man come to life again and flee, so that Erec and his wife are able to escape, the latter sitting on the neck of her husband's horse as they ride away. Erec tells her now that he is, at last, convinced of her love for him and that her trials are at an end. A rumor of Oringle's wicked conduct had reached Guivret le Petit and he hurries to Enid's rescue. As it happens, however, he meets Erec and Enid in the night — not knowing who they were — jousts with Erec and unhorses the latter easily, since he has been much weakened by his wounds. On learning his identity, Guivret takes his friend to his castle and, with the help of his (Guivret's) two sisters, cares for him until he is well enough to depart for his own country. On the day of their departure, however, Erec and Enid, accompanied by Guivret come to Brandigan, the superb and impregnable castle of King Evrain, which was situated on an island. But there was a peril connected with the place, viz., the adventure of the Joie de la Cour (Joy of the Court). In spite of Enid's anxiety and warnings from Guivret, Evrain, and the people, in general, Erec resolves to try this adventure, which was as follows: There was on the island an orchard of never-fading beauty — a sort of earthly Paradise — cut off from the surrounding world, not by any material obstacle, but by a wall of air, merely-through the power of necromancy. The fruit of this garden it was impossible to bring to the outside world. Erec penetrated the garden through its narrow entrance and observes there the impaled heads of his unsuccessful predecessors, with a fresh stake ready to receive his own head and a horn hanging on it. After leaving Evrain, Enid, and the rest, he follows a path which brings him to a sycamore, under which there is a bed and a beautiful girl lying upon it. Soon a knight appears, threatens him for approaching the girl, and then attacks him. After an obstinate combat, Erec is victor and announces his success by a blast on the horn. It turns out that his opponent was Mabonagrain — a nephew of Evrain — who had formerly lived at the court of Erec's father, and that the girl was a cousin of Enid's, who had bound her lover by a *don* never to leave the enchanted garden until a knight should appear who could vanquish him. The happiness of the people over the termination of the spell justified the name of the adventure — Joy of the Court. Erec, Enid, Mabonagrain, and his *amie,* all leave the garden now, rejoicing. Four days later Erec and his wife begin their journey to Arthur's court at Robais and, on their arrival in that city, they are cordially welcomed by the king and his consort. The court, however, moved later to Tintagel, and after a short sojourn there Erec hears of his father's demise. He acknowledges Arthur at once as his suzerain and begs him to come and crown him at his (Erec's) court. Arthur consents and the coronation, consequently, takes place at Nantes in Brittany, in the presence of a great throng of kings and nobility, both from the British Isles and from France, and amidst the most splendid festivities.

Tennyson's well-known *Geraint and Enid* (in later editions of the *Idylls of the King* divided into two parts, *Geraint and Enid* and *The Marriage of Geraint)* is based not on Chrétien's poem, but on the Welsh prose tale, *Geraint,* on whose relations to Chrétien see I, 108ff., above.

2. *Cliges.* Cp. I, 113ff.

3. *Lancelot (Conte de la Charrete).* Cp. I, 193ff.

4. Thomas's *Tristan.* Cp. I, 122ff. and I, 157ff.

5. *Yvain (Chevalier au Lion).* Cp. I, 95—6.

6. *Perceval (Conte del Graal).* Cp. I, 223 ff. and I, 290 ff.

7. *Li Biaus Descouneus (Le Bel Inconnu).* Edited by C. Hippeau: *Le Bel Inconnu* (Paris, 1860 — very incorrect — and by G. Perrie Williams: *Li Biaus Descouneus* (Oxford, 1915). 6228 lines. Author, Renaud de Beaujen; Dialect, Picard; Date probably, between 1185 and 1190. Only MS. known, XIV H 6 of the Musée Condé (Chantilly).

For bibliography see the conclusion of this article.

Arthur is holding court at Charlion (Caerleon) when a young knight (the hero) appears and asks a *don* (boon) of him. According to his custom in the romances, the king grants the boon before he knows what it is to be. The young knight will only give Biel Fil as his name, so that Arthur nicknames him *Li Biaus Descouneus* (The Beautiful Unknown). Just then a fair damsel, named Helie, appears accompanied by a dwarf, and begs the king for a champion to deliver her mistress, the daughter of King Gringras, from a spell, by performing the feat of the *fier baissier* (bold kiss). The hero at once claims the adventure from the king in fulfilment of his promise. Helie is greatly dissatisfied that so inexperienced a person should be assigned to the task and rides away with her dwarf. The Beautiful Unknown, however, with his squire, Robert, overtakes her, and on the advice of the dwarf, she reluctantly accepts his company. He soon has opportunities for convincing her of his qualifications for achieving high adventures: (1) At the Perilous Ford he overcomes Blioberis, its redoubtable defender, (2) the same night, in response to the cries of a girl (Clarie, Sagremor's sister) he rescues her from two giants whom he slays and in whose cave the party finds plentiful provisions (3) vanquishes three friends (Elins — or Heluins — de Graies, li Sires de Saies, and Willaumes de Salebrans) of Blioberis, who try to avenge his disgrace. In those days — fortunately for our hero — not more than one knight at a time would attack another knight. He is, therefore, able to slay Willaume, wounds Elin, and send the lord of Saies, as he had done Blioberis, to Arthur's court. So, too, with Orguillous de la Lande, who endeavored to recover from

Helie one of his hounds which she had appropriated. Our hero had, himself, vainly urged her to return the dog, but when she would not, felt constrained to defend her against the attacks of its master. — They come next to the castle of Becleus, where there was a tournament, with a sparrow-hawk as a prize. The knight who won this prize would turn it over to his lady and was supposed thereby to have vindicated for her the claim to superior beauty over the ladies of the rival knights. Our hero offers himself as the champion of Margerie, sister of Agolant, King of Scotland, whose lover had been slain in this contest — vanquishes the slayer, Gi(f)flet, son of Do, and sends him to Arthur's court. He next comes to the castle of the Isle d'Or (Golden Isle), whose mistress, La Pucele as Blances Mains (Girl with the White Hands), is versed in the seven arts, astronomy, etc. As events prove, she is really a fairy. The castle is indescribably beautiful, but at the head of the causeway by which it is reached there are 143 helmeted human heads impaled upon stakes. These are the heads of the knights who have failed to win the mistress of the castle, for, according to the custom of this stronghold, the successful suitor must have defended its approaches seven years against all comers, the victor in such contests being required to take the place of the vanquished and carry on the defence. No one, however, as yet had fulfilled this condition. When our hero slew Malgiers li Gris, its latest defender, the people manifested such joy as had not been known "since Jesus formed Adam." Our hero is entertained now splendidly in the castle, and its beautiful owner wishes to marry him — even tempts him by visiting his room in the middle of the night — but he sticks by his promise to deliver Helie's mistress. He next comes to the castle of Galigans, where, according to the custom of the place, he has first to overthrow its lord (Lampas), before he can enjoy its hospitality — then to the Gaste Cite (Waste City), a place of extraordinary beauty, which, however, has been deserted by its inhabitants — only at the palace he finds in the windows of the great hall jongleurs apparently playing on their musical instruments, a lighted candle before each. In this hall he has to joust with two knights. As he cuts off his second adversary's

head, smoke issues from it and the phantom jongleurs disappear,
leaving the hall in darkness. From a chest in the hall now a fearful
"wivre" (fabulous serpent) appears and from it a great light
streams forth. The creature propitiates our hero by its humility and,
before he is aware, it has kissed him and crawled back into the
chest, whereupon the hall becomes dark again. A voice now informs him that he is Guinglain, Gawain's son by Blancemal, the
fairy. He falls asleep, and, when he awakes in the morning, he
sees by his side a beautiful lady. It is the Blonde Esmeree (The
blonde, who is like refined gold — a daughter of King Gringras of
Wales), whom he has freed from enchantment through the kiss.
She tells him that she had been transformed by Evrain and Mabon —
the latter a great magician. The true name of the Waste City is
Senaudon (Snowdon). She offers herself to him as his wife and
he accepts her, provided Arthur will give his consent. The inhabitants of Senaudon now return to their city and sprinkle holy
water over it, to counteract the previous enchantments. — Notwithstanding the charms and wealth of Blonde Esmeree, Guinglain's heart is still with the lady of the Golden Isle, and so when
he and his new lady-love quit Senaudon for Arthur's court, he
tells Blonde Esmeree that he has a certain affair which he must
attend to before he can proceed to Arthur's court, and so turns
aside to visit the Isle. He meets the mistress of the latter on a
hunting party before he reaches her castle. She forgives him his
previous conduct, takes him to her castle, and puts him in a chamber
adjacent to her own, but tests his ardor by her tricks of magic,
before admitting him to her embraces, for, when he twice tries
to enter her room in the night, he seems to himself the first time
to have walked out on a narrow plank over deep waters and the
second time the roof appears to be falling in upon him. Both
times he arouses the whole castle by his screams. After this, however, the lady of the castle has him conducted to her bed by one
of her maidens and they spend the rest of the night together. She
tells him then how she had always loved him and kept watch over
him, had prompted Helie to go to Arthur's court, had announced
to him his name after the adventure of the *fier baissier*, etc. She

makes her barons, too, acknowledge him lord of the land. — In the meanwhile Blonde Esmeree had arrived at Arthur's court and obtained his consent to Guinglain's union with her. When her lover, however, still failed to appear, Arthur had a tournament proclaimed for the purpose of drawing him out of his concealment. Sure enough, a jongleur brings Guinglain news of the proclamation and he is eager to go, despite the opposition of his fairy-love. Owing to her supernatural powers, however, the latter knows that it is useless to resist his wishes, and so the next morning, on awakening, he finds himself lying in a wood with his squire and his arms by his side. He next rides on to the Castiel des Puceles (Maidens' Castle), where the tournament is to be held. A list of knights who participate in the affair is given and the jousts are described at great length. Guinglain is, of course, the victor in the tournament. They all adjourn now to London and then to Sinaudon (in Wales), where the marriage of the hero and Blonde Esmeree is celebrated.

In the opinion of the present writer, there is nothing specifically Celtic about this romance. It is filled with imitations of episodes and details in Chrétien's works — especially, the *Erec*. There has been much debate as to its relations to the cognate romances: 1. the Middle English *Libeaus Desconus* (composed about 1350), last edited by Max Kaluza, Leipzig, 1890. 2. the Italian Carduino (about 1375), edited by Pio Rajna as *I cantari di Carduino* in *Poemetti Cavallereschi*, Bologna, 1873, 3. the Middle High German *Wigalois* of Wirnt von Grafenberg (about 1210), edited by F. Benecke (Berlin, 1819), and by F. Pfeiffer, ibid., 1847. Besides the editions, see G. Paris, HLF, XXX, 171ff., H. Mennung, *Der Bel Inconnu des Renaut de Beaujeu in seinem Verhältnis zum Lybeaus Desconus, Carduino, und Wigalois* (Halle, 1890), W. H. Schofield, *Studies on the Libeaus Desconus*, Harvard *Studies and Notes in Philology and Literature*, IV (Boston, 1895), E. Philipot, "Un épisode d'Erec et Enide: La joie de la Cour. Mabon l'enchanteur," *Romania*, XXV, 258ff. (1896), and review of Schofield, ibid., XXVI, 290ff. (1897). Kaluza takes the French romance as the immediate source of No. 1; all the other scholars postulate a (lost) common source for the two. Philipot connects, however, *Li Biaus Descouneus* rather with the *Lanzelet* than with the *Perceval*, and, despite verbal borrowings of the former from *Erec*, denies (wrongly, in my judgment), its dependence on the latter, as far as the theme of the Joie de la Cour is concerned. Similar differences of opinion prevail as to the relations of *Carduino* and *Wigalois* to the French romance. For all these questions see Schofield's *Studies*. For the *Wigalois* and its sources, cp., particularly, F. Saran, "Ueber Wirnt von Grafenberg und den Wigalois," PBB, XXI, 253—420 (1896). Saran concludes (p. 412) that Wirnt had no knowledge of *Li Biaus Descouneus*, but followed a lost French romance, *Wigalois (Guiglois)*, of the twelfth century.

For an Irish parallel to the tricks which the fairy of the Isle d'Or plays on her lover in this romance, cp. Kittredge *Gawain and the Green Knight*, p. 265.

8. Robert de Boron's *Joseph* and *Merlin*, cp. I, 230ff.

9. Pseudo-Wauchier's continuation of Chrétien's *Perceval* (Conte del Graal). This occupies ll. 10602—21916 in Potvin's edition of the *Conte del Graal*. For authorship, date, etc. see I, 290ff. Its most significant episodes have already been analyzed in the text above, in one connection or another. The following outline is mainly intended to indicate the links that unite these episodes.

At the end of Chrétien's *Perceval* Gawain was at a castle (Chastel des Merveilles), where Arthur's mother (Ygerne) and Gawain's own mother and sister were then living. Gawain, however, had been separated from his mother since infancy and he recognized none of the three ladies. At the beginning of Pseudo-Wauchier's continuation Ygerne tells Gawain who she is and, also, who his mother and sister are, and Gwain, in turn, surprises Arthur by telling him that Ygerne is still alive, for Arthur has been under the impression that she had died thirty years before. It appears, however, that on Uther Pendragon's death Ygerne had got together much treasure and fled to this place, had had a castle erected there, and then sent for Gawain's mother, whose husband (Lot) had been slain. This lady came, gave birth to Clarisse (Gawain's sister) at the castle, and had lived there ever since. There is a fight now between Guiromelant, Clarisse's lover, and Gawain, but, on the girl's solicitation, Gawain stops the combat and gives her to Guiromelant, who now does homage to Arthur, like all the other barons of the *illes de mer*, except Brun de Branlant. Arthur, accordingly besieges Branlant. During this seven years' siege, Gawain and Yvain, pitying the distress of two beautiful girls among the besieged — Lore de Branlant and Ysaune de Carahais — induce Arthur to send food into the city, which prolongs the siege. Brun, however, finally submits to Arthur. During this siege Gawain, one day, comes upon Brandelis's sister in a tent in the forest and lies with her. Because of his renown, she had been in love with him before she ever saw him. Her father resents Gawain's act and attacks him, but is slain. Brandelis, immediately after, attacks him, too, but Gawain, enfeebled by a wound, received in the previous combat, begs Brandelis to adjourn the duel, which he consents to do. After Brun's submission, Arthur gives Ysaune de Carahais in marriage to Caraduel — father of Caradoc. Here begins, then, the interpolated *Livre de Caradoc (Karados)*, for which (with its *motifs* of the sorcerer's intrigue with Ysaune, the beheading game, Caradoc and the serpent, etc.) see I, 300 ff., above. — Next comes the episode which describes how Caradoc rescues Cador's sister Guimer (his future wife), from Aalardin and how they all go to Aalardin's tent, where there was a harp that sounded discords, whenever an unchaste girl approached. Swearing to be companions for life, Caradoc, Cador, and Aalardin proceed the next day to Arthur's court at Caerleon, where there is to be a tourney. The long and vapid description of this tourney in Potvin's text, ll. 13481—14943, is not in the Mons MS. and seems manifestly an interpolation in the *Livre de Caradoc* (itself an interpolation). It is the only part of Pseudo-Wauchier in which Perceval appears. — The story of the sorcerer's intrigue with Ysaune is here resumed and the episode of Caradoc and the serpent related. The next episode is that of the test of the chastity of wives by means of the drinking-horn, Bounef. If a man's wife is chaste he can drink from this horn without spilling any of its contents — otherwise he cannot. When Arthur insists on trying the horn, Guinevere endeavors to defeat the object of the test by praying that he may be wetted. Only Caradoc is successful in this test. — Arthur becomes melancholy over the thought that he has not rewarded his knights properly and summons them from every quarter to Caraheut for Whitsuntide. At a feast there he observes an empty seat (Gifflet's) at the table, falls into a revery, takes a knife from Ionet (his carver), rests the knife on a piece of bread and thoughtlessly wounds his hand slightly. On seeing the blood, he becomes conscious of his surroundings again, wraps his hand in a napkin to hide the blood, and tears drop from his eyes. When Gawain inquires the cause, he replies that it is because of the treason of his knights. The barons, offended at this speech, press for an explanation; they even follow him to his room, still demanding an answer from him, and Gawain breaks down the door. It turns out that their treason consists in their failure to rescue Gifflet from his prison in the Castel Orguellous. Acknowledging their wrong, Gawain etc. go to the siege of this castle. On the way Kay is humiliated, when he tries to carry off a roasted pea-cock *(paon roti)* from another castle. They next come to the Castiel de Lis, which Gawain recognizes as belonging to Brandelis, because he observes the latter's shield on the wall. In the castle everything was splendid, the table was laid out with delicious viands, etc., but no one was visible. Gawain warns Arthur that they must be on their guard, for they are in the castle of his (Gawain's) enemy — tells him[5] then how five years before he had ravished Brandelis's sister (somewhat later called Gloriete) and killed one of her brothers and had only escaped being killed by the other brother — Brandelis — by persuading him to adjourn

_____

[5] This is evidently a variant of the story, told above, concerning Gawain's relations with Brandelis's sister. There, however, the girl submits willingly to his embraces. Moreover, the resentful relative whom Gawain kills is, in the earlier passage, her father, not her brother. It looks as if, in the progress of the work, the author thought that he could improve on his first draft of these incidents, but, after composing a new version of them, neglected to cancel the old one.

their combat and conclude it before witnesses — since when they
had never met. Just then Kay, pursuing a hound out of the
castle, comes upon Brandelis in a garden, and the latter, hearing
that Arthur is in his castle, gladly rushes to the king and greets
him and his retinue effusively, but, on seeing Gawain, attacks him,
some of the men holding candles as they fight. His sister, however, brings in the little boy whom she had had by Gawain and puts
him between the combatants. Touched by the child's innocence,
the spectators implore Arthur to stop the fight. On the king's
appeal to him, Brandelis desists and becomes Arthur's man. Soon
after they reach the Castel Orguellous, Lucan is captured and
thrown into prison with Gifflet. Whilst hunting in the forest,
one day, Gawain's finds *Li Riches Sodoiers* (The Rich Soldier),
lord of this castle, lying under a tree, with his senses completely
benumbed, it would seem — the reason being that his lady-love
had failed to meet him at the time that she had promised. She
arrives a little later, however, and goes with her lover back to the
castle. This lord is subsequently vanquished in a joust by Gawain,
but, fearing lest the news of his abasement might cause the death
of his *amie*, he entreats the victor to act as if *he* had been vanquished
and to present himself to the girl in this assumed character. Gawain
acquiesces in this strange proposal and surrenders his sword to
the girl, after which she is sent to another castle, so that she may
not learn the truth. Li Riches Sodoiers now frees his prisoners,
tells Arthur the truth concerning his combat with Gawain, and
becomes the king's man. In the meanwhile, Gawain's son by
Gloriete has been abducted by unknown parties. Nevertheless,
Gawain leaves the search to the child's uncles and returns with
Gloriete and Gifflet to Britain, where he soon joins Guinevere
at the Castiel des Ormiaus (Castle of the Elms). At this point
begins the Grail adventure, the main features of which have already
been indicated above, I, 295 ff. — viz. the incident of the knight
who dies so mysteriously, declaring that it is Gawain's duty to
avenge him on his unknown slayer, since he (Gawain) is really
responsible for his death, Gawain's wanderings on this errand,
including the incident of the chapel and the bodiless hand, his

arrival at the Grail castle and his experiences there. — After these Grail adventures come the *enfances* of Gawain's son (whose abduction, however, still remains unexplained) — *inter alia*, his encounter with his father, neither, at first, knowing the other's identity. This, then, is followed by the incident of the swan-drawn boat, containing the body of a dead knight with a letter in its pouch begging the king to place the body in his (the king's) hall, but to let no one draw out the fatal truncheon (still in the mortal wound), unless he should promise by a thrust of this same truncheon and in the same part of the body to slay the person who gave the wound. (The dead man, we learn later, was King Guingamuer or Brangemuer — child of a mortal father and a fairy mother.) Gawain's brother, Karahes (Guerehes), who had himself, suffered humiliation at the hands of a little knight in the castle of the (unnamed) slayer, achieves this adventure and kills the slayer. After that he goes to the castle of the fairy-mother of the man whom he had avenged. The mother rejoices. When Karahes wakes up the next morning, he finds that (by the fairy's power) he has been borne to Caerleon in the same swan-drawn boat as the dead body of the fairy's son, and a girl is sitting by his bed. This girl goes up into Arthur's hall, and, on seeing the corpse there, falls into great grief, but declares that the dead man has now been avenged. With Arthur's consent, she has the corpse laid in the swan-drawn boat again and it is thus conveyed back to the fairy.

10. Here Pseudo-Wauchier ends and *Wauchier* takes up the story. He, in turn, is followed by Manessier and Gerbert, successively. In our chapter on the Grail we have indicated already all essential matters relating to the Grail in the 40,000 lines and upwards which these three continuators contributed to the *Conte del Graal*. There is really nothing else of interest in their work. In any event, there would be no commensurate benefit, if we should still further expand the bulk of this treatise by adding minute analyses of these interminable continuations. See, therefore, the abovementioned chapter for what is said in regard to Wauchier.

11. Béroul's *Tristan*, cp. I, 158, note 7.

12. *Meraugis de Portlesguez.* Edited by Matthias Fried-

wagner, *Meraugis von Portlesguez: altfranzösischer Abenteuer-*
roman von Raoul von Houdenc, zum ersten Mal nach allen Hand-
schriften herausgegeben (Halle, 1897). 5938 lines. Author, Raoul
of Houdenc (in the department of Seine-et-Oise) — Dialect, Isle-de
France (southwestern border). Date about 1200.
    G. Paris, HLF, XXX 220ff., E. Stengel, Vollmöller's *Jahres-*
bericht, VI, Teil, II, pp. 91ff. (1904), Caser Habemann, *Die lite-*
rarische Stellung des M. de P. in der altfranzösischen Epik, Göttingen, diss., 1908. G. Huet: Le Lancelot en prose et Meraugis
de Portlesguez, *Romania*, XLI, 518ff. (1912).
    Lidoine, the heroine, was daughter of the King of Cavalon in
Great Britain and succeeded to his kingdom. She was so celebrated
for her beauty and courtesy that people came from a great distance
to see her. She attends a tournament at Lindesores (probably
a corruption of Windesores = Windsor), which has been proclaimed
by the Lady of Landemore and in which the prize, a sparrow-hawk,
is to be awarded to the most beautiful woman present. Among the
participants in this tournament are two knights, Meraugis de Port-
lesges and Gorvains Cadruz, who had hitherto been devoted friends.
Both, however, fall in love with Lidoine — Gorvain on account
of her beauty, Meraugis, on account of her courtesy — and their
friendship thus turns to enmity. They fight a duel, but Lidoine,
hearing about it, comes and stops them and makes them agree to
submit their claims to Arthur's court at Cardoil during the Christmas festival. When the time arrives, however, only ladies are
allowed a voice in the decision. The case is argued with much
subtlety by the fair judges, but finally they all decide that Meraugis, in placing courtesy above beauty in love, has deserved the lady.
Gorvain wishes to renew the strife, but is compelled to submit and
Meraugis is "seized of" his mistress by a kiss, which at once in-
stils love of him into her heart. Nevertheless, she had already set
the condition that he must show himself worthy of her for a year
before she would consider marrying him — only now, however,
she resolves to accompany him on this year's wanderings. — Just
then an ugly dwarf turns up and reminds the king that a search
should be made for Gawain, who had gone on a quest for the Sword

with Strange Hangings (of Chrétien's *Perceval*). Meraugis undertakes the task and leaves the court, accompanied by Lidoine and the
dwarf. His first adventure is as follows: They come upon an old
woman who wears a golden circlet on her white hair. She has taken
the dwarf's horse away from him and he, in turn, predicts eternal
shame for Meraugis, unless Meraugis recovers it for him. The old
woman says that she will return the animal, if Meraugis will knock
down a shield which is hanging on a tree nearby. The young knight
does this, and she returns the horse, but, at the same time, heavy
groans begin to issue from a neighboring tent — in which, as it
turns out, there are three ladies. No one will explain the cause
of these groans and Meraugis goes on. He next overthrows a
knight Laquis de Lampagres, who, in fulfilment of a fantastic vow,
is attempting to defend a ford on bare horse-back, without saddle,
bridle or spurs. Meraugis learns from Laquis the mystery of the
shield and the groaning ladies. The shield is that of L'Outredote
(the One Feared Beyond Measure), who was so wicked that he
deliberately endeavored to promote wrong in every way. Having
fallen in love, however, he was forced by his lady-love to abstain
from all violence until somebody had first wronged him. Accordingly, he had hung up his shield in the hope that some one,
by striking it down, would release him from his constraint. Meraugis had done this, and the ladies were lamenting over the renewal
of L'Outredote's violence which they foresaw. In spite of his
protests, Meraugis now compels Laquis to go to the ladies and
remain with them until L'Outredote's arrival. L'Outredote, having
been informed by the girl who rode off with the lance in regard
to the insult to his shield returns to the tent and in a fight which
he forces upon Laquis blinds him in one eye and tells him that he
is going to kill him, after he has compelled him to guide him to
Meraugis. In the meanwhile, the dwarf has diverted Meraugis
from an enchanted glade, where even the bravest become cowards,
and taken him to King Amangon's court to be his champion in
a tournament. The victor in this tournament has the privilege
of choosing husbands for all the girls in the kingdom that year,
and the dwarf wishes to marry a hunchback damsel even more

hideous than himself. Meraugis, of course, wins in this affair and the dwarf gets his bride. In the meanwhile, Laquis and his captor had been seeking for Meraugis, and, after some difficulties, the former, being sent ahead by the latter, finds him and tells him of L'Out-redote. Meraugis, however, continues his quest for Gawain and, advised by the dwarf, goes to the *esplumeor Merlin* (Merlin's Retreat) to inquire about his friend. Here in a meadow, on top of an inaccessible rock, there are twelve young women who possess the gift of prophecy, and one of them answers the hero's questions from aloft. Though puzzled by the oracular terms in which her answer is couched, he follows her directions and goes to a cross-roads where the three roads that fork here are respectively named, according to an inscription in red letters, the Merciless Road, the Road Contrary to Reason, the Nameless Road. He follows the third of these roads and comes to a beautiful city by the sea, called first the Nameless City. When the blowing of horns an-nounces the approach of Meraugis and Lidoine, the inhabitants rush forth from their city with singing and every manifestation of joy, led by the seneschal, Meliadus. Meliadus wishes at once to take Meraugis to an isle which lies in sight of the city. He refuses, however, until he learns that a knight is occupying the isle, which is owned by a lady and that the joy of the people is over the prospect of a fight. Whoever wins in this combat will possess the isle and the lady. Meraugis crosses over and jousts with the strange knight. They are at first pretty evenly matched, but after midday the island-knight's strength waxes perceptibly. Before there is any decisive issue to the duel, however, the fact is disclosed that this knight is Gawain. The friends, therefore, lay aside their arms and greet each other cordially. It turns out that Gawain is held captive by the lady of the isle and has to fight all comers until some one slays him and succeeds to his office. Meraugis, however, suggests the following plot by which they are able to escape from the isle: They continue their duel until Meraugis is apparently slain; that night, however, he rises up, surprises the lady and her damsels in the castle, imprisons them, and the next day, clad in the lady's clothing, manages to obtain control of

a vessel which brings provisions to the island and thus escapes with
Gawain. They are shipwrecked in the harbor of Handitou, but
get to shore safely. In the meanwhile, Lidoine, thinking, like
everybody else, that her lover is dead, in deep grief, takes refuge
with a noble lady, Amice. On the other hand, Meraugis, being
unable to discover Lidoine, becomes almost insane. He and Gawain
now separate, vowing always to help each other. Whilst Meraugis
is engaged in a fight with Maret, L'Outredote passes by, and Meraugis's opponent consents to the postponement of their affair,
in order that Meraugis may pursue his deadliest enemy. Meraugis
follows L'Outredote into an enchanted garden, where he finds him
dancing and carrolling about a pine-tree with a number of girls.
    Our hero is about to attack his enemy, but, himself, falls under
the spell of the place and joins the carols, too. This releases, however, L'Outredote from the spell and he goes outside and waits for
Meraugis with the intention of attacking him. — Whilst Lidoine
is on her way home from Amice's dwelling, accompanied by the
latter, Belchis li Lois, under the guise of hospitality, gets her into
his castle and tries to force her to marry his son. Lidoine pretends
compliance, but sends Amice to Gorvain and to her seneschal,
Anchises li Ros, for aid. Gorvain comes with his own men and
hers. Belchis at first defeats Anchises — afterwards, however,
being assailed by Gorvain, flies to his castle, Monhaut, where he
is besieged by Gorvain. — In the meanwhile, another knight had
taken the place of Meraugis in the enchanted carols, but the latter,
though free, required some time to regain full possession of his
faculties. Whilst still in this condition, he proceeds on his journey,
meets L'Outredote, and, after a desperate fight, kills him, and cuts
off his right hand, which he had promised Laquis, but, himself,
becomes unconscious. Belchis's brother-in-law, Meliant de Lis, finds
him in this state and carries him to Monhaut, without knowing who
he is. After some days Meraugis is convalescent and learns where
he is—also, that Lidoine is under the same roof as himself and that
Gorvain is besieging the castle. Later on, whilst he is sitting in the
hall, with head shaved and, in his weakened condition, looking altogether like a fool, the ladies of the castle come in, and he and Lidoine,

recognizing each other, both faint. They manage, however, to conceal the cause of their emotion. — By this time Gawain has achieved the quest of the Sword of the Strange Hangings and returned to Arthur's court (held at Butost). Amice, who is there, lays on him the blame for Lidoine's misfortune. Accordingly, Gawain collects an army and a fleet and goes to Lidoine's rescue. From jealousy of Gorvain, Meraugis, as soon as he is well, resolves to assist the besieged side. He wishes, too, to measure his strength with Gawain's and issues forth for that purpose. He unhorses Calogrenant, but before his encounter with Gawain has had any decisive result, Gawain learns who he is and surrenders himself to him. Gawain, moreover, accompanies Meraugis back to the castle and there swears allegiance to him — so do Belchis and all his followers, save Meliant de Liz: — The battle with Gorvain is, at this point, renewed and Meraugis performs such deeds of valor that Lidoine pretends to be astounded that the fool she had seen in the hall was capable of them and asks to see him. As soon as the lovers are brought into each other's presence, they give themselves up to mutual embraces — much to Belchis's anger. Having pledged their allegiance, however, to Meraugis, Belchis's followers insist that Meraugis must have his lady-love — hence Belchis yields. On hearing of this, Gorvain abandons the siege, but challenges Meraugis to a duel at Arthur's court. The duel takes place, and, Gorvain having been vanquished, the two men become reconciled and renew their old friendship.

Concerning this romance, besides Friedwagner's introduction, cp., especially, G. Paris, HLF XXX, 220ff., and on the supposed Celtic episodes of Gawain's isle and the enchanted carols, F. Lot, *Romania*, XXIV, 325ff., and E. Philipot, *ibid.* XXV, 267, 269, 283, note 2. Their Celtic origin, however, is, in reality, very questionable. Friedwagner attempts, moreover, to identify the scene of the story with North Britain, but it is not at all likely that the author had any definite region in mind: he merely adopts the usual fanciful geography of the romances. Nothing in the present romance seems definitely Celtic, save perhaps one or two proper names, like *Gorvains Cadruz* (according to Lot op. cit., 326, = Welsh *Gwrvan Cadrawd*).

The whole complex of episodes in which the dwarf and L'Outredote figure is extravagant and insipid, and the romance is marred, furthermore, by some faults of construction. Note, particularly, the manner in which Gorvain, so prominent in the beginning, drops out of the action entirely for almost the whole of the remainder of the story — also, how Lidoine is almost completely forgotten by the poet in the account of the hero's wanderings down to his first combat with Gawain. Nevertheless, the *Meraugis* is, undoubtedly, one of the best of the Arthurian romances, outside of Chrétien. Especially noteworthy are the vivacity, grace and charm with which the debate of the ladies over the respective claims of Meraugis and Gorvain (ll. 855 ff.) is conducted. The incident of the Enchanted Carols (ll. 3663 ff.) is distinguished, in some degree, by the same qualities. Good too, is the episode (ll. 2815 ff.) of the Nameless City and Gawain's isle, and the account (ll. 4073 ff.) of Belchis's war with his enemies is, perhaps, the most effective description of warfare in the metrical romances of the Arthurian cycle. — The poem owes much to Chrétien, but little — and that not directly — to popular tradition. In turn, it was frequently imitated by subsequent writers — especially, in the prose romances. Cp., for example, pp. 224 below.

13. *La Vengeance de Raguidel.* First edited by C. Hippeau under the title, *Messire Gauvain ou La Vengeance de Raguidel* (Paris, 1862). This edition, however, is negligible, since the appearance of the one by Mathias Friedwagner (Halle, a. s. 1909): *La Vengeance de Raguidel.* 6182 lines. Author, Raoul — doubtless, identical with Raoul de Houdenc. Friedwagner has adopted the title which the author himself gives to the poem; the scribe of the Chantilly MS. however, calls it *Des Aniaus (On the Rings)*. Dialect, Isle-de-France (southwestern border) Date about 1200.

Besides Friedwagner's introduction cp. G. Paris; HLF, XXX, 45 ff., W. Zingerle, *Ueber Raoul de Houdenc und seine Werke* (Erlangen diss. 1880), Max Kaluza, *Ueber den Anteil des Raoul de Houdenc an der Verfasserschaft des V. Raguidel:* Festgabe *für G.*

Gröber, pp. 119ff. (Halle, 1899), Richard Rohde, *La V. Raguidel: Eine Untersuchung über ihre Beeinflussung durch Christian von Troyes und über ihren Verfasser.* Göttingen diss. (Hannover, 1904), M. Friedwagner, *Die V. Raguidel nach der Middleton-Handschrift* (Halle, 1918).

Arthur had passed Lent at Rouvelent (Ruddlan in Flintshire?), but at Easter held court at Caerleon). It was his custom not to eat before some adventure happened. One day he is greatly vexed because none happens, but orders his knights to proceed with their meal without him. That night, being sleepless, he rises and goes to the window and sees a ship with no visible crew come to shore before the palace. He goes down to the ship, alone, and finds in it a knight with a broken lance (truncheon) stuck in his body lying on his shield in a cart, with five rings on his fingers and a letter in his pouch. The letter calls for an avenger, but no one will be able to assume that rôle save the person who can pull the spear out of the corpse, and the vengeance must be executed with this same spear. Moreover, the avenger must have the aid of the knight who alone can draw the rings from the dead man's fingers. Kay, Bliobleris, Lancelot, and Tristan-Who-Never-Laughed try in vain to pull the spear out — only Gawain succeeds. Gawain, however, fails to draw away the rings; this is done by an unknown knight (really, Yder). Kay rides after this knight, but comes upon another knight who is being pursued by the one Kay is looking for. The latter slays his adversary and unhorses Kay, who is borne back to court, much humiliated. — Gawain now goes forth on his mission of vengeance. On seeking shelter for the night, he is directed by a herdsman to the castle of the Black Knight, with warnings, however, as to the owner's cruelty, of which the row of impaled heads before the castle furnish convincing proof. He sees nobody, when he first enters the castle, but partakes of an abundant meal which is set out on a table there. Whilst he is thus engaged, the Black Knight — Maduc le Noir — assails him, but unwarily consents to refrain from attacking him, until Gawain has eaten three morsels. Gawain, masticating these morsels very slowly, reaches out for his arms. His adversary, on horseback, now attacks Gawain, who is on foot, but Gawain kills his enemy's horse. In a moment, however, the Black Knight has mounted Gawain's own steed, Gringalet, whereupon Gawain persuades him to fight him on foot, for if Gringalet is killed and he (the Black Knight) is victor, he (the Black Knight) will have lost the finest horse in the world. In the end, Gawain vanquishes his opponent, who now explains his cruelty as due to an unfortunate experience in love: He had apparently won the love of the Pucele del Gaut Destroit (Maid of the Narrow or Difficult Wood), but in a tournament at her castle he had been vanquished by Gawain (after he, himself, had vanquished all his opponents) and his lady-love had then proclaimed Gawain her favored lover. Gawain, however, had eluded her advances. He knew that, if he could kill Gawain he would regain her love, but, having no acquaintance with the latter, he spared no one that he vanquished, lest Gawain might be among them. He agrees now to abandon his evil custom of giving no quarter, does Gawain homage, rides forth with him and meets with a party of his lady-love's men, who, in obedience to her command, have killed the famous white stag in his forest. These men endeavor to escape, but Gawain overtakes them, quiets their fears, and accepts their invitation to their mistress' castle. The lady of this castle, indignant on account of Gawain's former ignominious treatment of her, had arranged a window in her secret chapel with a sort of guillotine device by which she purposed killing him in a treacherous manner, but being deceived by one of her damsels into thinking that he was Kay, she did not recognize him and even told him, herself, of his previous conduct to her and of her consequently murderous intentions. He had, before this, unsuspectingly thrust his head through the window, but is henceforth on his guard. His brother, Gaheriet, was already imprisoned in this castle and was taken out every day to be scourged. At the suggestion of the lady's damsel, Marot, Gawain gets up very early the next morning on the pretext that he must continue his journey, but Marot keeps the door of the garden unlocked, so that he returns in time to rescue his brother, when the latter is led out for his daily beating. At the same time, Gawain discloses his identity.

He next flies to Maduc's castle, bearing with him Gaheriet, who is weak from his long incarceration, and Maduc learns now for the first time who had vanquished him a few days before. He aids Gawain and his brother, however, loyally, and Gawain, in the same spirit, refuses to look out for his own safety and abandons his host — only it is decided that he must escape from the castle to bring help from the outside. This is effected in a night-attack. Whilst Gawain and Gaheriet are on their way to get help, Gawain rescues a noble girl named Ydain from a would-be ravisher, Licoridon. Both rescuer and rescued fall in love with each other, and when the former is entertained at the latter's castle, they spend the night together. When the Maid of the Difficult Forest learns from Licoridon of Gawain's escape, she gives up the siege of Maduc's castle, and Maduc at once apprises Gawain of this by a messenger, who overtakes the latter, whilst he is *en route* to Arthur's court with Ydain. Somewhat further on Gawain learns from a knight of the recent mantle-test of the chastity of the ladies at Arthur's court, which only the *amie* of Caradeul (Caradoc) Briefbras stood successfully. When Gawain and Ydain join the court at Rouelent, Kay mockingly twits the former with having neglected to avenge the dead knight of the opening episode of the poem. As a matter of fact, Gawain had forgotten to take with him the broken spear (drawn from the corpse) with which alone the revenge could be accomplished. Kay intimates, too, that Ydain will prove untrustworthy, like all other women. Just then a hunchback knight, Druidain, appears at court and requests a *don* of Arthur. Arthur not only grants it, before knowing what it is to be, but compels his knights to bind themselves, also, to fulfill the boon. The *don* turns out to be a request that Ydain shall be given him. Gawain is angry and wishes to prevent the execution of the promise by force of arms. The hunchback is willing to fight the matter out on the spot with any knight, except Gawain — with Gawain he will only fight it out at another king's court. In the end, they decide to fight a duel at the court of Baudemagus a month hence. Kay again reproaches Gawain with delay in his original project of vengeance. Taking with him the truncheon which he had drawn from the corpse, Gawain now sets out for Baudemagus's court. On the way, a knight claims Ydain from him. When they agree to allow her to choose between them, she pretends to be indignant that Gawain should consent to accept such a solution of the dispute and surrenders herself to his rival. Her real motive, however, was a sensual one, which we will not describe here. After Ydain has journeyed some distance with her new lover, she forces him to go back and recover her two dogs, which she had left with Gawain. The lover proposes to Gawain that the dogs shall be permitted to choose whom they will follow, but Ydain will not agree to this, and so her lover has to sacrifice his life in a combat with Gawain. As soon as he has expired, his fickle *amie* overwhelms Gawain with manifestations of affection and disparages the dead man. Gawain receives her, however, rather coolly and makes her go ahead of him on his way to Baudemagus's court. In the duel between himself and Druidain there, he wins, but presents Ydain to the vanquished man. — After this Gawain resumes his quest to avenge the dead knight, and, as it chances, comes upon the ship which had brought the latter's corpse to Caerleon. He enters the vessel to inspect it, taking his steed in with him. Before he knows it, the ship sails away and takes him to a district of Scotland, apparently, uninhabited. Finally, he comes to a fine city. From a park near this city there issues forth a dwarf singing of Tristan and Iseult, of Paris and Helen, and he is followed by a lady whose clothes are turned wrong side outward and who is sitting on a horse with her face towards its tail. Gawain learns from her that she had loved a proud knight, named Raguidel (spelt here, Raguidan), whose deadliest enemy was Guengasonain, nephew of the King of Scotland. Now, a fay, named Lingrenote, had once held Guengasonain captive in the Nameless Castle, and, after dubbing him knight, had given him enchanted arms that no one could resist. Owing to his enchanted weapons, Guengasonian had slain Raguidel in combat, and the broken spear which gave the mortal thrust remained in the wound. Just after Raguidel's death, an unknown damsel appeared on the scene and comforted his disconsolate *amie* with the promise that her lover's death would be avenged ·by two men then living. This girl next had the body laid on the dead man's shield in a cart and taken to a haven, where it was transferred to a ship. She also put five rings on the fingers of the corpse and placed a letter in a pouch attached to it, calling for vengeance and stating the conditions for the successful execution of the same. The damsel then vannished and the vessel moved off. On the other hand, the dead knight's *amie* made the fantastic vow that she would wear only clothes turned inside out, etc., until her lover had been avenged. Gawain learns from her that the knight who drew the rings off Raguidel's finger was Yder and that he was in the forest of Tabroan — also, that Yder hates Guengasonain, not because he had killed Raguidel, but because the latter refused to give him his daughter — who loved Yder and whom Yder loved — declaring that she should marry no one save the man who should have slain him. Guengasonian, as Gawain still further learns, is always accompanied by a bear, for he knows that he can only be killed by the cooperation of two knights, and he wants a helper. Despite the girl's warnings that he can accomplish nothing alone, Gawain hunts for Raguidel's slayer and attacks him. At first he uses his own spear, instead of the truncheon that was necessary for success, but afterwards the truncheon — both without effect. His horse, maddened by a wound, throws its master and Guengasonain withdraws unharmed. In the meanwhile, Yder had seen the ship which had borne Gawain to Scotland, had recognized from certain signs that his friend was in the land, and had informed Raguidel's *amie* of the identity of her interlocutor (Gawain). He now arrived upon the scene just as Guengasonain is withdrawing and slays the latter's bear. The combat is about to be renewed when Guengasonain, of his own accord, offers to forego the advantage of his enchanted arms and armor and proposes that he and Gawain should fight it out with new equipment, as in an ordinary contest of bravery and skill, at the castle of Raguidel's *amie*. These proposals are accepted and Yder bears Guengasonain's message to his followers to bring him what he needs. Gawain slays his adversary and beheads him, whereupon, Raguidel having been avenged, his (Raguidel's) *amie* abandons the fantastic cus-

toms which she had adopted. By rights, Guengasonain's daughter
and his estates now belonged to Gawain, but, in response to Yder's
entreaties — her barons having given their consent — Gawain renounces her in favor of his friend. He leaves the happy pair in the
enjoyment of their honeymoon and travels slowly towards Arthur's
court. The bridal couple do not set out for the same destination
until eight days later, but they arrive the same day. The king
now learns how Raguidel has been avenged and the people of the
court award the credit for the exploit to Gawain.

This rambling romance is inferior in interest to the *Meraugis*.
It differs from the latter especially in its rather cynical attitude
towards women, and this difference, even more than some supposed
differences of language and metre, has caused certain eminent scholars to deny the identity of the Raoul who wrote it with Raoul de
Houdenc. Cp., for example, G. Paris, HLF. XXX, 48, Foerster,
Lancelot, p. CX, Gröber, *Grundriss*, II, I, 512. But the excessive
deference for the fair sex, in the spirit of the *amour courtois*, which
marks the *Meraugis*, may well have been put on, and the divergence just noted can hardly be regarded as an adequate ground for
denying the identity of authorship. The same thing applies to
the variant accounts of Yder's fight with the bear in the two poems.
This identity has been upheld by Friedwagner, and, before him,
by P. Meyer, *Romania*, XXI, 415 (1892). — Similarly, certain
scholars have seen two hands in the present romance, the line 3356
(just after Gawain and Gaheriet's escape from the castle) being
taken as the beginning of a second poet's work. On this controversy see Friedwagner's edition, pp. CXIff. I agree with this
editor that the poem is throughout the work of one man. For
the debate concerning the relative chronology of the *Meraugis* and
V. Raguidel cp. *op. cit.*, p. CLIII, including note. To the present
writer, the lines (1273ff., 3186ff.) in the latter concerning Meraugis plainly presuppose the former. What was said above of the
nomenclature and sources of the *Meraugis* is true, also, of the
V. Raguidel.

An abbreviated Dutch version *(De Wrake van Ragisel)* of
the *V. Raguidel* is preserved in the fourteenth century Dutch *Lance-*

lot Vol. II, Book III, ll. 11235—14136, and other fragments of the same version, apparently, have been discovered elsewhere. On editions of these Dutch versions and relation to our romance cp. Friedwagner, pp. CXCVIIf.

14. *La Mule sanz Frain (The Mule without a Bridle)*.

This is the title which is given to the romance by the scribe of the unique MS. No. 354 of the Bibliotheca Bongarsiana (Municipal Library) at Berne (Switzerland) and which is generally used in modern references to the poem. The author, himself, however, calls it, ll. 18f., "une aventure de la damoisele a la mure" — *mure* being a variant for *mule*. It was first edited by M. Meon in his *Nouveau Recueil de Fabliaux et Contes*, vol. I (Paris, 1823), and, separately, since by Boleslas Orlowski, *La Demoisele a la Mule, conte en vers du cycle arthurien par Paien de Maisieres* (Paris, 1911) and by Raymond Thompson Hill, as a Yale thesis, *La Mule sanz Frain, an Arthurian Romance by Paiens de Maisieres* (Baltimore, 1911). 1136 lines.

Besides the edition and G. Paris, HLF, XXX, 68f., cp. G. L. Kittredge, *A Study of Gawain and the Green Knight*, pp. 231—256 (Cambridge, 1916). Author, Paien de Maisieres. Dialect, Champagne. Date, early years of the thirteenth century.

A girl appears at Arthur's court on a bridleless mule, and craves a champion to recover for her the missing bridle. The rewards she promises the successful knight are "li baisiers et l'autre chose" (l. 107). The mule will bear him to the place where the bridle is kept. Kay first tries the adventure. He is taken by the mule, first, through a forest infested with lions, tigers, etc., which, out of reverence for the mule's mistress, however, do not molest him — rather kneel down before his mount — secondly, through a valley swarming with reptiles, and, thirdly (after he and his beast have refreshed themselves at a fountain), to a broad, deep, stream, which can only be crossed on an iron rod. Kay is afraid to traverse this and returns to Carduel, greatly downcast. — Gawain now undertakes the adventure and has the same experiences as Kay, until he reaches the stream — the Devil's River, as the author here calls it. He crosses, however, this stream and comes to the castle for which he is seeking. The row outside the castle, however, of impaled heads of unsuccessful champions is not encouraging. Moreover, as the castle is whirling about incessantly, it is difficult to penetrate. Nevertheless, Gawain accomplishes this, although the descending castle-gate lops off about one-half of the mule's tail. Inside, he at first finds nobody in the streets of the castle, but afterwards comes upon a dwarf. He questions the dwarf, but gets no answer. Then a shaggy *vilain* comes up out of a cave and, after taking him to a house, treats him in a hospitable manner and proposes to submit himself to decapitation that evening, if Gawain will do the same thing the next morning. Gawain consents, but the decapitated *vilain* picks up his head, walks off, and descends into his cave. The following day Gawain submits his neck in the same way, but, after testing his courage, the *vilain* lets him go free.

To win back the bridle, Gawain now has to overcome two lions, a knight, and two serpents. Having performed these exploits, he is conducted to the lady of the castle by the dwarf who had previously refused to speak to him. This lady it turns out was a sister of the girl who had been deprived of the bridle. She entertains him and offers to marry him, but he declines. Gawain is now given the bridle, and, as he quits the castle, observes that its inhabitants are out of their caves and are rejoicing, because they were free to occupy their houses once more, Gawain having killed the lions, etc., that had kept them terrified. After he had returned to court and restored the bridle to its owner, she bestowed many kisses upon him and rode away, although Guinevere and the rest urged her to remain.

At the beginning of his poem, the author expresses a preference for the old ways-very appropriately, for there is not an incident in his romance that had not already been used by his predecessors, especially, Chrétien and Chrétien's first two continuators. This being the case, there seems to us no need of discussing the work as if it embodied some Celtic tale. It is simply another instance of old *motifs* in a new combination — as it happens, of the most awkward kind.

There is, furthermore, no reason to doubt that G. Paris, Kittredge, etc., are right in regarding the episodes in *Diu Crône*, ll. 12601 ff., which correspond substantially to *La Mule sanz Frain*, as direct adaptations from the latter. Orlowski argues that they were derived from a common source. Furthermore, it seems safe to say that no folk-lore significance should be attached to the fact that the object lost was a bridle. Damsels in the romances had often been represented as riding on mules — so they actually do, not infrequently, in Spain down to the present day — and in an Arthurian romance a (rich) bridle would serve as well as anything else to start a knight off on a quest, should a lady desire it.

15. *Le Chevalier a l'Espee.* Edited, with this title, from the unique MS. 354 of the Bibliotheca Bongarsiana (Municipal Library) at Berne, (Switzerland) by the following scholars. 1. M. Meon: *Nonveau Recueil de Fabliaux et Contes*, I, 127 ff. (Paris, 1823), 2. W. J. A. Jonckbloet, *Roman van Walewein*, II, 35 ff. (Leiden, 1846—8), 3. Edward Cooke Armstrong, Johns Hopkins dissertation (Baltimore, 1900). 1206 lines. Author, unknown. Dialect Isle-de-France. (So Armstrong — not Picard, as Gröber, II, I, 519, states.) Date, first decade of the thirteenth century. HLF., XIX, 704 ff. — *Ibid.*, G. Paris, XXX, 67 f.

Gawain, overtaken by night in a forest, meets a knight who invites him to his castle the next day. He accepts and the host goes ahead to prepare for his reception. On his way to the castle Gawain is warned by shepherds that no one who goes there ever returns, but he pays no attention to these warnings. That night Gawain's host puts him in bed with his daughter and the bedfellows embrace and kiss one another. When Gawain, however, wishes to go further, the girl admonishes him of the danger he is incurring. At first he does not heed her — so a sword descends from above the bed and slightly wounds him. This happens twice, and Gawain thereafter desists from the effort. In the morning his host is surprised to find him alive — then gives him his daughter in marriage. After the wedding Gawain takes his wife away to see his friends. They had not gone far, however, before she wants her dogs, which she had neglected to bring with her — so Gawain goes back to fetch them, leaving her in the woods. On his return with the dogs, he beholds her going off with a new knight. He halts this knight, but when the girl is asked to choose between the two men, she chooses the stranger; on the other hand, the dogs follow Gawain. The girl then tells her new lover that she must have her dogs. When he demands them of Gawain, however, they turn away from him and the girl and still follow Gawain. Gawain and the knight now fight and the former is victorious. Seeing this, the girl wishes to return to Gawain, but he will not permit her and utters, at the same time, some sarcastic remarks on the ingratitude of women.

It will be observed that this romance, whose main merit is its brevity, consists obviously of two parts — the second of which (imitated from the *Vengeance de Raguidel*, ll. 4482ff.) is a sort of fabliau. G. Paris (p. 68) speaks of the tale embodied in the first part as, doubtless, of Welsh origin, but the *motif* (known in folk-lore studies as that of The Imperious Host) is, by no means, confined to Celtic lands. Cp. Kittredge's discussion of *The Carl of Carlisle* in his *Gawain and the Green Knight*, pp. 257ff. It was probably from the present romance that Heinrich von dem Türlin derived the similar episode in *Diu Crône*, ll. 8116ff. The author of the present romance mentions (l. 19) Chrétien de Troyes.

16. *Gliglois.* Preserved formerly in the unique MS. fr. L. IV, 33 (not 23, as G. Paris states), of the Royal Library at Turin. This MS. was virtually destroyed in the fire of January 26, 1904. The poem has not yet been edited and is known to scholars, in general, only through G. Paris's analysis, HLF, XXX, 161ff., which is based on W. Foerster's copy of the original MS. Its author is unknown. Paris says nothing concerning the dialect of the romance. He assigns it to the "deuxieme époque," of the Arthurian romances, by which he means, I presume, the early years of the thirteenth century. 2860 lines, according to W. Foerster, *Zs. f. rom. Ph. II, 78*, who calls it *Giglois*.

The hero is the son of a German noble who comes to Arthur's court and is turned over to Gawain for instruction in chivalry. Shortly thereafter, a girl who was appropriately named Beauty

— joint-heiress, with her sister, of the domain of Landemore — arrives there, too. She becomes an attendant on the queen and Gawain courts her, but she rejects him; nevertheless, he is urged by Guinevere to persevere. Consequently, he gets his squire, Gliglois, to enter her service, so that he may constantly keep his master in her mind, but the squire falls in love with the girl, himself. Gliglois is charged with the care of the falcons at the palace and one morning, whilst so employed in the palace garden, Beauty requests him to help her to lace up her *chemise*. Propinquity has its usual effect and the scene ends by the young man's making a declaration of love to her. Though really reciprocating his passion, she replies most scornfully and bids him never enter her presence again. He is fearfully downcast at this, but takes heart again, when he observes that she does not betray his audacity to Gawain. — The Lady of Proud Castle (Chatel Orgueilleux) holds a great tourney. Gawain goes there, hoping by his prowess to win Beauty's heart. Gliglois wanted to go, too, but Gawain ordered him to stay at home and take care of the hawks. On hearing that Gawain is to attend the tourney, Beauty objects to being in his company and resolves to stay at home, also, unless, as she tells Gliglois, some other knight will escort her. The squire gets the required escort for her, but afterwards decides to accompany them, himself, on foot. Owing to the hot weather, in the course of the day, he strips off successively his coat and his shoes — his feet were bleeding from the latter — but, notwithstanding his sufferings, his mistress shows herself pitiless toward him, reproaching him with not having stayed at home. She does not even allow the knight to lend him a horse. At a monastery, however, she paid a monk to compose a letter for her (in Latin) — the man made his living exclusively in this way — and she sends Gliglois with it and a ring to her sister, bidding him do whatever is set down in the letter. She now rejoins her escort and tells him that she has sent Gliglois home. When Gliglois reaches his destination, he gives the letter and the ring to Beauty's sister, who gets the chaplain to read the letter to her. As it turned out, the contents of this epistle were to the effect that the writer (Beauty) loved Gliglois above all

men and had been merely testing him by her seeming severity —
moreover, that she wishes her sister to do him all honor and equip
him for the tourney.   The sister complies with these instructions
and even serves him as an attendant — somewhat to the embar-
rasement of our hero.   After he has received from this lady the
arms of a knight, he appears to have been accepted as a member
of the order of knights, in every respect.   He goes *incognito* to the
tournament, wins the prize — a falcon which Beauty's escort had
put up — reveals his name to the queen and is adopted into Arthur's
retinue.   Beauty had by this time confessed her love for him to
the queen, whereupon Gawain drops his own suit in favor of his
former squire and the two young people are married.

It will be observed that the supernatural element is entirely
wanting in this romance.   Barring some of the conventional exag-
gerations of the *amour courtois*, it is a faithful picture of the
actual life of the time, and G. Paris commends it as one of the
best of the *genre*.   Both he and Foerster deny (properly, I believe) any connection between this poem and the *Bel Inconnu* group
of romances.   Schofield, however, *Studies on the Libeaus Desconus*,
pp. 180 ff., still maintained that such a connection existed.   Manifestly, this romance is not derived from a folk-tale.

17. *Yder*.   Edited by Heinrich Gelzer from the unique MS.
EE 426 of the University Library at Cambridge (England): *Der
altfranzösische Yderroman nach der einzigen bekannten Handschrift, mit Einleitung, Anmerkungen und Glossar, zum ersten
Male herausgegeben* (Dresden, 1913): Gesellschaft für romanische
Literatur, Band 31.   6769 lines preserved.   Author unknown.   His
language is that of Western Normandy and he wrote probably
in the second decade of the thirteenth century.   For Bibliography
see the end of this article.

The MS. is fragmentary at the beginning, but indications
in the poem enable us to reconstruct the missing narrative as follows: The hero is the offspring of an intrigue between Nuc, Duke
of Germany, and a noble lady at Cardoil.   After cohabitation they
break a ring into halves, each retaining a half (as a pledge of mutual
fidelity).   Nuc, however, deserts his mistress.   When Yder is seven-

teen years old, he goes in search of his father, but seeks him in vain
through many lands. — During these wanderings he falls in love
with Queen Guenloie at her capital, Carvain (Caerwent in Wales?).
She returns his love, but requires him to prove by feats of arms
that he is worthy of her. Leaving Carvain, he engages himself
as squire to a knight who had got lost in a wood, whilst hunting,
and slays two knights that assail his companion. From this point
on the narrative is preserved.

The knight turns out to be King Arthur. Yder, wishing
to be knighted and hoping for some opportunity to distinguish himself, goes to the king's court at Pomfret, but Arthur has forgotten
him. Moreover, he is a witness of Arthur's refusal to aid the Lady
of Maidens' Castle (Chastel as Puceles) against the Black Knight,
who is besieging her, on the ground that he (Arthur) must first
subdue the rebel, Talac de Rogemont. These incidents so disgust
our hero that he quits Arthur's court and is dubbed knight, at his
own request, by King Ivenant, whom he chances to meet. As
a condition, however, of granting him this favor, Ivenant requires
him to submit to the test of temptation from his wife at his castle.
In the sequel, Yder resists that lady's blandishments with even
unnecessary firmness, for by a well-directed kick in the stomach
he lays the temptress prostrate. When the husband hears of Yder's
behavior, he confers knighthood on the latter, who now proceeds
on his way. Luguein, son of a poor knight, at whose house Yder
spends the night, is accepted as the latter's spuire. Learning from
his squire that Talac de Rogemont's castle, which Arthur is bele-
aguering, is not far off, our hero owing to his grudge against the
king, resolves to go to Talac's assistance. The sweethearts of the
combatants were present to witness the fight — among them,
Guenloie, who had all along kept herself secretly informed as to
her lover's movements. Yder unhorses Kay (Quoi) and others in the
battle-defeats particularly an attempt of Kay's to destroy him —
and wins general admiration. Even Gawain finds his match in
him, but Kay, by a treacherous spear-thrust, leaves him for dead,
and Luguein carries him off the field. Discouraged by this loss,
Talac submits to Arthur. Guenloie is in despair when she comes

upon her wounded lover with Longuein, but, perceiving that he is not dead, she renders him first aid and has him taken to a nunnery, where a clever physician soon heals him. Arthur visits the nunnery and, supported by Gawain's entreaties, finally persuades Yder to become a knight of the Round Table.

In a hand-to-hand struggle, Yder overcomes a bear, which had invaded Guinevere's chamber, and hurls it into the castle moat through an open window.

Guenloie besieges Rogemont, because she thinks that her lover will come to Talac's aid and she will thus have a chance to see him. Arthur refuses to help Talac, but Gawain and Yvain, without letting Yder know, go to Talac's assistance. Angry at their secret departure, but not knowing where they are, Yder goes forth alone, escorts out of the forest a girl whose lover had been slain — he takes the corpse, also, along with them — but *en route* has an adventure at a castle — has words there — first with an insolent dwarf whom he finds roasting a crane on a spit, and then with the dwarf's master, named Cliges. Cliges and his lady, it turns out, had been in Guenloie's service, but the former had incurred her displeasure by censuring her for betraying too clearly her affection for Yder.

When Yder reaches Rogemont, Guenloie had raised the siege, but her own tent was still there, and a knight was courting one of her damsels, who was inclined to favor him — only he would not disclose his name to her. At the girl's request, Yder tries to force him to do so. In the combat a purse which contained the half-ring given by Yder's father to his mother at the time of his conception was cut away and fell to the ground. The anxiety to recover it which Yder displays leads to inquiries concerning the purse from his opponent, and, in the end, this opponent produces the other half of the ring and is thus revealed as Yder's father. They now leave Guenloie's damsel and go to seek Yder's mother by way of Cliges's dwelling and Arthur's court.

Arthur becomes jealous of Yder and Guinevere — proceeds indirectly to test her by asking her, if he, himself, were dead and she were compelled, on pain of death, to marry again, whom

would she choose. She, at last, answers reluctantly: "Yder". He
determines now to do away with his supposed rival — rides out
in search of adventures with Gawain, Yvain, Kay and Yder, being
all the while on the lookout to slay the last-named. They come
upon Guinloie, who tells them of a pair of giants in Malvern Wood,
near Worcester. These giants possess a wonderful knife and whoever brings her this knife may claim her hand in marriage. Arthur
and his knights go to this place, and after Kay, who was sent forward to reconnoitre, had been frightened almost to death by the
size of the monsters, the king ordered Yder to advance into the
house, hoping that he would be slain, but, as a matter of fact,
he slays both giants. When Yder is thirsty that night, however,
Kay gives him water from a poisoned spring and his body swells
up beyond recognition. Two sons of the King of Ireland chance
to be passing by. One of them (Miroet) has great skill in medi-
cine and saves Yder's life. When Miroet exposes at court the true
cause of our hero's illness, Gawain and Nuc wish to kill Kay, but
Yder arrives and, on Arthur's solicitation, generously establishes
peace.

Yder had brought off the giant's knife, so that Gueneloie
now consents to marry him and the two are wedded by the archbishop of Warwick. Their union removed all cause for Arthur's
jealous suspicions and he, accordingly, made Yder king. Gawain
now brought Yder's mother and grandmother to Carvain and the
hero's parents marry.

Of particular interest in Yder are ll. 2565 ff., the list of ancient
heroines (taken evidently from Ovid) who were the victims of
love, and ll. 3684 ff., a fierce denunciation of monks and the assertion that love is superior to religious observances.

William of Malmesbury's, *De Antiquitate Glastomiensis Ecclesiae*, Migne's *Patrologia Latina*, vol. 179, col. 1701 (reproduced
by Gelzer, pp. LIVf.), tries to connect Yder's bear-adventure with
the founding of Glastonbury abbey, but the passage is, doubtless,
a late interpolation, based on the present or some earlier French
Yder-romance. Cp. W. W. Newell, PMLA, XVIII, 496ff. (1903).
For an analysis and discussion of the *Yder* see, still further, G.

224   *Evolution of Arthurian Romance*

Paris, HLF, XXX, 199ff. Before bringing out his edition of
the *Yder*, Gelzer had already published a (Strassburg) dissertation
on the subject, which was later incorporated into the Introduction
to his edition. This dissertation is entitled: *Einleitung zu einer
kritischen Ausgabe des altfranzösischen Yderromans* (Halle, 1908).

18. Mannessier's continuation of Chrétien's *Perceval*, Cp.
I, 304 ff.

19. Gerbert's continuation of the same. Cp. I, 307 ff.

20. *Durmart*. Edited by Edmund Stengel from the unique
MS. 113 of the Municipal Library at Berne (Switzerland), *Li
Romane de Durmart le Galois. Altfranzösisches Rittergedicht, zum
ersten Mal herausgegeben. Bibliothek des Litterarischen Vereins
in Stuttgart*, CLVI (Tübingen, 1873). 15998 lines. Author,
unknown. Dialect, border of Normandy and Picardy. Date, probably second quarter of the thirteenth century.

Leonhard Kirchrath: *Li romans de Durmart le Galois in
seinem Verhältnisse zu Meraugis de Portlesguez und den Werken
Chrestiens de Troyes*. Marburg diss. 1884, G. Paris, HLF, XXX,
141 ff. Grober, II, I, 516 f.

Durmart's father, Jozefent, was a king in Gales (Wales) and
by his marriage with Andelise (a Danish princess) he had also
acquired the realm of Denmark. His capital is called "la blanche
cite en Gales." Our hero, in his youth, was turned over to a seneschal to be brought up, but a clandestine love-affair develops between him and the seneschal's pretty wife. Jozefent threatens to
cast his son off or imprison him, if he will not break off this
affair, but for a long while, however, the young man is deaf to
remonstrances and devotes his whole time to his *amie*. At length,
however, as he wearies of her, he becomes repentant, and returns
to his parents. — When Durmart was received into the order of
knighthood, a great feast was held in honor of the occasion. Now,
that day Durmart overhears a *vilain* exclaim on seeing him, "I never
saw such a marvel (as Durmart's beauty) but once before." On
inquiry, Durmart learns that the man is referring to the Queen of
Ireland. The *vilain* adds that Durmart and this lady should be
lovers. There are many queens, however, in Ireland and the *vilain*

knows neither the name nor the residence of this particular queen —
so is unable to guide the young prince to her. Nevertheless, Durmart, his fancy having been inflamed by the stranger's description
of her beauty, determines to seek her.[6] — On the first night of
his journey he comes upon a tree in a forest illuminated from top
to bottom with candles and a child at the top.[7] At the same time,
the voice of an invisible person bids him beware to obey its commands whenever this wonder is repeated. — He lands in Ireland,
inquires in vain concerning the queen, but, by chance, meets her,
without knowing who she is, and tells her of his love. She does
not make herself known to him, but promises to take him to the
object of his adoration. She first brings him to Landoc, where
Cardroain has proclaimed a contest, to prove that his *amie*, Ydain
de Landoc, is superior to the *amies* of all other knights, a sparrow-
hawk being the prize in this contest. On the road to Landoc, the
queen of Ireland guards Durmart, whilst he is asleep from the
attacks of a hostile big knight — whose name is Nogant, as we
learn later — and wakes him with three kisses. The queen had
expected this big knight to act as her champion in the contest,
but he shows the white feather, and it is finally Durmart who
slays Cardroain and wins for her the prize. He himself, however,
had been wounded in the fight, but is cured by a damsel whom he
comes upon in a red tent, playing chess with her brothers. He
overthrows Fel de la Garde, who had captured this damsel's lover,
Gladineaz, and sends him as a prisoner to his (Durmart's) mother.[8]
Our hero's mind is so full of his (as he imagined) unseen mistress
that he loses his way, and does not get back to the red tent, where
he had left the girl with the sparrow-hawk (really the queen). —

---

[6] J. Loth, *Mabinogion*, II[2], 98, says that love for a person one
has never seen is a Celtic *motif*. But it is found in folktales all over
the world. For the literature of the subject, cp. T. P. Cross, MPh.
XII, 598, note 4 and 612, note 3 (1915).
   [7] Imitated from Wauchier's continuation to Chrétien's *Perceval*,
LL, 34 412 ff.
   [8] It is a peculiar feature of this romance that the hero, here and
elsewhere, sends his prisoners to his mother.

He finds shelter, however, at the castle of Brun de Branlant. Here
he learns, for the first time, that the girl just mentioned was, really,
the Queen of Ireland. On quitting Brun de Branlant's castle, he
learns, still further, that Brun de Morois has seized Guinevere,
whilst she is under the protection of Yder, son of Nut, and carried
her off to his castle. Durmart goes to this place, vanquishes its
lord, and makes him surrender himself first to Guinevere, then
to Arthur, and next to his (Durmart's) mother. Finally, he is
to do homage to Arthur. Before his departure on these errands,
Brun treats his victorious adversary with the greatest friendliness.

Durmart next hears from Fel de la Garde of the Queen of Ireland's grief on finding herself separated from her lover (Durmart),
and, on Fel's advice, he decides to seek information concerning
her whereabouts at Glastonbury, where Arthur's court is assembled.
He crosses the sea for this purpose, and, contrary to a hermit's
warning, elects the most adventurous route to his destination —
conquers the fifty robber knights of Roche Brune (Brown Rock),
— visits the castle of the Ten Maidens (who, with their ten *amis*,
give their lives up to amusement), and participates, along with
Lancelot, Perceval, etc., in a two-days' tourney at the Blanches
Mores (White Moors). Geogenant, the handsomest and best knight
of the castle just mentioned, points out to Durmart the chief
knights in Arthur's host. Durmart, of course, wins the tourney,
but does not claim as his bride either of the girls whose fates were at
stake in this affair, his mind being still wholly occupied with the
Queen of Ireland, as we observe from his long soliloquy. On arriving at Glastonbury, he is warmly welcomed by Arthur, Guinevere,
etc., but will not become a knight of the Round Table, because
of his uncompleted quest for his ladylove. He overthrows here,
however, a knight, Gladain, who, like his whole train, is clad in
green and bears a green lance. — He next comes to the dominions
of the Queen of Ireland, which Nogant has recently devastated.
He (Nogant) is now besieging the queen, herself, in Limeri (Limerick), the principal warrior on her side being Procidas. Durmart joins Procidas's army at Limerick Mill near the town and
intelligence of her lover's arrival is soon conveyed to the queen.

In the first encounter, owing to Durmart's valor, victory falls to his side, and Nogant now calls King Arthur to his aid, on the pretext that the people who hold Limerick are infidels. Arthur, therefore, summons his vassals together, including Josefent, Durmart's father, and proceeds to Limerick. Here Kay receives as a boon from Arthur permission, with fifty knights, to make the first attack on the enemy. Durmart, however, unhorses him and wins the admiration of Gawain, Lancelot, etc., who make game of Kay. Josefent, recognizing the admired knight as his son, prevails upon Arthur to invite the Queen of Ireland and her barons to a parley. Angry at this, Nogant vilifies the queen still further — asserts that she does not believe in God, but, seeing that his falsehoods are unavailing, he evades a trial by combat by slipping away on a dromedary (in Ireland!). After his flight the Queen of Ireland — whose name, as we learn now for the first time, was Fenise — pardons his men. On the other hand, she tells Durmart that she will grant any boon that he may request of her and she proves as good as her word, when he asks for herself. The wedding is preceded by some rather broad jokes, on the part of the barons, in regard to the impending nuptials. In connection with his description of the ceremony itself, the poet argues against those who contend that a fine lover should not marry his *amie*. — Later on Durmart, pondering over the transitoriness of our life on earth, founds abbeys and performs all sorts of acts of beneficence. — Once again, still later, whilst lost in the forest during a hunt, he has the vision of the illuminated tree and the child (who bears five wounds in his hands and feet), and the voice of the invisible speaker declares that he will not comprehend the meaning of this vision, until he goes to Rome and confesses himself to the Pope. Accordingly, Durmart journeys to Rome, accompanied by his wife and parents, and he and his father deliver the city from the pagan army with which it is beset, at the time of their arrival, and they there confess themselves to the Holy Father, who expounds Durmart's vision as follows: The tree is the world, the candles (some of which were bright, and some not), are the people, the child is Christ. They all return now to Bangot (Bangor) in Gales

(Wales) and thence Durmart and his spouse pass over to Limerick, to take possession of their dominions in those parts. The poet concludes his work with a fervent eulogy of *largesse* and courtesy and a corresponding malediction upon their opposites.

As Stengel and Paris have observed, five divisions are distinguishable in the poem. The first of these, which ends with Durmart's abandonment of the seneschal's wife, is, as it were, the prologue to the romance, the last, which covers the incidents after his marriage, the epilogue. The author displays more skill than is usual in this *genre* in making the sparrow-hawk contest the centre of the story proper. In connection therewith the hero meets the other characters of most importance — the heroine and Nogant — but is not aware of their identity. Later, however, in succession, at turning-points in the development of the narrative, the identity of these two characters with the principal participants in the sparrow-hawk incident is revealed. By this handling of the story the interest of suspense is gained and at the same time, unity of plot.

Stengel emphasizes in the present romance the harmonious union of the ideals of mediaeval chivalry with Christian morality. He exaggerates, however, the ethical purpose of its author. The moral tone of the story, is, undeniably, purer than is the case with most writings of this class, but not more so, for instance, than in *Escanor*, and the pious end of the hero is, of course, merely a mediaeval convention.

The reader will have observed that the supernatural element is almost wholly absent from *Durmart*. It accords, doubtless, with this realistic tendency that the author has given us so many happy vignettes of actual contemporary manners. In particular, no other romancer, perhaps, has exerted himself in the same degree to portray his knights as practising the very last refinements of courtesy.

The best part of the poem is, unquestionably, its prologue — the picture of the youthful hero, sowing his wild oats in the affair with the seneschal's wife — the description of the life, devoted to pleasure the live-long day, which the couple lead together — then the growing coldness that results from satiety on the part of the lover — he does not even kiss his mistress at parting — and her resignation: "I was not the first to ask for love and I shall not be the last." This is one of the few episodes in Arthurian romance that might have been penned in any age.

21. *Li Chevaliers as Deus Espees.* The romance is so named at the end of the text in the unique MS. 12 603 (fonds fr., Bibl. Nat.), and this is the title adopted by Wendelin Foerster in the only edition (Halle, 1877) of the work that has been published. Nevertheless, it is sometimes called from its hero, *Meriadeus (Meriadeuc)*. 12353 lines. Author, unknown. Dialect, Isle-de-France (border of Picardy). Date, early part of the thirteenth century. It is earlier than the Pseudo-Robert prose *Merlin*-continuation (about 1235), for it is manifestly in imitation of the present work that Balaain in that romance is called "Li chevaliers as deus espees."

A. Mussafia, "Li Chevaliers as deus espees," *Zs. f. österreichische Gymnasien*, XXVIII, 197 ff. (1877), G. Paris, HLF, XXX, 237 ff., Gröber's *Grundriss*, II, 515 f., Robert Thedens, *Li Chevaliers as Deus Espees in seinem Verhältnis zu seinen Quellen, insbesondere zu den Romanen Crestiens von Troyes.* Göttingen diss. 1908.

Arthur holds high court in Cardueil at Pentecost. At his table sat ten kings and all his 366 knights, save Gawain, Tor (son of Ares), and Gifflet (Gierflet). A messenger from King Ris d'Outre-Ombre (Geoffrey of Monmouth's Ritho) comes in and demands, on his master's behalf, Arthur's beard. Ris wishes to add it to his mantle, which is woven from the beards of conquered kings. Arthur, of course, rejects the demand with indignation and prepares to go to Caradigan (here spelt, Garadigan, and identical with Cardigan in Wales) which Ris has been investing and which he actually captures before his messenger's return. Just after he has received this messenger's report, a dwarf appears before Ris, bringing him a rich horse-chain from his (Ris's) *amie*, the damsel of Yseland (for *Ireland?*) and summoning him to carry out his covenant with her, — viz. that he would send her Arthur as her prisoner. Ris now declares that he wants some one to take — by

night — the horse-chain to the Waste Chapel from which no one
had ever returned and bring back a portion of its altar-cloth: To
whoever should do this, he would grant any boon that such a person might ask. All are silent until the captive lady of Caradigan,
a beautiful girl, speaks up and offers to undertake the adventure.
Ris assents reluctantly to this and she rides away to the Waste
Chapel through a forest full of fearful sights and sounds — e. g.
she sees two fiends playing with the head of a dead man, in the
midst of thunder and lightning. After she reaches the chapel
(which we learn later is at the Fearful Castle) a weeping knight,
with the corpse of another knight, comes in, and, hiding behind
the altar, she observes him inter the body in the chapel and hears
him asseverate, as he does so, that no one will ever unloose the dead
man's sword, except some one of equal beauty and excellence. He
meets other weeping knights outside, assures them that he has
performed their dead lord's commands, and departs. The lady of
Caradigan now executes her commission, but, in addition, she removes the earth from the newly-buried corpse and ungirds the sword
attached to it and ties it to herself, after which she discovers, to
her astonishment, that she cannot again untie it. She now re-
calls, however, the words (cited above) of the weeping knight about
this sword. When she anounces her success at Ris's court, he is
fearful lest the boon she will ask for may be to wed him, but she
really petitions him for her inherited estates and he is obliged by
his promise to evacuate them. She goes now to Carduel to ask
a boon of Arthur, too, viz., that he should give her as her husband
the man who could unloose from her the sword which she had obtained at the Waste Chapel. Kay, Yvain, and Dodinel le Sauvage
fail in the attempt, but the following day the hero of the poem,
who, as we subsequently learn, was Meriadeuc (Meriadoc), son
of Bleheri, turns up, is admitted to knighthood on a previous re-
commendation of Gawain's and the third day succeeds in the test.
He had been a squire to Gawain, but his real name being unknown
to every one — himself included — Kay confers on him the nickname, "The Knight of the Two Swords," by which he is henceforth known. Immediately, however, after untying the sword, the

new knight rides off, nobody can say whither — much to the mortification of the Lady of Caradigan. Arthur despatches Yvain, Ellit, Sagremor (Saigremor), and Dodinel to fetch him back, but he unhorses them all. After this he attends various tournaments and is victor in all.

One day whilst Arthur is dining in his hall, a band of ten men, with loud lamentations, bring in a wounded knight and set him down before the king. The same thing is repeated with eight other wounded knights, yet still no one vouchsafes a word of explanation to the king or his courtiers. Next twenty men bring in a tenth wounded knight, who, after urgent solicitation and promises from Arthur that he would not be harmed, divulges the fact that he is King Ris and that the other knights are his followers — moreover, that the Knight of the Two Swords had vanquished them all and sent them to Arthur. This makes the Lady of Caradigan urge the king all the more eagerly to obtain the hero for her as her husband. After Ris and his men are cured, they proclaim their allegiance to Arthur and depart. At the same time Arthur sets out for Glamorgan (Clamorgan). Meeting Gawain on the way he tells him of our hero's exploits and after they have joined the queen at Glamorgan sends him in search of the young knight. Perceval, Yvain, etc., are to participate, also, in this quest. But before Gawain can quit Glamorgan, he rides out early one beautiful morning with no equipment save his lance and shield, and, as it happens, encounters Brien des Illes, whom his lady has declined to accept, until he has proved himself superior to Gawain (reckoned the best knight in the world). On learning Gawain's name — for, under no circumstances would Gawain ever conceal it, if questioned — Brien attacks him, despite his unarmed condition, and leaves him for dead on the field. Gawain, however, recovers himself sufficiently to climb upon his horse and ride back to Glamorgan. After having sent damsels to inquire why he did not appear at court, the king and queen go to him and on hearing of the story of his encounter and his wounding, they are filled with grief. The king now has to have his nephew guarded to prevent him from arising too soon from his

sick-bed to go in search of the knight who had wounded him. At
last, however, Gawain steals away from Glamorgan on this errand,
vowing, also, that he would not return until he had found the
Knight of the Two Swords. — At the end of the first day he comes
upon a pilgrim who gives him food. This man turns out to be
Brien's father and falls into deep dejection, on learning that Gawain
is still alive and that his son, accordingly, has not really won the
inheritance of the Lady (Queen) of the Isles. He is still incredulous, however, and determines to make inquiry in Britain. Next
Gawain is entertained by a hermit, who proves to be his enemy's
uncle and who, like the father, manifests profound disappointment
that Gawain is still alive. Indeed, the hermit, with the assistance of a *vilain*, was about to kill his guest, whilst the latter was
asleep, but, conscience-stricken at the last moment, refrains from
doing so. Gawain, the following day, meets a messenger of Brien's
who tells him of the impending wedding of his master and the
Queen of the Isles and, not knowing who he is, invites him to the
ceremony. On their way to the wedding, the two stop over at the
castle of a cousin of Brien's and he, too, is plunged in woe, on
hearing that Gawain is not dead. Indeed, he tries to kill Gawain,
but is unhorsed. — Gawain next comes to the castle of a knight-
governor of the Port-Castle — whose lands have been ravaged by
Gerneman of Northumberland, because this knight's daughter refused to marry him. Gerneman had given them a year's respite
to find a champion — otherwise at the end of that time, they
would have to surrender their estates and the girl be turned over
to his followers for outrage. Gawain has been struck with the girl's
beauty, and offers to be her champion, if she will grant him her
love. Undeterred by the spectacle of the impaled heads of 43
previous champions, he fights Gerneman and kills him. On his
return to the castle, the daughter of its lord brings him beautiful
clothing and ornaments and he, in turn, kisses her frequently.

That night the lady of the castle, herself, brought her daughter
to Gawain's chamber, but, after many ardent caresses, the girl denies
him the last favor, because she has dedicated her virginity, she
says, to Gawain, the best of all knights. Gawain now discloses

his identity to her, but she will not believe him until she has received confirmation of his statement at Arthur's court, and finally she leaves the room, still a virgin. The next day she goes to the court at Karahes (Garahes) and satisfies herself that her champion was, indeed, Gawain. In the interim, however, the latter had gone on to Rades, capital of the Lady of the Isles, where Brien's wedding and coronation were to be. When the people have assembled for the ceremony, Brien proclaims that he has killed Gawain. On hearing this declaration, the Knight of the Two Swords, who was in the throng, springs forward and wishes to avenge the slain man, since, as he affirms, he, himself, stands next to Gawain in excellence. But Gawain just then offers himself as really the slain man's proper successor. The two now fight to settle the matter and the younger combatant, astonished at his adversary's endurance, asks him his name. When he learns it, he ceases fighting and does homage to Gawain. The latter then denounces Brien's assertion in regard to his slaying of Gawain as a falsehood and challenges him to a combat. Gawain wins in this duel and despatches Brien as his prisoner to Arthur's court. Accompanied by the hero of the romance, Brien forthwith rides away without speaking to the Lady of the Isles, but to one of her men who rides after him he tells who he is. On learning that the victorious knight was really Gawain, the Lady vows that she will marry only him. — In the course of their journey, Gawain and his companion come upon a squire with a miserable horse, who tells the young man that his father had been killed by Gawain and that his mother wished him to avenge her dead husband. The Knight of the Two Swords then accuses his friend of the deed, but leaves him without attacking him, and wearing his father's shield, which he had received from the squire, rides on until he comes upon a sword lying on the ground and stained with fresh blood. These stains only become brighter when our hero tries to wipe them off.

There is a castle nearby, surrounded by a lake. At the request of a girl from this castle, he crosses the lake and is conducted to an orchard where the lady of the castle (really, his mother) sat grieving over her husband, who had been recently slain. She had sent a squire to summon her son (the hero of the poem) to avenge his father, but he had not yet returned. In the course of her talk it is revealed that this father was the man whom the Lady of Caradigan saw buried in the Waste Chapel-consequently, the sword which she had ungirded was the sword of our hero's father. The Knight of the Two Swords promises to avenge her. Just then the squire returns and observes by the shield which he had given the hero and which he now sees hanging up on the wall that the latter must be in the castle. This leads to a recognition of her son on the part of the lady of the castle. She tells him that his father was Bleheri, and that he is himself now lord of the Valleys of Blanquemore and the Lake of Jumeles — moreover, that Brien is really the person responsible for Bleheri's death, and that he is holding her daughter captive. Brien in his war with Bleheri, she avers, had trickily obtained the loan of Gawain from Arthur, the king having, as usual, granted a *don*, before he knew what it was to be. He (Brien) had then disguised Gawain in his own arms and sent him against Bleheri, with a fatal result for the latter. Bleheri had, before he expired, directed that he should be buried in the Waste Chapel, declaring that no one should have his sword, save the person who could gird it on or ungird it at will — moreover, that his son, whose name should be kept concealed from him, must avenge his death on Brien. She tells him, too, about the sword stained with blood, that it, — according to a letter that accompanied it — could only be unsheathed by a nameless knight — the most adventurous, etc., that ever was. The Knight of the Two Swords now quits his mother's castle, leaving behind him one of his three swords — the one that Arthur used in dubbing him. He comes first upon the wife of Menelais, lord of the Fearful Castle, a retainer of his father's, weeping over the body of her husband, whom Brien had slain. They carry this body to the Waste Chapel (which was at the Fearful Castle) and inter it, and when they leave the place, the young knight carries away the horse-chain which had been laid on the altar there by the Lady of Caradigan. They next come upon six more ladies, whose husbands Brien had slain, and the Knight of the Two Swords overcomes there six more of

Brien's knights and despatches them as prisoners to Arthur. When these prisoners report who had sent them, the Lady of Caradigan again urges Arthur to fulfill his promise and start in search of the man she loves, and Arthur does so. On the other hand Brien is indignant on hearing that our hero has rescued the ladies whose husbands he has killed, and goes in search of him. He finds him, but in the ensuing combat is killed. The Knight of the Two Swords and his companions now return to Fearful Castle — where the people rejoice over the news of Brien's death and hang his representatives — and he restores the lady of the castle to her slain lord's possessions. The other ladies he escorts to Arthur's court, but, on the way thither, comes to a convent, where his sister had taken the veil, to escape a marriage with Brien. This sister, whom he had never seen, he comforts with the news of Brien's death and relieves from the necessity of becoming a nun. At this juncture, the Knight of the Two Swords receives news that the king is in the forest searching for him. Consequently, in order to conceal his identity, he now calls himself "li chevaliers as dames" (Ladies' Knight). Seeking for Arthur in the woods, he comes upon Gifflet (Girflet), who makes some disparaging remark apropos of his new name, and is unhorsed in a joust on that account. After he has wandered in the forest for a day or two, one of Arthur's squires conducts him and his party to the spot where Arthur is encamped. The king is himself absent at the time, but the queen, who was reading a romance aloud to her knights and maidens, welcomes him. The Lady of Caridigan is, also, there and he falls in love with her. Nevertheless, he declines the queen's invitation to stay and so goes forth to earn still further his lady-love's esteem by new adventures — above all, he wishes to solve the mystery of the sword stained with blood. After his departure, Arthur arrives and is told by the queen of the young knight's visit. The ladies whom our hero had rescued were bound by a promise not to divulge his identity — not so, however, his sister, who reveals the fact that the Ladies' Knight and the Knight of the Two Swords are the same person and relates, moreover, his recent exploits. The king now hurries up the quest for the young knight, in order to forestall

a possible encounter between the latter and Gawain. — In the meanwhile our hero had heard from charcoal-burners concerning a knight
on a litter whom some ladies were attending at the Fountain of
Marvels in the forest, and sets out for this spot. Galien, Brien's
son, had begun, however, the siege of his (the hero's) mother at
Tygan about the same time, and Gawain, who is looking for the
Knight of the Two Swords, on learning this, goes to her assistance. With the aid of the men of Sandic — vassals of the be-
leaguered lady — he succeeds in penetrating Tygan. The next
day he slays Galien in single combat and the latter's forces then
surrender.

The lady is shocked when she is told that her deliverer is
her husband's slayer. She pardons him, however, and goes a part
of the journey with him when he leaves her castle — luckily so,
for she is thus able to stop a combat between Gawain and her son,
who, disbelieving the news of the former's services to his mother,
attacks him on the way. — After their reconciliation, Gawain
wishes the Knight of the Two Swords to go with him at once to
court, but the latter must first go to the Fountain of Marvels,
to solve the mystery of the stained sword. In the forest about
this fountain the two companions have various experiences — encounter a dwarf followed by a multitude of beasts — also, a company of huntsmen chasing a hart. Later they come to the tent
of these huntsmen's master, who is wounded. The knight who had
inflicted the wound upon him, however, leaves his sword behind and
tells him that this wound will not heal until the knight (hitherto nameless) whose name (Meriadeus) is inscribed on the sword
has struck him with it. The wounded man's wife had, accordingly,
had the sword, with an explanatory inscription attached to it, laid
where many adventurous knights were in the habit of passing.
This was the stained sword, and when our hero struck the wounded man (Gaus, son of the King of Norval) with it, the latter
was at once able to rise and the stains vanished from the weapon.
— About this time Li Rous du Val Perilleus (The Red One
of the Perilous Valley) was waging an unprovoked war on Arthur
and had occupied Dysnadaron, but the king had succeeded in sur-

rounding him in this city. The besieged knight now deserted his followers, slipping out of the city before day and escaping to his own country in which he held many of Arthur's subjects captive and which was virtually inaccessible to an enemy. After their lord's flight, his men surrendered to Arthur. Hearing of the affair of the Red Knight, Gawain and our hero started for his country, to set free the prisoners there, but they meet him in the forest and the younger knight unhorses him, obtains the means of liberating the captives, and sends him to Caradigan to present himself there to the Lady of Caradigan as a prisoner and with a horse-chain about his feet. This was the horse-chain which the Lady of Caradigan had, herself, laid on the altar of the Waste Chapel. After freeing the Red Knight's captives, Gawain and his companion return with them to the court at Caradigan on Ascension Day, and there the king, in fulfilment of his promise, gives the Knight of the Two Swords to his lady-love in marriage. Gawain, too, now enjoys the love of the daughter of the Lord of the Port. The Knight of the Two Swords and his bride were married by the Archbishop of Canterbury, and the bride's cloak had embroidered on it the history of Arthur from his conception down to the day of this ceremony. At the end of the poem we are told that her name was Lore.

This romance is better planned and better written than most works of its species. Noteworthy, too, is the fact that the author cultivates the trick of mystery in a manner that reminds one of the prose romances. As a matter of fact, it is doubtless later than the prose romances of the Vulgate cycle — the *Merlin*-continuation excepted — and the (not very important) points in which it resembles the Vulgate *Estoire del Saint Graal* may be due to imitation of the latter. Particularly spirited is the narrative of the battles around Tygan. Like his fellow-romancers, generally, the author makes free use of Chrétien. Among his sources, too, are Wace, *Li Biaus Descouneus, La Vengeance de Raguidel,* and *Durmart.*

22. *Fergus.* Edited by Francisque Michel for the Abbotsford Club: *Le roman des aventures de Frégus par Guillaume le Clerc,* trouvère du XIII⁰ siecle (Edingburgh, 1841), and by Ernst

Martin (from a much better MS.): *Fergus, Roman von Guillaume Le Clerc* (Halle, 1872). Author, Guillaume Le Clerc, who is not to be confounded with Guillaume le Normand. Dialect. probably, Isle-de-France. Date, about 1225. 6984 lines. G. Paris, HLF, XXX, 159f., W. Marquard, *Der Einfluss Kristians von Troyes auf den Roman "Fergus" des Guillaume le Clerc.* Göttingen diss. 1906.

Whilst holding court on St. John's Day at Karadigan (Cardigan), Arthur decides to begin a hunt for a certain white stag in the forest of Gorriendc (Geltsdale?) near Carduel (Carlisle). Having killed the animal, on their return from the chase, Arthur and his company pass by the dwelling of a rich peasant, named Soumilloit (Somerled, Smollet), who had married a woman of noble birth. Despite his wealth, this peasant would compel his two older sons to keep the sheep every day and the youngest, Fergus, to plow. — When Arthur and the knights of the Round Table pass through Soumilloit's place, Fergus, who is at the plow, like the countryman who is helping him, is much frightened by the spectacle of Arthur's train, but later recovers from his fears and wants to enter the king's service. He hurries home and advises his father of his desire. The father is on the point of chastising his son for his mad request, but is restrained by his wife and at last consents and bestows on his son his own suit of armor, which had not been used for 32 years, and a fine steed. The boy takes darts with him, too. Attacked *en route* to Arthur's court by four robbers, Fergus slays two and hangs their heads to his saddle-bow. On arriving at court (in Carduel), he tells the king that he wants to be one of his knights, which causes Kay, in mockery, to urge him to undertake an adventure which many of Arthur's knights had failed to achieve, viz, that of combating the Black Knight of the Black Mountain at Nouquetran (where Merlin long lived) and bring away the horn and wimple that hung upon a lion's neck there. Fergus, however, takes the matter seriously, and, having been adopted into Arthur's household, starts off on the adventure. That night, however, when he stops at the house of one of the king's chamberlains, his host, observing his rusticity and inadequate equipment, induces him to return with him the next day to Arthur's court, in order to obtain the proper arms, etc. and be formally knighted. This is done, and, in spite of the forebodings of Gawain and others concerning the issue of the enterprise which the inexperienced young man has undertaken, he sets out for the Black Mountain. On the way thither he spends the night at a castle, named Lidel (Liddell). Galiene, the niece, of its lord, falls desperately in love with the young visitor, and during the night she goes to his chamber and offers herself to him. Though smitten with her beauty, he declares that he must execute his present task before he can enjoy her favors, but that, if he survives the impending fight, he will return and become her lover. On approaching the Black Mountain, he ties his horse to an olive-tree (in Scotland!), hangs his shield upon it, too, and climbs to the top of the mountain, which was so lofty that you could see Ireland, England and Cornwall from its summit. The objects of his search were in a beautiful chapel. He first smashes to pieces a human automaton of brass at the door, enters and snatches away the horn and wimple from the neck of the lion, which proves to be an ivory image. He now comes out, blows the horn thrice, and remounts his steed. The Black Knight appears and is vanquished by Fergus, who spares his life on condition that he will take the horn and wimple to Arthur's court and announce himself there as his (Fergus's) prisoner. The hero next returns to Lidel, but finds every one there in dismay, because Galiene has fled, no one knows whither. Her uncle and Fergus have an amusing dialogue at cross-purposes, the former inquiring about Fergus's recent adventure, the latter answering with questions about Galiene. The young knight, now bitterly self-reproachful, avers that he will never rest until he has got news of her. — In his wanderings in search of her he has various adventures: 1. beats the hideous and insolent dwarf who guards the entrance of a tent-then vanquishes the lord of the tent, whom he taunts all through the fighting, and sends him and his *amie* to Arthur's court as his prisoners; 2. overthrows a robber-knight who holds people up at. a bridge and sends him, too, to Arthur's court; 3. kills thirteen out of a band of fifteen knights who, after giving Fergus food, try to rob him of his horse, and sends the survivors likewise, to Arthur. — In the meanwhile, Arthur thinks that Fergus has been killed at the Black Mountain and is reflecting how he may avenge him. Kay, on the other hand, rejoices with bitter jests over the young knight's supposed fate, but is discomfited when just then the various captives despatched by Fergus arrive at court. Fergus, himself, lives for sometime on the game that he is able to kill, but at length comes to a fountain near a chapel in the woods. If one drank of the waters of this fountain, one could have one's future perdicted by a dwarf that dwelt there. This dwarf told our hero that he would discover Galiene, if he could obtain the white shield at Dunostre (Dunothar in Kincardineshire) which was guarded by an old hag.

He journeys thither by way of the Castiel as Puceles (Maidens' Castle = Edinburgh) and embarks at Port la Roine (Queensferry). The sailors plan to rob him, but he disables all save the captain, who jumps into the sea, and is able to land at a Saracen town named Dunfremelin (Dunfermline). Thence he rides to Dunostre. The brilliant light which radiates from the shield there guides him to the castle. The giant hag defends the bridge with a scythe, but Fergus slays her. He next slays a *guivre* (monster serpent) and carries off the shield. He now returns to Port la Roine and the following day, as he rides on, learns from some herdsmen that he is in a country which belongs to Galiene and that she is now besieged at Roceborc (Roxburgh) by a certain king. Fergus proceeds to Roceborc, but *en route* kills a giant at Mont Dolerous, delivers two girls whom he had imprisoned, takes the giant's steed, which was as savage as its master, and rides away on it to the besieged castle. He attacks the besiegers, kills several of them, unhorses a nephew of the besieging king, and sends his horse to Galiene and retires to the forest at the close of the day. The next day Artofilas, the king's nephew-unhorsed by Fergus the previous day — induced his uncle to despatch him to Galiene with an insolent message ordering her to disperse her forces and to marry him (the uncle). In her anger Galiene imprudently replies that within eight days she would produce a champion who would outmatch any two knights that he could put into the field — otherwise, she would accept the terms of her enemy's message. Too late she regrets her folly, but Arondele, one of her maidens, consoles her with the promise that she (Arondele) will produce such a champion for her — either the unknown knight who, the day before, had so distinguished himself, or some knight of the Round Table. The girl first goes to Arthur's court (at Cardoil), but he is in deep dejection, partly because of Fergus's disàppearance and partly because all of his other chief knights are absent, seeking for Fergus. Arondele is in despair, since it seems impossible to obtain the needed champion, but on her way home, she passes by the castle where Fergus had a few days before slain the giant and where he was now again. Not knowing who he is, she tells him of Galiene's imprudent promise, and he decides to go to her mistress's aid, without disclosing, however, his purpose to the girl. He merely tells her that the knight who slew the giant was the same that did such execution among the besiegers and that he would doubtless turn up in time to defend Galiene. — When the appointed hour arrives and no succor is in sight, Galiene is about to commit suicide by springing from a castle window, but a mysterious voice restrains her and bids her look towards the forest. She does so and sees the whole woods illuminated by Fergus's shield which he had won at Dunostre. Though he had to fight both the king and his nephew, at the same time, Fergus succeeds in killing the latter and overthrowing the former, whom he spares, however, on the condition that in Galiene's presence he will renounce his claims to her inheritance and then go to Arthur's court. Immediately afterwards he again plunges into the forest. Galiene is convinced from her interview with the vanquished king that the victor is Fergus. This king reaches Arthur's court on Ascension Day, when all of Arthur's knights have returned from their quest, and he relates how Fergus had vanquished him. At this point the fool jumps up and prophesies that Kay will soon be a fisherman. Arthur is now so eager to see Fergus that he is about to go in quest of him, but, on the advice of the vanquished king, he decides that he had better proclaim a tournament to draw the young knight out of his concealment. Galiene hears of the proclamation, and, as she tells her barons, determines to go there for the purpose of finding a husband. The tournament is held at Gedeorde (Jedburgh) and Arthur has granted Kay the privilege of the first joust. Fergus, who is his opponent, ridicules him in the combat and throws him over into marshy ground, so that the fool's prediction is fulfilled: Kay has become a fisherman. After Kay, Fergus, also, unhorses Lancelot and on the following day Sagremor and the Black Knight. On the other hand, this second day he merely makes Perceval yield ground to him, because he is using the sword which Perceval gave him at the time that he (Fergus) was dubbed knight. Every night for a week, after the day's tournament, he would withdraw *incognito* into the forest. On Friday of the tournament week Galiene arrives at court, to ask the king for a husband and he promises her any one that she may choose. She wants Fergus and guesses that he is the unknown knight who has so distinguished himself in the present tournament. He retires, however, at the end of each day so how is he to be reached? It is settled as follows: The next day, when Fergus appears, Gawain meets him and requests him to come to Arthur. On learning who Gawain is, Fergus does him reverence and follows him to the king. Arthur now joins the hands of Fergus and Galiene and on St. John's Day the young couple are married at Roxburgh.

The influence of Chrétien's works — especially, the *Perceval* — is manifest in the *Fergus*. The romance is one of the feeblest specimens of its *genre,* its only original feature worth mentioning, perhaps, being the localization of the story in Scotland. Moreover, this localization is pretty exact and some of the places concerned are not prominent in the real Scotland. Still further, the hero and his father bear the names of actual Scottish chieftans of the twelfth century (second half) viz. Fergus of Galloway and Somerled, who ruled over Hebrides and Argyle. These circumstances, taken together with his remark in regard to how cleverly the Scotch nags are able to get over the bogs, appear to evince, on the part of the author, a personal knowledge of the country in which he has laid the scene of his story. Martin has, indeed, plausibly conjectured that the poem was written for Alan of Galloway, a powerful Scotch nobleman, who succeeded to his family estates in 1200.

23. *Hunbaut (Gawain et Humbaut, Humbaut).* The only edition is Hunbaut, *altfranzösischer Artusroman des XIII. Jahrhunderts, nach Wendelin Foersters Abschrift der einzigen Chantilly-Handschrift zum ersten Male kritisch bearbeitet von Jakob Stürzinger, aus dessen Nachlass ergänzt herausgegeben von Dr. Hermann Breuer:* Gesellschaft für Romanische Literatur, Band 35 (Dresden, 1914).

The unique MS. (second half of the thirteenth century) in the Musée Condé at Chantilly is the same that contains, also, the unique copies of *Li Biaus Descouneus, Fergus, Rigomer* and *L'Atre Perillos,* its press-mark (according to Miss G. P. Williams's edition of the *Li Biaus Descouneus,* p. XI) being XIV, H 6. The poem is a fragment of 3618 lines. Author, unknown. Dialect, Picard. Date, first half of the thirteenth century (probably, second quarter).

G. Paris, HLF, XXX, 69ff., G. L. Kittredge, *A Study of Gawain and the Green Knight,* pp. 61ff., 99ff.

Arthur is very fond of Hunbaut (one of his knights) and makes him sleep in his room, so that he may talk to him. Once, on Hunbaut's return to court, Arthur asks him: "Is there any one that does not acknowledge me as overlord?" Hunbaut answers, that there is still one king that does not. Arthur, accordingly, despatches Gawain to summon this king to his presence, although Hunbaut warns him that the monarch in question is unconquerable. Gawain wants company on his jorney and at the suggestion of his disgusted sovereign takes along with him his (Gawain's) sister, who sits on the neck of his horse. Afterwards the king regrets sending his nephew on such a dangerous expedition and consents to Hunbaut's request that he shall be allowed to go along with Gawain. Arthur even rides after the latter to admonish him concerning the risks which he will have to run. — Later Gawain decides that his sister must return to Caerleon and entrusts her to a *chevalier errant,* who is to escort her back. This man, however, is faithless to his trust and carries her off to his castle. — In the course of their journey, the two knights are entertained at a castle which lies on the edge of a country so wild that Hunbaut warns Gawain, he must eat his fill here, for they will be unable to get anything again for some time to come. He warns him, still further, against the daughter of the lord of this castle, who, as he happens to know, is already in love with Gawain (though she has never seen him). Gawain promises to be discreet, but is captivated with the girl, when he meets her, and the two exchange lovevows that night at the table. When they part for the night, the father[9] bids Gawain kiss his daughter; when Gawain, however, kisses her four times, instead of once, the father grows so angry that he orders his guest's eyes to be put out; later, owing to the protest of his followers, he revokes this command. That night the daughter comes to Gawain's room and stays with him until morning. — Gawain had been so occupied with the girl at the castle that he had neglected to eat anything — consequently, when, in passing through a forest the next day, he observes a lord and his *vallets* cooking venison, he is provoked by hunger to force himself upon them, and, when ordered away, he drives off this lord and his men and helps himself to their meal, whereupon Hunbaut predicts all sorts of dire censequences from this outrage. As a matter of fact, the lord does return with a hundred men to punish Gawain, but is persuaded by Hunbaut and his own followers that he was, himself, in the wrong. Gawain then accepts his invitation to go with him to his town, which, as it turns out, has a flourishing commerce with the Orient. From this port Gawain and Hunbaut sail for the land of the king who refuses to acknowledge Arthur's suzerainty. They land there, and, after two insignificant adventures, come to a rich city, at the entrance of which they find a hideous *vilain*, who is accustomed to challenge strangers on these terms: he will allow the stranger to cut off his head with his axe, provided the stranger will afterwards submit himself, also, to decapitation. Gawain accepts the challenge and cuts off the *vilain's* head, but defeats the enchantment by at once

---

[9] This is the Imperious Host *motif*, as in *Yder*, etc.

seizing and holding the *vilain's* trunk, so that he cannot get hold of his head again — consequently, the *vilain* dies.[10] Gawain and his companion now proceed to the castle of the king whom they are seeking. At its entrance Gawain kills a dwarf who blackguards him, then penetrates the place and delivers Arthur's summons to the monarch inside, who is so taken by surprise that the two invaders are able to escape before he gives orders for their seizure. — After returning to their own country, Gawain and Hunbaut recover a girl's lover and father for her from robber knights. Later Gawain compels a knight to marry a girl whom he had seduced on false pretences and abandoned. Next Gawain meets his brother Gaheries (Gaheriet), and the two journey on together, without mutual recognition. They finally have a fight, because Gaheries is unwilling to bestow upon a lady (Ydone) a kiss which, according to custom, is her due. Gawain wins and they recognize each other. — Gawain now goes in search of his sister and is soon joined in the quest by Lancelot, Sagremor, Kay and others. Even Arthur participates in this search. In doing so, at one time, he has to cross a broad river in a boat which had this peculiarity, that it would capsize, whenever an even number of passengers tried to use it. Luckily there were only eleven in the royal party. — Arthur and his men are entertained at the castle of the Maiden of Gaut Destroit (Narrow or Difficult Wood) who was in love with Gawain and kept an image of him constantly by her bedside. This image was so exact that it deceived Kay, Gifflet, and Yder, and altogether led to some curious misunderstandings. — Gawain overtakes his sister and her captor (Gorvain Cadrus) — vanquishes the latter and makes him take the former to Arthur's court and surrender himself to the king. Here the fragment breaks off.

This romance is agreeably written, but, apart from its variants of the Imperious Host and Beheading Game *motifs*, it possesses little originality. These variants were, no doubt, the author's

---

[10] This is, of course, a variant of the well-known Beheading Game *motif*. Cp. I, 88, above.

own inventions. He was plainly familiar with the works of Chrétien de Troyes (whom he mentions I. 187), Raoul de Houdenc,
and others, and, altogether, in his incidents deviates hardly at
all from the beaten paths.

24. *Les Mervelles de Rigomer.* Edited in two volumes by
W. Foerster and Hermann Breuer — vol. 1 (text) by Foerster,
vol. 2 (critical apparatus) by Foerster and Breuer — as vols. 19
and 39, respectively, of the publications of the Gesellschaft für
Romanische Literatur (Dresden, 1908—1915), under the title, *Les
Mervelles de Rigomer von Jehan: altfranzösischer Artusroman des
XIII. Jahrhunderts nach der einzigen Aumale-Handschrift in
Chantilly, zum ersten Mal herausgegeben.* 17271 lines preserved,
but about 1500 lines are wanting at the end.

The unique MS. of the romance[11] is No. 626 of the Musée
Condé. Author, Jehan (otherwise unknown). Dialect, that of Cam-
brai or Tournai. Date, thirteenth century — probably, second
quarter.

G. Paris, HLF, XXX, 86ff.; H. Kuhse, *Der Einfluss Raouls
von Houdenc auf den Roman "Les Mervelles de Rigomer."* Göttingen diss., 1914.

Arthur, holding court at Caerleon, observes, one day, his usual
custom of not eating until an adventure has occurred. A damsel,
however, soon appears and challenges his knights to seek adven-

---

[11] ll. 15923—17271 were once, also, preserved in the French
MS. 23 (l. IV. 33 — not 23, as G. Paris states) of the Royal Library
at Turin. This MS., however, as was remarked above, was virtually
destroyed in the fire which befell that library on Jan. 26, 1904.
Nevertheless, the fragment had already been edited by E. Stengel, *Die
Turiner Rigomer-Episode* (Greifswald, 1905), and it had been used,
also, by Eugen Pessen in his *Die Schlussepisode des Rigomerromanes:
Kritischer Text nebst einer Einleitung und Anmerkungen.* Heidelberg diss. (Berlin, 1907). Despite Pessen's contention, Paris and
Foerster were, doubtless, right in asserting that the Turin fragment
was copied directly from the Chantilly MS. Cp. on this episode, also,
Brugger, *Zs. f. frz. Spr. u. Litt.* XXX[2], 129ff. In the opinion of
the present writer, there is no sufficient ground for the view, which
has often been expressed, that this concluding episode was originally
an independent poem.

tures at Rigomer, the castle of her mistress (Dionise) in Ireland, promising them, at the same time, many delights there. Yvain del Leoniel and Sagremor follow her, but are each unhorsed by a knight a short distance from the court. — Lancelot now takes his turn. He does not catch up with the damsel, but reaches Ireland, and has some minor adventures, chief of which are: he is robbed by Savari of the Ruiste Valee (Wild Valley), who has designs on Ingle — known as the Flor Desiree (the flower which men longed for). Lancelot kills him. He afterwards vanquishes Macob Dicrac, who tried to disinherit his own aunt — also, later on overcomes six servants of the latter, and then his friend, Mauduin the Gardener (Savari's nephew), whose guest he (Lancelot) had been. Mauduin and his *amie* are sent by Lancelot to Guinevere. — Lancelot receives hospitality from a wild man, who tells him that he is now in the land of Brefeni (Brefny), which is contiguous to Conart (Connaught) and much more infested with robbers than the latter. He spends the next night in a house where a dead man is laid out in a bier and there is no living creature about, save a great quantity of cats that fill the house. After a long fight, Lancelot drives them out with a burning brand. The dead man rises up, but Lancelot hews him down with his sword and burns up the bier, to put an end to the enchantments of the place. Two girls then appear and provide him with food, drink, etc. — He next passes into Conart, meets Toplain (uncle of Flor Desiree), who had been bed-ridden from a wound in the head for 30 years, and, owing to a spell, can only keep alive, if strange knights visit him — had been wounded at Rigomer. Whilst Lancelot is at a *vilain's*, a knight who has had an eye knocked out at Rigomer comes in and tells about that stronghold. Lancelot enters now Tuesmomme (Desmond) and is directed to Rigomer by Buticostiaus, a treacherous knight, whose *amie* is with him. Next, whilst lodging with a poor man, Lancelot beats off an attack of robbers and the following night he spends in the dwelling of a woman so hideous that she frightens his steed. Her eyelids were so heavy that they had to be held up artificially. Journeying on, he again overcomes robber knights — later saves the daughter of Frion, King of Desmond (of which Cork is said to be the capital) from rape, but declines to marry her, though he leaves her *enceinte*. — All along, when, at the end of an adventure, Lancelot divulges his name, his interlocutors always express appreciation of his fame, but warn him against risking the perils of Rigomer. As he approaches the place, an unarmed knight advances towards him and tells him of the pleasures that will be his, if he will only enter Rigomer, disarmed. Lancelot rejects this condition, and, after jousting successfully with another knight, is brought by the unarmed knight to the bridge and the serpent. There he overthrows a white knight, then Li Chevaliers as Armes Trebles (a big knight with triple equipment), and sends the latter to Guinevere. He next beats back the serpent. Now begin the real "wonders of Rigomer," says the poet. — A magician is accustomed to imprison knights in the Fose Gobiene (Gobien Moat). One of his emissaries, a girl, deceives Lancelot into accepting arms which betray him into the magician's power — also a ring which causes him to forget everything. Thus Lancelot becomes the magician's captive.

At this point a new division of the romance commences, consisting of the narrative of the adventures of Gawain and other knights in their quest for Lancelot; for the various prisoners whom Lancelot had despatched to Guinevere had brought the news that he had gone to Rigomer. At the suggestion of Gawain, however, Arthur's knights do not begin the quest until the spring. At that season they assemble at the Gue de Blanc Espine (Whitethorn Ford) and, after some debate over the number of knights who shall participate in the quest, Gawain settles upon 56 as the proper number. They all go to Ireland. Gawain, however, is very soon lured into the castle of Gaudionet, whose brother he had slain. There, whilst he is disarmed, dames and damsels seize him and turn him over to Gaudionet for imprisonment. His companions, thinking that he had gone ahead of them to Rigomer, travel on and are attacked by a knight who mistakes them for the forces of his enemy. They reconcile this knight and his adversary. — Sagremor in a stag-chase comes upon Oringlaie, ravishes her, and leaves his pouch with her. Notwithstanding the outrage, she falls in love with him, but the affair was destined to bring about his death. — When Engrevain (Agravain) lodges at a castle, his host, Robert of Sotain Herber (Solitary Retreat) tells him of how a storm had recently swept away his (Robert's) *amie*. This lady Engravain subsequently discovers under a spell in a sort of earthly paradise within a mountain, where knights and maidens spend their time dancing and carolling. He leads a number of knights into the place and brings off the lady. — Bliobleheri vanquishes five knights and sends them to his companions. — A girl's accepted lover is disabled and so unable to joust on an appointed day against an objectionable rival, who is, moreover, assisted by another knight. Yvain puts on the disabled man's arms and wins his lady-love for him. — Gaudins li Bruns de le Montaigne rescues a girl from four giants who had wounded her lover. — Cliges of Greece has the adventure of the Astres Maleis (the Cursed Graveyard) and at the court of Morgan le Fay sees a knight apparently dead and about to be buried — also an empty tomb prepared for himself. After he has dined with a company of knights and ladies in a neighboring hall, they all go out into the graveyard, and he draws a truncheon out of the body of the knight who is apparently dead, whereupon the man springs up at once and challenges him. The knight had received his wound at Rigomer from Li Chevaliers as Armes Trebles and was in a state of delightful trance, as long as the truncheon remained in his body. He can only be killed by this truncheon, and it is with this weapon that Cliges finally despatches him. — Waheries (Gaheries) avenges a girl on a knight (Mal Ostagier) who had fed her lover's head to his falcon — a bird that lived exclusively on human heads — but she dies from grief. Arthur's knights arrive in sight of Rigomer. The unarmed knight bids them disarm, before entering the place, promising them all manner of delights, if they will do so. He tells them, too, of the captivity of Lancelot and seven others. Arthur's knights advance, still armed, and reach the serpent-guarded copper bridge. Just then they hear the blast of a horn, which is at once followed successively by a storm, by unendurable heat,

and by cold of equal severity. After this the knights of Rigomer, though protected by enchantment within the domain of
their castle, conceive such a scorn of the weakness of their opponents that they sally forth into the open. They get worsted,
however, and are only saved by a band of men who are dressed like
black monks, but have armor underneath. The members of this
band, at first, appear invulnerable and irresistible, but Arthur's
men soon discover that the secret of their strength is in their
hoods. At this point, still another band come to the aid of the
knights of Rigomer. This second band have dog-like counte-
nances, horned heads, and hairy bodies, and are swifter than horses.
The two sides now agree to a thirty days' tournament. Lorie of
the Roche Florie (Flowery Rock), a fairy who had long loved
Gawain, determines to deliver him from Gaudionet's prison, in
order that he may take part in this tournament and effects his
liberation through Gaudionet's daughter. She gives this girl a
drug to be administered to her father's household, whilst the father,
himself, and most of his men are away on a hunt. In return for
this favor, she brings about the marriage of the girl with the
young lover whom she favored as against the rich old man whom
her father desired to force upon her. Thus Gawain escapes and
rides away with Lorie towards Rigomer. On his way, he rescues
a girl from her captors by merely stating his name — overcomes
twelve knights and their lord, in succession: he had plucked a
flower from the latter's garden and custom required that a combat
against these odds should follow. Between the two adventures just
mentioned, Lorie had left him, with directions not to disclose his
identity at Rigomer. — Though warned by an Irish knight, Gawain
yields to the enticements of a bird called Willeri, which is endowed
with human speech and which also sings exquisitely, and turns
aside to the castle of Wanglent. Its lord, Bauduin, was jealous of
Rigomer, and had set up evil customs there that rivalled those
of the latter place. Gawain survives a succession of combats and
other adventures here — goes on towards Rigomer, of whose perils
he constantly hears more and more — comes upon a girl who is
watching a game of chess, played by automata of ivory and gold,

respectively, and overthrows two knights here. Being entertained at the castle of a certain knight, who is not aware of his identity, he learns from his host of the grief that prevails at Rigomer among his companions over his absence. On crossing into the domain of Rigomer two days later, he comes to a meadow in which the grass would lose its color and the dew fall, whenever a valiant knight entered it. These signs fail, however, when Gawain rode across it — hence everyone inferred that there was something extraordinary about him — that he was the knight destined to put an end to the enchantments of the place. Lorie had already arrived that morning and Gawain passes the night in her magnificent pavillion. During the following days he participates in the jousts and carries everything before him, so that people commonly remarked that here at last was the man to achieve the adventures of Rigomer. His success, however, excites the enmity of Arthur's knights, who did not know, however, that it was Gawain. On the morning of the last day of the tournament, Gawain, barely escapes an ambush set for him by Gaudoniet, whom he, in turn, captures. —

Then, through enchantment, all sorts of strange races come to the aid of Rigomer — people with beaks, people that run with incredible swiftness on one foot, etc. — A magical deluge of rain follows and the Britons fare so badly that they long for Gawain. The latter now proceeds to the copper bridge, but the serpent there, instead of attacking him, humbles himself before him. Moreover, the arts of the siren there have no effect on him, and the knight who comes forth from a cellar at his challenge rushes back at once, as soon as he sees him. In the kitchen of the palace Gawain finds Lancelot and his companions bereft of all intelligence and reduced to the condition of beasts. Under the influence of the magical ring Lancelot thought that the lady of the castle was his *amie*, but, as soon as this ring is pulled from his finger by Gawain, he regains his reason. Gawain, in the same way, breaks the spell of the other captives, who had been put to weaving, tilling the soil, etc. There are great rejoicings throughout the city, but Gawain still has to achieve the adventure of the falcon on the isle which is connected with Rigomer by a marvellous bridge, defended by copper giants, which only the best of all knights can cross. His achievement of this adventure is accompanied by signs and wonders. On his return to Rigomer, the people gather together before the castle and he sits in a rich chair as on a throne before them. — So, too, Dionise, Lady of Rigomer, who casts longing eyes at Gawain. Four kings offer him the crown of Islande (Ireland?) and he answers that he will take counsel about it. Shortly thereafter, Lorie announces to the throng that she is the hero's *amie* and he, himself, declares, much to Dionise's grief, that he has no intention of marrying and has decided to go home — affirms, however, that, by the expiration of a year, he will procure a suitable husband for Dionise. Lancelot and Gawain now return to Britain. Soon, however, a girl appears at court, whilst Arthur is waiting for an adventure, before eating, and wants a champion against Miraudiel, who is trying to compel her to marry him. Gawain is the first champion, but Miraudiel is so terrified at fighting this renowned warrior that he begs Gawain to remain in his prison until the day of the combat is passed. Out of pure courtesy, Gawain assents to this. Then Midomidas, son of King Lot of Galoee, claims the right to act as champion — unless a better one should present himself — on the principle that the last knight to arrive at court has the right to claim the first combat. But on the day of the fight, a knight appears at court, with execrable equipment and riding a wretched steed. He turns out, however, to be Lancelot and Midomidas yields the championship to him. Similarly, Miraudiel, recognizing Lancelot by a wound in his hand, recently healed, surrenders to him. Gawain is then freed and Midomidas is wedded to Dionise.

A cousin of the heiress of Quintefuele (Quintefeuille) tries to deprive her of her inheritance — so she sends a message to Arthur to the effect that she wants him as her champion and nobody else. His courtiers and spouse oppose the plan, but he insists on going. Gawain acts as his squire, when he takes his departure, and Arthur laughs at having the best knight in the world, he says, to hold his stirrup when he gets on his horse. Guinevere angers Arthur by disputing this statement and he threatens to behead her, unless she can prove that she is right, when he returns. Gawain expressed agreement with Guinevere's statement and promises to help her. — Lancelot accompanies Arthur on his journey, and when five robbers assail them he springs forward and disposes of each of them, before Arthur can do anything. They next pass through the Male Gaudine (Evil Wood), the haunt of innumerable beasts of prey and other creatures, which themselves, however, lived in deadly terror of a panther. When Lancelot determines that he will attack this animal, his attendants take flight — all, save one, who with his bow and arrows establishes himself with his back to a tree. Arthur, too, stands his ground. Lancelot next covers himself with linden branches as a protection against the flames which the panther breathes forth and inflicts severe wounds on the beast which cannot see his enemy, because of the branches. Moreover, Arthur and the valet, also, pierce him with a dart and arrows. The breath of the panther sets the bushes afire, but he at last succumbs to his wounds. Lancelot now swoons, and his companions, for a while, believe that he is dead, but a lady, clad in white, appears and cures him by anointing him from head to foot with a magical ointment. Arthur and the valet think, at first, that she is Mary Magdalen, or, perhaps, even the Virgin Mary, but it proves to be Lorie. — They go on to Quintefuele and in a duel there Arthur slays the knight who wished to disinherit his own cousin. After enjoying a feast at Quintefuele, Arthur and Lancelot proceed on their journey, but they had just reached a lovely valley, when the story breaks off.

Doubtless, in imitation of the latter part of the prose *Lancelot*, this romance, throughout, takes the form of a quest. We have here the usual superabundance of trivial adventures, but the ultimate aim of the quest is kept more steadily before the reader's mind than is usually the case with works of this nature, and the narrative is executed with greater *verve* than is customary in the later romances. An especially good piece of *diablerie* is Lancelot's adventure in the house which is haunted by spirits, in the form of cats, and the bird, Willeri, that "spoke several languages" is one of the happiest examples of this folk-tale figure. The author lays the scene of the quest in Ireland and adapts his nomenclature to this conception, but, after all, the Irish names of places which he employs are few and he knows nothing of that country, save that it is full of violence of all kinds — consequently, there is no necessity of assuming that he had any personal knowledge of it.

25. *Floriant et Floriete.* The only edition is *Floriant & Florete: A Metrical Romance of the Fourteenth Century, edited from a Unique Manuscript at Newbattle Abbey by Francisque Michel. Printed for the Roxburghe Club* (Edinburgh, 1873). Michel was, doubtless, in error in assigning this romance to the fourteenth century. The manuscript is of that date, but the poem, in all likelihood, was composed in the previous century, for it appears to be one of the sources of *Claris et Laris* (begun in 1268). 8270 lines preserved, but a few are missing at the end. Author, unknown. Dialect, Isle-de-France, it would seem. Date, probably third quarter of the thirteenth century.

Fully analyzed in HLF, XXVIII, 139ff., so that G. Paris, *op. cit.*, XXX, 60, devotes only three or four lines to it. Cp., besides, Gröber, II, II, 789f. and Arturo Graf's essay, *"Artu nell' Etna,"* in his *Miti, Leggende, e Superstizioni del Medio Evo*, II, 303ff. (2 vols. Turin, 1892—3).

Floriant is the posthumous son of Elyadus, a king of Sicily, and his wife, the daughter of King Clauvegris. Elyadus's seneschal, Maragot (Maragoz, Marigoz) being madly in love with the queen, who rejects his advances, treacherously murders his master on a hunt. He wants now to marry the widow, but she, having obtained a respite, on the plea of pregnancy, flies to Monreal, under the care of Omer, lord of that castle. In a forest, on the way, however, she gives birth to the hero of the romance, who is at once snatched away to Mongibel (Mount Aetna) by three sea-fairies, the chief of whom is Arthur's sister, Morgan. These fairies take the child to church, have him baptized, and name him Floriant. In the meanwhile, the seneschal usurps the crown of Sicily and prepares to lay siege to Monreal. — Floriant, under Morgan's care, is well-educated in the seven arts and in knighthood. She makes him a knight, tells him that he is of royal birth, and gives him a magic boat (independent of weather), the *cortine* of which is adorned with pictures from astronomy, the tale of Troy, and love-stories, and sends him to Arthur's court. *En route,* he delivers from captivity a number of Arthur's subjects who are held prisoners by Moradas and sends both captor and prisoners on ahead to Arthur's court at Cardigan — then kills a monster that had been devouring the maidens of the Ille as Puceles Beles, whose capital was La Blanche Cite, and despatches their queen (Alemandine), also, to Arthur's court. This queen arrives at Cardigan at Whitsuntide, whilst Arthur is waiting, according to his custom, for some adventure, before commencing his meal. On hearing of Floriant's exploit, the king (on Gawain's advice) proclaims a tournament, in order to attract him to it. In the meanwhile, Floriant delivers, still further, a number of girls from a knight, who, at his *amie's* command, was cutting off enough tresses from the girls whom he halted to make her a tent. (This knight, however, was not to blame, according to Arthur's courtiers, for he was merely obeying his *amie*). He next lands at a castle occupied by one of Arthur's foresters, and soon sees his magic boat speeding back across the sea, by itself, through Morgan's enchantment. Equipped with armor by the forester and with two of his (the forester's) sons accompanying him, Floriant goes to the tournament, joins the weaker side, is blackguarded by Kay, but unhorses some of Arthur's best knights.[12] Just at this moment, he receives a letter from Morgan informing him of his name and parentage and, also, of the fact that Maragot is besieging his mother. Arthur and his knights now offer the young man their assistance and embark for Sicily. On the way they touch at an island which is inhabited by Sathenes-horrible beasts with huge ears. When Maragot learns of Arthur's approach, he begs aid of the Emperor of Constantinople, the suzerain of Sicily, and the latter sails for Sicily with an army. A spy brings to Floriant's mother in Mon-

---

[12] The passage seems plainly imitated from the Vulgate *Mort Artu.* Cp. Bruce's edition, pp. 7 ff. The author includes (ll. 4767 f.) Galehaut and Mador among Arthur's knights, so he doubtless knew the prose *Lancelot.*

real news of the expected arrival of both Arthur and the Emperor.
The latter arrives first, but he does not oppose Arthur's landing,
because there would be no honor in winning a battle, when his
foe was at such a disadvantage. In the first battle between the
opposing hosts, which ends in the Emperor's retreat to Palermo,
Floriant, charging through the enemy's lines, chances to catch
a glimpse of Floriete, the Emperor's beautiful daughter, who had
accompanied him to Sicily, and the two fall in love with each
other at first sight. That night, both indulge in love-soliloquies
about each other. The following day our hero's mother meets
him and learns from him the full story of his abduction by the
fairies. — Floriant and Gawain are the leading knights in the
next encounter, and the sight of the former's exploit intensifies
Florete's passion for him. She has a heated altercation with some
other girls, who have also fallen in love with Floriant, and vows
that she will marry no one else. Floriant, on his part, in the
midst of the battle, in so overcome by the recollection of Florete's
beauty that he drops down on the battle-field and has to be taken
home by Gawain and others. Arthur visits him, but cannot ex-
tract from him the cause of his trouble. Gawain, however, is
more successful and encourages him to hopefulness, when he expresses himself in terms of despair in regard to his passion. Florete,
in the meanwhile, having witnessed her lover's collapse, feared
that he had been killed and took to her bed, which causes her
father great anxiety. On the suggestion of Blancardine, one of
her attendants, the princess now despatches a boy, named Jolis,
to ascertain the truth about her lover. Floriant sends a reply
that his fall was due to his love of Florete. Furthermore, through
the same messenger, it is arranged that Floriant and Gawain shall
meet Florete and Blancardine the same night in a *vergier*. The
couples spend that night and the succeeding nights together in
this place. A dwarf spies upon them and tells the emperor of
what is going on, but Jolis warns the lovers in time for them
to escape to Arthur's camp. The emperor is furious and attacks
Arthur's host without success. He then holds a parley with
Arthur, who tells him the truth about Maragot's treachery. There

follows a duel between Maragot and Floriant, and the former, being vanquished, confesses his murder of the latter's father. Still further, after the duel, Maragot is tried before a jury of twelve kings, and, in accordance with their verdict, he is drawn and quartered. A double wedding is now celebrated in Palermo with great splendor, the couples being, respectively, Floriant and Florete, Gawain and Blancardine. The festivities on this occasion lasted forty days.[13] — After this, Arthur, with Gawain and his bride, sails for London, which he reaches in fifteen days. — Floriant and his spouse remain in his kingdom of Sicily and in due time a son is born to them.[14] — For three years Floriant performs no feats of arms and overhearing, by accident, in the streets, some women criticizing him on this score, he resolves to seek adventures in Britain and his wife goes along with him.[15] They pass through Calabria and Apulia to the "port de Chipre" (the chief haven in his dominion), and, leaving all their knights behind them there, proceed by way of Rome to Britain, under disguised names, viz. Li Biaus Sauvages and la Plaisans de l'Ille, respectively. *En route*, he kills a dragon (seventeen feet long) and overcomes in combat a nobleman named Julian, whose wife, in marrying him, had made him promise that he would bring to her the head of her first husband's slayer. Not being acquainted with this slayer, the second husband was required to fight every knight that came along and compel him to tell his name. Accompanied by the vanquished man, Floriant goes to Rome and relieves the city, then besieged by pagans, killing the Sultan. He then sends Julien forward to Arthur at Camelot, but when Julien tells Arthur that his victorious adversary was Li Biaus Sauvages, the monarch does not know who this is. So, too, with the rest of the twenty knights

---

[13] This is, perhaps, the most elaborate and interesting description of such festivities in Old French romance. The musicians and *conteurs*, of course, are very prominent in it.

[14] The archbishop who baptizes the child names him *Froart*, because so many shields will be *frouez* (l. 6508) by him, when he is grown.

[15] The imitation of Chrétien's *Erec* is obvious.

whom he thus sends to Arthur, including Nabudan,[16] who had
attempted to carry off Florete. In the course of time, however,
Arthur begins to divine the truth. — Finally, Floriant and his
wife arrive in London at Whitsuntide, whilst the king is holding
his court there, and are cordially welcomed by all. Almost at the
same moment, however, comes intelligence of the death of Florete's
father and in a fortnight she and her husband set out for Constantinople, which they reach in fifteen days. Later they transfer their residence to Palermo. — One day Floriant is chasing
a big white stag and the animal after leading him to Morgan's castle
(Mongibel) vanishes there. It turns out that Morgan had sent the
stag for the express purpose of drawing him to this castle; for,
says the fairy, he was about to die, and she has now brought him
to a place where no one dies. Hither she will bring Arthur, too,
when he is mortally wounded. Floriant laments the absence of
Florete, but his lamentation is premature, for the same night
Morgan despatches three fairies to fetch her to the enchanted
castle. They found her asleep, after much grieving over her lost
husband, and they bore her back to Mongibel. — Here the fragment ends.

Notwithstanding some extravagances of the *amour courtois*
in the love-story, *Floriant et Florete* is one of the most pleasing
of the later metrical romances. It possesses the great advantage
that an incident, like the siege, with some semblance of reality
occupies the central position in the plot, instead of a series of
fantastic knight-errant adventures, as is ordinarily the case with
the romances. This feature of its construction gives solidity to
the narrative, as a whole, although even here episodes of the usual
kind, of course, are not entirely wanting. The supernatural element in the romance, moreover, is artfully disposed, for, in ser-
ving as a framework to the incidents of the hero's career, he is
brought up in fairyland and he returns there at the end to enjoy
immortality — it surrounds his whole story with the glamour of
the imagination. Morgan's fairy palace acquires, too, an added

---

[16] Very likely, a corruption of *Nabusardan* in the prose *Tristan*.

interest, perhaps, by being transferred to the brilliant atmosphere of the South and to so world-famous a mountain as Aetna.[17]

26. *Li Atres Perillox (Li Atre Perillos)* — i. e. *The Perilous Churchyard.* Edited anonymously[18] under the title, *Der Gefahrvolle Kirchof,* in the *Archiv für das Studium der Neueren Sprachen,* XLII, 135—212 (1868). 6667 lines.[19] Author, unknown. Dia-

---

[17] As Graf suggests in the above-mentioned essay, the Normans were doubtless responsible for the connection of Aetna with Arthurian traditions. Cp., further, on this subject I, 34, note 74, above. Manifestly, however, this connection was of literary origin. It was, doubtless, started by some noble reader of the romances in the latter part of the twelfth century. Other heroes of mediaeval romance, such as Huon of Bordeaux and Rainouart, had visited fairyland, and our author was, doubtless, familiar with these instances, for he appears to have had a wide acquaintance with earlier romances. His hero's end, however, was, most likely, suggested by Arthur's. Gröber, *loc. cit.* has called attention to the writer's borrowings from the *chansons de geste* in the matter of nomenclature. As a matter of fact, a glance at E. Langlois's *Table des Noms Propres de Toute Nature dans les Chansons de Geste Imprimées,* pp. 221 f. (Paris, 1904), will show how common the names of the hero and heroine (in variant forms) — especially the former — are in works of that class.

[18] According to Wasmuth, p. 5, the editor's name was Schirmer. This editor imagined that the MS. from which he printed the romance — MS. 1433, f. fr., Bibl. Nat. — was unique. G. Paris, however, pointed out, p. 79, that the poem is preserved, also, in MS. 2168 of the same collection and in the Chantilly MS. which contains the unique copy of *Libeaus, Descouneus, Fergus,* etc. A fourth MS., now lost, was listed in the old catalogues of the library of the French kings, and a study of the relations of the extant MSS. shows that still others must have once existed. Cp. Von Zingerle, p 274. Of the extant MSS. those in the Bibl. Nat. are closest to each other.

[19] This is the number in the printed text. None of the extant MSS. agree exactly in this regard. Von Zingerle, pp. 278 ff., prints an episode of 666 lines which occur just after line 3002 in MS. 1433 (and in this MS. alone). This episode, however, is worthless, and its linguistic peculiarities prove that it is not by the author of the original romance. — Because of the frequency of "Reicher Reim" in ll. 2791 —5718, E. Freymond, *Zs. f. rom. Ph.,* VI, 190, thought that they were interpolated. He suggested, indeed, that the whole romance had undergone redaction.

lect, Western Eure (Normandy). Date, Probably third quarter
of the fourteenth century.

G. Paris, HLF, XXX, 78ff., Theodor Wassmuth: *Untersuchungen der Reime des altfranzösischen Artusromans, Li Atre
Perillos.* Bonn diss. 1905. Wolfram von Zingerle: "Zum altfranzösischen Artusromane, Li Atre Perillos," *Zs. f. frz. Spr. u.
Litt.*, XXXVI[1], 274ff. (1910).

Whilst Arthur and his company are seated at the table, a
knight — later named Escanor de la Montaigne — rides into the
hall and carries off a damsel whom Arthur had recently appointed
boutilliere (female butler) and placed under Gawain's protection.
As the intruder leaves the hall, he insolently announces the road
that he is going to take and challenges any one to follow him. —
Gawain decides, however, strangely enough, that he will wait until
the feast is over, before he will pursue the abductor. Arthur is so
upset by the incident that he thrusts a knife into a loaf of bread,
leans on it in revery, and breaks the knife, before he knows it.[20]
He next expresses his disappointment at Gawain's conduct, and
Gawain replies that he had feared the king's disapproval, if he
sprang up abruptly from the table. Gawain now begins the pursuit of Escanor and soon meets Kay's horse without a rider, Kay,
himself, having been unhorsed in an attempt to rescue the *boutilliere.* — In the course of the pursuit Gawain encounters three
girls and a youth, who were under the false impression that they
had seen him slain by three knights. These same knights, moreover, had put out the youth's eyes, because he had tried to help
the supposed Gawain. Gawain promises to punish the offenders
and proceeds on his way, without disclosing his identity. He comes
next to a castle where it is not the custom to admit any one after
sunset, but the lord of the castle, who is bringing venison home
from a hunt, offers to take Gawain in, if he will leave his horse
(Gringalet), outside. Gawain, however, is unwilling to do this
and decides to spend the night in the neighboring churchyard,

---

[20] For this *motif* Cp. Pseudo-Wauchier, ll. 15892ff. and prose
Lancelot, III, 272ff. The former is probably our author's source.

despite the lord's warnings. Furthermore, he obtains a promise
from the lord that, if Escanor comes to the castle, he will not
admit him but will require him to turn over the damsel he has
abducted to his (the lord's) sister for the night.[21] This promise the
lord of the castle fulfills. — In the perilous churchyard that night
a girl issues from a tomb and tells Gawain how her step-mother
had bereft her of her reason and how a devil had restored it to
her on condition that she should give herself up to him. Accordingly, he was accustomed to shut her up in the tomb during the
day and visit her every night. Gawain fights this devil, strengthen-
ing himself from time to time by looking upon a cross in the
middle of the churchyard (as the girl had advised him), and, in
the end, cuts off his adversary's head. After this adventure, Gawain continues his pursuit of Escanor and overtakes him. Escanor's
strength increases with the sun[22] — up to noon it is equal to that
of three knights — then it declines until compline (evening prayer).
All this Gawain learns from the girl of the churchyard — also,
that his (Gawain's) mother, who possessed supernatural powers,
had predicted the achievements of her son and had urged him to
prowess — only, she had not mentioned Escanor, because of her
fear in regard to Gawain's encounter with him. Nevertheless, Gawain kills him. After Escanor's death, it turns out that the girl
whom he had abducted was, in reality, his accomplice and had been
sent to Arthur's court, so that he might provoke a quarrel with
Gawain. — On returning to Carduel with the two girls, Gawain
comes upon another girl who is in great distress over the loss of
her sparrow-hawk. He sends his two companions back to Carduel and goes with the new girl in quest of her bird, which leads
them on and on deep into the forest. This girl's lover, finding
her with Gawain, becomes jealous, seizes their horses, and leads
the animals away. His *amie* and Gawain are thus compelled to

---

[21] This *motif* is repeated later on in Gawain's pursuit of Escanor.
[22] As is well-known, this was originally the attribute of Gawain.
Cp. the examples in Bruce's edition of the *Mort Artu*, pp. 287 f. The
author of the present romance is doubtless responsible for its transfer
to Escanor.

spend that night — a stormy one — in the woods together and their relations on this occasion seem to prove that the lover's jealousy was not unnatural. The next day they obtain horses from a knight — Raguidel de l'Angarde, as he is later named — in exchange for the hawk, which, however, is taken merely as a pledge that Gawain owes him a favor for the future. Gawain's next encounter is with Espinogre, whose suit a girl had long rejected, but finally accepts, with the proviso that he shall prove himself superior to Gawain. Thinking that Gawain is dead, he agrees to this and his lady-love permits him to lie with her. Immediately afterwards, however, he deserts her. Gawain now vanquishes him and compels 'him to go back to his *amie*. Contrary to his custom, Gawain will not tell Espinogre his name — says that he has lost it and must now go in search of it (i. e. must do deeds, worthy of his name).

As a matter of fact, Gawain, in this part of the romance, is often called *Cil sans non* (the One without a Name). — In searching for Gringalet, Gawain meets a knight — afterwards called Cadre — who alternately laughs and cries. It turns out that the parents of this knight's *amie* are about to force her into a marriage with a rich man and that she has summoned her lover to come to her in this crisis. He laughs because he is to see her that day; he weeps because he will never see her again thereafter. In any event, he will have to fight twenty knights, before he can see her, and Gawain and Espinogre resolve to aid him in this combat. — The girl whose sparrow-hawk Gawain had caught and who had remained with him ever since now becomes hungry and thirsty, and Gawain has to force the young mistress of a neighboring castle to grant her food and drink. This inhospitable lady, as it happens, was Raguidel's *fiancée*, and, on Raguidel's requiring Gawain to get possession of her for him, in redemption of the pledge implied above, Gawain does so. She is at first angry with Gawain (whose identity she does not know), but when she discovers that the man to whom he hands her over is her bethrothed, she begs his (Gawain's) pardon. During this affair, Codrovain, a brother of the lady of the castle, rushes to his sister's aid and is unhorsed by Gawain. He is the jealous knight, the sparrow-hawk of whose *amie* Gawain

had recaptured and who had carried off Gringalet. Gawain now
recovers his steed and makes the knight forgive his *amie*. Codrovain's brothers are also about to assail Gawain, but Codrovain explains the situation and they now all agree to go with Gawain and
assist Cadre against the twenty knights. They defeat these knights
and Cadre regains his sweetheart, after which Gawain continues
his "search for his name." — At the castle where he next
stops, his host, Tristan-qui-ne-rit, labors under the prevalent false
impression that Gawain is dead: A knight, he says, had recently
come to his castle, and, later on, two of this knight's companions —
Li Orgellox Fae (The Proud One with Supernatural Powers) and
Goumeres — bearing Gawain's dismembered body. According to
the report of these knights, they were courting two girls who had
already dedicated their love to Gawain and Perceval, respectively,
although they had never seen those heroes, and had finally extorted
from the girls a promise that they would accept them (Li Orgellox
Fae and Goumeres), in case they succeeded in overthrowing Gawain and Perceval. The knights pretend to have slain Gawain
and Perceval and to be bringing the former's remains now to the
castle. Their host believes them and enchases in gold the right
arm of the supposed Gawain, just as if it were a saint's. Gawain
does not reveal his identity — nevertheless, he assures the lord
of the castle that Gawain is not dead. In the meanwhile, since
the girls in question deny that the dismembered corpse was Gawain's, their suitors offer to uphold the truth of their assertion
in combat against all comers. Espinogre overthrows Goumeres
and Gawain Li Orgellox Fae. The vanquished knights are taken
to court and Gawain, believing that he has accomplished enough
to have "found his name" again, tells who he is. It now turns
out that the three girls of Gawain's first adventure after leaving
court were identical with those whose love was sought by the two
vanquished knights and their companion and that these same
knights were responsible, also, for the blinding of the youth. In
response to Gawain's upbraidings, Li Orgellox Fae, who possesses
supernatural powers, resuscitates at Tristan's castle the slain knight

(le cortois de Huberlant)[23] whom he had palmed off as Gawain, and later, in the forest where Gawain had met the three girls, restores sight to the blinded youth. On their arrival at court, Arthur wishes to take vengeance on all who had boasted that they had slain Gawain, but Gawain tells the king of the covenant of peace which he and these men had agreed on and the king foregoes his wrath. The various knights now are united with their respective *amies* and the romance concludes with a description of the festivities on this occasion.

The author of this romance has planned his work with more forethought than is usual in this species of literature. For example, the full circumstances of Gawain's first adventure after he has left the court (the adventure of the three girls and the blinded youth) are not cleared up until the end of the poem. In his effort to produce the impression of mystery, no other romancer, moreover, has made such systematic use of the trick of holding back the names of the characters until the end of the particular episode in which they figure. The author's invention is above the average and his narrative flows easily, but perhaps the numerous descriptions of mediaeval hospitality which the poem contains, constitute, after all, its most interesting feature.[24]

27. *Claris et Laris*. Edited from the unique MS. 1447 (fonds fr., Bibl. Nat.) by Johann Alton: *Li Romans de Claris et Laris*, Bibliothek des Litterarischen Vereins in Stuttgart, CLXIX (Tübingen, 1884). 30369 lines. Author, an unknown minstrel. Dialect, Isle-de-France (Picard border). Date (begun), 1268.

---

[23] On the homeward journey Gawain has one of his innumerable fights with friends, in which the combatants are unaware of each other's identity. This time his adversary, a black knight, turns out to be Li Lais Hardis, who is engaged in a friendly quest for him.

[24] E. Brugger, H. Morf-*Festschrift*, p. 70, calls attention to the custom of the author of this romance of drawing characters from other romances — Espinogre from *Meraugis,* Raguidel from the *Vengeance Raguidel,* and Codrovain from *Durmart* — and ascribing to them new adventures. I see no ground for the same scholar's view that "Guiot's *Perceval*" was a source of the present romance. Cp. *Zs. f. frz. Spr. u. Litt.*, XXXI[2], 131, note 13.

G. Paris, HLF, XXX, 124ff., Gröber, II, 788f. Martin
Klose, *Der Roman von Claris und Laris in seinen Beziehungen zur
altfranzösischen Artuseik des XII. und XIII. Jahrhunderts: Beihefte zur Zs. f. rom. Ph.*, No. 63 (Halle, 1916).

The story of this tedious romance is as follows:
Claris was the son of a duke (presumably French), his friend,
Laris, was the son of the King of Germany. Laris's sister —
called variously in the poem, Lidoine, Ydoyne, Lidaine — had
married Ladon(t), an aged king of Gascony, although she, herself,
is young. Claris, who is in this king's service, falls in love with
her. After being knighted, the friends go forth on adventures.
They first overcome six robber knights, for whom a dwarf acts
as a decoy, and deliver Yvain—then, with Yvain's assistance, dispose
of a band of thirty robbers in an adjacent forest. — After this,
Claris is almost drowned, being in such a profound revery over
his ladylove, that he does not observe that his horse is taking him
into the river. — The companions next bring relief to a lady,
who is besieged by King Nador, and assist her in resisting the
siege (which is described at great length). — In the end, Claris
and Laris have a combat *à quatre* with Nador and his nephew,
Daton. The latter are vanquished and agree to give up the siege. —
The friends now liberate a number of knights, who are kept at
hard labor by two brutal scoundrels — and shortly thereafter they
perform the same service for Gawain and his *amie*, who had been
overpowered by four knights. In the course of this affair the
two knights, being temporarily separated, are so fearful for each
other's safety that they swoon. They next aid Carados, who had
foolishly offered to settle his claim to his lady-love as against a rival — Ladas de la Rochele — by a combat in which he should
have two men to help him and Ladas eight. The smaller number,
however, were victorious. — They now come to the forest of Broceliande, a list of whose marvels is posted at the point where they
enter it. They penetrate into the Castle Perilous, making their
way past a tower that burned perpetually, through doors that are
guarded by wild beasts, giants, etc., and they overcome the lord
of the place, who is a great sorcerer. Morgan le Fay, Arthur's

sister, next has them conducted to her enchanted palace — they
don't know where they are going — and there proffers them all
sensual delights, but avers that they will never be able to leave
the place. In the night Laris overhears his friend weeping, and,
on pressing him, learns that he is bemoaning the hopelessness of
his love for Ydoine, but Laris comforts him by promising to help
him to win his sister's favor. After this, Madoine, one of Morgan's
fairies, has an *amour* with Laris and betrays to him the means
of escaping from the enchanted palace. Having accomplished this,
the friends go to the Roche Perdue (Lost Rock), on top of which
there was a castle, built by Merlin, and vanquish the knights
of Matidas, who is lord of this castle. Assailed by wild beasts and
in the midst of a great storm, they journey on through the forest
until they come upon the castle of an old knight, who informs
them that King Thoas nearby is unjustly holding captive Kings
Loth, Marc, and Baudemagu, and the Duke of Montagu. After
freeing these men, the friends continue their journey until they
reach Arthur's court at Cardigan.

The king entertains them handsomely and issues the command that they shall be treated with honor wherever they go.
It does not suit the young men, however, to be constant objects
of attention. So they obtain from a hermit arms that belonged
to Kay and Gales li Chauz, for whom they are mistaken in a
tournament the next day, and again when they deliver Brandaliz
from Li Rous de la Gaudine (The Red one of the Forest), Laris
slaying the latter. They next kill a nest (so to speak) of eight
dragons. — Thereus, emperor of Rome, demands tribute of Arthur,
who refuses it. On learning from Brandaliz that Claris and Laris
are at his castle, Arthur and his queen ride thither, and solicit
their aid in the war. The friends gladly consent. In connection
with the account of the battle that follows we have long lists of the
knights that fought under the banners of Thereus and Arthur,
respectively. Arthur, of course, wins. Immediately afterwards the
companions have to return to Gascony, for the King of Spain,
who wishes to get possession of Ladon's wife, is besieging him in
Toulouse. Claris and Laris, however, with Gawain, Yvain, and

other Arthurian knights, effect the relief of the town and drive away the besieger and his forces. The queen now visits Claris, who had been wounded in the battle, and he makes love to her. When she rebukes him, he swoons and everybody thinks that he is dead, but, on Laris's advice, she kisses him and makes him well again. — The two friends now start for Britain with Gawain, etc. One night, *en route*, however, Madoine the fay, who is pregnant by Laris, seizes him, whilst he is asleep, and carries him to Morgan's fairy palace. In the meanwhile, Claris, searching for his friend, rescues a girl who is about to be ravished by Li Orguilleus de la Gaudine (The Proud One of the Forest), vanquishes two knights at a bridge, and, owing to the name of Our Lord on his sword, is able to deliver a girl from the power of the devil who was in love with her. Next follow, evidently, in imitation of the prose *Lancelot*, utterly commonplace adventures — two each — of Gawain, Yvain, Gaheriet, Brandaliz, Sagremor, Li Laiz Hardis, and — one, each — of Lucan, Kay, Bedivere and Agravain. The adventures of Yvain, Lucan and Kay end in their imprisonment, the first two in Thoas's castle, the third in Madoine's palace. — Claris, in quest of Laris, rescues a young girl from a hateful marriage with Bilas, an old duke, and, as the most loyal of knights, delivers Li Laiz Hardis and others from the enchantment of a singer. — Li Laiz Hardis next frees a lady from a dragon which has taken possession of her castle. — By the help of a *vilain*, Claris penetrates to the room in Morgan's palace where Laris is incarcerated. Along with Kay and the well-disposed *vilain*, they escape from the palace and come to Thoas's castle, where they liberate Yvain and Lucan, who, with Kay, return to Camelot. — Gawain is treacherously entrapped in a castle, but kills the owner and puts on his armor in which disguise he escapes. Gaheries and Brandeliz — the latter after an adventure with an old hag and her deformed lover — seek hospitality at Thoas's castle and are cast by him into dungeons. Claris and Laris, however, seize Thoas in the forest and after compelling him to set free Gaheries and Brandalis, despatch him to Arthur's court. — Sagremor's horse having been killed by a boar, he gets into an enchanted boat, with no one in it, and is brought to a deserted city, follows the voice of a girl who is singing a song, fights a knight, and is about to be attacked by other knights, when the girl protects him. Nevertheless, he is thrown into prison. — Claris and Laris have an encounter with Bedivere and a knight who has been deprived of his inheritance by his brother. When Bedivere recognizes them and they recognize him, they stop the fight and all four go against the unjust brother, who, after a combat, however, is reconciled to the rest. They next come to the castle where Sagremor is a captive, and in their honor, the lord of the castle liberates his prisoner. — Li Laiz Hardis attacks an envious knight for insulting language about the Round Table, but is overpowered, when a friend of his adversary joins in the combat, and is imprisoned. Claris and Laris, however, soon deliver him. — At Pentecost, Arthur holds a tournament to draw Claris and Laris out of their concealment. Gawain, Claris, and Laris resolve to attend it, but disguised in black arms (then, the sign of the first year of knighthood). They take sides against Arthur's men and vanquish them. Arthur's mortification, however, is relieved, when he hears who the victors are. Laris, having been wounded in the jousts, is attended by Marine, Yvain's sister, and becomes enamored of her. — Ladon dies and Savari(s), the king of Spain, invades Gascony, and by the treachery of certain noblemen, gets hold of the queen, Idoine, and has her shut up in Montjardin on the Spanish border. Claris and Laris, however, assisted by Gawain and others, come to the rescue, defeat Savari's host, kill him, and seize Montjardin, save the castle, but are at once themselves surrounded by a Spanish army. Lucan is despatched to Arthur for help. The king answers the appeal, comes with an army, and defeats the Spaniards and frees Ydoine, who is now married to Claris. Claris soon joins Arthur, however, and participates in the siege of Luiserne, which the Spaniards are finally forced to surrender. The whole land now submits to Claris and he is crowned king. Arthur next goes back to Britain and he is quickly followed by Claris and Laris, because the latter wishes to press his suit with Marine. Ydoine insists on accompanying them and leaves her infant child in charge of nurses. On their way through Gascony, a lustful knight, at whose castle they stop and who requires a new bed-fellow every night, first failing in an effort to seduce Ydoine, comes to her chamber at night to outrage her. Claris and Laris kill him and many of his followers, and the next morning endeavor to escape from the castle, but are driven back into it by the dead man's vassals — only Laris is left outside. Whilst wandering about disconsolate, Laris meets with Karados Brief-Bras and Kador. These kings and their men return with him and rescue his sister and her husband. Proceeding on their journey, they repel an attack which Lidas's mother causes to be made on them, cross successfully a river in a boat which, according to an inscription, will bear only perfectly loyal persons. When Ydoine, however, before landing, boasts of this as a proof that she has never caused her husband any trouble, she suddenly finds herself up to her breast in water. — When they first reach Camelot (Kamaalot), they are welcomed by Arthur and Guinevere and the rest, but Marine's absence makes Laris ill with disappointment. His case is even worse, when, on Ascension Day, as Arthur is holding court at Caerleon, news comes that Tallas of Denmark is besieging Urien with the purpose of forcing him to give him (Tallas) his daughter in marriage. Indeed, nothing can revive Laris from his swoon, until his sister, pretending to be Marine, bestows on him a kiss. Yvain, Laris, etc., now ride away to rescue Urien and Marine, but whilst they are on the way, Madoine almost breaks up the expedition by dressing up different people te represent Loth (Gawain's father) as dead, Urien as mortally wounded, and Ydoine as pursued by two knights, her purpose being to draw away Gawain, Yvain, and Claris, respectively, from the party. In this way, she is able to abduct Laris. Some of the knights whom she employs in this affair, however, later reveal the plot to Claris and he is able to rescue Laris. — Gawain, wandering in search of the men who were apparently carrying Loth's corpse, delivers from captivity certain knights. Yvain pursues the man who impersonated his father and had stolen his (Yvain's) steed — at the instance of a hermit, however, is reconciled to him, on learning that fairies had

compelled him to play this rôle. Yvain, by making the sign of
the cross, delivers a castle from a devil to whom its inhabitants
had been paying human tribute. — Claris and Laris overcome
and capture Moderas, who is trying to force a knight to surrender his daughter to him — make themselves at home in Olim-
piaus's castle, during the absence of its master and his vassals,
and, on the latter's return, escape, after a severe combat. Gawain
overtakes them at a forester's house and learns from them that
Loth is not dead. They now rescue Yvain, from some of Urien's
enemies. All four knights and their followers after this reach
Urien's city. In the battle that ensues Laris overthrows Tallas
in the presence of Marine, but is later, himself, knocked down in
the throng, whereupon his lady-love, thinking that he is dead,
falls into a deep swoon. — After Claris, Laris and their friends
have broken through the encircling host and joined Urien in the
city, the latter, in good faith, reports that his daughter is dead,
but Claris, suspecting the truth, resuscitates her by pretending
that he is Laris and kissing her — the exact counterpart of his
wife's trick on Laris. Laris is now called in and in the presence of Claris, he and Marine are formally betrothed. Laris
challenges Tallas to a personal combat and unhorses him, but the
fighting becomes general, until finally Urien's supporters re-enter
the city. At first, Marine will not speak to her lover, because
he had issued the above-mentioned challenge, without asking her
consent. Arthur now marches with his army to Urien's help. In
the battle that follows, Laris is missing (really is taken prisoner),
which fills Marine with despair, but thirty of Arthur's knights
go in quest of him. Arthur says that they must all meet at Clavent
on the Danish border a month hence. Claris and Gawain overcome knights (the second of them a robber), Yvain avenges four
girls, whose lovers have been slain by two brothers. These brothers,
in turn, were each endeavoring to win their widowed sister-in-
law's hand, the condition of success being that her new husband
should have avenged the death of the first. — Sagremor vanquishes
a knight, to whom, nevertheless, his lady-love remains loyal. Agravain wins the prize (a hawk) in a tourney, but is imprisoned in

a Danish castle. — Gaheries delivers a girl whom her jealous lover, on account of her supposed unchastity, kept immersed up to the waist in a cold spring, after which she and this lover are reconciled. — Guerrehes rescues a girl from a forced marriage, but will not, himself, wed her until he has discovered Laris. A valet, however, soon betrays him into the hands of Tallas, who imprisons him, with Laris. — Whilst Brandaliz, on his quest, is sleeping in the forest one night by the fire of an old man (really Merlin), a voice upbraids him for not consulting Merlin as to Laris's whereabouts and adds that he will not see Laris until he has been a prisoner, himself, for two months and Laris, by Merlin's counsel, delivers him. Sure enough, shortly thereafter, he becomes a prisoner, whilst trying to free a lady from the oppression of four *vilains*. — Karados kills a giant who is ravaging a district, but later becomes a prisoner in the same prison as Agravain. — After overcoming the lord of a castle which could only be reached by a bridge which was made of a magnet, Li Laiz Hardis winds up in the same prison as the two questers just named. — Claris comes to Merlin's fire and asks him where Laris is captive. Merlin tells him that Laris is in Denmark — tells him, moreover, how he must first liberate the imprisoned questers and adds directions as to how he is to deliver Laris, last of all, from his dungeon. —

He first frees Brandaliz. After having rescued a knight from four knights who were about to put out his eyes, Lucan is, himself, imprisoned with Agravain, etc. — Kay, on his way to Denmark, robs a squire of his master's steed. The master unhorses him and recovers the steed. Kay spends the night at an abbey, represents that a band of fourteen robbers had deprived him of his steed, receives another from the monks, but is afterwards thrown into the same prison as Lucan. Bedivere, too, is about to be imprisoned, when he is rescued by Claris and Brandalis. — Gales li Chaus meets a girl, who is carrying the head of her slain lover. — He kills the slayer and the girl ties the head of her dead lover's enemy to her horse's tail and rides away to her home, accompanied by Gales. Gales, however, is soon cast into the same prison as Lucan, etc. — Mordred is about to rape a girl, when her two brothers intervene and take him captive. Gawain, however, arrives opportunely and saves him. Gawain chides Mordred for his purposed outrage, after which there is a general reconciliation. The next day Gawain and Mordred meet Claris, Brandalis and Bedivere. — Yder puts up in an apparently empty castle, but in the night hears a lady lamenting. His arms are stolen from him the same night. When he meets Claris, etc., the following day, Mordred mocks at him, because of his unfurnished condition, and he retorts that Mordred would never dare to attempt to recover them, Mordred accepts the challenge, rides off to the castle, but has the same experience as Yder — only he loses his steed, in addition.

Claris now tries his luck — does not lay aside his arms and lie down by his steed, but keeps awake. The woful lady comes in and tells him that he has done right, for a magician has taken possession of the castle and the bed in which Yder and Mordred lay was enchanted, so that any one who occupied it fell at once into a profound slumber. Claris next vanquishes the magician, recovers his friends' belongings, and binds over the vanquished man never to enter the castle again. — The Black Knight is entertained at a castle, and, as champion of its lord, defeats a knight named Tantalis. He is, himself, however, captured by Tallas and imprisoned with Laris and Guerrehes. — A girl who is betrayed to a miller by her father, in anger, devotes herself and her father to the devil, who at once takes possession of the mill. Kador tries this adventure, but fails ignominiously. — So, too, Mordred, but the devil evacuates the premises, as soon as Claris appears. — The King of the Golden Circlet strays into the deserted city, where Gaheriet is imprisoned, and suffers the same fate. An inscription there declares that they will be kept fasting until "the true companion" (Claris) arrives and delivers them. — The King of Northumberland and Sagremor come to the castle of a knight, who is really a vassal of the former, although none of the parties know it. Sagremor vanquishes this lord's enemy, who has already killed two of his sons, and then reconciles the adversaries. They ride on to the deserted city where Gaheriet is imprisoned. Claris and his companions, also, soon arrive in this city. The spell that rested on the city was due to the fact that a great prelate had summoned its lord to confess himself and fast, but he had refused. In punishment therefor the lord is shut up in a subterranean vault. Receiving countless blows from invisible hands, Gawain and Claris rescue the repentant lord from this vault and undo the spell. After this, Claris and his eleven companions come to the hermitage where Merlin had commanded him to wait until the number grew to fifteen before he entered Denmark. — Elidus, King of Ireland, stops at the castle of a lady who falls in love with him, and on hearing him say that he had never loved but one woman, comes to his room in the night to inquire who was this woman; on learning that it is she, she spends the remainder of the night with him. — Galegantin punishes a knight for casting off a faithful dwarf, in favor of a false one, who had slandered his companion. — Kalogrenant comes to a bespelled castle where every one becomes like the thing he first sees on entering it. He first sees a girl, consequently he becomes like a girl. The next day he rides on to the Danish castle where Agravain is in prison, then to Tallas' castle where Laris is a captive, then, to the hermitage where Claris and his company are. Since he looks like a girl, the Danes do not molest him. On approaching the hermitage, however, Mordred, laboring under the same delusion as the rest, tries to rape him, but is worsted in the struggle and loses his horse to Kalogrenant, who now joins Claris, etc., tells them about Mordred and changes to male attire. — Erec, by a successful joust wins a crown and frees captives. — Cliges slays an insolent *vilain* and his wife, the latter being also a fierce participant in the combat. — Dodinel was a wag and by pleasantries avoids combats in his wanderings and palms himself off on Tallas as a minstrel. — Aglu (Eglu) Desvaus champions successfully the cause of certain nuns against a knight, who wishes to rob the convent of its property. — Tor, son of Ares, after vanquishing a knight who had spoken of Laris in a derogatory manner and protecting a girl against a dishonest uncle, who had tried to appropriate her estate to himself, is imprisoned with Agravain, etc. — The number of his company having grown to fifteen — the number required by Merlin's prophecy — Claris now moves against Tallas. They first deliver Agravain and his nine fellow-prisoners. At this castle they, also, clothe themselves as hermits (another of Merlin's requirements). They have moreover, colored their visages, so that they are not recognizable. — Li Biaus Mauves, in his quest for Laris, jousts successively with three women disguised as knights and unhorses all three. He, too, later falls into Laris's prison. — Bretiaus overcomes a knight who wrongly accuses him of having killed his wolf. He, also, comes to the castle where Laris is incarcerated.

Claris, Gawain, etc., disguised as hermits are admitted into Tallas's castle, seize it, and free Laris, etc. — Tallas takes flight, collects an army and besieges the castle. Moreover, his forces are augmented by those of his father, Saladin, and of Baraton, king of Russia. Madras (a squire) brings Arthur (in Britain) news of the predicament of Claris and his companions, whereupon the king, with a great host, marches to their rescue. Tallas's army is destroyed and he, himself, killed by Arthur. Arthur now consents to the marriage of Laris with Marine, and Yvain and Gawain go and fetch her to the wedding. Before they arrive, however, Madoine had made a last effort to prevent the marriage — having persuaded Marine by a trick that her lover was dead. Moreover, as the three are on their way back to Arthur's host, the fay gets them all into her power and takes them to her enchanted valley in the forest of Broceliande. She next goes to Laris, tells him where Marine is, and declares that he will never see her (Marine) again, unless he goes to this valley. He seizes her, however, and does not release her, until she has promised to set free her captives. She does this and they all come to where Arthur is encamped. The wedding was now celebrated and on the following day Arthur crowns Laris king of Denmark and then takes him and his bride first to Britain and next to Cologne where Laris's father, Henry, was emperor. The city however, was invested by Saris, King of Hungary, when Arthur and the rest arrive. Laris kills Saris and the Hungarians flee. Henry resigns his crown in favor of his son and all the characters now go to Cardigan with Arthur. Claris and Laris and their wives spend the winter there, but the next year move on to Gascony.

Both the length and structure of this mediocre and interminable poem were determined, in the main, by the prose romances — especially the *Lancelot*. The author adopts from that work the quest-form: A number of knights set out in search of another knight and the adventures of each are related. Inasmuch as each set of adventures is practically independent of the rest, the author can lengthen out his work at pleasure by simply adding to the number of questing knights or adventurers. Claris is more prominent in the first half of the romance, Laris in the second. Athis and Prophilias, Lancelot and Galehaut, served, doubtless, as models to this new exemplification of the friendship *motif*. The author uses all of Chrétien's romances, all the continuations of that writer's *Perceval*, and all the principal romances of Chrétien's successors. See Klose's detailed study of the subject. In point of morals, the poem is comparatively pure: it contains only two rather sensual passages, and both of these are brief.

28. *Sone de Nausay.* For the Holy Grail episodes in this romance, which do not, properly speaking, belong to the Arthurian cycle, see above.

29. *Escanor.* Only edition, *Der Roman von Escanor von Gerard von Amiens, herausgegeben von Dr. H. Michelant.* Bibliothek des Litterarischen Vereins in Stuttgart, No. 178 (Tübingen, 1886). 25936 lines are preserved, but a leaf, containing the beginning of the poem, is lost, and there are lacunae, also, after l. 8485 (1200 lines here wanting according to Michelant, 950 according to G. Paris) and after l. 9205 (according to G. Paris, two leaves are here missing). Author, Gerard of Amiens, Dialect, Picard. Date, about 1280.[25]

---

[25] We have three poems by Gerard: 1. *Escanor*, 2. *Meliacin*, 3. *Charlemagne*. G. Paris, *op. cit.* pp. 151f., dates them, respectively, 1280, 1286, 1290. *Meliacin* is similar to *Escanor* in the general character of its incidents, but is not connected with the Arthurian cycle. For an analysis of it, see G. Paris, *op. cit.*, pp. 171ff.

HLF, XIII, 133 ff., G. Paris, *ibid.*, XXXI, 151—205 (1893), Gröber, II, I, 786 f.[26]

Cador,[27] King of Northumberland, wants to marry his daughter, Andrivete (the heroine of the poem), to the best knight of the time, and in order to determine who this is, proclaims a tournament at Banborc (Bamborough), which many of Arthur's knights attend — among them Kay, who has a bitter tongue in *Escanor*, as in the other romances, but is here represented as a valiant and skilful knight, as he is not elsewhere in the French romances. On his way to the tournament Kay has encounters with Mordred and Dynadant (not knowing their identity) over the former's *amie*. On relating these affairs at Arthur's court (at Caerleon) afterwards, Dinadan (Dynadan) speaks with characteristic cynicism of women.

The inhabitants of Brittany want Gawain to rule over them, so he goes to that country with Gifflet as a companion, and restores tranquillity in the land. An enchantress, however, who is still hostile to him, lures him, by means of a hawk (ostoir), into an ambush in the depths of a forest, but the gift by which his strength increased up to midday and did not begin declining until after the ninth hour of the day stood Gawain in good stead, so that he overcame the ambush party, and the enchantress begged his pardon and gave him the bird, although she predicted that the devils would carry it off in two months. — Already, before the tournament was held, Kay had become deeply enamored of Andrivete and not much later she began to reciprocate his love. Among the knights

---

[26] For many valuable corrections to Michelant's edition, cp., too, A. Tobler, *Zs. f. rom. Ph.*, XI, 421 ff. — In his synopsis of the romance, G. Paris, *loc. cit.*, first analyses the story of Kay (Keu) and Andrivete and then (separately) that of Escanor.

[27] The poet pretends, ll. 61 ff., that Eleanor told him the story of his romance. This is probably a mere imitation of Chrétien's introduction to his *Lancelot*, and there can be no reasonable doubt that this story was of his own invention. It accords with this and not with his statement concerning his patroness that we find all through the work the usual appeal of the romancers to an imaginary *escrit* as his authority.

who took part in the jousts was the character who gives his title
to the poem, Li Biauz Escanor de la Blanche Montaigne, nephew
to Escanor le Grant — the latter an inveterate enemy of Gawain's
Both he and Kay were injured in the fighting. Kay, nevertheless,
bore himself so gallantly in the affair that, in the opinion of some,
he deserved the princess above all the other contestants. — After
the jousters have dispersed, because of his wounds, Kay lingers
on in Northumberland. He provokes Andrivete, however, by his
bashfulness about declaring his love to her. Cador, would have
gladly accepted Kay as his son-in-law — the Northumbrians, too,
generally favor Kay —, but his brother, Ayglin, tries to thwart
the plan, because he wishes to succeed Cador, himself. Finally,
much to Andrivete's chagrin, Kay returns to Arthur's court, without having made the expected declaration. — At Whitsuntide a
knight appears at Arthur's court and accuses Gawain of murdering
his cousin, and since Gawain is still absent, Lancelot, Yvain, etc.,
offer themselves as champions to defend him against the charge.
It is finally decided, however, that after forty days Gawain must
return and defend his own cause. The accuser — really Escanor
the Beautiful — then slips away without disclosing his name. —
After a while, Gawain and Gifflet return, and the former tells
the story of the *ostoir* (which he presents to the queen). Guinevere,
who loved Gawain better than she did any one, save her spouse,
invites the two knights to her chamber. On the way thither, Gawain
meets Li Biaus Descouneus (i. e. his natural son, Guinglain) and
learns his (Guinglain's) name now for the first time. The prospect of having to fight an adversary of whom he knows nothing
whatever so worries Gawain that the people begin to fear that the
accusation was wellgrounded. Indeed, towards the end, Arthur
has to exhort him, for his friends' sake, not to make a spectacle
of himself. — Before the expiration of the forty days, Gifflet's
brother, Galentivet — a mere squire — having procured the rustiest
and meanest equipment possible, goes forth to anticipate Gawain
in combating the latter's accuser. On the road he is abashed by
the successive bands of knights, damsels and ladies (the heads
of the last-named being bedecked with green garlands). All, ex-

cept the first band, as it turns out, belong to Escanor the Beautiful, whom (together with his lady-love) they extol to the skies. Finally the squire meets Escanor and his *amie* walking under a canopy of golden cloth and singing of love, like the preceding bands. The lines which are missing at this point must have told of an encounter between Galentivet and Escanor, in which the latter was overthrown and left for dead. The company bemoan their loss and charge Gawain with responsibility for the slaying of their lord, who, as they make known, was Gawain's accuser, in the first instance, and who was coming to Caerleon to fight with Gawain, according to his promise. Arthur has an honest investigation of the affair made, but without result. Gawain is deeply mortified that he should be the object of such suspicions, but Gifflet lets nobody into the secret of who was the real slayer. Kay sets out again for Northumberland and has, on the way, two commonplace adventures. Immediately after this there is another brief lacuna, in which the death of Cador, king of Northumberland, must have been told. Kay next learns the attempts of Andrivete's uncle, Ayglin, to supplant his niece in the succession and to marry her to a man of low birth. Kay stops at the castle of Yonet Alain, who manages to bring about a meeting of his guest and Andrivete there in which Kay tells his sweetheart that he will protect her, and she, on her part, avers that she will make him lord of the land. Kay, likewise, assures Yonet that he desires to marry Andrivete. He now rejoins Arthur's court and obtains the promise of the king and his knights that they will help him against Ayglin. In the meanwhile, by persuading Andrivete's relatives that she had been seduced by Kay and by other falsehoods, equally groundless, Ayglin had got possession of her person and was going to marry her off to a worthless man, but Yonet enables her to escape to Banborc, to which city her uncle then lays siege. Kay is preparing to start for Banborc, when he receives forged letters that purport to be from Yonet, but are really from Ayglin, stating that Andrivete had already married a nobody. In the meanwhile, however, Andrivete had fled from Banborc and was on her way to Caerleon, under the escort of Espinogre, whom she had come across by chance.

Shortly thereafter they meet Dinadan with whom Andrivete has a
tart exchange of words, because of the contempt which he expresses for fighting and women. Among other things, not being
aware of her identity, he observes that her sharpness of tongue
would make her a suitable *partie* for Kay, whose own lady-love
in Northumberland, he says, had recently betrayed him. Just
then Hector appears on the scene and unhorses both Espinogre and
Dinadan, which gives the latter occasion for some further very
sensible remarks on the folly of this eternal fighting. Dinadan,
moreover, is now eager to get rid of Andrivete, but out of perver-
sity, she continues to stick to him. At last, however, he effects
his escape, and she is so ill from vexation at his success that she
had to remain two weeks at a forester's. — By this time a *vallet,*
whom Kay has sent to Banbore to investigate the report about his
sweetheart, returns and states his conviction that the rumor is false.

Gawain and Gifflet now go to test the adventures of the *perron
Merlin,* and, although they performed some notable exploits there,
Gifflet is captured by followers of Escanor the Big, Gawain's old
enemy. The history of the enmity of these two was as follows:
This Escanor's father was a cruel giant and his mother a malicious
sorceress. Gawain and Escanor were born in the same hour. As
the latter was coming into the world, a cousin of his mother's who
was also skilled in necromancy, gained knowledge, through her art,
of Gawain's simultaneous birth and also, of the qualities which
the two children were destined, respectively, to develop: Gawain
was to be proud and mighty, Escanor strong, but cruel. Escanor's
mother, when he is grown up, tells him of Gawain's prowess,
which excites his jealousy — consequently, he seeks a combat with
Gawain. Gawain overthrows him and could have killed him but
spares him from courtesy. So mortified was the vanquished man
by this discomfiture that he lay in bed a whole year, and he now
seizes upon this affair of his nephew, Escanor the Beautiful[28]

---

[28] Escanor the Beautiful had married a rich princess, whose
father was dead, and at the wedding had vowed that he would go to
Britain and challenge the best knight there. The elder Escanor dis-
approved of his nephew's purpose and endeavored to make him promise

(baptized Escanor the Prophet after his father, Brun the Prophet), as an excuse for avenging himself on Gawain. The younger Escanor, by this time, however, had recovered from the wound,. which he had received in his encounter with Gifflet's brother. — Gawain, after recovering from his wounds, goes, accompanied by Gaheries, Kay, Lancelot,[29] etc., in quest of Gifflet, who is in prison at Traverses. Andrivete — who keeps herself concealed from Kay, until her good name is cleared — knows Gifflet's whereabouts and offers to guide Gawain, thither, on condition that he will be her champion, when she needs him. As a matter of fact, the person who had charge of Gifflet at Traverses was a cousin of Andrivete's — a queen — and she had fallen in love with her prisoner, who reciprocated her passion. There was, no question, therefore, of his not being treated well. Andrivete goes to her cousin's castle and later, returning to report to Gawain, finds Arthur and his followers in Norgales. — They had become entangled in a neighboring forest filled with wild beasts, etc., but had finally been hospitably received at the castle of Briant des Illes.[30] This Briant has a fairy, named Esclarmonde, as his *amie,* and she had decorated the room occupied by Arthur in the most magnificent manner, so that the king's companions aver, that even the enchanter,

---

that he would, at least, not challenge Gawain. This enraged, however, the young man and only rendered him more eager than ever to issue this very challenge — of which we have heard above.

[29] In the list of the questing knights at this point we have Percevaus (l. 14365) and Pellesvaus (l. 14389) enumerated as two different knights. Both, of course, are mere variants of Perceval's name. Similarly, ll. 18857 f. For other examples of this phenomenon in Arthurian romance, Cp. Bruce, MPh. XVI, 347 f. (1918). G. Paris, p. 168, suggests that Hector des Mares is similarly derived from Tor (through an hypothetical Hector), fils d'Ares. He was led to this conclusion, doubtless, by the observation that in *Escanor* Hector des Mares is sometimes called "Hector li fix le roi Arez" (ll. 4174, 5255, 14364) — and at least once (l. 4203), I might add, "fil le roi d'Escossuatre". This, however, is merely Gerard's individual blunder.

[30] To be sure, Briant does, in disguise, bring a false accusation against Gawain out of mere envy of the latter's fame. He is sufficiently chastised, however, when the latter unhorses him.

Vergil, had never made anything so wonderful. — At Gawain's request, Andrivete goes back now to Traverses, to comfort Gifflet, whilst Arthur gathers together his hosts to liberate him. The population of Norgales — whose king was away in Sorelois — and of the Isles which Briant ruled over were great raiders, so that Arthur avoided their country — a boggy one — on his way to Traverses, as much as he could, and they, on their side, were afraid of him and treated him with an honor that angered the absent king of Norgales.[31] — In the meanwhile, Andrivete, at Traverses, observing her cousin's weakness for Gifflet, had availed herself of the same to find opportunities for heartening the captive. Among the barons who assembled under the banners of the queen of Traverses, Briant des Illes counselled submission to Arthur, but the two Escanors vehemently espoused the opposite view, owing to their hatred of Gawain. Accordingly, when Yvain is sent by Arthur to demand Gifflet's release, the younger Escanor issues a challenge to Gawain to fight a duel with him, which the barons of his own side, however, prevent for the time being. The queen of the besieged city is, all this while, bent on marrying Gifflet, and, on that account, wishes to make peace with Arthur. There follows a description of Gifflet, who, on his part, runs through the whole gamut of a lover's hopes and fears — also, an address to him by Love. Andrivete perceives the mutual passion of the lovers, but continues to keep silent on the subject. — During the siege, Kay's messenger, who had been despatched a second time to Northumberland, returns and exposes to his master the whole plot of the forged letters. Kay, however, is still ignorant of Andrivete's presence in Britain and is in despair about her. — In the fighting around Troverses Gawain captures from the elder Escanor a valuable steed, named Gringalet, which had been presented to the younger Escanor by the fairy, Esclarmonde, and which had been lent by him to his uncle. The captured animal at

---

[31] Whilst Arthur was laying siege to Traverses, says our author, he would not let his men take anything from the inhabitants, without paying for it — hence they became well — disposed towards him and willingly furnish the greater part of his host with supplies.

first will not eat, but a maiden, Felinete, offers Gawain to cure him, provided Gawain should fulfill a boon for her. He consents, and she, accordingly, plucks a magical piece of cloth out of the creature's ear which the younger Escanor had made his valet put there whenever he was on a journey, in order to render unavailing any one else's possession of the steed. The favor which Felinete had expected to ask from Gawain, in requital, was that he should protect her relatives during the war, but what she actually asked for was that he should stop his combat with the younger Escanor; for this duel, after a long delay, had actually come off. Gawain, although, like his opponent, badly wounded in this affair, will not heed the girl's request, until Arthur intervenes and compels him to desist. Gifflet is now set free and Gawain wants to bring about a marriage between him and the queen of Traverses. —

Andrivete will not disclose her presence with Arthur's host to Kay until she is convinced that he is sorry for having hearkened to Ayglin's calumnies concerning her. Pending the settlement of this matter, she solicits Gawain's aid in avenging her on her uncle. Gawain consents to do so and gets her to agree that she will marry her lover, provided Arthur will restore her to her inheritance. The queen of Traverses had been a little suspicious of Andrivete's relations with Gifflet, but is now reassured. Arthur next declares that he will back Andrivete's claims to her inheritance and he teases Kay about the slanders he has uttered in regard to his mistress, to all of which Kay returns a bitter answer. Andrivete becomes a vassal of Arthur's. — Not long after this the two couples — Gifflet and his lady-love, Kay and Andrivete — are brought together by Gawain and marriages are arranged between them. — When the weddings have been celebrated, Arthur gets ready for the expedition against Ayglin. — News of these preparations disturb Ayglin greatly, but the people of Banborc are weary of war — especially, as Andrivete has disappeared from their sight — and they are about to deliver the town into Ayglin's hands, when Yonet arrests the ring-leaders. Nevertheless, he still has to appease the discontent of the people, by promising that before an appointed date he will discover Andrivete's whereabouts. Long before the day in question, however, her messenger arrives and enlightens him on this point. — In the sequel, it turned out that there was to be no conflict between Arthur and Ayglin, for, under the pressure of the Northumbrians, the latter had to surrender, and, after some rough handling and a brief imprisonment, he confessed his villainies and was pardoned. — The younger Escanor had gone with Arthur to Northumberland, but news of his wife's illness compels him to return home. She dies, however, before he gets back, and Gifflet uses this hour, in which grief has humbled the young knight's pride to inculcate upon him the lesson of self-control. Escanor is so impressed by Gifflet's words that he abdicates his throne, in favor of a cousin, and betakes himself to a hermitage. He gets there just in time to see angels bearing away the hermit's soul. Soon afterwards, two neighboring hermits come and bury their friend's body in the grave that he himself had prepared for this purpose. Escanor now confesses to one of these hermits and accepts his invitation to live with him. Before his own death, on the second anniversary of his entering the hermitage, he is rewarded with a vision of his wife, who had just been delivered from purgatory. His own interment, at the hands of his fellow-hermit, was attended by many wonders, the Virgin Mary being visibly present, with numerous saints and angels. — When the younger Escanor disappeared, the older Escanor, Gifflet, and his wife were much grieved over the matter, and the first-named of the three soon commenced a quest for his nephew. In the course of this quest, he is joined by an abbot, who was, likewise, strongly attached to the missing man. They come, at last, to the younger Escanor's grave, hold services there, and the abbot remains on the spot thenceforth as a hermit, so that a new head for his abbey has to be chosen. Gifflet's wife was so afflicted at the news of all this that her husband reproved her for her excessive manifestations of grief. At Gifflet's suggestion and accompanied by the elder Escanor, they now exhume the body of the dead man's wife and reinter it by his side. Moreover, Gifflet's wife had a fine house erected nearby, where, eventually, she, herself, died.

Escanor was written for Eleanor of Castile, wife of Edward I,

King of England. The character who gives its title to the poem
is borrowed from *L'Atre Perillos*. So, too, this character's enmity
with Gawain. G. Paris goes so far, indeed, as to speak of the
present romance as a sort of continuation of *L'Atre Perillos*. The
poem, as Michelant and Paris have observed, consists of two really separate stories — the Escanor-Gawain and Kay-Andrivete
stories, respectively — which are connected with one another merely
by the part that Andrivete plays as the intermediary between
Gawain and Gifflet. The worst fault of the romance, however,
is unquestionably its prolixity, which is most objectionable, perhaps, in the narratives of combats and in descriptions — e. g. of
the room occupied by Arthur in Briant's castle. Long soliloquies
and dialogues, which, of course, do not appear in a mere analysis
of incidents, like the above, and yet which make up a large part
of the work, furnish, besides, equally pertinent illustrations of
this same weakness. On the other hand, *Escanor* has its merits:
its author possesses a pleasing facility of style and his romance
gives a faithful and varied reflection of mediaeval life. The chief
personages in the story may be, in the main, as Paris remarks,
the stock characters of the *genre*, such as the highborn maiden
in love, the traitor, the loyal vassal, etc., but in more than one
episode these figures become well individualized; — e. g. that of
Yonet (the loyal vassal) in the passage (ll. 23548 ff.) where he holds
Banborc against the intrigues of Ayglin and the growing dis-
satisfaction of the masses. In the delineation of character, however, there is one capital failure to be registered against the author
— namely, Kay. It was a happy thought to represent Arthur's
seneschal, the scoffer and braggart, the chief comic figure of the
cycle, in the rôle of a lover. We all know the rich comedy which
Shakespeare extracted from a similar conception.[32] It seems, however, that the comic possibilities of the situation never even suggested themselves to Gerard. A slave, like his predecessors, to the
conventions of the *amour courtois*, he exploits his invention simply
to exemplify anew the power of love. Under this influence, Kay,

---

[32] That of Falstaff in the *Merry Wives of Windsor*.

accordingly, becomes a valiant knight, which contradicts the uniform tradition concerning the character in the romances, with no corresponding gain. — Much more successful than Kay is the figure of Dinadan — taken over from the prose *Tristan*[33] — whose cynical disparagement of women and protests against fighting as the highest function of man constitute signs of a growing reaction from the ideals of chivalry, in their more extravagant forms.

In addition to the above list of the metrical romances written before 1300, we have the following works of the same *genre* written after that date.

30. A romance which exists only in brief fragments in a MS. of about 1325, and which is, in all probability, itself, approximately of the same date. It is in the dialect of Champagne and by an unknown author. These fragments have been edited by E. Langlois, as "Fragments d'un roman de la Table Ronde," *Mélanges offerts à M. Emile Picot*, I, 383—389 (2 vols., Paris, 1913). Two kings, Ilas and Solvas, ride up before a king — doubtless, Arthur — who is seated, and the former renounces, for himself and his companions, their allegiance to the monarch. The king addressed does not understand what it is all about and, consequently, sits pensive. The barons, however, denounce the affair as an outrage, and, on the advice of Urien, the king pursues Ilas, etc. A fight is about to follow, but here the fragments end.[34]

---

[33] From the fact that Gerard does not represent Lancelot and Guinevere as lovers in this poem, G. Paris has drawn the unwarranted inference that he did not know the prose *Lancelot*. The names, Claudas, Claudin, Sorelois, — to say nothing of Hector des Mares — point, however, to a knowledge of that romance on the part of our author. He probably ignored this famous story of a British queen's adultery, no doubt, out of consideration for the particular British queen whom he was addressing. There is, to be sure, some rather frank and even coarse language in the poem, but such plain-spoken talk did not offend the taste of the Middle Ages. On the other hand, the conduct of the principal characters is, throughout, strictly moral. The picture of Briant des Illes, as Paris remarks, is probably based on the *Chevalier as Deus Espres*.

[34] Cp. the somewhat similar situation in the Vulgate *Mort Artu*, p. 71 (Bruce's edition) — also at the beginning of *Yder*.

31. *Méliador.* Only edition, *Méliador, par Jean Froissart: roman comprenant les poésies lyriques de Wenceslas de Bohème, Duc de Luxembourg et de Brabant, publié, pour la première fois par Auguste Longnon.* 3 vols. Société des Anciens Textes Français (Paris, 1895—1899). 30771 lines are extant, but the conclusion is missing. For a controversy on the subject of the date of the poem cp. G. L. Kittredge, "Chaucer and Froissart (with a discussion of the date of the Meliador," *Englische Studien,* XXVI, 321ff. (1899) and Longnon in his edition, III, 363ff. Both scholars agree that there were two redacations of the poem. Longnon dates, however, the first version before 1370, which is disputed by Kittredge.

The heroine, Hermondine, is the daughter of Hermond, King of Scotland, whose wife was a sister of Loth, lord of Montgries in Northumberland. The hero is Meliador,[35] son of Patris (Patrick), king of Cornwall, and he is, likewise, a knight of Arthur's court. Among the Arthurian knights that participate in the action, Sagremor is the most important.[36] The whole technique of the work is that of the prose romances, but the stock characters of the Arthurian cycle have little prominence in the story.[37]

---

[35] The name, as Longnon observes, I, p. LVIII, is, undoubtedly, a modification of *Meriadoc (Meriadeuc),* which we have found in older Arthurian romances.

[36] A peculiar feature of the romance is that one of its chief characters, Camel (a rival of the hero), is represented as a somnambulist.

[37] Gröber, II, I 790f. classifies the fragmentary *Brun de la Montaigne* (3926 decasyllabic lines in *laisses*) as an Arthurian romance, but its connection with the Arthurian cycle is of the slightest kind. See Paul Meyer's edition of the poem for the Société des Anciens Textes Français (Paris, 1875). At the commencement of the story, the infant hero is taken to a spring haunted by fairies in the forest of Bersillant (Broceliande), which is said to be a possession of Arthur's. There two of these supernatural ladies shower good gifts upon him, but a third, who is in a bad humor, because she did not have the first say in the matter, prophesies that he will suffer such misfortunes in love that he will deserve the name of "restor de Tristram" (l. 983) — i. e. New Tristan, and this name she at once confers upon him. Just at the end of our fragment, moreover, the writer

We have still further, one metrical romance of the Arthurian cycle in Provençal, viz., *Jaufre*, published by Raynouard, *Lexique Roman*, I, 48ff. (1836)[38] and analyzed HLF, XXII, 224ff. There is also a free translation of this poem by Mary Lafon: *Les Aventures du Chevalier Jaufre et de la Belle Brunissende traduites par Mary Lafon* (Paris, 1856), with illustrations by Gustave Doré. 11160 lines. Date, between 1222 and 1232. A. Stimming, "Der Verfasser des Roman de Jaufre" *Zs. f. rom. Ph.*, XII, 323ff. G. Paris, HLF, XXX, 215ff., Gröber, Band II, Abteilung 2, 8f.[39]

The romance opens with the common *motif* of Arthur's waiting for an adventure before eating. The adventure, however, does not occur until he has ridden out into the forest of Brocéliande, where one of his knights, endowed with magical powers, in the form of a strange beast, carries him off and drops him over a cliff. Nevertheless, his men catch him in cloths, so that he is not hurt. The same magician plays Arthur a similar trick near the end of the story, this time appearing in the form of a gigantic bird. Just after the first of these incidents, Taulat (Taulas) de Rougemont appears at court, and, as he says, in order to cast shame on Arthur strikes a knight dead in the presence of the queen (called here Gilaneier, as throughout the poem — doubtless, owing to a scribal blunder) and declares he will repeat the performance every year. Jaufre, son of Dovan, who had just come to court to beg Arthur to knight

brings his hero to a castle of Morgan le Fay's, but here the MS. breaks off. These few details hardly make this an Arthurian romance. The difference of metrical form should be, likewise, noted. The romance belongs to the late fourteenth century.

Cristal et Clarie, (late thirteenth century) mentioned by Gröber, *loc. cit.*, does not belong to our cycle. Cp. Hermann Breuer's edition, Gesellschaft für Romanische Philologie, vol. 36 (Dresden, 1915). So too with *Le Romans de la Dame a la Lycorne et du Biau Chevalier au Lyon* (first third of the fourteenth century), edited by Friedrich Gennrich for the same society as vol. 18 of the series (Dresden, 1908).

[38] A new edition by H. Breuer for the Gesellschaft für Romanische Litteratur was announced as in preparation a few years ago.

[39] For some minor contributions to the study of *Jaufre*, cp. Gröber, *loc. cit.*

him now — in spite of Kay's ridicule — undertakes to pursue
Taulat and punish him for his insolence. The adventures in which
he becomes involved during this pursuit are of the usual fantastic kind. The most noteworthy of them, perhaps, is the one
in which, by plunging to the bottom of a spring, he comes to
a fairy-land presided over by "la fee du Gibel" (i. e. Morgan).
In the course of his wanderings, he meets the heroine (the princess Brunesentz) and at a later time (though long before the end
of the story) he vanquishes Taulat and sends him to Arthur's court.

The poem was turned into French prose in the fourteenth
century, and this version, combined by a friar, Claude Platin, with a
prose version of *Li Biaus Descouneus*, was printed three times
in the first half of the sixteenth century. Platin, however, falsely
identified the hero of the romance with the Geoffroy de Mayence
of the *chansons de geste*. See p. 292, below, for the Spanish prose
romance: *Cronica de los nobles cavalleros Tablante de Ricamonte
y Jofre, hijo de Donasson* — first printed at Toledo in 1513 and
frequently since — which is principally noteworthy, because it
supplied suggestions to Cervantes for more than one episode in
Don Quixote, e. g. that of the *desdichados galeotes* (unfortunate
galley-slaves).[40]

---

[40] Cp. Lafon, pp. IX f.

Chapter II.
Portuguese and Spanish Versions
of Arthurian Romances.

The following versions (all in prose) of French romances of the Arthurian cycle in Portuguese and Spanish, respectively, have been preserved:

Portuguese.

1. *A Historia dos Cavalleiros da Mesa Redonda et da Demanda do Santo Graall.* Cp. I, 469, note 37, above.

2. *Liuro de Josep Abaramatia.*[1] Cp. I, 460, above.

3. *Estoria do Emperador Vespasiano.* This is the same as No. 2, apparently — only abbreviated. Cp. I, 460, above.

4. *Historia de Lancelote, Leonel e Galvan* (preserved in a unique MS. now in the Convento del Angel at Seville). No one has yet attempted to date this unpublished work or to describe its contents. The title, however, would seem to indicate that it is based on the Old French prose *Lancelot.*[2]

Spanish.

1. *El Baladro del Sabio Merlin.* Cp. I, p. 462, note 12, above.

2. Fragments of the *Joseph, Merlin* and *Demanda* preserved in the Madrid MS., Bibl. Real. 2 g. 5 (entitled *Leyes de Palencia*). Cp. I, 462, and note 12 *ibid.*, above.

3. *Lanzarote del Lago.* Versions of the Old French prose *Lancelot* in both Spanish (Castilian) and Catalan (both from the beginning of the fifteenth century) are extant, but have not been

---

[1] For notes on this book, cp. G. Baist, *Zs. f. rom. Ph.*, XXXI, 605 ff. (1907). Baist maintains that, after all, the Portuguese work may go back ultimately to a Spanish original.

[2] As to a Portuguese *Lancelot* (really the *Demanda*) and a supposed (really, non-existent) version in Provençal, cp. Foerster, *Der Karrenritter*, pp. XXV f. (Halle, 1899).

printed. Cp. A. Bonilla y San Martin's edition (1912) of No. 6, p. XXIX, and his *Las leyendas de Wagner en la literatura española, con un apendice sobre El Santo Grial en el* "Lanzarote del Lago" Castellano, pp. 47f. (Madrid, 1913). The MS. of the former Spanish version bears the date, 1414. In an appendix to the pamphlet just named, pp. 93—107, Bonilla prints extracts from this Spanish version and announces (p. 73, note 1) that his friend, D. Eduardo de Laiglesia, is preparing an edition of the whole work. The sixteenth century MS. 9611 (Aa 103, according to the old numbering) of the National Library at Madrid appears to be a copy of the MS. from which Bonilla gives excerpts. Klob, pp. 189ff., has described it and reproduced (p. 190, note 3) some of its rubrics.

4. *El Cuento de Tristan,* a fragmentary version of the earlier form of the French prose *Tristan,* preserved in the unique MS. Vatican, 6428 (fourteenth century). E. Monaci has published a facsimile of it, No. 6 in his *Fac-simili di antichi manoscritti* (Rome, 1881—1892).

5. *La Estoria del noble Vespasiano,*[3] the same as No. 3 in the Portuguese list above. It was first printed about 1490 and again in 1499.

6. *Libro del Esforçado Cauallero Don Tritsan de Leonis y de sus Grandes Fechos en Armas.* This Castilian adaptation of the Old French prose *Tristan* has been edited (Madrid, 1912) by A. Bonilla y San Martin from the earliest print of the work (Valladolid, 1501). For other early prints of the same, cp. Bonilla's edition, pp. LXIVff. The edition of 1528 (Seville) there described had already been printed by Bonilla in the same volume (pp. 339ff.) as the *Demanda del Sancto Grial.*

G. T. Northup seems to have proved that the Spanish prose versions of the *Tristan* romance are based on Italian versions. Cp. his articles, "The Italian Origin of the Spanish Prose *Tristram*

---

[3] In regard to this book, see Henry Thomas, *Spanish and Portuguese Romances of Chivalry,* p. 32 (Cambridge, 1920) — a work which has great bibliographical value for its subject, in general, but not for the Arthurian romances.

Versions," RR., III, 194ff., (1912) and "The Spanish Prose Tristram Source Question," MPh., 259ff. (1913).

7. *Cronica nuevamente emendada y añadida del buen caballero don Tristan de Leonis y del rey don Tristan de Leonis, el joven, su hijo* (Seville, 1534). Part I of this book is the same as No. 5, but Part II is the invention of a new (Spanish) author. The story of this part begins, in the approved style, at Arthur's court, but the majority of the adventures are laid in Spain. Cp. Menendez y Pelayo, *Origines*, I, p. CLXXXIII, note 3. Part II seems to be of very inferior quality.

In addition to the works just enumerated there appeared at Seville in 1576, *Historia de Perceval de Gaula, caballero de la Tabla Rotonda el cual acabó la demanda y aventures del Santo Grial*, but no copy of the work is known to exist. Bonilla is, doubtless, right in surmising that the book was a version of the 1530 (Paris) print of *Perceval le Gallois* or *Perlesvaus*, as it is commonly called. Cp. his above-mentioned pamphlet, p. 48.

For the Portuguese romances which I have listed above cp. C. Michaelis de Vasconcellos, Gröber's *Grundriss*, II Band, 2 Abteilung, pp. 213ff. (Strassburg, 1894), and for the Spanish, G. Baist, ibid., pp. 438ff. (1897) and Menendez y Palayo, *Origines de la novela*, I, pp. CLIXff. (Madrid, 1905). Much the fullest information about the Grail romances in both languages, however, is given by Otto Klob, "Beiträge zur Kenntniss der spanischen und portugiesischen Gral-Litteratur," *Zs. f. rom. Ph.*, XXVI, 169ff. (1901). Klob's essay, to be sure, is in many respects unsatisfactory. Cp. on the subject E. Brugger, *Zs. f. frz. Spr. u. Litt.*, XXIX[1], 118ff. (1905). There is no evidence, however, in favor of Brugger's view (p. 127) that the unprinted Spanish *Lanzarote del Lago* represents an hypothetical lost *Lancelot* of the pseudo-Robert de Boron (prose) cycle. The various extracts from it printed by Bonilla, pp. 73ff., are mere translations from the corresponding portions of the Vulgate *Lancelot*. Besides, as we have seen above, it is extremely doubtful whether a *Lancelot* was ever composed for the pseudo-Robert-de-Boron cycle. The fullest information about the Spanish *Tristan* romances is to be found in Bonilla's edition of the 1501 print of No. 6, above, pp. XXVIff.

Besides the romances which I have just named, Pascual de Gayangos in his "Catalogo Razonado de los Libros de Caballerias," *Biblioteca de Autores Espanoles*, XL, p. LXIII (Madrid, 1909 reprint), lists a *Triunfos de Sagramor em que se trataɏ os feitos dos cavalleiros da segunda Tavola Redonda*, Por Jorge Ferreyra Le Vasconcellos (Coimbra, 1554) and *Memorias das proezas da Segunda Tavola Redonda* (Coimbra, 1567). The latter, it seems, is, also, by Ferreyra de Vasconcellos. There is no "Second Round Table" in French romance, so that I presume that these two Portuguese books are the inventions of this author. *Ibid.*, Gayangos cites five separate editions of *La cronica de los nobles caualleros Tablante de Ricamonte y Jofre, hijo de don Asson*, the earliest being printed at Toledo in 1513. G. Paris (p. 217) speaks of the *Cronica* as a free imitation of *Jaufre*, but, according to the plausible conjecture of Menendez y Pelayo, *Origines*, I. p. CLXXXIV, this Spanish romance is based on a French prose version of the Provençal poem. Bonilla y San Martin has reprinted *Cronica* (from the edition published at Seville in 1564) in the same volume as the *Demanda*. See pp. 459ff. of that volume. This edition of 1564, used by Bonilla y San Martin, is not included in Gayangos's list of five editions.

Chapter III.
Italian Versions of Arthurian Romances.

The versions are in prose, unless otherwise indicated.

1. *Tristano* (latter part of the thirteenth century), preserved in a MS. of the Bibliotheca Riccardiana (Florence). Edited by E. G. Parodi, *Il Tristano Riccardiano* (Bologna, 1896), in the *Collezione di opere inedite o rare di scrittori italiani dal XIII al XVI secolo pubblicato per cura della R. commissione pe' testi di lingua nelle provincie dell' Emilia.*

2. *La Tavola Ritonda o L'Istoria di Tristano* (thirteenth century, but slightly later than No. 1, which is used in it) edited by Filippo-Luigi Polidori (2 vols. Bologna, 1864—1865) in the same collection as the preceding.

3. *Il Febusso e Breusso, poema ora per la prima volta pubblicato* (Florence, 1847). It is preserved in a MS. of the first half of the fourteenth century and was composed, doubtless, in that century. It is divided into six *Chantari* and is based on an episode in *Palamedes*.[1]

4. An unpublished poem, *La Morte di Tristano* (fourteenth century), by a minstrel of the lower classes. Cp. G. Bertoni, *Fanfulla della Domenica*, nos. 43, 46, 48 (Rome, 1915).

5. *La Vita di Merlino con le sue profezie* (last quarter of the fourteenth century). Printed first at Venice in 1480. This text, which is the Italian version of *Les Prophecies de Merlin* (cp. pp. 28ff., above) has been edited by Ireneo Sanesi under the title of *Storia di Merlino* (Bergamo, 1898). On the various MSS. and early prints, cp. Sanesi's introduction and Miss Paton, PMLA, XXVIII, p. 124 (1913).

---

[1] In the introduction to this edition the editor gives, pp. XCVII —CLXXIII, a *Frammento d'Antico Volgarizzamento di Girone il Cortese.*

6. *Li Chantari di Lancelloto* (first half of the fifteenth century). Cp. I, p. 449, above.

7. *Libro de battaglie di Tristano* (Cremona, 1492).

8. *Girone il Cortese* (probably first part of the sixteenth century), based on the 1501 edition of the French *Guiron le Courtois*. The Italian text was edited by Francesco Tassi (Florence, 1855).

9. *Gyrone il Cortese,* poem by Luigi Alamanni. First printed at Paris in 1548. Based on the French *Guiron le Courtois* (edition of 1501) and *Meliadus* (edition of 1528).

10. *Due libri dell' opere magnanime dei due Tristani* (2. vols., Venice, 1555). Translated, according to the author, from the Spanish. For the Spanish *Tristan* versions cp. pp. 289—91, above.

11. *L'illustre et famosa istoria di Lancillotto del Lago che fu al tempo del re Artu* (3. vols., Venice, 1557—8 and again 1558—9). Based on the 1533 (Paris) edition of the *Lancelot,* which like the other early prints, embraced, under this title, also, the *Queste and Mort Artu*[2] of the Vulgate cycle. Foerster, *Karrenritter,* p. XXV, mentions an 1862 reprint of this work, which I have not seen.

Besides the above, the sixteenth century witnessed the production of some Italian Arthurian poems which have a very slender connection, however, with mediaeval Arthurian traditions, being really independent compositions, e. g. Nicolo di Agostino's *Lo Innamorento di Lancellotto* (Venice, 1521—6) and Erasmo da Valvasone's *I quattro primi canti di Lancillotto* (Venice, 1580) — both poems. Cp. Polidori, I, pp. XXXIIff. on works of this character.

On the subject of the Italian Arthurian romances, cp. G. Melzi, *Bibliografia dei Romanzi di Cavaleria in versi e in prosa italiani* (3rd and best edition, Milan, 1865) — also, Polidori's edition of *La Tavola Ritonda,* I, pp. XXXIff.

---

[2] An Italian version (now lost) of the *Mort Artu* appears to have been in existence as early as 1279.

Chapter IV.
German Versions of Arthurian Romances.

Except where the contrary is stated, they are all in verse.

1. Eilhart von Oberge's *Tristrant* (about 1170). Edited by Franz Lichtenstein, *Quellen und Forschungen*, XIX (Strassburg, 1877).

2. Hartmann von Aue's *Erec* (shortly after 1191).

3. The same author's *Iwein* (about 1202). Cp. I, p. 124, above.

4. Ulrich von Zatzikhoven's *Lanzelot* (last decade of the twelfth century). Cp. I, 124, 208ff., above.[1]

5. Wolfram von Eschenbach's *Parzival* (about 1205). Cp. I, p. 124, above.

6. Wirnt von Grafenberg's *Wigalois* (shortly before 1210). Edited by G. F. Benecke (2 vols. Berlin, 1819) and by F. Pfeiffer (Leipzig 1847). Cp. pp. 197—8, above.

7. Gottfried von Strassburg's *Tristan* (about 1210). Cp. I, p. 162, note 12, above.

8. Wolfram's *Titurel* (between 1217 and 1220).

9. Heinrich von Türlin, *Diu Crône (Krône)* (shortly before 1220). Cp. I, p. 124, above.

10. *Manuel und Amande* (preserved in handwriting of the early fourteenth century, but date of composition undeterminable, although the poem belongs probably to the thirteenth century). Only fragments of this poem survive — 272 lines in all. Edited by Oswald Zingerle, "Manuel und Amande: Bruchstücke eines Artusromans," *Zs. f. d. A.*, XXVI, 297ff. (1882).

The hero, Manuel, is a Greek, and after his marriage to Amande, a Spanish princess, at Carduel, in Arthur's presence, he took his bride to Greece to live.

---

[1] For some recent studies of the *Lanzelet*, from the point of view of style, cp. J. L. Campion, MLN, XXXII, 416ff. (1917).

According to the author, Arthur's apparent death was the result of his fight with a monster cat — which was, it seems, at the same time, a fish. (Our fragments do not preserve the actual narrative of this combat, but this is the necessary inference from them.) Eleven years after his disappearance, his queen died of grief on his account and was buried at St. David's (in Wales). He, himself, however, returned subsequently and presided over the Round Table for twenty-five years longer.

On this poem Cp. G. Paris, HLF, XXX, 218ff. Paris places it in the twelfth century, but this is, doubtless, too early.

11. *Daniel von dem Blühenden Tal, ein Artusroman von dem Stricker, herausgegeben von Gustav Rosenhagen* (Breslau, 1894): Heft 9 of the *Germanistische Abhandlungen, begründet von Karl Weinhold, herausgegeben von Friederich Vogt*. 8482 lines. The incidents are of the same character as those in the French romances of the cycle[2] and G. Paris, in his discussion of the poem,[3] HLF, XXX, 136ff., was inclined to regard it as based on a French original. Rosenhagen, however, has shown that German sources account for everything in the romance and that Paris's hypothesis is, therefore, unnecessary. Most of the hero's adventures are in a sort of fairyland, called Cluse (i. e. the Enclosed Land) which is cut off from the rest of the world by mountains. It is only accessible through a tunnel, which, ordinarily, however, is closed by a stone. — The poem belongs, most likely, to the second decade of the thirteenth century.

12. Ulrich von Türheim's *Tristan* (about 1236). The text

---

[2] For example, at the beginning, Arthur is waiting for an adventure, before he will eat. The most original feature of the story is the fantastic beast which carries a banner in its mouth and which, as soon as this banner is removed, emits a horrible cry that, if continued, in a short time kills all that hear it. I observe in the *Dionysiaca*, XXVIII, 270ff., of the Greek poet, Nonnus (fourth century A. D.) that Halimedes, the Cyclops, killed twelve men by a single cry.

[3] Since the *Daniel* was then unpublished, Paris had to rely on the analysis of the poem in K. Bartsch's edition (Quedlinburg and Leipzig, 1857) of the same author's *Karl der Grosse*, pp. VIIIff.

will be found in the old editions of Gottfried's *Tristan* by Groote, Hagen and Massmann — e. g. in Massmann's, pp. 498—590 (Leipzig, 1843).[4] The work is a continuation of Gottfried, but the author follows especially Eilhart's version of his hero's story.

13. *Clies* (about the same time as the preceding), a German version of Chrétien's *Cliges*. Only some insignificant fragments survive and these are probably by Ulrich von Türheim. Cp. *Zs. f. d. A.*, XXXII, 123ff.[5]

14. *Segremors.* Only three small fragments of this romance survive. All three seem to have belonged originally to the same MS. (fourteenth century), but they are now preserved in three different libraries. Following are the editions of the fragments numbered according to what appears to have been their order in the original MS.

(1) Reinhold Köhler, "Bruchstücke eines Gedichts aus dem Artuskreise," *Germania*, V, 461—463 (1860). 144 lines: Segremor is going forth to fight Gawain. Malgrim (a dwarf) protests in vain that he (Segremor) is too young for such an undertaking. Niobe, Segremor's sweetheart, is in despair as he leaves — subsequently decides to go with him.

(2) Karl Regel, "Bruchstück eines Gedichts aus dem Kreise der Artussage," *Zs. f. d. A.*, XI, 490—500 (1859). 288 lines: Maurin wishes Segremor success in his impending combat (with Gawain, evidently) and Segremor rides away to Munpholie (Montpelier?). In his search for Gawain, Segremor comes upon Sirikirsan (lord of Boukovereye), who, according to the custom of his country, is holding the annual assembly of the young men and young women, respectively, who desire to marry that year. A series of

---

[4] J. L. Campion has a new edition in preparation. ·Cp. his *Das Verwandtschaftsverhältniss der Handschriften des Tristan Ulrichs von Turheim, nebst einer Probe des Kritischen Textes.* Johns Hopkins University diss., 1918.

[5] According to Rudolf von Ems, both Ulrich von Türheim and Konrad Fleck (about 1230) composed poems named *Clies.* For these allusions, cp. W. Foerster's large edition of Chrétien's *Cliges,* pp. XXVf. The extant fragments are more likely to be by Ulrich. Lachmann conjectured that Ulrich's *Clies* was a continuation of Fleck's.

jousts are held, and the victorious knights, in the order of their
success, have their choice of the girls. On an island of ideal beauty,
nearby, where it is always May, Karmente (manifestly, a fairy)
lives in a fine tower. Any knight who wanted her love had to
fight for her, but, if himself later overthrown by another knight,
had to yield his place to the victor. She is now, it seems, in Gawain's possession.

(3) Moriz Haupt and Heinrich Hoffmann: *Altdeutsche Blätter,*
II, 152—154 (Leipzig, 1840). At the end of a combat with
Segremor, Gawain surrenders. The citizens wish to rescue him,
but he forbids. The two knights constantly ride out together in
amicable fashion. Nevertheless, at the conclusion of the fragment,
the citizens are again preparing to intervene.

H. Suchier, "Anspielung an ein unbekanntes Gedicht (Segremors?)," *Germania,* XVIII, 115f. (1873), conjectured that there
is an allusion to this poem in Ulrich von Türheim's *Willehalm*
(written between 1261 and 1265). If this conjecture were correct,
we should have an approximate *terminus ad quem* for our romance,
but G. Paris, in his discussion of this romance, HLF, XXX, 261f.,
has pointed out that the allusion is probably to the German romance *Manuel und Amande.* Paris, *loc. cit.,* has pointed out, also,
what seem manifest imitations of *Meraugis de Portlesguez* in the
present poem. Some of the names, moreover — *Maurin,* etc., —
appear to be drawn from Wolfram's *Parzival. Segremors* was probably composed in the first half of the thirteenth century.

15. *Wigamur* (probably second quarter of the thirteenth century). — It occupies 62 pages (two columns to the page) in
*Deutsche Gedichte des Mittelalters, herausgegeben von Friederich
Heinrich von der Hagen und Dr. Johann Gustav Büsching,* vol. I
(2 vols., Berlin, 1808).

The hero's name is derived from *Guingamor,* the name of the
hero of Marie de France's well-known lay, but, as in the case of
Nos. 16—24 that follow, the story was substantially invented by
the author and is not based on any French original. Cp. G. Paris,
HLF., XXX, 269f., G. Sarrazin, *Wigamur, eine literarhisto-*

rische Untersuchung, vol. 35 (Strassburg, 1879) and *Zs. f. d. A.,* XXIV, 97.

16. *Edolanz* (about 1250). Only small fragments have been preserved. One fragment will be found in "Gawein: Drei Bruchstücke," *Altdeutsche Blätter von Moriz Haupt und Heinrich Hoffmann* [von Fallersleben],⁶ II, 148—152, others in Anton Schönbach's "Neue Bruchstücke des Edolanz," *Zs. f. d. A.,* XXV, 271f. (1881).

17. *Garel vom blühenden Tal, ein höfischer Roman aus dem Artussagenkreise von dem Pleier mit den Fresken des Garelsaales auf Runkelstein herausgegeben von Dr. M. Walz* (Freiburg i. B., 1892). 21310 lines. This poem, like the next two by the same author, was composed, it would seem, between 1260 and 1280.

18. *Tandareis und Flordibel, ein höfischer Roman von dem Pleiare, herausgegeben von Ferdinand Khull* (Graz, 1885). 18339 lines.

19. *Meleranz von dem Pleier, herausgegeben von Karl Bartsch* (Stuttgart, 1861): Bibliothek des Litterarischen Vereins in Stuttgart, LX. 12834 lines.

20. *Der jüngere Titurel.* Edited by K. A. Hahn (Quedlinburg and Leipzig, 1842). Composed by a Bavarian or Austrian poet named Albrecht (otherwise unknown) — probably in the third quarter of the thirteenth century. On this poem cp. *Zs. f. d. A.,* XXVII, 158ff. and Conrad Borchling's *Der jüngere Titurel und sein Verhältnis zu Wolfram von Eschenbach* (Göttingen, 1897). The author uses Wolfram's *Parzival* and *Titurel,* but no French romance.

21. *Lohengrin* (between 1276 and 1290), edited by Heinrich Rückert (Quedlinburg and Leipzig, 1858). 7670 lines, in 767 stanzas. Based on suggestions of Wolfram's poems — otherwise, invented by the author.

22. Albrecht von Scharfenberg (second of the thirteenth century). His poems are preserved only in partial fifteenth century redactions. See the next page.

---

⁶ Only the first of the fragments belongs to *Edolanz.* The second belongs to *Segremors;* the provenience of the third is doubtful.

23. Heinrich von Freiberg's *Tristan* (between 1285 and 1290). Edited by Alois Bernt (Halle, 1906).[7] 6890 lines. It continues Gottfried's *Tristan* and its sole sources for the story are Ulrich von Türheim, Gottfried, and Eilhart.[8]

24. *Gauriel von Muntabel* (shortly after 1300), by Konrad von Stoffeln. Edited by F. Khull (Graz, 1885).

25. *Parzifal*, composed by Claus Wisse and Philipp Colin (two citizens of Strassburg) between 1331 and 1336 as a continuation of Wolfram's *Parzival*. 36489 lines. Edited by Karl Schorbach as Vol. 5 (Strassburg and London, 1888) of the *Elsässische Litteraturdenkmäler aus dem XIV—XVII Jahrhundert, herausgegeben von Ernst Martin und Erich Schmidt*. As Colin tells us, a Jew, Sampson Pine, turned the French into German for the German poets. According to Schorbach, p. XLI, the sources of the poem are 1. the *Elucidation*, 2. Chrétien's *Perceval*, 3. Pseudo-Wauchier, 4. Wauchier, 5. Manessier.

26. Albrecht von Scharfenberg's *Merlin* (fifteenth century), which was based on a particular redaction of Robert de Boron's *Merlin* and the Vulgate *Estoire del Saint Graal* — in U. Fueterer's *Buch der Abenteuer*,[9] from which it has been edited by F. Panzer in his *Merlin und Seifrid de Ardemont von Albrecht von Scharfenberg in der Bearbeitung Ulrich Fuetrers, Bibliothek des Litterarischen Vereins in Stuttgart*, vol. 227 (1902).

27. A prose version, still unprinted, of the Old French prose *Lancelot* (in MSS. of the fifteenth and sixteenth centuries), which was, probably, composed in the thirteenth century, although this cannot be proved.[10]

---

[7] For older editions see introduction to this work, p. 19.

[8] S. Singer maintains, *Zs. f. d. Ph.*, XXIX, 73 ff., that Heinrich also used a French *Tristan* romance, but this view is refuted by Bernt, Introduction, pp. 168 ff. See, also, F. Wiegandt, *Heinrich von Freiberg in seinem Verhältnis zu Eilhart und Ulrich* (Rostock diss., 1879).

[9] The same work includes, also, a partial redaction of Albert's *Seifrid de Ardemont*, which contains Arthurian elements but cannot be reckoned an Arthurian romance. The *Seifrid*, in its original form, dated from the thirteenth century.

[10] The best authority on the subject of the German versions of

28. A prose redaction of No. 27 by Ulrich Fueterer (probably in last quarter of the fifteenth century). Edited by A. Peter in Bibliothek des Litterarischen Vereins in Stuttgart, vol. 175 (Tübingen, 1885).

29. A poetical version by Fueterer — based on his prose version and included in his *Buch der Abenteuer*.

30. *Tristan und Isolde* (prose version of Eilhart's *Tristrant*), first printed at Augsburg in 1484 and frequently since[11] — last edited by Richard Benz (Jena, 1912) in the series, *Die deutschen Volksbücher*. Cp., too, F. Pfaff's edition, *Tristrant und Isolde*, Bibliothek des Litterarischen Vereins in Stuttgart, vol. 152 (1881).

31. *Wigoleiss vom Rade* (prose version of Wirnt's *Wigalois)*, first printed at Augsburg in 1493 and more than once in the following century. Cp. J. G. T. Grässe, *Lehrbuch einer Literärgeschichte der berhümtesten Völker des Mittelalters, pp. 225f. Zweiter Band. Dritte Abtheilung* (Dresden and Leipzig, 1842). The work was composed in 1472.

32. A German poem (in couplets of irregular length), based on Wirnt's *Wigalois* and written in Hebrew characters. It is most commonly known as *Artus-Hof*. It exists in two MSS. of the sixteenth century and in printed editions of the seventeenth and eighteenth centuries and has latterly been edited by L. Landau, under the title of *Arthurian Legends or the Hebrew-German Rhymed version of the Legend of King Arthur: Teutonia*, Heft 21 (Leipzig, 1912).[12]

---

the prose *Lancelot* (which include, also, the *Queste* and *Mort Artu)* is A. Peter's "Die deutschen Prosaromane von Lanzelot", *Germania*, XXVIII, 129 ff. (1883).

[11] For the old editions, Cp. Lichtenstein's edition of Eilhart, pp. XVIIf.

[12] The first person who transliterated this version into German characters seems to have been Wagenseil in the edition of 1699 (Königsberg). There was also a Hebrew-German version of the same romance in ottava rima (Prag, 1652—1679). Lindau, p. XLI, derives this and the couplet version from a common (hypothetical) source, "Original Hebrew-German versions", of the fourteenth century. In his introduction this scholar discusses, too, Mediaeval Hebrew versions of

In addition to the German romances which I have listed, we have a small fragment of a Low German version of the Old French prose *Lancelot*. Cp. *Sitzungsberichte* of the Bavarian Academy of Sciences for 1896, pp. 313—316.

---

other romances of the period.   He does not, however, refer to the Hebrew *Mort Artu,* mentioned above.

Chapter V.
Dutch Versions of Arthurian Romances.

In the following list Nos. 2—9 were probably composed in the second half of the thirteenth century. Where the date is certain, this is definitely indicated.

1. *Roman van Walewein door Penninc en Pieter Vostaert uitgegeven door W. J. A. Jonckbloet* (2 parts, Leiden, 1846—8) 11198 lines. Date, probably about 1250. Discussed by G. Paris, HLF, XXX, 82—84, under the title, *Gauvain et l'Echiquier*. Jonckbloet and Paris regard it as translated from a French original. It is more probably an independent poem,[1] although the author may have used some French sources.

2. Jacob Van Maerlant: *Historie van den Grale* and *Merlijns Boeck,* edited as Jacob Van Maerlant's *Merlijn* by J. Van Vloten (Leiden, 1880). 10452 octosyllabic lines. Composed about 1261 and based on the Old French prose version of Robert de Boron's *Merlin.* For Lodewijc Van Velthem's continuation of this work, see No. 11, p. 306, below.

3. *Torec* (about 1262). Edited by Jonckbloet as part of No. 10 (see below), and, separately (Leiden, 1875), by Jan Te Winkel. A fragment of 3480 lines. G. Paris, in his discussion of the poem, HLF, XXX, 263 ff., regards it as based on a French original[2] — very likely, the French romance of the same name which was in the library of the Louvre in the fourteenth century.

4. *Ferguut.* Edited by L. G. Visscher (Utrecht, 1838) and by J. Verdam and Eelco Verwijs[3] (Groningen, 1882). 5589 lines.[4]

---

[1] This is the view of J. Te Winkel, Paul's *Grundriss,* II, I, p. 459 and G. Kalff, *Geschiedenis der Nederlandsche Letterkunde,* I, 119 (7 vols., Groningen 1906—1912).

[2] Kalff, *op. cit.,* I, 238, questions this, but Paris is, doubtless right.

[3] Verdam began the edition but died before completing it. Verwijs completed it.

[4] According to Verwijs, the portion after l. 2592 is by an in-

Translated from the French *Fergus*. The later edition constitutes a volume in the Bibliothek van Middelnederlandsche Letterkunde.

5. *Moriaen.* 4716 lines. Edited first by Jonckbloet (cp. No. 10, below) and, separately, by Jan Te Winkel, *Roman van Moriaen* (Groningen, 1882), in the same series as nos. 3 and 7. On this romance cp. G. Paris, HLF, XXX, 247ff., where it is called *Morien* — also Miss J. L. Weston's translation of it into English prose, *The Romance of Morien* (London, 1901). Unlike its editors, Paris and Miss Weston regard the poem not as an original composition, but as a translation from a lost French romance. In any event, it drew, at least, partly from French sources. On its connection with the Grail traditions, cp. I, 331, note 33, above.

6. *Die Wrake van Ragisel.* 2975 lines: a version of *La Vengeance Raguidel*. Edited by Jonckbloet. Cp. no. 10, below.

7. *Roman van den Riddere metter Mouwen.* Edited by Jonckbloet (cp. no. 10, below) and, separately, by Bertha M. van der Stempel (Leiden, 1914) in the same series as the preceding. According to the second editor, pp. XIIff., the source of the poem is the French romance, *Richars li Biaus*.[5] G. Paris has discussed the present romance, HLF, XXX, 121ff., under the title of *Le Chevalier à la Manche*.

8. *Walewein ende Keye.* 3668 lines. Edited by Jonckbloet. Cp., no. 10, below. For a discussion of this romance, which is probably based on a lost French original, cp. G. Paris, *op. cit.*, 84ff.

9. The romance (probably adapted from a lost French original) discussed by G. Paris, *op. cit.*, pp. 113ff. under the title, *Lancelot et la cerf au pied blanche*. 855 lines. It was edited by Jonckbloet as a part of No. 10, below.

10. *Roman van Lancelot*, edited by W. J. A. Jonckbloet (2 parts, The Hague, 1846—9).[6] Jonckbloet published under this

---

ferior hand. Kalff, pp. 113f., however, denies any difference of authorship.

[5] Edited by Wendelin Foerster (Wien, 1874).

[6] For a discussion of this vast compilation cp. Miss J. L. Weston, *The Legend of Sir Lancelot du Lac*, 147ff. (London, 1901). She

title the unique MS. which once belonged to Lodewijc Van Velthem and which consists of a collection of Arthurian romances in octosyllabic couplets. The MS. was originally divided into four books. The first of these books has been lost, but the remaining three contain a total of 87296 lines. Jonckbloet gives a separate numbering to the lines of each book. Thus Book II consists of 47262 lines, made up as follows: 1. ll. 1—36947: a metrical paraphrase of the last division of the French prose *Lancelot* — viz. the so-called *Agravain*. 2. ll. 36948—42546: a version of a part of Chrétien's *Perceval* (almost wholly the part which deals with Gawain's adventures). 3. ll. 42547—47262: *Moriaen*. Cp., No. 5, above.

Book III consists of 26980 lines, made up as follows:

(1) ll. 1—11160: a metrical paraphrase of the Vulgate *Queste del Saint Graal*.

(2) ll. 11161—14136: *Die Wrake van Ragisel*. Cp. no. 6, above.

(3) ll. 14137—14580: Two episodes in which Lancelot plays the chief *rôle*.[7] In the second, acting on information from Dodinel, Lancelot and Bohort rescue a maiden whom ruffian knights had bound to a tree, because she had aided Lionel in escaping from prison. The introduction of Lionel and Bohort into the story shows that the original author of this episode knew the prose *Lancelot*. Whether he was a Frenchman we cannot say.

(4) ll. 14581—18602: *De Ridder metter Mouwen*. Cp. No. 6 above.

---

greatly exaggerates, however, the value of the Dutch romances (or their French originals) in their relation to the development of Arthurian traditions. For the errors into which she has fallen in regard to its version of the *Mort Artu*, cp. I, 426 ff., notes 164, 166, 171, above.

[7] As regards the first, which is a sort of appendix to the *Vengeance Raguidel*, Guinevere had cut a sorry figure in the incident of the chastity-testing mantle and Lancelot was so sensitive on the subject that the sight of a mantle made him fighting mad. Now, he meets Yder with Belinette, and the latter is wearing a mantle, so he attacks Yder. After they have fought for some time, Bohort turns up and discloses Yder's identity to Lancelot, whereupon they stop the combat. —

(5) ll. 18603—22270: *Walewein ende Keye.* Cp. No. 8, above.

(6) ll. 22271—23125: The romance, named by G. Paris, *Lancelot et la cerf au pied blanc.* Cp. No. 9, above.

Book IV, which contains 13054 lines, is a metrical paraphrase of the Vulgate *Mort Artu.*

All the romances in the compilation published by Jonckbloet were probably composed in the second half of the thirteenth century or the first half of the fourteenth — more likely, the former. With the exception of the portions which were translated from the Vulgate cycle, its component parts were, doubtless, all independent of each other in their origin, and even these parts may have been by different authors.

11. Lodowijck Van Velthem's *Boec van Coninc Artur* (finished 1326). 25766 lines. Edited by J. Van Vloten in his edition of Van Maerlant's *Merlijn* (cp. no. 2, above), which poem it continues from l. 10453 to l. 36218 (end). Van Velthem's work is based on the so-called *Livre d'Artus (Merlin-* continuation) of the Vulgate cycle.[9]

The Scandinavian versions of the *matière de Bretagne* hardly require separate treatment in this place. Cp. on the subject E. Mogk, Paul's *Grundriss* II, I, 135, 147, — also, H. G. Leach, *Angevin Britain and Scandinavia,* ch. VI—IX (Cambridge, Mass., 1921). Besides the prose versions of Chrétien's *Yvain, Erec* and *Perceval (Inventssaga, Erexsaga, Parcevalssaga)* — the first of which dates from the early thirteenth century, the others from the early fourteenth — we have the *Tristamssaga* (cp., I, 162, 483ff., above), a prose version of Thomas's *Tristan,* composed in 1226 by an abbot, named Robert (otherwise unknown) — still further, the *Strengleikar* (see above), a version of French lays and the *Möttulssaga* (version of the story of the chastity-testing mantle) — both, probably, also by this same Robert — and a brief poem on Gawain called *Valverspattr* (early fourteenth century). All of the works

---

[9] The total number of Dutch romances is slightly higher than eleven, if we take into account the fragmentary version of Chrétien's *Perceval,* the paraphrases from the Vulgate cycle, and the isolated episodes included in No. 10.

which I have just enumerated were composed in Norwegian — Icelandic. There is, besides, however, a Swedish version of *Yvain*, executed it seems in 1303. This exhausts the list of the Arthurian materials in the Scandinavian languages which have been edited. Mogk, however, *op. cit.*, p. 135, refers (without naming them) to a number of Arth'urian compositions in those languages as still unpublished.

The Swedish metrical romance, *Duke Frederick of Normandy* (beginning of the fourteenth century) has sometimes been assigned to the Arthurian cycle, but its connection with that cycle is very slight. For an analysis and discussion of this poem, which is more probably adapted from a Low German than from a French original, see, especially, Edward Thorstenberg, "Duke Frederick of Normandy, an Arthurian Romance," MPh., VII, 395 ff. (1910).

Chapter VI.

Analysis of the Prose Vulgate Cycle.

1. L'Estoire del Saint Graal.

According to the introduction to this romance (pp. 3—12), the author is a hermit, who, fearing lest personal envy might impair the authority of his work, does not divulge his name. On Good Friday in 717 A. D. Christ appeared to him in a dream, and presented him with a little book (cp. *Revelation*, ch. X) which would dispel his doubts concerning the Trinity. The Savior declares that he (Christ) had written the book with his own hand, it being, indeed (119 f.), the only thing that he wrote after his resurrection. Our author found that the volume contained accounts of his (the author's) ancestors, of the Holy Grail and of certain unspeakably fearful things (left undefined). He swoons, is borne up into the heavens, beholds the Trinity, and has his doubts on that subject solved. He puts the book away with the *corpus domini*, but it disappears. Later he discovers it on the altar of a mysterious forest chapel. Obeying Christ's command, on the Monday following Easter Monday, he transcribes from the little volume the early history of the Holy Grail. (Here, p. 12, ends the Introduction.)

In the beginning of the romance proper we have the history of Joseph of Arimathea, his imprisonment, his liberation by Vespasian, and his setting forth on his travels with the Holy Grail — all drawn substantially from Robert de Boron (q. v., I, 230 ff., above) — only Hebron, Alain etc. are here omitted from the Grail company, which includes, however, a new character, viz. Josephe, Joseph's son. Josephe and his father, alone, are allowed to open the ark in which the Grail is carried. — The Grail company first arrives at Sarras, a heathen capital, whose king, Evalac, had recently been defeated by his former suzerain, Tholomer (= Ptolemy), king of Egypt. Joseph promises victory to the vanquished monarch, if he will adopt Christianity. The latter is puzzled by the doctrines of the Trinity and Incarnation — so, too, are his wise men. A vision, however, symbolizing these mysteries, impresses him. Christ, himself, now consecrates Josephe bishop of the land (p. 36).

In the war against Tholomer that ensues, Evalac's brother-in-law, Seraphe, fights valorously, but it is Christ who, in answer to Evalac's prayer and in the guise of a white knight, finally turns defeat into victory. Seraphe is then baptized under the name of Nascien, Evalac under the name of Mordrain. From curiosity, Nascien uncovers the Grail and is stricken thereby with blindness, but he is healed with drops from a bleeding lance, which, as Josephe prophesies, will not bleed again until the adventures of the Grail take place. Only the last of Nascien's line [i. e. Galahad] will ever behold the marvels of that vessel (p. 81). — Mordrain has a strange dream concerning Nascien's descendants and is then borne away by the Holy Ghost to an isle in the sea, once occupied by Forcaire, a pirate, who was hunted down by Pompey the Great. Here he is tempted by a devil and comforted by the Savior, both disguised. The people hold Nascien responsible for Mordrain's disappearance and imprison him. He is miraculously snatched from the prison, however, and set down on an island in the sea, the Turning Island (p. 114). A beautiful ship arrives here. On this ship Nascien finds a rich bed, a gold crown, a sword of fabulous workmanship (it had been King David's), but with cheap hangings of tow and hemp. On the bed there were, likewise, three spindles — red, white and green, respectively — made from scions (planted by Eve) of the Tree of Life. Having had a vision of the last of his line (Galahad), King Solomon, on his wife's advice, had had this ship built and the above-mentioned objects, intended for the descendant in question, placed on board, together with a letter which bids him heed Solomon's example and beware of women (p. 135). Solomon's wife put the hangings on the sword, but a damsel (Perceval's sister) was destined to replace them with costlier ones. Nascien, being sinful, was unworthy to enter the ship and is cast into the water. Later an old man interprets to him the allegorical meaning of the ship (Holy Church), the bed (eucharistic table) etc. — Nascien's ten-year old son, Celidoine, is, also, borne to an island in the ocean, the ruler of which is the pagan king Label. The boy predicts the king's impending death and converts him (p. 157). Label's subjects now set the young prophet adrift on a vessel which brings him to Solomon's ship. In the latter he fetches his father away from the Turning Island and takes Mordrain from another ship. Mordrain joins together the pieces of King David's sword, which had broken in the hands of the unworthy Nascien. By divine command, they all now transfer themselves to Mordrain's ship, and later come to a castle that belongs to a son of that monarch. Here the wives of Mordrain and Nascien are awaiting them — also, Label's daughter, whose experiences, including her conversion to Christianity and visit to the ruins of Hippocrates's palace,[1] had previously been told. Celidoine now, on the warning of a hermit, embarks on a vessel, which (as it turns out) takes him to Great Britain, whither Joseph and his company had just gone. Nascien, in search of Celidoine, comes to Solomon's ship (p. 201), learns in a dream about his own future and where his son is — also, sees in this dream his nine successive descendants and is told that the last of them (Galahad) is to be taken back to Sarras in this same ship.

In the meanwhile, Joseph's company had crossed the sea to Great Britain, the Grail-bearers walking on the water, Joseph, Bron (mentioned here, p. 209, for the first time), and others that were pure, on Josephe's shirt spread out on the sea (p. 211), the sinners in galleys. The ship to which Nascien has been mira-culously transferred from Solomon's ship now drifts to the port of embarkation of these sinners. Whilst Nascien is asleep, they get on board and sail away to Great Britain. On their arrival in that country they are welcomed by Josephe and his companions. Fed in a marvellous manner by the Grail, the Christians begin

---

[1] At this point (p. 171) is inserted an amusing *fabliau,* relating how a woman made a fool of the wise physician.

the conversion of Britain. The first convert is Duke Ganor, who is won over by Celidoine's arguments and Josephe's interpretation of a dream that the duke had had (p. 223). At Galafort, Ganor's capital, Joseph's son, Galahad (not the Grail knight) is born. Ganor's pagan liege lord, king of Northumberland, wages war on him and is slain by Nascien, but Joseph, Josephe and others, trying to convert Crudel, king of Norgales, are thrown into prison. — The same night Christ commands Mordrain to go to Britain, where Nascien, Ganor and others join him. In the battle that follows Crudel is killed, but Mordrain is grievously wounded. The next day Mordrain is punished with blindness and paralysis for endeavoring to see the Grail (p. 241). A celestial voice proclaims that he will be cured, only when the good knight (Galahad) visits him. He retires to a hermitage, turns it into an abbey, and endows it. — Josephe continues to preach the gospel. Among his ostensible converts is the Saracen king of Camelot, who, after Josephe's departure, however, kills twelve of his (Josephe's) relatives near a cross (hence called the Black Cross). Josephe has the heathen temples in Camelot demolished and St. Stephen's church erected instead. — Bron learns from Josephe that the vacant seat at the Grail table (occupied by Jesus at the Last Supper) will remain empty until it is filled by Christ or some one sent by Christ (p. 247). Moys, who tries to occupy it, is snatched away by fiery hands. Alain is consecrated by Josephe to succeed him as Grail-keeper after the latter's decease. He feeds their followers miraculously with a single fish which he had caught — hence the title of "Rich Fisher" is conferred on him and all subsequent Grail keepers. — After various supernatural experiences of Joseph and Josephe, including an allegorical vision of a stag (Christ) and four lions (the four evangelists), they come to Scotland. Crimes of Symeu and Chanaan, two sinners of the Grail company (p. 263), and miraculous signs at the tombs of the latter's victims and his own tomb (a fire which will not be extinguished, until Lancelot visits it). Peter, of the Grail company, ancestor of Gawain and his brothers, has his wound (received from Chanaan) healed on the isle of King Orcan, whose daughter he weds (p. 279). —

After missionary work, lasting fifteen years, Josephe dies (shortly after Joseph). He is first buried at Mordrain's abbey, but the corpse later is borne to Scotland to allay a famine and re-interred there. His brother, Galahad, king of Hocelice (later called Gales) and progenitor of Urien and Ivain, founds an abbey near the burning tomb of Symeu, the flames of which will not cease until the younger Galahad comes. — Alain succeeds Josephe as Grail-keeper (p. 286) and goes to the Terre Foraine, whose ruler, a leper, he heals and converts. This ruler, Alphasem, builds a castle for the Grail. Its name, Corbenic (Chaldee for "most holy vessel") appears miraculously over one of its doors. Alain and Alphasem soon died and Josue became the next "Rich Fisher." — A pagan king, Brulans, slew Lambor, fourth in descent from Josue, and thereby the "terre foraine" became the "terre gaste." Pelleam, Lambor's son and successor, being disabled by wounds, was called the "Maimed King" (p. 290). He, in turn, was succeeded by his son, Pelles, father of the younger Galahad's mother. — Nascien did not long survive Josephe and he was succeeded by Celidoine, who protected his people against famine and Saxon invasion. The throne descended ultimately to the older Lancelot (grandfather of Lancelot, Guinevere's lover), and then to Ban (father of the younger Lancelot). Two marvellous lions guarded the wonder-working tomb of the former, until they were killed by the younger Lancelot (p. 296).

2. Vulgate Merlin.

The opening division[2] of the Vulgate *Merlin* is a mere prose rendering of Robert de Boron's *Merlin*.[3] After the coronation of Arthur, however, there begins a long continuation (Sommer, II, 88, line 19—466) of that work which makes this branch, as a whole, the bulkiest of the romances of the Vulgate cycle, except the *Lancelot*. This continuation, as was said above, is intended to connect Robert's *Merlin* with the *Lancelot*, and consists, for

---

[2] Sommer, II, 3—88, line 18.
[3] Another text of this prose rendering will be found in the *Huth-Merlin*, I, 1—146.

the most part, of accounts of wars waged 1. by Arthur against other British chieftains, 2. by Arthur and these same chieftains against the Saxons. These narratives, however, are so intolerably commonplace, prolix, and monotonous that a bare indication of the contents of the main episodes of this kind will be sufficient for our present purpose.

The prose rendering of Robert's *Merlin* runs as follows:

When Christ, in the interval of three days between his death and resurrection, had descended into hell and had delivered from captivity there Adam and Eve and the rest, the devils were very angry and they took counsel together in order to determine how they might recover their power. They decide that they can best attain their ends through a man who, like Christ, should combine human and supernatural attributes, but the object of whose exertions should be the ruin of mankind, instead of their salvation. The evil spirits, consequently, send up to the earth one of their number who is capable of carnal intercourse with women, in order that he may beget upon some virgin the unholy offspring who is to execute their hellish designs. The fiend who has been appointed for this purpose already has under his influence a rich man's wife and he begins by destroying the husband's stock (at the wife's instigation) and reducing him to such despair that in an unwary moment he angrily devotes everything that belongs to him to the devil and withdraws himself from the society of men. The effects of this unhappy speech soon make themselves manifest, for the devil in question now strangles the man's son and causes the woman to hang herself (p. 5). The three daughters of the couple, however, still remain to be ruined: A young man, inspired by the fiend, seduces one of these, and she is condemned to die by being buried alive. Seeing that the devil is at work in the unfortunate family, a pious confessor goes to the surviving sisters and urges them to be virtuous. His exhortations are heeded by the elder of the two, but the younger, yielding to the evil suggestions of a woman whom the fiend possesses, becomes a strumpet. The holy man now renews his exhortations to the older sister and warns her, above all things, never to give way to impulses of wrath, for in such moments she would be at the mercy of the devil. The girl obeys, until one day her sister came with some vicious companions, accused her of illicit relations with the confessor, and finally beat her. The unfortunate victim forgets her confessor's injunction, falls into anger, locks herself up in her house, goes to bed, and falls asleep weeping. The fiend now sees his opportunity and cohabits with her whilst she is asleep. Remembering the occurrence next morning as if it were a dream, she goes to her confessor, who is at first incredulous, but when he perceives that she is telling the truth, he urges her to continue her virtuous life, gives her holy water to drink, makes the sign of the cross upon her, and commends her to God. The girl acts in accordance with his advice and, leading a uniformly pious and irreproachable life, affords the fiend no second opportunity. Hence the schemes of the devils are brought to naught, for, when her child is born, he inherits his father's supernatural powers, but not his wickedness (p. 12). When the mother's pregnancy had been observed, she had been arrested for unchastity, but the confessor had persuaded the judges not to put her to death at once for this offense, but to keep her in a tower until she had been delivered of her child. Immediately after the child's birth, he is baptized and named Merlin after his mother's father.

The excessively hairy body of the infant betrays his demonic origin — still more, the power of speech which he displays as soon as he is born, for as the mother weeps in expectation of her execution, he tells her that she will not suffer death on his account. At the public trial of his mother, the marvellous child defends her innocence and declares that he knows his own paternity much better than the judge on the bench who expresses doubts about the mother's story knows his, and he establishes the truth of this declaration by making the judge's mother confess that the father of the judge was not her lawful husband, but a priest. Merlin now tells the judges that a fiend was his (Merlin's) father.

After the trial was over, Merlin, who was not yet two years old, dictates to a learned clerk, Blaise, an account of Joseph of

Arimathea,[4] his companions, and the Grail — also, an account of the devils' plot to which he himself owed his existence. He later makes a prediction about his own future and foretells, besides, that Blaise will go to the region where the Grail company live and will there continue to write down what Merlin will dictate to him. The result of these dictations will finally be joined to the book of Joseph (Robert de Boron's *Joseph*) to form one book (p. 20).

Constant, an English king, has three sons, Maines (Moyne), Uther, and Pandragon (Pendragon). He, also, has an ambitious and unprincipled seneschal, named Vertig(i)er (Vortigern). Maines succeeds his father, but when he is defeated by the Saxons, his barons want Vertiger in his place, and, incited by the seneschal, kill their sovereign, in order that Vertiger may become king. When Vertiger is proclaimed king, the guardians of Uther and Pandragon take the young princes to an easterly land, whence their ancestors had come. In pretended anger, Vertiger now slays the men who had killed Maines, and a civil war between him and their friends ensues. He allies himself with the Saxons and marries the daughter of their chieftain Augis (Hangus=Hengist) — who is, later, killed. For his protection he wishes to build a strong tower, but the structure will not stand and his wise clerks are unable to fathom the cause. Each clerk, however, learns in a vision that a fatherless child, seven years old, is to be the cause of his (the clerk's) death. Accordingly, to save their own lives, they all agree to report that the foundations of the tower will never prove stable until they have been drenched with the blood of such a child as has just been described. The messengers who are sent forth to discover this child, after a long search, come upon Merlin and learn from him that he is the object of their search (p. 25). — Merlin now goes to Vertiger with the messengers, giving, *en route,* proofs of his supernatural powers, whilst Blaise retires to Northumberland. When Merlin arrives at the tower, he tells Vertiger

---

[4] Sommer's text here (p. 19) includes Nascien, but this is certainly a late insertion for Nascien was, indisputably, the creation of the author of the *Estoire.* Contrast with this the reading of the *Huth-Merlin,* I, 31.

how the clerks are planning to kill him, in order to save their own
lives, but asserts that the true cause of the instability of the tower
is a body of water about its foundations with a red and white dragon
in it — each of the creatures being under a big stone. When the
water is drawn off and the stones removed, the two dragons, just
as Merlin had predicted, fight each other and both perish in the
struggle (p. 33). Merlin explains, moreover, that the red dragon
signified Vertiger and the white one Constant's sons and that these
sons will be invading the kingdom in three days and that Vertiger
will fall in the ensuing war. The prophecy is fulfilled and Vertiger is consumed in the flames of the above-mentioned tower,
whereupon Pandragon becomes king. — Hearing of Merlin's
remarkable powers of divination, the new monarch sends for him.
The magician, however, meets the royal messengers as a beggar and
says that the king must come to Merlin. Pandragon, accordingly,
goes to Northumberland, and Merlin meets him at different times
in different shapes (pp. 38f.). After this (pp. 40-43), the
magician plays many more similar tricks upon Pandragon and
Uther. In admiration of his wisdom, they want him to stay with
them, and he consents — with the proviso, however, that he will
have to be absent very often. Shortly after this the king, as advised by Merlin, concludes peace with the Saxons on condition
that they shall evacuate the country. — A baron, jealous of Merlin's influence with the king, disputes the enchanter's wisdom,
and, in order to test him, in three different disguises, asks Merlin
in what manner he (the baron) is to die. The baron is triumphant
when each time Merlin gives a different reply, apparently irreconcilable with the others, but soon he loses his life in a manner
that shows that the contradiction was only apparent (p. 47).[5] —
The magician now retires to Northumberland to dictate an account of these recent happenings to Blaise. In the meanwhile,
the king is so struck with Merlin's prophetic powers that henceforth he has all of his predictions recorded. Thus the book of
Merlin's Prophecies came into existence. — Merlin foretells the

---

[5] The *motif* of the triple prediction is found already in the *Vita
Merlini*. Cp. I, 136—143, above, where the details are given.

return of the Saxons to the land to avenge Augis (Hengist); he
predicts, also, the death of either the king or his brother in the
conflict. The Saxons do return, but at Salisbury are utterly
destroyed by the brothers, who follow the prophet's sagacious advice, and Pandragon is killed in the battle, whereupon Uther —
adopting the name, Uther Pandragon — succeeds him (p. 52). —
Merlin by his art transfers from Ireland to the cemetery at Salisbury the great stones that are still there (i. e. the stones at Stone-
henge). He next tells Uther of the table of the Last Supper of
our Lord — likewise of the Grail table — and proposes that the
king shall establish a third — the Round Table. The three tables
are to symbolize the Trinity (p. 54). Uther assents and the Round
Table is founded in Carduel on the day of Pentecost (Whitsunday).
Merlin next selects fifty knights as the first company that are
to sit about it. He leaves vacant, however, one seat,[6] which is only
to be filled by the person (not yet born) who is to achieve the adventure of the Grail. As a matter of fact, a knight who was so
rash as to try to occupy the vacant seat at once disappeared. —
In a great Christmas feast at Carduel, Uther falls in love with
Ygerne, wife of the Duke of Tintagel (Tintaiol), and through
one of his nobles, Ulfin (Urfin), vainly endeavors to seduce the
lady by presents and messages. Finally (p. 61), Ygerne tells
her husband of the affair and he hastily takes her back to his own
dominions. The king summons him to return to court, and, when
he refuses, makes war on him. The duke is successful in defending
one of his castles against the king, whilst the duchess is in another
— Tintagel. The duke being still besieged, Uther rides to Tintagel, and having been made by Merlin's art identical in appearance with the duke, is able to penetrate Tintagel castle and beget
Arthur upon Ygerne (p. 68). On the day of Arthur's conception,
his father promises Merlin that, as soon as the child is born, it
is to be turned over to the enchanter. When Uther now rides
back to the castle in which the duke has been besieged, he learns that
the latter has been killed. The king's marriage to Ygerne follows

---

[6] This was to make the Round Table conform to the previous
tables, at each of which there had, also, been a vacant seat.

one month later[7] and, at the same time, Lothe, king of Orcanie, is married to a daughter (unnamed)[8] of Ygerne's by her first husband (p. 73). — When it becomes evident that Ygerne is going to give birth to a child before one is due — reckoning from the date of her marriage with Uther — she consents, in order to avoid scandal, that the child, as soon as it is born, shall be turned over to a person whom the king has selected. Thus the infant is at once put into Merlin's hands, and he, in turn, forthwith entrusts it to an excellent man named Antor (Auctor) to bring up (p. 76). The little boy is baptized with the name of Arthur (Artus). — In a new war with the Saxons Uther is slain and the land is left without a legitimate king. Merlin, however, advises the barons that, if they will assemble at Christmas, God will provide a proper successor to the crown. They adopt his advice and when they have come together at the appointed time, they behold before the church a block of stone with an anvil on it and in the anvil a sword fixed (p. 81). An inscription on the sword declared that the person who could draw it from the anvil would be king. The barons, week after week, try to achieve this, but none are successful. One day, at last, young Arthur, who has been sent by his foster-brother, Kay, to obtain a sword for him, after seeking one in vain, happens to pass by the stone and anvil and draws the sword from the latter, and gives it to Kay, who now claims to have performed this feat, himself. Kay finally, however, is compelled to confess the truth and restore the sword to the anvil. — Autor reveals to Arthur that the latter is not his son and makes him promise that, when he becomes king, he will appoint Kay his seneschal. — Again Arthur draws the sword from the anvil, but

---

[7] For the variant, "deux mois", cp. *Huth-Merlin,* I, 120.

[8] By way of digression, it is here said that from this daughter issued Gawain, Agravain, Guerrehes, Gaheries and Mordred — also, Morgan la Fee. Both Sommer's text (p. 73) and the *Huth-Merlin* credit Loth with another daughter. The former does not name her; the latter states that she was a bastard named Morgan(s), Morgan la Fee being called *Morgue* in this text. These are, of course, merely the oblique and nominative forms, respectively, of the same name. For such doublets, cp. Bruce, MPh., XVI, 67 f.

this time, in the presence of all the barons (p. 84). Nevertheless, because of what they imagine to be his low birth, the barons continue to postpone the coronation for many months, but, since in the course of time they become convinced that he is worthy of the crown, they at last permit the ceremony to be celebrated.

So far the prose rendering of Robert's *Merlin*. At this point[9] a continuator takes up the narrative.

At the beginning of the continuation the vassal kings of Arthur raise a revolt against him, because of his supposed humble origin. Merlin, in vain, enlightens them in regard to this matter — they persist in their rebellion. Arthur defeats them, but with a view to future contingencies, on Merlin's advice, he invites Ban of Benoic (Lancelot's father) and Bohort of Gaunes (Lancelot's uncle) to come to his aid, which they do. The rebel kings renew their attack and are again defeated. Moreover, whilst they are thus engaged, their own lands are invaded by the Saxons. They win a victory over the Saxons — especially through the valor of Gawain and his brothers (sons of Lot, king of Orcanie, and nephews of Arthur). In the meanwhile, adopting the counsel of Merlin, who desired that he should marry Guinevere, only child of Leodegan king of Carmelide (apparently in Scotland), Arthur, accompanied by Ban, Bohort, the knights of the Round Table etc., had gone to Carmelide to assist the king of that country against the Saxons and against Rion, king of the giants. In the battle which ensues near Carohaise, Arthur and his men put Leodegan's enemies to flight. (Interpolated in these accounts of the Saxon wars we have, pp. 128 f., an account of how Arthur begot Mordred upon his sister, Lot's wife, neither knowing who the other was — also, p. 149, how Leodegan on the same night begot both the true and the false Guinevere, lying in succession with his own wife and his seneschal's wife, respectively.) Arthur is attracted by Guinevere, who was the wisest, most beautiful and best beloved woman that had ever been in the land, with the exception of Elaine *sans per,* wife of Persides of Gazewilte, and the

---

[9] Sommer, II, 88, line 19 and, *Huth-Merlin,* I, 147, line 1.

daughter of Pelles de Listenois of Corbenic, niece of the Fisher
King (159).[10] — More battles (near Arundel) between the Saxons
and the rebel kings, during which Saigremor, a prince of Constantinople, after many encounters with the pagans, makes his way
safely to Camelot. In these conflicts Merlin plays a leading part,
availing himself often of his shape-shifting power, and resorting,
also, frequently to Blaise, who keeps a record of all that he (Merlin)
says. This *motif* of Merlin's visits to Blaise and dictating to the
latter accounts of his exploits runs all through the romance. Merlin
meets Viviane, daughter of a noble vavassor, named Dyonas (a
godson of the goddess, Diana), by a fountain in the forest, and
astounds her with his magical powers, through which he calls up
before her eyes phantom knights and ladies amusing themselves in
a beautiful orchard (209). She promises her love to the enchanter, on condition that he shall teach her some of his tricks
of magic.

After this Merlin returns to Leodegan's court, prophesies allegorically Lancelot's birth, and brings about the marriage of Arthur
and Guinevere (217). Arthur and his men now have a battle
with Rion and the Saxons and defeat them. In this battle Arthur
engages in personal combat with Rion, and, aided by Ban, overcomes him and captures his sword.

Guinebaut (brother of Bohort), who is skilled in enchantments, for the sake of a lady whom he loves, establishes the marvel
of the knights and ladies who are to dance unceasingly until the
knight who has never been false in love (Lancelot) breaks the
spell — likewise, another marvel, viz. self-playing chessmen, whom
no one, save the same knight, can checkmate (244 ff.).

Gawain and his companions come to meet Arthur. The latter
confers on him the highest rank in the kingdom next to himself —
dubs him knight, also, and presents him with his own sword,
Excalibur (253). During the festivities, Morgan le Fay makes
Merlin's acquaintance and learns from him many of his crafts
(254).

---

[10] On this passage cp. Bruce, MPh., XVI, 337 ff. (1918) and
RR, IX, 256 ff. (1918).

Arthur, accompanied by Merlin, Gawain and his army, now crosses the sea to aid Ban of Benoic in the defense of the latter's kingdom, which has been invaded by Claudas de la Deserte, Froille d'Alemaigne, and others. The fighting takes place at Trebes, on the river Loire (260). After a long struggle Ban's enemies are compelled to retreat with great losses and Claudas's own dominions are ravaged. Ban's consort (Helaine) has an allegorical dream of Arthur's future conflict with Galehaut and the part which her son, Lancelot, was destined to play in it. The dream is partially interpreted by Merlin (279 f.). Arthur and his allies go back to Great Britain, whilst Merlin goes to the court of Julius Caesar. Here he displays his supernatural powers in the Grisandole affair.[11] New battles occur between the rebel kings and the Saxons, in which the former get the worst of it. In Carmelide now Arthur weds Guinevere, and there follows a great tournament in which Gawain distinguishes himself most. The night of the wedding the relatives of the false Guinevere try to abduct the true Guinevere and substitute the false one as the bride. Merlin, however, brings the conspiracy to naught (308ff.) and the false Guinevere is exiled, together with the chief conspirator, Bertholais. When Arthur is returning to Logres with his bride, Lot, wishing to seize Guinevere, in order that he may recover his own wife by exchange, attacks him with a large force of men, but is unhorsed by his own son, Gawain. The identity of father and son, being revealed to each other, Gawain compels Lot to make his peace with Arthur and swear allegiance to him. A great feast is held at Logres, and here Arthur takes his oath that he will not sit down to dinner until some adventure is reported to him (320).[12] The knights of the Round Table vow that they will aid any damsel in distress. Gawain and his companions are accepted as the queen's knights and four clerks are appointed to chronicle their adventures. During the

---

[11] Sommer, II, 281 ff. For an analysis of this episode see I. 148 ff., above.

[12] For a list of occurrences of this *motif* in Arthurian romance see R. Zenker, *Zs. f. frz. Spr. u. Litt.*, XLV[1]. 102 ff. (1917). He cites sixteen romances in which it occurs.

tournament between the knights of the Round Table and the Queen's knights that follows, the former violate their agreement as to the kind of weapons that were to be used and the affair turns into a serious conflict. The aggressors are defeated and Gawain's wrath against them is appeased with difficulty through Guinevere's influence. — News of the arrival of the Holy Grail now spreads through Logres (334f.). Lot, accompanied by his sons, goes to the rebel kings to negotiate a reconciliation between them and Arthur. On the way, the Saxons, under King Clarion, attack him, but Gawain strikes down Clarion and takes possession of his famous horse, Gringalet (341). Lot and his sons, having rested at the house of a forester, named Minoras, proceed on their journey. They rescue from the Saxons Eliezer, Pelles's son, who was on his way to seek service under Gawain. Soon after this Gawain and Eliezer rescue a knight and a sister of the Lady of Roestoc from five scoundrels who had assailed them in the forest. They also aid Escan to vanquish the Saxons near Cambenic. Lot induces the rebel kings to declare a truce with Arthur (387).

Merlin summons knights from both Great and Little Britain to meet on Salisbury Plain. In the interim there had been a renewal of the clashes between the Queen's knights and the knights of the Round Table. The Saxons, hearing of the above-mentioned gathering of the hosts on Salisbury Plain, assemble near Clarence. There are battles near Garlot and Clarence between the Christians and the Saxons, in which the latter are severely defeated and driven out of the country (401). Merlin, Gawain, and Eliezer (who is dubbed knight by Gawain) are all prominent in these battles. Ban and Bohort start for home and pass by Agravadain's castle. Here Merlin brings about the cohabitation of Ban and Agravadain's wife, through which Hector is engendered.

Rion renews the war against Leodegan and desires to add Arthur's beard to the beards of the other kings that already adorn his mantle (412). Merlin, in the guise of a minstrel, appears at a great feast at Camelot. He summons the knights together and there ensues a battle between Rion and Arthur's men. Arthur

accepts Rion's challenge to a duel and kills him, whereupon the
dead king's followers do homage to the victor.

Merlin goes to Jerusalem and expounds a strange dream of
King Flualis there. He next visits Viviane and imprudently betrays more of his secrets to her. Thence he returns to Logres,
just when a beautiful lady arrives there with an ugly dwarf and
tricks Arthur into dubbing the latter. Luces, emperor of Rome,
sends an arrogant letter to Arthur, demanding tribute. Arthur
resents it, crosses the Channel, slays the giant of Mont St. Michel,
who is clad in an impenetrable serpent's skin, and is joined by Ban
and Bohort (431). Gawain, Ivain and Saigremor are sent as messengers to Rome, where, owing to Gawain's bold words, they get
into a fight in the emperor's presence. After Gawain has struck
off the head of the emperor's nephew, he and his companions are
chased back to Arthur's camp.

There is next an engagement between the Romans and Arthur's
host, which ends in the slaying of the emperor and the flight of
his men. Arthur now has his fight with the terrible cat of the
Lake of Lausanne.[13] News is brought to him of Leodegan's death.
He returns to Logres and is joyfully received by Guinevere.

Merlin informs Arthur that he (Merlin) must leave him forever (450). He tells Blaise the same thing, saying that he is going
to Viviane. Despite Blaise's protest, he departs. Viviane, through
blandishments, induces Merlin to impart to her secrets of witch-
craft by which she will be able to imprison a man forever. The
first use she makes of this knowledge is to put Merlin, himself,
under the spell. He imagines that he is in a bed in a beautiful
tower, and remains forever under the spell in this spot — in the
forest of Broceloande — where Viviane henceforth constantly visits him.

Gawain and thirty knights go in search of Merlin, each knight
riding in a different direction (453). There follow now adventures
of the dwarf, mentioned above, who overcomes various knights,
and, according to custom, sends them to Arthur's court. Gawain,

---

[13] On this episode (Sommer, II, 441ff.) cp. I, 41, note 9, above.

being in a revery, fails to salute a damsel whom he meets in the woods, and she pronounces as his punishment that he will for a time resemble the first man that he meets. This turns out to be the dwarf, who, himself, at the same instant recovers his natural form. Gawain, disconsolate on account of his transformation, decides to return to the court, and, in doing so, passes the place where Merlin is imprisoned. Merlin relates what has befallen him and declares that Gawain is the last person that will ever hear him speak (461). Gawain next rescues the damsel who was the cause of his transformation from two knights who are attacking her, and she restores him to his true form. The attack, however, had been pre-arranged as a test of Gawain. The former dwarf (Evadeam) becomes a knight of the Round Table.

3. Lancelot[14].

Ban has a son, first called Galahad and afterwards Lancelot. Claudas makes war upon him (Ban), with the help of the Romans, who thus conquer Gaul and capture the city of Benoic. The last city that Ban possessed (Trebes) is betrayed into the hands of the enemy by his deneschal (466).

Claudas of "la terre deserte" (Berri), which had been devastated by Aramont (Hoel), King of Lesser Britain, and Uterpendragon, makes war against his neighbor, King Ban of Benoic (Benoyc). Encouraged by a treacherous seneschal, Ban goes to Logres to seek Arthur's aid. As soon as he has gone, the seneschal surrenders Trebes (Ban's castle) to Claudas, who only takes possession, however, after a stout resistance on the part of Banin, Ban's godchild. Moreover, the treacherous seneschal is killed by Banin to the great joy even of Claudas. Ban had not proceeded far when he observed that Trebes, which Claudas had just occupied, was in flames. His heart breaks from grief at this culminating misfortune and he dies. His wife (Elaine), learning of his death, lays her little boy (Lancelot) down by a neighboring lake and goes to her husband, but before she can return, she sees a fairy plunge into the

---

[14] The romance fills vols. 3, 4, 5 in Sommer's series.

lake with the child in her arms. The sorrowful queen accepts now the invitation of a passing abbess to go with her to her convent, takes the veil, and becomes the head of the convent. Two days after Ban, King Bohort of Gannes (Ban's brother), dies, and his widow (Queen Evaine) flies from Claudas with her two little sons, Lionel and Bohort. Pharien, a nobleman who had been at enmity with her husband, seizes all three and is about to take them to Claudas, when, moved by her lamentations and by gratitude for a former favor, he resolves to retain the boys and bring them up himself. Evaine joins her sister (Elaine) and also becomes a nun (p. 19).

We are told now of Merlin's demon birth and of how the Lady of the Lake — the fairy who carried off the infant Lancelot — had beguiled him and imprisoned him forever through a spell which she had learned from him.[15] The lake was not a real one, but merely an illusion designed to conceal the fairy's abode (22).

Pharien's wife, who is Claudas's paramour, informs the latter as to the true identity of the two boys whom her husband is keeping. Pharien is about to return the boys to their mother, when Claudas begs him to retain them and promises to return to them their inheritance as soon as they are of age. He complies with the request of Claudas, who is now master of both Benoic and Gannes.

Two years later Claudas plans a war against Arthur, and, in disguise, visits the court of that monarch, in order to discover from direct observation the extent of the latter's power. He and his companion are much impressed with Arthur's court (33).

Lancelot grows up in the fairy's palace, gentle, generous, and brave. A friar (Adragain) informs the queens in the convent that their sons are alive. He goes also to Arthur's court to solicit his aid on behalf of these children and Arthur promises to redress their wrongs, as soon as he has quelled his rebellious barons.

Saraide, the friar's niece, goes as a messenger of the Lady

---

[15] The version of the "enserrement Merlin" in the Vulgate *Merlin* (Sommer, II, 450 ff.) is, doubtless, based on this passage. Cp. pp. 312 ff., above.

of the Lake to Claudas's court and upbraids him with keeping
Bohort's sons prisoners. Claudas, feeling the reproach, sends for
the boys. When they are received at court, Lionel, self-willed
and fearless, strikes Claudas in the face and knocks him down.
He and Bohort also kill Claudas's worthless son (Dorin). Saraide
converts the boys into greyhounds and two greyhounds into the
semblance of the boys, and the former are thus enabled to escape
and take refuge with the Lady of the Lake (57). Knights and
citizens, led by Pharien and his nephew (Lambegue), demand the
supposed children — really enchanted greyhounds — of Claudas,
who, refusing them, is besieged in his palace. Wounded and defeated, Claudas surrenders the supposed boys, who, at the moment,
however, that the real boys are disenchanted, assume their natural
form as dogs. The people believe that Claudas is playing a trick
upon them and has really killed the children. Pharien, however,
credits his protestations of innocence and takes his side in the fight
that ensues — also, later, when arms have been laid aside, protects him against the treachery of Lambegue and others (77) and
gets him to a place of safety.

Lionel and Bohort long for their masters, Pharien and Lambegue, and the Lady of the Lake sends a damsel for them. The
people imprison Pharien, because of Claudas's escape. Learning
from the damsel that the boys are safe, he advises that Lambegue
and a trustworthy knight (Leonce of Paerne) be sent to them.
He himself is to remain a prisoner until the people are satisfied
that the young princes are alive. Happy meeting of the two
knights with the children at the Lady of the Lake's and touches
that reveal the noble disposition of the child, Lancelot. The people
rejoice when they are convinced that Lionel and Bohort are safe,
but, distrusting Pharien's relations with Claudas, still keep him
in prison (p. 91). Claudas, breaking his promise to Pharien, besieges Gannes, and, when unarmed, is assailed by Lambegue, who
later, however, to save the town, voluntarily gives himself up to
Claudas. Peace now is concluded. Pharien goes to the Lake, is
reproached by Lionel for not having come earlier, and dies there.

When Lancelot is eighteen years old, the Lady of the Lake,

in great sorrow, has to prepare to let him seek admission into the
order of knighthood. She first instructs him at length in regard
to the high requirements of that order (pp. 112ff.). Crossing over
to Great Britain with Lancelot, his two cousins (Lionel and Bohort)
and others, on the way to Arthur's court, she meets the king in
a wood near Camelot and asks him to dub Lancelot on St. John's
Day. He consents, and the fairy, after warning the youth to say
that he does not know his name and, when once knighted, to commence his adventures without delay, returns home with Lionel,
Bohort, etc. Lancelot accompanies Arthur to Camelot, meets
Guinevere for the first time, and is thrilled by her beauty. Arthur
gives Lancelot the accolade, but before he can gird the sword on
the youth, the latter has performed his first exploit, viz. saves
the life of a strange knight by drawing a sword and lance-heads out
of his wounds and vowing, at the same time, to revenge him on
all who might aver that they loved the man who inflicted the
wounds better than the man who suffered them. (For the sequel
to this fantastic vow cp. pp. 174, 198, 208). Immediately after
this follows Lancelot's second adventure: The Lady of Nohaut,
being besieged by the King of Northumberland, asks Arthur for
succor. After much urging, Arthur permits the young knight
to try the adventure. On his departure, the queen grants his
petition that he might be allowed to call himself her knight, wherever he went. *En route* to rescue the Lady of Nohaut, he wins
three damsels in combat, requires a vanquished opponent to conduct them to Arthur's court and bring him back a sword from the
Queen. When he has girded this on, he is a full-fledged knight
(137). Lancelot and Kay (Kex) overthrow the two champions of
Northumberland, who now make peace.

Lancelot passes by the tomb of Leucan, nephew of Joseph
of Arimathea, vanquishes a knight at the Queen's Ford, and begins
the adventure of Dolorous Gard (143). Only the best knight
living, can do away with the evil customs and enchantments of
this strong castle (on the Humber). Lancelot overcomes all ob-
stacles and is master of the castle. In a cemetery nearby there
is a tomb with the inscription: "This slab will be raised by the

hand of no man save the one who shall conquer this dolorous castle, and his name is written beneath it." Lancelot lifts the slab, reads the inscription beneath, which runs: "Here will lie Lancelot of the Lake, son of King Ban of Benoyce" (152). Arthur and his court are amazed at the news of Lancelot's conquest and Gawain sets out to join him. After Lancelot's success the people entered the cemetery and put inscriptions — some true, some false — on the tombs. One of the latter causes a rumor that Lancelot was dead to be spread abroad. Gawain, Arthur and others were deceived thereby. Arthur and Guinevere go to Dolorous Gard and are deceived there by still other false inscriptions into the belief that Gawain and his companions were, also, dead. As a matter of fact, Brandus des Illes had treacherously lured them into a castle on an island in the Humber and shut them up there. Lancelot forces Brandus to give them up to him (167). He next receives the king and queen at Dolorous Gard, betrays his love for the latter by his absentmindedness and rides away, at the same time, sending Gawain and his companions, who do not know of their deliverer's identity, to thank the king and queen there the next day for what he (Lancelot) had done. On entering the castle, the royal pair are cautioned that they must not speak to anybody in it.

Arthur accepts Gawain's advice to challenge the *roi d'outre les marches de Galone* to an assembly in September and Gawain, himself, goes in quest of his deliverer (171). Lancelot, *incognito*, learns that the queen has summoned him and other knights to this assembly. After some minor adventures he arrives at the place of assembly. On the day of the conflict he puts on red armor, to keep from being recognized, performs striking feats of arms, but, being seriously wounded, is carried from the field. The assembly is to be renewed at a later date. The same evening Lancelot has himself borne away, after having been visited by Gawain, who does not learn, however, until the former has departed that this is the person whom he is seeking. Whilst Lancelot was on this journey, the Lady of Nohaut finds him sleeping under an elm (182) and takes him to her castle. Gawain learns from Brun(s) sans Pitie, whom he has overcome in combat, where Lancelot is, but Lancelot will not receive him, and Gawain's effort, under the guidance of a damsel, to discover Lancelot's name from the inscription on the underside of the slab of the tomb at Dolorous Gard is vain, since he cannot lift this slab. Gawain has experience of the treachery of Brun (p. 187, and, later, pp. 193 ff.).

Lancelot hears from a squire that the Queen is a captive at Dolorous Gard and that no one but the conqueror of that castle can liberate her. On arriving there, however, Lancelot is, himself, made captive and is only freed when he promises to terminate the enchantments of the place. He ought to have remained forty days at the castle after conquering it. Lancelot ends the enchantments and henceforth the castle is called Joyous Gard (192).

The assembly is renewed, Lancelot *(incognito)*, Gawain and his brothers being participants in it. A girl tells Gawain Lancelot's true name (196), which thus becomes known for the first time at Arthur's court. After the fight, by chance, Lancelot finds himself the guest of a knight whom his fantastic vow (see Sommer III, 127) requires him to fight. Both men lament the unfortunate situation, but the host is bound by a similar vow. In the fight Lancelot slays his adversary, but weeps over the necessity (199). — Arthur has allegorical dreams portending a misfortune near at hand and the interpretation offered by his clerks is very obscure (200).

Lancelot is so immersed in a revery concerning the queen that he hears no one, until he is prodded.

Arthur refuses Galehaut's (Galehot's) summons to become his man (201). On seeing the queen, Lancelot is so fascinated that he lets his horse go where he will. The animal takes him into the river and he is almost drowned (203). Daguenet, a foolish knight, led Lancelot's horse to Guinevere and pretended to have unhorsed the rider. The voice of the queen throws Lancelot again into a state of unconsciousness and his brief answers to questions are spoken as in a maze (205). He repeats this conduct later on (pp. 214, 237).

Lancelot, having killed the son of the Lady of Malehaut's

seneschal, voluntarily surrenders himself and is imprisoned by her
(210). Galehaut invades Arthur's kingdom. There are two assemblies (jousts) between their hosts. The Lady of Malohaut
(Malahaut) allows Lancelot to take part in these assemblies on his
promising to disclose his name to her soon and to return to prison.
To preserve his *incognito*, he uses in each assembly armor of a
different color (red, black and white, successively). When he leaves
the first assembly, Gawain and forty knights go in quest of him
(226ff.). In the meanwhile, a holy man (pp. 215ff.) rebukes
Arthur for his sins, gives him good moral advice, and interprets
the above-mentioned allegorical dreams (cp. pp. 199ff.). In the
second assembly Lancelot's achievements excite Galehaut's admiration to such a degree that, twice, when the former loses his
horse, Galehaut, though his foe, lends him his own (242f.) and,
after the joust is over, entertains him (244f.). The two become
devoted friends and the next day Lancelot puts on Galehot's armor.
But when Arthur and Gawain are filled with anxiety at the impending encounter with the superior host of the enemy, Galehaut,
moved by his love for Lancelot, goes to Arthur, kneels down before
him and begs forgiveness (249). The King is, of course, over-
joyed at this turn in events. When Galehaut goes back to his host,
he finds that Lancelot had spent the night in restlessness and
grief (on account of his passion for Guinevere). The next day the
king and queen learn that it was the black knight of the second
assembly who had brought about the peace between Galehaut and
Arthur (253). The queen, now much in love with Lancelot, ar-
ranges, through Galehaut, a meeting that evening with him. She
is accompanied to the rendezvous by Galehaut, the Lady of Malohaut and her attendant damsel, Lore de Carduel. Here Lancelot
confesses to Guinevere that he has loved her since he first saw her,
but, from timidity, does not ask her any favor. She kisses him
(263). She allows Galehaut to continue the friend of her lover
and Galehaut learns now for the first time from her the name of his
friend (hitherto withheld by Lancelot himself). The Lady of Malohaut acknowledges that she loved Lancelot, when he was her
prisoner, but that he did not reciprocate her affection (p. 266).

Now, on a hint which she gives to the queen, the latter brings Galehaut and herself together and the two become sworn lovers. Evening meetings of the four, after this, were frequent.

Galehaut now takes Lancelot with him to his kingdom, Sorelois, which is accessible only by two passages (269ff.). After returning to his own country, Arthur is plunged in a deep revery and in sorrow, because his knights had broken the vow which they had made after the first assembly not to cease their quest for the red knight of that contest (Lancelot), until they had found him (273). Gawain is told by Guinevere where Lancelot is and with nineteen other knights starts on the new quest, each going in a different direction. Gawain meets Hector and an insulting dwarf. Hector exhibits his prowess in various commonplace fights and Gawain delivers the Lady of Roestoc from her importunate suitor, Segurades (292ff.). This lady goes to court and takes with her Segurades, Hector, the dwarf, and the dwarf's niece, who is her cousin and Hector's lady-love. With great difficulty the queen and the Lady of Roestoc persuade the cousin to permit Hector to go in search of the knight who had delivered the Lady of Roestoc. A maiden brings from the Lady of the Lake a cleft shield which would never join together, until the love of the knight and lady (Lancelot and Guinevere) depicted on it attains its consummation. In the meanwhile Gawain had achieved different adventures among them, the saving of a knight afflicted with sores (through the ointment of a damsel) who turns out to be his own brother, Agravain — by furnishing some of his blood to bathe him in (315). To complete his cure the blood of the other best knight in the world (Lancelot) was also necessary. This was obtained later (p. 405).

Hector's adventures in quest of Gawain: he humbles Guinas de Blakestan, who is unjustly jealous of his sweetheart (325), unhorses the nephew of the lord of Falerne and his companion, succors Sinados de Windesores, whose wife's relatives warred upon him, because she had married him without their consent, comes to "L'Estroite Marche," where the custom prevailed that any knight hospitably received there had to devote half a day to the defence of the castle (337). Hector vanquishes Marganor, at the castle by

courtesy as well as valor and frees Yvain and Sagremor, who had
been captured by Marganor (349). The lord of the castle and
his daughter want Hector to marry the latter. He refuses, but
at his departure the girl gives him a magic ring which makes the
receiver love the donor. Through the machinations of a dwarf
Hector is imprisoned at Les Mares (355). He had killed one of
the sons of the lord of this castle and saved another (Ladomas).

Lancelot in Sorelois being love-sick for Guinevere, Galehaut
contrives a plan for his seeing her (357). In the meanwhile Gawain
resumes the quest for Lancelot and learns from a hermit where
his friend is. At Leverzerp he takes the side of the Duke of
Cambeninc against the King of Norgales, because his party is the
weaker — overcomes Gifflet, but the two then together assail
the men of Norgales and defeat them (364). They meet two girls,
one of whom repels Gawain's advances and the other accepts Gifflet's. The former (who loves Sagremor) promises Gawain, however, to lead him to her mistress, who is far more beautiful then
herself. Gawain champions successfully the cause of a vavassor
who had been falsely accused by a seneschal; in a combat recovers
Lionel's horse for him from a knight. (It was not permissible for
Lionel, a mere squire, to fight with a knight.) Lionel eludes Gawain's questions as to Lancelot's whereabouts (377). Gawain rescues Sagremor, whose peculiarities are described (381) and the
latter is united with the girl who loves him. This girl takes them
to the castle of the king of Norgales and that night guides Gawain
to the chamber of the king's daughter. The king detects Gawain
in bed with his daughter and tries to have him slain. With the assistance of the princess and Sagremor's *amie*, after some fighting,
he and Sagremor escape.

Hearing that Hector was in prison at Les Mares, the lord
of l'Estroite Marche, accompanied by Sinados and Marganor, set
out to liberate him, but already he had been freed, in order that
he might rescue Helaine sans Per, whose husband required her to
prove her assertion, uttered in a moment of anger, that her beauty
was superior to his bravery. Having vindicated the truth of the
lady's assertion, Hector proceeds in quest of Gawain.

Scotland being invaded by the Saxons and Irish (394), Arthur summons his hosts together. This gives the queen an opportunity to call Lancelot and Galehaut from Sorelois. They were to keep *incognito*, but Lancelot was to wear favors presented by the queen. Gawain conquers the entrance to Sorelois named the Pont Norgalois, and, as required by custom, has to defend it. Thus he and Hector fight, neither knowing the other. When he learns that Hector is his opponent, out of courtesy, he declares himself beaten: To keep Lancelot from fighting at the same place, Galehaut takes him to his own retreat in the Ille Perdue (399). Gawain and Hector force their way into this retreat and combat Lancelot and the King of the Hundred Knights, respectively. Both sides keep their names secret and do not recognize each other, until Lionel arrives on the scene, discloses Gawain's identity to Lancelot, and warns him that the queen has ordered that he (Lancelot) should show Gawain every consideration (403). Terror-stricken at having unwittingly disobeyed the queen's command, Lancelot fled from the field, but afterwards, on Galehaut's representations, kneeled down before Gawain and implored his mercy.

Lancelot, Galehaut, Gawain and Hector now join Arthur's army in Scotland and fight against the Saxons and Irish, who are worsted. The sight of Guinevere almost causes Lancelot to fall from his horse and he obeys her every wish. Camille, an enchantress of Saxon descent, who loves Arthur, entices him to a secret interview and imprisons him and his companion, Guerrehes. The same night Lancelot lies for the first time with Guinevere (411), and Galehaut with the Lady of Malehaut. The cleft in the shield sent by the Lady of the Lake closes, as the union of Lancelot and Guinevere is consummated. Camille entraps still further Lancelot, Galehaut, Gawain, and Hector, but releases the first, when he becomes insane. He returns to court and always obeys the queen, but continues demented until the Lady of the Lake comes and heals him (417). — Nine days after her departure, Lancelot, having enjoyed Guinevere's love, returns to the battle, in which Yvain and Yder had been the chief representatives of Arthur, and slays the giant Hagodabran, the mightiest of the

Saxon warriors (423). He desists from the fight, however, when
Lionel orders him to do so in Guinevere's name. Afterwards, cap-
turing Camille's tower, he liberates Arthur and the rest. On the
other hand, when Kay (Kex) destroys the books and boxes of
the enchantress, she commits suicide. Arthur and Guinevere both
shower favors on Lancelot and he consents to remain at court.
Moreover, Galehaut, who declares that he cannot live apart from
Lancelot, at his own request, is accepted as one of Arthur's companions. So too is Hector, whose deeds of arms had also been
greatly lauded. These two knights, with Lancelot, took their seats
that day at the Round Table (429) and clerks were summoned to
record their adventures. Three days before All Saints' Galehaut
takes his departure for Sorelois, being accompanied by Lancelot.
The queen, however, made them promise to be present at Camelot
on Christmas Day (430).

As Galehaut and Lancelot return to Sorelois,[16] the former is
filled with fear lest the latter may be drawn away from him by
the queen. He relates then to Lancelot two allegorical dreams
which he has had, pre-figuring that event. As further omens
of impending misfortune, Galehaut sees his best castle, L'Orguel-
louse Emprise, collapse before his eyes, and learns soon afterwards
that in a single night the same thing had happened to all the other
castles in Sorelois. He sends to Arthur for three of the wisest
clerks to expound his dreams (IV, 10), and Arthur sends him ten,
of whom Helyes of Toulouse is the wisest (24). Helyes, whose
speech includes a prophecy concerning Galahad as the Grail Winner
(27), interprets Galehot's dreams, and, among other things, makes
him understand that he (Galehaut) had only three years to live (34).

In the meanwhile, the court has been startled by a letter
from the false Guinevere,[17] accusing the true Guinevere of being
an impostor and of usurping her place as the king's consort. She
demands that Arthur shall return the Round Table (received from

---

[16] Here begins Sommer's Vol. IV.
[17] Cp. analysis of the Vulgate *Merlin,* pp. 312 ff., above.

her father, Leodegan), if he will not take her as his rightful wife. Gawain offers himself as the Queen's champion against Bertholai, champion of the false Guinevere. The king postpones a decision in the matter until he holds court at Bedingran at Candlemas (16). Galehaut soothes Lancelot's grief over this affair by telling him that, if Arthur now puts away Guinevere, he (Lancelot), will be able to marry her and that he, himself (Galehaut), will bestow Sorelois, the best of his kingdoms, on her (p. 17). In order to qualify himself better for the crown, he resolves on spending much time at Arthur's court and appoints Baudemagus, king of Gorre, regent in his absence. Gorre was accessible only by two bridges, one beneath the water, the other a sword-bridge, and Baudemagus had populated the land mainly with captives, seized whilst they were attempting to cross these bridges (40 f.) Meleagant, son of Baudemagus, is envious of Lancelot and wounds him in a tournament at Camelot on Christmas Day. On this occasion the queen has difficulty in disguising her passion for Lancelot (44).

The false Guinevere appears at Bedingran, according to the agreement, lures Arthur into the forest for a boar-hunt, and there he is captured by her men and carried off to Carmelide. She thoroughly infatuates Arthur by her wiles (50). Nothing having been heard of the king, the barons of Logres elect Gawain in his place until his fate can be ascertained. The missing king despatches messengers to his court, who tell where he is. In consequence, Guinevere, the barons, etc., go to Carmelide (54). There Arthur, supported by the barons of Carmelide, makes public proclamation that the true Guinevere has deceived him and the false Guinevere pleads that her rival may be put to death. Lancelot now offers to defend the queen's innocence in a judicial combat against any three knights. Galehaut, however, compels him to fight them singly (61) and he vanquishes all three. Urged by Bertholai to do so, Arthur permits the queen to accept Galehaut's offer of the kingdom of Sorelois (69), but wishes, in vain, to retain Lancelot. The queen goes to her new kingdom and receives the homage of the barons there (72).

Arthur's infatuation for the false Guinevere becomes worse

than ever. The pope rebukes him for his conduct when he refuses
to take back the true Guinevere, and lays Great Britain under an
interdict. During this period both the false Guinevere and
Bertholai are visited with paralysis (73) and their bodies begin to
decay. Gawain's reproaches touch Arthur's conscience in the matter
of the false Guinevere, but he continues to pine for her until in
consequence of severe illness he receives the sacrament from his
former chaplain, Amustan(s), now a hermit who, also, exacts a
confession of sin from him. The false Guinevere and Bertholai
likewise, confess their fraud to Amustan(s), and afterwards to
Arthur and the barons. The true Guinevere goes back, reluctantly,
to her husband, having been in Sorelois two years and a half.
Both Guinevere and Galehaut desire to keep Lancelot with them.
After returning for a while to Sorelois, he yields to the former's
request and stays at Arthur's court. — Arthur holds a great court
at London. Whilst Gawain, Yvain, Lancelot and Galeshin are in
a forest of marvels nearby, Carados of the Dolorous Tower carries
off Gawain (88). His companions separately go in search of him.
Galeshin learns from a cousin — the Lady of the White Castle —
who Gawain's captor is and how the Dolorous Tower can be penetrated; also, about a girl there, who will render him assistance. —
Lancelot lifts a wounded knight from a coffer as Yvain had failed
to do. This knight turns out to be the son of the wounded knight
(Trahan le Gai) of Lancelot's first adventure (see I, 414, above).
He had been put in the coffer by Carados's mother, an enchantress,
and only the best knight in the world could deliver him. — Yvain
rescues a squire, and, afterwards, with Lancelot's aid, Sagremor
and his sweetheart, whom knights of Norgales were maltreating,
because of the latter's share in Gawain's affair with the princess of that kingdom. — Lionel endeavors to go in search of Lancelot, but is held back by Galehaut. — News of Gawain's capture
is brought to the court by Trahan's son, Melian(s), and Arthur
resolves to deliver his nephew (104). — Galeshin prepares himself for the adventure of the Dolorous Tower by attempting the
less difficult adventures of overcoming the four fencers of Pin-
tadol and lifting the spell from Escalon le Tenebreus, where, owing

to an act of fornication committed in the church seventeen years before, the castle and church — but not the churchyard — had remained enveloped in darkness. Galeshin succeeds in the first adventure and fails in the second, which, however, is achieved by Lancelot (111). — All this while Gawain had been a prisoner in the Dolorous Tower, lying wounded in a dungeon, filled with poisonous vermin. Moreover, Carados's mother had envenomed his wounds. A damsel, who requites Carados's love with hate, kills the vermin with poisoned food and supplies Gawain with a healing ointment. — On the way to Carados's stronghold were the Chapel of Morgan (le Fay) and the enchanted valley, called "the valley from which there is no return" or "the valley of false lovers" (117). Morgan had laid it under a spell, because she had detected her lover there in an act of disloyalty to her with another woman. This spell could be undone only by a knight who was never false in love (Lancelot). Here Galeshin and Yvain became captives, but Lancelot slew the dragons and knights that guarded the place and broke the spell that rested on it. Morgan, however, treacherously bound Lancelot, whilst asleep, and imprisoned him. He will not give her, however, the ring presented to him by Guinevere. She lets him out on parole, that he may participate in the effort to free Gawain, but sends a girl with him, who is to try to make him unfaithful to the queen. The plot, however, fails. — Carados had left the Dolorous Tower, in order to bar Arthur's entry into the country through a certain narrow pass and he is followed up by Lancelot. Yvain and Galeshin, on the other hand, made an assault on the Dolorous Tower. Both, however, were captured, and only the intercession of the damsel who had befriended Gawain saved their lives (131). Lancelot attacks Carados's host from the rear and puts them to flight. He pursues and wounds Carados, but in attempting to seize the latter, both he and his enemy are borne within the precincts of Carados's castle. Carados could only be slain by a sword which he had committed to the above-mentioned damsel. This girl now gave the sword to Lancelot, whose own weapon was broken. Carados, seeing this act and knowing that he was doomed, tries at least,

to slay Gawain before he is, himself, slain, but Lancelot prevents
him and beheads him. He liberates his friends and they all go to
Arthur (with whom are Galehaut and Lionel) and present to him
Carados's head and the keys of his castle. In compliance with
Lancelot's petition, the king invests the damsel with the Dolorous
Tower, now called La Bele Garde or La Bele Prise, and she marries
Melian(s). — Lancelot goes back secretly to Morgan's prison and
she, having drugged him, obtains possession (140) of the ring
which Guinevere had presented him with and sends her damsel
to court with the ring. This messenger announces there that Lancelot was mortally wounded at the Dolorous Tower and will never
appear at court again. She also flings the ring into Guinevere's
lap before the king and the rest: Lancelot, she affirms, had returned it to the queen and exhorted the Knights of the Round
Table not to disgrace their lord, as he had done. The queen protests her innocence and Arthur declares that he would rather see
Lancelot Guinevere's husband than lose his companionship (142).

Galehaut, Lionel, and Gawain endeavor to discover Lancelot's
whereabouts by following Morgan's messenger, but she slips away
from them. Galehaut finds Lancelot's shield hanging on a pine
at Escalon, takes it away, is wounded in combats with knights that
pursue him, and is cured at a monastery. — Insignificant adventures of Gawain and Yvain, during which a friar warns the former
not to travel Saturday afternoon, save when it is unavoidable. —
Lionel is falsely informed that a fresh grave is that of Lancelot
recently killed, but another damsel takes him to a place whence he
can see Lancelot alive, and thence guides him to the monastery
where Galehaut was healed, but Galehaut had gone. — Morgan
tried to make Lancelot forget the queen, by drugging him into
strange dreams, but in vain. When he threatened to starve himself to death, she released him. — Lionel finds Galehaut and accompanies him to Sorelois. Later they return to Arthur's court.
Gawain and Yvain find Lancelot, too, fighting *incognito* in a
tournament and bring the news to the king. Lancelot seeks Galehaut in Sorelois and misses him. Crazed with distress, he fled
in the night in the scantiest attire and was soon reported dead.

When Galehaut hears this report, he will not eat for eleven days and finally from grief and disease expires. His nephew, Galehaudin, succeeds him (155).[18]

The Lady of Malehaut died soon after for love of Galehaut. — The Lady of the Lake discovers the mad Lancelot in the forest of Tintagel in Cornwall, cures him, and equips him with horse and arms. The queen still disbelieves the report of her lover's death. — Meleagant comes to court to challenge (the absent) Lancelot, declares that he will surrender the exiles of Gorre, if he is allowed to take Guinevere into the forest and maintain his possession of her against any knight. Kay (Kex) manages to secure the office of the queen's champion and is defeated, but Lancelot, who had witnessed the combat, sets out to rescue Guinevere. The killing of Lancelot's horses (one of them obtained from Gawain) prevents him from freeing her and he is compelled to continue the pursuit in a cart, although it was disgraceful for a knight to ride in such a vehicle (162) and he was therefore scoffed at and pelted with mud on the journey. At a castle near the boundary of Melagant's land he undergoes the adventure of the Perilous Bed (a fiery lance thrust towards the bed) and the next morning almost swoons when he sees Guinevere from his window. Gawain, who had joined him on the road, recognizes from this for the first time that the dejected knight is Lancelot. A damsel of the castle, on condition that they should, each, grant the first gift she might claim, shows them the two roads to the Terre Foraine (Baudemagus's kingdom) — one leading to the "pont perdu," the other to the "pont d'espee." Gawain takes the first, Lancelot the second. The damsel, who is anxious to discover Lancelot's identity, intercepts him *en route* and entertains him at a house where she tests both his courage and his continence. He emerges successful from both tests and overthrows a knight who has recently extorted a comb from Guinevere as toll for being permitted to pass over a causeway through a certain marsh. The sight of his mistress's hair in this comb, throws Lancelot into such an ecstasy that he almost swoons (172).

Having been halted by the damsel's suitor for a while, Lancelot

---

[18] Here begins the prose adaptation of Chrétien's *Lancelot*.

comes to a monastery. In the adjacent cemetery is the tomb of
King Galahad, son of Joseph of Arimathea: Lancelot lifts this
tomb from its place. He is unable, however, to open Symeu's
burning grave (in the cellar of a church). As Symeu's voice proclaims from the grave, only the Grail Winner can do this (175).
Monks bear Galahad's corpse to Gales (Wales) and the damsel,
having learned Lancelot's name, returns to her home. — Lancelot vanquishes four knights at the "pas de perrons," and helps a
band of the exiles of Gorre to defeat their oppressors. — Gawain
is guided to the "pont perdu" by the daughter of one of the exiles
(183). On the way thither he is victor in three different commonplace encounters (described at length). He crosses the "pont
perdu," on a submerged plank (193) and vanquishes Sephar,
who opposes him in the crossing. — Lancelot kills a knight, who
has vilified him, because he had ridden in a cart, and wishes to
exact toll of him, repels a treacherous attack of Meleagant's men
and reaches the chief city of Gorre, where Baudemagus and Guinevere witness his arrival from a tower (199). With eyes constantly
fixed on the queen, he crosses the "pont d'espee" (a sword with
the edge turned upwards), by pulling himself forward astride of
it. An accidental glance at the magic ring which he had received
from the Lady of the Lake drives away the lions which attack him
at the further end of this bridge. The good king, Baudemagus,
and Guinevere suspect Lancelot's identity and the former tries,
without effect, to dissuade Meleagant from fighting him. Lancelot takes off his helmet and shows who he is. In the duel the
sight of Guinevere distracts Lancelot, so that Kay (Kex) upbraids
him for his want of prowess (205). Consequently, Lancelot, ashamed of himself, attacks Meleagant with more vigor, but Baudemagus, seeing that his son is about to be vanquished, gets the
queen to intercede for him, so that Lancelot confines himself to
the defensive. Meleagant at last desists from fighting and surrenders the queen on condition that he and Lancelot shall fight
for her at Arthur's court. To the surprise of all, Guinevere now
treats Lancelot with disdain. Kay tells Lancelot that only Baudemagus has kept Meleagant from dishonoring Guinevere. — Lance-

lot, on his way to join Gawain, is, through a mistake, made captive
by Baudemagus's subjects. Both Lancelot and the queen are in
despair, owing to false rumors about each other's death. When
they at last meet, Lancelot learns the cause of her recent anger,
viz. his leaving London without her permission and the affair
of the ring which Morgan sent to court. — That night Lancelot
removes the bars of a window — wounding his hand, as he did
so, — enters Guinevere's chamber, and stays with her until the
approach of day. She tells him that Galehaut is dead. Stains of
blood on the queen's pillow, caused by Lancelot's wound, make Meleagant believe that she has cohabited with the wounded Kay (210).

Lancelot champions Kay's innocence in a duel and would
have killed Meleagant, but for the queen's intercession. — The
exiles of Gorre are now freed and Lancelot again starts to join
Gawain. Nevertheless, Meleagant, by means of a dwarf, lures him
into captivity and later sends to Guinevere a forged letter to the
effect that he is at Camelot. Accompanied by Gawain, she goes
thither, but is disconsolate on finding Lancelot not there. — The
king holds court in mid-August. Here there appears a cart drawn
by a miserable nag and driven by a dwarf. In the cart there was
a knight (Bohort) in bonds and wretchedly clad, who asked to be
delivered (p. 215). His arms were in the cart and his horse attached to it. His deliverer would have to take his place. Only
Gawain is willing to eat with the strange knight, for he remembers
that Lancelot rode in a cart. The knight departs, but returns soon
on horseback, upbraids Arthur's knights for their conduct, challenges them, and rides forth. Sagremor, etc., follow him and are all
unhorsed. The cart and dwarf reappear, this time with a damsel
(the Lady of the Lake) in the knight's place. She, too, rebukes
the court and proclaims that the bound knight was Bohort, who
now returns, as the damsel departs. The cart henceforth becomes
a vehicle of honor (218). — Arthur holds a tournament at Pome-
glay (near the boundary of Gorre). Lancelot is let out of prison
temporarily, so that he may attend the affair, *incognito*, — wins
every joust until the queen bids him do as badly as possible. He
acts thus until she bids him do his best. He now gains the prize

and returns to prison. Finally, he is released through the efforts
of Meleagant's half-sister, who hated Meleagant. Meleagant himself, having had Lancelot secretly imprisoned, thought now that
Guinevere would be his, since her champion would not be able
to appear. Being free, however, Lancelot goes to court, fights
the duel, and kills Meleagant, whose body is borne away in a
litter (227). — Lancelot is honored at court, hears about Bohort,
and has his own adventures recorded. On his way to Baudemagus's
capital to answer the challenge of a knight there, he vanquishes,
in succession, Margondes and Melyadus and despatches them to the
queen (who frees them), takes part with the "chastel as dames"
against the "chastel as puceles" in a tourney, the latter being
led by Lionel and Hector disguised (235). Bohort starts for Gorre
to aid Lancelot, succors the two sisters of Hongrefort, one of whom
their uncle, Galinde(s), Lord of the White Castle, desired to marry
to his seneschal. When the vanquished seneschal comes to this
girl she has him and his companion bound and shot from a man-
gônel into the camp of the besiegers. They fall dead before her
uncle's tent. Bohort, still further, slays Galinde's nephew, overcomes twelve of his knights in succession, and finally Galinde(s)
himself (251). Saraide, in the fight, tests Bohort's fidelity to
the Lady of the Lake and afterwards summons him to meet the
latter on the following Sunday. — Galinde's niece goes to seek
Bohort's forgiveness for her cruel execution of the seneschal. By
way of penance, she and her company rode horses that were without
manes or tails and they wore their garments turned inside out. —
    King Agrippe's daughter had killed many of King Vadalon's
men by poisoning a well and he had punished her by fixing two iron
bands about her body. Bohort removes these bands and goes to
revenge her on Vadalon (258). A tournament was to be held at
the Castel de la Marche, in honor of the anniversary of King
Brangoire's coronation. On his way thither, Bohort overthrows
and wounds a knight (Gawain's brother, Agravain) who denied
that Lancelot was superior to Gawain. Bohort wins the tournament for Brangoire's party and, consequently, has to occupy the
golden chair in a pavilion and be served by the twelve next-best

knights. According to custom he must now choose a damsel for his wife — also, one for each of the twelve knights. Having vowed perpetual chastity, he disappoints Brangoire's daughter, who loves him passionately, by making no choice for himself. The knights now make fantastic vows before the princess as to the expoits which they will accomplish in her honor. That night the princess's nurse, by a magic ring, makes Bohort love her mistress and go to her (the princess's) chamber. The fruit of their cohabitation was Helain le Blanc, Emperor of Constantinople. Bohort was not conscious of what he had done until, on returning to his own room, he accidentally rubbed off the magic ring (270). — Journeying still further, he saves the damsel of Glocedon, whom four men were about to drown, evades her cousin, the damsel of Hongrefort, but is followed by the two girls (274). — Lancelot rescues Meleagant's sister, who was about to be burned at Florega by the latter's people for her part in the latter's death. On his way to Florega Lancelot comes upon Galehaut's tomb (in an abbey), guarded by five knights. He beats off these knights, opens Galehaut's tomb, has the body taken to Joyous Gard, and gets Saraide to take Galehaut's sword to Bohort. He, himself, rides to Baudemagus's court to fight a would-be avenger (Argondras) of Meleagant's death, meets a girl, who, afterwards, dies for love of him, overthrows certain knights, including one in red armor, and rescues his host's brother. He spends a night at Banin's castle, hears his praises from the old man, but conceals his identity (289). At Huidesan he finds Baudemagus, kills Maleagant's champion in a duel, and is affectionately treated by Baudemagus, although he is suspected by the latter of having slain his son (Meleagant). Lancelot overthrows a knight (Patrides) of Brangoire's castle, who was trying to fulfill a vow, made to the princess there, and compels him to bear to Baudemagus the message that Lancelot had killed Maleagant and begged pardon for the act. Instructed by an old woman, he learns at Joyous Gard of a magnificent tomb in the chapel there and in this he buries Galehaut. Hence he proceeds to Camelot. — Bohort rescues Lambegue(s) from a vengeful father and receives from Saraide Galehaut's sword. Whilst all three are

being entertained at the castle of a cousin of the damsels of Hongrefort and Glocedon, the latter arrive, and the first of the two damsels
is pardoned by Bohort for killing the seneschal.   Bohort, Lambe-
gue(s), and Saraide reach Joyous Gard after Lancelot's departure,
and Bohort continues the quest of his cousin alone. — Patride(s)
delivers Lancelot's message to Baudemagus and the latter learning
from his baron that Meleagant's body is at the Castle of Four
Stones, goes thither and with great grief had him interred in
a hermitage.

A year later whilst Arthur and his consort are hunting
in the forest of Camelot, Bohort *(incognito)* carries off the
queen (301) after having unhorsed Kay, Sagremor and Dodinel,
her defenders. On the other hand, Lancelot, though pierced in
the side, wounds and unhorses Bohort. At this point an old damsel
claims the fulfilment of his (Lancelot's) promise and he has to
quit the place of combat and accompany her. The queen, Dodinel,
and Sagremor take the wounded Bohort to the Fairies' Fountain and the last two then go to Mathamas's house in search
of food. On the way, Sagremor beats an insolent dwarf, delivers
Calogrenant, and has a series of fights on behalf of a girl. At
Mathemas's house he is thrown into prison but is fed by his
captor's daughter. — Dodinel protects a damsel whom the dwarf
of Malruc the Red had tried to kiss — in doing so overthrows
Malruc and sends him on parole to Guinevere (315) — later, falls
into a stream and is captured (319). — Lancelot, following the
old damsel, has to give up his arms to a knight, as he had previously promised, and this knight (Griffon des Malx Pas) in Lancelot's armor unhorses Kay and kills Malruc. — On Arthur's return
from the forest he hears what has happened to Lancelot and is
prostrated with grief. Gawain and nine knights go in quest of
Lancelot. They make their first halt at the Black Cross (321).
(Here follows shortened account of the Black Cross according to the
Estoire, I, 244ff.) In the forest they come upon a knight (Elyzer,
son of Pelles) with two swords. One of them is broken and blood
drops from its point. Gawain and the rest cannot mend the sword.
It was the one with which Joseph of Arimathea was wounded

(325ff., shortened from *Estoire*, I, 252ff.). — Agloval rescues a knight from Griffon and tells Kay of the quest for Lancelot, which Kay joins. Gawain frees Sagremor and Hector Dodinel. Hector, too, joins the quest, but the knights all make search separately (334). At the tournament of the Mill Castle Gawain espouses the cause of Thanaguis's sweetheart, but is unhorsed by Hector disguised as a red knight. Both he and Hector fail to achieve the adventure of the churchyard in which there is a burning tomb, surrounded by twelve tombs (not burning), with a sword standing upright on each. Only Lancelot can accomplish this. — Gawain comes to the Grail castle or palace (342) tries vainly to deliver a girl from a bath of scalding water, is entertained in the castle by its maimed king, sees a dove flying through the hall, with a censer in its beak, then a maiden bearing the Grail, which supplies the most delicious viands and odors conceivable. A dwarf prevents him from leaving the palace. He lies down armed on the Adventurous Bed and is wounded there by a flaming lance. He has an allegorical vision of Arthur's future wars with Lancelot and Mordred and sees twelve damsels kneeling, weeping, and praying before the door where the dove had entered. He fights with a knight and swoons from exhaustion. A great storm shakes the palace and Gawain hears angelic voices and sees again the maiden and the Grail. Darkness envelops the palace and he feels himself seized, carried out to the courtyard, and bound there to a cart. The next morning an old woman drives the cart through the town, whilst the people hoot and cast missiles at him. Having passed a bridge, she unties him and tells him that the castle is named Corbenic (347). A hermit later explains to him that this castle is the Grail Castle and interprets his vision to him. — Hector slays the cruel Marigart le Rous and delivers from his prison a lady (cousin of Lancelot) guarded by lions. — Yvain is, likewise, victor in two minor encounters. — Gawain and his four brothers are described (358f.) and two adventures of Mordred's are related, viz. a fight over a dwarf and his seduction of a girl, who was the *amie* of his host.

When Agravain had left the companions of the quest, he rode for a week without meeting with any adventure worth mentioning.[19] Then he avenges a girl for her dead lover on Druas, who guarded a hill and whose father Gawain had slain. Agravain slays Druas, but the latter's brother, Sornehan, later unhorses him and imprisons him. His life, however, is saved on the intercession of Sornehan's niece. Guerrehes makes love to the daughter of an old knight, whom he had rescued, but she rejects him and expresses an ardent love for Lancelot (12). He helps his host to repulse a night attack of twenty men on the castle, rides away, and comes upon three ladies (sixty, forty, and twenty years old, respectively) by a fountain. The oldest of the three had been forced to yield her daughter to a hateful knight. Guerrehes rescues the girl and then seeks her love. She was in love, however, with another man and refuses him, adding to her refusal reproaches concerning Guerrehes's disloyalty to his own *amie* (22). The youngest of the three ladies had incensed her detestable husband by comparing him disadvantageously with Lancelot (16f.), and Guerrehes goes to her castle to punish this husband. Sagremor, also, arrives there soon after. The jealous husband, with the aid of his relatives, plots against their lives, but they are themselves slain (27). Sagremor goes off with a maiden in search of her brother, Agloval, and Guerrehes comes at night to four pavilions, goes to bed with a woman (a cousin of Lancelot's) who thinks that he is her husband. The husband, believing that his wife was voluntarily an adulteress, assails Guerrehes and is killed. Guerrehes carries off the reluctant wife and compels her to cohabit with him, but she finally gets rid of him by entering a nunnery (32f.). A week later at Druas's hill ("tertre as caitis," p. 47) he is overthrown by Sornehan and incarcerated

---

[19] Here begins Sommer's Vol. V, which contains the last division of the *Lancelot*, often called (without manuscript authority) the *Agravain*. The opening of this division, as will be observed, presupposes that Agravain was already one of the company who were in the quest for Lancelot. No mention of him in this connection, however, had hitherto been made. It seems as if the original text of the *Lancelot* must have been altered at this point. See, on the subject, Bruce, RR, X, 64 ff. (1919).

along with his brother, Agravain. The victor's niece, however, owed a favor to Guerrehes and made them comfortable in prison. — Gaheriet (Gaheries) undertakes to right the wrongs of a girl, a vassal of the Lady of Roestoc, in a matter of inheritance against her brother-in-law, Guidan — on the way thither, vanquishes Guinae, who was eager to measure his strength with Gawain, and frees Brandelis, who had got into trouble with a jealous knight (41) — also, compels a knight to apologize to a dwarf, and arrives at Roestoc — is victorious over Guidan, who drowns himself in despair (46). He learns of the captivity of Agravain and Guerrehes from a girl, vanquishes Sornehan at the hill (henceforth called Agravain's Hill) and liberates them. — The three brothers assist Duke Calles and his nephews against his six sons, who, in a quarrel over a question of inheritance had killed their brother-in-law and were besieging their father (53). Agravain nearly ruins the duke's cause by his rashness — is captured but afterwards exchanged. His brothers and the duke, however, win the battle, in which one of Calles's sons is slain by Gaheriet. — Arthur and Guinevere believe that Lancelot is dead and express this belief to Lionel, when he returns to court. In lieu of Lancelot and Gawain, Bohort goes as champion of the Lady of Galvoie and begins, at the same time, with Lionel the quest for Lancelot. They were confidants of the queen and she regrets their departure. — Confined to her bed from grief over Lancelot, the queen has a dream of Lancelot in bed with a beautiful maiden and later she tries to embrace the dream-figure of Lancelot. She sends a girl-messenger to the Lady of the Lake, praying her to come to her for Lancelot's sake (65). — Lancelot, now well again, rescues a girl from her ravisher and sends her grateful sister to court to announce that he is alive. On receiving this news, Guinevere rapidly recovers. — Lancelot and the old damsel come upon a knight and two girls — one of them, the knight's sister — by a spring, which is full of venom, because of two serpents that live in it. Lancelot is poisoned by the water and his body swells up. The knight's sister, who had fallen deeply in love with our hero, saves his life by her skill, but he loses his hair and his nails (73). Bohort and Lionel discover their cousin in this condition and the former proceeds on his errand to the Lady of Galvoie. Lionel, on the other hand, gives Lancelot the ring which Guinevere had sent the latter and takes back to her some of his hair and news of his illness. — In order to see her lover, the queen, on Lionel's advice, has a tournament proclaimed for the octaves of St. Magdalene's Day, in the expectation that he will attend it. Lionel carries back Guinevere's greetings to Lancelot and hears from the knight's sister a confession of her love for her patient. The girl, herself, is now ill for this reason and cannot continue her ministrations to Lancelot— consequently, he, too, is growing worse. Lionel remonstrates with the sick man for not saving his own life and the girl's by promising her his love (79), but he will not do so without Guinevere's leave. Lionel comforts the girl by declaring that Lancelot will be her knight, should she heal him, and goes back to Camelot. The queen sends a message by him to Lancelot, bidding her lover act in such a manner, as to save both his life and the girl's. In the end, his benefactress, whose passion is not of a carnal nature, is contented, when Lancelot merely promises to be her knight, without detriment to Guinevere's claims, and exchanges tokens with her (84). — Lionel and Lancelot assist Calles's sons to defeat their father. The latter kills Calles and overthrows Gaheriet, not knowing who he is. He has the three brothers (all prisoners) released. He has now satisfied the claims of the old damsel and goes on with Lionel.

Whilst Lancelot is asleep under an apple-tree, a big knight, Terican, unhorses Lionel and bears him away, as he has already done many other Arthurian knights, Agloval, Sagremor, Kay, and others, hanging up their shields, etc., on pine trees near a spring. Shortly after Lionel, Hector suffers the same fate (91). — The Queen of Sorestan, Morgan le Fay (who did not recognize Lancelot on account of his short hair), and Sebile seize the sleeping Lancelot and imprison him in the "Chastel de la Charete." He angers them by speaking contemptuously of their love. The daughter of the Duke of Rochedon, who is in charge of the captive, is about to be forced into a hateful marriage with the brother of her hereditary enemy, the Queen of Sorestan. She releases Lancelot, on condition that he shall frustrate this marriage. He goes to a tournament between Baudemagus and the King of Norgales and, on his journey thither, he comes upon Meleagant's sister in a convent. She summons her father and in the joyful meeting between the two, Lancelot promises Baudemagus to fight *(incognito)* on the latter's side. He redeems his promise, overthrows Mordred, Mador de la Porte, and Galehodin, who had won the previous tourney, and drives the men of Norgales before him. He avoids recognition and rides away into the forest (102). A lady, whose husband had fought against Lancelot in the tournament, invites him to her castle, saying that the next day she would show him the most beautiful thing (Pelles's daughter) that he had ever seen. Lancelot accepts and on the morrow is taken to Corbenic. He delivers the girl from the tub of scalding water (cp. Gawain's failure, above), slays a fire-spitting serpent and is welcomed at the Grail castle by Pelles. Like Gawain, he sees the dove, and the damsel who carries the Grail (108). With Pelles's consent, Brisane, nurse of Pelles's daughter, manages to bring about the cohabitation of Lancelot and her charge at a neighboring castle (Castel de la Casse). By means of a magic potion, she deludes him into the idea that he was in bed with Guinevere. Thus Galahad is engendered.[20]

The purpose of the plot was that a hero might be begotten to deliver the Terre Foraine from the evils which had come upon it from the Dolorous Stroke (110). The next morning Lancelot wishes to kill Pelles's daughter on account of the deception, but, touched by her beauty and by her pleas for compassion, foregoes his wrath. Whilst in search of Lionel, he saves from rape the girl that had healed him, learns that Hector is his bastard half-brother, having been begotten by Ban upon the daughter of the "Sires des Mares." He unhorses Hector's uncle, meets Hector's mother, and, despite warnings of its dangers, enters the "Forest Perdue," from which no one had ever returned. In this forest he succumbs to the spell of the enchanted carols (123). — Not

---

[20] For discussion of this cardinal episode of the Grail romances cp. F. Lot, *Étude sur le Lancelot en prose*, p. 217 (Paris, 1918) and Bruce, RR, IX, 364ff. (1918).

knowing each other, Bohort and Yvain fight over a dog which Yvain's damsel has taken from a dwarf. They stop on learning each other's identity. Bohort, hearing from the dwarf about Lancelot's participation in Baudemagus's recent tournament and, also, of the impending tournament at Camelot, decides to go thither. — In order to free a dwarf, Yvain binds himself to kiss an old woman, but, to get out of this predicament, beats down a shield — of the giant, Mauduit, as it turns out — in a pavilion. Mauduit, enraged, slays many people in his quest of Ivain. Ivain, in turn, seeks for the giant, but is captured by five knights and imprisoned in a castle, the lady of which befriends him, because his father had once done hers a favor (138). — In a duel with Mariales Bohort champions the Lady of Galvoie in a matter of inheritance, at Corbenic, before Pelles. He vanquishes his foe, and on Lancelot's account, is hospitably entertained at the Grail castle. There he beholds the Grail, cared for by a niece of Pelles, since his daughter was disqualified now for the office by her loss of virginity (141f.).

Bohort next comes to a small church, kept by a hermit. This hermit, who in his early life had been one of the elder Bohort's knights, tells him of the prediction, made by another hermit at Lancelot's baptism, in regard to Lancelot's future greatness — also, how the elder Bohort had built this church in commemoration of his escape from destruction at the hands of King Cerses. Later Bohort is reproached by one girl for not having faced the dangers of the Adventurous Palace at Corbenic and rescues from two knights another girl's brother and hawk (147). — The girl who had healed Lancelot tells Gawain that she had recently seen him (Lancelot). In the meanwhile Lancelot, as the best and handsomest of knights, had undone the spell of the knights and ladies who danced and carolled incessantly in the Forest Perdue, and of the invincible automatic chessmen. This chessboard he sends to Guinevere. The above-mentioned enchantments had been established by a brother (Guinebaut) — now dead — of Lancelot's father. — Thirty knights attack Lancelot, beat him and throw him into a well, full of snakes and vermin (155). The daughter of the lord of the castle rescues him, but she and Lancelot are afterwards beaten unmerci-

fully by her father and his men. In the fight Lancelot kills
many of these men and the father breaks his neck. The daughter,
unaware of her father's death, flies with Lancelot, carrying off
much treasure with her. On the way, Lancelot avenges the death
of a maiden on her slayer (a knight), by compelling him to bear
her corpse to Camelot, and submit to execution there, if the queen
and the ladies consider this desirable. In case they pardon him,
he is to repeat the same performance at the courts of Baudemagus
and Norgales. — Lancelot had lost sight of the girl with the
treasure, but later rescues her from her brother and three knights,
who had pursued her and were about to burn her. Accompanied
by this girl, Lancelot arrives at the Chastel de la Charrete on the
day when the daughter of the Duke of Rochedon was to be forced
to wed the brother of the Queen of Sorestan. Lancelot frustrates
the marriage and the cowardly (intended) bridegroom slinks away
(166). — The damsel who was accompanying Lancelot brings
letters from him to Guinevere, and later messages back and forth
between the two, whereby the queen learns her lover's purpose of
appearing, *incognito*, in red armor at the tournament. Certain
envious knights of the Round Table resolve to fight against which-
ever side Lancelot should espouse. Lancelot fights on the same
side as Baudemagus and against Gawain and Bohort, who, like
Arthur, do not recognize him. He performs marvels of prowess
and the king expresses bitter regret that Lancelot is not there to
oppose the wonderful new knight (175f.). When Lancelot, however, finds himself facing the queen, he is so stricken by her beauty
that he has to be taken off the field — hence Arthur's men again
get the upper hand. The queen, alarmed, despatches Bohort to
Lancelot with the command that the latter, if not wounded, should
come to her that night. In the interim, she attacks the damsel who
cured Lancelot of the poisoned water, but her jealousy is allayed,
when she learns of the true relations of this girl to Lancelot.
Gawain and others agree that the red knight (really Lancelot) is
superior to Lancelot. Guinevere resents Ydier's criticism of her
lover and, consequently, through Bohort, induces Baudemagus to
challenge Arthur to another assembly. — Lancelot spends two

nights with the queen and on the second visit she equips him with white armor and Bohort with red for the coming tournament (185). Some four thousand knights, including the Emperor of Germany and King of Norgales, take part in the assembly. Lancelot unhorses Gawain and Gaheriet and chases the other knights of the Round Table from the field. Having revealed his identity, at the king's request, he is cordially welcomed at court. Baudemagus and other high personages are beaten at chess by the automatic chessmen — only Lancelot wins against them. — Clerks now record Lancelot's adventures in a separate book (found at Salisbury after Arthur's death) — likewise, Gawain's (191f.). — Lancelot, Bohort, Baudemagus (now made a knight of the Round Table), etc. begin a quest for the knights who had not returned from the search for Lancelot. Before Lancelot's departure, however, he has an interview with the queen in which she laments that his sin with her would keep him from achieving the Grail quest and gives him a ring presented to her by the Lady of the Lake, which had the power of dispelling enchantments. The first exploit of the questers is to rescue Mordred from Maten and his band of ruffians at the Tour de la Blanche Espine, burning at the same time both tower and town; the next was to liberate Yvain from the dungeon of the Castel del Trespas. He had been shut up there, because he had aroused the anger of the giant, Mauduit, and thus brought many ills on the country. The next day Bohort slays Mauduit (203). —

The companions now separate, but agree to reassemble on All Saints' Day at the Castel del Trespas. — Lancelot is seeking for Lionel. A damsel takes him to the castle of Terrican (Carados's brother), where the latter is in prison — along with Agloval, Sagremor, and others — but exacts from him the promise that he will follow her, whenever she summons him. After a long combat Lancelot kills Terrican, who was bringing in a new captive — the wounded Gaheriet. Summoned by the damsel, he has to leave the liberation of the prisoners to Gaheriet. After these have been set free, Gaheriet, Agloval, etc., go their several ways, in quest of Lancelot (210). — Lancelot kills a robber-knight who had appropriated the damsel's palfrey, and getting on the trail of

Hector, kills, furthermore, a peasant robber, and two giants so strong that they disdained the use of weapons. One of Morgan's emissaries (a girl), however, now entices him into a house in the Forest Desvoiable, and there he is imprisoned. Whilst he is under the influence of a narcotic, Morgan blows a powder into his nose, which deprives him of his senses (216). Thus he had been in prison for a month before he knew it. One day he sees through the window a man painting the history of Aeneas's flight from Troy. Lancelot borrows some of his colors and paints on the wall of his room the main events in his affair with Guinevere. Morgan (herself, in love with Lancelot) is glad that he is betraying himself in this manner. — Gawain renews the quest for Lancelot, learns from the Queens del Parc (whose brother had been one of Terrican's captives) about Lancelot's exploits and from Baudemagus of the rendezvous on All Saints' Day at the Castel del Trepas, goes there, but Lancelot (being in prison) does not turn up. They agree to meet at the same place on Magdalen's Day, but on that day there is still no news of Lancelot. After two winters and one summer of captivity, Lancelot breaks the bars out of his window, to gather a rose, which reminded him of the queen. Being once out, he procures armor and rides away (223). — Lionel was a prisoner in the Castel d'Estrangot, where Vagor held him on a charge of treason. Lancelot goes thither to deliver him. On the way, a knight, wounded with an arrow, which no one but the best knight in the world can draw out of him, not knowing who Lancelot is, refuses to let him remove it. Lancelot gets the news about Agloval etc. from the wounded Baudemagus at this knight's house and rides to L'Ille Estrange (variant, Estrangot), where Lionel is in prison. The King (Vagor) allows him to see Lionel, who is still disabled by his wound, so that he cannot fight with Marabron (Vagor's son) the next day. (As the result of a Potiphar's wife incident, Lionel had killed Marabron's brother and now had to defend his innocence against Marabron). Lancelot takes Lionel's place in the duel, vanquishes his opponent, and compels him to retract the slander about Lionel (231). — Lancelot next comes to the abbey of La Petite Aumosne — so named, because of the small dole which a Scotch king, Heliser (one of Joseph of Arimathea's converts), who had voluntarily embraced a beggar's life, had received there. Lancelot leaves the wounded Lionel in this abbey and proceeds to the castle of the Tertre Deuee, founded by Clochide(s), who, for the protection of his wife, would permit nobody to approach it. Bohort, however, had overthrown Clochide(s) and was defending the hill in his stead. He had already vanquished and imprisoned, among others, Gawain, Yvain, Hector — all *incognito*. Lancelot is getting the best of Bohort, when he recognizes by a sword of Galehot's the identity of his adversary. Bohort now sets his prisoners free (242).

Obeying a vision, Lancelot slips away to achieve the adventure of his (paternal) grandfather's tomb in the Perilous Forest. This grandfather (the elder Galahad) had been treacherously beheaded at a boiling spring by a (wrongly) jealous cousin. His bleeding tomb was watched over by two lions. Lancelot kills the lions and lifts the head from the boiling spring, but, as he learns from a hermit, his sins disable him from attempting the other adventures (248). — Later he and a squire see in the Perilous Forest a white stag conducted by four lions. Here, too, a knight, Sarras of Logres, tells Lancelot (whom he does not know) of Galahad's birth (251). After avenging Sarras on Belias, he dispatches the former to the court with a message that he will be at Camelot on Whitsunday. — The damsel whom the queen had sent to the Lady of the Lake was delayed, *en route*, at a convent by illness. Whilst passing through Gannes, Claudas detains her and is provoked by her answers to his inquiries with regard to Lancelot, Lionel, and Bohort. To prevent Claudas from seeing the letter she is carrying, the girl gives it to a dwarf, who throws it into the river. The seneschal, however, observes him, as he does so, and the messenger and her attendants are, therefore, committed to prison. Claudas now sends two squires to Great Britain as spies. One of them is so impressed by the splendor of Arthur's court that he does not return to Claudas, and a year later tells the queen of her messenger's misfortune. He bears then a letter from Guinevere to Claudas, demanding the girl's release and threatening vengeance in case of non-compliance. Expressing contempt both for her and for her "lecher" (Lancelot), Claudas returns defiance to the queen (263). — Lancelot is attacked by a black knight (Belias's brother), pursues him into a castle, kills him, his father, and others and liberates, also, Mordred, who was imprisoned there. — In response to a message from Lancelot, Gawain and his companions at the *Tertre Deuee* set out to Camelot, in order that they may be present there on Whitsunday. On their way, they come to Peningue (a castle of Galehodin's), where a tournament is in preparation. Calling themselves poor knights of Norgales, they determine to take part in the affair. Before the assembly, however, they save Agloval from knights who were trying to revenge the death of one of Galehodin's relatives and kill several of his pursuers. Galehodin is at first angry over the slaughter of these men, but accepts Gawain's explanation and rejoices to meet him (276). — Lancelot and Mordred see in the Perilous Forest, by moonlight, the stag and four lions pass before them. In riding after the animals they are suddenly attacked by two knights and their horses taken from them; they recover them, however, later. A hermit tells them that only the Grail Winner will be able to understand the vision of the stag and lions. Mordred unhorses two knights. He and Lancelot hear at a vavasor's about the tournament of Peningue and determine to go there. In the forest nearby they come upon a rich tomb and a priest kneeling before it.[21] The priest angers Mordred by telling him of his incestuous birth and of his future wickedness and evil end and is killed by him (284 f.). Lancelot and Mordred, in the tournament, fight against Galehodin's party, which includes Gawain, Lionel, Bohort, and Hector, and Lancelot performs wonderful feats of arms. Only at the end, however, are Bohort and Hector convinced of his true identity. Bohort follows him from the field and the two have a joyful meeting. When the others hear later who he is, they are disappointed that they did not recognize him. They now start for Camelot, bearing Mordred, who had been wounded by his own brothers (291). After rescuing from robbers the son and daughter

---

[21] On this episode cp. Bruce, RR., IX, 382 ff. (1918).

of the King of a Hundred Knights, Bohort gets separated from
Lancelot and, in his wandering, comes again to Corbenic (296).
He overthrows Brunout who loved Pelles's daughter and was waiting there for a chance to attack Lancelot. He, also, sees Galahad
(now two years old) and learns that the child is Lancelot's. He
again beholds the Grail and its wonders and he spends two nights
in the Adventurous Palace, where he has all sorts of fantastic
experiences, comprising an allegorical vision of the wars that
brought about the destruction of the Round Table.[22] — After two
insignificant adventures, Lancelot, now in search of Bohort, saves
Kay (Kex) one night from pursuing knights, and the next morning by mistake puts on Kay's armor. He is, accordingly, mistaken for Kay and assailed by various knights, including Sagremor, Hector, Yvain and Gawain, all of whom he unhorses. —
He comes upon the damsel who had healed him and in the same
place meets Brangoire's daughter and her little son, whose father
was Bohort (311). Lancelot apologizes for Bohort's not visiting her and offers himself as her knight. — Gawain, Bohort and
the rest return to Camelot in time for the Whitsunday (435, A.D.)
service there in St. Stephen's cathedral. In the distribution of
gifts, according to individual merit, Bohort is the most favored
knight. Kay, arriving in red armor, is at first mistaken for Lancelot. He tells, however, the incident of Lancelot's unintentional exchange of arms, and Gawain and his companions now know who
really struck them down in the armor of the supposed Kay. Lancelot arrives and in the joust that follows, through an inadvertence,
is unhorsed by Gawain (318). He is treated with honor by Arthur.

Arthur, crowned, goes with the queen and his nobles to
St. Stephen's church. A picture on the wall there of a serpent
reminds Lancelot of the slain priest's interpretation of Arthur's
allegorical prophetic dream (Sommer, V, 284) about his death by

---

[22] On this second visit of Bohort's to the Grail castle cp. Bruce,
RR, IX, 385 ff. (1918). The description is more complicated here than
is the case with any of the other descriptions of visits to the same
castle in the *Lancelot*. Note, too, that in this passage Pelles's father,
and not Pelles, is the Fisher King, as well as the Maimed King.

the serpent (Mordred). Not one of the 150 knights of the Round Table is absent. At this juncture, Brumant, Claudas's nephew, in fulfilment of a foolish vow, tries to occupy the vacant seat (the Perilous Seat) at the Round Table, reserved for Galahad, and is consumed in doing so (320f.). — Guinevere learns from Lance‧ lot about his imprisonment at Morgan's hands and tells him of Claudas's insulting message. He resolves to avenge her and, at the same time, recover his patrimony. Baudemagus and Arthur promise to aid him with all their power. Two spies bring news of all this to Claudas, who gets ready for war, although the majority of the knights, subject to him, leave him for Great Britain (330f.). Through liberality, however, he attracts to himself a large number of knights and, besides, he gains the Romans as allies. His step-son, Claudin, commands his army. Arthur has the adventures of Lancelot, Bohort and the rest recorded (Lancelot's in a separate volume). Guinevere learns from Lancelot about Mordred's slaying the priest and about the latter's prophecy — only Lancelot suppressed the fact that Mordred was Arthur's son. — Arthur, whose host had been now strengthened by the forces of Brangoire, Carados and others, first subdues Flanders and then invades Gaul. They capture Pinegon, but Serses, who was in command there escapes and tells of the castle's fall. Claudas's seneschal advises a surprise raid upon the enemy. Claudin leads the attack successfully, and he returns with many captives to Claudas's base, the Chastel del Cor (p. 342). — In the great battle before this castle that now ensues, Claudas's army is beaten. Claudas, himself, brings reinforcements from Gannes which enable it to rally, but they are afterwards pushed back to Gannes by Bohort's division. At this point Claudas exchanges Lionel, whom he had captured, for his nephew, Chanart (355). Lancelot's mother and the Lady of the Lake (now married to a knight) come to the camp in search of Lancelot. The latter observes the Roman host in hiding and informs Bohort.

Consequently, when the Romans delivered what they imagined would be a surprise attack, Arthur's men were ready for them. The battle lasted a week (361) — then a truce was de-

clared, in order that the combatants might bury their dead. On
the expiration of the truce, the battle before Gannes is renewed,
and Gawain, Bohort, and Hector make Claudin and Chanart prisoners. A truce is again proclaimed and Baudemagus (captured by
the Romans before the first truce) is exchanged for Claudin and
Chanart (369). — In response to a message from Yvain, Lancelot,
with Arthur and a new host, goes to Gaul, the crown to which is
now claimed by Frolle d'Alemaigne. Arthur asserts that his claim
is superior and invests Lancelot with the kingdom and summons
its barons to do him (Lancelot) homage. Being worsted in battle,
Frolle challenges Arthur to a duel. He (Frolle) is killed in this
affair, and when Claudas hears of his ally's death, he abandons
hope and takes flight by night (375). When Arthur and Lancelot
arrive, Claudin surrenders Gannes to them. Here Lancelot's mother
welcomes her son, but dies a week later at her abbey. — Hector
becomes king of Benoic and Lionel of Gaul, but Lancelot and
Bohort refuse crowns, and return to Camelot with Arthur before
Whitsuntide, at which time Arthur holds a great court. Pelles's
daughter, with Brisane and young Galahad, attends it somewhat
to Lancelot's dismay (378) and is made much of there. Brisane
again brings about a cohabitation of Lancelot with Pelles's
daughter. Guinevere detects him in the act and drives him away
from Camelot. He bids the city farewell in a touching apostrophe
and soon becomes demented from grief (381). Indignant at the
queen's conduct, Bohort reproaches her and quits Camelot, taking
Hector and Lionel with him, to go in quest of his cousin. Gawain,
Yvain and many others soon join, also, in this quest, which lasted
two years. Perceval (now fifteen years old) accompanies his
brother, Agloval, to court, with the purpose of getting knighted
383ff.). He does not let his mother know of his intention until
he is already on the way. She dies when she hears of it, and the
squire, who brought the message, is killed by an enemy of Agloval's, before he can overtake the brothers on his return journey.
Perceval is dubbed knight by Arthur at Carduel and a damsel,
hitherto mute, assigns him to the seat on the left of the Perilous
Seat (reserved for Galahad at the Round Table); Bohort is to

occupy the one on the right. She did not speak again, until she received the *corpus domini* four days later on her death-bed. Stung by remarks of Kay's and Mordred's, Perceval sets forth on adventures (in quest of Lancelot). By one stroke of the sword, he severs the chain with which a jealous husband had bound Patrides (Baudemagus's son). Next he fights Hector. Neither knows the other, until they both have been desperately wounded. As they were lying near each other, in agony, a vision of the Grail heals them both (p. 392). Hector explains to his companion what the Grail is and Perceval vows to dedicate himself to the quest of it.

Bliant takes the mad Lancelot, chained to his bed, to his (Bliant's) castle and cures his physical ills. Lancelot, in turn, saves Bliant's life, when the latter is pursued by two knights into Lancelot's room in the castle (397). Lancelot, still insane, is wounded by a boar, is cared for by a hermit, and finally wanders to Corbenic. There he seeks shelter in a stable and amuses the people by his gambols. A cousin of Pelles dresses the madman in a squire's garments, but even then Pelles does not know him. On finding him asleep in a garden, however, Pelles's daughter did recognize him. Pelles has him bound and carried into the Adventurous Palace, and during the night he is healed by the Holy Grail (400). At his own request, he is now taken to a castle on an island in the sea, where Pelles's daughter and her maidens keep him company. Here he gives himself up to grief every day when he looks towards Logres. Under the title of "Li Cheualiers Mesfais," he proclaims through a dwarf that he will joust against all comers. He is victor in many encounters and acquires the reputation of being the best knight in the world. Pelles's daughter and her attendants led such a merry life there that the island became known as the "Isle of Joy." Perceval and Hector hear about the wonderful knight and determine to try their luck with him in jousting. It is a drawn contest between Lancelot and Perceval. Learning at last who Perceval is, Lancelot discloses his own identity. Pelles's daughter now entertains the two stranger knights and Hector tells Lancelot of Guinevere's desire that her lover should return to court. Thus, after a sojourn of four years on the island,

Lancelot rejoins Arthur and the rest at Caerleon, stopping at Corbenic *en route*. The child Galahad is put in a convent not far
from Camelot, the abbess of which was Pelles's sister. When the
boy was eighteen years old, a neighboring hermit, one day, after
Easter, announced to Arthur that at Whitsuntide the young knight
who was to achieve the Grail adventures would come to court
and occupy the Perilous Seat (409).

4. La Queste del Saint Graal [23].

On Whitsunday Eve a damsel comes to Camelot and, in the
name of Pelles, summons Lancelot to follow her. She takes him
to a convent in the woods where Galahad had been brought up.
He finds Bohort and Lionel there, dubs Galahad (whose identity
is unknown to him, but is suspected by Bohort and Lionel) and
returns the next day with his cousins of court.[24] They observe there
from an inscription on the Perilous Seat that it is to be occupied
that day (Whitsunday, 454, A.D.) by its master. — Arthur is
about to sit down to dinner, when he is reminded by Kay that
custom forbids his doing so until some adventure had happened.
The adventure, however, is not long delayed. A stone with a
sword fastened in it is reported to be floating on the river. On the
handle of the weapon there is a declaration that only the best
knight in the world can wield it. Gawain and Perceval fail in the
trial and Lancelot holds back (p. 7). Suddenly the doors and
windows of the hall shut of themselves, but it remains light inside.
Then, an old man, clad in white, leads in a knight in red armor
without shield or sword, and introduces him as a descendant of
David and of Joseph of Arimathea. The knight (Galahad) occupies the Perilous Seat and his name at once appears on it.
Guinevere, when she hears of the young stranger, guesses that
this is the son of Lancelot and Pelles's daughter. Galahad now
draws the above-mentioned sword from the stone. — In honor of

---

[23] This is printed in Sommer, VI, 3—199.
[24] On discrepancies between the end of the Lancelot and the
commencement of the Queste, cp. Bruce, RR, X, 114 ff. (1919).

the quest for the Holy Grail which is about to commence Arthur holds a great tournament. In this affair Galahad, though shield-less, unhorses all the other participants, save Lancelot and Perce-val. That evening, as the knights of the Round Table were sitting at table together, there was a clap of thunder, and an intense light in the hall — then the Holy Grail, covered with white samite, was borne in by invisible hands. It filled the palace with delicious odors and satisfied each knight with the kind of food he most desired (13). After that it vanished. The sacred vessel, how-ever, had not fully revealed itself to the companions: Gawain, therefore vows that he will go in quest of it, and the others offer a similar vow — much to Arthur's consternation, who fears now that he is about to lose a large number of his knights. Many of the ladies intended to accompany the knights, but the hermit, Nascien, warns the latter that this would be a sin and admonishes them, moreover, to confess their sins before they start on the quest: — Arthur wishes to prevent the quest, but this proves impossible. Beginning with Galahad, the (150) knights all swear not to return to court until they have learned the truth about the Grail. As Lancelot parts with the queen, she upbraids him for leaving her. The knights begin the quest together and are all entertained at Vagan's castle together, but after that they sepa-rate (20). On the fifth day Galahad comes to a white (Cistercian) abbey (where, as it was told in the *Estoire del Saint Graal*, Nascien was buried) and meets there Baudemagus and Yvain the Bastard. At this abbey a marvellous white shield with a red cross on it is kept — the shield by virtue of which Mordrain overcame the pagan Tholomer. Baudemagus tries to carry it off, but a white knight (Christ) unhorses and wounds him and sends the shield to Galahad by a squire. Galahad now achieves the adventure of removing the armed corpse of a knight from a devil-haunted tomb. The whole adventure has a symbolical significance, which is expounded to Galahad by a monk (28ff.). Galahad, accompanied by Melian (son of the king of Denmark), leaves the abbey. Melian, how-ever, parts with Galahad, picks up a gold crown, which he found on a chair in the forest, and is severely wounded for this by a

knight, who, later, is, himself, wounded and put to flight by
Galahad. The symbolical significance of this adventure, too, is
explained by a monk (32 ff.). Galahad leaves the disabled Melian
at the abbey and next conquers, against great odds, the Castle
of Maidens, delivering the captive girls there (37). — First, Gawain, and, then, Gaheriet come to the castle where Melian lay
wounded. The two are joined further on by Yvain and all three
together slay the seven wicked brothers who had fled from the
Castle of Maidens (38). A hermit chides Gawain for his sin-
fulness — particularly for his neglect of the confessional — but
recognizes that these admonitions, in the case of such a hardened
sinner, are lost labor. — Lancelot and Perceval are unhorsed by
Galahad (neither side knowing the other). They separate, and
Lancelot comes to a dilapidated chapel, but furnished with a rich
altar and a silver chandelier inside. He falls asleep by a cross,
not far from the chapel, and has a vision of a knight in a litter.
In answer to the knight's prayers, God sends the Holy Grail, which
heals him. The sacred vessel and the chandelier, which had accompanied it, now return to the chapel, and the knight, wondering that Lancelot had slept through all these marvels, takes the
latter's equipment and joins in the Grail quest. When Lancelot
awakes, he discovers that the things seen in his vision had actually happened. Moreover, a stern voice from the chapel rebukes
him for his sins and bids him begone. In a spirit of profound
despondency and self-reproach, he comes to a hermit's chapel in
the woods. In response to the hermit's exhortations, Lancelot confesses all his sins, including even his adulterous relations with
Guinevere. — Perceval's aunt, once the queen of the Terre Gastee,
lived as a religious recluse in the forest near the spot where he
and Lancelot parted company. From her he learns that the knight
who had unhorsed him was Galahad — also, that his mother is dead.
    She describes to him (54 ff.) too, the origin of the Grail table[25]
and the Round Table which were both similar to the table of

---

[25] This account differs in some important details from the account
of the same matter, given in the *Estoire del Saint Graal*, Sommer,
I, 216.

the Last Supper. Merlin, she says, reserved the Perilous Seat at the Round Table for the future master of that table (Galahad). She compares Galahad to Christ and expounds the allegorical significance of each detail that marked his first appearance at Arthur's court. She, also, cautions Perceval that he must keep chaste, if he is to achieve the Grail quest. — At the service in a monastery Perceval sees an old lamed king (Mordrain) on a couch receive the sacrament. The priest tells Perceval of how Mordrain (now four hundred years old) was wounded and how, receiving no sustenance, except from the holy wafer, he was waiting to be healed by the Grail Winner that was to be (62). After Perceval left the priest, he is assailed by twenty armed men and rescued by Galahad *(incognito)*. His steed having been killed, he tries in vain to get another. — A seeming woman, really a devil, supplies him with a black charger, which carries him off with miraculous speed — finally plunging into a body of water. Here Perceval involuntarily makes the sign of the cross and the animal vanishes. In the morning he perceives that he is on a mountain surrounded by the sea. Observing a fight between a lion and a serpent over the former's cub, he wins the lion's gratitude by killing the serpent, and the grateful beast spends the night by his side, but in the morning is gone. During the night two women come to him in a vision. The younger woman, mounted on a lion, warns him that on the morrow he is to have an encounter with the most redoubtable champion in the world; the older reproaches him for killing the serpent. — A man, in the garb of a priest, visits Perceval's isle next day and interprets to him the allegorical import of his dream (73 f.). After this good man (Christ) had sailed away in his ship, a fallen angel, in the form of a woman, tempts Perceval to carnal sin. Only his making accidentally the sign of the cross again saves him and drives away the demon. Perceval, contrite, stabs himself in the thigh as a castigation for his sin. The good man returns now and explains to Perceval the true meaning of the history of herself which this demon had given him. The visitor then vanishes and a voice bids Perceval enter the ship, which will take him to Galahad and Bohort (82). — Lancelot receives

admonitions from the hermit, especially on the subject of the necessity of chastity and of confessing one's sins, and goes on his
journey. After being upbraided by a squire in the forest for his
adultery he comes upon another hermit, just as he is exorcising
a devil from the corpse of an old man that is lying before his
dwelling. The hermit relates to Lancelot the marvellous circumstances of the hermit-knight's death (he had been killed by vengeful knights) and they are to bury him the next day. In the meanwhile, he (the hermit) enumerates Lancelot's virtues before he
sinned with Guinevere and how the devil now had got him into
his power — compares, also, the Grail quest to the wedding feast
in the Gospel (*St. Matthew,* XXII, 1ff.): "For many are called,
but few are chosen" (91). At this point Lancelot declares himself repentant and happier from his repentance. He puts on haircloth, promises the hermit that he will confess his sins every week,
and departs. A damsel on a white palfrey exhorts him to persevere in repentance. That night he has a strange vision (relating
really to his ancestors and to his son, Galahad). The following
day he comes to a third hermit and confesses his sins to this
holy man, who expounds to him his latest dream. He proceeds
on his journey, and takes the part of the black knights in a tournament against their opponents, the white knights, because the former
seems the weaker side. He proves himself the most skillful of all
the combatants, but his side loses and he is led away into the forest
in a state of the deepest dejection (p. 101). A female recluse here
interprets to him the allegorical meaning of the tournament and
his defeat. He next arrives at the Lake Marchoise, where a black
knight, rising out of the water, kills his horse. Thus Lancelot
is cut off without food in a trackless forest. — After fruitless
wanderings, Gawain and Hector come to a ruined chapel in the
woods, and are visited there by dreams that symbolize the vain
efforts of themselves and their associates to attain the Grail. On
their way to the hermitage of Nascien, who interprets these dreams
to them (111ff.), Gawain kills Yvain (Ywain), the Bastard, not
knowing who he is. — An old man of religion impresses upon
Bohort the necessity of confession and repentance, gives him a

white garment to put on under his scarlet one, hears the penitent's confession and absolves him (120). Henceforth he adopts ascetic practices in regard to food, drink and sleep. He champions King Amans's daughter, whose elder sister has dealt unjustly with her in regard to her inheritance, overcomes the latter's knight (Priadan le Noir), and establishes the younger sister's rights. Later he sees Lionel being tortured by two knights and, at the same moment, another knight carrying off a maiden into the thick of the wood. Despite his love for his brother, he saves the damsel first — then returns to rescue Lionel, who, however, has disappeared.

The devil, disguised as a priest, gives a false interpretation of certain dreams which Bohort had had, and otherwise tempts him with pretended women, really devils, but an accidental sign of the cross causes them all to vanish. He receives now from an abbot a true exposition of the signification of his dreams (131ff.). At a hermitage the following day Bohort finds Lionel, who upbraids his brother for having deserted him, and is only prevented from killing the unresisting Bohort by the intervention of Calogrenant. Lionel kills Calogrenant (138) and again attacks Bohort, who, at last, is on the point of defending himself, when a flame from heaven parts the two. Obeying a voice, Bohort goes to the sea and embarks on a ship, on which he later rejoices to discover Perceval. — Galahad, *incognito*, vanquishes and wounds Gawain in a tourney, stops at a hermitage near Corbenic, and is conducted thence in the night by a damsel to the ship on board which were Bohort and Perceval. The three recount their adventures to each other (p. 143). This vessel, with miraculous celerity, bore them to a desert, fourteen days' journey from Logres. There on the exhortation of the damsel, they all transfer themselves to a magnificent, but deserted ship (Solomon's ship), and the damsel reveals herself as Perceval's sister. As described already in the *Estoire* (cp. p. 309, above) there was in this vessel a beautiful bed and on this bed King David's sword, half-drawn from its scabbard. Only the bravest of the brave (Galahad) could draw it. Perceval's sister relates the story of the Dolorous Stroke made with this sword (147), and explains the inscriptions on the

sword, one as applying to Mordrain, the other to Pellinor, the
Maimed King.[26] The origin of the three staves of different colors
which make part of the bed is told (pp. 151ff.).[27] The three companions, still further, looked there upon the crown and upon an
almsbag in which they found a scroll confirming all that Perceval's sister had told them. Moreover, Perceval's sister now replaced
the tow and hemp, which had constituted the hangings of David's
sword, with other hangings, made of her own hair and braided
with jewels. She called the sword with its new ornament
"L'Espee as Estraingnes Renges" (the Sword with the Strange
Hangings) and the sheath "Memoire de Sanc" (Memory of Blood).
At the request of Bohort and Perceval, Galahad allowed the damsel
to gird the sword on him and he, who was himself perfectly free
from all carnal sin, now vows to be the knight of Perceval's sister,
who was, also, dedicated to a life of perpetual chastity (p. 163).

All four sail away in the ship and land near the castle of Carte-
lois. There Galahad, Bohort and Perceval slay the wicked sons
of Count Ernol(s), and Christ assures the first-named, though
a priest, that he (Galahad) has avenged him (Christ) by this
act and bids him go and heal the Maimed King. — In a forest
nearby they meet with the stag (Christ) and four lions (four
Evangelists) and in a hermit's chapel witness a change of the
five beasts into forms that symbolize more definitely their true
significance, as expounded by the hermit. They next have a fierce
encounter with certain knights who are seeking to obtain blood
from a virgin princess, wherewith to cure the leprous lady of
their castle. During a truce, which is to last overnight, Perceval's sister, being told of the motive of their assailants, voluntarily yields the needed blood, but dies therefrom. In accordance
with her own desire, her body is laid out in a ship and thrust

---

[26] On Pellinor as the Maimed King see Bruce, "Pelles, Pellinor
and Pellean in the Old French Arthurian Romances", MPh., XVI,
337 ff. (1918), where earlier discussions of the character are taken
into account — also, F. Lot's *Lancelot*, p. 242 ff., note 8.

[27] This merely repeats the history of these three staves, given
in the *Estoire*. Cp. Sommer, I, 124 ff.

out to sea with a scroll by its side, setting forth her history (172).
Shortly after the departure of the three companions, a storm arose
which destroyed the castle. This was a divine retribution for the
slaughter of the twelve virgin princesses, who had been killed
there and whose graves were in an adjacent churchyard. Bohort
first left his companions to rescue a flying knight and then these
companions separated. — By God's grace, Lancelot is directed
to the ship which bore the dead body of Perceval's sister, and
learns from the scroll who the girl was and what was her history.
He stays in the vessel and is later joined by Galahad. Living
thus in this vessel for upwards of six months, they achieve many
adventures together, until, at last, God sends Galahad a white
charger with the command that he should now go and finish the
adventures of Logres. The ship brings Lancelot to the Grail castle
one night after midnight (179). Lancelot goes through the rooms
of the castle, not knowing where he is. Through the open door
of a room, which he is warned not to enter, he is permitted to
behold the Grail and a priest celebrating the mass before it. The
priest seems to Lancelot to sink under the weight of the *corpus
domini;* consequently, praying for pardon of his disobedience, he
hurries to the priest's assistance, but falls into a trance, which
lasts fourteen days (corresponding to his fourteen years of sin).
Whilst in this condition, he sees many spiritual secrets. On his
return to consciousness he learns that the castle is Corbenic and
that his quest is ended; still, he will not desist from the penance
of wearing hair-cloth. Pelles tells him of the death of Galahad's
mother (182). On the fifth day after this, the Holy Grail is
feeding its votaries, when the doors of the palace close, of themselves, to exclude Hector, who endeavors to force an entrance, but
has to withdraw amid the jeers and maledictions of the people. —

Lancelot now quits Corbenic and comes to the tomb of Baudemagus, at an abbey of white monks (Cistercians). An inscription on
this tomb declares that the dead man beneath was slain by Gawain.
Lancelot next passes the tombs of Chanaan's brothers, and thence
returns to court. — Galahad visits Mordrain's abbey, and the latter,
whose wounds are healed by their visit, expires contented. He

achieves, moreover, the adventures of the boiling fountain and the burning tomb (Symeu's). The next day he meets Perceval and for five years they wander together, before they reach the Grail castle. During these years they brought to an end nearly all the adventures of Logres. Finally Bohort joins them and they all arrive at Corbenic, to the great joy of Pelles (p. 187). Bohort and Perceval are unable to unite the pieces of the broken sword, with which Joseph was wounded, but Galahad succeeds. A voice warns all who have no right to sit at Christ's table to withdraw. Thus, besides the three questers, only three members of the Corbenic household (Pelles, his son, Eliezer and his niece) were left in the hall. To these are soon added three knights from Gaul, three from Ireland, and three from Denmark. Afterwards four damsels bring in on a bed the Maimed King, who expresses his confidence that with Galahad's coming his sorrow will be relieved and that he will die. The voice now commands all present (including the nine knights), save the questers, to depart. A bishop is brought down from heaven by four angels in a rich chair and seated at the Grail table. Letters on his forehead say that he is Josephe. The angels make preparations for the mass, which is conducted by Josephe, the Holy Grail being in the centre of the table. Josephe kisses Galahad and then bids him kiss the other questers. Finally, having assured them that they would be fed and rewarded by the Savior, he vanishes (190). Christ, with bleeding hands and feet, now rises out of the Holy Grail, feeds them from the Grail and declares that this vessel is the dish of the Last Supper. They will see it more clearly in the Spiritual Palace at Sarras. He next sends the twelve knights abroad into the world to preach the Gospel. Obeying Christ's command, Galahad heals the Maimed King with blood from the lance. This king now retires to an abbey of white monks and performs many miracles. —

That night a voice bids the twelve knights depart. Galahad, Bohort and Perceval go to the sea, where they find Solomon's ship, and on it the Holy Grail. The sacred vessel was thus lost forever to the people of Logres, because of their sins. Galahad, remembering his happiness at the Grail ceremony, longs for death, and God

promises him that his desire will be fulfilled. — The ship arrives
at Sarras and the knights carry the Holy Grail to the Spiritual
Palace, where Our Lord had consecrated Josephe the first bishop
(194). The vessel that bore the body of Perceval's sister arrived
at Sarras at the same moment as Solomon's ship. A lame beggar,
who, in compliance with Galahad's request, helps to carry the
Holy Grail from the waterside to the palace, is miraculously cured
thereby. Perceval's sister is buried in the palace. Escorant, King
of Sarras, disbelieves what the three companions tell him concerning the Grail and keeps them in prison for a year, during which
period they were fed by the holy vessel. Escorant dies and on his
deathbed Galahad, Bohort and Perceval grant him forgiveness for
his injustice towards them. Against Galahad's will, he is elected
to succeed Escorant. One year thereafter, in the Spiritual Palace,
they find Josephe kneeling before the Grail He removes the
cover from the vessel, so that Galahad at last sees clearly the object
of his desires. He prays now for death, receives the sacrament and
expires. Angels bear his soul to heaven. At the same time Bohort
and Perceval saw a hand reach down from heaven and lift the
Grail and the lance up thither. From that day to this nobody
has ever beheld them again. Galahad was buried where he died.
Perceval and Bohort went into a hermitage and there, some fourteen months later, Perceval, too, expired and was interred by his
sister's side. Bohort now returned to Arthur's court. His welcome at court was all the warmer, because every one had supposed
that he was dead. Arthur had the adventures of the Holy Grail
as related by Bohort recorded and the record was kept in the
abbey at Salisbury. For King Henry's sake, Walter Map drew
thence his book on the Holy Grail, which book King Henry had
translated from Latin into French (199).

5. La Mort Artu.

King Henry wished to hear how the knights mentioned in
the *Queste* ended their careers — hence Walter Map wrote this last
division and called it *La Mort al roi Artu* (p. 203). — On Bohort's
return from Sarras, the people at Arthur's court welcomed him

with joy, but they were deeply grieved by the news of the death
of Galahad and Perceval. Arthur had the adventures of each
quester written down. It turned out that twenty-two of the knights
who were engaged in this adventure had been slain. Gawain reluctantly acknowledges that, of these, he had killed eighteen, including Baudemagus — doubtless, he says, owing to his sins. —
In order to prevent his knights from losing the practice of arms,
the king proclaims a tournament at Winchester. In the meanwhile,
Lancelot had forgotten the vows which he had made during the
quest for the Holy Grail and within a month after his return
to court had resumed his adulterous relations with Guinevere
and in a more reckless spirit than ever. Wishing to attend the
tournament *incognito*, Lancelot feigned indisposition and bade his
kinsmen go without him. When Agravain, who hated Lancelot,
became aware of this, he suspected that Lancelot was really remaining behind for the purpose of a clandestine meeting with the
queen. Consequently, he informs Arthur of Lancelot's intrigue
with Guinevere and of what he imagines to be Lancelot's true
motive for not accompanying his kinsmen to Winchester. Arthur
is incredulous and will not follow the matter up. Nevertheless,
to test the truth of Agravain's suspicions, he bids the queen stay
at Camelot. Lancelot now tells Guinevere why he had feigned
illness, and, with one squire, rides by night to Winchester. On
the way, he stops at a castle (Escalot) which Arthur is on the point
of leaving, after having spent the previous night there. Despite
Lancelot's effort to conceal his identity, the monarch recognizes
him. The lord of the castle, a rich vavassor, has two sons, one
of whom cannot attend the tournament. To preserve his *incognito*,
Lancelot exchanges armor with this young man. He permits his
host's other son to go with him to the assembly, and he also consents, though with dismay (remembering the queen), to wear a
token (a sleeve) of his host's daughter in the combat and be her
knight. They journey by night and put up at the house of the
young knight's aunt, a mile from Winchester. Lancelot decides
to assist the outsiders, since their opponents (including Bohort,
Lionel and Hector) are more numerous (210). After performing

many feats of valor — particularly against his chief adversaries, Hector and Bohort — Lancelot wins the prize for his side and rides back to the house of his companion's aunt, where, owing to a wound, he is confined for six weeks. Gawain and Gaheriet make a futile effort to discover the victor, concerning whose identity Arthur drops vague hints.

Arthur now proclaims another tournament, which is to be held at Taneborc[28] a month hence. On his return to Camelot, the king, with Gawain and others, again stops at Escalot. The Maid of Escalot learns from Gawain that the knight who wore her token had won the prize in the assembly. Gawain makes love to the Maid, who piques him by her answer that she is already in love with a knight not inferior to him. When she shows him the shield which her knight had left behind him in the exchange of arms, Gawain recognizes that it is Lancelot's and tells her that she has a right to be proud of her conquest (217). Wondering that Lancelot has been willing to bestow his love upon a girl of lower rank than himself, Gawain bids her greet her (supposed) lover on his behalf. — Arthur tells Gawain of Agravain's accusations against Lancelot, but both are convinced that the charges are false. — On their arrival at Camelot, the king and Gawain merely say that it was a knight in red with a sleeve on his helmet who won the tourney. Guinevere, however, learns from Gifflet that this knight is Lancelot and she falls into a fury of jealousy. She expresses her rage to Bohort, who now learns for the first time that his cousin had been his adversary at Winchester. The queen's jealousy is fostered still further by Lancelot's prolonged absence from Camelot. Gawain then tells her that Lancelot is lingering at Escalot, because of his love for the Maid of Escalot. The queen expresses herself to Bohort very bitterly with respect to Lancelot's fancied disloyalty. Much offended at this, Lancelot's kinsmen quit the court and, after a fruitless search, proceed to Taneborc, in the hope that they may find him at the tournament there. — The Maid of Escalot goes to her aunt's and nurses Lancelot during his illness. She is desperately in love with

---

[28] On Taneborc (Edinburgh) see Bruce, *Mort Artu*, p. 271.

him, however, and receives her death-blow, when he tells her that
he has already bestowed his heart elsewhere (226). Lancelot's
wound prevents him from attending the tournament at Tanebore,
but he sends greetings to the queen and Gawain by a squire: the
jealous Guinevere, however, does not credit the squire's report about
Lancelot's illness. — After carrying off the honors of the day,
Lancelot's relatives begin again their quest for him, whilst Arthur
proclaims still another assembly at Camelot, a month hence, with
the purpose of drawing him out of hiding. In order to get rid
of the importunate inquiries of Bohort, etc., as to Lancelot's whereabouts, the squire had misdirected them. When they discover the
deception, following Gawain's advice, they all go to Escalot. Hence
the son of the vavasor of Escalot conducts them to Lancelot. The
latter now learns for the first time that it was Bohort who had
wounded him. The knights stay with him until he is well, but
they do not let him know of the queen's anger. — On his way
back to Camelot, Arthur lingers at Tauroc and, losing his way
in the neighboring forest, is lured by Morgan to her palace (235).
There she shows him the pictures of the history of Lancelot's love-
affair with Guinevere, painted on the walls of his room by the
former.[29] This Morgan did, in order to revenge herself on Guinevere. — Lancelot, having recovered, returns to Camelot with his
companions. In his last conversation with the Maid of Escalot, she
foretells her death from unrequited love. — Being still jealous,
the queen feigns illness and will not see Lancelot. Bohort upbraids
her with her conduct and advises Lancelot to absent himself from
the court until she summons him back. On Arthur's return, he
was pleased to hear of Lancelot's brief stay at court, for this seemed
to confute the suspicions which he had imbibed at Morgan's palace. — A knight named Avalon, who hated Gawain with a mortal
hate, seeing the queen seated by the latter at dinner, handed her
some poisoned apples, with the idea that she, in turn, would present them to Gawain.[30] She actually gave them, however, to Gaheries de Karaheu, who, after eating them, dropped dead on the

---

[29] Cp. above.
[30] On this episode see Bruce, *Mort Artu*, pp. 274 ff.

spot (248). In the general opinion, Guinevere was guilty of murder
and so the inscription on the dead man's tomb recorded that she
had poisoned him. — About this time Lancelot was accidentally
wounded by a huntsman in the forest and was compelled to remain
at a hermit's for medical treatment.

In the meanwhile the tournament at Camelot came off
and Bohort won the prize after which he went immediately
in search of the absent Lancelot. — Mador de la Porte learns
about the death of his brother, Gaheries, from the epitaph
on the tomb and makes public accusation against the queen
that she had killed him. None of the knights present offer
to defend Guinevere — consequently, Arthur grants her a respite
of forty days in which to find a champion. She regrets now that
she has alienated Lancelot's kinsmen (256). — The Maid of Escalot
has died, and, in compliance with her directions, her body is laid
in a barge with a scroll in her hand and allowed to drift down
stream to Camelot. Arthur, accompanied by Gawain, goes on board
the barge and reads the scroll in which the Maid had set forth
that her loyal but unrequited love for the best knight in the world
(Lancelot) was the cause of her death. Gawain sees from this
that he had suspected Lancelot wrongly of loving the girl. Arthur
has her buried in St. Stephen's church and an inscription put on
the tomb, reciting the manner of her death (259). — After Lancelot's wound was almost well again, he hears from a knight in the
forest concerning Guinevere's peril. Hector and Bohort join him
thereafter and are sent by him to court to ascertain the queen's
disposition towards him. Bohort refuses to be the queen's champion and on account of her treatment of his cousin, derives a
malicious pleasure from her present predicament. Gawain and
other knights are convinced of her guilt and will not respond to
Arthur's appeals on her behalf. Finally, when Guinevere be-
seeches Bohort again, he promises to be her champion, in case
no better knight presents himself. — On the day appointed, Lancelot, known only to Bohort and Hector, appears as the queen's
champion. He is victor and Mador surrenders his sword. After
the queen's acquittal, she and Lancelot renew their *amours*, and in

so reckless a manner that Gawain and his brothers all become
cognizant of the intrigue. One day as they were discussing the
matter together, Arthur chanced to come upon them, and, having
overheard a remark of Agravain's, demanded of them that they
should tell him what they were talking about. At first, they all
refuse, but, finally Agravain, under threats of violence, reveals
the truth to the king. On Agravain's suggestion, it is agreed that
the next day Arthur, with some of his knights, shall go on a hunt
and that, when Lancelot tries to take advantage of his absence,
to visit the queen, Agravain, Guerrehes and Mordred shall proceed
to catch him in the act. Notwithstanding the warnings of Gawain
as to the danger of this enterprise, which he and Gaheriet decline to
have any part in, Arthur adopts the plan. He treats Lancelot so
coldly that evening that Bohort expresses the belief to his cousin
that Agravain or Morgan has betrayed him. — Agravain's plot is
carried out: the two lovers are caught in the queen's chamber
together, but, on Bohort's advice, Lancelot had carried his sword
with him. Consequently, he is able to slay one of Agravain's party
and puts the rest to flight. Lancelot, Bohort, and Hector now
take refuge in the woods, not far away, and wait there, in order
to save Guinevere, when need should arise. The next day the
barons condemn Guinevere to die — only Gawain threatened to
renounce his allegiance to Arthur, should the latter allow the sentence to be carried out. She is to be burned at the stake and
Agravain with forty knights is to prevent any rescue. The queen
had been already led forth, when Lancelot and his companions,
having heard, through a squire, of the impending execution, charged
into the procession. Lancelot slew Agravain and Gaheriet (the
latter, without knowing who he was) and Bohort, Guerrehes (281).
After a consultation, they take Guinevere to Lancelot's castle,
Joyous Gard. Arthur is horrified on being told of the death of
his nephews and he puts an embargo on the ports of his kingdom,
to keep Lancelot from escaping. Gawain and Arthur both utter
laments over the body of Gaheriet, especially, and swoon from
grief. After the funeral of the dead brothers, Arthur vows vengeance on Lancelot and decides to besiege Joyous Gard, but, before

starting on his expedition, he fills the 72 vacant seats at the
Round Table.

In the meanwhile, Lancelot was preparing for the siege,
having summoned knights to his aid from Benoic, Sorelois,
and other lands. — When Arthur arrives before Joyous Gard,
Lancelot sends him a message by a damsel, offering to prove his
innocence in a combat with any two of the king's knights, or to
submit the matter to the judgment of Arthur's court (295). Gawain, however, exasperated by his brother's death, hardens his
uncle's heart against these offers, although the damsel reminds him
of his prophetic vision at Corbenic.[31] Bohort and Hector, with a
band of men, had been placed in ambush and they attack Arthur's
host the next day, at the same time that Lancelot sallied forth
from the castle. When night fell, there had been no decisive
result. — Lancelot's men renew the contest early on the morrow and
Bohort is severely wounded. Lancelot merely covers himself, when
attacked by Arthur — otherwise, does not defend himself. Even
when Hector has unhorsed the king and wishes to slay him, Lancelot will not permit him and remounts his sovereign courteously,
which touches Arthur deeply (306). — The siege had lasted two
months when the Pope, hearing of Arthur's marital troubles, intervened and threatened him with an interdict, if he did not take
back his lawful spouse. Arthur is willing to do so and Lancelot
is ready to return her, notwithstanding the urgent advice of Bohort
to the contrary. The queen, too, consents to go back on condition
that her consort will allow Lancelot and his people to return to
their own country unmolested. The next day Lancelot hands her
back to the king. At the instigation of Gawain, who vows in-
cessant war, until he has avenged Gaheriet, Arthur will not promise Lancelot to refrain from attacking him in his (Lancelot's) own
country. Before leaving Logres, Lancelot has his shield (afterwards venerated as a relic by the people) hung up in St. Stephen's
at Camelot. He also sends treasures to the clergy there, soliciting
their prayers. Having set sail for his native land, he bids a

---

[31] Cp. I, 416, above.

touching farewell to Logres (p. 314). After they have reached
their destination, Lancelot bestows the kingdom of Benoyce on
Bohort, that of Gannes on Lionel, keeping Gaul for himself. —
Still incited by Gawain, the next spring Arthur invades Gaul and
wages war on Lancelot. Before sailing, he accepts Mordred's offer
to guard the queen and the kingdom during his absence. Near
Gannes an old lady on a white palfrey predicts Arthur's failure
to capture that city and reminds Gawain of the vision which he
had seen at Corbenic foreshadowing his death in this war.[32] There
were now bloody encounters between Arthur's and Lancelot's men,
but there was no decisive victory for either side. — In the meanwhile, Mordred ingratiates himself with high and low in Logres
by every means and resolves to marry the queen (321). Accordingly, he forges a letter which pretends to be from Arthur and
in which the king, mortally wounded, is made to request the barons
to elect Mordred as his successor and turn over Guinevere to him
as his wife. The barons proceed to comply with the terms of
this request, but Guinevere objects. Obtaining the aid of her
cousin, Labor, to whom she communicastes the secret of Mordred's
incestuous birth,[33] she shuts herself up with a band of men in the
Tower of Logres and successfully holds out against Mordred (327).
Furthermore, she despatches a squire to Gaul, in order to ascertain
the truth about Arthur, and, in case the latter is dead, to beg
Lancelot for aid. — About this time Gawain challenges Lancelot
to settle the matters at issue between the two armies by a duel.
Lancelot reluctantly accepts, provided Gawain will present sureties
that he will keep his covenant. At the meeting where this agreement is executed, Arthur and Lancelot wish to avoid further strife,
and the latter shows that he still loves his comrade-in-arms, but
Gawain is implacable. Even the protests of Yvain and the general
condemnation of his own side leave him unmoved (pp. 336 f.).
The combat takes place the next day. Although they had fought
fiercely for hours, with only a brief interval of rest, as noon approached, to Lancelot's amazement, Gawain became as fresh as

---

[32] Cp. above.   [33] Cp. I, 441, above.

if he had not fought at all. This was due to the gift which God had conferred on him at the time of his baptism, in answer to the prayer of the hermit who baptized him: according to this gift, Gawain's strength always increased towards midday (340). Nevertheless, Lancelot held out against him, until his strength fell again to the normal.

The fight continued until vespers and Lancelot could have easily slain his opponent, who, though exhausted, refused to yield, but, out of old affection, he spared him, and, at last, is excused by Arthur from further combat. Gawain has suffered an especially bad wound on the head. — Arthur now goes to the city of Meaux (in Gaul), where Gawain begins to recover, and here learns that the Romans are moving through Burgundy to attack him (345). The emperor of the Romans tells Arthur's envoys that he has come to avenge the death of Froille d'Alemaigul (slain by Arthur in a previous war) and to claim tribute from their king. Adopting Gawain's advice, Arthur attacks first. Gawain kills the emperor's nephew and Arthur the emperor, but the old wound which Gawain had received in his duel with Lancelot bursts open and, in the end, proves mortal. Just after his victory over the Romans, Arthur receives his wife's message in regard to the treason of Mordred and hurries back to Logres (349). As Gawain feels himself dying, he relents in his bitterness towards Lancelot and advises Arthur to send for his old friend to aid him against Mordred. — Mordred, by this time, had so confirmed his hold on the barons that they consented to support him in his war against Arthur. Raising the siege of Guinevere's tower, he advances against the king, whereupon the queen flees to a convent in a forest. — Shortly after Arthur's host has landed at Dover, Gawain expires. Before his death, he warns Arthur against combating Mordred and begs that the epitaph on their common grave should record that he and Gaheriet had been killed by Lancelot, through their own fault. Arthur's sorrow over his dead nephew is boundless. The lord of Beloe slays his wife from jealousy on account of the grief which she displays over the death of Gawain. The body is finally interred in St. Stephen's at Camelot. — In

a vision the spirit of Gawain again urges his uncle not to meet
Mordred and to send for Lancelot. Arthur, however, feeling that
he has wronged Lancelot, is ashamed to do so.

On the way to meet Mordred, the king has still another vision, in which he sees himself dashed from Fortune's
Wheel. An archbishop, whom he consults about these dreams,
discovers impending evil in them, but Arthur will not heed
his advice to turn back. Later, on Salisbury Plain, the archbishop observes Merlin's inscription on a rock there, foretel-
ling a battle on this plain by which the kingdom of Logres
will be orphaned, and reads it to Arthur. The king spurns
an insolent demand of Mordred's that he shall quit the country
(363). In the ensuing battle Arthur's army is inferior in numbers to Mordred's which embraces Saxon, Irish, Scotch, and Welsh
divisions. Towards the end of the battle, which lasted all day,
on Arthur's side, only the king, Lucan, and Gifflet are left alive.
Arthur and Mordred now wound each other mortally and Lucan
and Gifflet mount the former on a horse and take him to the
Black Chapel. The next day the king kills Lucan unintentionally
by his embrace and rides away to the sea with Gifflet. There they
dismount and Arthur sends Gifflet with the sword, Excalibur,
to throw it into a neighboring lake. Gifflet is tempted by the
rich weapon and twice returns with the false statement that he
has cast it in, but finally in each instance has to confess the un-
truth. The third time he really throws it in, and a hand, rising
from the lake, seizes the weapon, brandishes it three times, and
disappears with it (380). At Arthur's command, Gifflet now leaves
him, but from a hill, not far distant, sees Morgan, the king's sister,
come in a boat full of ladies, and bear her brother away.

They buried him at the Black Chapel, as Gifflet discovered three
days afterwards, when he came upon the two tombs there — one Arthur's and the other Lucan's. Gifflet turned hermit, but, himself, died
eighteen days later. Mordred's sons now make themselves masters
of the kingdom. — Having heard of Arthur's end, Guinevere
takes the veil and dies shortly thereafter. Lancelot and his kinsmen
return to Logres and at Winchester overthrow and slay Mordred's

sons, but Lionel is killed in the battle (385 f.). From the battle-field Lancelot rode away aimlessly, mourning for the queen and Lionel, until he came to a hermitage, on top of a rocky mountain, where he finds the Archbishop of Canterbury and his own cousin, Blyobleris. He, too, becomes a hermit here. After the battle at Winchester, Bohort went back to his own country, but Hector rode about Logres, in quest of Lancelot, until he found him in his hermitage. Hector now devotes himself to the service of God and joins his half-brother in the hermitage. Four years later, he dies and is entombed there.

Not long thereafter, Lancelot, too, dies, having besought his companions on his death-bed to bury him at Joyous Gard, with Galehaut. The archbishop, who was sleeping outside of the her-mitage at the time of Lancelot's passing away, first knew of the event through a vision of angels carrying his friend's soul to heaven. Lancelot's body was buried at Joyous Gard, as he had desired and, owing to the warning of a hermit, Bohort arrived at the castle the very day of the obsequies. He took Lancelot's place in the hermitage and continued to live there the remainder of his life.

Thus Master Walter Map ends the history of Lancelot. Any one who should pretend to relate anything more on the subject will be lying (391).

Chapter VII.
A Select Bibliography of Arthurian Critical Literature.

The following bibliographical list corresponds to Parts I, II, and III of the present treatise. Among the metrical romances, consequently, it includes only those that were written by Chrétien, by the continuators of his *Perceval*, and by Robert de Boron. The bibliography of the other French metrical romances will be found in Part IV of this work; so, too, with the bibliography of all the Arthurian romances in the various continental languages, except French. The writer has purposely omitted from the following list works on the Arthurian theme which, in his opinion, are without value; on the other hand, he has endeavored to list all books, articles, etc. — especially, of the last sixty or seventy years — that seem to constitute substantial contributions to our knowledge of the subject.

As regards the arrangement of the titles in any particular section of the list, the texts are given first — then, as a rule, general works on the subject — after that, special articles, etc., approximately in the same order as is observed in the discussion of the subjects in question in the main division of the treatise. The list does not embrace publications that deal simply with matters of style or textual criticism. Moreover, no book-reviews are recorded, save those that seemed to possess the value of original contributions to the subject.

We have the following special works on the Arthurian theme: Joseph Ritson, *The Life of King Arthur (London, 1825)*, M. W. Maccallum, *Tennyson's Idylls of the King and Arthurian Story from the XVIth century* (London and New York, 1894) — which, notwithstanding its title, contains 108 pages on the mediaeval literature of the subject; — S. H. Gurteen, *The Arthurian Epic (ibid.,*

1895) — a worthless book; — Howard Maynadier, *The Arthur of the English Poets* (Boston and New York, 1907) — more than half devoted to the Middle Ages; — W. Lewis Jones, *King Arthur in History and Legend* (Cambridge, 1911). It did not enter, however, into the plan of these writers to give copious lists of the critical literature of the subject. Up to the present, accordingly, the most valuable bibliographical aids in the study of the *matière de Bretagne* have been G. Paris's lists in the *Histoire Littéraire de la France*, Vol. XXX, pp. 111 ff. (1888) and *Manuel*, pp. 296 ff. (fifth ed., 1914), the citations in Gröber's *Grundriss*, Band II, Abt. I, pp. 491 ff., 785 ff., 996 ff. (1898—1902), and, above all, the admirable reports on publications relating to the mediaeval romances and Celtic literature which appeared periodically in Karl Vollmöller's *Kritischer Jahresbericht über die Fortschritte der Romanischen Philologie*, covering the years 1890—1912. These reports were prepared by such authorities as E. Freymond, A. Hilka, J. Loth, L. C. Stern, etc.

Part I (Traditions, Chronicles, Lays and Romances)

For editions of Gildas and Nennius, cp. I, pp. 5—7, above. For fuller bibliographies of these two writers cp. R. H. Fletcher's *Arthurian Material in the Chronicles*, pp. 2 f. and 8 f., note, respectively. For the articles of A. Anscombe and A. Wade-Evans, attacking the authenticity of Gildas, and replies to the same, cp. II, p. 49, note 11.

Annales Cambriae, edited by Egerton Phillimore from MS. Harley, 3859, in *Y Cymmrodor*, IX, 152 ff. (1888). Phillimore's text is reproduced by J. Loth, *Les Mabinogion*[2], II, 370 ff. (Paris 1913).

For other pre-Geoffreyan chronicles cp. I, p. 11, note 22, above.

William of Malmesbury, Gesta Regum Anglorum, edited by William Stubbs, Rolls Series, 2 vols. (London, 1887—1889).

John Rhys, Celtic Britain (third edition, London, 1904).

W. H. Dickinson, Arthur in Cornwall (London, 1900).

H. M. Chadwick, The Origin of the English Nation (Cambridge, 1907).

R. H. Fletcher, The Arthurian Material of the Chronicles, especially those of Great Britain and France: Harvard *Studies and Notes in Philology and Literature*, X (Boston, 1906).

Ernst Windisch, Das Keltische Britannien bis zu Kaiser Arthur: Des **XXIX** Bandes der Abhandlungen der Philologisch-Historischen

Klasse der Königl. Sächsischen Gesellschaft der Wissenschaften No. VI (Leipzig, 1912).

Adolf Holtzmann, Artus, Franz Pfeiffer's *Germania*, XII, 257 ff. (1867).

J. S. Stuart-Glennie, Arthurian Localities: Introduction to Part III (1869) of the E. E. T. S. edition of the Middle English prose *Merlin* (Original Series, No. 36).

Arthur de la Borderie, L'Historia Britonum attribuée à Nennius et l'Historia Britannica avant Geoffroi de Monmouth (Paris and London, 1883).

Pio Rajna, Gli eroi Brettoni nell' onomastica Italiana, *Romania*, XVII, 161 ff., 355 ff. (1888). — Cp. H. Zimmer, Göttingische Gelehrte Anzeigen, Oct. 1, 1890, pp. 830 f., note.

   For the critical literature concerning the Arthurian figures on the Porta della Pescheria of the Modena Cathedral, cp. I, p. 14 f., above.

G. Heeger, Über die Trojanersagen der Britten (Munich, 1886).

Heinrich Zimmer, review of G. Paris's *Romans ens vers du cycle de la Table Ronde (Histoire littéraire de la France*, vol. XXX) in *Gött. G. A.*, Oct. 1, 1890.

John Rhys, Studies in the Arthurian Legend (Oxford, 1891).

H. Zimmer, Nennius Vindicatus (Berlin, 1893).

E. W. B. Nicholson, King Arthur and Gildas, *The Academy*, Oct. 12, 1895.

L. Duchesne, Nennius Retractatus, *Revue Celtique*, XV, 174 ff. (1894).

Richard Thurneysen, review of H. Zimmer's *Nennius Vindicatus* in *Zeitschrift für deutsche Philologie*, XXVIII, 80 ff. (1895).

L. Duchesne, L'Historia Britonum, *Revue Celtique*, XVII, 1 ff. (1896).

R. Thurneysen, review of Mommsen's edition of Gildas and Nennius, *Zs. f. celt. Ph.*, I, 157 ff. (1896).

W. W. Newell, Doubts concerning the British History attributed to Nennius, PMLA, XX, 622 ff. (1905).

A. Nutt, Celtic and Mediaeval Romance: Popular Studies in Mythology, Romance and Folklore, No. 1 (London, 1899).

Jessie L. Weston, King Arthur and his Knights, a Survey of Arthurian Romance, *ibid.*, No. 4 (1899).

Ferdinand Lot, Nouvelles études sur la provenance du cycle arthurien, Romania, XXX, 1 ff. (1901).

Abbé de la Rue, Essais historiques sur les bardes, les jongleurs, et les trouvères normands et anglo-normands (3 vols., Caen, 1834).

San Marte (A. Schulz), Gottfried's von Monmouth Historia Regum Britanniae mit literar-historischer Einleitung und ausführlichen Anmerkungen, und Brut Tysylio, altwälsche Chronik in deutscher Übersetzung (Halle, 1854).

J. E. Lloyd, History of Wales down to the Edwardian Conquest, II, 524 (2 vols. Oxford, 1911).

Sir Frederick Madden, The Historia Britonum of Geoffrey of Monmouth, *The Archaeological Journal*, XV, 299 ff. (1858).

H. Zimmer, Bretonische Elemente der Arthursage des Gottfried von Monmouth, *Zs. f. frz. Spr. u. Litt.*, XII¹, 231 ff. (1890).

H. L. D. Ward, article on Geoffrey of M., Catalogue of Romances in the Department of MSS. in the British Museum, I, 203 ff. (1893).

H. L. D. Ward, Postscript to the article upon Geoffrey in the Catalogue of Romances, Vol. I (1883), *Anglia*, XXIV, 383 ff. (1901).

W. Lewis Jones, Geoffrey of Monmouth, *The Transactions of the Honorable Society of Cymmrodorion*, Session, 1898—99, pp. 52 ff.

R. H. Fletcher, Two Notes on the *Historia Regum Britanniae* of Geoffrey of Monmouth, PMLA, XVI, 461 ff. (1901).

— on Geoffrey in *The Arthurian Material in the Chronicles*, etc., pp. 43 ff. (1906).

E. Windisch, on Geoffrey in *Das Keltische Britannien bis zu Kaiser Arthur*, pp. 123 ff. (Leipzig, 1912).

F. Zarncke and B. Ten Brink, Über das Verhältnis des Brut y Tysylio zu Galfrid's Hist. Reg. Brit., Ebert's *Jahrbuch für englische und romanische Philologie*, V, 249 ff. (1863).

W. W. Newell, Arthurian Notes, MLN, XVII, 277 f. (1902).

H. Tausendfreund, Vergil und Gottfried von Monmouth (Halle, 1913). Halle diss.

Paul Feuerherd, *Geoffrey of Monmouth und das Alte Testament* (Halle, 1915). Halle diss.

Hertha Brandenburg, Galfrid von Monmouth und die frühmittelenglischen Chronisten (Berlin, 1918). Berlin diss.

H. Salter, Geoffrey of Monmouth and Oxford, *English Historical Review*, XXXIV, 382 ff. (1919).

A. Leitzmann, Bemerkungen zu Galfrid von Monmouth, *Archiv f. d. Studium der neueren Sprachen*, Vol. 134, pp. 373 ff. (1916).

Der Münchener Brut: Gottfried von Monmouth in französischen Versen aus der einzigen Münchener Handschrift zum ersten Mal herausgegeben von Konrad Hoffmann und Karl Vollmöller (Halle, 1877).

Geffrei Gaimar: L'Estorie des Engles, edited by T. D. Hardy and C. T. Martin for the Rolls Series (2 vols. London, 1889).

Otto Wendeburg, Ueber die Bearbeitung von Gottfried von Monmouths Historia Regum Britanniae in der HS. Brit. Mus. Harl. 1605 (Braunschweig, 1881). Erlanger diss.

Le Roman de Brut par Wace, poete du XII⁰ siècle publié pour la première fois ... par Le Roux de Lincy (2 vols. Rouen, 1836—1838).

E. Du Méril, La vie et les ouvrages de Wace, Ebert's *Jahrbuch für romanische und englische Literatur*, I, 1 ff. (1859).

G. Paris, *Romania*, IX, 592 ff. (1880)[1].

B. Ten Brink, Wace and Galfrid von Monmouth, Ebert's *Jahrbuch*, IX, 241 ff. (1868).

Albert Ulbrich: Über das Verhältnis von Wace's Roman de Brut zu seiner Quelle, der Historia Regum Britanniae des Gottfried von Monmouth, *Romanische Forschungen*, XXVI, 181 ff. (Erlangen, 1908).

Annette B. Hopkins, The Influence of Wace on the Arthurian Romances of Crestien de Troies (Menasha, Wis. 1913). Chicago diss.

Leo Waldner, Wace's Brut und seine Quellen (Karlsruhe, 1914). Jena diss.

Katharina Schreiner, Die Sage von Hengest und Horsa: Entwickelung und Nachleben bei den Dichtern und Geschichtsschreibern Englands. *Germanistische Studien*, Heft 12 (Berlin, 1921).

Layamon's Brut or Chronicle of Britain; a Poetical Semi-Saxon Paraphrase of The Brut of Wace, now first published from the Cottonian Manuscripts in the British Museum, accompanied by a Literal Translation, Notes, and a Grammatical Glossary, by Sir Frederic Madden. Published for the Society of Antiquaries of London (3 vols. London, 1847)[2].

R. Wuelcker, Über die Quellen Layamons, PBB, III, 524 ff. (1876).

P. Branscheid, Über die Quellen des stabreimenden Morte Arthure, *Anglia, Anzeiger*, VIII, 179 ff. (1885).

A. C. L. Brown, The Round Table before Wace, [Harvard] *Studies and Notes in Philology and Literature*, VII, 183 ff. (1900).

— Welsh Traditions in Layamons Brut, MPh., I, 95 ff. (1903).

R. H. Fletcher: Did Layamon make any use of Geoffrey's Historia? PMLA, XVIII, 91 ff. (1903).

R. Imelmann: Layamon, Versuch über seine Quellen (Berlin, 1906).

J. D. Bruce: Some proper names in Layamon's Brut, not represented in Wace or Geoffrey of Monmouth, MLN, XXVI, 65 ff. (1911).

— The Development of the Mort Arthur Theme in Mediaeval Romance, RR, IV, 403 ff. (1913) — particulary, pp. 451 ff. [3].

---

[1] For a full bibliography of Wace's life and writings cp. Miss A. B. Hopkins's thesis named below — especially, p. 10, note 24 a.

[2] For full bibliographies of Layamon, cp. B. S. Monroe, JEGcPh., VII, no. 1, pp. 139 ff. (1908), and J. E. Wells, *A Manual of the Writings in Middle English* 1050—1400, 792 ff. (Yale University Press, 1916). I give above only the publications that are important for the sources.

[3] On the so-called Martin of Rochester, cp. I, 29, note 59, above.

Frances Lytle Gillespy, Layamon's Brut: a Comparative Study in Narrative Art, *University of California Publications in Philology*, III, 361 ff. (1916).
R. H. Fletcher, Some Arthurian Fragments from Fourteenth Century Chronicles, PMLA, XVIII, 84 ff. (1903).

William F. Skene The Four Ancient Books of Wales (2 vols. Edinburgh, 1868).
J. Rhys and J. Gwenogvryn Evans, The Text of the Mabinogion and other Welsh tales from the Red Book of Hergest (Oxford, 1887).
J. G. Evans, The White Book Mabinogion, Welsh Tales and Romances reproduced from the Peniarth Manuscripts. (Pwllheli, 1909 — though dated 1907).
The Mabinogion from the Welsh of the Llyfr Coch o Hergest (The Red Book of Hergest) in the Library of Jesus College, Oxford, translated with Notes by Lady Charlotte Guest (reprint, London, 1877).
— with notes by Alfred Nutt (London and New York, 1902).
J. Loth, Les Mabinogion du Livre Rouge de Hergest avec les variants du Livre Blanc de Rhydderch, traduits du gallois, etc. (second edition, 2 vols. Paris, 1913).
    For the bibliography of the controversy concerning the relations of the Mabinogion to the French romances — especially, Chrétien's, cp. II, 63-4, above.
Chapters on *Die keltischen Literaturen* in the volume, entitled *Die romanischen Literaturen mit Einschluss des Keltischen* (Berlin and Leipzig, 1909) in Paul Henneberg's cooperative work, *Die Kultur der Gegenwart*.
H. D. Arbois de Jubainville, Cours de littérature celtique (9 vols., Paris — earlier volumes undated, vol. 9 dated 1900).
G. Paris, *Histoire littéraire de la France*, XXX, 7 ff. (Paris, 1888).
— review of the same by H. Zimmer, *Gött. G. A.*, Oct. 1, 1890.
Thomas Stephens, The Literature of the Kymry (second edition, London, 1876).
M. Wilmotte, L'évolution du roman français aux environs de 1150: Académie Royale de Belgique (Bruxelles). Bulletins de la Classe des Lettres, etc. 1903, pp. 327 ff. — and the *Note Additionelle* thereto, pp. 475 ff.
G. Ehrismann, Märchen im höfischen Epos, PBB, XXX, 14 ff. (1905).
H. Zimmer, Über direkte Handelsverbindungen Westgalliens mit Irland im Altertum und frühen Mittelalter, *Sitzungsberichte der Königl. Preuss. Akademie der Wissenschaften, Philos.-Hist. Klasse* for 1909, pp. 363 ff., 430 ff., 543 ff., 582 ff. — for 1910, pp. 1031 ff.

386   *Evolution of Arthurian Romance*

H. Zimmer, Auf welchem Wege kamen die Goidelen vom Kontinent nach Irland? *Abhandlungen* of the same Academy for 1912.
— Der Kulturhistorische Hintergrund in der altirischen Heldensage, *Sitzungsberichte der Königl. Preuss. Akademie der Wissenschaften, Philos.-Hist. Klasse*, 1911, IX, 174 ff. — reviewed by J. Vendryes, *Revue Celtique*, XXXII, 232 ff. (1911).

E. Faral, Recherches sur les sources latines des contes et romans courtois du moyen age (Paris, 1913). — reviewed by M. Wilmotte, *Romania*, XLIII, 110 ff. (1914) and F. M. Warren, MLN, June, 1914.

W. W. Newell, King Arthur and the Round Table (2 vols., Boston, 1897).

F. M. Luzel: De l'authenticité des chants du Barzaz-Breiz de M. de la Villemarqué (Paris, 1872).

John Rhys, The Origin and Growth of Religion as illustrated by Celtic Heathendom: Hibbert Lectures for 1886 (London, 1888).

San Marte (A. Schulz), Die Arthur-Sage und die Mährchen des rothen Buchs von Hergest: Bibliothek der gesammten deutschen National-Literatur, Abt. II, Band 2 (Quedlinburg and Leipzig, 1842).
— Beiträge zur bretonischen und celtisch-germanischen Heldensage *op. cit.*, Band 3 (ibid. 1847).

W. Golther, Zur Frage nach der Entstehung der bretonischen oder Artus-Epen, *Zs. für vergleichende Literaturgeschichte, Neue Folge*, III, 211 ff. (1890).
— Beziehungen zwischen französischer und keltischer Literatur im Mittelalter, *ibid.*, pp. 409 ff.

H. Zimmer, review of A. Nutt's *Studies on the Legend of the Holy Grail, Gött. G. A.*, June 10, 1890.
— Beiträge zur Namenforschung in den altfranzösischen Arthurepen, *Zs. f. frz. Spr. u. Litt.*, XIII', 1 ff. (1891).

Franz Pütz, Zur Geschichte der Entwicklung der Artursage, *Zs. f. frz. Spr. u. Litt.*, XIV', 161 ff. (1892).

F. Lot, Celtica, *Romania*, XXIV, 321 ff. (1895).
— Études sur la provenance du cycle arthurien, *ibid.*, 497 ff., XXV, 1 ff. (1896).
— Nouvelles études sur la provenance du cycle arthurien, *ibid.* XXVIII, 1 ff. 321 ff. (1899), XXX, 1 ff. (1901).

J. Loth, Le roi Loth des romans de la Table Ronde, *Revue Celtique*, XVI, 84 ff. (1895).

Jessie L. Weston, The Legend of Sir Gawain (London, 1897). Grimm Library, no. 7.

Ernst Brugger, Ueber die Bedeutung von Bretagne, Breton, in mittelalterlichen Texten, *Zs. f. frz. Spr. u. Litt.*, XX', 79 ff. (1898).

E. Phillimore's note on the triads in the Middle English *Merlin*, Part IV, p. XCVIII, note 3, Early English Text Society (London, 1899).

Wendelin Foerster, Introductions to his editions of Chrétien's romances — especially, the one to *Der Karrenritter (Lancelot) und das Wilhelmsleben (Guillaume d'Angleterre) von Christian von Troyes* (Halle, 1899).

E. Freymond, Artus' Kampf mit dem Katzenungetüm: Sonderabzug aus: Beiträge zur romanischen Philologie, Festgabe für Gustav Gröber (Halle, 1899).

John Rhys, Celtic Folklore, Welsh and Manx (2 vols., Oxford, 1901).

E. Anwyl, The Four Branches of the Mabinogi, *Zs. f. celt. Ph.*, I, 277 ff. (1896), II, 124 ff. III, 123 ff.

John Rhys's Preface to *Le Morte D'Arthur* by Sir Thomas Malory in the Everyman's Library edition (2 vols., London, 1906).

W. J. Gruffydd, The Mabinogion, *Transactions of the Honourable Society of Cymmrodorion*, Session 1912—1913.

Josef Baudis, The Mabinogion, *Folk-Lore*, XXVII, 31 ff. (1916).

J. Loth, Contributions à l'étude des romans de la Table Ronde (Paris, 1912). — continued *Revue Celtique*, XXXIV, 365 ff. (1913), XXXVII, 317 ff. (1917—1919).

Gideon Huet, Notes d'histoire littéraire I. Le témoignage de Wace sur les fables arthuriennes, *Moyen Age*, XIX, 234 f. (1916).

B. de Roquefort, Poésies de Marie de France, poète anglo-normand du XIIIᵉ siècle, Vol. I (Paris, 1819).

Karl Warnke, Die Lais der Marie de France . . . mit vergleichenden Anmerkungen von Reinhold Köhler (second edition, 1900)[4].

E. Höpffner, Marie de France: Les Lais, Bibliotheca Romanica, No's. 274, 275, 277, 278 (Straßburg, 1921).

F. Wolf, Ueber die Lais, Sequenzen und Leiche (Heidelberg, 1841).

Edith Rickert; Marie de France, Seven of her lays done into English (London and New York, 1901).

Wilhelm Hertz, Spielmannsbuch (fourth edition, Stuttgart and Berlin, 1912).

John Charles Fox, Marie de France, *English Historical Review*, XXV, 303 ff. (1910).

— Mary, Abbess of Shaftesbury, *ibid.*, XXVI, 317 ff. (1911).

Emil Winkler, Französische Dichter des Mittelalters II: Marie de France: Kaiserl. Akademie der Wissenschaften in Wien, Philo-

---

[4] For editions of the anonymous lays, see below. For bibliographies of the lays, in general, see the introduction to Warnke's edition.

sophisch-historische Klasse, *Sitzungsberichte,* 188. Band, 3. Abhandlung (Wien, 1918).

Giulio Bertoni, Maria di Francia, *Nuova Antologia*, Sept. 1, 1920.

Emil Schiött, L'amour et les amoureux dans les lais de Marie de France (Lund, 1889).

J. Bédier, Les lais de Marie de France, *Revue des deux Mondes,* CVII, 835 ff. (Oct. 15, 1891).

W. H. Schofield, Chaucer's Franklin's Tale, PMLA, XVI, 405 ff. (1901).

Pio Rajna, Le origini della novella narrata dal Frankeleyn nei *Canterburg Tales* del Chaucer, *Romania*, XXXII, 204 (1903).

Lucien Foulet, Marie de France et les lais bretons, *Zs. f. rom. Ph.,* XXIX, 19 ff. (1905).

— English Words in the *Lais* of Marie de France, MLN, XX, 109 ff. (1905).

— The Prologue of Sir Orfeo, *ibid.,* XXI, 46 ff. (1906).

— Le Prologue du *Franklin's Tale* et les lais bretons, *Zs. f. rom. Ph.,* XXX, 698 ff. (1906).

— Marie de France et la légende de Tristan, *ibid.,* XXXII, 161 ff., 257 ff. (1908).

— Thomas and Marie in their relation to the *conteurs,* MLN, XXIII, 205 ff. (1908).

P. Voelker, Die Bedeutungsentwickelung des Wortes Roman, *Zs. f. rom. Ph.,* X, 485 ff. (1887).

G. Paris, Les romans en vers du cycle de la Table Ronde, *Histoire Littéraire de la France,* XXX, 1 ff. (Paris, 1888).

Gustav Gröber, *Grundriss der romanischen Philologie,* II. Band, 1. Abteilung, pp. 491 ff. (1898), 785 ff. (1901).

M. Wilmotte, Les origines du roman breton, *Moyen Age,* IV, 186 ff. (1891).

J. Loth, Des nouvelles théories sur l'origine des romans arthuriens, *Revue Celtique,* XIII, 475 ff. (1892).

Fritz Seiffert, Ein Namenbuch zu den altfranzösischen Artusepen, Teil I (Greifswald, 1882).

F. Lot. Glastonbury et Avalon, *Romania,* XXVII, 553 ff. (1897).

F. M. Warren, The Island of Avalon, MLN, XIV, 93 f. (1899).

Lucy Allen Paton, Studies in the Fairy Mythology of Arthurian Romance: Radcliffe College Monographs, No. 13 (Boston, 1903).

E. Brugger, Beiträge zur Erklärung der arthurischen Geographie I, Estregales, *Zs. f. frz. Spr. u. Litt.,* XXVII¹, 69 ff. (1904), II, Gorre, XXVIII¹, 1 ff. (1905).

A. C. L. Brown, *The Round Table before Wace.* [Harvard] *Studies and Notes in Philology and Literature,* VII, 183 ff. (1900).

Lewis F. Mott, The Round Table, PMLA, **XX**, 231 ff. (1905).
— review of the same by Brugger, *Zs. f. frz. Spr. u. Litt.*, **XXIX²**, 238 ff. (1906).
Jessie L. Weston, A hitherto unconsidered aspect of the Round Table, Mélanges offerts à M. Maurice Wilmotte (Paris, 1910).
A. Nutt and Kuno Meyer, The Voyage of Bran (2 vols. London, 1895-7): Grimm Library, No. 6.
Carrie A. Harper, Carados and the Serpent, MLN, **XIII**, 417 ff. (1898).
G. Paris, Caradoc et le Serpent, *Romania*, **XXVIII**, 214 ff. (1899).
F. Lot, Caradoc et Saint Paterne, *ibid.* 508 ff.
G. Huet, Le chateau tournant dans la Suite du Merlin, *Romania*, **XL**, 235 ff. (1911).
G. Paris, Cliges, *Journal des Savants*, Feb., June, July, August, December, 1902 — reprinted, *Mélanges G. Paris*, **I**, 229 ff. (Paris, 1910).
G. L. Kittredge, Arthur and Gorlagon: [Harvard] *Studies and Notes*, **VIII** (1903).
— A Study of Gawain and the Green Knight (Cambridge, Mass., 1916).
Axel Ahlström, Sur l'origine du Chevalier au lion, *Mélanges de philologie romane dediés a Carl Wahlund* (Macon, 1896).
A. C. L. Brown, Iwain, a Study in the Origins of Arthurian Romance: [Harvard] *Studies and Notes*, **VIII** (1903). — Cp. Nitze's review, MLN, **XIX**, 82 ff. (1904).
— The Knight of the Lion, PMLA, **XX**, 673 ff. (1905).
— Chrétien's „Yvain", MPh., **IX**, 109 ff. (1911).
— On the Independent Character of the Welsh Owain, RR, **III**, 143 ff. (1911).
Rudolf Zenker, Forschungen zur Artusepik, I, Ivainstudien (Halle, 1921)⁵.

For Arthurian romance in Irish and Gaelic, cp. **I**, 92 ff. and notes, above.
J. C. Hodges, Two Otherworld Stories, MLN, **XXXII**, 280 ff. (1917).

Ch. Potvin, Bibliographie de Chrestien de Troyes: comparaison des manuscrits de Perceval le Gallois (Bruxelles, Leipzig, Gand, Paris, 1863).
W. W. Comfort, Eric and Enid by Chrétien de Troyes (London and New York, 1913) — translation of *Erec, Cliges, Yvain,* and *Lancelot,* in Everyman's Library — pp. 373—377 (Select Bibliography of Works relating to Chrétien de Troyes)⁶.

---

⁵ For a full bibliography of Chrétien's *Yvain*, cp. Zenker, pp. XXIff.
⁶ This is the best bibliography of Chrétien that we have. It includes works on text-criticism, grammar, style, etc, as the bibliography in the present treatise does not.

Christian von Troyes: Sämtliche Werke, nach allen bekannten Handschriften herausgegeben von Wendelin Foerster. The volumes in
the series are numbered: I, *Cliges*, II, *Yvain*, III, *Erec*, IV,
Lancelot and *Guillaume d'Angleterre*. They were all published
at Halle and are enumerated under the headings of the respective
romances that now follow [7].

For publications on Chrétien's romances in their relation to
the *Mabinogion*, cp. II, 62 f., above.

W. L. Holland, Crestien von Troies, eine literaturgeschichtliche Untersuchung (Tübingen, 1854).

H. Emecke, Chrestien von Troyes als Persönlichkeit und als Dichter.
Strassburg diss., 1893.

Otto Schulz, Die Darstellung psychologischer Vorgänge in den Romanen
des Kristian von Troyes (Halle, 1903).

F. M. Warren, Some Features of Style in Early French Narrative
Poetry (1150—1170), MPh., III, 179 ff. (1905), 513 ff. (1906),
IV, 655 ff. (1907).

Wendelin Foerster, Kristian von Troyes, Wörterbuch zu seinen sämtlichen Werken (Halle, 1914).

E. Faral, Recherches sur les sources latines des contes et romans
courtois du moyen âge (Paris, 1913).

Andreas Capellanus, De Amore Libri Tres, edited by E. Trojel (Copenhagen, 1892).

W. A. Neilson, The Origins and the Sources of the Courts of Love:
[Harvard] Studies and Notes, VI (Boston, 1899).

E. Wechssler, Frauendienst und Vassalität, *Zs. f. frz. Spr. u. Litt.*,
XXIV[1], 158 ff. (1902).

— Das Kulturproblem des Minnesangs: Studien zur Vorgeschichte der
Renaissance. Band I (Halle, 1909) [8].

— reviewed by Karl Vossler in LB. March, April, 1911.

Myrrha Borodine, La femme et l'amour au XIIe siècle d'après les
poèmes de Chrétien de Troyes (Paris, 1909).

M. Wilmotte, Rodlieb, notre premier roman courtois, *Romania*, XLIV,
373 ff. (1916—1917).

T. F. Crane, Italian Social Customs in the Sixteenth Century and their
influence on the literatures of Europe, ch. I (New Haven, 1920).

Philomena, conte raconté d'après Ovide par Chrétien de Troyes publié
. . . par C. De Boer (Paris, 1909).

F. E. Guyer, The Influence of Ovid on Crestien de Troyes, RR, XII,
97 ff., 216 ff. (1921).

---

[7] Foerster's editions of Chrétien's Works have supplanted all previous
ones. He did not edit, however, the *Chansons* or the *Perceval*.

[8] Only one volume has appeared up to date (Feb. 1922).

For the influence of the French romances of antiquity on Chrétien, among others, cp. the Göttingen dissertations listed I, 111 and note 18, above.

Erec et Enide, edited by Immanuel Bekker, *Zs. f. d. A.*, X, 373 ff. (1856), and by Wendelin Foerster in a large form (Halle, 1890) and in a small form (second edition, *ibid.* 1909). — For *Erec* literature, cp. II, 63 ff. and notes, above.

G. Cohen, Zum Text des Erec, *Zs. f. frz. Spr. u. Litt.*, XXXVIII[1], 97 f. (1911).

E. Philipot, Un episode d.Erec et Enide: la joie de la cour, *Romania*, XXV, 258 ff. (1896).

W. Meyer Lübke, Crestien von Troyes Erec und Enide, *Zs. f. frz. Spr. u. Litt.*, XLIV [1], 129 ff.

W. Küchler, Über den sentimentalen Gehalt der Haupthandlung in Crestien's Erec und Ivain, *Zs. f. rom. Ph.*, XL, 83 ff. (1919).

Cliges, edited by W. Foerster in a large form (Halle, 1884) and in a small form (third edition, *ibid.*, 1910).

J. L. Weston, The Three Days' Tournament, a Study in Romance and Folk-Lore: Grimm's Library, No. 15 (London, 1902).

C. H. Carter, better discussion of the same *motif* in his article, *Ipomedon, Haverford Essays*, pp. 237 ff. (Haverford, 1909).

A. G. van Hamel, Cliges et Tristan, *Romania*, XXXIII, 465 ff. (1904).

— Bydrage tot de vergelijking van Cliges en Tristan, *Taal en Letteren*, XIV, 193 ff. (1904).

F. Settegast, Byzantinisch-Geschichtliches im *Cliges* and *Yvain*, *Zs. f. rom. Ph.*, XXXII, 400 ff. (1908).

W. Foerster, Randglossen zum Athisroman, *ibid.*, XXXVI, 727 ff. (1912).

Le Conte de la Charrette (Lancelot), edited by W. J. A. Jonckbloet as an Appendix to Part II (The Hague, 1849) of his edition of the Dutch *Roman van Lancelot,* and by W. Foerster under the title, *Der Karrenritter* in the volume, *Der Karrenritter (Lancelot) und das Wilhelmsleben (Guillaume d'Angleterre) von Troyes* (Halle, 1899). — For *Lancelot* literature, cp. II, 397-8, below.

Yvain, edited by W. L. Holland (first ed. 1862, third ed. 1886 and reprinted Berlin, 1902) and by W. Foerster, *Der Löwenritter (Yvain)* in large form (1887) and in small form (fifth edition revised by A. Hilka, 1921). — For *Yvain* literature, cp. II, 389, above.

O. M. Johnston, The Episode of Yvain, the Lion, and the Serpent in Chrétien de Troies, *Zs. f. frz. Spr. u. Litt.*, XXXI[1], 157 ff. (1907).

O. M. Johnston, The Fountain Episode in Chrétien de Troies' *Yvain*, *Transactions and Proceedings of the American Philological Association*, vol. XXXIII, pp. LXXXIIIf. (1902).

W. A. Nitze, A New Source of the *Yvain*, MPh., III, 267 (1905). — The Fountain Defended, *ibid.*, XII, 145 ff. (1909).

Louise B. Morgan, The Source of the Fountain-Story in the *Ywain*, MPh., VI, 331 ff. (1909).

G. L. Hamilton, Storm-making Springs: Studies on the Sources of the *Yvain*, RR, II, 315 ff. (1911), V, 213 ff. (1914).

H. Sparnaay, Ueber die Laudinefigur, *Neophilologus*, III, 122 ff. (1918). — Laudine bei Crestien und bei Hartmann, *ibid.*, IV, 310 ff. (1918).

Marianne Mörner, Le terminus a quo du Chevalier au Lion, *Archivium Romanicum*, III, 95 f. (1919).

Elise Richter, Die künstlerische Stoffgestaltung in Chrestiens Ivain, *Zs. f. rom. Ph.*, XXXIX, 385 ff. (1918).

Conte del Graal *(Perceval)*, edited by Ch. Potvin in his *Perceval le Gallois ou le Conte du Graal*, Part 2, vols. 1 and 2 (6 vols. Mons, 1866—1871), and by G. Baist (Freiburg, 1909 and 1912 — an undated and unedited reproduction of the text of MS. 794, f. français, Bibl. Nat.). — For *Perceval* literature cp. II, 401—404, below.

Paul Steinbach, Über den Einfluss des Crestien de Troyes auf die altenglische Literatur, Leipzig diss. 1885.

F. L. Critchlow, Arthur in Old French Poetry, not of the Breton Cycle, MPh., VI, 477 ff. (1909).

W. M. Stevenson, Der Einfluss des Gautier d'Arras auf die altfranzösische Kunstepik, insbesondere auf den Abenteuerroman, Göttingen diss., 1910.

W. H. Schofield, Studies on the Libeaus Desconus, [Harvard] *Studies and Notes*, IV (Boston, 1895).

Anna Hunt Billings, A Guide to the Middle English Metrical Romances: *Yale Studies in English*, IX (New York, 1901).

John Edwin Wells, A Manual of the Writings in Middle English, 1050—1400. Ch. I (New Haven and London, 1916). — First Supplement thereto *(ibid.*, 1919).

W. F. Skene, Four Ancient Books of Wales (2 vols. Edinburgh, 1868).

Die Sagen von Merlin, mit alt-wälschen, bretagnischen, schottischen, italienischen und lateinischen Gedichten und Prophezeiungen Merlins, der Prophetia Merlini des Gottfried von Monmouth und der Vita Merlini, lateinischem Gedichte aus dem dreizehnten Jahrhundert, herausgegeben und erläutert von San Marte (Halle, 1853).

G. Paris, *Huth-Merlin*, I, 1—146 (Paris, 1886) — prose version of
   Robert's *Merlin*. — See his Introduction for a discussion of the
   French romances on Merlin.

H. O. Sommer, Le Roman de Merlin or the Early History of King
   Arthur, pp. 1—92 (London, 1894) and Vulgate Version of the
   Arthurian Romances, II, 1—88 (Washington, D. C. 1908) —
   another text of the prose version of Robert's *Merlin*.

E. Brugger, Mitteilungen aus Handschriften der altfranzösischen Prosaromane Joseph und Merlin, nebst textkritischen Erörterungen,
   Romanische Forschungen, XXVI, 1 ff. (Erlangen, 1909).

H. L. D. Ward: Article on *Vita Merlini* in the Catalogue of Romances
   in the Department of Manuscripts in the British Museum, I,
   278 ff. (1883).

— Lailoken (or Merlin Silvester), *Romania*, XXII, 504 ff. (1893).

P. Phillimore, Additional Notes to J. E. Lloyd's *Welsh Place-Names*,
   Y Cymmrodor, XI, 15 ff. (1892).

William Edward Mead, Outlines of the History of the Legend of
   Merlin: Introduction to Part IV of the Middle English Prose
   Merlin. E. E. T. S. (London, 1899).

F. Lot, Études sur Merlin, *Annales de Bretagne*, XV, 324 ff., 505 ff.
   (1900).

— Nouvelles études sur le cycle arthurien, *Romania*, XLV, 1 ff.
   (1918—1919).

A. C. L. Brown, Barinthus, *Revue Celtique*, XXII, 339 ff. (1901).

E. Brugger, L'Enserrement Merlin: Studien zur Merlinsage, *Zs. f. frz.
   Spr. u. Litt.*, XXIX[1], 56 ff. (1906), XXX[1], 169 ff. (1906),
   XXXI[1], 239 ff. (1907), XXXIII[1], 145 ff. (1908), XXXIV[1],
   99 ff. (1909), XXXV[1], 1 ff. (1909).

L. A. Paton, Merlin and Ganieda, MLN, XVIII, 163 ff. (1903).

— The Story of Grisandole, PMLA, XXII, 234 ff. (1907).

— The Story of Vortigern's Tower — an Analysis: Radcliffe College
   Monographs, No. 15 (1910).

G. H. Maynadier, Merlin and Ambrosius, *Kittredge Anniversary Papers*,
   pp. 119 ff. (Boston and London, 1913).

Francisque Michel, Tristan, recueil de ce qui reste des poèmes relatifs
   a ses aventures composés en françois, en anglo-normand et en
   grec dans les XII. et XIII. siècles (London, 3 vols., 1835—9).

Le roman de Tristan par Thomas, poème du XIIe siècle publié par
   Joseph Bédier (2 vols. Paris, 1903—1905). Société des Anciens
   Textes Français. Cp. review by W. Golther, LB, XXVIII, 61 ff.
   (1907).

Le roman de Tristan par Béroul et un anonyme publié par Ernest Muret (Paris, 1903) SATF.

Béroul: Le roman de Tristan, poème du XIIe siècle édité par E. Muret (Paris, 1913). Les Classiques Français au Moyen Age.

Les deux poèmes de La Folie Tristan publiés par Joseph Bédier (Paris, 1907). SATF.

Eilhart von Oberge, herausgegeben von Franz Lichtenstein: QF, XIX (Strassburg and London, 1877).

H. Degering: Neue Funde aus dem zwölften Jahrhundert: ein bruchstück der urfassung von Eilharts Tristrant, PBB, XLI, 513 ff. (1916).

Gottfried's von Strassburg *Tristan,* edited by Reinhold Bechstein (third edition, Leipzig, 1890), by W. Golther (*ibid.* 1889), by Karl Marold (*ibid.* 1906 — text only)[9].

Eugen Kölbing, Die nordische und die englische Version der Tristan-Sage (2 Parts, Heilbronn, 1878—1882).

Saga af Tristram ok Isönd samt Möttuls Saga (edited by G. Brynjulfson). Copenhagen, 1878.

E. Kölbing, Tristrams Saga ok Isondar (Heilbronn, 1878).

G. P. McNeill: Sir Tristrem (Edinburgh, 1886). Scottish Text Society.

J. Loth, L'"Ystoria Trystan" et la question des archetypes des romans de la Table Ronde, Académie des Inscriptions et Belles-Lettres: Comptes Rendus des Séances de l'Année 1913. Bulletin de Mars-Avril.

— L'Ystoria Tristan et la question des archetypes, *Revue Celtique,* XXXIV, 365 ff. (1913).

T. P. Cross, A Welsh Tristan Episode, [University of North Carolina] *Studies in Philology,* XVII, 93 ff. (1920).

J. H. Lloyd, O. J. Bergin and G. Schoepperle, The Reproach of Diarmaid, *Revue Celtique,* XXXIII, 41 ff. (1912).

— The Death of Diarmaid, *ibid.* 157 ff.

J. Bédier: Roman de Tristan et Iseut, traduit et restauré (Paris, 1900, and often since).

Tristan und Isolde von Gottfried von Strassburg, neu bearbeitet von Wilhelm Hertz (fifth edition. Stuttgart and Berlin, 1907).

Fritz Vetter, La légende de Tristran d'après le poème français de Thomas et les versions principales qui s'y rattachent (Marburg, 1882). Marburg diss.

---

[9] For older editions of Gottfried and literature of the subject, cp. Golther's *Tristan und Isolde,* p. 165, note 1. For a good bibliography of Gottfried, cp. Bruno Dittrich's *Die Darstellung der Gestalten in Gottfrieds Tristan,* pp. V ff., Greifswald diss. 1914.

A Select Bibliography of Arthurian Critical Literature 395

W. Soederhjelm, Sur l'identité du Thomas auteur de Tristan et du
Thomas auteur de Horn, *Romania*, XV, 575 ff. (1886).

Francesco Novati, Un nuovo ed un vecchio frammento del *Tristran*
di Tommaso, *Studj di filologia romanza*, II, 390 ff. (1887).

L. Foulet, Thomas and Marie in their relation to the conteurs, MLN,
XXIII, 205 ff. (1908).

S. Singer, Thomas Tristan und Benoit de Saint Maure, *Zs. f. rom.
Ph.*, XXXIII, 729 ff. (1909).

A. Hilka, Der Tristanroman des Thomas und die Disciplina Clericalis,
Zs. f. frz. Spr. u. Litt., XLV¹, 38 ff. (1917).

R. S. Loomis, Tristram and the House of Anjou, MLR, XVII, 24 ff.
(1922).

J. Knieschek, Der čecische Tristram und Eilhart von Oberge, Sitzungsberichte der Wiener Akademie der Wissenschaften, Philos.-histo-
rische Klasse, Vol. 101, pp. 319 ff. (1882).

— Der čechische Tristram und seine deutschen Vorlagen, Mitteilungen des Vereins für Geschichte der Deutschen in Böhmen
XXII, 226 ff. (1884).

— Der tschechische Tristram (German translation), *Zs. f. d. A.*, XVI,
261 ff. (1884).

J. Bédier, La mort de Tristan et Iseut, d'après le m. fr. 103 de la
Bibliothèque nationale comparé au poème allemand d'Eilhart
d'Oberg. *Romania*, XV, 481 ff. (1886).

E. Muret, Eilhart d'Oberg et sa source française, *Romania*, XVI,
288 ff. (1887).

G. Huet, Sur un episode du Tristan d'Eilhart d'Oberge, *Romania*,
XXXVI, 50 ff. (1907).

E. Gierach, Zur Sprache von Eilharts Tristrant, Prager *Deutsche
Studien*, IV (1908).

A. Bossert, Tristan et Iseult, poème de Gotfrit de Strasbourg comparé
à d'autres poèmes sur le meme sujet. Paris thesis (Paris, 1865).

— La légende chevaleresque de Tristan et Iseult: essai de littérature
comparée (Paris, 1902).

Richard Heinzel, Gottfrieds von Strassburg Tristan und seine Quelle,
Zs. f. d. A., XIV, 272 ff. (1869).

F. Piquet, L'originalité de Gottfried de Strasbourg dans son poème
de *Tristan et Isolde:* étude de littérature comparée: Travaux et
Mémoires de l'Université de Lille. Nouvelle Série, I, *Droit-
Lettres* — Fascicule 5 (Lille, 1905).

W. Lutoslawski, Les Folies de Tristan, *Romania*, XV, 511 ff. (1886).

H. Morf: Le Folie Tristan du ms. de Berne, *ibid.*, pp. 558 ff.

E. Hoepffner, Das Verhältniss der Berner *Folie Tristan* zu Berols
Tristandichtung, *Zs. f. rom. Ph.*, XXXIX, 62 ff. (1917).

E. Hoepffner, Die Berner und die Oxforder Folie, *ibid.*, **XXXIX**, 551 ff. (1918), 672 ff. (1919).

— Die Folie Tristan und die Odyssee, *ibid.*, **XL**, 232 ff. (1919).

G. Paris, Note sur les romans relatifs à Tristan, *Romania*, **XV**, 597 f. (1886).

—— Tristan et Iseut, *Revue de Paris*, April 15, 1894.

—— Cliges, *Journal des Savants*, June, 1902.

W. Golther, Die Sage von Tristan und Isolde (Munich, 1887).

— Zur Tristansage, *Zs. f. rom. Ph.*, **XII**, 348 ff. (1888).

— Die Jungfrau mit den goldenen Haaren: Studien zur Literaturgeschichte, M. Bernays gewidmet (Leipzig, 1893).

— Bemerkungen zur Sage und Dichtung von Tristan und Isolde, *Zs. f. frz. Spr. u. Litt.*, **XXII**[1], 1 ff. (1900).

— Tristan und Isolde in den Dichtungen des Mittelalters und der Neuzeit (Leipzig, 1907).

— review by E. Muret, *Zs. f. frz. Spr. u. Litt.*, **XXXVII**[2], 167 ff. (1911).

W. Röttiger, Der heutige Stand der Tristanforschung. Programm des Wilhelm-Gymnasiums zu Hamburg (Hamburg, 1897).

Max Deutschbein, Studien zur Sagengeschichte Englands. I, Wikingersagen (Cöthen, 1906).

Jakob Kelemina, Untersuchungen zur Tristansage (Leipzig, 1910).

R. Zenker, Die Tristansage und das persische Epos von Wis und Ramin, *Romanische Forschungen*, **XXIX**, 321 ff. (Erlangen, 1911).

J. Loth, Contributions à l'étude des romans de la Table Ronde (Paris, 1912), made up of articles (most of them on the *Tristan* legend) which originally appeared in the *Revue Celtique*, **XXX**, 270 ff. (1909), **XXXII**, 296 ff., 407 ff., 421 ff. (1911), **XXXIII**, 249 ff., 258 ff., 403 ff. (1912). — For a valuable review of Loth's book, cp. A. Smirnov, *Romania*, **XLIII**, 121 ff. (1914). — After the publication of his volume, Loth continued the *Contributions* in the *Revue Celtique*, **XXXIV**, 365 ff. (1913), **XXXVII**, 317 ff. (1917—9).

Gertrude Schoepperle: Tristan and Isolt, a Study of the Sources of the Romance. New York University, Ottendorfer Memorial Series of Germanic Monographs, No. 4 (2 vols. Frankfurt a. M. and London, 1913).

— reviews by F. Lot, *Romania*, **XLIII**, 126 ff. (1914), W. Golther, *Deutsche Literaturzeitung*, **XXXV**, 670 ff. (1914), W. A. Nitze, JEGcPh., **XIII**, 444 ff. (1914), and J. D. Bruce, MLN, **XXIX**, 213 ff. (1914).

F. M. Warren, Tristan on the Continent before 1066, MLN, **XXIV**, 37 f. (1909).

Gertrude Schoepperle, The love-potion in *Tristan and Isolt, Romania,*
XXXIX, 277 ff. (1910).
— The Island Combat in *Tristan,* Radcliffe College Monographs,
no. 15, pp. 27 ff. (1910).
— Isolde Weisshand am Sterbebette Tristans, *Zs. f. deutsche Philo-
logie,* XLIII. 453 ff. (1911).
E. Brugger, Zum Tristan-Roman, *Archiv für das Studium der neueren
Sprachen,* CXXIX., 134 ff., 375 ff. (1912), CXXX, 117 ff.
(1913).
J. J. Meyer, Isoldes Gottesurteil in seiner erotischen Bedeutung (Berlin,
1914).
　For the bibliography of allusions to Tristan and Iseult in
mediaeval literature and of the use of their story in the deco-
rative arts, cp. I, 163, note 13, above.
L. Sudre, Les allusions à la légende de Tristan dans la littérature du
moyen age, *Romania,* XV, 534 ff. (1886).
C. Appel: Tristan bei Cercamon? *Zs. f. rom. Ph.,* XLI, 219 ff. (1921).
J. L. Deister, Bernart de Ventadour's Reference to the Tristan Story,
MPh., XIX, 278 ff. (1922).

W. Foerster, Der Karrenritter (Lancelot) und das Wilhelmsleben
(Guillaume d'Angleterre) von Christian von Troyes (Halle, 1899).
— review by W. Golther, *Zs. f. frz. Spr. u. Litt.,* XXII², 1 ff.
(1900).
— Introduction to Foerster's Chrétien *Wörterbuch* (Halle, 1914).
Ulrich von Zatzikhoven's *Lanzelet,* edited by K. A. Hahn (Frankfurt
a. M. 1845).
H. O. Sommer, The Prose *Lancelot:* Vols. III (1910), IV (1911),
V (1912), of *The Vulgate Version of the Arthurian Romances*
(Washington, D. C.).
W. A. Nitze, *San et matiere* dans les oeuvres de Chrétien de Troyes,
Romania, XLIV, 14 ff. (1915).
Paul Märtens, Zur Lanzelotsage, Boehmer's *Romanische Studien,*
557 ff. (1880).
G. Paris, Études sur les romans de la Table Ronde: Lancelot du Lac,
Romania, X, 465 ff. (1881), XII, 459 ff. (1883).
J. Rhys, Studies in the Arthurian Legend (Oxford, 1891).
J. L. Weston, The Legend of Sir Lancelot du Lac (London, 1901).
— review by W. W. Greg, *Folk-Lore,* XII, 486 ff. (1901).
　For articles concerning Melwas, Cp. I, 197, note 11, above.
A. C. L. Brown, The Grail and the English Sir Perceval, MPh. XVI,
559 ff. (1919), XVII, 361 ff. (1919) — discusses the *Lanzelet,*
also.

R. Thurneysen, Zu Wilhelm von Malmesbury, *Zs. f. rom. Ph.*, XX, 316 ff. (1896).

F. Lot, Glastonbury et Avalon, *Romania*, XXVII, 529 ff. (1898).

— Mélanges d'Histoire Bretonne (Paris, 1907).

W. W. Newell, William of Malmesbury on the Antiquity of Glastonbury, PMLA, XVIII, 459 ff. (1903).

E. Brugger, Beiträge zur Erklärung der arthurischen Geographie: II, Gorre, *Zs. f. frz. Spr. u. Litt.*, XXVIII[1], 1 ff. (1905).

Laura Hibbard, The Sword Bridge of Chrétien de Troyes and its Celtic Original, RR, IV, 166 ff. (1913).

J. D. Bruce, Human Automata in Classical Tradition and Mediaeval Romance, MPh., X, 511 ff. (1913).

H. R. Patch, Some Elements in Mediaeval Descriptions of the Otherworld, PMLA, XXXIII, 601 ff. (1918).

M. B. Ogle: The Perilous Bridge and Human Automata, MLN, XXXV, 129 ff. (1920).

Part II (The Holy Grail)

Francisque Michel, Le Roman du Saint Graal (Bordeaux, 1841) — contains Robert de Boron's *Joseph* and unfinished *Merlin*. Michel's edition was reprinted by the Comte de Douhet in Abbé Migne's *Dictionnaire des légendes du christianisme*, cols. 454 ff. (Paris, 1855) and by F. J. Furnivall as an appendix to Vol. I of his *Seynt Graal or Sank Ryal* (2 vols. London, 1861—3), printed for the Roxburghe Club.

Ch. Potvin, Perceval le Gallois ou le Conte du Graal (6 vols., Mons, 1866—1871).

G. Baist, Crestiens von Troyes Contes del Graal (Percevaus li galois): Abdruck der Handschrift Paris, français, 794, mit Anmerkungen und Glossar (Freiburg i. B.). Undated, but issued first in 1909 and then in 1912. On the numerous errors of the first issue see R. Weeks's review, RR. II, 101 ff. (1911).

E. Hucher, Le Petit Saint Graal en prose on Joseph D'Arimathie in *Le Saint Graal*, I, 209 ff., 277 ff. (3 vols. Le Mans and Paris, 1875—8) — from two different MSS.

Georg Weidner, Der Prosaroman von Joseph von Aramathia (Oppeln, 1881) — another edition of the prose version of Robert de Boron's *Joseph*.

For Modern French prose paraphrases of Robert's *Joseph.*, cp. P. Paris, RTR, I, 123 ff. (Paris, 1868) and E. Hucher, *op. cit.*, I, 156 ff. (Le Mans and Paris, 1875).

For bibliography of the prose Grail-romances — Estoire del Saint
Graal, Queste del Saint Graal, Didot-Perceval, Perlesvaus, etc.,
— cp. pp. 406ff., below [10]

J. B. B. Roquefort, Dictionnaire de la langue romane (Paris, 1808)
— article, *Graal.*

Le Roux de Lincy, Essai sur l'abbaye de Fécamp (Rouen, 1840).

F. Zarncke, Zur Geschichte der Gralsage, PBB. III, 327 ff. (1876).
Adolph Birch-Hirschfeld, Die Sage vom Gral, ihre Entwicklung und
dichterische Ausbildung in Frankreich und Deutschland im 12.
und 13. Jahrhundert (Leipzig, 1877).

E. Martin, Zur Gralsage (Strassburg, 1880). QF, XLVII.

G. Paris, Perceval et la légende du Saint Gral: Société Historique et
Cercle Saint-Simon, Bulletin, no. 2 (Paris, 1883).

R. Heinzel, Über die französischen Gralromane, *Denkschriften* of the
Vienna Academy, *Philos.-Hist. Klasse*, Vol. XL (Vienna, 1891).

G. Baist, Arthur und der Gral, *Zs. f. rom. Ph.*, XIX, 326 ff. (1895),
XX, 320 f. (1896).

— Zu Robert de Boron, *ibid.*, XXXII, 231 (1908).

— Parzival und der Gral (Freiburg i. B., 1909): Prorektoratsrede.

— review of the preceding by A. Nutt, *The Academy*, May 7, 1910.

R. Thurneysen, Zu William von Malmesbury, *Zs. f. rom. Ph.*, XX,
316 ff. (1896).

Edward Wechssler, Die Sage vom heiligen Gral in ihrer Entwicklung
bis auf Richard Wagner's Parsifal (Halle, (1898). Cp. J. F.
D. Blöte's review *Zs. f. d. A.*, Anzeiger, XLIII, 350ff.

— Untersuchungen zu den Graalromanen, *Zs. f. rom. Ph.*, XXIII,
135 ff. (1899).

W. W. Newell, The Legend of the Holy Grail and the Perceval of
Crestien of Troyes (Cambridge, Mass., 1902) — reprint of articles,
originally published in the *Journal of American Folk-Lore*, X,
117 ff. 299 ff. (1897).

F. Lot, Glastonbury et Avalon, *Romania*, XXVII, 529 ff. (1898).

— Mélanges d'Histoire Bretonne, pp. 277 ff. (Paris, 1907).

W. W. Newell, William of Malmesbury on the Antiquity of Glastonbury, PMLA, XVIII, 459 ff. (1903).

Willy Staerck, Über den Ursprung der Grallegende (Tübingen, 1903).

— review by Konrad Burdach, *Deutsche Literaturzeitung*, XXIV,
3050 ff. (Dec. 12, 1903).

Arthur Edward Waite, The Hidden Church of the Holy Grail (London,
1909) — a fantastic book.

----

[10] I purposely omit from the above list, as destitute of value, various
writings on the Grail, such as those of Sebastian Evans, J. S. Tunison,
G. Wardle, and others.

Rose J. Peebles, The Legend of Longinus: Bryn Mawr College Mono-
graph Series, IX (1911).
— review by A. C. L. Brown, MLN, XXVIII, 28 ff. (1913).
G. B. Woods, A Reclassification of the Perceval Romances, PMLA,
XXVII, 524 ff. (1912).
W. Foerster, Chrétien *Wörterbuch* (Halle, 1914).
Lizette Andrews Fisher, The Mystic Vision in the Grail Legend and
in the Divine Comedy: Columbia Studies in English and Comparative Literature (New York, 1917).
— review by W. A. Nitze and E. H. Wilkins, MPh., XVI, 433 ff
(1918).

Alfred Nutt, The Aryan Expulsion — and Return-Formula, *Folk-Lore
Record*, IV, 1 ff. (1881).
— Studies on the Legend of the Holy Grail, with especial reference
to the hypothesis of its Celtic Origin (London, 1888).
— review of the preceding by G. Paris, *Romania*, XVIII, 588 ff.
(1889), and by H. Zimmer, *Göttingische Gelehrte Anzeigen*,
June 10, 1890.
— Les derniers travaux allemands sur la légende du Saint Graal,
Revue Celtique, XII, 181 ff. (1891).
— The Legends of the Holy Grail: Popular Studies in Mythology,
Romance and Folklore, no. 14 (London, 1902).
— Recent Grail Literature, *The Academy*, May 7, 1910.
A. C. L. Brown, Balin and the Dolorous Stroke, MPh., VII, 203 ff. (1909).
— The Bleeding Lance, PMLA, XXV, 1 ff. (1910).
— Notes on Celtic Cauldrons of Plenty and the Land-Beneath-the-
Waves, *Kittredge Anniversary Papers* 235 ff. (Boston and
London, 1913).
— From Cauldron of Plenty to Grail, MPh., XIV, 385 ff. (1916).
Kuno Meyer, An Old Irish Parallel to the Motive of the Bleeding
Lance, *Eriu*, VI, 156 f. (1912).
R. B. Pace, Death of the Red Knight in the Story of Perceval, MLN,
XXXI, 53 ff. (1916).
— *Sir Perceval* and the *Boyish Exploits* of Finn, PMLA, XXXII,
598 ff. (1917).
Esther C. Dunn, The Drawbridge of the Grail Castle, MLN, XXXIII,
399 ff. (1918).
J. L. Weston, Sir Gawain at the Grail Castle (London, 1903):
Arthurian Romances unrepresented in Malory's "Morte D'Arthur",
No. 6.
— Wauchier de Denain and Bleheris (Bledhericus), *Romania*, XXXIV,
100 ff. (1905).

J. L. Weston, The Legend of Sir Perceval (2 vols. London, 1906—9): Grimm Library, No. 6.

— reviews of the preceding: of Vol. I, by W. Golther, *Zs. f. vergleich. Literaturgeschichte,* XVIII, 135 ff., of Vol. II, by F. Lot, *Bibliothèque d'École des Chartes,* LXX, 566 ff. (1909), and of both by E. Brugger, *Zs. f. frz. Spr. u. Litt.,* XXXI², 122 ff. (1907), XXXVI², 31 ff. (1910), and by J. F. D. Blöte, *Zs. f. d. A., Anzeiger,* XXXII, 24 ff. (1908), XXXIV, 242 ff. (1910).

— Sir Gawain and the Lady of Lys (London, 1907): same series as first title, No. 7.

— The Grail and the Rites of Adonis, *Folk-Lore,* XVIII, 283 ff. (1907).

— The Quest of the Holy Grail (London, 1913).

— From Ritual to Romance (Cambridge, 1920).

Edward Owen, A note on the identification of Bleheris, *Revue Celtique,* XXXII, 5 ff. (1911).

W. J. Gruffyd, Bledhericus, Bleddri, Breri, *ibid.,* XXXIII, 180 ff. (1912).

W. A. Nitze, Glastonbury and the Holy Grail, MPh., I, 247 ff. (1903).

— The Fisher King in the Grail Romances, PMLA, XXIV, 365 ff. (1909).

— The Castle of the Grail — an Irish Analogue, *Studies in Honor of A. Marshall Elliott,* I, 19 ff. (2 vols. Baltimore, undated).

— The Sister's Son and the Conte del Graal, MPh., IX, 291 ff. (1912).

— Concerning the Word *Graal, Greal,* MPh., XIII, 681 ff. (1916).

— The Glastonbury Passages in the *Perlesvaus,* [Univ. of North Carolina] *Studies in Philology,* XV, 7 ff. (1918).

Hugo Waitz, Die Fortsetzungen von Chrestiens *Perceval la Gallois* nach den Pariser Handschriften (Strassburg, 1890).

For Miss Weston on Wauchier (and Pseudo-Wauchier) see list of her Grail writings, above.

Paul Meyer, Wauchier de Denain, *Histoire littéraire de la France,* XXXIII, 258 ff. (1906).

A. Rochat, Über einen bisher unbekannten Percheval li Gallois (Zürich, 1855).

F. Kraus, Über Girbert de Montreuil und seine Werke (Erlangen, 1897). Würzburg diss.

M. Wilmette, Gerbert de Montreuil et les écrits qui lui sont attribués, Académie Royale de Belgique: *Bulletin de la Classe des Lettres,* etc. pp. 166 ff. (1900).

J. Bédier and J. L. Weston, Tristan Menestrel: extrait de la continuation de Perceval par Gerbert, *Romania,* XXXV, 497 ff. (1906).

James Orchard Halliwell, The Thornton Romances: the Early English
Metrical Romances of Perceval, Isumbras, Eglamour, and Degrevant
(London, 1844). Camden Society.

J. Campion and F. Holthausen, Sir Perceval of Gales (Heidelberg and
New York, 1913): Alt- und Mittelenglische Texte, herausgegeben
von L. Morsbach und F. Holthausen B[an]d 5.

W. Golther, Chrestiens conte del graal in seinem Verhältnis zum
wälschen Peredur und zum englischen Perceval, *Sitzungsberichte*
of the Bavarian (Munich) Academy, *Philos.-hist. Klasse*, II,
174 ff. (1890).

Paul Steinbach, Über den Einfluss des Crestien de Troies auf die altenglische Literatur. Leipzig diss. 1885.

Carsten Strucks, Der junge Parzival in Wolframs von Eschenbach
"Parzival", Crestien's von Troyes "conte del gral", im englischen
"Syr Percyvelle" und italienischen "Carduino" (Borna-Leipzig,
1910). Münster diss.

R. H. Griffith, Sir Perceval of Galles (Chicago, 1911). Chicago thesis.
— reviews of the preceding by J. D. Bruce, RR, IV, 125 ff. (1913),
and by E. Brugger, *Zs. f. frz. Spr. u. Litt*, XLIV², 137 ff.
(1917).

A. C. L. Brown, The Grail and the English Sir Perceval, MPh., XVI,
553 ff. (1919), XVII, 361 ff. (1919), XVIII, 661 ff. (1921).

Wolfram's *Parzival* is, of course. discussed in all histories of German
literature (Scherer's, etc.) — moreover, in all the leading treatises
on the Grail which I have already listed (Birch-Hirschfeld's, Nutt's,
Wechsslers', Miss Weston's, etc.). Cp. too, the *Perceval* studies
(listed above) by Miss Weston, Griffith and A. C. L. Brown. —
There are special Wolfram bibliographies by G. Bötticher, Die
Wolfram-Literatur seit Lachmann, mit kritischen Anmerkungen
(Berlin, 1880), and by F. Panzer, Bibliographie zu W. von E.
(Munich, 1896). For a good select bibliography on the subject,
cp. E. Wechssler, Die Sage vom heiligen Gral, pp. 193 ff. (Halle,
1898).

Wolfram's von Eschenbach Parzival und Titurel, herausgegeben von
Karl Bartsch (3 parts, Leipzig, 1875 – 7): Franz Pfeiffer's
Deutsche Classiker des Mittelalters, IX, X, XI.

— the same, herausgegeben und erklärt von Ernst Martin (2 parts,
Halle, 1900—1903)¹¹: Germanistische Handbibliothek, begründet
von Julius Zacher, IX, 1. 2.

---

¹¹ An anastatic reproduction of Part I (text) was, also, issued at Halle
in 1920. For older editions of Wolfram's works — especially, K. Lachmann's
(first published in 1833) — cp. Martin, I, pp. 1 ff.

Wolfram's von Eschenbach the same, herausgegeben von A. Leitzmann (Halle, 1902, et seq.).

A. von Siegenfeld, Das Landeswappen Steiermarks (Graz, 1901).

— review of the same by A. Schönbach, *Zs. f. d. A., Anzeiger,* XXVII, 149 ff. (1903).

Johann Baptist Kurz, Heimat und Geschlecht Wolframs von Eschenbach (Ansbach, 1916).

R. Lück, Ueber die Abfassungszeit des Parzival. Halle diss. 1878.

John Orr, Les oeuvres de Guiot de Provins (Manchester, 1915): Publications de l'Université de Manchester: Série française, No. I.

G. A. Heinrich, Le Parcival de Wolfram d'Eschenbach et la légende du Saint-Graal (Paris, 1855).

San Marte (A. Schulz), Ueber die Eigennamen im Parzival des Wolfram von Eschenbach, *Germania,* II, 385 ff. (1857).

— Wolfram von Eschenbach und Guiot von Provins, *ibid.,* III, 445 ff. (1858).

— Parzivalstudien I—III (Halle, 1861—62).

— Sein oder Nichtsein des Guiot von Provence, *Zs. f. deutsche Ph.,* XV, 385 ff. (1883).

— Zur Gral- und Arthursage, *ibid.,* XVI, 129 ff. (1884).

K. Bartsch, Die Eigennamen in Wolframs Parzival und Titurel, *Germanistische Studien,* II, 114 ff. (Vienna, 1875).

Alfred Rochat, Wolfram von Eschenbach und Chretiens de Troyes, *Germania,* III, 81 ff. (1858).

T. Urbach, Über den Stand der Frage nach den Quellen des Parzival. Program (Zwickau, 1872).

Karl Simrock, Parcival und Titurel: Rittergedichte von W. von Eschenbach, übersetzt und erläutert (fifth ed., Stuttgart, 1876).

F. Zarncke, Zur Geschichte der Gralsage, PBB, III, 304 ff. (1876).

— Der Graltempel, *Abhandlungen* of the Royal Saxon Academy of Sciences, V, 477.

G. Bötticher, Zur Frage nach der Quelle des Parzival, *Zs. f. deutsche Ph.,* XIII, 385 ff. (1882).

Otto Küpp, Die unmittelbaren Quellen des Parzival von Wolfram von Eschenbach, *ibid.,* XVII, 1 ff. (1885).

G. Bötticher, Das Hohelied vom Rittertum, eine Beleuchtung des Parzival nach Wolframs eigenen Andeutungen (Berlin, 1886).

W. Hertz, Sage vom Parzival und dem Gral (Breslau, 1892).

Paul Hagen, Parzivalstudien, *Germania,* XXXVII. 74 ff. (1892).

— Der Gral (Strassburg, 1900), QF, LXXXV.

— Untersuchungen über Kiot, *Zs. f. d. A.,* XLV, 187 ff. (1901).

— Wolfram und Kiot, *Zs. f. deutsche Ph.,* XXXVIII, 198 ff. (1906).

Cp. E. Brugger's review of this article, *Archiv f. d. St. der n. Spr.* CXVIII, 230 ff. (1907).

R. Heinzel, Über Wolframs von Eschenbach Parzival, *Sitzungsberichte* of the Vienna Academy, 1894. Philos.-hist. Classe, Band 130.

J. L. Weston, Parzival, a Knightly Epic (London, 1894).

— The Legends of the Wagner Drama (*ibid.*, 1896).

Ludwig Grimm, Wolfram von Eschenbach und die Zeitgenossen, I. Teil. Zur Entstehung des Parzival. Leipzig diss. 1897.

J. Lichtenstein, Zur Parzivalfrage, PBB, XXII, 1 ff. (1897).

W. Hertz, Parzival von Wolfram von Eschenbach, neu bearbeitet (second ed. Stuttgart, 1898).

E. Wechssler, Zur Beantwortung der Frage nach den Quellen von Wolframs Parzival, Festgabe für Eduard Sievers, pp. 237 ff. (Halle, 1896).

— Die Sage vom heiligen Gral (*ibid.*, 1898).

Albert Nolte, Der Eingang des Parzival, Marburg diss., 1899.

— Die Composition der Trevrezent-Scenen, *Zs. f. d. A.*, XLIV, 241 ff. (1900).

S. Singer, Über die Quelle von Wolframs Parzival, *Zs. f. d. A.*, XLIV, 321 ff. (1900).

— Wolframs Stil und der Stoff des Parzival, *Sitzungsberichte* of the Vienna Academy of Sciences, 1918, — *Philos.-histor. Classe,* Band 180, Abhandlung 4.

A. Leitzmann, Untersuchungen über Wolframs Titurel, PBB, XXVI, 93 ff. (1901).

J. L. Weston, The Romance of Morien (London and New York, 1901)[12].

A. B. Faust, The Ninth Book of Wolframs Parzival, MPh., I, 275 ff. (1903).

J. F. D. Blöte, Zum lapsit exilis, *Zs. f. d. A.*, XLVII, 101 ff. (1903).

E. Brugger, Alain de Gomeret, ein Beitrag zur arthurischen Namenforschung: Sonderabdruck aus . . . Festgabe für Heinrich Morf (Halle, 1905).

F. Wilhelm, Ueber fabulistische Quellenangaben, PBB, XXXIII, 286 ff. (1908).

W. Golther, Parzival und der Gral in deutscher Sage des Mittelalters und der Neuzeit: Universitätsvortrag, Rostock, 1910: Zur deutschen Sage und Dichtung, pp. 154 ff. (Leipzig, 1911).

P. S. Barto, The Schwanritter-Sceaf Myth in Perceval le Gallois ou le Conte du Graal, JEGcPh., XIX, 190 ff. (1920).

For bibliography of the Swan-Knight (Lohengrin) story, cp. G. Paris, *Manuel*[5], p. 289, J. F. D. Blöte, Das Aufkommen des clevischen

---

[12] For further discussions of Morien cp. I, 331, note 33; II, 304, above.

Schwanritters, *Zs. f. d. A.*, XLII, 1 ff. (1898), W. Golther, *Romanische Forschungen*, II; G. Poisson, L'origine celtique de la légende de Lohengrin, *Revue Celtique*, XXXIV, 182 ff. (1913).

J. Loth, *Peredur* in *Les Mabinogion*[1], II[2], 47 ff. (1913).

J. G. Evans, The White Book Mabinogion (Pwllheli, 1907).

W. Golther, Chrestiens conte del graal in seinem Verhältnis zum wälschen Peredur und zum englischen Sir Perceval: *Sitzungsberichte* of the Munich Academy, 1890, *philos.-philolog. und historische Classe*, I, 174 ff.

J. Rhys, Studies in the Arthurian Legend (Oxford, 1891).

Mary R. Williams, Essai sur la composition du roman gallois de Peredur, Paris thesis, 1909.

— review of the preceding by R. Thurneysen, *Zs. f. celt. Ph.*, VIII, 185 ff. (1912).

M. Goldschmidt, Sone de Nausay: Bibliothek des Litterarischen Vereins in Stuttgart, CCXVI (Tübingen, 1899).

S. Singer, Über die Quelle von Wolframs Parzival, *Zs. f. d. A.*, XLIV, 321 ff. (1900).

K. Nyrop, Sone de Nansai et la Norvège, *Romania*, XXXV, 555 ff. (1906).

J. L. Weston, Notes on the Grail Romances, *Romania*, XLIII, 403 ff. (1914).

G. H. F. Scholl: Diu Crône: Bibliothek des Litterarischen Vereins in Stuttgart, XXVII (Stuttgart, 1852).

A. N. Wesselofsky, Der Stein Alatyr in den Localsagen Palästinas und der Legende vom Gral, *Archiv für slavische Philologie*, VI, 33 ff. (1882).

— Zur Frage über die Heimath der Legende vom heiligen Gral, *ibid.*, XXIII, 321 ff. (1901).

M. Gaster, The Legend of the Holy Grail, *Folk-Lore*, II, 50 ff., 198 ff. (1891), including note appended by A. Nutt to Gaster's second article.

Paul Hagen, Der Gral (Strassburg, 1900), QF No. 85.

Willy Staerk, Über den Ursprung der Gral-Legende (Tübingen and Leipzig, 1903).

Theodor Sterzenbach, Ursprung und Entwickelung der Sage vom heiligen Gral. Münster diss. 1908.

Ludwig Emil Iselin, Der morgenländische Ursprung der Grallegende (Halle, 1909).

Leopold von Schroeder, Die Wurzeln der Sage vom heiligen Gral. *Sitzungsberichte* of the Vienna Academy, 1910, *Philos.-histor. Classe*, Band 166, 2. Abhandlung. — For reviews of this work, cp. I, 357 f., notes 4, 5, above.

Victor Junk, Gralsage und Graldichtung des Mittelalters, *ibid.*, Band 168, Abhandlung 4. (1911).

Julius Pokorny, Der Ursprung der Arthursage: Mitteilungen der anthropologischen Gesellschaft in Wien, vol. 39 (1909).

Fra Gaetano da Teresa, Il Catino di Smeraldo Orientale, Gemma consagrata da N. S. Gesù Cristo nell' Ultima Cena degli Azimi, etc. (Genoa, 1726)[13]

Part III (The Prose Romances)

Georg Phillips, Walter Map, ein Beitrag zur Geschichte König Heinrichs von England und des Lebens an seinem Hofe: *Sitzungsberichte* of the Vienna Academy of Sciences. Philos.-histor. Klasse, X, 319 ff. (1853).

H. L. D. Ward, article on Map, Catalogue of the Romances in the Department of Manuscripts in the British Museum, I, 734 ff. (1883).

C. L. Kingsford, article on Map, Dictionary of National Biography.

J. Bardoux, De Walterio Mappio (Paris, 1900).

James Hinton, Walter Map's *De Nugis Curialium*, its plan and composition, PMLA, XXXII, 81 ff. (1917).

Henry Bradley, Notes on Walter Map's *De Nugis Curialium*, English Historical Review, XXXII, 393 ff. (1917).

H. Oskar Sommer, The Vulgate Version of the Arthurian Romances (7 vols. plus Index, The Carnegie Institution, Washington, D. C.). Vol. I, L'Estoire del Saint Graal[14] (1909); Vol. II, L'Estoire de Merlin (1908)[15]; Vols. III (1910), IV (1911), V (1912), Le Livre de Lancelot del Lac; VI, Les Aventures ou La Queste del Saint Graal, La Mort le Roi Artus (1913); VII, Supplement: Le Livre d'Artus (1913); Index of Names and Places to Volumes I—VII (1916).

Der altfranzösische Prosaroman von Lancelot del Lac: Versuch einer kritischen Ausgabe nach allen bekannten Handschriften, by pupils

---

[13] For the various traditions concerning this vessel, cp. I, 374 ff., above.

[14] This romance has often been called — without manuscript authority — the *Grand Saint Graal*.

[15] Both Vols. I and II really appeared in 1910.

of Professor Eduard Wechssler, in the *Marburger Beiträge zur Romanischen Philologie.* The following issues have appeared up to date (Feb. 1922): Heft II (1911): Erste Branche: La Reine as Granz Dolors, edited by G. Brauner; Heft VI (1912): Zweite Branche: Les Enfances Lancelot (1. Teil) by H. Becker; Heft VIII (1912): Zweite Branche: Les Enfances Lancelot (2. Teil), and dritte Branche: La Doloreuse Garde (1. Teil), by H. Bubinger; Heft XIX (1916): Vierte Branche: Galehout, by A. Zimmermann [16].

F. J. Furnivall, Seynt Graal or the Sank Ryal (2 vols. Printed for the Roxburghe Club, London, 1861—3). — The French text here given was reprinted in Vols. 20, 24, 28, 30 of the Publications (Extra Series) of the Early English Text Society.

— La Queste del St. Graal (for the same club, *ibid.,* 1864).

Eugène Hucher, Le Saint Graal ou le Joseph d'Arimathie: Première Branche des Romans de la Table Ronde (3 vols. Le Mans and Paris, 1875—8). In Vol. I are printed Robert de Boron's *Joseph* (prose version) and the *Didot-Perceval,* in Vols. II and III, the *Estoire del Saint Graal (Grand St. Graal)* of the Vulgate cycle.

H. Oskar Sommer, Le Roman de Merlin or the Early History of Arthur (London, 1894).

J. D. Bruce, Mort Artu, an Old French Prose Romance of the XIIIth century, being the Last Division of Lancelot du Lac (Halle, 1910).

Paulin Paris, Les Romans de la Table Ronde (5 vols., Paris, 1868—77).

H. O. Sommer, Le Morte Darthur by Syr Thomas Malory (3 vols., London, 1889—91).

J. D. Bruce, The Middle English Stanzaic Le *Morte Arthur* (Harleian MS. 2252). E. E. T. S., Extra Series, No. 88 (1903).

— The Middle English Metrical Romance Le Morte Arthur (Harleian MS. 2252): Its Sources and its Relation to Sir Thomas Malory's Morte Darthur, *Anglia,* XXXIII, 67 ff. (1900).

Walter De Gray Birch, Li Chantari di Lancelotto (London, 1874).

Paulin Paris, Les manuscrits françois de la Bibliothèque du Roi (7 vols., Paris, 1836—48).

G. Gröber, Grundriss der Romanischen Philologie, Band II, Abt. I, pp. 996 ff. (1902).

P. Paris, Le Saint Graal, *[Estoire],* Romania, I, 457 ff. (1871).

---

[16] For a criticism of the first issue of this edition in which the plan of the whole is set forth, cp. E. Brugger, *Zs. f. frz. Spr. u. Litt.,* XL², 37 ff. (1912).

A. Birch-Hirschfeld, Die Sage vom Gral (Leipzig, 1877).

A. Nutt, Studies on the Legend of the Holy Grail (London, 1888).

J. Rhys, Studies in the Arthurian Legend (Oxford, 1891).

R. Heinzel, Über die französischen Gralromane (Vienna, 1891): *Denk-schriften* of the Vienna Academy of Sciences. *Philos.-hist. Classe.* Band XL.

E. Wechssler, Die Sage vom heiligen Gral (Halle, 1898).

— Untersuchungen zu den Graalromanen, *Zs. f. rom. Ph.,* XXIII, 135 ff. (1899).

J. L. Weston, The Legend of Sir Lancelot du Lac (London, 1901): Grimm Library, No. 12.

— The Legend of Sir Perceval (2 vols. *ibid.,* 1906—9): Grimm Library, .Nos. 17 and 19.

E. Brugger, L'Enserrement Merlin, *Zs. f. frz. Spr. u. Litt.* XXIX[1], 56 ff. (1906), XXX[1], 169 ff. (1906), XXXI[1], 239 ff. (1907), XXXIII[1], 145 ff. (1908), XXXIV[1], 99 ff. (1909), XXXV[1], 1 ff. (1909).

J. D. Bruce, Arthuriana, RR, III, 173 ff. (1912).

— The Development of the Mort Arthur Theme in Mediaeval Romance, *ibid.* IV, 403 ff. (1913).

— Pelles, Pellinor, and Pellean in the Old French Arthurian Ro-mances, MPh., XVI, 113 ff., 337 ff. (1918).

— Galahad, Nascien, and Some Other Names in the Grail Romances, MLN, XXXIII, 129 ff. (1918).

— Mordrain, Corbenic, and the Vulgate Grail Romances, *ibid.,* XXXIV, 385 ff. (1919).

— The Composition of the Old French Prose *Lancelot.* RR, IX, 241 ff. 353 ff. (1918), X, 48 ff., 97 ff. (1919).

F. Lot, Étude sur le Lancelot en prose (Paris, 1918): Bibliothèque de l'École des Hautes Etudes. Fascicule 226. — It includes two essays (appendices) at the end by Mme. Lot-Borodine. These have since been reprinted in her volume, *Trois Essais sur le Roman de Lancelot du Lac et la Quête du Saint Graal* (Paris, 1919).

— reviews by J. D. Bruce, RR, X, 377 ff. (1919), and A. Pauphilet, *Romania,* XLV, 521 ff. (1917—1919).

M. Lot-Borodine, Les deux conquérants du Graal: Perceval et Galaad, *Romania,* XLVII, 41 ff. (1921), and in her volume just men-tioned.

Albert Pauphilet, Études sur la Queste del Saint Graal attribuée à Gautier Map (Paris, 1921).

Paul Märtens, Zur Lanzelotsage, Boehmer's *Romanische Studien,* V, 643 ff. (1880).

A Select Bibliography of Arthurian Critical Literature 409

G. Paris, Études sur les romans de la Table Ronde, *Romania*, X, 465 ff. (1881), XII, 459 ff. (1883).

G. Huet, Le Lancelot en prose et *Meraugis de Portlesguez*, *Romania*, XLI, 518 ff. (1912).

E. Freymond, Zum Livre d'Artus, *Zs. f. rom. Ph.*, XVI, 90 ff. (1912).
— Beiträge zur Kenntnis der altfranzösischen Artusromane in Prosa, *Zs. f. frz. Spr. u. Litt.*, XVII¹, 1 ff. (1895).

H. O. Sommer, The Structure of Le Livre d'Artus and its Function in the Evolution of the Arthurian Prose-Romances (London and Paris, 1914).

G. Paris and Jacob Ulrich, Merlin, roman en prose du XIIIᵉ siècle, publié avec la mise en prose du poème de Merlin de Robert de Boron, d'après le manuscrit appartenant à M. Alfred H. Huth (2 vols. Paris, 1886): Société des Anciens Textes Français)

Karl von Reinhardtstoettner, A Historia dos Cavalleiros da Mesa Redonda e da Demanda do Santo Graall (Berlin, 1887).
— review by G. Paris, *Romania*, XVI, 582 ff. (1887).

Adolfo Bonilla y San Martin, Libros de Caballerias: Primera Parte: Ciclo arturico = Ciclo carolingio: pp. 3—162, El Baladro del Sabio Merlin, Primera Parte de la Demanda del Sancto Grial; pp. 163—338, La Demanda del Sancto Grial con los maravillos Fechos de Lanzarote y de Galaz, su Hijo, Segunda Parte de la Demanda del Sancto Grial (Madrid, 1907): Nueva Biblioteca de Autores Españoles.

E. Wechssler, Über die verschiedenen Redaktionen des Robert von Borron zugeschriebenen Graal-Lancelot-Cyklus (Halle, 1895). Habilitationsschrift.

Otto Klob, Beiträge zur Spanischen und Portugiesischen Graal-Literatur, *Zs. f. rom. Ph.*, XXVI, 169 ff. (1902).
— Dois Episodios da Demanda do Santo Graal, *Rivista Lusitana*, VI, 332 ff. (1910).

H. O. Sommer, The Queste of the Holy Grail forming the third part of the trilogy indicated in the *Suite du Merlin*, Huth MS., *Romania*, XXXVI, 369 ff., 543 ff. (1907).
— Galahad and Perceval, MPh., V, 55 ff., 181 ff. (1907), 291 ff. (1908).
— Zur Kritik der altfranzösischen Artus-Romane in Prosa, *Zs. f. rom. Ph.*, XXXII, 327 ff. (1908).
— Die Abenteuer Gawains, Ywains und Le Morholts mit den drei Jungfrauen aus der Trilogie (Demanda) des Pseudo-Robert de Borron (Halle, 1913): *Beihefte zur Zs. f. rom. Ph.*, No. 47.

E. Vettermann, Die Balen-Dichtungen und ihre Quellen (Halle, 1918):
Beihefte zur Zs. f. rom. Ph., No. 60.
A. Pauphilet, La Queste du Saint Graal du MS. Bibl. Nat. Fr. 343,
Romania, XXXVI, 591 ff. (1907).
K. Pietsch, MS. 2—G—5 of the Palace Library at Madrid, MPh.,
XI, 1 ff. (1903).
— Madrid Manuscript of the Spanish Grail Fragments, *ibid.*, XVIII,
147 ff. (1920), 591 ff. (1921).

Editions of the Didot-Perceval: E. Hucher, Le Saint Graal, I, 415 ff.
(La Mans and Paris, 1874) and J. L. Weston, Legend of Sir
Perceval, II, 9 ff. (London, 1909). — Cp. E. Brugger's review
of the latter, *Zs. f. frz. Spr. u. Litt.*, XXXVI², 31 ff. (1910).
Walter Hoffmann, Die Quellen des Didot-Perceval. Halle diss. 1905.
H. O. Sommer, Messire Robert de Borron und der Verfasser des Didot-
Perceval (Halle, 1908): *Beihefte zur Zs. f. rom. Ph.*, No. 17.
— review by E. Brugger, *Zs. f. frz. Spr. u. Litt.*, XXXVI², pp. 7 ff.
(1910).
F. Lot, Nouvelles Études sur le cycle arthurien, *Romania*, XLV,
16 ff. (1917—1919).
Ch. Potvin, Perlesvaus, in Vol. I (Mons, 1866) of his *Perceval le
gallois ou le Conte du Graal.*
Sebastian Evans, The High History of the Holy Grail (2 vols. London,
1898): The Temple Classics.
John Thomas Lister, Perlesvaus, Hatton Manuscript 82, Branch I.
(Menasha, Wis., 1921): University of Chicago thesis.
For the *Perlesvaus* consult the treatises (named above) on the Grail
by Birch-Hirschfeld and Heinzel, Miss Weston's *Sir Lancelot*
and *Sir Perceval* books — also, Brugger's articles, entitled
L'Enserremeut Merlin, in *Zs. f. frz. Spr. u. Litt.*, — parti-
culary, XXIX¹, 77 ff. (1905) — and Sommer's article, "The
Queste of the Holy Grail". *Romania*, XXXVI (1907). Cp.,
besides, on the date of the romance, II, 154, note 24, above.
Robert Williams, Y Seint Greal [Welsh version of 1. the Vulgate
Queste, 2. Perlesvaus] . . . edited with a translation and glos
sary (London, 1876).
E. Wechssler, Handschriften des Perlesvaus, *Zs. f. rom. Ph.*, XX,
80 ff. (1896).
W. A. Nitze, The Old French Grail Romance, Perlesvaus (Baltimore,
1902): Johns Hopkins University diss.
— Glastonbury and the Holy Grail, MPh., I, 247 ff. (1903).
— The Glastonbury Passages in the Perlesvaus. [University of North
Carolina] *Studies in Philology*, XV, 7 ff. (1918).

W. A. Nitze, On the Chronology of the Grail Romances, MPh., XVII, 151 ff. (1919), 605 ff. (1920).

G. Baist, Parzival und der Gral (Freiburg i. B., 1909): Prorektoratsrede.

J. L. Weston, Notes on the Grail Romances, *Romania*, XLIII, 403 ff. (1914).

— The Perlesvaus and the Vengeance Raguidel, *ibid.*, XLVII, 349 ff. (1921).

J. D. Bruce, Arthuriana, RR, III, 173 ff. (1912) — particularly the section. "Arthur's Son, *Lohot*", pp. 179 ff.

— The Development of the Mort Arthur Theme in Mediaeval Romance, *ibid.*, IV, 403 ff. (1913).

G. Huet, Deux personnages arturiens [Lohot and Dodinel le Sauvage], *Romania*, XLIII, 100 ff. (1914).

E. A. Hall, Spenser and Two Old French Grail Romances, PMLA, XXVIII, 539 ff. (1913).

E. Löseth, Tristanromanens gammelfranske prosahaandskrifter. University of Christiania thesis. 1888.

— Le roman en prose de Tristan, le roman de Palamède et la compilation de Rusticien de Pise: analyse critique d'après les manuscrits de Paris (Paris, 1890): Bibliothèque de l'École des Hautes Études.

— Le Tristan et le Palamède des manuscrits français du British Museum (Christiania, 1905): Videnskabs-Selskabets Skrifter, II, Hist.-Filos. Klasse, 1905, No. 4.

John Colin Dunlop: History of Prose Fiction: a New Edition, revised with Notes, Appendices and Index by Henry Wilson (2 vols., London, 1896).

F. Polidori: La Tavola Ritonda o l'istoria di Tristano (2 parts, Bologna, 1864—5).

Ernst Schürhoff, Über den Tristan-Roman des Jean-Maugin. Halle diss. 1909.

J. D. Bruce, A Boccaccio Analogue in the Old French Prose Tristan, RR, I, 384 ff. (1910).

For the bibliography of the only Greek Arthurian romance, cp. II, 295, above.

H. O. Sommer, edition of Malory's *Morte Darthur*, III, 295 ff. (1891).

Ireneo Sanesi, Storia di Merlino (Bergamo, 1898): Biblioteca storica della letteratura, III.

L. A. Paton: Notes on Manuscripts of the *Prophecies de Merlin*, PMLA, XXVIII, 121 ff. (1913).

G. Paris, article on *Le Chevalier du Papegau*, HLF, XXX, 103 ff. (1888).

Ferdinand Heuckenkamp, Le Chevalier du Papegau (Halle, 1896).

F. Saran, Ueber Wirnt von Grafenberg und den Wigalois, PBB, XXI, 253 ff. (1896).

J. D. Bruce, Historia Meriadoci and De Ortu Waluuanii; Two Arthurian Romances of the XIIIth century in Latin Prose (Göttingen and Baltimore, 1913). Hesperia: Schriften zur englischen Philologie, herausgegeben von Hermann Collitz und James W. Bright, Ergänzungsreihe, 2. Heft [17].

Margaret Shove Morris, The Authorship of the *De Ortu Waluuanii* and the *Historia Meriadoci*, PMLA, XXII, 599 ff. (1908).

Paul Meyer, Les Enfances Gauvain: fragments d'un poème perdu, *Romania*, XXXIX, 1 ff. (1910).

Pio Rajna, Le Fonti dell' Orlando Furioso (second edition, Florence, 1900).

Henri Hauvette, Luigi Alamanni (Paris, 1903).

Giulio Bertoni, Nuovi Studi su Matteo Maria Boiardo (Bologna, 1904).

---

[17] For the earlier editions of these romances by the same editor, cp. II, 33, note 1, above.

Index of Critics.

Index of Subject=Matter.

416, 418, 432. — II, 152, 162, 321 (in Vulgate *Merlin*), 324 ff. (in *Lancelot del Lac*)

Claudin, II, 357, 358

Clerk's Tale, Chaucer's, I, 63, 110

Cliges, by Chrétien de Troyes, I, 67, 100, 101 f., 112, 113 ff. (analysis), 116 ff. (as *Anti-Tristan* cp. 205), 155, 193, 211, 212, 220, 247, 248-9, 251, 253, 315, 319

Clinschor, I, 338

Clovis (and variants), I, 405

Colomba, Columba (Saint), I, 6, 131

Comandemenz Ovide, Les, by Chrétien, I, 101-2

Compilation of Rusticiano da Pisa. See *Rusticiano da Pisa*.

Conal(l), I, 83, 89

Conan (of Brittany), I, 140

Conchobar, I, 52, 83, 98, 173

Condwiramurs, Perceval's wife in Wolfram, I, 316, 325, 334

Constant, English king, II, 315

Constantine, Arthur's successor, I, 33, 439, 440

Constantinus, I, 3

Conte de la Charette (= Lancelot) by Chrétien de Troyes, I, 67. See *Lancelot*.

Conte del Brait, I, 460, 474, 476, 477, 479, 480-482 (main discussion), 487

Conte del Graal (= Perceval) by Chrétien and his continuators, I, 67, 219, 229, 292, 308, 342, 399, 410. — II, 73. See *Perceval*.

Conversions of Clovis, Constantine, Edwin, Ethelbert, I, 390

Copper Castle, The, II, 15

Cor, Le, I, 61, 64, 66. — II, 183

Corbenic (= Corbeni, Corbiniacum), I, 393 f., 402, 407 f., 410, 414, 416, 446. — II, 312, 345, 356, 359 (in prose *Lancelot*), 365, 367, 375, 376

Corbie, I, 393 f.

Cornwall, I, 431

Cotovatre, I, 228

Count Ernol(s), II, 366

Count of Nantes, II, 71

Crestien de Troyes (= Chrétien de T.), I, 37. See Chrétien de Troyes

Crestiiens li Gois, I, 302

Cristal et Clarie, II, 287

Cristan (mistaken for Tristan), I, 177

Crône (Krône), Diu, by Heinrich von dem Türlin, I, 88, 124, 206, 207, 346 ff. (main discussion)

Cronica de los nobles cavalleros Tablante de Ricamonte y Tofre, hijo de Donasson, II, 288, 292

Cronos, I, 277

Crudel, II, 311

Cuchulinn's Sick Bed, I, 94, 96. — II, 75

Cuchull(a)in, I, 52, 77, 83, 84, 89, 94, 96, 97, 98, 99, 108, 189, 248, 249, 270. — II, 103

Cundrie, I, 338

Cuneda, I, 200

Cwy, I, 43

Cymbeline, I 19

Dabraida, I, 6

Daguenet, II, 329

Dameisele as Petites Mances, La, I, 229

Danain of Maloaut (Maloanc), II, 24

Dante, I, 106, 417

Daras, I, 485

Date of the Battle of Badon Hill. See Badon Hill.

David, King of Israel, I, 402 f. (ancestor of Galahad, 492. — II, 360

David's Sword, the Grail Sword, I, 375, 384 f., 391. — II, 365-6

De Antiquitate Ecclesiae Glastoniensis, I, 12, 262-267, 356

Death of Cuchullin, I, 77

Death of Diarmaid, The, I, 172, 174

Decameron (Boccaccio's), I, 65

Deirdre, I, 173

De la Queste etc., by René of Anjoù, II, 41

Demanda (Portuguese), I, 424, 460, 461, 469, 470, 471, 472, 474, 477, 480. See, also, *Portuguese Versions of Arthurian Romances*.

Demanda (Spanish), I, 460-2, 469-473, 475, 480, 481. — II, 138. See, also, *Spanish Versions of Arthurian Romances*.

Demetia, I, 134

Denis Pyramus, I, 66

De Hugis Curialium, by Walter Map. I, 370 f.

Deorham, battle of, II, 48, 49

De Ortu Waluuanii, I, 441. — II, 33-38 (main discussion), 57, 157

Bibliographischer Nachtrag.

Auf Wunsch des Verlages, der das treffliche Werk des allzufrüh der Artus- und Gralforschung entrissenen James Douglas Bruce infolge der Zeitumstände nur in einem unveränderten Abdruck aufs neue der Fachwelt unterbreiten kann, habe ich es unternommen, zu dem bibliographischen Teile die wichtigsten Nachträge zu liefern, die sich etwa bis 1927 erstrecken. Es konnte nicht in unserer Absicht liegen, durch Verarbeitung dieses Stoffes etwa in Form von kurzen Exkursen Bruce's Ausführungen zu ergänzen oder gar in einigen Punkten zu bessern. Da alles bei ihm nach einem bestimmten Plane ausgearbeitet ist, trägt es eben den Charakter seiner Eigenart. Auch wäre eine solche Aufgabe fast eine Versuchung gewesen, größere Teile von einem anderen Standpunkte aus durchzuarbeiten und so der Absicht des Verfassers entgegen zu wirken. Bruce's Werk ist seiner ganzen Bedeutung nach und in seiner praktischen Brauchbarkeit bereits so anerkannt, daß jüngst Wolfgang Golther in seinem größeren Werke 'Parzival und der Gral' (1925) nicht nur Bruce's Grundsätze anerkannte, sondern auch für die Bibliographie auf Bruce's Verzeichnisse verweisen konnte. Außerdem hat es Gustav Rosenhagen in der siebenten Auflage (1927) der Parzivalübersetzung von Wilhelm Hertz übernommen, den gesamten Stoff, der sich auf die Gralforschung bezieht, in einem besonderen Nachtrage kritisch darzustellen. So konnte meine Aufgabe wesentlich einfacher ausfallen. In meiner Neuedition von Chrestien's Graldichtung nebst den Fortsetzungen auf Grund aller bekannten Handschriften, die nahezu fertig vorliegt, hoffe ich all jenes beizubringen, was sich auch seit dem Erscheinen dieses Werkes für die Gralforschung an neuen Gesichtspunkten ergeben hat.

Alfons Hilka (Göttingen)

Allgemeines.

J. Bédier et P. Hazard, Histoire de la littérature française illustrée, Paris s. d., t. I., p. 18: Les romans bretons; p. 23: Marie de France: les lais; p. 38: Les romans de la Table ronde; p. 40: Le cycle de Saint Graal.

J. Bédier, A. Jeanroy et F. Picavet, Histoire de la nation française, t. XII, Paris s. d., p. 271: La littérature française au XIIe siècle (L'aristocratie dans les provinces du Nord, sa culture et ses goûts. — La littérature d'imagination, ses sources et ses caractères. — Les romans bretons. — p. 357: Les récits romanesques en vers; romans arthuriens, d'aventures et de mœurs. — Le roman en prose; Lancelot du Lac).

L. A. Hibbard, Mediaeval Romance in England. A Study of the Sources and Analogues of the non-cyclic Metrical Romances, New York 1924. Rez. MLR. 20 (1925), 339 (C. Brett); *MLN.* 41 (1926), 406 (K. Malone); Z. f. rom. Ph. 46 (1926), 500 (A. Hilka); Anglia, Beibl. 36 (1925), 332 (G. Binz).

H. Schneider, Heldendichtung, Geistlichendichtung, Ritterdichtung, Heidelberg 1925, *Geschichte der deutschen Literatur, hgb. A. Köster u. J. Petersen* I, p. 238: Chrestien de Troyes; p. 247: Tristansage; p. 261: Hartmann von Aue; p. 271: Wolfram von Eschenbach; p. 279: Gralforschung; p. 280: Kyotfrage; p. 287: Gottfried von Straßburg; p. 307: Lancelet des Ulrich von Zatzikhoven. Rez. LGRPh. 47 (1926), 145 (G. Ehrismann).

Fr. Schürr, Das altfranzösische Epos, München 1926, p. 299: Die Umbildung des epischen Stiles; p. 338: Gautier d'Arras und der Abenteuerroman; p. 354: Die bretonische Stoffwelt; p. 366: Die Lais der Marie de France; p. 388: Tristanromane; p. 408: Kristian von Troyes; p. 428: Der heilige Gral. Rez. Rom. 52 (1926), 559 (M. Roques); RR. 18 (1927,) 346 (H. F. Muller); Neoph. 12 (1927), 223 (J. J. Salverda de Grave); Nph. Mttg. 28 (1927), 113 (H. Wallenskoeld).

W. Schwarzkopff, Sagen und Geschichten aus dem alten Frankreich und England, München 1925. Rez. Z.f.rom.Ph. (A. Hilka); MLN. 41 (1926), 546 (T. F. Crane).

E. Tegethoff, Französische Volksmärchen, Jena 1923, p. 36: Parzival in der Graalsburg; p. 42: Ivain; p. 137: Aus den Lais der Marie de France.

Fr. Vogt, Geschichte der mittelhochdeutschen Literatur. I. Teil: Frühmittelhochdeutsche Zeit. Blütezeit I: Das höfische Epos bis auf Gottfried von Straßburg. 3. Aufl. Berlin u. Leipzig 1922, p. 210: Der Artusroman und Hartmann von Aue; p. 257: Wolfram von

Eschenbach und der Gral; p. 316: Gottfried von Straßburg. Rez.
LGRPh. 47 (1926), 145 (G. Ehrismann).

Altfranzösische Kunstepik (Allgemeines).

S. F. Barrow, The Medieval Society Romances. Diss. Columbia University, New York 1924 (The machinery of courtly love. — Courtly love and society).

E. R. Goddard, Women's Costume in French Texts of the eleventh and twelfth centuries, Baltimore 1927, *Johns Hopkins Studies in Romance Literature and Language* 7.

St. Hofer, Studien zum höfischen Roman, *ZFSL.* 46 (1923), 386: Die Voraussetzung des höfischen Epos. — Der Inhalt des höfischen Epos. — Die höfischen Ideale im Epos. — Die neue Romantechnik. — Die Vorläufer. — Erec, der erste höfische Roman. *ZFSL.* 47 (1925), 193: Minnesang und Epos. — Übereinstimmungen mit dem Volksepos.
ZFSL. 47 (1925), 267: Die Entstehung der Liebe. — Das Herz im Motiv. — Amor als Person. — Die Konkretisierung der Minne: Die Liebe als Krankheit, das Wesen der Krankheit, Unheilbarkeit, Dauer und Stärke, die Heilung. — Die Verehrung der Herrin in Frankreich. — Die Abstrakta des Minnesanges im Epos. — Der Minnedienst.

Artussage (Allgemeines).

M. W. Beckwith, A note on Punjab Legend in relation to Arthurian Romance, *Medieval Studies in memory of Gertrude Schöpperle Loomis,* Paris and New York 1927, 50.

A. C. L. Brown, The Irish Elements in King Arthur and the Grail, *Medieval Studies in memory of Gertrude Schöpperle Loomis,* Paris and New York 1927, 95.

A. C. L. Brown, A note on the Nugae of G. H. Gerould's „King Arthur and Politics", *Speculum* 2 (1927), 449.

— James Douglas Bruce, 1862—1928, *MPh.* 20 (1922/23), 338.

J. D. Bruce, The Evolution of Arthurian Romance from the Beginnings down to the Year 1300, 2 vols., Göttingen 1923. Rez. LGRPh. 46 (1925), 5 (W. Golther); Z.f.rom.Ph. 46 (1926), 492 (A. Hilka); *MLN.* 39 (1924), 482 (G. H. Maynadier); JEGPh. 23 (1924), 582 (R. S. Loomis); *MLR.* 20 (1925), 209 (J. L. Weston); *MPh.* 22 (1924/25), 99 (W. Nitze).

J. D. Bruce, Mordred's incestuous birth, *Medieval Studies in memory of Gertrude Schöpperle Loomis,* Paris and New York 1927, 197.

E. K. Chambers, Arthur of Britain, London 1927.

N. H. Clement, The Influence of the Arthurian Romances on the five books of Rabelais, Berkeley, California 1926, *University of California Publications in Modern Philology* 12, 3 (1926), 147. Rez. JEGPh. 26 (1927), 271 (Arthur C. L. Brown).

P. Deschamps, La légende arthurienne à la cathédrale de Modène et l'école lombarde de sculpture romane, Paris 1926. Rez. Rom. 53 (1927), 445 (M. Roques).

A. G. van Hamel, Koning Arthur's vader, *Neoph.* 12 (1926), 34.

L. Hibbard Loomis, Arthur's Round Table, *PMLA.* 41 (1926), 771. Rez. MPh. 25 (1927), 242 (A. C. L. Brown).

R. Sh. Loomis, The Story of the Modena Archivolt and its mythological roots, *RR.* 15 (1924), 266.

— Medieval Iconography and the Question of Arthurian Origins, *MLN.* 40 (1925), 65.

— Romance and Epic in the romanesque art of Italy, *Nuovi Studi medievali* 2 (1926), 105.

— The Date, Source, and Subject of the Arthurian Sculpture at Modena, *Medieval Studies in memory of Gertrude Schöpperle Loomis,* Paris and New York 1927, 209.

— Celtic Myth and Arthurian Romance, New York 1927. Rez. MLN. 42 (1927), 560 (W. A. Nitze); Rom. 53 (1927), 401 (F. Lot).

J. Loth, L'historicité d'Arthur d'après un travail récent, *Rev. celt.* 42 (1925), 306.

F. P. Magoun, An Index of abbreviations in Miss Alma Blount's unpublished „Onomasticon Arthurianum", *Speculum* 1 (1926), 190.

Kemp Malone, Artorius, *MPh.* 22 (1924/25), 367.

— The Historicity of Arthur, *JEGPh.* 23 (1924), 463.

J. J. Parry, Modern Welsh Versions of the Arthurian Stories, *JEGPh.* 21 (1922), 572.

— An Arthurian Parallel, *MLN.* 39 (1924), 307.

M. Schlauch, Literary Exchange between England and Sicily, *RR.* 14 (1923), 168 (p. 174: Artus im Ätna).

Fr. Schürr, Das Aufkommen der matière de Bretagne im Lichte der veränderten literarhistorischen Betrachtung, *GRM.* 9 (1921), 96.

S. Singer, Die Artussage, Bern u. Leipzig 1926. Rez. ZFSL. 50 (1927), 161 (E. Brugger); 46. Anzg. zur Z.f.d.A. 64 (1927), 43 (J. F. D. Blöte).

E. van der Ven Ten Bensel, The Character of King Arthur in English Literature, Amsterdam 1925. Rez. MLN. 42 (1927), 417 (John J. Parry).

E. H. Waller, A Welsh Branch of the Arthur Family-Tree, *Speculum* 1 (1926), 344.

Chroniken und Artussage.

E. Faral, Geoffrey de Monmouth, les faits et les dates de sa biographie, *Rom.* 53 (1927), 1.

M. Förster, War Nennius ein Ire?, *Finke-Festschrift*, Münster 1925, 36. Rez. Rev. celt. 42 (1925), 451.

G. Hall Gerould, King Arthur and Politics, *Speculum* 2 (1927), 33.

Acton Griscom, The Date of Composition of Geoffrey of Monmouth's Historia; new manuscript evidence, *Speculum* 1 (1926), 129.

A. H. Krappe, Note sur un épisode de l'Historia Britonum de Nennius, *Rev. celt.* 41 (1924), 181.

F. Liebermann, Die angebliche Entdeckung einer brythonischen Geschichte aus der Römerzeit: Galfrid von Monmouth und Tysylio, *ASNS.* 144 (1922), 31.

— Nennius der Britenhistoriker, *ASNS.* 152 (1927), 218.

F. Lot, De la valeur historique du De excidio et conquestu Britanniae de Gildas, *Medieval Studies in memory of Gertrude Schöpperle Loomis,* Paris and New York 1927, 229.

H. Matter, Englische Gründungssagen von Geoffroy of Monmouth bis zur Renaissance, Heidelberg 1922, *Angl. Forschungen* 58.

W. A. Nitze, Geoffrey of Monmouth's King Arthur, *Speculum* 2 (1927), 317.

J. J. Parry, Geoffrey of Monmouth and Josephus, *Speculum* 2 (1927), 446.

E. T. Sage, Giraldus Cambrensis and Petronius, *Speculum* 2 (1927), 203.

R. Thurneysen, Zum Geburtsjahr des Gildas, *Z.f.celt.Ph.* 14 (1923), 13.

Wace.

St. Hofer, Wace und die höfische Kunst, *Z.f.rom.Ph.* 43 (1923), 221.

M. M. Jirmounsky, Essai d'analyse des procédés littéraires de Wace, *Rev. d. l. rom.* 65 (1925), 261.

Gaimar.

A. Bell, Le Lai d'Haveloc and Gaimar's Haveloc Episode edited, Manchester 1925. Rez. MLR. 22 (1927), 476 (W. K. Pope).

Marie de France und Laisdichtung.

E. Brugger, Eigennamen in den Lais der Marie de France, *ZFSL.* 49 (1927), 201 u. 381.

H. Gelzer, Mabon, *ZFSL.* 47 (1925), 73.

E. Höpffner, La tradition manuscrite des Lais de Marie de France, *Neoph.* 12 (1926), 1 u. 85.

E. Levi, Maria di Francia e le abbazie d'Inghilterra, *Arch. Rom.* 5 (1921), 472. Rez. Neoph. 24 (1923), 54 (A. Wallenskoeld).

E. Levi, Sulla cronologia delle opere di Maria di Francia, *Nuovi Studi medievali* 1 (1923), 40.

— Troveri ed abbazie, Firenze 1925, *Archivo Storico Italiano* 192£, 1. Rez. Rom. 53 (1927), 283 (M. Roques); Z.f.rom.Ph. 46 (1926), 503 (A. Hilka).

— Maria di Francia, Eliduc. Riveduto nel testo, con versione a fronte, introduzione e commento, Firenze 1924, *Biblioteca Sansoniana straniera* 33. Rez. Z. f. rom. Ph. 46 (1926), 503 (A. Hilka); Neoph. 10 (1924), 63 (J. J. Salverda de Grave); Neuph. Mttg. 26 (1925), 59 (A. Wallenskoeld).

E. Lommatzsch, Le lai de Guingamor. — Le lai de Tydorel, Berlin 1922, *Rom. Texte* 6. Rez. ASNS. 144 (1923), 301 (O. Schultz-Gora).

J. P. Mc Keehan, Guillaume de Palerne: a medieval „best seller“, *PMLA*. 41 (1926), 785 (zum Bisclavret und zur Werwolfsage).

M. B. Ogle, The Orchard Scene in Tydorel and Sir Gowther, *RR.* 13 (1922), 37.

J. J. Salverda de Grave, Marie de France et Enéas, *Neoph.* 10 (1924), 56.

K. Warnke, Die Lais der Marie de France, mit vergleichenden Anmerkungen von R. Köhler nebst Ergänzungen von J. Bolte und einem Anhang 'Der Lai von Guingamor' hgb. von P. Kusel, Halle 1925, *Bibl. norm.* 3. Rez. ZFSL. 49 (1927), 116 (E. Brugger); ASNS. 148 (1925), 316 (O. Schultz-Gora); Z.f.rom.Ph. 46 (1926), 314 (A. Hilka); RR. 16 (1925), 95 (H. F. Muller); MPh. 23 (1925/26), 233 (W. A. Nitze); Neoph. 11 (1926), 141 (E. Höpffner).

— Vier Lais der Marie de France, nach der Hs. des Brit. Mus. Harl. 978 mit Einl. und Glossar hgb., Halle 1925, *Sammlung rom. Übungstexte* 2.

M. Wilmotte, Marie de France et Chrétien de Troyes, *Rom.* 52 (1926), 353.

Merlinsage.

H. Gelzer, Der Silenceroman von Heldris de Cornuelle, *Z.f.rom.Ph.* 47 (1927), 87.

J. J. Parry, The Date of the Vita Merlini, *MPh.* 22 (1924/25), 413.

— The Vita Merlini, Urbana 1925, *University of Illinois Studies in Language and Literature* 10, 3. Rez. ZFSL. 50 (1927), 368 (E. Brugger); Speculum 1 (1926), 353 (J. S. P. Tatlock); JEGPh. 26 (1927), 423 (R. Loomis).

L. Allen Paton, Les Prophecies de Merlin, edited from Ms. 593 in the Bibl. municipale of Rennes, New York 1926/27, 2 vols.

Tristansage.

V. de Bartholomaeis, Tristano, gli episodi principali della leggenda in versioni francesi, spagnuole, e italiane, Bologna s. d. Rez. Rom. 49 (1923), 134 (A. Jeanroy).

E. Brugger, Loenois as Tristan's Home, *MPh.* 22 (1924/25), 159. Rez. LGRPh. 46 (1925), 215 (W. Golther).

— Der Dichter Bledri-Bleheri-Breri, *ZFSL.* 47 (1925), 162.

T. P. Cross, A Welsh Tristan Episode, *Studies in Phil.* 17 (1920), 93. Rez. Rev. celt. 38 (1920), 81 (J. Vendryes).

J. L. Deister, Bernhart de Ventadour's Reference to the Tristan Story, *MPh.* 19 (1922), 287.

J. Gombert, Eilhart von Oberg und Gottfried von Straßburg, Beitrag zur Tristanforschung, Rotterdam 1927.

A. G. van Hamel, Tristan's combat with the dragon, *Rev. celt.* 41 (1924), 331.

G. L. Hamilton, Tristram's coat of arms, *MLR.* 15 (1920), 425.

B. Jansen, Tristan und Parzival, ein Beitrag zur Kulturgeschichte des Mittelalters, Diss. Utrecht 1923.

A. Jeanroy, Quelques corrections au texte du Tristan de Béroul, *Mélanges de philologie et d'histoire offerts à M. Antoine Thomas par ses élèves et ses amis,* Paris 1927, 227.

M. M. Jirmounsky, Quelques remarques sur la datation du „Tristan" de Thomas, *Arch. Rom.* 11 (1927), 210.

J. Kelemina, Geschichte der Tristansage nach den Dichtungen des Mittelalters, Wien 1923. Rez. Rom. 51 (1925), 597 (E. Faral); LGRPh. 46 (1925), 149 (W. Golther).

R. Sh. Loomis, Tristram and the House of Anjou, *MLR.* 17 (1922), 24.

— The Romance of Tristram and Ysolt by Thomas of Britain, transl. from the Old French and Old Norse, New York 1923. Rez. JEGPh. 23 (1924), 609 (J. J. Parry); LGRPh. 45 (1924), 313 (W. Golther); MPh. 21 (1923/4), 441 (L. E. Winfrey); PMLA. 38 (1923), 492 (H. G. Leach).

— Bleheris and the Tristram Story, *MLN.* 39 (1924), 319.

— Problems of the Tristan Legend: Bleheris; the Diarmaid parallel and Thomas' date, *Rom.* 53 (1927), 82.

E. Løseth, Le Tristan et le Palamède des manuscrits de Rome et de Florence, Kristiania 1924. Rez. ZFSL. 48 (1926), 325 (E. Brugger); Z.f.rom.Ph. 46 (1926), 504 (A. Hilka).

F. Lot, Encore Bleheri-Breri, *Rom.* 51 (1925), 397.

— Sur les deux Thomas, poètes anglo-normands du XIIe siècle, *Rom.* 53 (1927), 176.

M. Lot-Borodine, Tristan et Lancelot, *Medieval Studies in memory of Gertrude Schöpperle Loomis,* Paris and New York 1927, 21.

J. Loth, L'épée de Tristan, *Comptes rendus de l'Académie des Inscriptions et Belles-Lettres de l'année* 1923, p. 117. Rez. Rev. celt. 40 (1923), 489 (J. Vendryes).

E. S. Murrell, Girart de Roussillon and the „Tristan" Poems, Chesterfield 1926. Rez. Rom. 53 (1927), 443 (M. Roques).

E. Nickel, Studien zum Liebesproblem bei Gottfried von Straßburg, Königsberg 1927, *Königsberger deutsche Forschungen,* H. 1.

F. Ranke, Die Allegorie der Minnegrotte in Gottfrieds Tristan, *Schriften der Königsberger Gelehrten Gesellschaft,* Jahr 2, Geisteswissenschaftliche Klasse, H. 2, Königsberg 1925. Rez. LGRPh. 48 (1927), 93 (A. Götze); 46. Anzeiger zur Z.f.d.A. 64 (1927), 46 (J. F. D. Blöte).

— Tristan und Isolde, München 1925, *Bücher des Mittelalters.* Rez. Z.f.rom.Ph. 46 (1926), 506 (A. Hilka); LGRPh. 47 (1926), 344 (W. Golther); MLN. 41 (1926), 546 (T. F. Crane); MLR. 22 (1927), 112 (R. Priebsch); 45. Anz. zur Z. f. d. A. 63 (1926), 179 (G. Ehrismann).

— Isoldes Gottesurteil, *Medieval Studies in memory of Gertrude Schöpperle Loomis,* Paris and New York 1927, 87.

J. H. Scholte, Eine Interpretationsfrage bei Gottfried von Straßburg, *Neoph.* 9 (1924), 172.

O. Schultz-Gora, Zum ersten Straßburger Tristanfragment, *ASNS.* 151 (1926), 95.

K. Sneyders de Vogel, Tristan et Iseut, d'après des publications récentes, *Neoph.* 1 (1916), 81.

R. Thurneysen, Eine irische Parallele zur Tristansage, *Z.f.rom.Ph.* 43 (1926), 385.

W. A. Tregenza, The ʽRoman de Renart' and the Tristan Poems, *MLR.* 19 (1924), 301.

J. Vendryes, Gertrude Schöpperle (Mrs. Roger Loomis), *Rev. celt.* 40 (1923), 238.

E. Vinaver, Etudes sur le Tristan en prose. Les sources, les manuscrits, bibliographie, critique, Paris 1925. Rez. Z.f.rom.Ph. 46 (1926), 511 (A. Hilka); Nph.Mttg. 27 (1926), 109 (A. Långfors); MLR. 22 (1927), 230 (C. Johnson); LGRPh. 48 (1927), 406 (W. Golther).

— Le roman de Tristan et Iseut dans l'oeuvre de Thomas Malory, Paris 1925. Rez. Z.f.rom.Ph. 46 (1926), 511 (A. Hilka); MLR. 22 (1927), 97 (E. K. Chambers); LGRPh. 48 (1927), 406 (W. Golther).

E. Vinaver, The Love Potion in the primitive Tristan Romance, *Medieval Studies in memory of Gertrude Schöpperle Loomis*, Paris and New York 1927, 75.

C. C. Wright, „A entercer le pur Tristan" (Folie Tristan d'Oxford, Bédier's ed. l. 846), *RR.* 12 (1921), 290.

Ille et Galeron.

Fr. A. G. Cowper, The new Manuscript of Ille et Galeron, *MPh.* 18 (1921), 601.

— The Sources of Ille et Galeron, *MPh.* 20 (1922/23), 35.

Chrestien de Troyes.

G. Cohen, Crestien de Troies, sa vie et son oeuvre, *Revue des cours et conférences* 1926/27.

P. Fabrick, La construction relative dans Chrétien de Troyes, Diss. Amsterdam, Paris 1924. Rez. Z.f.rom.Ph. 46 (1926), 495 (A. Hilka).

E. Gamillscheg, Chrestien li Gois, *ZFSL.* 46 (1923), 183.

L. M. Gay, The Chronology of the earlier works of Crestien de Troyes, *RR.* 14 (1923), 47.

Ch. Grimm, Chrestien de Troyes's Attitude towards woman, *RR.* 16 (1925), 236.

F. E. Guyer, The Influence of Ovid on Crestien de Troyes, *RR.* 12 (1921), 97 u. 216. Rez. MLR. 17 (1922), 431 (J. Orr), dazu Entgegnung 18 (1923), 240 (Guyer).

St. Hofer, Beiträge zu Chrestiens Werken, *Z.f.rom.Ph.* 41 (1921), 408: Zur Datierung des Erec. — Ovidiana und Minnelyrik. — Zur Karre. — Zur Abfassungszeit des Gralromans.
Z.f.rom.Ph. 42 (1922), 343: Wace's Brut und Erec. — Wace und Cligés. — Karre und Lai Yonec.

E. Höpffner, Crestien de Troyes und Guillaume de Machaut, *Z.f.rom. Ph.* 39 (1919), 627.

U. T. Holmes, Chronology of Chrétien de Troyes' Works, *RR.* 16 (1925), 43.

F. H. Titchener, The Romances of Chrétien de Troyes, *RR.* 16 (1925), 165.

Erec.

H. Sparnaay, Zu Erec-Gereint, *Z.f.rom.Ph.* 45 (1925), 53.

— Die Mabinogionfrage, *GRM.* 15 (1927), 444.

A. Taylor, The Motif of the vacant Stake in Folklore and Romance, *RR.* 9 (1918), 21.

R. Zenker, Weiteres zur Mabinogionfrage, *ZFSL.* 48 (1926), 1: Der Erec des Hartmann von Aue in seinem Verhältnis zu Chrétiens Erec und zu dem Mabinogi von Gereint. Mit zwei Exkursen: 1. Fée Morgain (Fata Morgana) = irisch Morrigan. 2. Zum Lanzelet des Ulrich von Zatzikhoven (Fortsetzung). *ZFSL.* 48 (1926), 386: Die altnordische Erexsaga.

— Erekiana, *RFg.* 40 (1927), 458.

Cligés.

A. Franz, Die reflektierte Handlung im Cligés, *Z. f. rom. Ph.* 47 (1927), 61.

Yvain.

A. Gilchrist Brodeur, The grateful Lion, *PMLA.* 39 (1924), 485.

W. Förster, Kristian von Troyes, Yvain (der Löwenritter) hgb. Zweite unveränderte Aufl. mit einem Nachwort von A. Hilka, Halle 1926, *Rom. Bibl. Textausgabe.* Rez. ZFSL. 50 (1928), 480 (E. Brugger); ASNS. 152 (1927), 314 (O. Schultz-Gora).

F. E. Guyer, Some of the Latin Sources of Yvain, *RR.* 14 (1923), 286.

C. B. Lewis, The Function of the Gong in the Source of Chrestien de Troyes' Yvain, *Z. f. rom. Ph.* 47 (1927), 254.

E. Sattler, Das Märchen vom „Retter in der Not" in Chrestiens „Yvain" und in der Egilssaga, *GRM.* 3 (1911), 669.

E. S. Sheldon, Notes on Förster's Edition of Yvain, *RR.* 10 (1919), 233; 12 (1921), 297.

H. Sparnaay, Zu Yvain-Owein, *Z. f. rom. Ph.* 46 (1926), 517.

R. Zenker, Ivain im Torverließ, *Z. f. d. A.* 62 (1925), 49.

Gralsage (Allgemeines).

K. Burdach, Vorspiel. Gesammelte Schriften zur Geschichte des deutschen Geistes I, 1: Mittelalter, Halle 1925, p. 161: Longinus und der Gral (1903). — p. 165: Der Ursprung der Grallegende (1903). — p. 174: Der Judenspieß und die Longinussage (1916). — p. 217: Der Longinusspeer in eschatologischem Lichte (1920). Rez. 46. Anz. zur Z.f.d.A. 64 (1927), 140 (J. Schwietering); Nph. Mttg. 27 (1926), 207 (H. Suolahti); Mus. 34 (1927), 69 (J. van Dam).

W. Golther, Parzival und der Gral, Stuttgart 1925. Rez. Z.f.rom.Ph. 46 (1926), 497 (A. Hilka); 45. Anz. zur Z.f.d.A. 63 (1926), 185 (J. F. D. Blöte); Dt. Litztg. 1927, 151 (G. Rosenhagen).

R. Koechlin, Les ivoires gothiques, Paris 1924, 3 vols. Rez. Rom. 52 (1926), 566 (M. Roques).

R. Palgen, Der Stein der Weisen, Quellenstudien zum Parzival, Breslau

1922. Rez. Zs.f.rom.Ph. **43** (1923), **497** (A. Hilka); **42.** Anz. zur Z.f.d.A. **60** (1923), 105 (J. F. D. Blöte).

J. A. Robinson, Two Glastonbury Legends: King Arthur and St. Joseph of Arimathea, Cambridge 1926. Rez. Anglia, Beiblatt 38 (1927), 133.

Rohr, Parzival und der heilige Gral, eine neue Deutung der Symbolik der Graldichtungen, Hildesheim 1922. Rez. LGRPh. **46** (1925), 214 (W. Golther).

H. Sparnaay, Verschmelzung legendarischer und weltlicher Motive in der Poesie des Mittelalters, Groningen 1922. Rez. Rom. **53** (1927), 283 (M. Roques); LGRPh. **47** (1926), 7 (K. Wagner); **43.** Anz. zur Z.f.d.A. **61** (1924), 63 (G. Ehrismann); JEGPh. **23** (1924), 591 (A. H. Krappe); Z.f.rom.Ph. **43** (1923), 499 (A. Hilka).

F. Witte, Die Sage vom heiligen Gral und die Liturgie, *Z. f. christl. Kunst* **26** (1913), 103.

Chrestien's Conte del Graal.

A. C. L. Brown, Did Chrétien identify the Grail with the Mass, *MLN.* **41** (1926), 226.

J. H. Scholte, Der rote Ritter, *Neoph.* **5** (1920), 115.

Peredur.

G. Le Roux, Le roman de Pérédur, texte gallois traduit en breton, avec une traduction française d'après J. Loth, Rennes 1923. Rez. Rev. celt. **41** (1924), 260 (J. Loth).

L. Mühlhausen, Untersuchung über das gegenseitige Verhältnis von Chrestiens Conte del Graal und dem kymrischen Prosaroman von Peredur, *Z. f. rom. Ph.* **43** (1923), 465.

— Ein Beitrag zur Mabinogionfrage: Peredur — Perceval, GRM. **10** (1922), 367.

L. Weißgerber, Die Hss. des Peredur ab Efrawc in ihrer Bedeutung für die kymrische Sprach- und Literaturgeschichte, *Z.f.celt.Ph.* **15** (1925), 66. Rez. ZFSL. **48** (1925), 326 (E. Brugger).

— Angebliche Verwirrungen im Peredur, RFg. **60** (1927), 483.

J. L. Weston, Notes on the Grail Romances: Caput Johannis, Caput Christi, *Rom.* **49** (1923), 273.

R. Zenker, Zu Perceval-Peredur, *GRM.* **11** (1923), 240.

— Nochmals Peredur-Perceval, *RFg.* **40** (1926), 251.

Sir Perceval.

A. C. L. Brown, The Grail and the English Sir Perceval, *MPh.* **16** (1918/19), 553; 17 (1919/20), 361; 18 (1920/21), 201 u. 661; 22 (1924/25), 79 u. 113. Rez. LGRPh. **46** (1925), 283 (W. Golther); MLR. **21** (1926), 78 (A. Bell); JEGPh. **25** (1926), 133 (J. J. Parry).

Wolfram's Parzival.

E. K. Heller, Wolfram's Relationship to the Crestien Mss., *MLN.* 41 (1926), 520.

W. Hertz, Parzival von Wolfram von Eschenbach, mit einem Nachtrag von Gustav Rosenhagen, 7. Aufl., Stuttgart u. Berlin, 1927.

E. Karg-Gasterstädt, Zur Entstehungsgeschichte von Wolframs Parzival, Halle 1925. Rez. 45. Anz. zur Z.f.d.A. 63 (1926), 141 (J. F. D. Blöte); ASNS. 152 (1927), 279 (Th. Frings)'; MLR. 21 (1926), 336 (M. Fr. Richey); JEGPh. 25 (1926), 452 (E. K. Heller).

Georg Misch, Wolframs Parzival, eine Studie zur Geschichte der Autobiographie, *Dt. Vierteljahrsschrift für Litwiss. u. Geistesgesch.* 5 (1927), 213.

F. Neumann, Wolfram von Eschenbachs Ritterideal, *Dt. Vierteljahrsschrift für Litwiss. u. Geistesgesch.* 5 (1927), 9—24.

M. Ramondt, Zur Jugendgeschichte des Parzival, Neoph. 9 (1923), 15.

M. F. Richey, Gahmuret Anschevin, a Contribution to the Study of Wolfram von Eschenbach, Oxford 1923. Rez. Z.f.d.Ph. 51 (1926), 124 (G. Rosenhagen); 44. Anz. zur Z.f.d.A. 62 (1925), 23 (J. F. D. Blöte); MLR. 20 (1925), 99 (E. Purdie).

— Schionatulander and Sigune. An Episode from the Story of Parzival and the Graal as related by Wolfram von Eschenbach, interpreted and discussed, London 1927.

G. Röthe, Der Dichter des Parzival, Rektoratsrede, Berlin 1924.

A. Schreiber, Neue Bausteine zu einer Lebensgeschichte Wolframs von Eschenbach, Frankfurt 1922. Rez. Z.f.rom.Ph. 44 (1924), 744 (G. Müller) u. 750 (A. Hilka); LGRPh. 48 (1927), 252 (G. Ehrismann); 45. Anz. zur Z.f.d.A. 63 (1926), 9 (F. Ranke); MLR. 18 (1923), 360 (M. F. Richey).

Robert de Boron.

G. Huet, La chronologie dans l'œuvre de Robert de Boron, *MA.* 32 (1921), 138.

W. A. Nitze, The Date of Robert de Borron's „metrical Joseph", *The Manly Anniversary Studies in Language and Literature,* Chicago 1923, 300. Rez. Rom. 53 (1927) 445 (M. Roques).

— The Identity of Brons in Robert de Borron's Metrical Joseph, *Medieval Studies in memory of Gertrude Schöpperle Loomis,* Paris and New York 1927, 135.

— Robert de Boron, Le roman de l'Estoire dou Graal, Paris 1927, *Les Classiques fr. du moyen âge* 57.

Chrestien's Gralfortsetzer und die Elucidation.

E. Brugger, Bliocadran, the Father of Perceval, *Medieval Studies in memory of* Gertrude Schöpperle Loomis, Paris and New York 1927, 147.

R. J. Peebles, The Children in the Tree, *Medieval Studies in memory of Gertrude Schöpperle Loomis,* Paris and New York 1927, 285.

J. L. Weston, Who was Brian des Illes?, *MPh.* 22 (1924/25), 405.

M. Williams, Gerbert de Montreuil, la continuation de Perceval, t. I, v. 1-7020, Paris 1922, *Les Classiques fr. du moyen âge* 28; t. II, v. 7021-14078, Paris 1925, *Les Classiques fr. du m. âge* 50.

Prosagralromane.

A. Pauphilet, Le roman en prose de „Perceval", *Mélanges d'histoire du moyen âge offerts à M. F. Lot par ses amis et ses élèves,* Paris 1925, 603.

J. L. Weston, The Perlesvaus and the Story of the Coward Knight, *MPh.* 20 (1922/23), 379.

— The Relation of the Perlesvaus to the cyclic Romances, *Rom.* 51 (1925), 348.

E. Anitchkof, Le Galaad du Lancelot-Graal et les Galaads de la Bible, *Rom.* 53 (1927), 388.

A. Beaunier, Les nouveaux romans de la Table Ronde, *Rev. des deux mondes,* 94e année, t. 22 (1924), 205.

J. D. Bruce, The Development of the Mort Arthur Theme in Mediaeval Romance, *RR.* 4 (1913), 403. Rez. ZFSL. 47 (1925), 98 (E. Brugger).

L. Gilson, La mystique de la grâce dans la Queste del Saint Graal, *Rom.* 51 (1925), 321.

F. J. Johnson, Grenoble Ms. 866, *MLR.* 22 (1927), 322 (enthält ein Fragment der Estoire del Saint Graal, vgl. H. O. Sommer, The Vulgate Version of the Arthurian Romances I (1909), 93.

F. Lot, L'épée de Lancelot du Lac, *Rom.* 50 (1924), 99.

— L'origine du nom de Lancelot, *Rom.* 51 (1925), 423.

M. Lot-Borodine, Le double esprit et l'unité du „Lancelot" en prose, *Mélanges d'histoire du moyen âge offerts à M. F. Lot par ses amis et ses élèves,* Paris 1925, 477.

M. Lot-Borodine et Gertrude Schöpperle, Lancelot el Galaad mis en nouveau langage, avec une introduction par R. Loomis, New York 1926.

E. S. Murrel, Some new Arthurian Manuscripts in the Bodleian Library, *MLR.* 22 (1927), 87.

A. Pauphilet, La Queste del Saint Graal, roman du XIIIe siècle, Paris 1923, *Les Classiques fr. du moyen âge* 33.

A. Pauphilet, Sur les mss. de la Mort d'Artus, *Mélanges de phil.
et d'histoire offerts à M. A. Thomas par ses élèves et ses amis,*
Paris 1927, 341.

H. O. Sommer, The Structure of Le Livre d'Artus and its Function
in the Evolution of the Arthurian Prose Romances, London and
Paris 1914. Rez. ZFSL. 47 (1925), 319 (E. Brugger).

J. L. Weston, The relative Position of the 'Perceval' and 'Galahad'
Romances, *MLR.* 21 (1926), 385.

Sonstige Artusromane.

Li Biaus Desconneüs. U. T. Holmes, Renaut de Beaujeu, *RR.* 18
(1927), 334.

Claris et Laris. L. Jordan, Der Roman de Claris et Laris, ein
Sprachdenkmal des oberen Moseltals aus dem Jahre 1268, *Arch.
Rom.* 9 (1925), 5.

Fergus. E. Brugger, „Huon de Bordeaux" and „Fergus", *MLR.* 20
(1925), 158.

L. Jordan, Zum altfranzösischen Fergusroman, *Z.f.rom.Ph.* 43 (1923), 154.

O. Schultz-Gora, Zum Text des Fergus, *Z.f.rom.Ph.* 44 (1924), 102.

Galeran de Bretagne. L. Foulet, Jean Renart, Galeran de Bretagne,
roman du XIIIe siècle, Paris 1925, *Les Classiques fr. du moyen
âge* 37.

L. Foulet, Galeran et Jean Renart, *Rom.* 51 (1925), 76.

— Galeran et les dix compagnons de Bretagne, *Rom.* 51 (1925), 116.

Ch. V. Langlois, La vie en France au moyen âge de la fin du XIIe
au milieu du XIVe siècle d'après des romans mondains du temps,
Paris 1924, 1.

Sir Gawain and the Green Knight. M. Förster, Der Name des
Green Knight, *ASNS.* 147 (1924), 194.

E. v. Schaubert, Der englische Ursprung von Sir Gawain and the Green
Knight, *Engl. Studien* 57 (1923), 330.

J. R. R. Tolkien and E. V. Gordon, Sir Gawain and the Green Knight,
edited, Oxford and New York 1925. Rez. MPh. 23 (1925/26),
246 (J. R. Hulbert); MLN. 41 (1926), 397 (R. J. Menner); MLR.
22 (1927), 451 (C. Brett); JEGPh. 26 (1927), 248 (O. E. Emer-
son); ASNS. 149 (1925), 172 (O. Schultz-Gora).

Historia Meriadoci and De Ortu Walwanii. E. Brugger, Zu
Historia Meriadoci und De Ortu Walwanii, *ZFSL.* 46 (1923), 247
u. 406.

P. Rajna, Sono il De ortu Walwanii e l'Historia Meriadoci opera di
un medesimo autore?, *Medieval Studies in memory of Gertrude
Schöpperle Loomis,* Paris and New York 1927, 1.

Hunbaut. A. Hilka, Plagiate in altfranzösischen Dichtungen, 47 (1924), 60. Rez. Rom. 51 (1925), 443 (A. Långfors). *ZFSL.*

Jaufre. H. Breuer, Jaufre, ein altprovenzalischer Abenteuerroman des XIII. Jahrhunderts hgb., Göttingen 1925, *Ges.f.rom.Lit.* 46. Rez. ASNS. 150 (1926), 305 (O. Schultz-Gora); MLR. 21 (1926), 455 (H. J. Chaytor).

H. Breuer, Zum altprov. Abenteuerroman Jaufre, *Z. f. rom. Ph.* 46 (1926), 411.

— Berichtigungen zur Ausgabe des Jaufre, *Z.f.rom.Ph.* 46 (1926), 80.

— Jaufre, altprov. Abenteuerroman des XIII. Jahrhunderts hgb., Halle 1927, *Sammlung rom. Übungstexte* 12.

Sone de Nansai. Ch.-V. Langlois s. o., p. 286.

Yder. St. Hofer, Zum Yderroman, *Z.f.rom.Ph.* 42 (1922), 108.

Vgl. für Artusromane auch A. Hilka, Die anglonormannische Kompilation didaktisch-epischen Inhalts der Hs. Bibl. nat. nouv. acq. fr. 7517, *ZFSL.* 47 (1925), 423.

Anteil Italiens.

E. G. Gardner, Arthurian Matter in the „Mare amoroso", *MLR.* 20 (1925), 329.

— The Holy Graal in Italian Literature, *MLR.* 20 (1925), 443.

J. Gombert, Entlegene Spuren des Tristan im Dekameron?, *Neoph.* 7 (1922), 136.

E. F. Griffiths, Li Chantari di Lancellotto, edited with an introduction, notes and glossary, Oxford 1924. Rez. Z.f.rom.Ph. 45 (1925), 349 (B.Wiese); ASNS. 149 (126), 320 (O. Schultz-Gora); MLR. 20 (1925), 214 (E. G. Gardner).

Anteil Spaniens.

Ph. St. Barto, The subterranean Grail Paradise of Cervantes, *PMLA.* 38 (1923), 401.

P. Bohigas Balaguer, El „Lanzarote" español del manuscrito 9611 de la Bibl. Nacional, *Rev. de fil. esp.* 11 (1924), 282.

— Los textos españoles y gallego-portugueses de la Demanda del santo Grial, Madrid 1925, *Rev. de fil. esp.*, Anejo VII.

— Más sobre el „Lanzarote" español, *Rev. de fil. esp.* 12 (1925), 60.

W. J. Entwistle, A note on Fernán Pérez de Guzmán ‘Mar de historias’, cap. 96 (Del santo grial), *MLR.* 18 (1923), 206.

— Geoffroy of Monmouth and Spanish Literature, MLR. 17 (1922), 381.

— The Adventure of „Le cerf au pied blanc" in Spanish and elsewhere, *MLR.* 18 (1923), 435.

— The Arthurian Legend in the Literatures of the Spanish Peninsula,

London and Toronto 1925. Rez. MLR. 21 (1925), 333 (E. G. Gardner); Rev. de fil. esp. 13 (1926), 294 (P. Bohigas); MPh. 24 (1927), 481 (G. T. Northup).

K. Pietsch, The Madrid Manuscripts of the Spanish Grail Fragments, *MPh*. 18 (1920/21), 147 u. 591.

— Spanish Grail Fragments. El Libro de Josep Abarimatia; La Estoria de Merlin; Lançarote, edited from the unique manuscript, vol. I: Texts; II: Commentary, *The Modern Monographs of the University of Chicago* 1924/25. Rez. ASNS. 151 (1926), 155 (F. Krüger); Nph. Mttg. 27 (1926), 115 (O. J. Tallgren); Rom. 53 (1927), 441 (M. Roques); LGRPh. 47 (1926), 366 (L. Spitzer); MLR. 20 (1925), 357 (W. J. Entwistle); MPh. 24 (1927), 355 J. E. Gillet); Rev. de fil. esp. 11 (1924), 428 (P. Bohigas y J. Vallejo) u. 13 (1926), 67 (P. Bohigas).

H. Thomas, Spanish and Portuguese Romances of Chivalry, Cambridge 1920. Rez. MPh. 21 (1923/24), 223 (G. T. Northup); Z.f.rom.Ph. 44 (1924), 764 (A. Hilka); Rev.d.l.rom. 62 (1923), 446 (J. Ronjat).